Lecture Notes in Computer Science 16229

The series Lecture Notes in Computer Science (LNCS), including its subseries Lecture Notes in Artificial Intelligence (LNAI) and Lecture Notes in Bioinformatics (LNBI), has established itself as a medium for the publication of new developments in computer science and information technology research, teaching, and education.

LNCS enjoys close cooperation with the computer science R & D community, the series counts many renowned academics among its volume editors and paper authors, and collaborates with prestigious societies. Its mission is to serve this international community by providing an invaluable service, mainly focused on the publication of conference and workshop proceedings and postproceedings. LNCS commenced publication in 1973.

Étienne André · Jingyi Wang · Naijun Zhan
Editors

Formal Methods and Software Engineering

26th International Conference on Formal Engineering Methods, ICFEM 2025 Hangzhou, China, November 10–13, 2025 Proceedings

Springer

Editors
Étienne André
Université Sorbonne Paris Nord
Villetaneuse, France

Jingyi Wang
Zhejiang University
Hangzhou, China

Naijun Zhan
Peking University
Beijing, China

ISSN 0302-9743 ISSN 1611-3349 (electronic)
Lecture Notes in Computer Science
ISBN 978-981-95-4212-3 ISBN 978-981-95-4213-0 (eBook)
https://doi.org/10.1007/978-981-95-4213-0

This Springer imprint is published by the registered company Springer Nature Singapore Pte Ltd.
The registered company address is: 152 Beach Road, #21-01/04 Gateway East, Singapore 189721, Singapore

Preface

This volume contains the papers presented at The 26th International Conference on Formal Engineering Methods (ICFEM 2025), organized by Zhejiang University, China, and held in Hangzhou, China, during November 10–13, 2025.

To constitute the program of ICFEM 2025, we composed a Programme Committee of 49 renowned scientists from all over the world. We received a total of 58 abstract submissions, which resulted in 47 full-paper submissions from 14 different countries. Each submission went through a rigorous single-blind review process in which the papers were reviewed by at least three PC members. Following a discussion phase lasting two weeks, we selected 20 papers, yielding an acceptance rate of 43%, for presentation during the conference and inclusion in these proceedings. The conference featured keynotes by Jifeng He (East China Normal University, China), Jim Woodcock (University of York, UK), Mariëlle Stoelinga (University of Twente, Netherlands), and Yongwang Zhao (Zhejiang University, China). We hereby thank these invited speakers for having accepted our invitation. As before, ICFEM 2025 also contained a Journal-First Track and Doctoral Symposium Track. There were 2 submissions for the former, and 1 for the latter; all were accepted. The 2 accepted papers for journal-first submissions were invited to present at the conference, and the accepted paper for the doctoral symposium is also included in these proceedings. There was also a workshop "PIFI Day on the Design of AI-Enabled Safety-Critical Systems" (Nov. 7–11) collocated with ICFEM 2025.

We are grateful to all involved in ICFEM 2025, in particular the PC members and sub-reviewers for their accurate and timely reviewing, all authors for their submissions, and all attendees of the symposium for their participation. We also thank the excellent local organization and publicity teams.

We are very grateful to our sponsors: the Huawei Technologies Co. Ltd, Ant Research, the Zhejiang University, the Zhejiang University NGICS Platform, the Chinese Academy of Sciences, and in particular its Institute of Software, and the National Natural Science Foundation of China. Finally, we thank Springer for publishing these proceedings and we acknowledge the support from EasyChair in assisting us in managing the complete process from submissions to these proceedings to the program.

September 2025

Étienne André
Jingyi Wang
Naijun Zhan

Organization

Program Committee

Yamine Ait Ameur	IRIT/INPT-ENSEEIHT, France
Jie An	Institute of Software, Chinese Academy of Sciences, China
Étienne André	Université Sorbonne Paris Nord, France
Lei Bu	Nanjing University, China
Yufan Cai	National University of Singapore, Singapore
Jialun Cao	Hong Kong University of Science and Technology, China
Mingshuai Chen	Zhejiang University, China
Yuqi Chen	ShanghaiTech University, China
Thao Dang	CNRS/VERIMAG, France
Naipeng Dong	National University of Singapore, Singapore
Alexandre Duret-Lutz	EPITA Research Lab (LRE), France
Osman Hasan	National University of Sciences and Technology, Pakistan
Zhe Hou	Griffith University, Australia
Fuyuki Ishikawa	National Institute of Informatics, Japan
Swen Jacobs	CISPA Helmholtz Center for Information Security, Germany
Niu Jun	Faculty of Information Science and Engineering, Ningbo University, China
Sun Jun	Singapore Management University, China
Tsutomu Kobayashi	Japan Aerospace Exploration Agency, Japan
Regine Laleau	Paris-Est Créteil University, France
Didier Lime	École Centrale de Nantes, France
Dominique Mery	Université de Lorraine, France
Munyque Mittelmann	University of Naples Federico II, Italy
Rosemary Monahan	Maynooth University, Ireland
Jun Pang	University of Luxembourg, Luxembourg
Julie Parreaux	Université de Rennes, France
Srinivas Pinisetty	Indian Institute of Technology Bhubaneswar, India
Jakob Piribauer	TU Dresden, Germany
Chris Poskitt	Singapore Management University, Singapore
Partha Roop	University of Auckland, New Zealand

Kristin Yvonne Rozier	Iowa State University, USA
Adenilso Simao	ICMC/USP, Brazil
Fu Song	Chinese Academy of Sciences, China
Jeremy Sproston	University of Turin, Italiy
B. Srivathsan	Chennai Mathematical Institute, India
Jing Sun	University of Auckland, New Zealand
Meng Sun	Peking University, China
Sofiène Tahar	Concordia University, Canada
Jean-Pierre Talpin	Inria, France
Cong Tian	Xidian University, China
Elena Troubitsyna	KTH Royal Institute of Technology, Sweden
Doğan Ulus	Boğaziçi University, Turkey
Masaki Waga	Kyoto University, Japan
Bow-Yaw Wang	Academia Sinica, Taiwan
Jingyi Wang	Zhejiang University, China
Zhiwu Xu	Shenzhen University, China
Pengfei Yang	Southwest University, China
Naijun Zhan	Peking University, China
Min Zhang	East China Normal University, China
Peixin Zhang	Singapore Management University, Singapore
Xiyue Zhang	Department of Computer Science, University of Oxford, UK
Yedi Zhang	National University of Singapore, Singapore
Zhenya Zhang	Kyushu University, Japan
Peter Ölveczky	University of Oslo, Norway

Additional Reviewers

Anand, Ayush
Ashraf, Sobia
Bukhari, Syed Ali Asadullah
Chan, Julian
Chatterjee, Sobhan
Chen, Xi
Guo, Xiao
Kim, Moon
Li, Mengze
Li, Zhiyang
Lin, Tengjie
Liu, Hengjie
Luan, Xiaokun
Parrot, Rémi
Rashid, Adnan
Sarwar, Muhammad Bilal
Turrini, Andrea
Wang, Jiawan
Wang, Zhongyi
Wei, Zeming
Zhang, Xianhao

Invited Papers

Unifying Probability within Universal Matrix Framework

Jifeng He

East China Normal University, Putuo, Shanghai, 200062 China
jifeng@sei.ecnu.edu.cn

Abstract. In the world at large, probabilism offers a simple, fast and unbiased choice between alternatives. Its use therefore provides an alternative to a time or space intensive computation for resolving a choice. For not only is its use efficient in both those senses, but it may provide a symmetrical algorithm where no efficient non-probabilistic symmetric algorithm exists. However, the price to be paid for these worthwhile benefits is that some probabilistic algorithms meet their ideal specifications with only high probability.

Probabilistic techniques have been used in mathematics for over two centuries. However, only in 1955 was the foundation laid for probabilistic algorithms, in the form of probabilistic Turing machines. In the 1970s Monte Carlo methods (e.g. primality testing) became popular. Since then, the use of probabilism has burgeoned in Computer Science. It has been used, for example to defeat an input adversary and hence to improve average-case efficiency; to overcome difficulties due to symmetry; in efficient symmetrical distributed algorithms; and in quantum algorithms.

One approach to using formal methods to reason about probabilistic programs would be to use a standard (non-probabilistic) method to reason about the non-probabilistic aspects of the program and then to use probability theory to 'graft on' an argument about the probabilistic behavior. I follow this approach by extending a standard formal method to embrace probability, thus achieving a homogeneous unified method. I will show how to use universal matrices to specify both non-probabilistic and probabilistic behaviors in the same framework. I take as implicit that programs are specified and verified by step-wise derivation. The basis in either case is the same: a refinement relation. Moreover, to promote the use of laws, as distinct from semantic reasoning. A semantic model shows a set of laws to be sound; a set of laws encapsulates properties of a semantic model. I will show that both methods can be more readily automated (by simple calculation), more easily appreciated by practitioners, and build an existing algebraic facility.

UTP and Institutions: A Semantic Foundation for Formal Engineering Methods

Jim Woodcock

University of York, Heslington, York, YO10 5DD UK
jim.woodcock@york.ac.uk

Abstract. Unifying Theories of Programming (UTP) and Institutions are two of the most influential frameworks for giving rigorous semantics to programming languages and specification logics. Each has distinctive strengths: UTP excels at computational reasoning, refinement, and the laws of programming within a unified relational model; the institution framework excels at logic independence, heterogeneous specification, and meta-theoretic results at scale. In this talk, I demonstrate how we can integrate these complementary approaches to construct trustworthy systems. I begin by contrasting the challenges that UTP solves but Institutions struggle with, and vice versa, illustrated with examples from the refinement calculus, healthiness conditions, heterogeneous logic translation, and the satisfaction condition. I then combine the two perspectives: UTP theories are wrapped as Institutions, enabling heterogeneous reasoning while retaining UTP's calculational power. This combination provides a pathway toward a semantic foundation that unifies intra-paradigm refinement with inter-paradigm logic-independence. The practical relevance of this integration is clear: modern systems are increasingly heterogeneous and safety-critical, spanning autonomous vehicles, cyber-physical systems, security protocols, and AI assurance. By combining UTP and Institutions, we move closer to the vision of formal engineering methods: rigorous semantic theory serving engineering practice, which is at the heart of ICFEM's mission.

TRust^2: Towards Formally Verified Toolchain of Rust Language in Isabelle/HOL

Yongwang Zhao

Zhejiang University, Hangzhou, 310007 Zhejiang, China
zhaoyw@zju.edu.cn

Abstract. Rust has emerged as a prominent systems programming language that uniquely combines high performance with strong memory-safety guarantees, making it particularly suitable for safety-critical domains such as operating systems and blockchain technologies. However, ensuring the correctness of Rust programs remains a significant challenge, primarily due to its complex language features—including the ownership model, lifetimes, and the complicated borrow checking mechanisms. Formal verification provides a rigorous methodology to address these challenges. Tools such as Verus and Kani have been developed for this purpose and have been successfully applied to verify real-world Rust systems.

This talk introduces **Trust^2** (website: https://trust2proj.github.io/), an open project aimed at building a formally verified toolchain for Rust using Isabelle/HOL. The toolchain is designed to incorporate formal semantics, program verifiers, static analyzers, verified compilers, and certified code generators for Rust. **Trust^2** is structured into three layers:

- *Semantic Foundation:* Mechanizing the semantics of Rust and its intermediate representations, e.g., Mid-level Intermediate Representation (MIR), in Isabelle/HOL, forming a basis for formal reasoning about Rust programs;
- *Verified Toolchain:* Developing Rust-focused verification tools leveraging existing backends (e.g., Isabelle/HOL and Z3) and formal techniques such as separation logic, abstract interpretation, and symbolic execution;
- *Industrial Applications*: Applying the verified toolchain to real-world systems written in Rust, including operating systems, virtual machines, compilers, and blockchain platforms.

Our ongoing work aligns with the three-layer architecture of **Trust^2**. At the semantics layer, we are formalizing the semantics of Rust MIR in Isabelle/HOL. At the toolchain layer, we are establishing a bidirectional translation between Isabelle/HOL and Rust: *Isabelle2Rust* extends Isabelle/HOL's code generator to output Rust code, while *Rust2Isabelle* leverages the Charon + Aeneas framework to derive Isabelle/HOL models directly from Rust source code. At the application layer, we have formally modeled and verified correctness properties of critical components within the Solana blockchain platform using Isabelle/HOL.

Looking forward, our research will pursue two main directions. The first is to develop a formal specification language for Rust, accompanied by tool support for translating these specifications into Isabelle/HOL for further verification. The second is to verify the correctness of the translation passes between Rust and Isabelle/HOL, for instance, through translation validation techniques.

Are Dynamic Fault Trees Essentially Agent-Based Models? A Vision from Maintenance Optimization

Marielle Stoelinga[1,2]

[1] Formal Methods and Tools, University of Twente, Enschede, the Netherlands
m.i.a.stoelinga@utwente.nl
[2] Department of Software Science, Radboud University, Nijmegen, the Netherlands

Abstract. Fault trees are a classical formalism for dependability analysis. Their extensions—for example dynamic fault trees and fault maintenance trees—incorporate temporal order, spare management, inspections, and repairs. I will argue that such models are, to some extend, *agent-based models*: components and maintenance policies behave as autonomous agents whose interactions generate emergent availability and cost.

Keywords: Fault trees · Dynamic fault trees · Fault maintenance trees · Agent-based modeling · Statistical model checking

1 Introduction

Fault Trees Analysis. Fault trees (FTs) are a long-standing, industry-standard technique for dependability analysis [1, 7, 8]. They describe how basic events (component failures) combine through logical gates to cause a system-level failure. Classical FTs are static and combinatorial, focusing on minimal cut sets and probability calculations. Over time, many extensions have emerged. This paper considers two important extensions: *Dynamic fault trees (DFTs)* enrich the formalism with temporal and causal operators such as priority gates, spares, and functional dependencies, enabling the modeling of sequence- and order-sensitive failures [2, 3]. *Fault maintenance trees (FMTs)* further extend the approach by incorporating component degradation phases, inspection modules, and repair strategies, making it possible to analyze and optimize reliability-centered maintenance policies [4, 5].

Fault Tree Extensions as Agent-based Models. I argue that extended FTs (DFTs and FMTs) are ABMs in disguise. Components, spares, and maintenance policies behave as autonomous entities; their local rules and stochastic timings give rise to emergent availability and cost. In earlier work [4–6], I have modeled these DFTs and FMTs as a network of probabilistic timed automata and used statistical model checking to compare several maintenance strategies. In this paper, I will showcase the agent perspective through a railroad maintenance case study, demonstrating how FTs-as-ABMs enrich both dependability modeling and formal methods.

References

1. IEC 61025: Fault tree analysis (FTA) (2006). Standard
2. Boudali, H., Crouzen, P., Stoelinga, M.: Dynamic fault tree analysis using input/output interactive Markov chains. In: Proceedings DSN. IEEE (2007)
3. Dugan, J.B., Bavuso, S.J., Boyd, M.A.: Dynamic fault-tree models for fault-tolerant computer systems. In: IEEE Transactions on Reliability, vol. 41, pp. 363–377 (1992)
4. Ruijters, E., Guck, D., Drolenga, P., Stoelinga, M.: Fault maintenance trees: Reliability centered maintenance via statistical model checking. In: Proceedings RAMS. IEEE (2016)
5. Ruijters, E., Guck, D., van Noort, M., Stoelinga, M.: Reliability-centered maintenance of the electrically insulated railway joint via fault tree analysis: A practical experience report. In: Proceedings DSN (2016)
6. Ruijters, E.J.J., Guck, D., Drolenga, P., Peters, M., Stoelinga, M.: Maintenance analysis and optimization via statistical model checking: Evaluating a train pneumatic compressor. In: Agha, G., Van Houdt, B. (eds.) Quantitative Evaluation of Systems. QEST 2016. LNCS, vol. 9826, pp. 331–347. Springer, Cham (2016). https://doi.org/10.1007/978-3-319-43425-4_22
7. Stoelinga, M., Ruijters, E., Krčál, P.: Concise Guide to Fault Tree Analysis: Models, Methods and Algorithms. Springer, Cham (2025). To appear
8. Vesely, W.E., Goldberg, F.F., Roberts, N.H., Haasl, D.F.: Fault Tree Handbook with Aerospace Applications. NASA Office of Safety and Mission Assurance (2002)

Contents

Formal Verification of Physical Layer Security Protocols for Next-Generation Communication Networks

Kangfeng Ye[1(✉)], Roberto Metere[1], Jim Woodcock[1,2,3], and Poonam Yadav[1]

[1] University of York, York, UK
{kangfeng.ye,roberto.metere,jim.woodcock,poonam.yadav}@york.ac.uk
[2] Southwest University, Chongqing, China
[3] Aarhus University, Aarhus, Denmark

Abstract. Formal verification is crucial for ensuring the robustness of security protocols against adversarial attacks. The Needham-Schroeder protocol, a foundational authentication mechanism, has been extensively studied, including its integration with Physical Layer Security (PLS) techniques such as watermarking and jamming. Recent research has used ProVerif to verify these mechanisms in terms of secrecy. However, the ProVerif-based approach limits the ability to improve understanding of security beyond verification results. To overcome these limitations, we re-model the same protocol using an Isabelle formalism that generates sound animation, enabling interactive and automated formal verification of security protocols. Our modelling and verification framework is generic and highly configurable, supporting both cryptography and PLS. For the same protocol, we have conducted a comprehensive analysis (secrecy and authenticity in four different eavesdropper locations under both passive and active attacks) using our new web interface. Our findings not only successfully reproduce and reinforce previous results on secrecy but also reveal an uncommon but expected outcome: authenticity is preserved across all examined scenarios, even in cases where secrecy is compromised. We have proposed a PLS-based Diffie-Hellman protocol that integrates watermarking and jamming, and our analysis shows that it is secure for deriving a session key with required authentication. These highlight the advantages of our novel approach, demonstrating its robustness in formally verifying security properties beyond conventional methods.

Keywords: Physical Layer Security · Formal Verification · Watermarking and Jamming · Needham-Schroeder Protocol · Diffie-Hellman Protocol · Communicating Sequential Processes · Isabelle/HOL

1 Introduction

Classic cryptographic methods [27] assume the computational hardness of inverting one-way trapdoor functions (e.g., prime factoring or discrete logarithm) and the limited computational power of adversaries. Adversaries that can use a sufficiently powerful quantum computer would employ techniques based on Shor's

É. André et al. (Eds.): ICFEM 2025, LNCS 16229, pp. 1–21, 2026.
https://doi.org/10.1007/978-981-95-4213-0_1

algorithm [38] to break (invert) the above functions efficiently. As quantum computers are currently limited in the number of qubits required to attack deployed systems, a temporary mitigation is to use longer keys, which necessitate more complex key generation and management. This extra complexity will also need more computational power and cause delays, translating into a waste of resources and making it difficult or even impossible to be deployed in resource-constrained, power-limited, or latency-sensitive devices, typical of next-generation networks, such as 6G. Modern networks, indeed, demand enhanced security requirements [33] for highly diverse applications. An example are demands for strict quality of service (QoS), such as ultra-low latency and extreme high reliability (e.g., for extended reality and remote surgery), highly dynamic and heterogeneous wireless networks, massive number of low-cost Internet of Things (IoT) sensor devices, and evolving threats from Machine Learning (ML) and Artificial Intelligent (AI) in 6G, Physical Layer Security (PLS) [30,49] is emerging as a complementary approach to add an extra layer security. In this context, providing security guarantees at the physical layer significantly reduces the need for the above complications.

PLS aims to secure wireless communication at the physical layer (the lowest network layer) by exploiting the inherent characteristics and randomness of the wireless communication channel itself, such as fading, noise, interference, dispersion, and diversity. PLS is based on information-theoretic security or unconditional security, a paradigm of security that focuses on the fundamental limits of information leakage as defined by information theory [37]. It aims to provide security that is provably unbreakable regardless of the eavesdropper's computational resources, such as Shannon's perfect secrecy [37], weak secrecy [42] and strong secrecy [12] (or statistical independence and asymptotically secure). PLS can resist some physical layer attacks such as spoofing, eavesdropping, and jamming (while conventional cryptography is not able to do so), can be keyless [23] (so no complex key management), and is quantum-resistant (because it is not based on computational hardness). Additionally, it has low computational complexity and latency, making it intrinsically suitable for IoT devices and heterogeneous wireless networks in 6G.

While a large amount of work in PLS focuses on secrecy, PLS techniques for achieving authentication have also received considerable attention. For example, Soderi et al. [41] proposed the watermark-based blind physical layer security (WBPLSec) approach to achieve both secrecy and message integrity (i.e., authenticity with proper protocols). The method combines watermarking [11,24], where the sender embeds a watermark or authentication information in a content signal to create a covert channel based on a shared secret, with jamming, where the legitimate receiver selectively interferes with parts of the signal so that only it can recover the message while eavesdroppers cannot.

Notwithstanding its considerable potential, formal verification of PLS mechanisms constitutes an underdeveloped area of research. Traditional cryptographic security protocols have benefited from formal verification with useful tools such as FDR [17], Isabelle [34], Maude-NPA [15], AVISPA [2], ProVerif [8], and Tamarin-prover [3], (1) to discover attacks [1,26]; (2) to identify missing or weak assumptions [5]; (3) to propose fixes or improvements to protocols [5,26,29]; and

(4) to guarantee correctness [4,6]. These formal security analysis methods primarily focus on higher-layer cryptographic protocols. PLS protocols, however, operate in the lower-layer physical layers and use different security mechanisms from cryptography. Therefore, it is highly beneficial to formally verify PLS protocols before their vulnerabilities and missing assumptions are discovered after their deployment.

A recent work [10] has leveraged ProVerif [8], a security verification tool, to verify the secrecy of a WBPLSec-based variant (called NSWJ) of the Needham-Schroeder protocol [32]. Their verification approach, however, is carried out by formal verification experts in that specific language. *Protocol designers still cannot use the approach to inspect and verify the protocols by themselves.* In this regard, our recent work [48] provides more accessibility to formal verification through sound animation. This limits the intervention of experts and allows designers to either manually explore or automatically verify cryptographic protocols. In such a workflow, formal experts use a variant of Communicating Sequential Processes (CSP) [20,36], called the Interaction Trees [44] (ITrees) based CSP (ITrCSP) [16,46], to model security protocols in the theorem prover Isabelle/HOL [34]. Then, Isabelle can automatically generate Haskell code that, when compiled, provides a lightweight model checker or animator requiring no more expert intervention. However, this work only supports the Dolev-Yao attack model [14], the ad-hoc framework for each protocol (each protocol has a different fundamental message theory), and a terminal interface (users at least need a PC or workstation to run animators). Physical layer security is defined in terms of a different attacker model, so we extended [48] to model it.

Based on the context, this work is guided by the following research questions: **RQ1** (PLS): How to extend the ITrCSP-based framework to support PLS and its related attack model for verification? **RQ2** (Generic and generalisation) Can the ITrCSP-based framework be general to model all different attack models and security protocols in a generic message theory? **RQ3** (Case studies) What different insights can we get if we conduct a more thorough analysis of NSWJ? Can WBPLSec be used to implement the Diffie-Hellman algorithm? What benefits can PLS bring? **RQ4** (Accessibility) Can the framework be made even more accessible to a wider range of stakeholders, such as non-professional groups like students and the general public?

In this paper, we present our work that addresses these questions. Our novel contributions here are as follows: (1) a general sound animation framework to support both classic cryptography and PLS techniques, built on a generic and polymorphic message theory; (2) a more scalable implementation of intruder's message inference rules by constraining build-up messages into all the possible messages that legitimate agents can receive, instead of the naive implementation of [48] to build up all possible messages from inference rules; (3) a comprehensive analysis of NSWJ by considering not only secrecy but also authenticity in both passive and active attacks when the adversary could be within or out of the jamming ranges of each legitimate participant, to confirm the result of secrecy with [10] but contradicts the interpretation of authenticity from [10]; (4) a new WBPLSec-based DH protocol (DHWJ) to fix the man-in-the-middle attack and achieve authenticity; (5) a new web interface to make our animation more accessible and user-friendly, in addition to the terminal interface. All definitions in this paper are mechanised and show an icon () that links to the corresponding repository artefacts[1].

The remainder of this paper is organised as follows. We review related work in Sect. 2, introduce sound animation and WBPLSec in Sect. 3, and present the modelling of security protocols in our generic framework in Sect. 4. And in Sect. 5, we describe the modelling of NSWJ and DHWJ in our framework, then present the web interface and discuss verification results in Sect. 6. Finally, in Sect. 7, we conclude and discuss future work.

2 Related Work

Formal Verification of Security Protocols. Model checking and theorem proving tools, such as Casper [25], FDR [17,26], Isabelle [34,35], Maude-NPA [15], AVISPA [2], ProVerif [8], and Tamarin-prover [3], have been commonly used to formally verify security protocols. These tools require users to have an in-depth level of knowledge in formal verification, and thus are not accessible to general protocol designers. Instead, the work presented in this paper provides a more accessible approach using sound animation, allowing protocol designers to interact, inspect, and verify protocols through interfaces, as well as to perform automated verification. Similar to our work, SPAN [9] is an animation tool and can be used by designers. But its soundness is not guaranteed.

Formal Verification of PLS. Formal verification for physical-layer security protocols is a relatively new area. To the best of our knowledge, the work from Costa et al. [10] is the only one that focuses on this topic. In their work, the standard ProVerif language was extended with functions to model and analyse WBPLSec-based protocols symbolically. Furthermore, an attack model for WBPLSec was implemented, and their work demonstrated that NSWJ with WBPLSec is secure (in terms of secrecy) against active attackers within the jamming range and insecure otherwise. Their work formally demonstrates the sufficiency of watermarking and jamming to ensure secrecy and authenticity. Inspired by [10], our work verifies WBPLSec and its based NSWJ protocol, in the same scenarios and under the same common principles, such as its attack model and assumptions. Conversely, our work goes beyond to comprehensively analyse all *four scenarios*, where the eavesdropper is located at different positions in terms of Alice's and Bob's jamming ranges, under both *passive and active attacks*. The analysis provides previously undiscovered results: *authenticity is preserved even when the eavesdropper is outside the jamming range (and thus, the loss of secrecy)*. We also propose a new variant (DHWJ) of DH, based on WBPLSec, and conduct a comprehensive analysis of it. The other benefit of our work, if compared to theirs, is the *accessibility* of verification to protocol designers. It is worth noting that *the capability to understand and debug protocols* is crucial for protocol designers too, especially in new areas such as PLS.

[1] We assume basic knowledge of Isabelle/HOL from interested readers to understand these definitions and theorems.

Table 1. Comparison of related work where ○ for no, ● for yes, and * for comments.

Related work	Primitives		Attack		Sound	Verification				UI	
	Crypt	PLS	DY	PLS		DBG	UGV	Reach	Feas	Term	Web
Tamarin	●	○	●	○	●*	○	○	●	○	●	●*
ProVerif	●	○	●	○	●*	○	○	●	○	●	○
Costa et al. [10]	●	●	●	●	●*	○	○	●	○	●	○
SPAN [9]	●	○	●	○	○	●	○	●	○	●	●
Ye et al. [48]	●	○	●	○	●	●	●	●	●	●	○
This work	●	●	●	●	●	●	●	●	●	●	●

Acronym Crypt: cryptography; Attack: attack models; DY: Dolev-Yao; DBG: debugging; Reach: reachability check; Feas: feasibility check; Term: terminal interface; UGV: user-guided verification.

As a result, we demonstrate how our analysis facilitates a deeper understanding of the protocol, as it contradicts one of the conclusions in [10], as mentioned previously.

Sound Animation. For another comparison, ITrCSP has been applied to animate robotic control software [46] modelled in RoboChart [31,45] and security protocols [48], and demonstrate functional correctness through manual interaction and automatic checking. Our work is also based on ITrCSP and extends [48] in three aspects: a general modelling framework, the WBPLSec security protocol, and a web user interface. The sound animation approach presented in [48] primarily focuses on two case studies. Its modelling framework in ITrCSP and Isabelle is not generic. Thus, every protocol has an ad-hoc message theory in Isabelle. Our work presents a generic and polymorphic message theory, enabling all protocols to share a common message framework. Additionally, each protocol can be instantiated for specific configurations. This will be discussed in Sect. 4. We also extend the modelling framework to support a new attack model for WBPLSec in addition to the Dolev-Yao model. WBPLSec-based protocols, such as NSWJ and DHWJ, can be modelled and verified in the same framework. From an interface aspect, we develop a new web interface to allow users to easily configure properties, verify, and view their interactions with models and counterexamples.

Summary. Table 1 summarises the comparison of this work with others in modelling primitives and attack models, soundness, verification, and interfaces. It is worth noting that (1) the claimed soundness in Taramin and ProVerif is not formally verified, unlike our work where the soundness is guaranteed by Isabelle/HOL; and (2) Taramin has a web interface for its interactive proof mode, but not intended for designers.

3 Background

ITrCSP and Sound Animation. Animation models interactions of reactive systems with their environment through events. We utilise Interaction Trees [44]

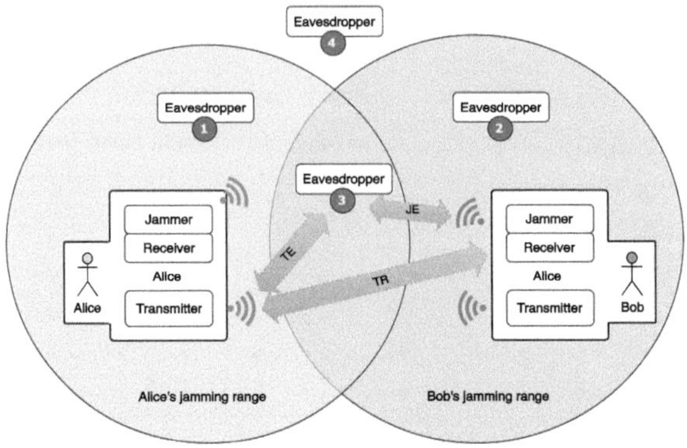

Fig. 1. An illustration of WBPLSec with two legitimate agents (Alice and Bob) and an eavesdropper in different spatial locations in terms of the agents' jamming ranges. There are four combinations of locations, denoted as Eve1, Eve2, Eve3, and Eve4.

(ITrees), which allow for a formal specification to be associated with both abstract and executable denotational semantics [43], as coinductive tree structures. This enables the construction of denotational and operational semantics, facilitating both reasoning and implementation. Using ITrees, Foster et al. [16,46] gave semantics to a deterministic version of CSP process algebra [20,36], called ITree-based CSP or ITrCSP, and mechanised it in Isabelle/HOL [34] to allow automatic generation of Haskell code from a CSP model for animation. The basic processes and operators of ITrCSP are summarised in [48, Table 1]. Further details about their definitions, semantics, and implementation in Isabelle/HOL can be found in [16,46].

The animation is sound thanks to ITree's executable semantics and Isabelle's code generator [19], which translates executable ITree definitions in HOL logic to target functional languages (such as Haskell). Soundness is not a formally proved property here, but the simple and unbroken link from operational semantics of CSP, to (corecursive) definitions of CSP operators in ITrees, and the final Haskell code through an equational logic-based code generator (all in Isabelle/HOL) ensures its soundness. We illustrate this link in [47, Appendix A].

PLS: Watermarking and Jamming. Soderi et al. [41] proposed WBPLSec, which combines watermarking [11,24] with jamming (based on iJAM [18] but improved the data rate from half to full) for secure communication. During the transmission, the source clear message and the watermarked signal (from a part of the source message) are transmitted in two independent paths, either embedded both signals in a narrow-band channel [41] or two different visible lights (the blue light and the red light) in visible light communication (VLC) [40]. Figure 1 illustrates the concept of WBPLSec schematically. We consider two legitimate agents, Alice and Bob, and one eavesdropper (Eve) in various locations (Eve 1, 2, 3, and 4) in terms of the jamming ranges (the two large circles in the diagram) of Alice and Bob. Each of the legitimate agents is equipped with a transmitter and a receiver which contains a jammer. There are three kinds of links depicted in the diagram: TR for the transmitter-receiver link, TE for the transmitter-eavesdropper link, and JE for the jammer-eavesdropper link. Considering a scenario where Alice wants to send a confidential message m to Bob, the WBPLSec approach works as follows:

S1. the transmitter of Alice modulates m to get the host regulated signal x_S of length N, of which the first N_w samples x_w are selected to use direct sequence spread spectrum (DSSS) for watermarking (by using the pseudo-noise PN code c_w to spread the x_w to decorrelate the host signal with the watermark later) to get the spread-spectrum (SS) watermark w;
S2. the transmitter embeds w in x_S to get x'_S and sends it;
S3. then the receiver Bob uses his jammer to jam M (where $M \leq N_w$) samples over x'_S to get an intentionally interfered and corrupt $\hat{x}_S$;
S4. Bob can extract the watermark $\hat{x}_w$ from the received signal (via the TR link) by using an additional DSSS demodulator based on the same PN code c_w;
S5. Bob's receiver then removes corrupted jammed samples from $\hat{x}_S$ and replaces them with unjammed samples from $\hat{x}_w$;
S6. if Eve, such as Eve 2, is within the jamming range of Bob, Eve is not able to construct clean messages from $\hat{x}_S$ (received through the JE link) because she does not know c_w;
S7. otherwise, if Eve is out of the jamming range of Bob, she can receive the watermarked signal x'_S through the TE link and understand the clean message x_S.

To ensure secrecy and integrity, Alice and Bob share a common secret, N and c_w, beforehand and never send the secret over the network. Bob will use another PN code for his transmitter, which Alice is also aware of in advance.

The security of WBPLSec-based protocols is highly dependent on the location of the eavesdropper. To minimise the information leakage, the location of legitimate agents, their transmission and jamming powers need to be considered. One possible solution is to ensure that jamming fully covers the transmission area. This is feasible if the receiver (such as an edge node) is more powerful or visible light in VLC is restricted in an area (for example, by walls). Another solution is to use reconfigurable intelligent surfaces (RIS) to dynamically direct transmission signals towards legitimate receivers and then direct jamming signals to cover that transmission area, thereby forming a secure region [39].

4 Modelling of Security Protocols

Our framework supports the symbolic modelling of both classic cryptographic and PLS protocols. The formalization of cryptography and the Dolev-Yao attack model [14] have already been described in [48]. For this reason, this section presents our formalization of PLS protocols in excruciating detail, instead of cryptography.

Assumptions. For WBPLSec, we assume

AS1. As a sender, each legitimate agent has a unique secret code used for watermarking.
AS2. As a receiver, each legitimate agent knows the unique secret codes which the corresponding senders use for watermarking, and the agent then uses the code to jam the communication from these senders.
AS3. The intruder (or Eve)[2] does not know or guess the secret codes that legitimate agents use for watermarking and jamming.
AS4. The intruder may have her code for watermarking, but her code is not known to any legitimate agents.
AS5. These secret codes are never transmitted over the network.

Network Model. A network model describes how different agents and the intruder communicate through proper (secure or public) channels. For WBPLSec, we employ a different network model than that used for cryptography [48] because watermarking and jamming differ from conventional cryptography: they establish a secure region (based on locations), whereas cryptography enforces security through encryption, hashing, and other primitives. In the new network model, each legitimate agent sends a watermarked message $wm = \mathsf{wat}(m, bA_w)$ using its watermarking bitmask bA_w (corresponding to the secret code, as with [10]). The intruder has no jammer because she always tends to hear more information instead of interfering, and will receive wm. Its receiver relays wm to Bob, and at the same time, it sends a jammed message $jm = \mathsf{jam}(wm, bB_j)$ (using Bob's jamming bitmask bB_j) to the main body of the intruder if the intruder is within the jamming range of Bob. Otherwise, the receiver sends wm to the intruder. This way, the intruder will hear the jammed and watermarked message or just the watermarked message, depending on her location. More details will be given later when we discuss the modelling of NSWJ using Fig. 3.

Attack Models and Inference Rules. In WBPLSec, Eve is usually passive. She captures transmitted signals and tries to learn more knowledge from them. In this paper, we also consider an active Eve who can send fake messages to legitimate agents. The information she can derive and the messages she can convey are controlled by inference rules based on her current knowledge. Such rules are defined in Table 2 where K, a set of messages, denotes Eve's current knowledge. Rules are divided into two groups: *breakdown* rules, where $(K \vdash_{\Downarrow} m)$ denotes a message m can be derived from K using one of member, unpairing, decryption, digital verify, watermarking, and jamming rules; and *build-up* rules, where $(K \vdash_{\Uparrow} m)$ denotes a message m can be derived from K using one of member, pairing, encryption, digital sign, and watermarking rules. We note that the Dolev-Yao cryptographic inference rules are also supported and included in the table to make our inference more general.

As with [10], $\mathsf{wat}(m, n) = \mathsf{wat}(m', n')$ only if $m = m'$ and $n = n'$. That means the same watermarked messages can be generated only if watermarking applies

[2] We use *Intruder* in the modelling of security protocols and only use *Eve* when discussing WBPLSec in general.

Table 2. Intruder message inference rules: breakdown and build-up rules.

Name	Id	Premises	Break down	Build up
Member	Mb	$m \in K$	$K \vdash_{\Downarrow} m$	$K \vdash_{\Uparrow} m$
Pairing	Pa	$m \in K \wedge m' \in K$		$K \vdash_{\Uparrow} (m, m')$
Unpairing	Up	$(m, m') \in K$	$K \vdash_{\Downarrow} m \wedge K \vdash_{\Downarrow} m'$	
Enc/Sign	Enc	$m \in K \wedge k \in K$		$K \vdash_{\Uparrow} \{m\}_k$
Dec/Verify	Dec	$\{m\}_k \in K \wedge k^{-1} \in K$	$K \vdash_{\Downarrow} m$	
Water-marking	Wat1	$\mathsf{wat}(m, b) \in K$	$K \vdash_{\Downarrow} m$	
	Wat2	$m \in K \wedge b \in K$		$K \vdash_{\Uparrow} \mathsf{wat}(m, b)$
Jamming	Jam	$\mathsf{jam}(\mathsf{wat}(m, b), b') \in K \wedge b' \in K \wedge \exists x \bullet b' \frown x = b$	$K \vdash_{\Downarrow} \mathsf{wat}(m, b)$	

to the same message using the same bitmask. Also, $\mathsf{jam}(m, 0) = m$ denotes that jamming using an empty bitmask is like no jamming. Particularly, the jamming rule defines that if jamming a watermarked message using the prefixing bitmask b' of the watermarking bitmask b, the watermarked message can be recovered when b' is known. Here, we treat a bitmask as a sequence of bits and use the sequence concatenation $\frown$ to establish that b' is the prefix of b. This corresponds to M and N_w in S3.

Informally, if the intruder sits within the jamming range of a receiver A, she can only hear jammed watermarked messages. According to AS3 and the inference rule Jam in Table 2, she cannot derive the watermarked messages from the learned messages. So, secrecy is preserved. However, if she sits outside the jamming range but still within the transmission range of the sender, she may still be able to hear watermarked messages. According to the Wat1 inference rule, she can derive clear messages from the watermarked messages. So, secrecy is violated. According to AS3, in both cases, message integrity is maintained because the intruder cannot forge a watermarked message without knowledge of its secret code. An active intruder can build up all messages from her knowledge using the build-up rules. And then she can fork or send these (possibly watermarked using her secret code) messages to the network. According to AS4, the messages are neither expected nor accepted by legitimate agents because the secret code is unknown to other agents. Indeed, there is little difference between passive and active attack models.

Message Data Types. We define a generic message type which is parametric in the sizes of various entities in messages, such as agents, nonces, keys, bitmasks, and modulo exponent bases. We require these entities to be finite for the sake of the executable nature of animation. This generic type is achieved through a data type `fsnat`, defined below, for a finite set of natural numbers. Consequently, each entity (from a finite set of n entities) can be numbered from 0 to $n - 1$.

```
typedef (overloaded) ('n::len) fsnat = "0..<LENGTH('n)::nat set"
```

The `fsnat` is a polymorphic type with one type variable `'n` of class `len`. The `len` class is equipped with a `LENGTH` function to get its size. So the new type `'n fsnat` is isomorphic to a finite set of natural numbers from 0 to the size of 'n minus 1. This type comes with a pair of functions nat_of_fsnat and fsnat_of_nat to convert from fsnat to a natural number or from a natural number to a fsnat. To facilitate the construction of such a 'n fsnat value, we define nmk () function to construct a 'n fsnat value from its input natural number x. Then a variety of data types can be defined using fsnat.

```
datatype ('n::len) dagent = Agent (ag:"'n fsnat") |Intruder |Server
datatype ('k::len,'s::len) dkey = Kp "fsnat['k]" | Ks "fsnat['s]"
datatype ('bm, 'bl) dbitmask = Null | Bm  "'bm fsnat" "'bl fsnat"
```

Participants or agents are modelled using 'n dagent where 'n is the number of legitimate Agents except an Intruder and a Server. In the definition, ag is a function to extract the agent number from an Agent. If such a function is applied to Intruder or Server, an exception will be raised in the generated code. Nonces (of type dnonce) and modulo exponent bases (dexprg) are just fsnat and their definitions are omitted here. Keys (of dkey) are either public by the constructor Kp or private by the constructor Ks.

Bitmasks (of type dbitmask) contain an additional Null for an empty bitmask. The type has two type variables 'bm and 'bl to represent the number of bitstrings and the maximum length of a bitstring used for watermarking or jamming. Additionally, this data type is instantiated to partial order, so any two bitmasks can be compared using $\leq$. And two bitmasks bm1 $\leq$ bm2 if either (1) bm1 is empty, or (2) both bm1 and bm2 are not empty (such as Bm b1 l1 and Bm b2 l2), their bitstrings are equal (b1=b2), and their lengths are less than or equal (l1$\leq$l2). This is to implement the abstract prefix relation in Table 2 to derive the watermarked message from its jammed counterpart.

Based on these types, a message type is defined below where only a few constructors are shown and the complete definition is given in [47, Appendix B].

```
datatype ('a, 'n, 'k, 's, 'g, 'bm, 'bl::len) dmsg = ...
  | MBitm   (mbm:"('bm, 'bl) dbitmask")                    b_m _ _
  | MWat    (mwm:"T dmsg") (mwb:"T dmsg")                 {|_|}^w_
  | MJam    (mjm:"T dmsg") (mjb:"T dmsg")                 {|_|}^j_
```

All messages for communication on channels are of the polymorphic type dmsg with 6 type variables to represent the numbers of agents ('a), nonces ('n), public keys ('k), private keys ('s), modulo exponent bases ('g), and bitmasks ('b). T in the definition above is a shorthand for ('a, 'n, 'k, 's, 'g, 'bm, 'bl::len). Messages can be agent's identities of type dagent (with the constructor MAg), nonces (with MNon), public and private keys (with MK), pairing of two messages (with MPair), modulo exponent bases (with MExpg), modulo exponentiation (with MModExp), bitmasks (with MBitm), watermarking (with MWat), and jamming (with MJam). To simplify and shortening formulas, we introduce the notations $\langle m_1, m_2\rangle$, $g_m\ n$, m^e, $b_m\ nl$, $\{\!|m|\!\}_b^w$, and $\{\!|m|\!\}_b^j$ to denote them respectively.

Message Inferences. In Isabelle, we define a function breakm () for the breakdown rules in Table 2 to derive a list of messages from a given list for the sake of implementation in Haskell. The `breakm` is defined on another function `break_lst`. We omit the details of these functions here for simplicity.

For the build-up rules, [48] uses `buildm` to construct all possible messages by these rules. The number of these messages is usually huge. It is time-consuming and space-consuming, and has a significant impact on performance. To address this issue, we propose a solution that considers only the possible acceptable messages from all legitimate agents and disregards other unacceptable messages. This is a reasonable assumption because the transmission of these unacceptable messages will not change the behaviour of all legitimate agents.

For the approach, we first define a function `buildable m ms` to return whether a message `m` can be constructed from a set `ms` of messages using the build-up rules. Then `filter_buildable xs ms` returns a list of messages, of which each message is from `xs` and buildable from `ms`. This improves the inference performance dramatically in animation.

Generally, when the intruder hears a new message, she attempts to break it down using her existing knowledge and updates it accordingly. Then, if modelling an active attack, she will construct all buildable messages from her up-to-date knowledge using the `filter_buildable` function and send them to the network.

Signals. We declare signals to specify properties. The definition `dsig` is the same as [48] and omitted here.

Channels. Channels for communication are grouped in a definition `chan` below, where seven channels (with their corresponding message types) are declared.

```
datatype T chan =
  env  :: "'a dagent×'a dagent"
  send :: "'a dagent×'a dagent×'a dagent×T dmsg"
  recv :: "'a dagent×'a dagent×'a dagent×T dmsg"
  cjam :: "T dmsg"    sig   :: "('a, 'n) dsig"
  leak :: "T dmsg"    terminate :: "unit"
```

We extend the traditional channels `send` and `recv` in [48] with an additional component such as `M` in `send!(A, M, B, m)` to denote the medium through which the message is sent or received. If `M` is the `Intruder`, then it denotes a message through a public and insecure channel. Otherwise, it implies the use of a private channel (so the intruder cannot hear such a message). With this additional component, we can model both public and private channels. And `hear` and `fake` (or `relay`) are just synonyms to `send` and `recv`. The channel `cjam` relates to jamming communications. The channels `sig`, `leak`, and `terminate` are used to signal the stages which the protocol is on. Eventually, they are used to specifying security protocols. For example, secrecy is specified using `leak` events and authenticity is specified through signals `StartProt` and `EndProt` on channel `sig`. The `terminate` event indicates a successful completion of a protocol run.

In brief, our formalization establishes structured inference rules to determine what an intruder can know or do, while models, watermarking, and jamming restrict their capabilities through physical-layer security techniques.

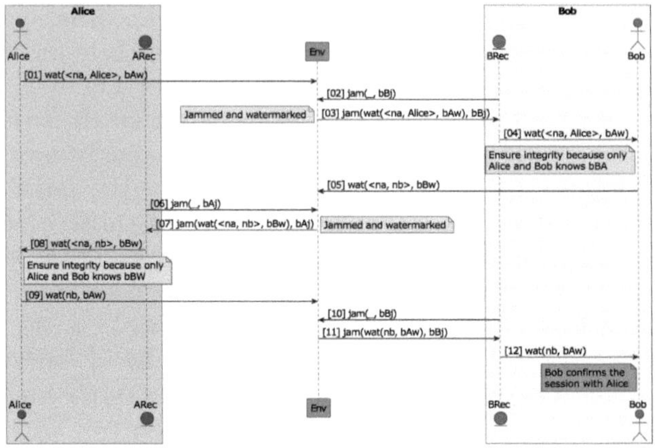

Fig. 2. The messages between Alice and Bob for NSWJ.

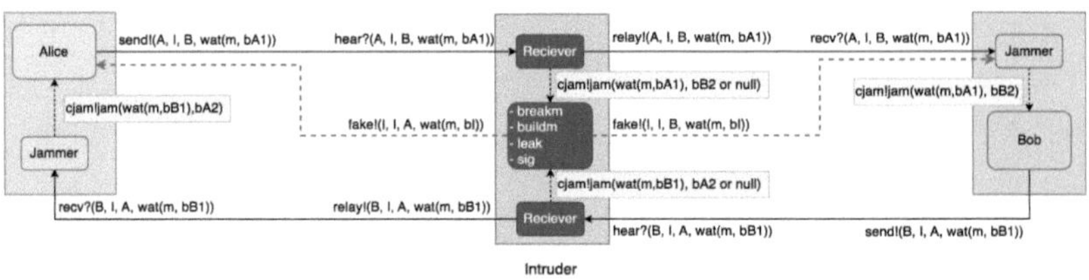

Fig. 3. The modelling of NSWJ in ITree-based CSP.

5 Needham-Schroeder and Diffie-Hellman Protocols

The Needham-Schroeder protocol [32] is used to establish mutual authentication between two parties (such as Alice and Bob) over an insecure or public network, utilizing either symmetric or asymmetric encryption. In this paper, we consider a variant of NSPK, referred to as NSWJ here, which utilizes watermarking and jamming (instead of asymmetric encryption) to achieve secrecy and authenticity, similar to [10]. We illustrate the message exchange between Alice and Bob for both NSPK and NSWJ below, where the asymmetric encryption in NSPK is replaced by watermarking in NSWJ.

$$
\begin{array}{ll}
\quad\quad NSPK & \quad\quad NSWJ \\
A \rightarrow B : \{\!|(na, Alice)|\!\}^{a}_{pk_B} & A \rightarrow B : \{\!|(na, Alice)|\!\}^{w}_{bA_w} \\
B \rightarrow A : \{\!|(na, nb)|\!\}^{a}_{pk_A} & B \rightarrow A : \{\!|(na, nb)|\!\}^{w}_{bB_w} \\
A \rightarrow B : \{\!|nb|\!\}^{a}_{pk_B} & A \rightarrow B : \{\!|nb|\!\}^{w}_{bA_w}
\end{array}
$$

We further illustrate the detailed message exchange in NSWJ in Fig. 2, where ARec and BRec represent the receivers of Alice and Bob, respectively. Alice starts the session by sending a watermarked message (01) to the environment Env (i.e., the secure region) containing a nonce na and her identity, using her watermarking bitmask. BRec starts to jam (02) Alice's watermarked message using Bob's jamming bitmask and receives the (03) jammed watermarked message from the environment. BRec can recover the watermarked message because BRec knows the jamming code and sends it (04) to Bob. Bob can confirm this message is from Alice because it is watermarked using Alice's bitmask. Afterwards, Bob sends (05) back Alice's nonce na and his nonce nb to Env. Similarly, ARec will jam (06) the message, receive (07) the jammed and watermarked message, recover the watermarked message from Bob, and send (08) it to Alice. Alice confirms the integrity of the message and sends (09) nb back to Bob. BRec will jam (10), receive (11), recover, and send (12) it to Bob. Finally, Bob can confirm he has established a secure session with Alice if Eve is only within the jamming range of Alice and Bob.

Figure 3 schematically depicts the modelling of NSWJ in ITrCSP. We model Alice, Bob, and the intruder as three processes. Both Alice and Bob contain a jamming receiver (or jammer), and the intruder includes a receiver (Fig. 3 splits the receiver into two elements for better visualisation of connections). Alice and Bob `send` messages to the intruder and receive messages on the `recv` channel from the intruder. The intruder `hears` messages that are sent by Alice or Bob and can `fake` messages (if he is an active attacker) that Alice and Bob will receive. The receiver of the intruder will relay the received watermarked messages to intended agents (such as Bob), and jam the messages using the bitmasks (such as `bB2`) of their intended agents (or a `Null` bitmask) if he is in the jamming range (or out of the range) and send the jammed messages to the intruder through the `cjam` channel. While the intended agents receive the relayed watermarked messages, the jammer jams the messages using his jamming bitmask (such as `bB2`) and sends the messages to the agents (such as Bob). This way, we can flexibly model the location of the intruder, and his location will not affect the message Bob receives, because the intruder's receiver will jam the watermarked messages accordingly based on his location. We note that the `cjam` channel is represented by a dashed line, indicating that jamming is an internal behaviour and will be hidden from the modelled protocol in CSP.

The main body of the intruder, represented as a box in the middle, describes its main behaviour: breaking down heard messages, building up new fake messages, and sending them to the network (if it is active), leaking secrets if the secrets are within its knowledge, or dealing with signals.

To model the protocol in Isabelle using ITrCSP, we first define a *configuration* of this protocol, which includes the instantiation of message types as follows.

```
type_synonym max_agents = 2; max_nonces = 4; max_bm = 3;
   max_bm_len = 2; max_pks = 1; max_sks = 1; max_expg = 1
type_synonym dagent = "max_agents dagent"
```

First, we define type synonyms, such as `max_agents`, as a numeral type 2 and use these synonyms to instantiate polymorphic data types, `dagent`, etc. We give the same names to type synonyms of these concrete types. When we refer to these types in the rest of the paper, we mean the specific types mentioned in this section. In this protocol, we define three bitmasks, each with a length of up to 2 (`max_bm_len`). The protocol is configured below.

```
abbreviation "Alice ≡ Agent (nmk 0) :: dagent"
abbreviation "Bob ≡ Agent (nmk 1) :: dagent"
abbreviation "nonmap ≡ {Alice↦ nmk 0, Bob↦nmk 1, Intruder↦nmk 2}"
abbreviation "bmmap ≡ {Alice↦Bm (nmk 0) (nmk 1),
  Bob↦Bm (nmk 1) (nmk 1), Intruder↦Bm (nmk 2) (nmk 1)}"
```

Such a configuration maps the legitimate agents Alice and Bob to the agent, nonce, and bitmask indices, where the constructors like `nmk` are used to make an instance of `fsnat`. The location of an intruder is defined in terms of jamming ranges and configured using the map below.

```
datatype deve = Eve1 | Eve2 | Eve3 | Eve4
abbreviation "evemap eve ≡ case eve of
   Eve1 ⇒ {Alice↦T, Bob↦F} | Eve2 ⇒ {Alice↦F, Bob↦T} |
```

The `evemap` configures the location (among four, see Fig. 1) of the intruder (`eve`) based on where the intruder is within the jamming range of Alice and Bob (where `T` for True and `F` for False). Then we use these configurations to define the jamming process (`jamming`) for Alice and Bob, the jamming process (`jammingI`) for the intruder, the process (`PAlice`) for Alice, the process (`PBob`) for Bob, and the process (`PIntruder`) for Intruder where her initial knowledge is taken into account. We discuss the definition of `PAlice` more below and omit the details of other processes here for simplicity.

$$PAlice \mathrel{\widehat=} \big(\big(Initiator(\_) \parallel_{jevents} jamming(\_) \big) \setminus jevents \big) \llbracket \{ Terminate \} \rhd skip$$

`PAlice` is a parallel composition of an `Initiator` (see [48] for details) for the behaviour of Alice, and `jamming` over the jamming events (`jevents`) with these events hidden. This process can be terminated using the CSP exception operator over the `Terminate` channel. Finally, the protocol NSWJ is composed of the processes for Alice, Bob, and the intruder in response to appropriate events.

$$\mathtt{NSWJ} \mathrel{\widehat=} \big(PAlice \parallel_{TermEvent} PBob \big) \parallel_{ABIEvents} PIntruder$$

This is the process used to generate an animator for the protocol.

The Diffie-Hellman (DH) [13] protocol aims to establish a shared secret between two agents using agreed-upon information over an insecure network. It is commonly used to derive new session keys. DH is based on modular exponentiation $g^a \bmod p$ where g is the base, a is the power or exponent, and p is the modulus. In [48], we model the DH with three messages: (1) $A \rightarrow B : g^{na}$ and B computes $k_B = g^{na^{nb}}$, (2) $B \rightarrow A : g^{nb}$ and A computes $k_A = g^{nb^{na}}$, (3) $A \rightarrow B : \{\!|t|\!\}^s_{k_A}$ where t is a secret and the superscript s denotes a symmetric encryption, and B decrypts it using k_B to get t. Using sound animation, it is easy to demonstrate a man-in-the-middle attack where secrecy is not preserved.

Next, we consider a variant of DH, called DHWJ, which uses watermarking and jamming. It is composed of four messages: (1) $A \to B : \{\!|g^{na}|\!\}^{w}_{bA_w}$ and B computes $k_B = g^{na^{nb}}$, (2) $B \to A : \{\!|g^{nb}|\!\}^{w}_{bB_w}$ and A computes $k_A = g^{nb^{na}}$, (3) $A \to B : \{\!|\{\!|t|\!\}^{s}_{k_A}|\!\}^{w}_{bA_w}$ and B decrypts it using k_B to get t, (4) $B \to A : \{\!|\{\!|t|\!\}^{s}_{k_B}|\!\}^{w}_{bB_w}$ and A decrypts it to confirm B knows t. The message exchange and protocol configuration () are similar to those of NSWJ and are omitted here for simplicity.

6 Verification and Evaluation

In Isabelle, we can automatically generate the Haskell code for the NSWJ and DHWJ protocols. To facilitate the automatic or manual exploration of the design to check secrecy and authenticity, we developed a new web interface[3] in addition to the terminal interface (as presented in [48]) to directly visualise sequence diagrams of animation and counterexamples (attacks), as illustrated in [47, Appendix C]. The verification algorithm underneath interfaces is the depth-first exploration of the event space up to specified steps for a protocol design. The terminal interface provides users with manual exploration, automatically exhaustive or random reachability check in terms of trace properties, or feasibility check of a specified sequence of events or trace. Random exploration and feasibility check are not yet implemented in the web interface. It, however, supports sessions and enables designers to (simultaneously) manually explore or exhaustively check reachability and view counterexamples visually in sequence diagrams, as shown in Fig. 2. Graphical visualisation of protocols as sequence diagrams has been demonstrated in [28]; however, their approach is design-oriented rather than analysis-oriented, and their diagrams are manually created, whereas our diagrams are dynamically updated. We could not extend it, as manually created diagrams lack the precise execution semantics needed for automated visualisation and attack simulation.

While the web interface provides no more verification features than the terminal interface functionally, the diagrammatic view of counterexamples helps designers easily follow their interactions with animators and identify problems. Additionally, verification is more easily configured through the web interface, allowing for the selection of intruder location and properties to check. For both protocols, the web interface will enable users to select which location of Eve to animate and verify, manually animate the protocol, automatically verify secrecy and correspondence properties such as authentication, or combine manual exploration with an automatic check for user-guided verification. More details about the web interface can be found in [47, Appendix C].

Using the interfaces, we analysed NSWJ and DHWJ, along with their cryptographic counterparts, NSPK3 and DH, in terms of secrecy and authenticity. Table 3 shows verification results in the presence of an active intruder and NSWJ

[3] The source code is available at https://github.com/RandallYe/Animation_of_Security_Protocols/tree/master/animation-web-ui.

Table 3. Comparison of verification results: NSPK vs. NSWJ, and DHWJ vs. DH in the presence of an active intruder, except the specific NSWJ† for a passive intruder.

Properties	NSPK	NSWJ				NSWJ Passive†				DH	DHWJ			
		E1	E2	E3	E4	E1	E2	E3	E4		E1	E2	E3	E4
Secrecy	○	○	○	●	○	○	○	●	○	○	○	○	●	○
Authenticity for Alice	●	●	●	●	●	●	●	●	●	○	●	●	●	●
Authenticity for Bob	○	●	●	●	●	●	●	●	●	○	●	●	●	●

in the presence of a passive intruder. The results of NSPK and DH are already discussed in [48]. It is not surprising that secrecy is only satisfied in the scenario of Eve3 (E3 in the table) because Eve can only hear jammed messages from both Alice and Bob (so she cannot derive clear messages). Authenticity for both Alice and Bob is preserved when using WBPLSec due to the watermarking feature. We note that DH is not an authentication protocol and usually other mechanisms such as digital signature, hash, trusted certificate authority (CA), and message authentication code (MAC) are required to achieve both secrecy and authenticity such as in the Unified model and MQV [7], SIGMA [21] and HMQV [22]. With PLS, we demonstrate that both properties can be achieved without such a mechanism, regardless of Eve's location.

While the ProVerif analysis in [10] uses an active intruder, we consider both active and passive intruders. Our animation shows that whether the intruder is active or passive makes no difference in terms of secrecy and authenticity. If a property is held in the passive model, it is also held in the active model and vice versa. This is related to As4 where neither Alice nor Bob knows the Intruder's watermarking bitmask, and therefore neither Alice nor Bob will accept the watermarked (inferred) message from the Intruder. This should not be surprising because watermarking can ensure message integrity.

Although the result of NSWJ in [10] is correct and consistent with ours, we argue that their speculation "WBPLSec, in which the receiver, besides the sender, also plays an active role in the communication, so keeping authenticity between the enrolled parties" is not accurate. It is recognized that the real problem with NSPK is its second message $\langle na, nb \rangle$, sent by Bob to Alice, which contains no information about Bob's identity (authenticity is not guaranteed). This permits a man-in-the-middle to forward such a message to Alice, making her believe it originated from the intruder (while Bob generated it). To support that, the fix [26] appends Bob's identity to the second message. We conclude that NSWJ ensures authenticity not due to jamming, but instead to watermarking, thanks to its implicit integrity guarantee. This evidence suggests that our formalism can enhance the understanding of protocols and their security mechanisms for designers.

To evaluate performance, we ran all the verification on the same MacBook Pro laptop. For both the original NSPK and its corrected version [26], it took about 1 s (s) in Tamarin and about 200 milliseconds (ms) in ProVerif to verify all secrecy and authenticity properties. It took about 4 s in our tool for each property. For the NSWJ version in [10], ProVerif uses 186 ms to prove four secrecy properties when considering Eve3. For the same protocol, our tool uses less than 1 s to verify each secrecy or authenticity property when considering the same eavesdropper location Eve3. However, it will take about 7 s to verify each secrecy property when considering other eavesdropper locations and about 9 (or 33) seconds to verify an authenticity property when considering Eve1 or Eve2 (or Eve4). So, it takes longer for our tool to verify properties, which is due to the executable nature of our approach to achieve accessibility for designers. The verification of the Diffie-Hellman protocols, including DH and DHWJ is similar.

In a nutshell, we successfully address all research questions. We extended our framework to support both the Dolev-Yao and PLS attack models, and verified two PLS-based security protocols (RQ1). We generalised a message theory to be generic. So security protocols using different primitives and attack models can be modelled and verified in the same framework (RQ2). We proposed DHWJ. With a thorough analysis of NSWJ and DHWJ using our approach, we found that authenticity is due to the watermarking (as we expect) and is preserved in all scenarios, even when secrecy is compromised. That is one benefit that PLS can bring (RQ3). We developed a web interface and used it to verify both the cryptographic-based and PLS-based WJ and DH protocols. Indeed, this can be carried out by a wide range of stakeholders (RQ4).

7 Conclusion and Future Work

This paper presents a formal verification framework for Physical Layer Security protocols based on sound animation with graphical interface to improve accessibility. Our work builds upon the formalism by [48], based on ITrCSP and implemented in Isabelle/HOL. We further extend its generality by supporting both cryptographic and PLS protocols, by improving its intruder's message inference rules, and by introducing a new web interface. We apply our framework to model and verify the WBPLSec-based Needham-Schroeder protocol proposed in [10]. We further integrate watermarking and jamming techniques into the Diffie-Hellman protocol, and our analysis shows that the proposed protocol preserves both secrecy and authenticity when a new session key is derived.

Our work has limitations. We verify protocols through the exploration of event trees using animators. The event trees could be too big to be exhaustively explored for complex security protocols. For the same reason, our tool needs a longer time to verify these protocols. So, scalability is still a challenge. Our current approach reduces the intervention from formal experts, which is still needed to model security protocols in Isabelle initially. They need to write CSP processes for each legitimate agent and a process for the intruder, consider what messages these processes can send and receive, and then compose the processes together through corresponding events. With significant additional effort, improvements would require to (1) design or utilise a domain-specific language (DSL) by designers to capture their protocols, properties, and attack models; (2) automatically transform the DSL models to ITrCSP in Isabelle; and (3) automatically generate animators.

Following [10], we consider a simplified scenario where the jamming signal remains consistent within a given distance, and no signal is received beyond this distance. In reality, the jamming signal and transmission signal are degraded as the distance increases. We use this assumption to simplify scenarios in terms of the eavesdropper's location: either within the jamming range or outside the range. One of our future projects is to consider more complex scenarios.

Future work will also focus on verifying more cryptographic protocols, such as the Mesh Commissioning Protocol (MeshCoP) for the Thread network and variants of Diffie-Hellman protocols, such as the STS, ISO, and SIGMA protocols [21], and the Ephemeral Diffie-Hellman Over COSE[4], and other PLS protocols.

We also plan to deploy our verified case studies on a public website, allowing researchers, engineers, or students in security to explore and verify protocols interactively using our sound animation.

Acknowledgements. The EPSRC and DSIT support this work through the Communications Hub for Empowering Distributed Cloud Computing Applications and Research (CHEDDAR) under grants EP/X040518/1, EP/Y037421/1 and EP/Y019229/1. We thank Michele Sevegnani, Yue Gu, and Sana Hafeez from the University of Glasgow, Dalal Alrajeh, and Zhi Zhang from Imperial College London for their helpful comments on an early version of the manuscript.

References

1. Arapinis, M., et al.: New privacy issues in mobile telephony: fix and verification. In: Proceedings of the 2012 ACM Conference on Computer and Communications Security, CCS 2012, pp. 205–216. Association for Computing Machinery, New York (2012). https://doi.org/10.1145/2382196.2382221
2. Armando, A., et al.: The AVISPA tool for the automated validation of internet security protocols and applications. In: Etessami, K., Rajamani, S.K. (eds.) CAV 2005. LNCS, vol. 3576, pp. 281–285. Springer, Heidelberg (2005). https://doi.org/10.1007/11513988_27
3. Basin, D., Cremers, C., Dreier, J., Sasse, R.: Symbolically analyzing security protocols using tamarin. ACM SIGLOG News **4**(4), 19–30 (2017). https://doi.org/10.1145/3157831.3157835
4. Basin, D., Cremers, C., Dreier, J., Sasse, R.: Tamarin: verification of large-scale, real world, cryptographic protocols. IEEE Secur. Priv. Mag. (2022). https://doi.org/10.1109/msec.2022.3154689. https://hal.science/hal-03586826
5. Basin, D., Dreier, J., Hirschi, L., Radomirovic, S., Sasse, R., Stettler, V.: A formal analysis of 5G authentication. In: Proceedings of the 2018 ACM SIGSAC Conference on Computer and Communications Security, CCS 2018, pp. 1383–1396. Association for Computing Machinery, New York (2018). https://doi.org/10.1145/3243734.3243846

[4] https://datatracker.ietf.org/doc/rfc9528/.

6. Bhargavan, K., Blanchet, B., Kobeissi, N.: Verified models and reference implementations for the TLS 1.3 standard candidate. In: 2017 IEEE Symposium on Security and Privacy (SP). IEEE (2017). https://doi.org/10.1109/sp.2017.26
7. Blake-Wilson, S., Menezes, A.: Authenticated Diffe-Hellman key agreement protocols. In: Tavares, S., Meijer, H. (eds.) SAC 1998. LNCS, vol. 1556, pp. 339–361. Springer, Heidelberg (1999). https://doi.org/10.1007/3-540-48892-8_26
8. Blanchet, B.: Modeling and verifying security protocols with the applied pi calculus and proverif. Found. Trends® Priv. Secur. **1**(1–2), 1–135 (2016). https://doi.org/10.1561/3300000004
9. Boichut, Y., Genet, T., Glouche, Y., Heen, O.: Using animation to improve formal specifications of security protocols. In: 2nd Conference on Security in Network Architectures and Information Systems (SARSSI 2007), pp. 169–182 (2007)
10. Costa, G., Degano, P., Galletta, L., Soderi, S.: Formally verifying security protocols built on watermarking and jamming. Comput. Secur. **128**, 103133 (2023). https://doi.org/10.1016/j.cose.2023.103133. https://www.sciencedirect.com/science/article/pii/S0167404823000433
11. Cox, I., Miller, M., McKellips, A.: Watermarking as communications with side information. Proc. IEEE **87**(7), 1127–1141 (1999). https://doi.org/10.1109/5.771068. https://ieeexplore.ieee.org/document/771068
12. Csiszár, I.: Almost independence and secrecy capacity. Probl. Peredachi Inf. **32**(1), 48–57 (1996)
13. Diffie, W., Hellman, M.: New directions in cryptography. IEEE Trans. Inf. Theory **22**(6), 644–654 (1976). https://doi.org/10.1109/TIT.1976.1055638
14. Dolev, D., Yao, A.: On the security of public key protocols. IEEE Trans. Inf. Theory **29**(2), 198–208 (1983). https://doi.org/10.1109/TIT.1983.1056650
15. Escobar, S., Meadows, C., Meseguer, J.: A rewriting-based inference system for the NRL protocol analyzer and its meta-logical properties. Theoret. Comput. Sci. **367**(1–2), 162–202 (2006). https://doi.org/10.1016/j.tcs.2006.08.035
16. Foster, S., Hur, C.K., Woodcock, J.: Formally verified simulations of state-rich processes using interaction trees in Isabelle/HOL. In: Haddad, S., Varacca, D. (eds.) 32nd International Conference on Concurrency Theory (CONCUR 2021). Leibniz International Proceedings in Informatics (LIPIcs), vol. 203, pp. 20:1–20:18. Schloss Dagstuhl – Leibniz-Zentrum für Informatik, Dagstuhl, Germany (2021). https://doi.org/10.4230/LIPIcs.CONCUR.2021.20. https://drops.dagstuhl.de/entities/document/10.4230/LIPIcs.CONCUR.2021.20
17. Gibson-Robinson, T., Armstrong, P., Boulgakov, A., Roscoe, A.W.: FDR3 — a modern refinement checker for CSP. In: Ábrahám, E., Havelund, K. (eds.) TACAS 2014. LNCS, vol. 8413, pp. 187–201. Springer, Heidelberg (2014). https://doi.org/10.1007/978-3-642-54862-8_13
18. Gollakota, S., Katabi, D.: Physical layer wireless security made fast and channel independent. In: 2011 Proceedings IEEE INFOCOM, pp. 1125–1133 (2011). https://doi.org/10.1109/INFCOM.2011.5934889. https://ieeexplore.ieee.org/document/5934889
19. Haftmann, F., Nipkow, T.: Code generation via higher-order rewrite systems. In: Blume, M., Kobayashi, N., Vidal, G. (eds.) FLOPS 2010. LNCS, vol. 6009, pp. 103–117. Springer, Heidelberg (2010). https://doi.org/10.1007/978-3-642-12251-4_9
20. Hoare, C.A.R.: Communicating Sequential Processes. Prentice-Hall Int. (1985)
21. Krawczyk, H.: SIGMA: the 'SIGn-and-MAc' approach to authenticated Diffie-Hellman and its use in the IKE protocols. In: Boneh, D. (ed.) CRYPTO 2003.

LNCS, vol. 2729, pp. 400–425. Springer, Heidelberg (2003). https://doi.org/10.1007/978-3-540-45146-4_24
22. Krawczyk, H.: HMQV: a high-performance secure Diffie-Hellman protocol. In: Shoup, V. (ed.) CRYPTO 2005. LNCS, vol. 3621, pp. 546–566. Springer, Heidelberg (2005). https://doi.org/10.1007/11535218_33
23. Kumar, M.S., Ramanathan, R., Jayakumar, M.: Key less physical layer security for wireless networks: a survey. Eng. Sci. Technol. Int. J. **35**, 101260 (2022). https://doi.org/10.1016/j.jestch.2022.101260. https://www.sciencedirect.com/science/article/pii/S2215098622001690
24. Li, X., Yu, C., Hizlan, M., Kim, W.T., Park, S.: Physical layer watermarking of direct sequence spread spectrum signals. In: MILCOM 2013 - 2013 IEEE Military Communications Conference, pp. 476–481. IEEE, San Diego, CA, USA (2013). https://doi.org/10.1109/MILCOM.2013.88. http://ieeexplore.ieee.org/document/6735668/
25. Lowe, G.: Casper: a compiler for the analysis of security protocols. In: Proceedings 10th Computer Security Foundations Workshop, pp. 18–30 (1997). https://doi.org/10.1109/CSFW.1997.596779. https://ieeexplore.ieee.org/document/596779
26. Lowe, G.: Breaking and fixing the Needham-Schroeder public-key protocol using FDR. In: Margaria, T., Steffen, B. (eds.) TACAS 1996. LNCS, vol. 1055, pp. 147–166. Springer, Heidelberg (1996). https://doi.org/10.1007/3-540-61042-1_43
27. Menezes, A.J., Vanstone, S.A., Oorschot, P.C.V.: Handbook of Applied Cryptography, 1st edn. CRC Press, Inc., USA (1996). https://doi.org/10.1201/9780429466335
28. Metere, R., Arnaboldi, L.: Automating cryptographic protocol language generation from structured specifications. In: Proceedings of the IEEE/ACM 10th International Conference on Formal Methods in Software Engineering, pp. 91–101 (2022). https://doi.org/10.1145/3524482.35276
29. Miller, R., Boureanu, I., Wesemeyer, S., Newton, C.J.P.: The 5G key-establishment stack: in-depth formal verification and experimentation. In: Proceedings of the 2022 ACM on Asia Conference on Computer and Communications Security, ASIA CCS 2022, pp. 237–251. Association for Computing Machinery, New York (2022). https://doi.org/10.1145/3488932.3517421
30. Mitev, M., Chorti, A., Poor, H.V., Fettweis, G.P.: What physical layer security can do for 6G security. IEEE Open J. Veh. Technol. **4**, 375–388 (2023). https://doi.org/10.1109/OJVT.2023.3245071. https://ieeexplore.ieee.org/document/10044975/?arnumber=10044975
31. Miyazawa, A., Ribeiro, P., Li, W., Cavalcanti, A., Timmis, J., Woodcock, J.: Robochart: modelling and verification of the functional behaviour of robotic applications. Softw. Syst. Model. **18**(5), 3097–3149 (2019). https://doi.org/10.1007/s10270-018-00710-z
32. Needham, R.M., Schroeder, M.D.: Using encryption for authentication in large networks of computers. Commun. ACM **21**(12), 993–999 (1978). https://doi.org/10.1145/359657.359659. https://dl.acm.org/doi/10.1145/359657.359659
33. Nguyen, V.L., Lin, P.C., Cheng, B.C., Hwang, R.H., Lin, Y.D.: Security and privacy for 6G: a survey on prospective technologies and challenges. IEEE Commun. Surv. Tutor. **23**(4), 2384–2428 (2021). https://doi.org/10.1109/COMST.2021.3108618
34. Nipkow, T., Wenzel, M., Paulson, L.C.: Isabelle/HOL: a proof assistant for higher-order logic. Springer (2002). https://doi.org/10.1007/3-540-45949-9
35. Paulson, L.C.: Mechanized proofs of security protocols: Needham-Schroeder with public keys. Technical report, University of Cambridge (1997). https://doi.org/10.48456/tr-413

36. Roscoe, A.W.: Understanding Concurrent Systems. Texts in Computer Science. Springer (2011). https://doi.org/10.1007/978-1-84882-258-0
37. Shannon, C.E.: A mathematical theory of communication. Bell Syst. Tech. J. **27**(3), 379–423 (1948). https://doi.org/10.1002/j.1538-7305.1948.tb01338.x. https://ieeexplore.ieee.org/document/6773024/?arnumber=6773024
38. Shor, P.: Algorithms for quantum computation: discrete logarithms and factoring. In: Proceedings 35th Annual Symposium on Foundations of Computer Science, pp. 124–134 (1994). https://doi.org/10.1109/SFCS.1994.365700
39. Soderi, S., Brighente, A., Turrin, F., Conti, M.: VLC physical layer security through RIS-aided jamming receiver for 6G wireless networks. In: 2022 19th Annual IEEE International Conference on Sensing, Communication, and Networking (SECON), pp. 370–378 (2022). https://doi.org/10.1109/SECON55815.2022.9918547. http://arxiv.org/abs/2205.09026
40. Soderi, S., De Nicola, R.: 6G networks physical layer security using RGB visible light communications. IEEE Access **10**, 5482–5496 (2022). https://doi.org/10.1109/ACCESS.2021.3139456
41. Soderi, S., Mucchi, L., Hämäläinen, M., Piva, A., Iinatti, J.: Physical layer security based on spread-spectrum watermarking and jamming receiver. Trans. Emerg. Telecommun. Technol. **28**(7), e3142 (2017). https://doi.org/10.1002/ett.3142. https://onlinelibrary.wiley.com/doi/abs/10.1002/ett.3142
42. Wyner, A.D.: The wire-tap channel. Bell Syst. Tech. J. **54**(8), 1355–1387 (1975). https://doi.org/10.1002/j.1538-7305.1975.tb02040.x. https://ieeexplore.ieee.org/document/6772207
43. Xia, L.Y.: Executable denotational semantics with interaction trees. Ph.D. thesis, University of Pennsylvania (2022)
44. Xia, L.Y., et al.: Interaction trees: representing recursive and impure programs in Coq. Proc. ACM Program. Lang. **4**(POPL) (2019). https://doi.org/10.1145/3371119
45. Ye, K., Cavalcanti, A., Foster, S., Miyazawa, A., Woodcock, J.: Probabilistic modelling and verification using RoboChart and PRISM. Softw. Syst. Model. **21**(2), 667–716 (2022). https://doi.org/10.1007/s10270-021-00916-8
46. Ye, K., Foster, S., Woodcock, J.: Formally verified animation for RoboChart using interaction trees. J. Log. Algebraic Methods Program. **137**, 100940 (2024). https://doi.org/10.1016/j.jlamp.2023.100940
47. Ye, K., Metere, R., Woodcock, J., Yadav, P.: Formal Verification of Physical Layer Security Protocols for Next-Generation Communication Networks (extended version) (2025). https://arxiv.org/abs/2508.19430
48. Ye, K., Metere, R., Yadav, P.: User-guided verification of security protocols via sound animation. In: Software Engineering and Formal Methods, pp. 33–51. Springer (2024). https://doi.org/10.1007/978-3-031-77382-2_3
49. Zhang, S., Zhu, D., Liu, Y.: Artificial intelligence empowered physical layer security for 6G: state-of-the-art, challenges, and opportunities. Comput. Netw. **242**, 110255 (2024). https://doi.org/10.1016/j.comnet.2024.110255. https://www.sciencedirect.com/science/article/pii/S1389128624000872

Automata-Based Steering of Large Language Models for Diverse Structured Generation

Xiaokun Luan, Zemin Wei, Yihao Zhang, and Meng Sun(✉)

School of Mathematical Sciences, Peking University, Beijing, China
{luanxiaokun,sunm}@pku.edu.cn, {weizeming,zhangyihao}@stu.pku.edu.cn

Abstract. Large language models (LLMs) are increasingly tasked with generating structured outputs. While structured generation methods ensure validity, they often lack output diversity, a critical limitation that we confirm in our preliminary study. We propose a novel method to enhance diversity in automaton-based structured generation. Our approach utilizes automata traversal history to steer LLMs towards novel structural patterns. Evaluations show our method significantly improves structural and content diversity while maintaining comparable generation efficiency. Furthermore, we conduct a case study showcasing the effectiveness of our method in generating diverse test cases for testing open-source libraries.

Keywords: Large language models · Structured generation · Diversity

1 Introduction

Large language models (LLMs) have demonstrated remarkable capabilities in a wide range of tasks [7,22,25,28], leading to their rapid adoption across various domains. As LLMs are increasingly integrated into complex systems, such as AI agents [9,24] and automated code generation [3,14], the demand for reliable and precisely formatted outputs has become critical. These downstream applications often require LLMs to produce outputs that strictly adhere to predefined structures, such as JSON schemas, API call formats, XML documents, or formal specifications, which are essential for ensuring parsability, correctness, and interoperability in complex systems. However, standard LLM generation cannot guarantee consistently structured outputs due to issues like hallucination [10], lack of adherence to instructions [13], and inconsistency across multiple outputs [21].

Structured generation techniques have emerged to ensure that LLM outputs conform to specified structural requirements [15]. Prominent examples include tools like Outlines [26], SGLang [31], and XGrammar [6], which leverage finite automata or pushdown automata to guide the token selection process. Invalid tokens not conforming to the specified grammar are filtered out, ensuring that

É. André et al. (Eds.): ICFEM 2025, LNCS 16229, pp. 22–41, 2026.
https://doi.org/10.1007/978-981-95-4213-0_2

the generated outputs adhere to the desired structure. While these approaches have been widely adopted for enforcing output validity, their primary focus has been on correctness. The diversity of the generated structured outputs, however, often remains overlooked.

The importance of diversity is well-recognized in unconstrained LLM generation [5,29], where it fosters creativity and broader coverage of potential responses. This need is equally pertinent in structured generation downstream applications. For instance, in software testing, a diverse set of structured test cases (e.g., API call sequences, configuration files) is crucial for achieving high test coverage and uncovering edge cases. Similarly, AI agents can benefit from diverse structured plans to enhance their adaptability and robustness in complex environments. However, the diversity of the outputs from the current state-of-the-art structured generation methods has not been thoroughly explored. Our preliminary study investigates this question by analyzing outputs from the popular structured generation method Outlines. We observe that the generated samples exhibit limited diversity, tending to repeat common structural patterns. This finding highlights that existing methods, even when paired with sampling strategies like adjusting temperature, may not effectively explore the full space of valid, diverse structured allowed by the constraints. This lack of diversity can hinder the performance of downstream applications, as they may rely on a wide range of structured outputs to function effectively.

To bridge this gap, we propose a novel approach to enhance diversity in regular expression constrained generation. Our core idea is to leverage the history of exploration within the guiding automaton during the generation process. Specifically, we monitor the states and transitions traversed by the LLM. This historical information is then used to adaptively adjust the LLM's token selection probabilities, encouraging the model to explore less frequented paths within the automaton. To maintain generation quality and prevent unproductive exploration, our method incorporates a penalty mechanism to discourage looping in local states and a dynamic range adjustment factor to ensure appropriate guidance intensity. Our methodology, while targeted at finite automata and regular expressions, is generalizable to pushdown automata and context-free grammars.

Evaluations of our proposed method demonstrate significant improvements in both structural diversity and content diversity compared to baseline method. These gains are achieved while maintaining a substantial portion (approximately 88%) of the baseline generation efficiency. We also conduct ablation studies to confirm the effectiveness of our method under various settings. Furthermore, the case study on generating test cases for testing open-source libraries illustrates that our method can produce diverse test cases that achieve a higher code coverage compared to those generated by the baseline method.

The main contributions of this paper are as follows:

1. A novel method to enhance diversity in automaton-based structured generation, which systematically encourages the LLM to explore less frequented paths within the guiding automaton.

2. A comprehensive evaluation of our method against the baseline method, demonstrating significant improvements in output diversity while maintaining comparable generation efficiency.
3. A case study on generating diverse test cases for testing open-source libraries, showcasing the practical applicability of our method in real-world scenarios.

2 Background

In this section, we provide a brief overview of large language model generation and structured generation. Later, we describe the notations and concepts of deterministic finite automata used in our work.

2.1 Large Language Model Generation

Large language models generate text by predicting the next token in a sequence following an autoregressive manner. This process starts with a prompt, and a token is sampled from the model's predicted distribution and appended to the input. The generation continues until an end-of-sequence token `EOS` is produced or a maximum length is reached.

Formally, given a vocabulary $\mathcal{V}$ and an input sequence $x = (x_1, x_2, \ldots, x_n) \in \mathcal{V}^n$, the language model M returns a logit vector z for the next token, which is then converted into a probability distribution over the vocabulary $\mathcal{V}$ using the softmax function. The next token x_{n+1} is sampled from the distribution $\text{softmax}(z)$, defined as follows.

$$z = M(x_1, x_2, \ldots, x_n), \tag{1}$$

$$x_{n+1} \sim \text{softmax}(z), \text{ where } \text{softmax}(z)_i = \frac{e^{z_i}}{\sum_{j=1}^{|\mathcal{V}|} e^{z_j}}. \tag{2}$$

Sampling temperature T controls the randomness of the sampling process by scaling the logits before applying softmax, i.e., $\text{softmax}(z/T)$. The higher the temperature, the more uniform the distribution becomes, leading to more diverse outputs. For simplicity, we use $x_{1:n} :- (x_1, x_2, \ldots, x_n)$ to denote the sequence of tokens generated so far.

2.2 Structured Generation

Structured generation methods impose constraints on the generation process to ensure adherence to the given grammar. At each step, tokens that do not conform to the grammar are masked out, and their logits are set to $-\infty$, ensuring that invalid tokens are never sampled. Formally, let G be a grammar defining a set of valid strings over the vocabulary $\mathcal{V}$. Given a sequence $x_{1:n} \in \mathcal{V}^n$, the structured generation process can be described as follows.

$$z = M(x_{1:n}), \tag{3}$$

$$z' = \text{mask}(x_{1:n}; G) + z, \tag{4}$$

$$x_{n+1} \sim \text{softmax}(z'), \tag{5}$$

where $\text{mask}(x_{1:n}; G) \subseteq \mathcal{V}$ is a vector of the same size as z consisting of zeros for valid tokens and $-\infty$ for invalid tokens. Valid tokens $\mathcal{V}_{\text{valid}}(x_{1:n}; G)$ is determined by the grammar G and the current sequence $x_{1:n}$ to obtain the mask, i.e.,

$$\text{mask}(x_{1:n}; G)_i = \begin{cases} 0, & \text{if the } i\text{-th token } w_i \in \mathcal{V}_{\text{valid}}(x_{1:n}; G), \\ -\infty, & \text{otherwise.} \end{cases} \tag{6}$$

Therefore, the logits of valid tokens are preserved, while the logits of invalid tokens are set to $-\infty$ in z', ensuring that their probabilities are zero. The grammar G can be defined in various ways, such as regular expressions and context-free grammars.

To efficiently implement the masking process, finite state automata and push-down automata can be used to represent the grammar and determine the valid tokens at each step. Specifically, the current state (and the stack) of the automaton is maintained during the generation process. When a new token is sampled, the automaton transitions to a new state (and updates the stack) based on the sampled token. The valid tokens for the next step can then be determined by the current state (and stack) of the automaton. Since the vocabulary is finite, the token-level transition table can be pre-computed to enable efficient masking.

2.3 Deterministic Finite Automata

Deterministic finite automata (DFA) are a type of finite state machine that can be used to recognize regular languages. A DFA $\mathcal{A}$ is defined as a 5-tuple $(Q, \Sigma, \delta, q_0, F)$, where Q is a finite set of states, Σ is the alphabet (set of input symbols), $\delta : Q \times \Sigma \to Q$ is the transition function, which maps a state and an input symbol to the next state, $q_0 \in Q$ is the initial state, and $F \subseteq Q$ is the set of accepting states. The language defined by the DFA is the set of strings that lead to an accepting state when processed by the automaton, i.e., $L(\mathcal{A}) = \{w \in \Sigma^* \mid \delta^*(q_0, w) \in F\}$, where δ^* is the extended transition function inductively defined as $\delta^*(q, \epsilon) = q$ and $\delta^*(q, wa) = \delta(\delta^*(q, w), a)$ with ϵ being the empty string.

Given a state q and a string w, we denote the sequence of states visited when processing w in state q as $\text{States}(q, w) = (q_1, \ldots, q_m)$ with $q_i = \delta^*(q, w[:i])$, where $w[:i]$ is the prefix[1] of w of length i. Similarly, we denote the sequence of transitions taken during the processing of w as $\text{Transitions}(q, w) = (t_1, t_2, \ldots, t_m)$, where $t_i = (q_{i-1}, w[i], q_i)$ is the transition from state q_{i-1} to state q_i on input symbol $w[i]$. We assume that the alphabet Σ consists of all input symbols that make up tokens in the vocabulary $\mathcal{V}$, i.e., $\mathcal{V} \subseteq \Sigma^*$. In the following, we will use w_i to denote some string, e.g., a token in the vocabulary $\mathcal{V}$, and w_i with square brackets $w_i[j]$ to denote the j-th symbol in w_i.

To efficiently guide the LLM generation process, one needs to first pre-compute the subset of valid tokens for each state of the DFA and construct a token transition table. For this purpose, we first introduce the concepts of *live*

[1] Square brackets (e.g., $w_i[j]$ and $w[i:j]$) are for string indexing (0-based) and slicing.

states and *dead states*. A state q is considered *live* if there exists a path from q to an accepting state, and it is *dead* if there is no such path. We denote the set of live states as Q_{live} and the set of dead states as Q_{dead}. The set of valid tokens that can be generated from a given state q is defined as the subset of the vocabulary that can lead to a live state, i.e., $\mathcal{V}_{\text{valid}}(q) = \{w \in \mathcal{V} \mid \delta^*(q, w) \in Q_{\text{live}}\}$. Based on this, we can construct a token transition table T, where each entry $T(q, w)$ contains the next state after processing the token w from state q, i.e., $T(q, w) = \delta^*(q, w)$.

3 How Diverse Is Structured Generation?

3.1 A Preliminary Study

Although structured generation methods guarantee that the generated outputs adhere to the given grammar, not all desirable outputs in the grammar can be generated in practice. This is due to the fact that the sampling process is stochastic and influenced by the model's prediction, which in turn relies on the training data that may impose biases.

In this section, we conduct a preliminary study to investigate the diversity of structured generation. We select representative, non-trivial regular expressions as constraints, and generate 1000 samples for each grammar using a state-of-the-art structured generation method. To evaluate the diversity of the generated samples, we measure finite automata coverage and count Distinct N-grams. We also briefly examine the effect of varying sampling temperature on output diversity. In the rest of this section, we present the details of our experimental setup and findings.

3.2 Sample Generation

Two regular expressions are selected for our study: G_{email} [17] and G_{color} [11], which are designed to capture *all* valid email addresses and CSS color codes, respectively. These grammars are not as simple as they may seem, as they also cover many edge cases, such as using IPv4 in email addresses and various color formats in CSS. The minimal DFA for each grammar has 43 and 1309 states, and 1594 and 7495 transitions, respectively. The complete regular expressions are provided in Appendix 7.

We use Qwen2.5-1.5B-Instruct, a 1.5 B parameter LLM, to generate 1000 samples for each constraint, following the structured generation method proposed by Willard et al. [26]. This method, implemented in the popular Python library `outlines` [2] (over 11k GitHub stars at the time of writing), has proven to be effective for such tasks. The rationale of this method has been presented in Sect. 2. We adopt the default multinomial sampling strategy with a temperature of 1.0 and 1.5, representing the normal and high sampling temperatures, respectively. All samples are generated independently with a maximum length of 18 tokens, which is sufficient to cover most valid cases.

3.3 Diversity Evaluation

We evaluate the diversity of the generated samples from two perspectives: structural diversity and content diversity. Regarding structural diversity, we measure the coverage of DFA states and transitions by the generated samples. Specifically, we compile the regular expression into a minimal DFA and then count the number of unique states and transitions that are visited by these samples. Intuitively, the more diverse the samples are, the more structural patterns they will cover, leading to a higher coverage of states and transitions. On the contrary, a low coverage indicates that some states and transitions are never reached by the given samples, suggesting that the model is not fully exploring the grammar. Formally, given a minimal DFA $\mathcal{A} = (Q, \Sigma, \delta, q_0, F)$ and a set of samples $S = \{s_i\}_{i=1}^n$ generated by the model, we introduce the following metrics to measure the coverage of the DFA states and transitions:

$$\text{StateCov}(S) = \frac{|\bigcup_{i=1}^n \text{States}(q_0, s_i)|}{|Q|}, \tag{7}$$

$$\text{TransCov}(S) = \frac{|\bigcup_{i=1}^n \text{Transitions}(q_0, s_i)|}{|\{(q, a, q') \in Q \times \Sigma \times Q \mid \delta(q, a) = q'\}|}, \tag{8}$$

where $\text{States}(q_0, s_i)$ and $\text{Transitions}(q_0, s_i)$ are the sequences of states and transitions traversed by the minimal DFA $\mathcal{A}$ when processing the sample s_i.

To evaluate content diversity, we use the commonly used Distinct N-grams metric [12], which counts the number of unique n-grams in the samples. Formally, given a set of samples S, the Distinct N-grams metric is defined as follows:

$$\text{Distinct}{-}n(S) = |\{s[i{:}i+n] \mid s \in S, |s| \geq n, 0 \leq i \leq |s| - n\}|. \tag{9}$$

This metric captures the local sequence variety of the generated samples. The greater the Distinct$-n$ value, the more diverse the samples are.

3.4 Results and Findings

Table 1. Diversity evaluation results of preliminary study.

Metric	G_{email}		G_{color}	
	Temp. 1.0	Temp. 1.5	Temp. 1.0	Temp. 1.5
StateCov (%)	18.60	23.26	16.96	31.55
TransCov (%)	20.45	20.83	7.59	12.26
Average length	53.6	68.4	15.3	12.8
Distinct-2	1610	1558	458	635
Distinct-3	10 172	12 526	1295	1991

The main results of our preliminary study are reported in Table 1, where we additionally report average length of the generated samples. Clearly, the finite automata coverage values for both grammars are relatively low, indicating that the model has not fully explored the DFA even though it has generated 1000 samples. Regarding the Distinct N-grams metric, the Distinct−2 and Distinct−3 values seem satisfactory. But when considering the average length of the generated samples, the Distinct N-grams values are not as impressive as they appear, suggesting that there are many repeated patterns in the generated samples. For example, there are about 53 600 bigrams in the generated email addresses, but only about 3% of them are unique.

Theoretically, increasing the sampling temperature can make the sampling process more random, which helps the model explore more edge cases. However, as shown in Table 1, the DFA coverage of states and transitions have not improved significantly when we increase the sampling temperature to 1.5. Most edge cases in the grammars are still not covered, despite that we have used a relatively high temperature. For example, the regular expression G_{email} allows using double quotes in the local part of the email address (e.g., `"user"@example.com`), but none of the generated samples contain this case. Similarly, the regular expression G_{color} allows using HSL and HSLA color formats (e.g., `hsl(120, 100%, 50%)`) and the `lch` and `lab` functions, which are also absent in the generated samples.

The results of our preliminary study indicate that the state-of-the-art structured generation method is not fully exploring the grammar, leading to a lack of diversity in the generated samples. Increasing the sampling temperature cannot significantly improve the diversity of the generated samples. This is due to the model's tendency to follow its prediction based on natural language modeling rather than fully considering the grammar constraints. Such lack of diversity may significantly limit the applicability of structured generation methods in scenarios where diverse outputs are desired.

4 Method

4.1 Overview

The lack of diversity in structured generation arises from the model's non-awareness of the legal paths under the grammar constraints, especially those that are rare in the natural language context. To improve the diversity of structured generation, we encourage the model to explore different paths in the automata by adjusting the logits based on history transitions. This is achieved by keeping track of the transitions made by the model during the entire generation process to identify valid paths in the grammar that are rarely explored. In addition, we penalize the tokens that lead to frequently visited states to avoid looping into local optima. The adjustment terms are adaptively scaled based on the range of the logits to avoid over-penalizing or over-rewarding the tokens.

Algorithm 1 summarizes the overall process of our method, where the main difference between our method and the standard structured generation method is

Algorithm 1: Diversity-enhanced Structured Generation

Input: The number of samples n, a minimal DFA $\mathcal{A} = (Q, \Sigma, \delta, q_0, F)$ of the given regex, a token transition table T, a hyperparameter γ
Output: A set of generated samples $S = \{s_i\}_{i=1}^{n}$

```
S = {};
Initialize global transition counter C and local state counter C_loc;
for i = 1 to n do
    q ← q_0;
    s_i ← ε;
    Reset local state counter C_loc;
    while True do
        z ← M(prompt + s_i);
        Compute the range(q, z) and adjust(q);
        z'_j = z_j + mask(q)_j + γ · range(q, z) adjust(q)_j for all j;
        Sample a token w from the distribution Softmax(z');
        if w is EOS then
            break;
        s_i ← s_i + w;
        C_loc(q_{j+1}) ← C_loc(q_{j+1}) + 1 for each q_j ∈ States(q, w);
        q ← T(q, w);
    C(q_j, q_{j+1}) ← C(q_j, q_{j+1}) + 1 for each q_j ∈ States(q_0, s_i);
    S ← S ∪ {s_i};
return S
```

that we adjust the logits based on history transitions. The adjustment is achieved by maintaining two counters during the generation process. In the following, we describe the main components of our adjustment terms in detail.

4.2 Encouraging Exploration

Suppose a minimal DFA $\mathcal{A} = (Q, \Sigma, \delta, q_0, F)$ of the given regular expression and its corresponding token transition table T are constructed. By design, the minimal DFA ensures that ambiguities and overlapping transitions are resolved. Recall that a token transition $T(q, w)$ makes several transitions to the next state $\delta^*(q, w)$ after generating a new token w, going through a sequence of states States(q, w). If there are two adjacent states q_i and q_{i+1} in this sequence and there have never been any transition moving from q_i to q_{i+1} during the whole generation process, then we can encourage the model to sample the token w in state q so that a new path is explored. Intuitively, the less such a state pair appears in the whole generation process, the more we should reward the model to sample it, thus potentially increasing the structural diversity of the generated samples.

To achieve this, we maintain a global transition counter C to keep track of the number of times each state bigram (i.e., state pair) has been taken during the whole generation process. Formally, C is a mapping from a state pair to the number of times it has been taken, i.e., $C : Q \times Q \to \mathbb{N}$. $C(q, q')$ is initialized to zero at the beginning of the generation process. This counter is updated after a valid sample s is generated[2], where $C(q_i, q_{i+1})$ is incremented by one for each state pair (q_i, q_{i+1}) in the sequence $\text{States}(q_0, s)$. With such a global counter, we can encourage the model to explore infrequently visited paths by adjusting the logits of the next token. Specifically, assume the current state is q and the valid tokens are $w_1, w_2, \ldots, w_k \in \mathcal{V}_{\text{valid}}(q)$. For each token transition $T(q, w_i)$, we measure if it is worth exploring by quantifying the least frequently visited state pair in its transition sequence $\text{States}(q, w_i)$, defined as follows:

$$E(q, w_i) = \min_{q_j \in \text{States}(q, w_i)} C(q_j, q_{j+1}). \tag{10}$$

Intuitively, $E(q, w_i)$ represents how many times the least frequently visited state bigram has been taken in the transition sequence of w_i from state q. To encourage the model to explore such less frequently visited paths, we add a reward term $\text{reward}(q)$ to the logits of the next token, defined as follows:

$$\text{reward}(q)_i = \begin{cases} \dfrac{\log\left(1 + \sum_{j=1}^{k} E(q, w_j)\right)}{1 + E(q, w_i)}, & \text{if } w_i \in \mathcal{V}_{\text{valid}}(q), \\ 0, & \text{if } w_i \notin \mathcal{V}_{\text{valid}}(q), \end{cases} \tag{11}$$

where k is the number of valid tokens in state q. The reward term $\text{reward}(q)$ is added to the logits of the next token x_{n+1}, so that as the model generates more samples, the reward term will favor under-explored paths and thus increasing the diversity of the generated samples.

4.3 Avoiding Looping Into Local Optima

However, as the global transition counter C is only updated after a valid sample is generated, it may result in a situation where the model repeatedly predicts a token that leads back to the same state. For example, after generating a few samples, the reward term may favor certain token w_i in state q that leads to the same state q again, thus causing the model to loop into local optima and fail to reach accepting states.

To avoid this, we introduce a local state counter $C_{\text{loc}} : Q \to \mathbb{N}$ to keep track of the number of times each state has been visited during the generation process of a single sample. Therefore, C_{loc} is similar to C, except that it is reset to zero at the beginning of each sample generation and updated after a new token is sampled. We similarly introduce $m(q, w_i)$ to denote the maximum number of times a state has been visited in the state sequence of a valid token w_i from state q, defined as follows:

$$m(q, w_i) = \max_{q_j \in \text{States}(q, w_i)} C_{\text{loc}}(q_j). \tag{12}$$

[2] Invalid samples are possible due to reaching maximum tokens before generating the `EOS` token.

Based on this, we employ a penalty term penalty(q) to adjust the logits of the next token, defined as follows:

$$\text{penalty}(q)_i = \begin{cases} \beta(1 + m(q, w_i)), & \text{if } w_i \in \mathcal{V}_{\text{valid}}(q), \\ 1, & \text{if } w_i \notin \mathcal{V}_{\text{valid}}(q), \end{cases} \tag{13}$$

where β is a hyperparameter that controls the intensity of the penalty. The reward term reward$(q)_i$ is divided by the penalty term penalty$(q)_i$ before being added to the logits, i.e.,

$$\text{adjust}(q)_i = \frac{\text{reward}(q)_i}{\text{penalty}(q)_i}. \tag{14}$$

Therefore, the penalty term will prevent the model from repeatedly predicting the same token that leads to the same state, even if the reward term favors it.

4.4 Adaptive Scaling

To better adapt the reward and penalty terms to the varying scale of the logits, we introduce an adaptive scaling method to adjust the reward and penalty terms based on the range of the logits and a hyperparameter γ, i.e.,

$$z_i' = z_i + \text{mask}(q)_i + \gamma \cdot \text{range}(q, z)\ \text{adjust}(q)_i, \tag{15}$$

where z_i is the original logits of the token w_i, mask$(q)_i$ is the mask term for the token w_i, and range(q, z) is the range of the logits in state q, defined as the difference between the maximum and minimum logits of valid tokens in state q:

$$\text{range}(q, z) = \max_{w_i \in \mathcal{V}_{\text{valid}}(q)} z_i - \min_{w_i \in \mathcal{V}_{\text{valid}}(q)} z_i. \tag{16}$$

This adaptive scaling method allows the model to adjust the reward and penalty terms based on the scale of the logits, thus avoiding over-penalizing or over-rewarding the tokens. Meanwhile, the hyperparameter γ controls the strength of the adjustment, serving as a lever to balance exploration and exploitation. A higher γ value amplifies the reward for less-frequented paths, encouraging the model to generate more diverse outputs. Conversely, a lower γ value leads the model to rely more on its original high-confidence predictions, effectively refining and improving upon the quality of more probable outputs.

5 Evaluation

This section evaluates the proposed method for enhancing diversity in structured generation. We compare its performance with a state-of-the-art baseline, Outlines, focusing on diversity and generation efficiency. Ablation studies are conducted to further assess the method's performance under high-temperature settings and evaluate the contribution of each component. Finally, we present a case study showcasing the practical application of our method in generating diverse test cases for testing open-source libraries. Our implementation is publicly available[3].

[3] https://github.com/luan-xiaokun/diverse-structured-generation.

5.1 Experimental Setup

Grammar and Language Model. We conduct our experiments on four regular expressions, including G_{email}, G_{color}, G_{json}, and G_{bomb}. The first two, G_{email} and G_{color}, were introduced in our preliminary study in Sect. 3. They represent common real-world formats with intricate standardized rules and many edge cases. The third grammar, G_{json}, describes a simple JSON object with three fields (i.e., name, gender, age) and represents a common application scenario in structured generation. Finally, G_{bomb} serves as a negative constraint, allowing any string except those containing the word "bomb" (case-insensitive). Such negative constraints are essential for applications like content moderation and safety filtering. The complete regular expressions are provided in Appendix 7.

We use Qwen2.5-1.5B-Instruct, a 1.5 B instruction fine-tuned large language model, for structured generation in our experiments. Unless otherwise specified, we adopt a default multinomial sampling strategy with a temperature of 1.0. The max length of the generated samples is set to 18 tokens, except for G_{json}, which is set to 54 tokens. This setting is sufficient for the grammars we are using. The prompts used for the generation are as follows:

- G_{email}: Give me an email address.
- G_{color}: Give me a CSS color code.
- G_{json}: Give me a JSON object, which has three fields: name (a string), gender (male or female), age (an integer).
- G_{bomb}: Tell me how to make a bomb.

Baseline and Hyperparameters. We compare our method with the state-of-the-art baseline method Outlines. The hyperparameters β and γ of our method are set to 3 and 0.5, respectively. Both methods use the same default multinomial sampling strategy with a temperature of 1.0 unless otherwise specified. For each experiment, we generate 1000 samples per grammar using both our method and the baseline method on a platform with an NVIDIA GeForce RTX 3060Ti GPU and an AMD Ryzen 9 7900X CPU with 32 GB memory.

Evaluation Metrics. We employ two sets of metrics to evaluate structural and content diversity. For structural diversity, we measure the DFA state coverage StateCov, transition coverage TransCov, and path coverage PathCov of the generated samples, where the path coverage is defined as the ratio of the number of unique state bigrams covered by the generated samples to the total number of state bigrams in the DFA. For content diversity, we use the Distinct N-grams and the Vendi score [8], a commonly used metric for evaluating the diversity of datasets. The Vendi score requires a semi-definite similarity function over the samples, which is a similarity function for strings in our case. We adopt the weighted-degree kernel with shifts kernel [16] as the string similarity function, which considers the number of common substrings between two strings.

Table 2. Structural diversity evaluation results.

Grammar	DFA Size	StateCov (%)		TransCov (%)		PathCov (%)	
		Baseline	Ours	Baseline	Ours	Baseline	Ours
G_{email}	43 / 1594	18.60	**95.35**	20.45	**31.56**	13.68	**77.78**
G_{color}	1309 / 7495	16.96	**62.49**	7.59	**24.94**	9.12	**42.05**
G_{json}	216 / 10 192	31.94	**56.48**	2.04	**6.66**	12.60	**33.11**
G_{bomb}	12 / 1213	50.00	**83.33**	12.12	**28.69**	27.45	**70.59**

Table 3. Content diversity evaluation results.

Grammar	Average Length		Distinct-2		Distinct-3		Vendi Score	
	Baseline	Ours	Baseline	Ours	Baseline	Ours	Baseline	Ours
G_{email}	53.6	51.8	1610	**1670**	10 172	**10 333**	702.1	**707.7**
G_{color}	15.3	11.1	458	**679**	1295	**2039**	98.0	**169.9**
G_{json}	56.8	53.6	354	**1639**	657	**2881**	14.7	**56.3**
G_{bomb}	82.6	79.5	1080	**2025**	4335	**5655**	477.0	**491.5**

5.2 Performance Comparison

Diversity Enhancement. We first evaluate the performance of our method and the baseline method in terms of structural and content diversity. The results are shown in Table 2 and Table 3, respectively, where the DFA size n/m indicates that the minimal DFA has n states and m transitions. We use bold font to highlight the best results between the two methods for each grammar. Our method significantly outperforms the baseline method in terms of both structural and content diversity across all four grammars. The DFA state coverage, transition coverage, path coverage, and the Vendi score of our method are improved by 45%, 12%, 40%, and 90% on average compared to the baseline method. The average length of the generated samples is slightly lower than that of the baseline method, which is expected since our method encourages the model to explore more diverse paths.

As the minimal DFA has a dead state dedicated to handle invalid inputs, achieving 100% state coverage is impossible. Taking this into account, our method has covered all live states in the DFA of G_{bomb}. Another figure worth noting is that the transition table of G_{json}'s DFA are very dense, with 10 192 transitions in total. This is due to the regex of G_{json} has a dot-star pattern, which allows any character to appear in the string. Consequently, its transition coverage is relatively low compared to the other three grammars.

Efficiency Analysis. The proposed method has a higher computational overhead than the baseline method due to the additional logits adjustment step. We

Table 4. Tokens generated per second of our method and the baseline method.

Grammar	Baseline (TPS)	Ours (TPS)	Percentage
G_{email}	**33.44**	32.80	98.09%
G_{color}	**34.39**	31.49	91.57%
G_{json}	**23.64**	18.16	76.82%
G_{bomb}	**25.69**	22.60	87.97%

analyze the efficiency of our method by measuring the number of tokens generated per second (TPS) and compare it with the baseline method. Table 4 shows the TPS of both methods for each grammar and the percentage of TPS of our method compared to the baseline method. The results show that our method is slower than the baseline method, with an average TPS of 88.8% of the baseline method. This is mainly caused by the computation of the reward term and the penalty term. However, considering the gain in diversity, the trade-off is acceptable.

5.3 Ablation Studies

Table 5. Structural diversity evaluation results under temperature 1.5.

Grammar	StateCov (%)		TransCov (%)		PathCov (%)	
	Baseline	Ours	Baseline	Ours	Baseline	Ours
G_{email}	23.26	**90.70**	20.83	**32.56**	17.95	**76.92**
G_{color}	31.55	**61.65**	12.26	**24.18**	16.78	**40.68**
G_{json}	33.33	**56.48**	3.87	**6.76**	14.34	**32.04**
G_{bomb}	75.00	**83.33**	30.26	**35.94**	50.98	**74.51**

Table 6. Content diversity evaluation results under temperature 1.5.

Grammar	Average Length		Distinct-2		Distinct-3		Vendi Score	
	Baseline	Ours	Baseline	Ours	Baseline	Ours	Baseline	Ours
G_{email}	68.4	63.6	1558	**1814**	12 526	**12 585**	792.0	**802.8**
G_{color}	12.8	11.3	635	**720**	1991	**2166**	143.1	**158.4**
G_{json}	59.1	61.7	1132	**2604**	3127	**5570**	65.4	**121.8**
G_{bomb}	89.6	85.8	5154	**6805**	15 375	**17 812**	819.8	**841.5**

Table 7. Perplexity of generated samples constrained by G_{bomb}.

Temperature	Baseline (PPL)	Ours (PPL)
1.0	54.6	138.0
1.5	55133.3	81 710.8

High-Temperature Generation. To evaluate the performance of our method under high-temperature settings, we re-generate the samples with a temperature of 1.5. The results are shown in Table 5 and Table 6. As expected, the diversity of samples generated by baseline method improves compared with the default temperature setting. However, our method still outperforms the baseline method in terms of both structural and content diversity. Interestingly, all the metrics of our method slightly decrease compared to the default temperature setting. This occurs because our method and temperature scaling represent two distinct, competing forces for promoting diversity. Our method directly manipulates logits to widen their range, while temperature scaling smooths the final probability distribution. When $T > 1$, this smoothing effect partially counteracts our explicit logit adjustments, leading to the observed slight decrease in diversity. Therefore, the slight decrease in the diversity of our method compared with the default temperature setting is expected.

We further analyze the perplexity of the generated sampled constrained by G_{bomb} to assess the quality of the generated samples, since G_{bomb} is the only grammar that allows natural language generation among the four grammars. The perplexity is calculated using another larger model, Phi4-mini-instruct, which is a 4 B instruction fine-tuned LLM. Intuitively, a lower perplexity indicates that the generated texts are more natural and fluent. The results are shown in Table 7, where the perplexity of the generated samples under temperature 1.5 is significantly higher than that under temperature 1.0 for both methods. Such significant quality drop is not acceptable for natural language generation. As a result, although the baseline method could achieve a higher diversity with a higher temperature, the generated samples are neither of high quality nor diverse. On the other hand, our method achieves a good balance between diversity and quality under the default temperature setting.

Table 8. Ablation study on the effectiveness of each component.

Components	DFA Coverage (%)			Distinct-2	Distinct-3	Vendi Score
	StateCov	TransCov	PathCov			
All	62.49	24.94	42.05	679	2039	169.9
No reward(q)	15.30	7.20	8.20	463	1213	93.7
No penalty(q)	—	—	—	—	—	—
No range(q, z)	23.50	9.40	12.70	461	1278	96.8

Component Analysis. We conduct an ablation study to analyze the effectiveness of each core component of our method, including the reward term reward(q), the penalty term penalty(q), and the logits range adjustment factor range(q, z). We remove one component at a time and evaluate the performance of the modified method on the G_{color} grammar. Table 8 shows the results of the ablation study.

We first remove the reward term by setting reward$(q)_i = 1$ for all i. As expected, the performance drops significantly, even a bit lower than the baseline method. This demonstrates that the reward term is essential for our method to enhance diversity. After removing the penalty term by setting penalty$(q)_i = 1$ for all i, we observe that the generation process becomes unstable and that the model struggles to generate valid samples. As more samples are generated, the model tends to repeat certain patterns (e.g., "oklch(18.27777...") that quickly reach the max token limit, resulting in a very low success rate on generating valid samples. Therefore, we conclude that the penalty term is crucial for the stability of our method, as it avoids the model from getting stuck in a local optimum. We further remove the logits range adjustment factor. The structural diversity metrics are slightly better than the baseline method, and the content diversity metrics are on par with the baseline method. This indicates that without the adaptive scaling provided by the logits range factor, the strength of the adjustment is insufficient to significantly improve diversity. In summary, all three components contribute to the overall performance of our method.

5.4 Case Study: Test Case Generation

Table 9. Branch coverage of generated test cases.

Grammar	Library	LoC	Branch Coverage (%)	
			Baseline	Ours
G_{email}	`email_validator`	792	46.19	**59.08**
G_{color}	`webcolors`	441	78.04	**83.18**

To evaluate the effectiveness of our method in downstream tasks, we conduct a case study on using LLMs to generate test cases for testing open source third-party libraries. We select two popular Python libraries, `email_validator` [23] and `webcolors` [4], which are mainly used for validating email addresses and converting CSS color codes, respectively.

We utilize the generated samples of G_{email} and G_{color} generated by baseline and our method to test these libraries. The branch coverage of the generated test cases is reported in Table 9. The results show that our method achieves a higher branch coverage than the baseline method with 12.89% and 5.14% improvement on `email_validator` and `webcolors`, demonstrating its effectiveness in generating diverse test cases. As most generated samples are valid, they cannot trigger part of the library's logic intended to handle invalid inputs. On the other hand, some samples adhere to the given regular expressions but are not valid in the default context of the library, which contributes to the branch coverage. For example, the `email_validator` library does not accept IPv4 addresses in the email field by default[4], but such variations are valid according to the regex.

To summarize, the proposed diversity-enhanced structured generation method can generate more diverse test cases than the baseline method, which is beneficial for improving the branch coverage of the generated test cases.

6 Related Work

6.1 Large Language Model Structured Generation

Structured generation is proposed to improve the quality of LLM-generated outputs by enforcing constraints during the generation process. Various methods have been developed to facilitate structured generation, including Guidance [1], Outlines [26], XGrammar [6], and SGLang [31]. Among them, Guidance employs a template-based approach, where users define templates with placeholders and the model fills in the placeholders with generated tokens. In contrast, Outlines proposes a finite state machine-based approach to mask invalid tokens based on the current automaton state, and it supports both regular expressions and context-free grammars (CFGs). XGrammar focuses on building an engine for efficient CFG-constrained generation through token mask caching and other various optimization techniques. SGLang functions as a domain-specific language embedded in Python, featuring a rich front end for defining structured tasks and a highly optimized back end for efficient execution. Except for Guidance's template system, these prominent methods are fundamentally based on finite automata or pushdown automata. Their primary distinctions often lie in the specific optimization strategies for their generation and the expressiveness of the primitives they offer to users. Consequently, while these methods differ in usability and generation efficiency, they have generally not prioritized the diversity of the generated structured outputs, often yielding a limited range of structural variations. Our proposed method is orthogonal to these existing engines and front ends, allowing for easy integration into them to enhance their output diversity.

6.2 Diversity Enhancement in Text Generation

Diversity is widely recognized as a critical attribute of high-quality text generation. Before the widespread adoption of LLMs, the importance of diversity was already acknowledged, and various methods were proposed to promote it. For instance, Shi et al. [20] employed inverse reinforcement learning to learn a reward function that encourages diverse outputs. Xu et al. [27] proposed Diversity-Promoting Generative Adversarial Networks that assign lower reward for repetitive text and higher reward for novel generations. Following the advent of LLMs,

[4] Such feature is only supported when a corresponding option is turned on.

increasing sampling temperature has been a common heuristic to boost output diversity, though often at the expense of coherence or factual accuracy [5]. The trade-off between diversity and other quality aspects is a recurring theme in text generation research. For example, Shao et al. [18] introduced a controllable text generative model based on Conditional Variational Autoencoders to manage this balance via a tunable hyperparameter. Zhao et al. [30] presented a novel method called LoFT to enhance diversity while maintaining faithfulness in logical table-to-text generation. To generate long and diverse text outputs from structured data, Shao et al. [19] proposed a Planning-based Hierarchical Variational Model, which segments input data into a sequence of groups and generates sentences for each group. Our approach is complementary to these methods, specifically targeting the enhancement of diversity in automaton-based structured generation.

7 Conclusion and Future Work

In this paper, we identified the limitation of state-of-the-art structured generation methods in producing diverse outputs. To enhance diversity, we proposed a novel method that encourages LLMs to explore new paths in the automata by leveraging the history of traversed states and transitions. Our evaluations demonstrated that our method significantly improves both structural and content diversity while maintaining comparable generation efficiency. We also conducted ablation studies to show that simply increasing sampling temperature in standard structured generation is insufficient for achieving substantial diversity improvements and could degrade output quality. Our case study on generating structured test cases for software testing further illustrated the practical benefits of our approach. Our findings highlight the importance of exploring the full space of valid structured outputs and suggest that our method can be a valuable addition to existing structured generation techniques.

For future work, we plan to generalize our method to more expressive Context-Free Grammars (CFGs) and develop adaptive strategies for the exploration-exploitation trade-off. Furthermore, integrating with parser combinators could enable application to general-purpose programming languages, enhancing tasks like automated code generation.

Acknowledgments. This work was supported by the National Key R&D Program of China under Grant 2022YFB2702200, National Natural Science Foundation of China (Grant No. 62172019), and Beijing Natural Science Foundation (Grant Nos. QY24035, QY23041).

Appendix

The regular expressions G_{email}, G_{json}, and G_{bomb} used in our study are provided in the following listings. G_{color} is exceptionally complex as it covers various color formats. Therefore, we provide a GitHub repository link[5] that contains the complete G_{color} expression instead of including it here.

[5] https://github.com/Kyza/color-regex/.

```
(?:[a-z0-9!#$%&'*+/=?^_`{|}~-]+(?:\.[a-z0-9!#$%&'*+/=?^_`{|}~-]+)*|\"(?:[\x01
-\x08\x0b\x0c\x0e-\x1f\x21\x23-\x5b\x5d-\x7f]|\\[\x01-\x09\x0b\x0c\x0e-\x7f])
*\")@(?:(?:[a-z0-9](?:[a-z0-9-]*[a-z0-9])?\.)+[a-z0-9](?:[a-z0-9-]*[a-z0-9])?
|\[
\bUnALT{}(?:(?:(2(5[0-5]|[0-4][0-9])|1[0-9][0-9]|[1-9]?[0-9]))\.)
    ↪{3}(?:(2(5[0-5]|[0
-4][0-9])|1[0-9][0-9]|[1-9]?[0-9])|[a-z0-9-]*[a-z0-9]:(?:[\x01-\x08\x0b\x0c\x
0e-\x1f\x21-\x5a\x53-\x7f]|\\[\x01-\x09\x0b\x0c\x0e-\x7f])+)\eUnALT{}
\]
```

Listing 1. The regular expression G_{email}.

```
\{\s*\"name\":\s*\"(?:.+?)\",\s*\"gender\":\s*\"(?:fe)?male\",\s*\"age\":\s*
\d+\s*\}$
```

Listing 2. The regular expression G_{json}.

```
(?:[^bB]|[bB][^oO]|[bB][oO][^mM]|[bB][oO][mM][^bB])+
```

Listing 3. The regular expression G_{bomb}.

References

1. Guidance ai: Guidance: A guidance language for controlling large language models. https://github.com/guidance-ai/guidance. Accessed 11 May 2025
2. dottxt ai: Structured text generation. https://github.com/dottxt-ai/outlines. Accessed 11 May 2025
3. Austin, J., et al.: Program synthesis with large language models (2021). https://doi.org/10.48550/arXiv.2108.07732. https://arxiv.org/abs/2108.07732
4. Bennett, J.: A library for working with HTML/CSS color formats in Python. https://github.com/ubernostrum/webcolors. Accessed 11 May 2025
5. Chung, J., Kamar, E., Amershi, S.: Increasing diversity while maintaining accuracy: Text data generation with large language models and human interventions. In: Rogers, A., Boyd-Graber, J., Okazaki, N. (eds.) Proceedings of the 61st Annual Meeting of the Association for Computational Linguistics (Volume 1: Long Papers), pp. 575–593. Association for Computational Linguistics, Toronto (2023). https://doi.org/10.18653/v1/2023.acl-long.34
6. Dong, Y., et al.: XGrammar: flexible and efficient structured generation engine for large language models (2024). https://arxiv.org/abs/2411.15100
7. Du, Z., et al.: GLM: general language model pretraining with autoregressive blank infilling. In: Muresan, S., Nakov, P., Villavicencio, A. (eds.) Proceedings of the 60th Annual Meeting of the Association for Computational Linguistics, vol. 1: Long Papers, pp. 320–335. Association for Computational Linguistics, Dublin (2022). https://doi.org/10.18653/v1/2022.acl-long.26. https://aclanthology.org/2022.acl-long.26/
8. Friedman, D., Dieng, A.B.: The Vendi score: a diversity evaluation metric for machine learning. Trans. Mach. Learn. Res. (2023). https://openreview.net/forum?id=g97OHbQyk1
9. Guo, T., et al.: Large language model based multi-agents: a survey of progress and challenges. In: Larson, K. (ed.) Proceedings of the Thirty-Third International Joint Conference on Artificial Intelligence, IJCAI-24, pp. 8048–8057. International Joint Conferences on Artificial Intelligence Organization (2024). https://doi.org/10.24963/ijcai.2024/890

10. Ji, Z., et al.: Survey of hallucination in natural language generation. ACM Comput. Surv. **55**(12) (2023). https://doi.org/10.1145/3571730
11. Kyza: Pattern matching and extracting color code formats using RegEx. https://github.com/Kyza/color-regex/. Accessed 11 May 2025
12. Li, J., Galley, M., Brockett, C., Gao, J., Dolan, B.: A diversity-promoting objective function for neural conversation models. In: Knight, K., Nenkova, A., Rambow, O. (eds.) Proceedings of the 2016 Conference of the North American Chapter of the Association for Computational Linguistics: Human Language Technologies, pp. 110–119. Association for Computational Linguistics, San Diego (2016). https://doi.org/10.18653/v1/N16-1014
13. Lou, R., Zhang, K., Yin, W.: Large language model instruction following: a survey of progresses and challenges. Comput. Linguist. **50**(3), 1053–1095 (2024). https://doi.org/10.1162/coli_a_00523
14. Nijkamp, E., et al.: CodeGen: an open large language model for code with multi-turn program synthesis. In: The Eleventh International Conference on Learning Representations (2023). https://openreview.net/forum?id=iaYcJKpY2B_
15. OpenAI Platform: Structured model outputs (2024). https://platform.openai.com/docs/guides/structured-outputs?api-mode=responses. Accessed 12 Aug 2025
16. Rätsch, G., Sonnenburg, S., Schölkopf, B.: RASE: recognition of alternatively spliced exons in c.elegans. Bioinformatics **21**(1), 369–377 (2005). https://doi.org/10.1093/bioinformatics/bti1053
17. Resnick, P.: Internet message format. RFC 5322 (2008). https://doi.org/10.17487/RFC5322. https://www.rfc-editor.org/info/rfc5322
18. Shao, H., et al.: Controllable and diverse text generation in e-commerce. In: Proceedings of the Web Conference 2021, WWW '21, pp. 2392–2401. Association for Computing Machinery, New York (2021). https://doi.org/10.1145/3442381.3449838
19. Shao, Z., Huang, M., Wen, J., Xu, W., Zhu, X.: Long and diverse text generation with planning-based hierarchical variational model. In: Inui, K., Jiang, J., Ng, V., Wan, X. (eds.) Proceedings of the 2019 Conference on Empirical Methods in Natural Language Processing and the 9th International Joint Conference on Natural Language Processing (EMNLP-IJCNLP), pp. 3257–3268. Association for Computational Linguistics, Hong Kong (2019). https://doi.org/10.18653/v1/D19-1321. https://aclanthology.org/D19-1321/
20. Shi, Z., Chen, X., Qiu, X., Huang, X.: Toward diverse text generation with inverse reinforcement learning. In: Proceedings of the 27th International Joint Conference on Artificial Intelligence. IJCAI'18, pp. 4361–4367. AAAI Press (2018)
21. Stureborg, R., Alikaniotis, D., Suhara, Y.: Large language models are inconsistent and biased evaluators (2024). https://doi.org/10.48550/arXiv.2405.01724. https://arxiv.org/abs/2405.01724
22. Sun, Y., et al.: ERNIE 3.0: large-scale knowledge enhanced pre-training for language understanding and generation (2021). https://arxiv.org/abs/2107.02137
23. Tauberer, J.: A robust email syntax and deliverability validation library for Python. https://github.com/JoshData/python-email-validator. Accessed 11 May 2025
24. Wang, G., et al.: Voyager: an open-ended embodied agent with large language models. Trans. Mach. Learn. Res. (2024). https://openreview.net/forum?id=ehfRiF0R3a
25. Wang, H., et al.: LEGO-prover: neural theorem proving with growing libraries. In: The Twelfth International Conference on Learning Representations (2024). https://openreview.net/forum?id=3f5PALef5B

26. Willard, B.T., Louf, R.: Efficient guided generation for large language models (2023). https://doi.org/10.48550/arXiv.2307.09702. https://arxiv.org/abs/2307.09702
27. Xu, J., Ren, X., Lin, J., Sun, X.: Diversity-promoting GAN: a cross-entropy based generative adversarial network for diversified text generation. In: Riloff, E., Chiang, D., Hockenmaier, J., Tsujii, J. (eds.) Proceedings of the 2018 Conference on Empirical Methods in Natural Language Processing, pp. 3940–3949. Association for Computational Linguistics, Brussels (2018). https://doi.org/10.18653/v1/D18-1428, https://aclanthology.org/D18-1428/
28. Yu, L., et al.: MetaMath: bootstrap your own mathematical questions for large language models. In: The Twelfth International Conference on Learning Representations (2024). https://openreview.net/forum?id=N8N0hgNDRt
29. Zhang, H., Duckworth, D., Ippolito, D., Neelakantan, A.: Trading off diversity and quality in natural language generation. In: Belz, A., Agarwal, S., Graham, Y., Reiter, E., Shimorina, A. (eds.) Proceedings of the Workshop on Human Evaluation of NLP Systems (HumEval), pp. 25–33. Association for Computational Linguistics, Online (2021), https://aclanthology.org/2021.humeval-1.3/
30. Zhao, Y., Qi, Z., Nan, L., Flores, L.J., Radev, D.: LoFT: enhancing faithfulness and diversity for table-to-text generation via logic form control. In: Vlachos, A., Augenstein, I. (eds.) Proceedings of the 17th Conference of the European Chapter of the Association for Computational Linguistics, pp. 554–561. Association for Computational Linguistics, Dubrovnik (2023). https://doi.org/10.18653/v1/2023.eacl-main.40. https://aclanthology.org/2023.eacl-main.40/
31. Zheng, L., et al.: SGLang: efficient execution of structured language model programs (2024). https://doi.org/10.48550/arXiv.2312.07104. https://arxiv.org/abs/2312.07104

LLM-SYM: Integrating Symbolic Methods and Large Language Models for Automated Theorem Proving

Yifan Wu[1,2], Yanhong Huang[1,2(✉)], and Jianqi Shi[1,2]

[1] National Trusted Embedded Software Engineering Technology Research Center, East China Normal University, Shanghai, China

[2] Software Engineering Institute, East China Normal University, Shanghai, China

yhhuang@sei.ecnu.edu.cn

Abstract. Interactive theorem provers (ITPs) are crucial tools in formal verification, enabling researchers to ensure software reliability and safety in critical systems. While effective, the process of writing proofs using ITPs is costly, involving repetitive tasks. Techniques for automating proofs using symbolic methods and machine learning have been proposed, but both have limitations: symbolic methods struggle with higher-order logic, while machine learning requires extensive training data. Although large language models (LLMs) are increasingly used in software engineering for tasks such as code generation, their effectiveness in theorem proving is hindered by a lack of sufficient training data and the iterative nature of proof generation. To overcome these challenges, we introduce LLM-SYM, an end-to-end framework that integrates symbolic methods with LLMs, enhancing LLMs' theorem-proving capabilities through fine-tuning. Our approach extracts proof information from human-constructed proofs and employs symbolic methods to rewrite low-level proofs. We enhance data with tactics history and use curriculum sorting to optimize learning. We developed an interactive proof search agent to explore and verify tactics. Testing LLM-SYM on CompCert project reveals improvements over existing methods, and ablation experiments confirm the effectiveness of components within our approach.

Keywords: Theorem Proving · Coq · Large Language Models(LLM)

1 Introduction

Interactive theorem provers (ITPs) like Coq [30], Isabelle [22], and Lean [21] are essential tools for formal verification in software systems, widely used in computer science to ensure semantic guarantees. They provide a rigorous framework for defining and verifying program behavior, significantly reducing software error likelihood. ITPs operate by users stating theorems and incrementally constructing and verifying each logical step, with each step mechanically checked by the

É. André et al. (Eds.): ICFEM 2025, LNCS 16229, pp. 42–59, 2026.
https://doi.org/10.1007/978-981-95-4213-0_3

tool to ensure correctness. This method is particularly effective for complex logical and mathematical structures, offering higher reliability and security than traditional methods. Researchers have used ITPs to ensure software reliability and safety in critical areas such as compilers [17], hardware design [25], and operating system kernels [5].

However, writing mathematical proofs in ITPs is not easy. On one hand, it requires users to have specialized knowledge, and on the other hand, the proving process involves a lot of repetitive and tedious work. The cost is substantial when using interactive theorem provers for complex system verification. For example, the verification of the CompCert C compiler [17] required six person-years.

Many proof automation techniques have been proposed to reduce the effort required by ITPs, primarily divided into symbolic methods [6,16,23] and machine learning methods [7,8,26,27]. Symbolic methods leverage previously established theorems and automated theorem provers like Z3 [20] to automate proofs. Despite their effectiveness, they are limited in handling higher-order and inductive reasoning, restricting their ability to prove complex theorems. Machine learning methods use models to predict the next proof step in a heuristic-guided search process, which requires substantial training data [7,8,26].

In recent years, large language models (LLMs) have gained popularity for their ability to comprehend and generate human-like text, adapt to diverse tasks, and enhance productivity by automating complex processes, making them valuable in various software engineering fields such as code generation [12]. Regrettably, LLMs lack proficiency in theorem proving, and even the most advanced LLMs struggle to generate formal proofs effectively [19]. This limitation can primarily be attributed to the shortage of theorem-proving-related data in the training datasets of most mainstream LLMs. Furthermore, theorem proving inherently involves an iterative process that requires ongoing feedback at each step to refine and correct the proof as it progresses. Without this feedback loop to guide the models, LLMs fail to effectively handle the complexities and nuances of formal proof generation.

To address the challenges mentioned above, we propose *LLM-SYM*, an end-to-end framework that combines symbolic methods and LLMs. Our approach involves fine-tuning existing large general-purpose models to enhance their performance in the theorem proving. Specifically, we extract proof tactics and the proof environment from existing human-constructed proofs as raw training data. During this process, to prevent trivial details from affecting the model's learning, we employ symbolic methods to rewrite low-level proofs. We enhance the data with logical continuity information through data augmentation with tactics history. Additionally, curriculum sorting is utilized to improve the model's learning performance on new tasks. We design an interactive proof search agent to facilitate the exploration and verification of proof tactics within dynamic environments. We test *LLM-SYM* on a famous verification project called CompCert [17], achieving improvements over existing methods. Furthermore, a set of ablation experiments demonstrated the effectiveness of each component of our approach.

Our main contributions are as follows:

- We propose *LLM-SYM*, a novel proof automation framework that integrates symbolic methods and LLMs.
- We experimented with our method on CompCert, demonstrating better performance compared to existing methods.

This paper is organized as follows: Sect. 2 provides an overview of interactive theorem proving in Coq and hammer. Section 3 details the framework of our approach. Section 4 covers the experimental setup and discusses the results of our evaluation. Section 5 introduces recent related work. Finally, Sect. 6 concludes our work.

2 Preliminaries

2.1 Interactive Theorem Proving in Coq

The Coq proof assistant [30] is a popular interactive theorem prover(ITP), which is widely used for creating machine-verified proofs of mathematical theorems and validating software systems. It enables users to build these proofs interactively using tactics. In Coq, the proof state consists of one or more unproven goals. Each goal comprises a conclusion, which is the statement to be proven, and a local context containing named hypotheses, variables, and local definitions used to prove the conclusion. For ease of description, we collectively refer to all items in the local context as hypotheses. Unless otherwise specified, hypotheses are assumed to point to the current goal. To better introduce the basic usage of Coq, we demonstrated the proof process for the associativity of addition on natural numbers, as shown in Fig. 1. The proof begins by introducing the quantified variables a, b, and c into the context using the `intros` tactic. Then, `induction` is performed on a, splitting the proof into two cases: the base case and the inductive case. In the base case, where $a = 0$, the goal $(0+b)+c = 0+(b+c)$ is simplified using the `simpl` tactic and solved by `reflexivity`. In the inductive case, assuming the inductive hypothesis $a' + b + c = a' + (b + c)$ for some a', the goal $(Sa' + b) + c = Sa' + (b + c)$ is simplified and rewritten using `rewrite IH` to substitute the inductive hypothesis, followed by solved with `reflexivity`. This step-by-step process demonstrates the use of induction and rewriting tactics in Coq to construct a formal proof of the associativity of addition for natural numbers.

2.2 Hammer

To simplify the process of constructing proofs, Coq has a powerful symbolic method called CoqHammer [6] and provides a tactic called `hammer`. It initially uses machine learning to retrieve lemmas that serve as premises, which can assist in solving the current goal. Secondly, it translates proof goals into first-order logic form and solves them using automated theorem prover(ATPs), including

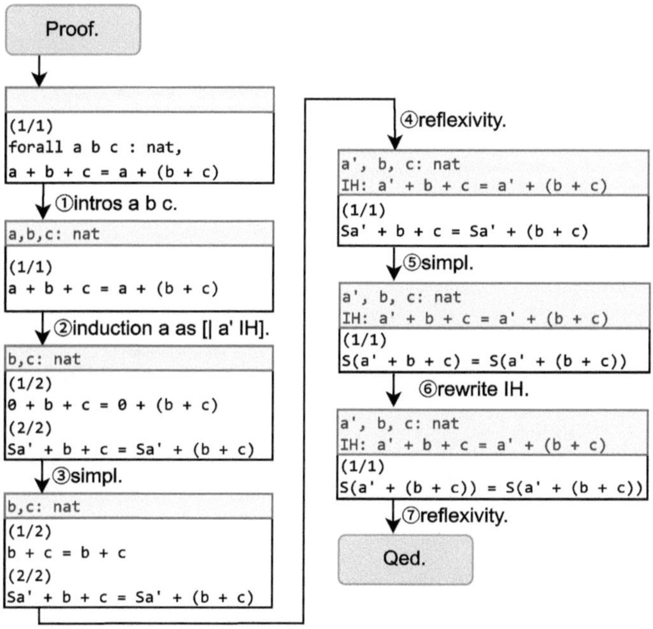

Fig. 1. The procedure of proving addition's associativity: gray sections show hypotheses, white sections outline goals, and arrows depict tactics.

Vampire [24], CVC5 [3], Eprover [1], and Z3 [20]. Thirdly, if an ATP successfully solves the problem, hammer reconstructs the proof in Coq.

Despite their power, hammers do have limitations. They cover only a subset of the reasoning capabilities of ITPs. For example, they generally do not handle proof tactics that require structural reasoning, such as `induction`, which is crucial for proving properties of recursively defined structures or functions. This limitation means that while hammers can efficiently solve many straightforward goals, they may struggle with or be unable to directly prove more complex theorems.

3 Approach

Figure 2 provides an overview of *LLM-SYM*, which integrates several components to enhance automated proof search within a Coq proof environment. The system starts by extracting training data using hammer, which is then augmented with historical information. The augmented data is sorted by difficulty to form a curriculum, facilitating a progressive learning strategy. The training data is used to fine-tune a model called Qwen2.5-14B-Chat [32], optimizing it for theorem proving task. An interactive proof search agent executes tactics in the Coq environment, synthesizes prompts, and receives feedback to adjust its approach. This agent communicates with the finetuned model by sending prompts and incorporating the model's responses to advance the proof search.

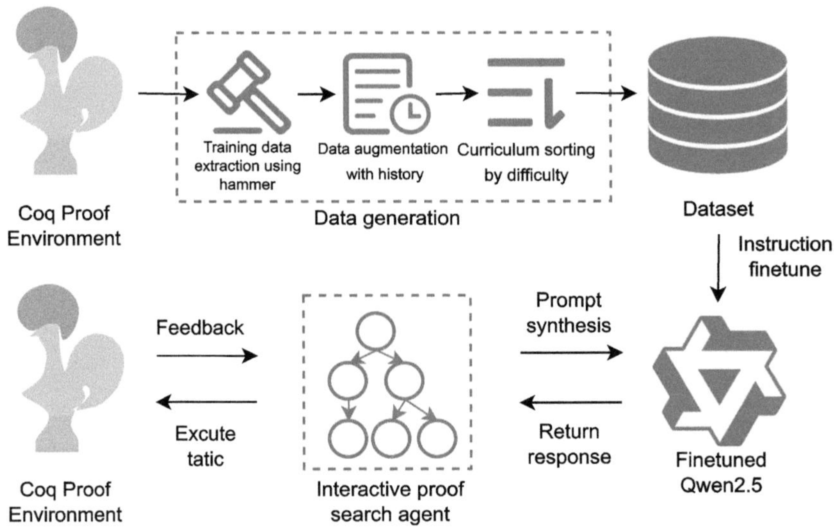

Fig. 2. The overview of *LLM-SYM*.

3.1 Training Data Extraction

Starting from existing human-constructed proofs, we use the symbolic method known as hammer to handle the proof details, thereby extracting the data needed for fine-tuning. Algorithm 1 presents the training data extraction procedure. The input to the procedure is a theorem statement T and a list of original tactics TL. The output is a list L of datapoints during the successful proof attempt. Each datapoint is a dictionary that includes a proof state, a tactic applicable, and other information in that proof state. We use the notation $|L|$ to denote the length of the list L and $L \circ t$ to represent appending the element t to the end of the list L.

Initially, the algorithm sets up an empty list L to store the records and initializes the proof environment with the given theorem T. An index i, used to indicate the original tactic which could be applied, is initialized to 0. The main loop of the algorithm continues until there are no remaining goals in the proof state. Within each iteration, the algorithm collects the current proof state and attempts to solve the goals using hammer. If hammer fails, the algorithm appends the environment and original tactic to the list L. It then executes the tactic and advances the index i. If hammer successfully solves the goals, the proof state and hammer tactic are appended to L . The algorithm checks if there are remaining goals. If goals persist, the algorithm will adjust to find the tactics originally meant to address these sub-goals. The algorithm continues this process of executing tactics, recording proof state until all goals are solved. Finally, it returns the complete list of tactic and environment records L.

Algorithm 1. Training data extraction algorithm

```
Input:A theorem statement T, a list of original tactic TL
Output:A list of datapoint from one theorem L
function EXTRACTION(T, TL)
    L ← empty_list
    Coq.init_env(T)
    i ← 0
    while |Coq.goals| > 0 do
        dict ← empty_dictionary
        dict.hypothesis ← Coq.hypothesis
        dict.goals ← Coq.goals
        error ← Coq.execute(hammer)
        if error then
            dict.tactic ← TL_i
            Coq.execute(TL_i)
            i ← i + 1
        else
            dict.tactic ← hammer
            gn ← |Coq.goals|
            if gn > 0 then
                Coq.execute(Undo)
                while |Coq.goals| ≠ gn do
                    Coq.execute(TL_i)
                    i ← i + 1
        L ← L ∘ dict
    return L
```

3.2 Data Augmentation with History

We observed a significant correlation between different tactics in the proving process. For example, after applying *induction*, the first goal can often be automatically solved using the *hammer* tactic. So we add historical tactic information to each datapoint to capture the logical continuity between tactics.

In Coq, after completing a subgoal, the proof of the next subgoal automatically begins, which means these adjacent tactics are not fully logically related. Instead, we need to identify the actual previous tactic for the next subgoal, which is the reason the subgoal was generated. A stack is used to handle this situation, with its top storing the index of the previous tactic for the next subgoal (if a next subgoal exists). The stack-based approach is theoretically supported by its effectiveness in handling state transitions and facilitating backtracking, akin to depth-first search algorithms, which excel at systematically navigating extensive search spaces. This method optimizes computational efficiency by preserving a coherent reasoning path, reducing redundant computations, and enabling the model to swiftly return to prior states without the need to recompute entire paths.

Algorithm 2 describes the procedure of the data augmentation. The input is a list L of datapoints, and the output is an augmented list of datapoints. The algorithm initializes an empty stack S and sets the history of the first datapoint L_1 to an empty list. It then iterates through each datapoint L_i from the second one, calculating the difference d between the current goals size and the previous goals size. If $d < 0$, which means a subgoal has finished, it pops an index from the stack and assigns it to *pre*; otherwise, it sets *pre* to $i - 1$ and pushes i-1 onto the stack for d times. The history of L_i is updated by concatenating the history of L_{pre} with the tactic from L_{pre}. Finally, it returns the augmented list L.

Algorithm 2. Data augmentation algorithm

Input:List of datapoint from one theorem L
Output:List of augmentative datapoint from one theorem L
function PROVE(TL)
    $S \leftarrow empty\_stack$
    $L_0.history = empty\_list$
    for $i = 1$ to $|L|$ **do**
        $d \leftarrow |L_i.goals| - |L_{i-1}.goals|$
        if $d < 0$ **then** ▷ previous tactic finish a subgoal
            $pre \leftarrow S.pop()$
        else
            $pre \leftarrow i - 1$
            for $i = 1$ to d **do** ▷ push onto stack if generats subgoals
                $S.push(i - 1)$
        $L_i.history = L_{pre}.history + L_{pre}.tactic$
    return L

3.3 Curriculum Sorting

Due to the limited exposure of LLMs to the task of automated theorem proving during their pre-training, they lack familiarity with this task. Inspired by curriculum learning [4], we apply a method called curriculum data sorting to facilitate the progressive learning of this new task by LLMs. The essence of curriculum data sorting is to enhance the model's learning process by incrementally increasing task complexity. Theoretically, this approach can be linked to the dynamics of gradient descent, where starting with simpler problems helps establish a stable gradient flow, reducing the risk of erratic updates that might occur if complex problems are introduced too early. This can lead to smoother convergence and potentially faster learning rates. Additionally, insights from transfer learning suggest that solving simpler problems first allows the model to develop generalizable features that are beneficial for tackling more complex tasks, enhancing the model's ability to transfer knowledge across different problem domains. We use the length of the current proof tactic as an indicator of the theorem's difficulty level and rearrange the data in ascending order based on the difficulty of the corresponding theorems. By adopting this technique, LLMs can gradually adapt to the increasing complexity of the task, thereby enhancing their overall performance.

3.4 Instruction Fine-Tuning

After constructing training data, we perform the instruction fine-tuning on Qwen2.5-14B-Chat [32] using the LoRA [11] method for the time efficiency. Qwen2.5-14B-Chat is a language model designed to handle complex reasoning and language understanding tasks. With 14 billion parameters, it is capable of processing large amounts of data and generating coherent, contextually relevant responses. It excels in applications requiring nuanced interpretation and precise execution of instructions. The provided instruction consists of the proof state along with the history of tactics. The desired output is a Coq proof tactic. Detailed experimental settings are described in Sect. 4 .

3.5 Interactive Proof Search Agent

Research indicates that the capability of LLMs in formal reasoning is frequently underestimated [13]. To better leverage LLMs' capability in proving Coq theorems, inspired by Copra [29], we propose an interactive proof search agent. This agent organizes the current proof goal, hypothesis, historical tactics of the proof, and error cases into prompts to enable LLMs to continuously interact with Coq.

Algorithm 3 outlines the search procedure employed by our agent to prove a given theorem statement T. Initially, the environment is set up. Two lists, $L_{history}$ and L_{fail} are initialized empty to manage tactic history and failed tactics in one state. A stack S is initialized empty to restore $L_{history}$ and L_{fail} when backtracking to a previous state. The agent iteratively synthesizes prompts using the current goals, hypotheses, tactic history, and failed tactics. Then the prompts are given to LLM to generate a tactic. The tactic is executed, and the agent checks whether the proof is completed successfully by monitoring whether there are remaining goals. If the execution results in errors, the agent appends the failed tactic to L_{fail}. If the number of errors in a state reaches a threshold t, it employs a backtracking mechanism by restoring a previous state from the stack and executing an undo tactic. The current state is saved to the stack if no errors occur, updating $L_{history}$ with successful tactics and resetting L_{fail}. The search loop continues until the theorem is proved or the maximum number of queries is reached, ensuring an efficient exploration of tactics through strategic error handling and state management.

Algorithm 3. Search procedure in our agent

```
Input: A theorem statement T
procedure SEARCH(T)
    L_history, L_fail ← empty_list
    S ← empty_stack
    Coq.init_env(T)
    for i = 1 to k do                               ▷ a maximum of k queries for one theorem
        p ← PROMPTSYNTHESIS(Coq.goals,Coq.hypothesis,L_history,L_fail)
        tactic ← PARSETACTIC(LLM(p))
        error ← Coq.execute(tactic)
        if |Coq.goals| = 0 then
            break                                   ▷ proof finish successfully
        else if error then
            L_fail ← L_fail ∘ tactic
            if |L_fail| > t then                    ▷ a maximum of t queries for one state
                L_history, L_fail ← S.pop()
                Coq.execute(Undo)
        else
            S.push((L_history, L_fail ∘ tactic))    ▷ save the search state
            L_history ← L_history ∘ tactic
            L_fail ← empty_list
```

4 Evaluation

4.1 Set up

In this work, we evaluate formal reasoning capabilities using CompCert [17], a prominent compiler verification project implemented in Coq. CompCert is well-known for its rigorous machine-checked proofs that ensure the source and compiled C code behave identically. Following prior work [33], we performed a similar dataset split by using the 508 theorems from 12 Coq files as the test set, while all remaining files were used for training.

We apply the aforementioned data extraction algorithm on the training set, ultimately constructing approximately 22,000 datapoints. This process is completed on a workstation equipped with a GTX 1080 Ti (11 GB VRAM), an Intel i9-7960X CPU, and 64GB of memory, taking a total of 50 h. We performed instruction fine-tuning on Qwen2.5-14B-Chat [32] using the LoRA [11] method to improve time efficiency. [1] Using a learning rate of 1E-5 and 1,000 initial warm-up steps, the training process is completed in approximately 3 h on a server equipped with two 4090 GPUs. After completing the training, we deploy the fine-tuned model on the same workstation used for the data extraction process. We employ temperature sampling with a temperature parameter of T = 0.5 to generate outputs from the language model. For the parameters in the search process, we set the maximum number of queries for one theorem k to 60, and the maximum number of queries for one state t to 5. These values were chosen

[1] Training sample details are provided in the appendix.

based on heuristic observations to balance computational efficiency and proof success rates.

Our experiments are compared with two state-of-the-art proof automation methods: *Proverbot9001* [26], *PALM* [19]. *Proverbot9001* uses recurrent neural network [10] to capture proof state characteristic features. *PALM* uses LLMs to generate proof and uses symbolic methods to fix the proof generated by LLM. According to its introduction, *PALM* exhibits generalizability across LLMs of different sizes. Considering cost factors, we have consistently used *GPT-3.5* [2] as LLM in our replication.

To demonstrate *LLM-SYM*'s generalizability across LLMs of varying sizes, we also evaluate it using Qwen2.5-7B and Qwen2.5-3B.

4.2 Results

Table 1 displays the number and percentage of theorems each approach can successfully prove. Compared to existing methods, *LLM-SYM* shows a significant improvement in success rate, proving 43.6% and 10.9% more theorems than *Proverbot9001* and *PALM*, respectively. The results in Table 1 also show that while theorem proving capability decreases with fewer parameters, *LLM-SYM* still outperforms other baselines, indicating its generalizability.

Table 1. Theorems demonstrated by each approach.

Approach	Proofs Solved	Success Rate
Proverbot9001	133/508	26.2%
PALM	172/508	33.9%
***LLM-SYM*(14B)**	**191/508**	**37.6%**
LLM-SYM(7B)	187/508	36.8%
LLM-SYM(3B)	178/508	35.0%

To analyze the performance of each approach in more detail, Fig. 3 presents a Venn diagram depicting the theorems proven by each method. All approaches are capable of proving 230 theorems, the majority of which (83%) can be proven by *LLM-SYM*. Additionally, *LLM-SYM* uniquely proves 24(10.4%) theorems that none of the other approaches can demonstrate. These data clearly demonstrate that *LLM-SYM* can prove a wide range of theorems.

In our analysis of the complexity of theorems that *LLM-SYM* proves, we use the number of tactics in the original proofs as a proxy metric for theorem complexity. As shown in Fig. 4, we group the theorems in the test set based on the number of tactics in the original proofs and distinguish between successfully proven and those not successfully proven by *LLM-SYM*. With an average of 4.35 tactics and a median of 4, it is evident that *LLM-SYM* is more effective with shorter proofs. This is understandable because longer proofs may involve more complex proof tactics and frequently use assertions to introduce assumptions during the proof process, which can be challenging for *LLM-SYM*.

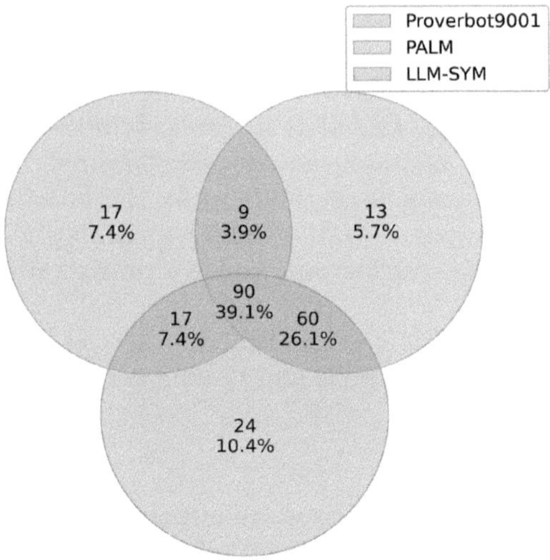

Fig. 3. Venn diagram

On average, *LLM-SYM* takes 49.9 s to successfully prove a theorem. The average number of queries is 4.08, and the average number of backtracks is 0.08, which means approximately one backtrack occurs every 50 queries. This indicates that *LLM-SYM* is generally efficient.

4.3 Ablation Studies

Table 2. Theorems demonstrated by each variant.

Approach	Proofs Solved	Success Rate
***LLM-SYM*(14B)**	**191/508**	**37.6%**
w/o hammer in data extraction	42/508	8.3%
w/o data augmentation with history	174/508	34.3%
w/o curriculum sorting	161/508	31.7%
w/o backtracking in search procedure	179/508	35.2%

Due to the low GPU cost of *LLM-SYM*, we performed an extensive ablation study to assess the effectiveness of its components. We created three variants for *LLM-SYM*: the first one does not use the hammer tactic during data extraction; the second one does not use data augmentation with history; the third one does not use curriculum sorting; the last one does not use backtracking mechanism in search procedure. Aside from these differences, each variant remains consistent with *LLM-SYM*.

The results are presented in Table 2. In general, removing any component from our framework results in a significant drop in performance compared to

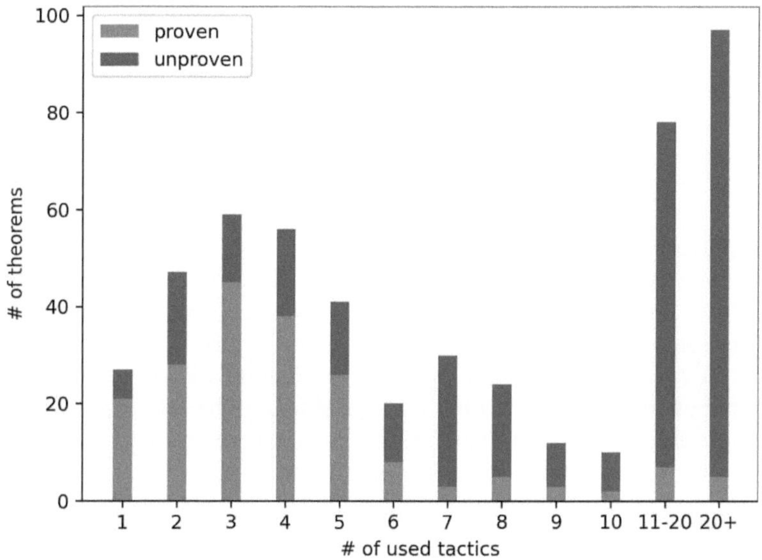

Fig. 4. Distribution of theorems that are proven or not proven by *LLM-SYM*, categorized by the number of tactics in the original proofs.

the full framework, demonstrating that the modules we propose are not mere combinations but work synergistically to improve performance.

The ablation study indicates that the data simplified through hammer tactic is better suited for fine-tuning LLMs. By reducing complexity and filtering out irrelevant information, hammer tactic helps create a cleaner and more focused dataset. This makes it easier for LLMs to learn and generalize, resulting in improved performance in proof tasks. Removing data augmentation with historical context results in a decline in performance, which we believe is due to the lack of learning in LLMs regarding the continuity features of proof tactics. Eliminating curriculum sorting also leads to performance deterioration. By delaying the introduction of lengthy and difficult examples, curriculum sorting helps prevent disruptions in learning and promotes a more gradual training progression. Furthermore, disabling backtracking in the search procedure will result in a decreased success rate because using incorrect tactics can lead to a new goal that is more difficult or even impossible to prove.

4.4 Case Studies

Although *LLM-SYM* is effective, it is unable to prove 62.4% of the theorems in our dataset. To understand the reasons for *LLM-SYM*'s failures, we randomly selected 50 theorems that *LLM-SYM* fails and carried out a manual categorization and examination. Table 3 presents the two primary reasons.[2] Then we show an illustrative example for each type of failure.

[2] Since a theorem can fail for multiple reasons, the percentage of reasons exceeds 100%.

Table 3. The reasons for *LLM-SYM*'s failures.

Reason	Number	Rate
Requiring necessary premises	37/50	74%
incorrect compound tactic	23/50	46%

An important reason for *LLM-SYM*'s failure (74%) is the lack of necessary premises. For example, as shown in the Fig. 5, the proof gets stuck due to the absence of the required premise named `genv_public_add_globals`.

Another reason for *LLM-SYM*'s failure is the incorrect compound tactic. As illustrated in the Fig. 6, the manual proof used semicolons to combine tactics. After `destruct op`, it handled all 33 subgoals using `inv H0; hammer`, automatically completing each proof. *LLM-SYM* couldn't generate correct compound tactic due to the unknown subgoal proof environment.

```
Theorem globalenv_public:
  forall p, genv_public (globalenv p) = prog_public p.

  (* Human written proof *)
  unfold globalenv; intros.
  rewrite genv_public_add_globals. auto.

  (* LLM-SYM generated proof *)
  intros. unfold globalenv.
  hammer.
```

Fig. 5. A failure case that requires the necessary premises.

```
Lemma eval_unop_lessdef:
  forall op v1 v1' v,
  eval_unop op v1 = Some v -> Val.lessdef v1 v1' ->
  exists v', eval_unop op v1' = Some v' /\ Val.lessdef v v'.

  (* Human written proof *)
  intros.
  destruct op; inv H0; hammer.

  (* LLM-SYM generated proof *)
  intros.
  destruct op; hammer.
```

Fig. 6. A failure case of an incorrect compound tactic.

5 Related Work

Various machine learning-based techniques have been developed to automate formal proof generation for interactive theorem provers (ITPs). Tree-LSTM [28] models proof states using abstract syntax trees (ASTs) and searches for proofs via depth-first search. ASTactic [33] was the first deep learning-based proof generation technique for ITPs, and subsequent techniques have enhanced its performance. For instance, TacTok [8] not only models proof states but also incomplete scripts for more context. Diva [7] enlarges the search space by combining models trained with varying hyperparameters and data orderings. Proverbot9001 [26] uses an RNN with engineered features to predict tactics and arguments, employing advanced search algorithms like A-star and several pruning techniques to improve efficiency. Thor [15] augments the PISA [14] dataset with SledgeHammer [23] invocations and trains a model to guide hammer usage during proofs.

Recently, there has been growing interest in applying large language models (LLMs) to formal verification. Draft, Sketch, and Prove (DSP) [13] translates informal proofs into formal sketches using LLMs and fills in the details with automated theorem provers. Copra [29] leverages GPT-4 in a depth-first search process, relying on LLMs' capabilities to avoid errors and improve theorem proving success. PALM [19] is a generate-then-repair approach that uses LLMs to create initial formal proofs and then employs symbolic methods to iteratively fix lower-level errors, significantly improving theorem proving success rates. These methods use general large language models (LLMs) for formal verification, improving theorem proving success rates by translating informal proofs, employing depth-first search, and iteratively repairing errors. However, as these LLMs are not specifically designed for interactive theorem proving tasks and have limited opportunities to write proofs during the pre-training phase, they still face challenges in handling complex proof details and ensuring the reliability of automated reasoning. Some researchers have attempted to use fine-tuning techniques to enhance the capabilities of large models for specific tasks. Baldur [9] fine-tunes Minerva [18] for proof generation and repair, using extensive sampling from a large dataset. TheoremLlama [31] is an end-to-end framework that transforms a general-purpose LLM into a Lean4 expert by generating aligned NL-FL datasets and employing advanced training techniques, significantly improving theorem proving accuracy over existing baselines. Unlike existing methods, our approach combines symbolic methods with fine-tuning LLM, enhancing learning outcomes by using symbolic methods to manage proof details.

6 Conclusion

In conclusion, our research demonstrates the effectiveness of LLM-SYM, an innovative framework that integrates symbolic methods with large language models to enhance theorem-proving capabilities. By extracting proof information from human-constructed proofs and utilizing symbolic methods to rewrite low-level proofs, we obtain data suitable for fine-tuning LLMs. The inclusion of tactics history and curriculum sorting further optimizes the learning process. Our interactive proof search agent effectively explores and verifies tactics. Evaluation using the CompCert project shows that LLM-SYM surpasses existing proof automation methods. The results of ablation experiments confirm the efficacy of the components within our framework, highlighting LLM-SYM's potential to significantly advance interactive theorem proving in formal verification.

Future work will focus on expanding the dataset and refining the proof generation process to further improve accuracy and robustness. Additionally, to address the limitation of needing specific premises, we plan to enhance the interactive proof search agent with theorem retrieval capabilities. This will enable the agent to effectively leverage existing lemmas, thereby streamlining the proof process. Furthermore, we plan to explore how the approach will generalize to other theorem provers beyond Coq, such as Lean and Isabelle. This will involve systematically extracting training data from these libraries and adapting our framework to accommodate their unique syntactic and semantic features. We will redesign the proof search agent to ensure compatibility with these environments, focusing on effective iterative proof construction.

Acknowledgment. This work is supported by National Natural Science Foundation of China Projects (No.92370201), and National Key Research and Development Program(No.2022YFB3305200)

Appendix

Each of the training samples consists of three parts: System prompt, instruction, and the model's response. Figure 7 presents an example of instruction and model response. Figure 8 shows the system prompt, which serves as the guideline provided to the model to generate responses.

```
Goals to prove:                                                        instruction
[GOALS]
[GOAL] 1
slot_valid f Outgoing ofs ty = true
[HYPOTHESES] 1
[HYPOTHESIS] B : (typealign ty | ofs)
[HYPOTHESIS] A : ofs >= 0
[HYPOTHESIS] H : In (S Outgoing ofs ty) (regs_of_rpairs (loc_arguments sg))
[HYPOTHESIS] sg : signature
[HYPOTHESIS] ty : typ
[HYPOTHESIS] ofs : Z
[HYPOTHESIS] f : Linear\\.function
[END]
[STEPS]
[STEP] intros.
[STEP] exploit loc_arguments_acceptable_2; eauto.
[STEP] intros [A B].
```

```
[RUN TACTIC]                                                           response
unfold slot_valid.
[END]
```

Fig. 7. An example of instructions and model responses

You are a proficient formal theorem-proving agent in Coq. You can predict the next proof step given the current proof state, relevant definitions, and some possible useful lemmas/theorems. The proof state is described in the following format:
1. All the goals are described under `[GOALS]` keyword. Each goal within the `[GOALS]` is described under the keyword `[GOAL] i`, where `i` is a positive integer. For example, `[GOAL] 1`, `[GOAL] 2`, etc.
2. Within each `[GOAL] i` keyword, the goal is described as a human-readable serialized version of the proof state as shown while running `coqtop` command. Each goal, might also accompany some hypotheses, which are described under the keyword `[HYPOTHESES] i`. Each hypothesis within `[HYPOTHESES]`, starts with the prefix `[HYPOTHESIS]`.
3. Sometimes `[GOALS]` can have description about the proof state like `Proof finished`, `There are unfocused goals`, `Not in proof mode`, etc. The description is described under the keyword `[DESCRIPTION]`.
4. Finally, `[STEPS]` keyword is used to describe proof-steps used so far. Several lines will appear under this keyword, each proof step starts with the prefix `[STEP]`, and is a valid Coq tactic ending with a `.`. For example, `[STEPS]\n[STEP]intros a.\n[STEP]induction a.`.
5. Sometimes, `[INCORRECT STEPS]` keyword optionally used to describe proof-steps which should `NOT` be generated. Several lines will appear under this keyword, each incorrect proof step starts with the prefix `[STEP]`, and is a valid Coq tactic ending with a `.`. For example, `[INCORRECT STEPS]\n[STEP]apply mul_assoc.\n[STEP]rewrite <- H.`.
6. There is also an optional `[LAST STEP]` keyword which describes the proof-step generated last time. If the proof-step was incorrect, then it is also followed by error message from Coq environment. For example, `[LAST STEP]reflexivity.[ERROR MESSAGE]Error: In environment\nn : nat\nUnable to unify \"n\" with \"n + 0\".`. If the proof-step was correct then it is followed by the keyword `[SUCCESS]`. For example, `[LAST STEP]reflexivity.[SUCCESS]`. Don't generate the last proof-step again if it was NOT successful.
7. Sometimes there can be errors in the format of the generated response. This is reported using the keyword `[ERROR]` followed by the error message. For example, `[ERROR]\nInvalid response:\n'Great! The proof is complete.', \nStopping Reason: 'stop'.\n Please respond only in the format specified.[END]`. This means that the response generated by you was not in the specified format. Please follow the specified format strictly.

If you think you know the next proof step, then start your response with `[RUN TACTIC]` followed by the next proof-step which will help in simplifying the current proof state. For example, `[RUN TACTIC]destruct c.[END]`. Generate exactly ONE proof-step. Multiple proof steps are more error prone, because you will not get a chance to see intermediate proof state descriptions. Make sure that the proof step is valid and compiles correctly with Coq. You are able to use the tactic `hammer`, which is a powerful tactic which can automatically prove goals via calls to external SMT solvers. You should attempt `hammer` when a goal seems relatively straightforward to prove but may require many steps. However, it is important to note that when using the hammer, it must not violate Rule 5 and Rule 6.

Fig. 8. System prompt.

References

1. Eprover (2024). http://www.eprover.org
2. Gpt-3.5-turbo (2024). https://platform.openai.com/docs/models/gpt-3-5-turbo
3. Barbosa, H., et al.: cvc5: a versatile and industrial-strength SMT solver. In: TACAS 2022. LNCS, vol. 13243, pp. 415–442. Springer, Cham (2022). https://doi.org/10.1007/978-3-030-99524-9_24
4. Bengio, Y., Louradour, J., Collobert, R., Weston, J.: Curriculum learning. In: Proceedings of the 26th Annual International Conference on Machine Learning, pp. 41–48 (2009)
5. Chen, H., Wu, X., Shao, Z., Lockerman, J., Gu, R.: Toward compositional verification of interruptible os kernels and device drivers. In: Proceedings of the 37th ACM SIGPLAN Conference on Programming Language Design and Implementation, pp. 431–447 (2016)
6. Czajka, z., Kaliszyk, C.: Hammer for coq: automation for dependent type theory. J. Autom. Reason. **61**(1–4), 423–453 (2018). https://doi.org/10.1007/s10817-018-9458-4

7. First, E., Brun, Y.: Diversity-driven automated formal verification. In: Proceedings of the 44th International Conference on Software Engineering, pp. 749–761 (2022)
8. First, E., Brun, Y., Guha, A.: Tactok: semantics-aware proof synthesis. Proc. ACM Program. Lang. **4**(OOPSLA), 1–31 (2020)
9. First, E., Rabe, M., Ringer, T., Brun, Y.: Baldur: whole-proof generation and repair with large language models. In: Proceedings of the 31st ACM Joint European Software Engineering Conference and Symposium on the Foundations of Software Engineering, pp. 1229–1241 (2023)
10. Grossberg, S.: Recurrent neural networks. Scholarpedia **8**(2), 1888 (2013)
11. Hu, E.J., et al.: Lora: low-rank adaptation of large language models. ICLR **1**(2), 3 (2022)
12. Hu, Y., et al.: Qualityflow: an agentic workflow for program synthesis controlled by llm quality checks. arXiv preprint arXiv:2501.17167 (2025)
13. Jiang, A.Q., et al.: Draft, sketch, and prove: guiding formal theorem provers with informal proofs. arXiv preprint arXiv:2210.12283 (2022)
14. Jiang, A.Q., Li, W., Han, J.M., Wu, Y.: Lisa: language models of isabelle proofs. In: 6th Conference on Artificial Intelligence and Theorem Proving, pp. 378–392 (2021)
15. Jiang, A.Q., et al.: Thor: wielding hammers to integrate language models and automated theorem provers. Adv. Neural. Inf. Process. Syst. **35**, 8360–8373 (2022)
16. Kaliszyk, C., Urban, J.: Hol (y) hammer: online atp service for hol light. Math. Comput. Sci. **9**, 5–22 (2015)
17. Kästner, Det al.: CompCert: practical experience on integrating and qualifying a formally verified optimizing compiler. In: ERTS 2018: Embedded Real Time Software and Systems. SEE (2018). http://xavierleroy.org/publi/erts2018_compcert.pdf
18. Lewkowycz, A., et al.: Solving quantitative reasoning problems with language models (2022). https://arxiv.org/abs/2206.14858
19. Lu, M., Delaware, B., Zhang, T.: Proof automation with large language models. In: Proceedings of the 39th IEEE/ACM International Conference on Automated Software Engineering, pp. 1509–1520 (2024)
20. de Moura, L., Bjørner, N.: Z3: an efficient SMT solver. In: Ramakrishnan, C.R., Rehof, J. (eds.) TACAS 2008. LNCS, vol. 4963, pp. 337–340. Springer, Heidelberg (2008). https://doi.org/10.1007/978-3-540-78800-3_24
21. de Moura, L., Kong, S., Avigad, J., van Doorn, F., von Raumer, J.: The lean theorem prover (system description). In: Felty, A.P., Middeldorp, A. (eds.) CADE 2015. LNCS (LNAI), vol. 9195, pp. 378–388. Springer, Cham (2015). https://doi.org/10.1007/978-3-319-21401-6_26
22. Nipkow, T., Wenzel, M., Paulson, L.C.: Isabelle/HOL: A Proof Assistant for Higher-Order Logic. Springer-Verlag, Heidelberg (2002)
23. Paulson, L.C., Blanchette, J.C.: Three years of experience with sledgehammer, a practical link between automatic and interactive theorem provers. In: Sutcliffe, G., Schulz, S., Ternovska, E. (eds.) IWIL 2010. The 8th International Workshop on the Implementation of Logics. EPiC Series in Computing, vol. 2, pp. 1–11. EasyChair (2012).https://doi.org/10.29007/36dt
24. Riazanov, A., Voronkov, A.: The design and implementation of VAMPIRE. AI Commun. **15**(2,3), 91–110 (2002)
25. Russinoff, D.M.: Formal verification of floating-point hardware design. Springer, **10**, 978–3 (2022)

26. Sanchez-Stern, A., Alhessi, Y., Saul, L., Lerner, S.: Generating correctness proofs with neural networks. In: Proceedings of the 4th ACM SIGPLAN International Workshop on Machine Learning and Programming Languages, pp. 1–10 (2020)
27. Sanchez-Stern, A., First, E., Zhou, T., Kaufman, Z., Brun, Y., Ringer, T.: Passport: improving automated formal verification using identifiers. ACM Trans. Program. Lang. Syst. **45**(2), 1–30 (2023)
28. Tai, K.S., Socher, R., Manning, C.D.: Improved semantic representations from tree-structured long short-term memory networks. arXiv preprint arXiv:1503.00075 (2015)
29. Thakur, A., Wen, Y., Chaudhuri, S.: A language-agent approach to formal theorem-proving. arXiv preprint arXiv:2310.04353 (2023)
30. The Coq Development Team: The Coq reference manual – release 8.19.0 (2024). https://coq.inria.fr/doc/V8.19.0/refman
31. Wang, R., et al.: Theoremllama: transforming general-purpose llms into lean4 experts. arXiv preprint arXiv:2407.03203 (2024)
32. Yang, A., et al.: Qwen2. 5 technical report. arXiv preprint arXiv:2412.15115 (2024)
33. Yang, K., Deng, J.: Learning to prove theorems via interacting with proof assistants. In: International Conference on Machine Learning, pp. 6984–6994. PMLR (2019)

Modeling and Analysis of Cyber-Physical Systems in the Hybrid π-Calculus Using Extended Sequence Diagrams

Xiong Xu[1], Jixiang Miao[1,2], Shuling Wang[1(✉)], and Jean-Pierre Talpin[3]

[1] National Key Laboratory of Space Integrated Information System, Institute of Software, Chinese Academy of Sciences, Beijing, China
wangsl@ios.ac.cn
[2] University of Chinese Academy of Sciences, Beijing, China
[3] INRIA, Rennes, France

Abstract. Digital infrastructures, grids, and networks heavily rely on Cyber-Physical Systems (CPSs) endpoints in a context of mobile computing, referred to as mobile CPSs, including applications such as smart cities, intelligent transportation systems, and unmanned vehicles. Most of such systems are safety-critical, i.e., any error may result in catastrophic consequences. Mobile CPSs represent a novel computing paradigm, and their inherent complexity and interdisciplinary nature pose significant challenges to system design beyond the limits of state-of-the-art separation of concerns. Model-Based Design (MBD) is a key approach to mitigate the complexity of safety-critical systems. However, it lacks adequate modeling and analysis techniques to tame mobile CPSs. To address this gap, this paper proposes an extension of sequence diagrams, as found in SysML/UML, to facilitate an accurate, graphical representation of the deeply-coupled mobile, parallel, and hybrid behaviors (i.e., the entangled interplay of discrete and continuous behaviors). To ensure the correctness of the designed models, we propose a set of transformation rules that convert the (graphical and hence, by nature, informal) extended sequence diagram to a formal representation using the hybrid π-calculus, thereby enabling formal verification using, e.g., bisimulation-based model checking. Finally, we provide a case study where we employ extended sequence diagrams to model the scenario of the handover protocol of a train control system and formalize it into a hybrid π-calculus model using the proposed transformation rules.

Keywords: CPS · MBD · Sequence diagrams · Hybrid π-calculus · SysML/UML · Mobile computing and communication

1 Introduction

With the rapid development of 5G, 6G, real-time wireless, and integrated air-space-ground networks, an era of ubiquitous computing is emerging [2,6,7] featuring the integration of social, digital, and physical worlds. The fundamental characteristics of this paradigm include the interconnection of all entities,

É. André et al. (Eds.): ICFEM 2025, LNCS 16229, pp. 60–78, 2026.
https://doi.org/10.1007/978-981-95-4213-0_4

software-defined everything, universal programmability, and natural interactions among humans, machines, and physics. The dynamic environments, diverse requirements, and complex physical scenarios introduced by mobile computing necessitate that hardware resources, data resources, software platforms, and applications possess flexible, software-defined capabilities, dynamic topologies, adaptability, mobile interoperability, and natural interaction capabilities. Cyber-Physical Systems (CPSs) in the context of mobile computing, referred to as *mobile CPSs*, represent a novel computing paradigm whose significance has been widely recognized. In particular, the design of safety-critical CPSs spans multiple disciplines, including computer science, control theory, applied mathematics, communication theory, and artificial intelligence. Their inherent complexity and interdisciplinary nature pose great challenges to system design.

Model-Based Design (MBD) has become a popular approach in the design and development of complex safety-critical systems. Its primary advantage lies in the "divide and conquer" strategy to address the inherent complexities of CPSs, thereby enhancing both the efficiency and reliability of system design. This strategy is embodied through two dimensions: horizontal composition/decomposition and vertical abstraction/refinement. In the horizontal dimension, MBD facilitates the integration of heterogeneous models, resulting in modeling techniques with heightened expressive capabilities. For example, AADL models and Simulink/Stateflow models can be composed at the graphical modeling level [25], leveraging each other's strengths. In the vertical dimension, it supports the analysis of models at different levels of abstraction, ranging from intuitive graphical models to rigorous formal models [10], and ultimately to executable code [21]. By adhering to the orthogonal design principles, MBD effectively alleviates the complexity of system modeling, ensuring a more manageable and robust development process.

However, we observe a lake of dedicated modeling and analysis methods for mobile CPSs. As complex heterogeneous systems, mobile CPSs integrate discrete computational, control, and communication processes while deeply embedding the continuous evolution of the physical world. In the context of mobile computing, these systems must consider the openness, uncertainty, and variability of the context, including challenges posed by device diversity, network dynamics, and resource constraints. These characteristics impose significant hurdles for effectively modeling CPSs. Moreover, in mobile computing, the entities interacting with the system exhibit heterogeneity and diverse interaction modalities, resulting in intricate causality chains that may alter safety. Capturing the complex behaviors of such systems accurately and comprehensively represents a formidable challenge. Current modeling techniques, however, often adopt a narrower focus on either hybrid behavior modeling or on mobile computing and communication, which limits their ability to capture such intricate interactions and dynamic evolution within the system and between the system and its environment.

To address these challenges, we propose an extension of sequence diagrams, as used in SysML/UML, to enable accurate and intuitive graphical representations of complex, deeply coupled mobile, parallel, and hybrid behaviors—specifically, the entangled interplay between discrete and continuous dynamics. To ensure the correctness of the designed model, we introduce a set of transformation rules that convert the extended sequence diagram—which is graphical and inherently informal—into a formal representation based on the hybrid π-calculus [23], a recently proposed formalism capable of capturing deeply coupled mobile, parallel, and hybrid behaviors of mobile CPSs. This formalization facilitates verification and analysis of the modeled system.

We start by introducing the preliminaries on sequence diagrams and the hybrid π-calculus in Sect. 2. Section 3 presents the extended sequence diagrams and Sect. 4 translates the extended sequence diagram to the hybrid π-calculus. The case study is shown in Sect. 5. Finally, Sect. 6 reviews related works and positions our contributions accordingly, followed by the conclusion in Sect. 7.

2 Preliminaries

2.1 Sequence Diagrams

Sequence diagrams are used to depict the process of message passing and collaboration among system components over time. They include core elements such as lifelines, messages, and combined fragments. Lifelines represent individual instances participating in an interaction by exchanging messages with other lifelines. Time progresses downward along a lifeline, such that events occurring higher up happen before those lower down on the same lifeline. Messages serve as the fundamental units of communication between lifelines. Combined fragments provide a mechanism to express control logic within interactions. Among them, `option`, `alternative`, `loop`, and `parallel` are the most commonly used in practice. The `alt` fragment represents conditional branching, similar to an `if-then-else` construct. The `opt` fragment denotes optional execution of a single branch, akin to an `if` statement without an `else`. The `loop` fragment indicates repeated execution of a specific interaction sequence. The `par` fragment specifies parallel execution of multiple interaction branches. We also consider `break` and `critical` fragments. A `break` fragment represents an interruption of the normal flow in order to execute an exceptional sequence, such as error handling. A `critical` region denotes a section of interaction that must be executed atomically.

2.2 Hybrid π-Calculus

The hybrid π-calculus [23], as a conservative extension to Robin Milner et al.'s traditional π-calculus [15], can formally capture both mobile computing and communication as well as hybrid behavior in infrastructures where the network topology and its communicating entities evolve continuously in the physical world.

$$
\begin{array}{llll}
\pi ::= \tau & \text{(Silent)} & \mathtt{P} ::= \sum_{i\in I} \pi_i.\mathtt{P}_i & \text{(Sum)} \\
\quad \mid x(\boldsymbol{y}) & \text{(Input)} & \quad \mid (\nu x)\mathtt{P} & \text{(Restriction)} \\
\quad \mid \overline{x}\langle \boldsymbol{e} \rangle & \text{(Output)} & \quad \mid \mathtt{P}\|\mathtt{P}' & \text{(Parallel)} \\
\quad \mid [B] & \text{(Guard)} & \quad \mid !\mathtt{P} & \text{(Replication)} \\
\quad \mid \{\boldsymbol{e}_0 \mid \dot{\boldsymbol{v}} = \boldsymbol{e}\&B, \mathcal{R}\}(\boldsymbol{y}) & \text{(Continuous)} & &
\end{array}
$$

The syntax of the hybrid π-calculus consist of prefixes π and processes $\mathtt{P}$. A sum $\sum_{i \in I} \pi_i.\mathtt{P}_i$ represents a non-deterministic choice, where sub-terms guard a process $\mathtt{P}_i$ by a prefix π_i, which can be a silence τ, an input $x(\boldsymbol{y})$, an output $\overline{x}\langle \boldsymbol{e} \rangle$, a Boolean clause $[B]$, or a continuous clause $\{\boldsymbol{e}_0 \mid \dot{\boldsymbol{v}} = \boldsymbol{e}\&B, \mathcal{R}\}(\boldsymbol{y})$. The empty sum ($I = \emptyset$) stands for inaction and is written as process $\mathtt{0}$. The restriction of a name x to the scope of $\mathtt{P}$ is denoted $(\nu x)\mathtt{P}$ and subject to we adopt Barendregt's conventions. Replication is denoted by $!\mathtt{P}$ and parallel composition by $\mathtt{P} \| \mathtt{P}'$. The term $\{\boldsymbol{e}_0 \mid \dot{\boldsymbol{v}} = \boldsymbol{e}\&B, \mathcal{R}\}(\boldsymbol{y}).\mathtt{P}$ denotes a continuous process. From left to right, it consists of a vector of expressions $\boldsymbol{e}_0$ representing the initial state of the ODE's variables $\boldsymbol{v}$ and $\boldsymbol{e}$ its vector field which we require to be locally Lipschitz-continuous. The Boolean condition B defines the domain constraints (range or boundary) on the continuous variable. Once B is violated by the state of the ODE, e.g., c, its evolution stops immediately and its continuation $(\boldsymbol{y}).\mathtt{P}$ is applied to the final state c, reducing to $\mathtt{P}\{\mathsf{c}/\boldsymbol{y}\}$. We omit $(\boldsymbol{y})$ if $\boldsymbol{y}$ are not free in the continuation $\mathtt{P}$. Finally, the set $\mathcal{R} \subseteq \{v, \overline{v} \mid v \in \boldsymbol{v}\}$ is called the ready set or interface of the ODE. It declares the channel names which can be sensed or actuated by discrete processes. We omit B if it is **true** and omit $\mathcal{R}$ if it is $\emptyset$.

3 Extended Sequence Diagrams

Interactions and activities in sequence diagrams are typically described using informal methods such as natural language. This section aims to refine these informal descriptions into more formal representations. Overall, these refinements include: assignment (Sect. 3.1), communication (Sect. 3.2), continuous evolution (of the physical environment, Sect. 3.3), sensation and actuation (interactions between controlling processes and the physical environment, Sect. 3.4), and timing constraints (Sect. 3.5). For clarity, we adopt `PlantUML` [18] to describe sequence diagrams, and the extension to sequence diagrams introduced in this section will also be presented using `PlantUML` syntax (Sect. 3.6).

3.1 Assignment

Each participant $\mathtt{p}$ can assign values to its local variables: $\mathtt{p} \rightarrow \mathtt{p} : x := e$, where e is an arithmetic expression evaluated and assigned to the variable x. For multiple assignments, we can employ the notation $\mathtt{p} \rightarrow \mathtt{p} : \boldsymbol{x} := \boldsymbol{e}$, where $\boldsymbol{x}$ and $\boldsymbol{e}$ are vectors of variables. Note that assignments such $\mathtt{p} \rightarrow \mathtt{q} : x := e$, where $\mathtt{p} \neq \mathtt{q}$, are considered invalid, as it is generally not permissible for one participant to directly modify a variable belonging to another participant. Instead, such assignments between participants can be facilitated through communication, which will be detailed in the following discussion (Sect. 3.2).

3.2 Communication

Participants can interact through communication, which can be classified into two modes: synchronous and asynchronous. In synchronous communication, if one party is not ready to proceed, the other must wait. In contrast, asynchronous communication employs a buffer or queue between the sender and receiver. In this paper, we focus on synchronous communication: $\mathtt{p} \rightarrow \mathtt{q} : ch(\boldsymbol{x} := \boldsymbol{e})$, where $\mathtt{p} \neq \mathtt{q}$. It specifies that participant p sends expressions $\boldsymbol{e}$ to participant q via channel *ch*, while q receives them through the same channel, storing them in variables $\boldsymbol{x}$. This implies that vectors $\boldsymbol{x}$ (used for reception) and $\boldsymbol{e}$ (sent) must have the same length.

It is worthy noting that messages transmitted over a channel can themselves be channels (higher-order communication). For example, $\mathtt{p} \rightarrow \mathtt{q} : ch(x := ch')$ signifies that participant p transfers ownership of channel ch' to participant q. Afterward, q can communicate with other participants via ch', a mechanism referred to as mobile communication. Such higher-order communication is prevalent in mobile CPSs.

3.3 Continuous Evolution

In CPSs, physical entities, such as trains, undergo continuous evolution, which is typically modeled using ODEs. Therefore, we extend sequence diagrams by introducing ODEs. Concretely, the continuous evolution of a physical entity (participant) p is modeled as an activity, referred to as a *continuous activity*, annotated (`note`) with an ODE, as shown below:

$$\begin{array}{l}\texttt{activate p}\\ \texttt{note Loc of p}: \texttt{«ode»}\ \{\boldsymbol{e}_0 \mid \dot{\boldsymbol{v}} = \boldsymbol{e}\&B\}\\ \texttt{Frag}\\ \texttt{deactivate p}\end{array}$$

where `Loc` ::= `left` | `right` | `over` denotes the position of the ODE relative to the activity in the diagram, and `Frag` contains the interactions (sensation and actuation in Sect. 3.4) of p with other participants. In this context, participants performing continuous evolution are referred to as *physical participants*, whereas those interacting with physical participants are termed *discrete participants*.

The above notation specifies that participant p `activates` a continuous evolution described by $\{\boldsymbol{e}_0 \mid \dot{\boldsymbol{v}} = \boldsymbol{e}\&B\}$, where the physical variables $\boldsymbol{v}$ start from the initial condition $\boldsymbol{e}_0$ and evolve according to the ODE $\dot{\boldsymbol{v}} = \boldsymbol{e}$. Once the evolution reaches the boundary of B, i.e., the boundary condition B is violated, the evolution terminates, i.e., the continuous evolution is `deactivated`.

After the deactivation, we use $\boldsymbol{v}'$ to represent the values of the physical variables $\boldsymbol{v}$ at the termination of the ODE. For example, $\mathtt{p} \rightarrow \mathtt{q} : ch(\boldsymbol{x} := \boldsymbol{v}')$ after `deactivate p` means that p sends the final values of the ODE to q via channel *ch*; and `note Loc of p` : `«ode»` $\{\boldsymbol{v}' \mid \dot{\boldsymbol{v}} = \boldsymbol{e}'\&B'\}$ after `deactivate p` indicates that p has activated another continuous evolution starting from the final values ($\boldsymbol{v}'$) of the preceding one.

3.4 Sensation and Actuation

As discussed in Sect. 3.3, physical participants may interact with discrete participants during their continuous evolution. Specifically, a discrete participant may sense (read) and/or actuate (write) certain physical variables of a physical participant to perform the control. For example, a base station can read the real-time position and velocity of a train (sensation) within its coverage area and subsequently adjust the train's acceleration (actuation) based on the sensed data to ensure safety. Therefore, we extend sequence diagrams by introducing two types of interactions: sensation and actuation.

Sensation is modeled using the following notation: $\mathtt{p} \rightarrow \mathtt{q} : \texttt{«sense»}\ x := v$, where $\mathtt{p} \neq \mathtt{q}$. It specifies that participant `p` senses the current value of the physical variable v of participant `q` and stores the sensed value in variable x. This indicates that `p` is a discrete participant while `q` is a physical one. Actuation is similarly modeled as: $\mathtt{p} \rightarrow \mathtt{q} : \texttt{«actuate»}\ v := e$. This indicates that `p` modifies the value of the physical variable v to e.

3.5 Delay

In plant-control models, the control component typically operates periodically. For example, a train's controller may periodically read its state (sensation) and perform corresponding actions to regulate its motion (actuation). This periodic behavior can be effectively captured using delay constructs, which may occur within specific loops. In an extended sequence diagram, delay behaviors can be represented using a `delay` activity, defined by `activate p note Loc of p:delay(d) deactivate p` to mean that participant `p` delays for d time units.

3.6 Syntax of Extended Sequence Diagrams

Each ESD starts with `@startuml` and ends with `@enduml`. The interactions are structured using `Frag`ments, which can include basic operations (assignment, communication, sensation, and actuation), continuous activities, `alt`ernatives, `opt`ions, `loop`s, `break`s, `par`allel compositions, and `critical` regions. Additionally, to enhance the expressiveness of the model, we extend each `alt`ernative with an index $[i]$ and a participant `p` responsible for evaluating the *cond*ition. Concretely, the fragment $\texttt{alt}[i]\ \mathtt{p} : \mathit{cond}\ \texttt{Frag else Frag}'\ \texttt{end}$ means that this is the i-th `alt` fragment and the evaluation of its *cond* is performed by `p`. In other words, `p` selects the branch of the `alt` fragment to execute, while the index $[i]$ distinguishes different `alt` fragments. Similarly, we extend `opt` and `loop` by adding an index $[i]$ and associating them with a participant `p`.

In summary, the PlantUML syntax of the extended sequence diagram (ESD) is specified by the following grammar:

$$
\begin{aligned}
\texttt{ESD} &::= \texttt{@startuml Frag @enduml}\\
\texttt{Frag} &::= \emptyset \mid \texttt{p} \rightarrow \texttt{p} : x := e\ \texttt{Frag} \mid \texttt{p} \rightarrow \texttt{q} : ch(\boldsymbol{x} := \boldsymbol{e})\ \texttt{Frag}\\
&\mid \texttt{p} \rightarrow \texttt{q} : \texttt{«sense»}\ x := v\ \texttt{Frag} \mid \texttt{p} \rightarrow \texttt{q} : \texttt{«actuate»}\ v := e\ \texttt{Frag}\\
&\mid \texttt{activate Note p Frag deactivate p Frag}\\
&\mid \texttt{alt}[i]\ \texttt{p} : cond\ \texttt{Frag ALT} \mid \texttt{opt}[i]\ \texttt{p} : cond\ \texttt{Frag end Frag}\\
&\mid \texttt{loop}[i]\ \texttt{p} : cond\ \texttt{Frag end Frag} \mid \texttt{break Frag end}\\
&\mid \texttt{par Frag PAR} \mid \texttt{critical Frag end Frag}\\
\texttt{ALT} &::= \texttt{else Frag end Frag} \mid \texttt{else}\ cond\ \texttt{Frag ALT}\\
\texttt{PAR} &::= \texttt{else Frag end Frag} \mid \texttt{else Frag PAR}\\
\texttt{Note} &::= \texttt{note Loc of p} : \texttt{«ode»}\ \{\boldsymbol{e}_0 \mid \dot{\boldsymbol{v}} = \boldsymbol{e} \& B\}\\
&\mid \texttt{note Loc of p} : \texttt{delay}(d)\\
\texttt{Loc} &::= \texttt{left} \mid \texttt{right} \mid \texttt{over}
\end{aligned}
$$

4 Translation to Hybrid π-Calculus

Sequence diagrams serve as graphical models that enable users to model systems intuitively. However, ensuring the correctness of established models poses a significant challenge. By transforming these informal models into formal ones, we enable formal verification based on rigorous mathematical theories, which ensures the safety and reliability of system models. Among numerous formal methods, hybrid π-calculus stands out for its ability to represent both the hybrid behavior and the mobile communication (higher-order communication, Sect. 3.2) of CPSs. Therefore, this section presents the rules for translating extended sequence diagrams into hybrid π-calculus processes.

Specifically, the translation can be represented as a function $\mathfrak{T}(\texttt{ESD}) = \texttt{P}$, where ESD denotes an extended sequence diagram and P represents the corresponding hybrid π-calculus process for ESD, i.e., the formal representation of ESD. To define the translation function $\mathfrak{T}$, we introduce an auxiliary function $\mathcal{T}(\texttt{Frag}, \mathcal{P}) = \{\texttt{p} : \texttt{P}_\texttt{p}\}_{\texttt{p} \in \mathcal{P}}$, which takes a Fragment of the ESD as input, and outputs a mapping $\{\texttt{p} : \texttt{P}_\texttt{p}\}_{\texttt{p} \in \mathcal{P}}$, where $\mathcal{P}$ is the set of all the participants involved in the ESD. The function $\mathcal{T}$ is defined through a set of transformation rules. We begin with the base case in which the interaction fragment is empty. In this case, each participant performs no action, denoted by the inaction 0, i.e., $\mathcal{T}(\emptyset, \mathcal{P}) = \{\texttt{p} : \texttt{0}\}_{\texttt{p} \in \mathcal{P}}$. The remaining translation rules are presented below. All of them have been implemented in Python[1].

4.1 Assignment

For an assignment prefixed fragment, denoted $\texttt{q} \rightarrow \texttt{q} : x := e\ \texttt{Frag}$, if the hybrid π-calculus process of each participant can be derived from Frag, then the

[1] https://github.com/Jixiang-Miao/ESD-to-HpC.

assignment is added as the prefix to the process $\mathtt{P_q}$ of the participant $\mathtt{q}$:

$$\frac{\mathcal{T}(\mathtt{Frag}, \mathcal{P}) = \{\mathtt{p} : \mathtt{P_p}\}_{\mathtt{p}\in\mathcal{P}}}{\mathcal{T}\,(\mathtt{q} \to \mathtt{q} : x := e\ \ \mathtt{Frag}, \mathcal{P}) = \{\mathtt{q} : \langle x := e\rangle.\mathtt{P_q}\} \cup \{\mathtt{p} : \mathtt{P_p}\}_{\mathtt{p}\in\mathcal{P}\setminus\mathtt{q}}}$$

Since the hybrid π-calculus does not include an assignment operation, we introduce $\langle x := e\rangle$ as syntactic sugar for assignments in this section. We first define an auxiliary process Memory to manage the storage of the variable x, initialized to a value y:

$$\mathtt{Memory} \triangleq\ !a(y).(\overline{x'}\langle y\rangle.\overline{a}\langle y\rangle + x'(z).\overline{a}\langle z\rangle)$$

A hybrid π-calculus process can "activate" a Memory location by invoking $\overline{a}\langle e\rangle$. This renders a behavior similar to allocating a space in memory for the variable x and to storing the value e into it. Subsequently, the process can read the value of x from the "memory" using $x'(x)$, and it can also store a new value e' into x using $\overline{x'}\langle e'\rangle$. Here is an example illustrating the operations "allocation", "load", and "store" on the Memory:

$$\begin{aligned}\overline{a}\langle e\rangle.x'(x).\overline{x'}\langle x+1\rangle\|\mathtt{Memory} &\to x'(x).\overline{x'}\langle x+1\rangle\|(\overline{x'}\langle e\rangle.\overline{a}\langle e\rangle + x'(z).\overline{a}\langle z\rangle)\|\mathtt{Memory}\\ &\to \overline{x'}\langle e+1\rangle\|\overline{a}\langle e\rangle\|\mathtt{Memory}\\ &\to \overline{x'}\langle e+1\rangle\|(\overline{x'}\langle e\rangle.\overline{a}\langle e\rangle + x'(z).\overline{a}\langle z\rangle)\|\mathtt{Memory}\\ &\to \overline{a}\langle e+1\rangle\|\mathtt{Memory}\\ &\to (\overline{x'}\langle e+1\rangle.\overline{a}\langle e+1\rangle + x'(z).\overline{a}\langle z\rangle)\|\mathtt{Memory}\end{aligned}$$

Given a hybrid π-calculus process P containing assignments, the first occurrence of an assignment $\langle x := e\rangle$ should hence be replaced with $\overline{a}\langle e\rangle$, while subsequent assignments $\langle x := e'\rangle$ should be replaced with $\overline{x'}\langle e'\rangle$. Then, a "load" operation for x, denoted $x'(x)$, must be inserted before every free occurrence of x in the process. This transformation is formally captured by the function $\mathcal{A}_x$. Consequently, any process P that only contains assignments to the variable x is equivalent to $(\nu a, x')\,(\mathcal{A}_x(\mathtt{P})\|\mathtt{Memory})$, where $(\nu a, x')$ indicates that the names a and x' are bound and therefore hidden (or inaccessible) from the environment.

4.2 Communication

The communication prefix $\mathtt{q} \to \mathtt{q}' : ch(\boldsymbol{x} := \boldsymbol{e})$ indicates that participant q sends expressions $\boldsymbol{e}$ to participant $\mathtt{q}'$ via channel ch. Consequently, the corresponding process prefix for q is $\overline{ch}\langle\boldsymbol{e}\rangle$. Participant $\mathtt{q}'$ receives the expressions from channel ch and stores them to variables $\boldsymbol{x}$. Therefore, the corresponding process prefix is $ch(\boldsymbol{x})$. This is illustrated by the following rule:

$$\frac{\mathcal{T}(\mathtt{Frag}, \mathcal{P}) = \{\mathtt{p} : \mathtt{P_p}\}_{\mathtt{p}\in\mathcal{P}}}{\mathcal{T}\left(\begin{matrix}\mathtt{q} \to \mathtt{q}' : ch(\boldsymbol{x} := \boldsymbol{e})\\ \mathtt{Frag}\end{matrix}, \mathcal{P}\right) = \{\mathtt{q} : \overline{ch}\langle\boldsymbol{e}\rangle.\mathtt{P_q}, \mathtt{q}' : ch(\boldsymbol{x}).\mathtt{P_{q'}}\} \cup \{\mathtt{p} : \mathtt{P_p}\}_{\mathtt{p}\in\mathcal{P}-\{\mathtt{q},\mathtt{q}'\}}}$$

4.3 Continuous Evolution

As described in Sect. 3.3, the continuous evolution of physical participants is modeled as continuous activities:

$$\texttt{activate q note Loc of q}: \texttt{«ode»}\ \{e_0 \mid \dot{\boldsymbol{v}} = e\&B\}\ \texttt{Frag deactivate q}$$

where physical participant q evolves according to the ODE $\{e_0 \mid \dot{\boldsymbol{v}} = e\&B\}$, and the interaction fragment **Frag** contains the sensation and actuation between this ODE and discrete participants. Therefore, we first analyze the interactions of participant q within **Frag** to compute the ready set of its ODE (see Sect. 2.2 for details). This ready set defines the interface through which the ODE interacts with discrete participants. The computation of the ready set is formalized as a function $\mathfrak{R}(\mathtt{q}, \mathtt{Frag}) = \mathcal{R}$. Specifically, If q is not involved in the interactions of **Frag**, the corresponding ready set is empty: $\mathfrak{R}(\mathtt{q}, \emptyset) = \emptyset$. If a physical variable v of q is sensed by some discrete participant, the corresponding output action $\overline{v}$ is included in the ready set. Symmetrically, if a physical variable v of q is actuated by a discrete participant, the corresponding input action v is included in the ready set.

Based on the aforementioned ready set construction rules, continuous activities can be translated according to the following rule:

$$\frac{\mathcal{R} = \mathfrak{R}(\mathtt{q}, \mathtt{Frag}) \cap \{v, \overline{v} \mid v \in \boldsymbol{v}\} \quad \mathcal{T}(\mathtt{Frag\ Frag'}, \mathcal{P}) = \{\mathtt{p} : \mathtt{P_p}\}_{\mathtt{p} \in \mathcal{P}}}{\mathcal{T}\left(\begin{array}{l}\mathtt{activate\ q} \\ \mathtt{note\ Loc\ of\ q:} \\ \quad \texttt{«ode»}\ \{e_0 \mid \dot{\boldsymbol{v}} = e\&B\} \\ \mathtt{Frag} \\ \mathtt{deactivate\ q} \\ \mathtt{Frag'}\end{array}, \mathcal{P}\right) = \begin{array}{c}\{\mathtt{q} : \{e_0 \mid \dot{\boldsymbol{v}} = e\&B, \mathcal{R}\}(\boldsymbol{v}').\mathtt{P_q}\} \\ \cup \\ \{\mathtt{p} : \mathtt{P_p}\}_{\mathtt{p} \in \mathcal{P} \setminus \mathtt{q}}\end{array}}$$

where $\boldsymbol{v}'$ denote the values of the physical variables $\boldsymbol{v}$ at the termination of the ODE. The premise $\mathcal{R} = \mathfrak{R}(\mathtt{q}, \mathtt{Frag}) \cap \{v, \overline{v} \mid v \in \boldsymbol{v}\}$ indicates that the ready set $\mathcal{R}$ forms a valid interface for the ODE $\{e_0 \mid \dot{\boldsymbol{v}} = e\&B\}$.

4.4 Sensation and Actuation

The sensation prefix $\mathtt{q} \rightarrow \mathtt{q'} : \texttt{«sense»}\ x := v$ indicates that participant q reads the current value of the physical variable v from participant q′ and assigns it to variable x. Consequently, the prefix of the process corresponding to q is $v(x)$, leading to the following rule:

$$\frac{\mathcal{T}(\mathtt{Frag}, \mathcal{P}) = \{\mathtt{p} : \mathtt{P_p}\}_{\mathtt{p} \in \mathcal{P}}}{\mathcal{T}\left(\begin{array}{l}\mathtt{q} \rightarrow \mathtt{q'} : \texttt{«sense»}\ x := v \\ \mathtt{Frag}\end{array}, \mathcal{P}\right) = \{\mathtt{q} : v(x).\mathtt{P_q}\} \cup \{\mathtt{p} : \mathtt{P_p}\}_{\mathtt{p} \in \mathcal{P} \setminus \mathtt{q}}}$$

where participant $\mathtt{q'} \in \mathcal{P} \setminus \mathtt{q}$ is a physical participant, and its translation rules were introduced in Sect. 4.3.

The actuation prefix $\mathtt{q} \rightarrow \mathtt{q}'$: **«actuate»** $v := e$ is dual to the sensation prefix above. It indicates that participant $\mathtt{q}$ updates the value of the physical variable v of the physical participant $\mathtt{q}$ to e, leading to the following rule:

$$\frac{\mathcal{T}(\mathtt{Frag}, \mathcal{P}) = \{\mathtt{p} : \mathrm{P}_\mathtt{p}\}_{\mathtt{p}\in\mathcal{P}}}{\mathcal{T}\left(\begin{array}{l}\mathtt{q} \rightarrow \mathtt{q}' : \texttt{«actuate»}\ v := e\\ \mathtt{Frag}\end{array}, \mathcal{P}\right) = \{\mathtt{q} : \overline{v}\langle e\rangle.\mathrm{P}_\mathtt{q}\} \cup \{\mathtt{p} : \mathrm{P}_\mathtt{p}\}_{\mathtt{p}\in\mathcal{P}\backslash\mathtt{q}}}$$

4.5 Delay

The `delay` activity of participant $\mathtt{q}$ is translated to a `wait` prefix:

$$\frac{\mathcal{T}(\mathtt{Frag}, \mathcal{P}) = \{\mathtt{p} : \mathrm{P}\}_{\mathtt{p}\in\mathcal{P}}}{\mathcal{T}\left(\begin{array}{l}\mathtt{activate\ q}\\ \mathtt{note\ Loc\ of\ q} : \mathtt{delay(d)}\\ \mathtt{deactivate\ q}\\ \mathtt{Frag}\end{array}, \mathcal{P}\right) = \{\mathtt{q} : \mathtt{wait(d)}.\mathrm{P}_\mathtt{q}\} \cup \{\mathtt{p} : \mathrm{P}_\mathtt{p}\}_{\mathtt{p}\in\mathcal{P}\backslash\mathtt{q}}}$$

where notation $\mathtt{wait(d)} \triangleq (\nu t)\{0 \mid \dot{t} = 1 \& t < \mathrm{d}\}$ is syntactic sugar for representing delay in the hybrid π-calculus (Sect. 2.2).

4.6 Alternative

For the sake of clarity, the `alt` fragment considered in this section only includes two branches, mirroring an `if-then-else` structure, and the method can naturally be extended to `alt` fragments with more branches. Suppose that the condition *cond* of the `alt` fragment is evaluated by participant $\mathtt{q}$. Based on the result of this evaluation, $\mathtt{q}$ sends corresponding signals to other participants within the fragment, thereby scheduling them to perform interactions in either the **true** or **false** branch.

It is important to note that $\mathtt{q}$ should not schedule physical participants, but it can schedule the interactions of those discrete participants to sense and actuate physical participants in different `alt` branches. We define a function DisP that takes an interaction fragment `Frag` as input and returns the set of all discrete participants involved in `Frag`. This leads to the following rule:

$$\frac{\begin{array}{c}\mathcal{T}(\mathtt{Frag\ Frag}'', \mathcal{P}) = \{\mathtt{p} : \mathrm{P}_\mathtt{p}\}_{\mathtt{p}\in\mathcal{P}} \quad \mathcal{T}(\mathtt{Frag}'\ \mathtt{Frag}'', \mathcal{P}) = \{\mathtt{p} : \mathrm{P}'_\mathtt{p}\}_{\mathtt{p}\in\mathcal{P}}\\ \mathrm{DisP}(\mathtt{Frag}) = P \quad \mathrm{DisP}(\mathtt{Frag}') = P' \quad P \cup P' = \{\mathtt{q}, \mathtt{p}_1, \cdots, \mathtt{p}_k\}\end{array}}{\mathcal{T}\left(\begin{array}{l}\mathtt{alt}[i]\ \mathtt{q} : cond\\ \quad \mathtt{Frag}\\ \mathtt{else}\\ \quad \mathtt{Frag}'\\ \mathtt{end}\\ \mathtt{Frag}''\end{array}, \mathcal{P}\right) = \begin{array}{c}\left\{\mathtt{q} : \left(\begin{array}{l}\mathtt{if}\ cond\ \mathtt{then}\\ \quad \overline{\mathtt{alt}_{i,1}}.\cdots.\overline{\mathtt{alt}_{i,k}}.\mathrm{P}_\mathtt{q}\\ \mathtt{else}\\ \quad \overline{\mathtt{alt}'_{i,1}}.\cdots.\overline{\mathtt{alt}'_{i,k}}.\mathrm{P}'_\mathtt{q}\end{array}\right)\right\}\\ \cup\\ \{\mathtt{p}_j : \mathtt{alt}_{i,j}.\mathrm{P}_{\mathtt{p}_j} + \mathtt{alt}'_{i,j}.\mathrm{P}'_{\mathtt{p}_j}\}_{1\le j\le k}\\ \cup\{\mathtt{p} : \mathrm{P}_\mathtt{p}\}_{\mathtt{p}\in\mathcal{P}-(P\cup P')}\end{array}}$$

where notation $\texttt{if } B \texttt{ then P else Q} \triangleq [B].\texttt{P} + [\neg B].\texttt{Q}$ is syntactic sugar of conditional in the hybrid π-calculus (Sect. 2.2).

Participant $\texttt{q}$ evaluates the value of the Boolean expression *cond*. If the result is **true**, it schedules (via $\overline{\texttt{alt}_{i,j}}$) the interactions of other discrete participants $\texttt{p}_i$ in $\texttt{Frag Frag}''$ (denoted $\texttt{P}_{\texttt{p}_j}$), where $1 \leq j \leq k$, and then executes its own interactions in $\texttt{Frag Frag}''$ (denoted $\texttt{P}_\texttt{q}$). Otherwise (if **false**), it schedules (via $\overline{\texttt{alt}'_{i,j}}$) the interactions of $\texttt{p}_j$ in $\texttt{Frag}'\ \texttt{Frag}''$ (denoted $\texttt{P}'_{\texttt{p}_j}$), and then executes its own interactions in $\texttt{Frag}'\ \texttt{Frag}''$ (denoted $\texttt{P}'_\texttt{q}$).

4.7 Option

An $\texttt{opt}$ fragment is a special case of an $\texttt{alt}$ fragment, analogous to the $\texttt{if-then}$ construct. Formally, $\mathcal{T}(\texttt{opt}[i]\ \texttt{q} : \mathit{cond}\ \texttt{Frag end Frag}', \mathcal{P})$ is equivalent to

$$\mathcal{T}\,(\texttt{alt}[i]\ \texttt{q} : \mathit{cond}\ \texttt{Frag else } \emptyset\ \texttt{end Frag}', \mathcal{P})$$

4.8 Loop

Assume that the condition *cond* of the $\texttt{loop}$ fragment is evaluated by participant $\texttt{q}$. Similar to the $\texttt{alt}$ fragment discussed in Sect. 4.6, $\texttt{q}$ can only schedule the interactions of discrete participants within the $\texttt{loop}$ fragment, but not those of physical participants. This leads to the following translation rule:

$$\frac{\mathcal{T}(\texttt{Frag}, \mathcal{P}) = \{\texttt{p} : \texttt{P}_\texttt{p}\}_{\texttt{p}\in\mathcal{P}} \quad \mathcal{T}(\texttt{Frag}', \mathcal{P}) = \{\texttt{p} : \texttt{P}'_\texttt{p}\}_{\texttt{p}\in\mathcal{P}} \quad \text{DisP}(\texttt{Frag}) = P = \{\texttt{q}, \texttt{p}_1, \cdots, \texttt{p}_k\}}{\mathcal{T}\left(\begin{array}{l}\texttt{loop}[i]\ \texttt{q} : \mathit{cond} \\ \quad \texttt{Frag} \\ \texttt{end} \\ \texttt{Frag}'\end{array}, \mathcal{P}\right) = \left\{\begin{array}{c}\texttt{q} : \mu\texttt{loop}_i.\left(\begin{array}{l}\texttt{if } \mathit{cond} \texttt{ then} \\ \quad \overline{\texttt{loop}_{i,1}}.\cdots.\overline{\texttt{loop}_{i,k}}.\texttt{P}_\texttt{q}.\overline{\texttt{loop}_i} \\ \texttt{else} \\ \quad \overline{\texttt{loop}'_{i,1}}.\cdots.\overline{\texttt{loop}'_{i,k}}.\texttt{P}'_\texttt{q}\end{array}\right) \\ \cup\{\texttt{p}_j : !(\texttt{loop}_{i,j}.\texttt{P}_{\texttt{p}_j} + \texttt{loop}'_{i,j}.\texttt{P}'_{\texttt{p}_j})\}_{1\leq j\leq k} \\ \cup\{\texttt{p} : \texttt{P}_\texttt{p}\}_{\mathcal{P}-P}\end{array}\right\}}$$

where $\mu x(\boldsymbol{y}).\texttt{P}@\langle \boldsymbol{e}\rangle \triangleq (\nu x)\,(\overline{x}\langle \boldsymbol{e}\rangle \| !x(\boldsymbol{y}).\texttt{P})$ is syntactic sugar for expressing recursion in the hybrid π-calculus (Sect. 2.2), and particularly, $\mu x.\texttt{P} \triangleq \mu x().\texttt{P}@\langle\rangle$.

At each iteration, participant $\texttt{q}$ checks whether the condition *cond* holds. If **true**, it schedules (via $\overline{\texttt{loop}_{i,j}}$) the interactions of other discrete participants $\texttt{p}_j$ within the $\texttt{loop}$ body $\texttt{Frag}$ (denoted $\texttt{P}_{\texttt{p}_j}$), where $1 \leq j \leq k$. After that, it executes its own interactions within the $\texttt{loop}$ body (denoted $\texttt{P}_\texttt{q}$) and initiates the next iteration of the loop (via $\overline{\texttt{loop}_i}$). Otherwise, it schedules (via $\overline{\texttt{loop}'_{i,j}}$) the interactions of $\texttt{p}_j$ in $\texttt{Frag}'$ (denoted $\texttt{P}'_{\texttt{p}_j}$), indicating the $\texttt{end}$ of the $\texttt{loop}$. It then proceeds to execute its own post-loop interactions, denoted $\texttt{P}'_\texttt{q}$.

When translating a $\texttt{break}$ fragment nested inside a $\texttt{loop}$, the containing $\texttt{loop}$ fragment, denoted $\texttt{loop}[i]\ \texttt{q} : \mathit{cond}\ \texttt{Frag end}$, must first be modified as follows:

- Insert the assignment $\mathtt{q} \rightarrow \mathtt{q} : \mathit{break}_i := 0$ immediately before the `loop`;
- Update the `loop` condition to $\mathit{cond} \wedge \mathit{break}_i = 0$;
- Append the assignment $\mathtt{q} \rightarrow \mathtt{q} : \mathit{break}_i := 1$ right after the `break` fragment.

After these modifications, the following translation rule applies:

$$\mathcal{T}\,(\mathtt{break\ Frag\ end\ Frag}', \mathcal{P}) = \mathcal{T}\,(\mathtt{Frag}, \mathcal{P})$$

4.9 Parallel

The `par` fragment in sequence diagrams reflects interleaving: interactions within the same fragment must preserve their order, whereas those in different parallel fragments may occur in any order. Therefore, we assume that the `par` fragment does not involve physical participants, since parallel continuous behaviors are typically executed synchronously rather than in an interleaved manner.

Similar to the `alt` fragment introduced in Sect. 4.6, we consider for clarity the parallel composition of only two fragments; however, the approach can naturally be extended to cases involving multiple parallel fragments. Additionally, we assume that each `par` fragment is composed of assignments (Sects. 3.1 and 4.1), communications (Sects. 3.2 and 4.2), and `critical` regions. These `critical` fragments may also include more complex structures, such as nested `alt`, `loop`, or even sub-`par` fragments.

We define the auxiliary function $\mathcal{T}_1$, which selects the first interaction of the first `par` fragment to execute, and then returns the translation result based on this selection. Concretely,

- $\mathcal{T}_1(\mathtt{par}\ \emptyset\ \mathtt{else\ Frag\ end\ Frag}', \mathcal{P}) = \mathcal{T}(\mathtt{Frag\ Frag}', \mathcal{P})$
- $\mathcal{T}_1(\mathtt{par\ p} \rightarrow \mathtt{p} : x := e\ \mathtt{Frag\ else\ Frag}'\ \mathtt{end\ Frag}'', \mathcal{P})$
  $= \mathcal{T}(\mathtt{p} \rightarrow \mathtt{p} : x := e\ \mathtt{par\ Frag\ else\ Frag}'\ \mathtt{end\ Frag}'', \mathcal{P})$
- $\mathcal{T}_1(\mathtt{par\ p} \rightarrow \mathtt{q} : ch(\boldsymbol{x} := e)\ \mathtt{Frag\ else\ Frag}'\ \mathtt{end\ Frag}'', \mathcal{P})$
  $= \mathcal{T}(\mathtt{p} \rightarrow \mathtt{q} : ch(\boldsymbol{x} := e)\ \mathtt{par\ Frag\ else\ Frag}'\ \mathtt{end\ Frag}'', \mathcal{P})$
- $\mathcal{T}_1(\mathtt{par\ critical\ Frag\ end\ Frag}'\ \mathtt{else\ Frag}''\ \mathtt{end\ Frag}''', \mathcal{P})$
  $= \mathcal{T}(\mathtt{critical\ Frag\ end\ par\ Frag}'\ \mathtt{else\ Frag}''\ \mathtt{end\ Frag}''', \mathcal{P})$

If the first fragment is empty, i.e., `par` $\emptyset$ `else Frag end` (i.e., a case without any parallel structure), this simplifies to just `Frag`. If the first fragment is a `critical` region, the interactions within the region should be executed atomically. Based on $\mathcal{T}_1$, the translation rule for `par` fragments is given as follows:

$$\frac{\mathcal{T}_1\,(\mathtt{par\ Frag\ else\ Frag}'\ \mathtt{end\ Frag}'', \mathcal{P}) = \{\mathtt{p} : \mathtt{P}\}_{\mathtt{p} \in \mathcal{P}} \quad \mathcal{T}_1\,(\mathtt{par\ Frag}'\ \mathtt{else\ Frag\ end\ Frag}'', \mathcal{P}) = \{\mathtt{p} : \mathtt{P}'\}_{\mathtt{p} \in \mathcal{P}}}{\mathcal{T}\,(\mathtt{par\ Frag\ else\ Frag}'\ \mathtt{end\ Frag}'', \mathcal{P}) = \{\mathtt{p} : \mathtt{P} + \mathtt{P}'\}_{\mathtt{p} \in \mathcal{P}}}$$

The function $\mathcal{T}_1(\mathtt{par\ Frag\ else\ Frag}'\ \mathtt{end\ Frag}'', \mathcal{P})$ returns the translation result obtained by selecting the first interaction (or the first `critical` region) of the `Fragment`. Similarly, $\mathcal{T}_1(\mathtt{par\ Frag}'\ \mathtt{else\ Frag\ end\ Frag}'', \mathcal{P})$ returns the translation result of selecting the first interaction (or the first `critical` region) of the $\texttt{Frag}'$. Combining these two results with the nondeterministic choice operator (+) reflects the interleaving nature of the `par` fragment.

It is important to ensure that both operands of the + operator are in the form of a sum. Specifically, if both $\texttt{P}$ and $\texttt{P}'$ are already sums (i.e., represented as $\sum_{i\in I} \pi_i.\texttt{P}_i$), then $\texttt{P} + \texttt{P}'$ directly forms a sum; if $\texttt{P}$ is a sum but $\texttt{P}'$ is not, a silent prefix τ should be added to $\texttt{P}'$, resulting in $\texttt{P} + \tau.\texttt{P}'$; if $\texttt{P}'$ is a sum but $\texttt{P}$ is not, the prefix τ should instead be added to $\texttt{P}$, yielding $\tau.\texttt{P} + \texttt{P}'$; finally, if neither $\texttt{P}$ nor $\texttt{P}'$ is a sum, both must be prefixed with τ, leading to $\tau.\texttt{P} + \tau.\texttt{P}'$.

4.10 Start and End

The start marker (`@startuml`) and end marker (`@enduml`) denote a complete `ESD`, i.e., `ESD` ::= `@startuml Frag @enduml`, according to the syntax in Sect. 3.6. If the hybrid π-calculus processes for each participant can be derived from the `Frag`, i.e., $\mathcal{T}(\texttt{Frag}, \{\texttt{p}_1, \cdots, \texttt{p}_n\}) = \{\texttt{p}_1 : \texttt{P}_1, \cdots, \texttt{p}_n : \texttt{P}_n\}$, then the hybrid π-calculus process of the `ESD` is the parallel composition of all $\texttt{P}_i$s:

$$\frac{\mathcal{T}(\texttt{Frag}, \{\texttt{p}_1, \cdots, \texttt{p}_n\}) = \{\texttt{p}_1 : \texttt{P}_1, \cdots, \texttt{p}_n : \texttt{P}_n\}}{\mathfrak{T}(\texttt{@startuml Frag @enduml}) = \texttt{P}_1 \| \cdots \| \texttt{P}_n}$$

5 Case Study

We model a successful handover scenario of the train control system's protocol, as introduced in [23], using the extended sequence diagram proposed in Sect. 3. We then formalize this model into a hybrid π-calculus process, adhering to the translation rules specified in Sect. 4. The scenario involves two adjacent track sectors and a train. Initially, the train is positioned at the starting point of the left sector and moves under its control. The left sector periodically reads the train's real-time position and velocity (sensation) and, based on this information, computes an acceleration. This newly computed acceleration is then sent to the train (actuation) to regulate its continuous movement. The train's motion is governed by a set of ODEs, until it arrives at the terminus.

Upon reaching the handover point of the left sector, the left sector initiates a handover request to the right sector. In this scenario, we assume that the right sector is available and thus responds with "yes". Subsequently, the left sector transfers the train's physical variables—position (p), velocity (v), and acceleration (a)—to the right sector. At this point, the handover is successfully concluded, and the right sector assumes control of the train using the received variables. In essence, the control of the train is transferred from the left sector to the right one (mobility). Similarly, the right sector will periodically sense and actuate the train until it reaches the handover point of the right sector. At this juncture, the right sector sets the train's acceleration to -1 m/s^2, causing it to come to a stop before reaching the end of the right sector. The extended sequence diagram for this scenario is illustrated in Fig. 1, where the control periods for

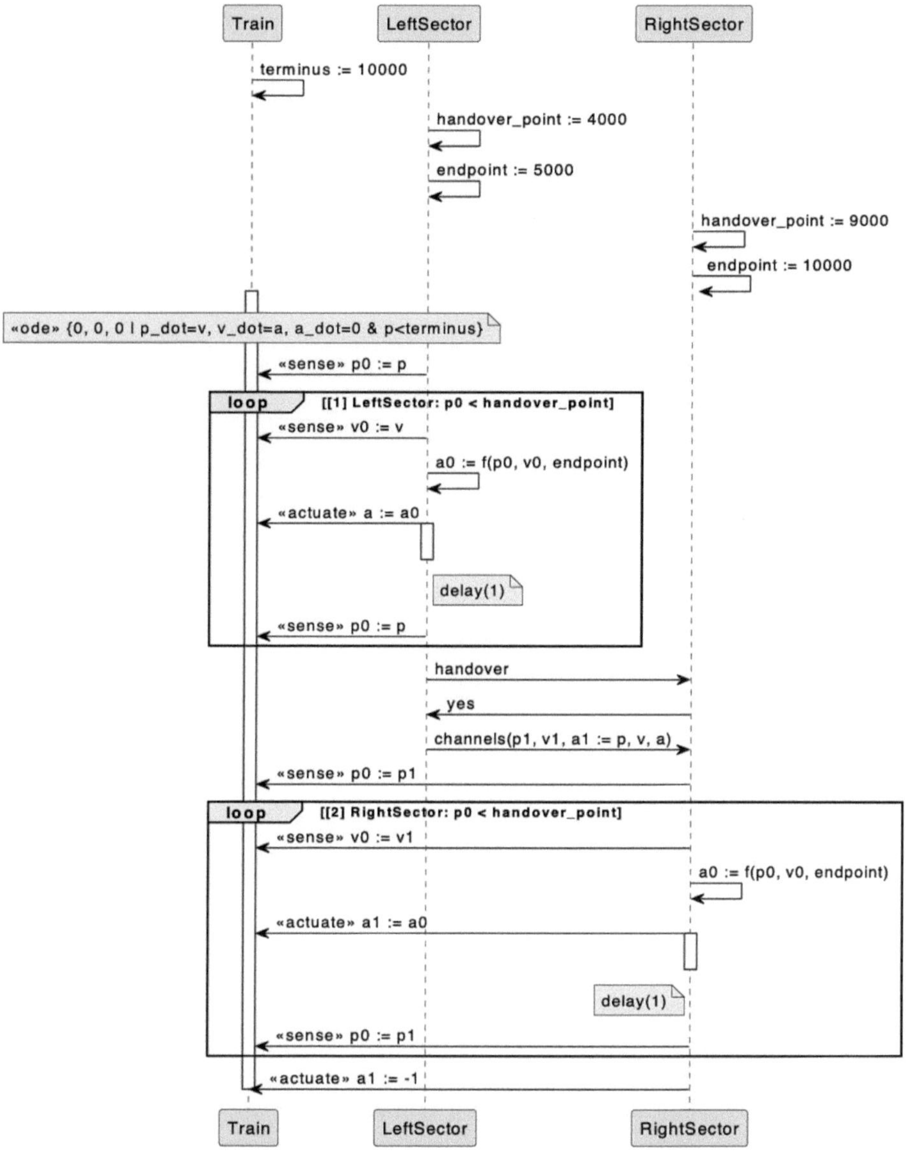

Fig. 1. The `ESD` of the successful handover scenario in `PlantUML`.

both the left and right sectors are set to 1 s, and the control algorithm is denoted by the function f.

The function f takes as inputs the real-time position (p_0) and velocity (v_0) of the train, along with the *endpoint* of the sector containing the train, and outputs a safe acceleration for the train. More specifically, f first checks whether it is safe for the train to run at the maximum acceleration (1 $\mathrm{m/s^2}$) during the next control period (1 s). If so, it outputs the maximum acceleration. Otherwise, it checks whether it is safe for the train to maintain its current speed. If this is safe, it outputs 0. Otherwise, it outputs a deceleration of -1 m/s^2 to prevent the train from entering an unsafe region, i.e., crossing the *endpoint* of the current sector or exceeding the velocity limit of 40 m/s. Further details of the function f can be found in the case study presented in [23,24].

By applying the translation rules defined in Sect. 4, the hybrid π-calculus process of the extended sequence diagram in Fig. 1 is derived as follows:

$$
\begin{aligned}
\texttt{System} &\triangleq \texttt{Train} \| \texttt{LeftSector} \| \texttt{RightSector} \\
\texttt{Train} &\triangleq \langle terminus := 10000\rangle . \left\{ \begin{array}{l} 0 \mid \dot{p} = v \\ 0 \mid \dot{v} = a \ \ \& \ p < terminus, \{\overline{p}, \overline{v}, a\} \\ 0 \mid \dot{a} = 0 \end{array} \right\} \\
\texttt{LeftSector} &\triangleq \langle handover\_point := 4000\rangle . \langle endpoint := 5000\rangle . p(p_0). \\
&\quad \mu loop_1 . \left(\begin{array}{l} \texttt{if } p_0 < handover\_point \texttt{ then} \\ \quad v(v_0).\langle a_0 := f(p_0, v_0, endpoint)\rangle . \overline{a}\langle a_0\rangle . \\ \quad \texttt{wait}(1).p(p_0).\overline{loop_1} \\ \texttt{else } \overline{handover}.yes.\overline{channels}\langle p, v, a\rangle \end{array} \right) \\
\texttt{RightSector} &\triangleq \langle handover\_point := 9000\rangle . \langle endpoint := 10000\rangle . \\
&\quad handover.\overline{yes}.channels(p_1, v_1, a_1).p_1(p_0). \\
&\quad \mu loop_2 . \left(\begin{array}{l} \texttt{if } p_0 < handover\_point \texttt{ then} \\ \quad v_1(v_0).\langle a_0 := f(p_0, v_0, endpoint)\rangle . \overline{a}_1\langle a_0\rangle . \\ \quad \texttt{wait}(1).p_1(p_0).\overline{loop_2} \\ \texttt{else } \overline{a}_1\langle -1\rangle \end{array} \right)
\end{aligned}
$$

The System model serves as a formal representation of the informal graphical model illustrated in Fig. 1. For this formal model, some analysis and verification can be conducted. For instance, we can define the formal specification (SPEC) of this scenario using the hybrid π-calculus as follows:

$$
\begin{aligned}
\texttt{SPEC} &\triangleq (\nu p, v)\,((\texttt{ACC.Steady.DEC}) \| \texttt{Observer}) \\
\texttt{ACC} &\triangleq \{0, 0 \mid \dot{p} = v, \dot{v} = 1 \ \& \ p < 800\}(p_1, v_1) \\
\texttt{Steady} &\triangleq \{p_1, v_1 \mid \dot{p} = v, \dot{v} = 0 \ \& \ p < 9200\}(p_2, v_2) \\
\texttt{DEC} &\triangleq \{p_2, v_2 \mid \dot{p} = v, \dot{v} = 0 \ \& \ p < 10000\} \\
\texttt{Observer} &\triangleq \{0 \mid \dot{x} = v \ \& \ p < 10000\}
\end{aligned}
$$

Since the handover is successful in this scenario, the train smoothly runs from the left sector to the right one, and its evolution consists of three stages: accelerating for 800 meters (ACC), then maintaining a Steady speed until it is 800 meters away from the terminus, and finally decelerating until it comes to a stop (DEC). An additional process, Observer, monitors the evolution of the train and calculates its location using a free variable x by sensing the recorded velocity v of the train without actuating the dynamics of the train.

We also use the Observer to observe dynamics of train. Specifically, we obtain $\texttt{System}' \triangleq (\nu p, v, a, handover, yes, no, channels, c)(\texttt{System} \| \texttt{Observer})$, where the channels and variables we do not wish to observe are hidden using ν, and we can demonstrate that $\texttt{System}'$ and $\texttt{SPEC}$ are in some weak bisimulation, i.e., $\texttt{System}' \approx \texttt{SPEC}$, following the method used in [23].

6 Related Works

Yoshida et al. [3,12] use sequence diagrams informally to depict communication protocols in distributed systems, particularly in multiparty session types. Although lacking formal semantics, these diagrams effectively illustrate interaction structures and improve understanding, highlighting the potential for their formalization to support rigorous analysis. Grosu et al. [9] introduced Hybrid Sequence Charts (HySCs), which provide a synchronous semantic framework for hybrid systems sharing time and continuous variables. However, HySCs have limited expressiveness for complex continuous dynamics and may fail to capture detailed system behaviors. Li et al. [13] proposed a formal semantics for UML sequence diagrams by representing their abstract syntax as hierarchical trees and defining a consistency-checking mechanism with class and state diagrams. This approach, however, struggles with timing constraints and concurrency, limiting its applicability in complex real-time systems. In terms of model transformation, several studies have translated sequence diagrams into executable or analyzable formal models, such as PROMELA [14], Timed Automata Network [11], CCS [17], Petri nets [5] and Clock Constraint Specification Language [4], enabling formal verification. More recently, Zhao et al. [28] proposed KBX, a formal bidirectional transformation (BX) framework for verified model synchronization. As an application, they derive a BX between UML Sequence Diagrams and HCSP by first specifying a unidirectional transformation from HCSP to UML. However, their work only supports a limited subset of UML constructs and lacks mobility. Xu et al. [25] proposed a framework that integrates AADL with Simulink/Stateflow, referred to as AADL$\oplus$S/S, along with a method for translating the combined model into HCSP. This translation enables subsequent simulation and verification [20]. The verified HCSP model can then be translated into SystemC [26] and C [21]. Implemented as part of the toolchain MARS 2.0 [27], this framework supports the transformation from graphical AADL$\oplus$S/S models to formal HCSP models, and ultimately to executable code. Our work will extend this framework by adding SysML formal modeling and analysis for broader industrial applicability.

In terms of verification tools, Vince et al. [16] leveraged five specialized tools for SysML v2 formal analysis and verification. Each tool, already integrated with SysML v2, employs distinct verification approaches (such as model checking and theorem proving) targeting different verification objectives. David et al. [8] proposed a method to formalize real-time extensions of UML state machine diagrams into Hierarchical Timed Automata (HTA) and translate HTA into flat timed automata for verification with UPPAAL. Rahim et al. [19] generated PNML documents from activity diagrams and converted them into CPNTools models to analyze safety and liveness properties. Lima et al. [14] implemented an automatic translation from UML sequence diagrams to PROMELA, enabling simulation and temporal property verification via the SPIN model checker. Similarly, Messaoud et al. [1] used Zenon, an automated theorem prover in FoCaLiZe, to verify formal models. Wu et al. [22] proposed simulating hybrid SysML models within the DEVS framework, allowing engineers to perform verification using DEVS-based tools without requiring deep expertise in DEVS theory, thereby improving modeling and verification efficiency.

Our work presents the first extension of sequence diagrams of SysML/UML with hybrid behavior and mobile communication, enabling them to model mobile CPSs. Based on this extension, we translate the extended sequence diagrams into the hybrid π-calculus models. In other words, we provide a formal semantics for the extended sequence diagrams based on the hybrid π-calculus, thereby supporting analysis and verification at the level of formal models. We plan to integrate our work into the toolchain MARS 2.0 [27], supporting MBD for CPSs in the context of mobile computing.

7 Conclusion and Future Works

In this paper, we proposed an extension of sequence diagrams in SysML/UML to better capture the complex behaviors inherent in mobile CPSs, including mobile computing and computation and hybrid behavior, i.e., the interplay between discrete behavior and continuous dynamic. To ensure the correctness of safety-critical systems modeled by the extended sequence diagram, we introduced a set of transformation rules that translate the (graphical) extended sequence diagram into a formal representation based on the hybrid π-calculus. This approach bridges the gap between intuitive modeling and formal verification, supporting the MBD paradigm that is essential for developing safe and reliable CPSs.

For future works, we intend to develop a simulator for the hybrid π-calculus. This simulator will facilitate the visual observation of the execution of hybrid π-calculus models generated from extended sequence diagrams, aiding in the identification of potential flaws in the design of mobile CPSs. Additionally, we aim to develop automatic or interactive provers for the hybrid π-calculus, thus enabling formal verification of extended sequence diagrams. We will also investigate the code generation from (verified) hybrid π-calculus models, reflecting the vertical dimension of MBD, i.e., the transformation from intuitive graphical models to rigorous formal representations, and ultimately to executable code.

Acknowledgments. This work is funded by the Natural Science Foundation of China under grant No. 62402479, 62432005, 62192732, and the President's International Fellowship Initiative of the Chinese Academy of Sciences.

References

1. Abbas, M., Rioboo, R., Ben-Yelles, C., Snook, C.F.: Formal modeling and verification of UML activity diagrams (UAD) with FoCaLiZe. J. Syst. Archit. **114**, 101911 (2021). https://doi.org/10.1016/J.SYSARC.2020.101911
2. Bengler, K., et al.: A references architecture for human cyber physical systems, part II: fundamental design principles for human-CPS interaction. ACM Trans. Cyber Phys. Syst. **8**(1), 3:1–3:27 (2024). https://doi.org/10.1145/3622880
3. Bettini, L., Coppo, M., D'Antoni, L., De Luca, M., Dezani-Ciancaglini, M., Yoshida, N.: Global Progress in Dynamically Interleaved Multiparty Sessions. In: van Breugel, F., Chechik, M. (eds.) CONCUR 2008. LNCS, vol. 5201, pp. 418–433. Springer, Heidelberg (2008). https://doi.org/10.1007/978-3-540-85361-9_33
4. Chen, X., Mallet, F., Liu, X.: Formally verifying sequence diagrams for safety critical systems. In: TASE 2020, pp. 217–224. IEEE (2020).https://doi.org/10.1109/TASE49443.2020.00037
5. Cunha, E., Custódio, M., Rocha, H., Barreto, R.S.: Formal verification of UML sequence diagrams in the embedded systems context. In: SBESC 2011, pp. 39–45. IEEE Computer Society (2011). https://doi.org/10.1109/SBESC.2011.18
6. Damm, W., et al.: A reference architecture of human cyber-physical systems - part III: semantic foundations. ACM Trans. Cyber Phys. Syst. **8**(1), 4:1–4:23 (2024). https://doi.org/10.1145/3622881
7. Damm, W., et al.: A reference architecture of human cyber-physical systems - part I: fundamental concepts. ACM Trans. Cyber Phys. Syst. **8**(1), 2:1–2:32 (2024). https://doi.org/10.1145/3622879
8. David, A., Möller, M.O., Yi, W.: Formal Verification of UML Statecharts with Real-Time Extensions. In: Kutsche, R.-D., Weber, H. (eds.) FASE 2002. LNCS, vol. 2306, pp. 218–232. Springer, Heidelberg (2002). https://doi.org/10.1007/3-540-45923-5_15
9. Grosu, R., Krüger, I., Stauner, T.: Hybrid sequence charts. In: ISORC 2000, p. 104. IEEE Computer Society (2000).https://doi.org/10.1109/ISORC.2000.839517
10. Guo, P., Zhan, B., Xu, X., Wang, S., Sun, W.: Translating a large subset of stateflow to hybrid CSP with code optimization. J. Syst. Archit. **130**, 102665 (2022). https://doi.org/10.1016/J.SYSARC.2022.102665
11. Han, D., Xing, J., Yang, Q., Wang, H., Zhang, X.: Formal sequence: extending UML sequence diagram for behavior description and formal verification. In: COMPSAC Workshops 2016, pp. 474–481. IEEE Computer Society (2016). https://doi.org/10.1109/COMPSAC.2016.118
12. Honda, K., Yoshida, N., Carbone, M.: Multiparty asynchronous session types. In: Proceedings of the 35th Annual ACM SIGPLAN-SIGACT Symposium on Principles of Programming Languages, pp. 273–284 (2008)
13. Li, X., Liu, Z., He, J.: A formal semantics of UML sequence diagram. In: ASWEC 2004, pp. 168–177. IEEE Computer Society (2004). https://doi.org/10.1109/ASWEC.2004.1290469
14. Lima, V., Talhi, C., Mouheb, D., Debbabi, M., Wang, L., Pourzandi, M.: Formal verification and validation of UML 2.0 sequence diagrams using source and destination of messages. In: SSV 2009. ENTCS, vol. 254, pp. 143–160. Elsevier (2009). https://doi.org/10.1016/J.ENTCS.2009.09.064
15. Milner, R.: The polyadic π-calculus: a tutorial. In: Logic and Algebra of Specification, pp. 203–246. Springer, Heidelberg (1993). https://doi.org/10.1007/978-3-642-58041-3_6

16. Molnár, V., et al.: Towards the formal verification of SysML v2 models. In: MODELS (Companion) 2024, pp. 1086–1095. ACM (2024).https://doi.org/10.1145/3652620.3687820
17. Peng, T., Ding, G.: Formal specification and automated verification of UML2.0 sequence diagrams. In: GrC 2012, pp. 370–375. IEEE Computer Society (2012). https://doi.org/10.1109/GRC.2012.6468641
18. PlantUML Team: PlantUML. https://plantuml.com/en/
19. Rahim, M., Hammad, A., Boukala-Ioualalen, M.: Towards the formal verification of SysML specifications: translation of activity diagrams into modular Petri nets. In: ACIT 2015, pp. 509–516. IEEE (2015). https://doi.org/10.1109/ACIT-CSI.2015.97
20. Sheng, H., Bentkamp, A., Zhan, B.: HHLPy: practical verification of hybrid systems using Hoare logic. In: FM 2023. LNCS, vol. 14000, pp. 160–178. Springer, Cham (2023). https://doi.org/10.1007/978-3-031-27481-7_11
21. Wang, S., Ji, Z., Xu, X., Zhan, B., Gao, Q., Zhan, N.: Formally verified C code generation from hybrid communicating sequential processes. In: ICCPS 2024, pp. 123–134. IEEE (2024).https://doi.org/10.1109/ICCPS61052.2024.00018
22. Wu, X., Yan, X., Li, X., Wang, Y.: Simulating hybrid SysML models: a model transformation approach under the DEVS framework. J. Supercomput. **79**(2), 2010–2030 (2023). https://doi.org/10.1007/S11227-022-04654-6
23. Xu, X., et al.: HpC: a calculus for hybrid and mobile systems. Proc. ACM Program. Lang. **9**(OOPSLA1), 1158–1183 (2025). https://doi.org/10.1145/3720478
24. Xu, X., et al.: HpC: a calculus for hybrid and mobile systems - full version. CoRR abs/2501.09430 (2025). https://doi.org/10.48550/ARXIV.2501.09430
25. Xu, X., Wang, S., Zhan, B., Jin, X., Talpin, J., Zhan, N.: Unified graphical co-modeling, analysis and verification of cyber-physical systems by combining AADL and Simulink/Stateflow. Theor. Comput. Sci. **903**, 1–25 (2022). https://doi.org/10.1016/J.TCS.2021.11.008
26. Yan, G., Jiao, L., Wang, S., Wang, L., Zhan, N.: Automatically generating SystemC code from HCSP formal models. ACM Trans. Softw. Eng. Methodol. **29**(1), 4:1–4:39 (2020). https://doi.org/10.1145/3360002
27. Zhan, B., et al.: Mars 2.0: a toolchain for modeling, analysis, verification and code generation of cyber-physical systems. CoRR abs/2403.03035 (2024). https://doi.org/10.48550/ARXIV.2403.03035
28. Zhao, J., Zhao, Y., Yao, P., Zeng, F., Zhan, B., Ren, K.: KBX: verified model synchronization via formal bidirectional transformation. ACM Trans. Softw. Eng. Methodol. **34**(2) (2025). https://doi.org/10.1145/3696000

Neural-Symbolic System Control Adjustment Based on Runtime Verification

Hongxu Zhu, Wanwei Liu[(✉)], and Ji Wang

College of Computer Science and Technology, National University of Defense Technology, Changsha, China
{zhuhongxu,wwliu,wj}@nudt.edu.cn

Abstract. Neural-Symbolic Systems (NSSs) have been widely deployed in safety-critical domains. However, due to the inherent uncertainty and opaqueness of DNNs, there is an increasing demand for security assurance. In this work, we propose an adjustment framework based on runtime verification (RV, for short) to ensure NSS compliance with given signal temporal logic (STL) properties. To identify unsafe control signal in time, we utilize Runge-Kutta method to predict the system trajectory under scrutiny at discrete time-steps. Our framework also supports the switching of control signals upon violation of safety properties. This capability is achieved through the deployment of predictive strategies, including the construction of a state tree and forward-search algorithms, enabling the system to dynamically select and switch to alternative control signals in real time. We conduct an evaluation on publicly available control systems. The evaluation results show that our method successfully repairs critical safety issues, and significantly improves the reliability of NSSs.

Keywords: Neural-symbolic system · Runtime verification · Control adjustment

1 Introduction

Neural-symbolic systems (NSSs) [3], a.k.a, neural-networks controlled cyber-physical systems (CPSs), which utilize both neural networks and cyber controllers to maintain behaviors of particular mechanical systems, have been broadly deployed into diverse real-world applications. In these systems, the neural modules are employed to transform high-dimensional signals from the physical world into compressed information for the control module. Subsequently, the control module issues specific control signals to guide the subsequent operation of the system.

This work is supported by the National Key R&D Program of China No. 2022YFA1005101, the National Natural Science Foundation of China under Grant No. 62032019 and No. 61872371.

É. André et al. (Eds.): ICFEM 2025, LNCS 16229, pp. 79–96, 2026.
https://doi.org/10.1007/978-981-95-4213-0_5

With their immense potential, NSSs are increasingly adopted in various safety-critical domains such as aerospace [9], autonomous driving [14], and healthcare monitoring [10]. Therefore, ensuring the reliability and safety of NSSs in such contexts has become increasingly urgent. However, NSSs still face several distinctive challenges. For example, the opacity of these systems and the difficulty in formally verifying their behavior can result in inappropriate actions under certain conditions [19].

To address this issue, earlier research proposed various solutions. A portion of the research focuses on testing NSS with the aim of identifying potential hazardous states, employing methods such as falsification [11,20] and runtime verification [3]. Related research in complex CPS safety assurance has explored efficient runtime verification paradigms. For systems with unpredictable dynamics, techniques have shifted from exhaustive state-space analysis toward targeted validation of critical operational scenarios [1]. Further development proposes an incremental online verification technique for dynamic CPS. The method identifies the differential constraints between the current and previous verification problems, and then leverages incremental linear programming techniques to efficiently solve the new constraint set by reusing the solution basis from the previous cycle [2].

Nevertheless, effectively adjusting unsafe control signals âĂŞ crucial for enhancing NSS reliability and mitigating risks from improper decisions âĂŞ remains understudied. A common approach is neural network (NN) repair to improve NN performance through adversarial training or parameter adjustments [13]. However, these methods are primarily suited for white-box policies, where internal network states are known and modifiable, making them less applicable to opaque, black-box policies with unknown or immutable structures. To mitigate the risk of adverse decision-making, existing methods often transform the control repair process into a multi-objective optimization problem, but typically enable only single-step control adjustments [18]. In addition, these optimization techniques generally incur substantial computational costs. Given the extensive deployment of NSS in safety-critical environments, unsafe control commands can lead to dangerous behaviors, resulting in failures or even harm. These challenges significantly impede the further development and deployment of NSS in various fields.

In this paper, we present our preliminary efforts towards addressing this challenge with the introduction of CABRV (Control Adjustment Based on Runtime Verification), a novel framework aimed at automating the repair process for NSSs in safety-critical contexts. Given predefined safety constraints, the CABRV framework aims to detect instances of noncompliance by analyzing potential future states of the system through a methodical sampling and predictive trajectory analysis. Following the identification of potentially hazardous behaviors, CABRV employs methodologies to adjust control decisions accordingly. When faced with an execution scenario that violates the safety criteria, CABRV performs a retrospective analysis, exploring alternative control strategies to determine the most effective corrective actions that ensure the operation of the system aligns with the specified safety requirements.

The contributions of this paper are summarized as follows:

- First of all, we propose a novel approach that leverages real-time status information from the model during operation to evaluate and predict system safety. This approach also informs subsequent adjustments when necessary, ensuring that corrective actions are guided by current operational insights.
- Second, we introduce an online control adjustment strategy that uses the prediction algorithm to generate safer actions in real time through alternative control strategies.
- Last but not least, we perform an experimental evaluation on 4 instances of NSSs. The evaluation results demonstrate the effectiveness of our approach.

2 Preliminaries

In this paper, we refer to $\mathbb{B} = \{0, 1\}$ as the set of boolean values, $\mathbb{R}$ as the set of real numbers, and $\mathbb{T} = \mathbb{R}_{\geq 0}$ as the time set. A *signal* describing an evolution of a variable is a function $x : \mathbb{T} \to \mathbb{R}$, and an *m-ary signal vector* is $\boldsymbol{x} = (x_1, x_2, \ldots, x_m)^{\mathrm{T}}$, where $x_1, x_2, \ldots, x_m$ are signals. If the context is not ambiguous, we write x_t instead of $x(t)$, and $\boldsymbol{x}_t$ instead of $(x_1(t), x_2(t), \ldots, x_m(t))^{\mathrm{T}}$.

2.1 Neural Networks

Deep neural networks (DNNs) are hierarchical models composed of multiple layers of neurons. Each layer transforms its input data through a linear operation followed by a nonlinear activation function. Formally, given an input vector $\boldsymbol{x} \in \mathbb{R}^D$, the output of the l-th layer is computed as:

$$\boldsymbol{h}^{(l)} = \sigma\left(\boldsymbol{W}^{(l)}\boldsymbol{h}^{(l-1)} + \boldsymbol{b}^{(l)}\right),$$

where $\boldsymbol{W}^{(l)}$ and $\boldsymbol{b}^{(l)}$ are the learnable weight matrix and bias vector of layer l, $\boldsymbol{h}^{(l-1)}$ is the output from the previous layer (with $\boldsymbol{h}^{(0)} = \boldsymbol{x}$), and $\sigma(\cdot)$ denotes a nonlinear activation function (e.g., ReLU, Sigmoid, or Tanh).

The *depth* of a DNN refers to the number of hidden layers. The final output layer typically uses a task-specific activation function (e.g., softmax for classification or linear for regression), enabling the model to learn complex, high-level feature representations through successive nonlinear transformations.

2.2 Neural-Symbolic Systems

In this subsection, we briefly recall the representation method in [3] to define a neural-symbolic system, which is constituted with a set of signals and control functions. Among them, the signals include the following categories:

- *Environmental-signals* $\boldsymbol{v} = \{v_1, v_2, \ldots, v_n\}$, are used to represent information perceived from the environment.
- *Input-signals* $\boldsymbol{x}$, a subset of $\boldsymbol{v}$, being the inputs for the neural system.
- *Output-signal* $\boldsymbol{y} = \{y_1, y_2, \ldots, y_k\}$, which are the outputs of the AI module.
- *Control-signal* $\boldsymbol{c} = \{c_1, c_2, \ldots, c_m\}$, are discrete and are used to guide the behaviors of the system at each time step, and we require $\boldsymbol{y}$ and $\boldsymbol{c}$ to be disjoint.

An NSS further includes three control functions, described as follows:

- *Physical control* f, described by a differential equation $\dot{\boldsymbol{v}} = f(\boldsymbol{v}, \boldsymbol{y}, \boldsymbol{c}, t)$, describes how the environmental signal of the system evolves.
- *Neural mapping* Ψ, can be thought of as a function $\boldsymbol{y} = \Psi(\boldsymbol{x})$. Even though we may not know exactly how Ψ operates internally, we can always use it to generate an output for any valid input.
- *Cyber control* δ, is defined by the equation $\boldsymbol{c}' = \delta(\boldsymbol{v}, \boldsymbol{y}, \boldsymbol{c}, \Delta t)$, which computes the control signal $\boldsymbol{c}'$ for the subsequent time step Δt.

For the sake of convenience in subsequent discussions, $\boldsymbol{w}_t = \{\boldsymbol{v}_t, \boldsymbol{y}_t, \boldsymbol{c}_t\}$ will be referred to as the NSS state at time t. A *trajectory* τ is a sequence of NSS states (i.e., $\tau = \{\boldsymbol{v}_t, \boldsymbol{y}_t, \boldsymbol{x}_t\}_{t\in\mathbb{T}}$).

2.3 Signal Temporal Logic

In this paper, to express NSS specifications, we use *Signal Temporal Logic* (STL), which syntax is recursively defined as following BNF

$$\varphi ::= \top \mid \mu \mid \neg\varphi \mid \varphi \vee \varphi \mid \varphi \mathsf{U}_I \varphi,$$

where $\mu ::= g(\boldsymbol{z}) \gtrsim 0$, $\gtrsim \in \{>, \geq\}$ is a comparison operator, g is a continuous function over the variable signal vector $\boldsymbol{z}$. U_I is the until operator with an interval I, which is a subset of $\mathbb{T}$, being in the form $[t_1, t_2]$, $[t_1, t_2)$, $(t_1, t_2]$ or (t_1, t_2), where $t_1 \leq t_2$ are in $\mathbb{T}$, and for t in $\mathbb{T}$, $t + I$ is the set $\{t + t' \mid t' \in I\}$. For convenience, we can also define more temporal operators: eventually ($\mathsf{F}_I\varphi \overset{\text{def}}{=} \top\mathsf{U}_I\varphi$), always ($\mathsf{G}_I\varphi \overset{\text{def}}{=} \neg\mathsf{F}_I\neg\varphi$), and historically ($\varphi\mathsf{R}_I\psi \overset{\text{def}}{=} \neg(\neg\varphi\mathsf{U}_I\neg\psi)$).

For a given trajectory $\tau := \tau_{0:T}$ and $t \in \mathbb{T}$, we define the qualitative semantics of an STL formula φ as follows:

$$\begin{aligned}
\tau, t \models \mu \quad & \Leftrightarrow g(\tau_t) \gtrsim 0 \\
\tau, t \models \neg\varphi \quad & \Leftrightarrow \neg(\tau, t \models \varphi) \\
\tau, t \models \varphi \vee \psi & \Leftrightarrow (\tau, t \models \varphi) \vee (\tau, t \models \psi) \\
\tau, t \models \varphi \mathsf{U}_I \psi & \Leftrightarrow \exists t' \in I \text{ s.t. } \tau, t + t' \models \psi \wedge \forall t'' \in [t, t + t'), \tau, t'' \models \varphi
\end{aligned}$$

To quantitatively measure the degree of satisfaction for a given safety specification, we employ the quantitative robust semantics $[\![\varphi]\!]_{\tau,t}$, which maps a STL formula φ, a NSS trajectory τ, and time t to a real number by induction as follows [5]:

$$\begin{aligned}
[\![\top]\!]_{\tau,t} &= \infty \\
[\![g(\boldsymbol{z}) \gtrsim 0]\!]_{\tau,t} &= g(\boldsymbol{z}) \\
[\![\neg\varphi]\!]_{\tau,t} &= -[\![\varphi]\!]_{\tau,t} \\
[\![\varphi \vee \psi]\!]_{\tau,t} &= \max\{[\![\varphi]\!]_{\tau,t}, [\![\psi]\!]_{\tau,t}\} \\
[\![\varphi \mathsf{U}_I \psi]\!]_{\tau,t} &= \sup_{t' \in I+t} \min\left\{[\![\psi]\!]_{\tau,t'}, \inf_{t'' \in [t,t')} [\![\varphi]\!]_{\tau,t''}\right\}
\end{aligned}$$

An STL formula φ is considered *strict* if all its atomic subformulas μ of φ are of the form $g(\boldsymbol{z}) > 0$ when φ is equivalently written in a negative normal form. In fact, we have the following claim for the relation between qualitative and quantitative satisfaction.

Theorem 1. *For every strict STL formula φ, trajectory τ and $t \in \mathbb{T}$, we have: $\tau, t \models \varphi$ if and only if $[\![\varphi]\!]_{\tau,t} > 0$.*

A positive or negative value of $[\![\varphi]\!]_{\tau,t}$ indicates whether the specification is satisfied or violated, with higher values signifying stronger satisfaction or violation.

2.4 Runge-Kutta Methods

Runge-Kutta methods constitute a family of iterative numerical algorithms widely used for the temperal discretization of ordinary differential equations (ODEs). These methods provide approximate solutions to the initial value problems (IVPs), which are formulated as follows:

$$y'(t) = f(t, y(t)), \quad y(t_0) = y_0$$

where f is a known function, $y(t)$ is the unknown function to be determined, $y'(t)$ denotes the derivative of y with respect to t, and y_0 is the initial condition.

A general *s-stage* Runge-Kutta method (where s denotes the number of slope evaluations per step) for solving the above IVP can be written as:

$$y_{n+1} = y_n + \Delta t \sum_{i=1}^{s} b_i k_i$$

where Δt is the step size between consecutive points t_n and t_{n+1}, b_i are weights, and the increments k_i are described as:

$$k_i = f\left(t_n + c_i \Delta t, y_n + \Delta t \sum_{j=1}^{s} a_{ij} k_j\right)$$

for $i = 1, 2, \ldots, s$, with coefficients a_{ij}, b_i, and c_i that define a specific Runge-Kutta method. The method is *explicit* when $a_{ij} = 0$ for $j \geq i$ (allowing sequential computation of k_i), and *implicit* otherwise.

The coefficients of Runge-Kutta methods are typically derived by matching Taylor series expansions of the numerical solution with the exact solution's Taylor expansion. The *order* of a Runge-Kutta method is defined as the highest-degree Taylor polynomial that the method replicates exactly for polynomial solutions. For a h-order method, the *local truncation error* (LTE) behaves as $\mathcal{O}(\Delta t^{h+1})$. Although LTE decreases rapidly with reduced step size, the *global truncation error* (GTE) accumulates over successive integration steps. Crucially, even when individual LTEs are small, repeated application of the method can propagate and amplify errors, potentially causing significant deviation from the exact solution. Direct estimation of GTE is challenging as it requires knowledge of the exact solution, which is generally not available.

3 The Control Adjustment Framework

3.1 Problem Formulation

In this work, we consider an NSS, defined by the following components:

$$\begin{cases} \dot{\boldsymbol{v}} = f(\boldsymbol{v}, \boldsymbol{y}, \boldsymbol{c}, t) \\ \boldsymbol{y} = \Psi(\boldsymbol{x}) \\ \boldsymbol{c}' = \delta(\boldsymbol{v}, \boldsymbol{y}, \boldsymbol{c}, \Delta t) \end{cases} .$$

At time step t, the system state is denoted as $\boldsymbol{w}_t = \{\boldsymbol{v}_t, \boldsymbol{y}_t, \boldsymbol{c}_t\}$. The neural mapping Ψ processes $\boldsymbol{v}_t$ to generate output $\boldsymbol{y}_{t+1}$, after which the cyber control δ produces the control signal $\boldsymbol{c}_{t+1}$. Execution of this control signal advances the environmental signal to $\boldsymbol{v}_{t+1}$. Consequently, the state at $t+1$ becomes $\boldsymbol{w}_{t+1} = \{\boldsymbol{v}_{t+1}, \boldsymbol{y}_{t+1}, \boldsymbol{c}_{t+1}\}$.

The system trajectory $\tau = \{\boldsymbol{w}_0, \boldsymbol{w}_1, ..., \boldsymbol{w}_T\}$ over T time steps originates from the initial state $\boldsymbol{w}_0$. Our framework is designed to ensure that the system trajectory satisfies the given STL specification φ. In other words, the quantitative robust semantics $[\![\varphi]\!]_{\tau,t}$ must be positive.

However, as a consequence of factors including inadequate training or over-fitting, neural mapping Ψ may yield erroneous outputs that result in the control function δ generating faulty control signals. To preempt violations, we need to anticipate hazardous control signals during runtime, and dynamically adjust signals before violations occur. Therefore, the CABRV framework operates cyclically as follows:

(1) At the current time point $t = t_0$, we first predict the trajectory τ of the system within the time span T according to the system state $\boldsymbol{w}_{t_0}$, and analyze whether the trajectory will cause the property φ to be violated.
(2) If the NSS trajectory τ is predicted to be unsafe, we subsequently determine an adjustment time point t_r for the control signal and generate an alternative control signal c'_{t_r} that will allow the system to return safe.

(3) After adjustment, the NSS continues to operate according to the original control procedure and repeats steps (1) and (2).

Refer to Fig. 1 for a diagram that illustrates the runtime workflow. Additional details are provided in the following subsection.

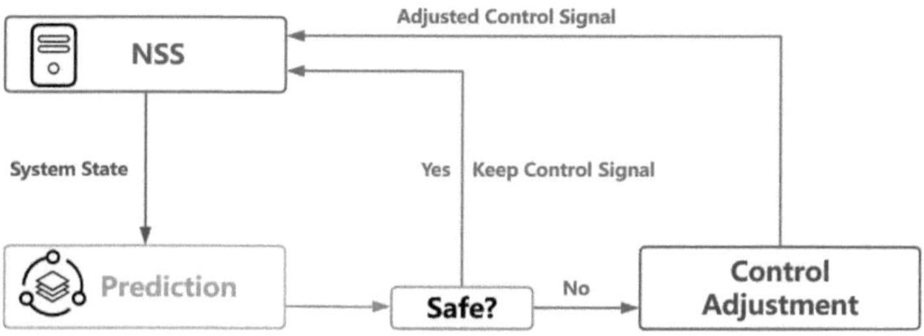

Fig. 1. CABRV Runtime workflow

3.2 Unsafe Control Signal Positioning

The core challenge in the CABRV is accurately identifying unsafe control signals in real time while minimizing computational overhead. This section elaborates on our prediction-based method for detecting risky control signals and determining the optimal intervention time.

In this paper, we employ the STL quantitative robustness function to evaluate the extent to which a given system output trajectory satisfies safety constraints. However, since the future state of the system in the expected time span is unknown until the execution comes to an end, a prediction of the future state of the system is needed at runtime to obtain an approximate trajectory of the operation. To address this, we introduce a Runge-Kutta (RK) based prediction algorithm that estimates the future system trajectory from current NSS state $\boldsymbol{w}_0$. The RK method is ideal for this task due to its balance between precision and efficiency, particularly for the ODE-governed physical control function f.

When the control signal c of NSS remains near-constant over a period of time Δt, the physical control f can be approximated as constant. This permits RK method over the time interval Δt and utilizes the result to represent $\boldsymbol{w}_{t_0+\Delta t}$. Our prediction approach allows for fine-tuning the Runge-Kutta method's parameters to enhance prediction accuracy and computational efficiency. By presetting thresholds ϵ_v and ϵ_c, the system can autonomously modify the algorithm's order and adapt the step size to better align with the specific NSS. These adjustments are contingent on whether the actual errors surpass the set thresholds. To estimate the local truncation error e_v in state prediction, we use the half-step method as follows:

Algorithm 1: Prediction algorithm

Input : NSS $S(f, \Psi, \delta)$, State $\boldsymbol{w} = \{\boldsymbol{v}, \boldsymbol{y}, \boldsymbol{c}\}$, Current time t, Time span T, Error tolerance $\epsilon = \{\epsilon_v, \epsilon_c\}$

Output: Trajectory τ

Initial RK time step Δt, order $h = 1$, and $\tau = [(t, \boldsymbol{w})]$;
while $t<T$ **do**
    $\boldsymbol{v}', e_v = RK(f, \boldsymbol{v}, t, \Delta t, h)$;
    $y' = \Psi(v)$;
    $c' = \delta(\boldsymbol{v}, \boldsymbol{y}, \boldsymbol{c}, \Delta t)$;
    if $e_v < \epsilon_v \cdot \frac{\Delta t}{T}$ *and* $e_c = \|\boldsymbol{c}' - \boldsymbol{c}\|_\infty < \epsilon_c$ **then**
        $t = t + \Delta t$;
        $\boldsymbol{w} = \{\boldsymbol{v}', \boldsymbol{y}', \boldsymbol{c}'\}$;
        τ.append($\boldsymbol{w}$)
    end
    $\Delta t, h = Adjust(\Delta t, h, e_v, e_c, \epsilon)$;
end
return τ

- Compute the state $\boldsymbol{v}'_1$ at $t + \Delta t$ using one full step of size Δt.
- Compute the state $\boldsymbol{v}'_2$ at $t + \Delta t$ using two half-steps of size $\Delta t/2$.
- Calculate the error: $e_v = \|\boldsymbol{v}'_1 - \boldsymbol{v}'_2\|_\infty$.

This error estimate enables adaptive control of the step size and the order of the RK method. The adjustment of the step size and order is as follows:

- First, the step size Δt is adaptively adjusted , decreased if $e_c > \epsilon_c$ or increased if $e_c < \epsilon_c$, to preliminarily estimate its upper bound.
- Then, if $e_v \ll \epsilon_v \cdot \frac{\Delta t}{T}$, the order h is decreased by one to refine the computational efficiency.
- And if $e_v > \epsilon_v \cdot \frac{\Delta t}{T}$, the step size Δt is adjusted using the formula $\Delta t_{\text{new}} = \Delta t \cdot \left(\frac{\epsilon_v \cdot \Delta t}{e_v \cdot T}\right)^p$, where p is a moderating parameter, usually between 0.2 and 0.8, depending on the order of the Runge-Kutta method used. When $e_v \gg \epsilon_v \cdot \frac{\Delta t}{T}$, the order h is increased additionally.

Note that the prediction algorithm begins execution at time t_0, and we assume that its computation time is negligible. Furthermore, when the system actually reaches the generated trajectory time point t, we perform a check. Let $\widehat{\boldsymbol{w}}_t$ be the corresponding actual state values, and until it detects $\|\boldsymbol{w}_t - \widehat{\boldsymbol{w}}_t\|_\infty > \epsilon$, where ϵ represents a preset error threshold. Then any subsequent predicted trajectory will be discarded, and we will immediately perform a new prediction over the time horizon T with current NSS state $\boldsymbol{w}_t$, i.e., re-execute Algorithm 1 with setting $t_0 = t$.

3.3 Adjusted Control Signal Generation

Using the prediction algorithm described in Sect. 3.2, we obtain the predicted trajectory τ starting from initial time t_0 and compute the STL score $[\![\varphi]\!]_{\tau,t}$ at each time point $t \in [t_0, t_0+T]$ using the quantitative robustness function. When an unsafe trajectory is identified at time t_w (i.e., $[\![\varphi]\!]_{\tau,t_w} \leq 0$), the control signal adjustment process is initiated. This section details two distinct strategies for generating an adjustment time point $t_r \in [t_0, t_w)$ and a corresponding alternative control signal c'_{t_r}: *State-Tree-Based Multi-Criteria Optimization* and *Forward-Search Adjustment.*

State-Tree-Based Multi-Criteria Optimization. To enable immediate switching to safe control signals upon detecting safety violations,we construct a *state tree* during trajectory prediction. This tree encapsulates multiple control decision paths, providing alternatives for runtime adjustment.

The tree originates from a root node representing the initial system state $\boldsymbol{w}_{t_0}$, with depth extending to the prediction horizon T. At each time step t, every node branches into k child nodes corresponding to feasible control signals: one generated by the nominal control function δ and $k-1$ alternatives sampled uniformly from the system's permissible control space $[-c_{max}, c_{max}]$. Subsequent states are computed using a low-precision Runge-Kutta method to balance computational efficiency and accuracy. To maintain tractability, the tree undergoes pruning to eliminate branches that either lead to immediate STL violations (indicated by $[\![\varphi]\!]_{\tau,t}$) or exhibit robustness scores significantly worse than their sibling branches. This pruning process carefully balances the exploration of potential control strategies with the computational constraints of real-time operation, ensuring both safety and performance are upheld.

Following the construction of the state tree, when a safety violation is detected at time t_w, the framework initiates a backtracking through the state tree to evaluate candidate adjustment points t_r. For each candidate, we first calculate the robustness improvement $\Delta\rho = [\![\varphi]\!]_{\tau',t_r} - [\![\varphi]\!]_{\tau,t_r}$, where τ' denotes the trajectory generated under alternative control signals. We then perform multi-criteria optimization using the composite score:

$$score = \alpha_1 \frac{t_w - t_r}{T} + \alpha_2 \Delta\rho + \alpha_3 \left(1 - \frac{\|c_{t_r} - c'_{t_r}\|_\infty}{c_{max}}\right)$$

This score balances three key factors: the timing of intervention (weighted by α_1), the degree of safety improvement (weighted by α_2), and the magnitude of control signal deviation (weighted by α_3), ensuring a balanced trade-off between early response, safety enhancement, and system stability. These values may conflict with each other, meaning that improving one might come at the expense of another. Therefore, the result of the weighted scoring provides a relatively optimal choice with linear time complexity. The candidate adjustment (t_r, c'_{t_r}) with the highest composite score is selected.

The weighting parameters α_1, α_2, and α_3 play a critical role in balancing the factors. These parameters are application-specific and context-dependent. Initially, the parameters are typically set manually based on domain expertise, the relative importance of each objective for the specific system and safety property, and preliminary experimentation. Subsequently, as the CABRV framework operates and accumulates historical data from previous control adjustments, these parameters can be automatically refined and adapted.

Theorem 2. *Given a prediction horizon T and a branch factor k (number of candidate control signals per step), the time complexity of the state-tree-based adjustment strategy is $\mathcal{O}(k^T)$*

In this strategy, the state tree has $\mathcal{O}(k^T)$ potential nodes. Evaluating the multi-criteria score for each candidate node $\mathcal{O}(T \cdot k)$ requires operations. The overall complexity is $\mathcal{O}(T \cdot k + k^T) = \mathcal{O}(k^T)$, still dominated by exponential growth in T or k. While the score provides a systematic way to explore alternative control signals, its computational overhead may become prohibitive for real-time systems with strict latency constraints.

Forward-Search Adjustment. To address the time limitation, we introduce a greedy forward search strategy with early termination, which prioritizes efficiency while maintaining safety guarantees. This approach is based on the following key observations:

- *Early adjustments yield greater impact:* Control signals applied closer to the initial time t_0 exert a more profound influence on the overall system trajectory. Correcting errors proactively at this stage prevents violations from occurring, rather than requiring reactive fixes later.
- *Early adjustments enhance stability:* Modifications made earlier allow the system to adapt its behavior more smoothly. This avoids disruptive and abrupt changes that could destabilize the system or trigger secondary violations.
- *Early adjustments optimize computation:* Given the impracticality of exhaustively evaluating all possible adjustments, prioritizing early interventions focuses computational resources on the most impactful corrections. Crucially, if an early adjustment effectively mitigates the predicted violation, it circumvents superfluous evaluation of later time points.

Upon detecting a safety violation at time t_w (indicated by $[\![\varphi]\!]_{\tau,t_w} \leq 0$), our framework initiates a forward-search adjustment process starting from the initial time t_0 and progresses through each subsequent time point. For each step, the algorithm checks k candidate control signals. The method sequentially examines each candidate control signal in chronological order, seeking the first adjustment point t_r that simultaneously satisfies two critical conditions: the adjusted control signal c'_{t_r} must improve the trajectory's robustness score ($\Delta\rho = [\![\varphi]\!]_{\tau',t_r} - [\![\varphi]\!]_{\tau,t_r} > 0$), and must postpone the safety violation to a later time $t'_w > t_w$. This forward-search approach ensures computational efficiency by terminating immediately upon finding the first valid adjustment, avoiding the overhead associated with exhaustive backward searches or complex optimization procedures.

Theorem 3. *Given a prediction horizon T and a branch factor k , the time complexity of the forward-search adjustment strategy is $\mathcal{O}(k \cdot T)$.*

4 Case Study

In this section, we present the experimental results of the proposed method on different NSSs provided by Zhu et al. [21]. All experiments were conducted on a machine equipped with an Intel Core i5-12400F CPU and 16GB of RAM.

4.1 System Description

The case study involves following NSSs:

- **Pendulum**: This system models a pendulum attached to a frictionless joint. A torque is applied to maintain stability. The safety requirements mandate that the tilt angle $|\eta|$ must remain below 90° and the angular velocity ω must be less than $\pi/2$ rad/s.
- **Cart Pole**: This system features a cart with a pole balanced vertically on top. The initial state varies after each reset. The cart must move left or right under the applied force u to keep the pole upright. Safety requires: the pole's angle η from vertical must be less than 90°, the cart's displacement δ from the origin must stay within 0.3 m, and the cart's velocity $|v_1|$ and the pole's angular velocity $|v_2|$ must be below 0.3 m/s and 0.5 m/s, respectively.
- **Self Driving**: This system controls a vehicle to track a predefined path. Its state is two-dimensional $[\eta, d]$, where η is the angle between the direction of the car and the road centerline, and d is the lateral distance from the front of the car to the centerline. The control signal δ adjusts the steering angle. Formally, the system is safe if the heading angle $|\eta|$ stays below 90° and the lateral distance $|d|$ remains under 2.0 m.
- **Lane Keeping**: This system maintains a vehicle between lane markers and centered in a possibly curved lane. Safety is ensured if the distance d to the preceding vehicle is less than 0.9 m.

The physical control functions governing these systems range from linear to polynomial. Four distinct pre-trained neural mappings trained using Deep Deterministic Policy Gradient (DDPG) [12] are employed to manage the NSSs and satisfy their time-related constraints. The AI module parameters and the formal safety specifications for each NSS are detailed in Table 1.

Parameter Configuration. The quantitative robustness semantics are computed utilizing a pre-existing tool, RTAMT[16]. Based on the prior bisection search and the actual runtime performance of the system, we established $\Delta t = 0.01$ s. We performed 1000 sampling iterations with different initial values within the feasible initial value interval of the NSSs to generate 1000 different trajectories. To mitigate the impact of randomness, we repeat each experiment 10 times and report the average results.

Table 1. AI Parameters and specifications of NSSs.

NSS	AI Parameters			Safety Specification
	Inputs/Outputs	Layers	Neurons	
Pendulum	2/1	3	[280,240,200]	$\mathsf{G}_{[0,200]}(\|\eta\| < 90° \wedge \|\omega\| < \pi/2)$
Cart Pole	4/1	3	[300,250,200]	$\mathsf{G}_{[0,200]}(\|\eta\| < 90° \wedge \|\delta\| < 0.3 \wedge$ $\|\eta_1\| < 0.3 \wedge \|\eta_2\| < 0.5)$
Self Driving	2/1	3	[300,250,200]	$\mathsf{G}_{[0,200]}(\|\eta\| < 90° \wedge \|d\| < 2.0)$
Lane Keeping	4/2	2	[240,200]	$\mathsf{G}_{[0,200]}(\|d\| < 0.9)$

4.2 Experiment Results

Our evaluation aims to answer the following research questions:

RQ1: Can the approximated trajectory obtained through the prediction algorithm accurately verify the system's safety during operation?
RQ2: How efficient is the online control signal adjustment strategy of CABRV?
RQ3: Does CABRV effectively improve the safety of NSS?

The experimental evaluation primarily compares the performance of the original NSS controller against its operation under the CABRV framework. This self-comparison approach was necessitated by the novelty of CABRV's core contribution trajectory prediction and real-time control signal adjustment. To the best of our knowledge, there is no directly comparable baseline that performs online control signal switching guided by predicted STL robustness scores without requiring preparatory steps (e.g., model abstraction or data collection) for the same class of NSSs.

For **RQ1**, in order to a comprehensive evaluation, for different NSSs, the time span of the predicted trajectories is consistent with their specifications. And the error tolerance for control signal ϵ_c is set to one percent of the control signal range (i.e., $\epsilon_c = 0.01 \cdot (c_{max} - c_{min})$), while varying error tolerance thresholds ϵ_v are applied in different experimental budgets, denoted by **TT**.

We focus on the following metrics:

- **False positive count (FP)**: The number of trajectories predicted to be unsafe that were actually safe.

- **False negative count (FN)**: The number of trajectories predicted to be safe that were actually unsafe.
- **Average prediction trajectory length (TL)**: The average number of discrete time steps predicted for a trajectory.
- **Prediction error rate (PE)**: The overall error rate of the predictions.
- **Average time (Time)**: The average computational time required to generate a single predicted trajectory.

Our experimental results are shown in Table 2. The results demonstrate a clear trade-off between prediction accuracy and computational cost. As the tolerance threshold (ϵ_v) becomes stricter, the prediction error rate generally improves. This enhanced accuracy comes at the cost of increased computation time and longer predicted trajectory lengths, as the algorithm requires more steps and potentially higher-order RK methods to meet the tighter error bound.

Table 2. The performance of the trajectory prediction algorithm.

NSS	TT	FP	FN	TL	PE (%)	Time (s)
Pendulum	0.0015	20.2	6.4	33.0762	2.66	0.0331
	0.0010	19.3	0.2	37.1897	1.95	0.0371
	0.0005	7.8	2.0	44.8438	0.98	0.0451
Cart Pole	0.003	31.2	1.8	158.2998	3.30	0.0947
	0.002	26.4	1.4	185.2536	2.78	0.1108
	0.001	11.6	0.2	186.7780	1.18	0.1123
Self Driving	1.00	7.0	0.0	13.4410	0.70	0.0095
	0.70	6.2	0.0	13.6452	0.62	0.0095
	0.40	4.0	0.0	13.8878	0.40	0.0096
Lane Keeping	0.07	12.6	6.6	174.3362	1.92	0.0358
	0.06	6.4	8.4	184.2992	1.48	0.0460
	0.05	6.0	8.0	190.5066	1.40	0.0897

For **RQ2**, we generate 100 initial states that would lead to errors in each of the four NSSs, and then conduct control signal adjustment experiments on these initial states using State-Tree-Based Multi-Criteria Optimization (**STB-MCO**), because its exhaustive nature provides an upper bound on the potential performance of the adjustment generation mechanism. The hyperparameters for these experiments are the tolerance threshold ϵ_v and the number of random control signal branches k. The adjustment strategy of CABRV was evaluated based on the *Number of adjustments* (NA), which is the average count of applied alternative signals, and the *Adjustment efficiency*, which measures the percentage of successful adjustments. The results are shown in Table 3.

The experimental results for RQ2 demonstrate that the control adjustment strategy of the CABRV framework is effective. The framework consistently generates and applies alternative control signals in response to predicted violations.

More importantly, most of these interventions are successful, preventing safety breaches without introducing new violations. This confirms the practical utility of the adjustment mechanism. The results also reveal that the strategy's performance can be tuned through its parameters. A stricter prediction tolerance threshold generally leads to more precise and necessary adjustments, thereby improving effectiveness.

Table 3. The adjustment efficiency of **STB-MCO**.

NSS	TT	CS	NA	AE (%)
Pendulum	0.0010	3	95.6	25.4
		5	95.8	30.4
	0.0005	3	98.8	50.4
		5	99.0	59.2
Cart Pole	0.0030	3	100.0	84.2
		5	100.0	87.2
	0.0020	3	98.8	88.0
		5	100.0	93.0
Self Driving	1.0	1	97.1	63.5
		3	100.0	92.1
	0.7	1	97.3	63.7
		3	100.0	92.7
Lane Keeping	0.5	1	70.2	63.7
		3	78.0	69.0
	0.1	1	73.8	64.7
		3	79.1	70.6

For **RQ3**, We run these subject NSS over 1000 initial states, with (1) the original controller, (2) the controller monitored by CABRV using State-Tree-Based Multi-Criteria Optimization (**STB-MCO**), and (3) the controller monitored by CABRV using Forward-Search Adjustment (**FSA**), respectively. The experimental results for RQ3 are shown in Table 3, including the safety rates of these systems and the average time cost.

The results for RQ3 provide a validation of the CABRV framework's effectiveness. The most significant finding is a substantial improvement in safety rates across all tested systems when either adjustment strategy is activated, compared to the original, unmonitored controller. A key trade-off between the two adjustment strategies is evident. The State-Tree-Based Multi-Criteria Optimization (STB-MCO) method consistently achieves the highest safety performance. In contrast, the Forward-Search Adjustment (FSA) strategy offers a reduction in computational overhead, making it a highly efficient alternative (Table 4).

Table 4. The performance of different adjustment strategy in CABRV.

NSS	Safety Rate (%)			Time Cost (s)	
	Original	STB-MCO	FSA	STB-MCO	FSA
Pendulum	84.7	90.1	87.8	0.714	0.286
Cart Pole	82.1	91.5	91.3	1.103	0.751
Self Driving	96.5	99.1	98.7	0.336	0.016
Lane Keeping	96.4	97.3	97.3	0.835	0.349

5 Related Work

Although with the rapid development of AI, NSSs are increasingly replacing traditional cyber-physical systems [4,6], there is relatively little work on verifying and repairing for NSS. Currently, most research focuses on the formal verification of these NSSs, as it provides rigorous safety guarantees. Techniques such as reachability analysis [7,17] have been widely explored and are considered highly effective in validating AI controllers. These approaches excel in providing strong offline guarantees, often requiring detailed system models for analysis. Another approach to formal verification involves constraint-solving methods, including DLV [8]. In contrast, falsification is seen as a more scalable alternative compared to verification, a point supported by empirical research [15] that examined the performance of model checking versus testing in NSS. Despite this, current falsification studies primarily address NSS with conventional controllers and often overlook the unique architecture of neural networks.

For control signal adjustment, the NSS policies are often designed for decision making tasks, including neural mapping and cyber control. This makes control signal adjusting particularly complex, as the process must account for high-dimensional, continuous state and action spaces, as well as the intricate system dynamics. One way to solve this problem is to first adjust the data collection method according to the characteristics of the actual task and then update the policy through retraining. For example, [13] propose a framework that involves the collection of trajectory data, using signal diagnostic tools to identify potential risk periods. It then uses a genetic algorithm to generate repaired trajectories, creating a safeguarded dataset that can be used to retrain the policy. Such methods focus on improving the underlying policy offline through data-driven refinement. CABRV offers a complementary online strategy, designed to provide immediate safety corrections at runtime without requiring policy retraining or model updates.

The work most similar to our research is [18], both of our studies focus on control signal adjustment. In their approach, they utilize a DNN model to predict the STL scores of the NSS and generate the repaired signals through a BIM-based optimization that is guided by the predicted STL scores. This work presents a valuable approach using learned models for prediction and optimization for repair. CABRV shares the goal of runtime adjustment but employs a different technical foundation: it utilizes physics-based simulation (Runge-Kutta) for trajectory prediction and explores strategies to identify potentially earlier and more effective intervention points, while also incorporating mechanisms like adaptive step sizing and pruning for computational efficiency.

6 Conclusion

In this paper, we present CABRV, a novel framework for runtime control adjustment in NSSs based on runtime verification. CABRV addresses the critical challenge of ensuring safety in NSSs by predicting potential unsafe trajectories using the Runge-Kutta method and dynamically adjusting control signals. Our approach not only identifies violations of safety properties in real-time but also generates alternative control signals to maintain system safety with minimal performance overhead. The experimental evaluation on industry-level NSSs demonstrates the effectiveness of CABRV. The results showed that our framework significantly reduces safety violations while maintaining computational efficiency. Specifically, the prediction algorithm achieved high accuracy in identifying unsafe trajectories, and the control adjustment strategy successfully mitigated risks in real time. Future work will expand the scope of evaluation to include a wider range of STL formula types, including those with nested time operators and complex signal constraints, to further demonstrate the versatility and adaptability of the CABRV framework in different application scenarios.

References

1. Bu, L., Wang, Q., Ren, X., Xing, S., Li, X.: Scenario-based online reachability validation for cps fault prediction. IEEE Trans. Comput. Aided Des. Integr. Circuits Syst. **39**(10), 2081–2094 (2019). https://doi.org/10.1109/TCAD.2019.2935062
2. Bu, L., Xing, S., Ren, X., Yang, Y., Wang, Q., Li, X.: Incremental online verification of dynamic cyber-physical systems. In: 22nd Design, Automation and Test in Europe Conference and Exhibition, DATE 2019, pp. 782–787. Institute of Electrical and Electronics Engineers Inc. (2019). https://doi.org/10.23919/DATE.2019.8715003
3. Deng, S., Liu, W., Zhang, M.: Runtime verification of neural-symbolic systems. In: International Symposium on Dependable Software Engineering: Theories, Tools, and Applications, pp. 293–309. Springer, Heidelberg (2024). https://doi.org/10.1007/978-981-96-0602-3_16
4. Deshmukh, J.V., Kapinski, J.P., Yamaguchi, T., Prokhorov, D.: Learning deep neural network controllers for dynamical systems with safety guarantees. In: 2019 IEEE/ACM International Conference on Computer-Aided Design (ICCAD), pp. 1–7. IEEE (2019). https://doi.org/10.1109/ICCAD45719.2019.8942130
5. Donzé, A., Maler, O.: Robust satisfaction of temporal logic over real-valued signals. In: International Conference on Formal Modeling and Analysis of Timed Systems, pp. 92–106. Springer, Heidelberg (2010). https://doi.org/10.1007/978-3-642-15297-9_9

6. Ferlez, J., Sun, X., Shoukry, Y.: Two-level lattice neural network architectures for control of nonlinear systems. In: 2020 59th IEEE Conference on Decision and Control (CDC), pp. 2198–2203. IEEE (2020). https://doi.org/10.1109/CDC42340.2020.9304079
7. Huang, C., Fan, J., Li, W., Chen, X., Zhu, Q.: Reachnn: reachability analysis of neural-network controlled systems. ACM Trans. Embed. Comput. Syst. (TECS) **18**(5s), 1–22 (2019). https://doi.org/10.1145/3358228
8. Huang, X., Kwiatkowska, M., Wang, S., Wu, M.: Safety verification of deep neural networks. In: International Conference on Computer Aided Verification, pp. 3–29. Springer, Heidelberg (2017). https://doi.org/10.1007/978-3-319-63387-9_1
9. Izzo, D., Märtens, M., Pan, B.: A survey on artificial intelligence trends in spacecraft guidance dynamics and control. Astrodynamics **3**(4), 287–299 (2019). https://doi.org/10.1007/s42064-018-0053-6
10. Kamruzzaman, M.: New opportunities, challenges, and applications of edge-AI for connected healthcare in smart cities. In: 2021 IEEE Globecom Workshops (GC Wkshps), pp. 1–6. IEEE (2021). https://doi.org/10.1109/GCWkshps52748.2021.9682055
11. Liang, Z., et al.: Credit assignment for trained neural networks based on Koopman operator theory. Front. Comp. Sci. **18**(1), 181324 (2024). https://doi.org/10.1007/s11704-023-2629-4
12. Lillicrap, T.P., et al.: Continuous control with deep reinforcement learning. Comput. Sci. (2015). https://doi.org/10.48550/arXiv.1509.02971
13. Lyu, D., et al.: Autorepair: automated repair for AI-enabled cyber-physical systems under safety-critical conditions. arXiv preprint arXiv:2304.05617 (2023). https://doi.org/10.48550/arXiv.2304.05617
14. Muhammad, K., Ullah, A., Lloret, J., Del Ser, J., de Albuquerque, V.H.C.: Deep learning for safe autonomous driving: current challenges and future directions. IEEE Trans. Intell. Transp. Syst. **22**(7), 4316–4336 (2020). https://doi.org/10.1109/TITS.2020.3032227
15. Nejati, S., Gaaloul, K., Menghi, C., Briand, L.C., Foster, S., Wolfe, D.: Evaluating model testing and model checking for finding requirements violations in simulink models. In: Proceedings of the 2019 27th ACM Joint Meeting on European Software Engineering Conference and Symposium on the Foundations of Software Engineering, pp. 1015–1025 (2019). https://doi.org/10.1145/3338906.3340444
16. Ničković, D., Yamaguchi, T.: RTAMT: online robustness monitors from STL. In: International Symposium on Automated Technology for Verification and Analysis, pp. 564–571. Springer, Heidelberg (2020). https://doi.org/10.1007/978-3-030-59152-6_34
17. Tran, H.D., et al.: Star-based reachability analysis of deep neural networks. In: International Symposium on Formal Methods, pp. 670–686. Springer, Heidelberg (2019). https://doi.org/10.1007/978-3-030-30942-8_39
18. Wang, R., Zhou, Z., Song, J., Xie, X., Xie, X., Ma, L.: Mortar: a model-based runtime action repair framework for ai-enabled cyber-physical systems. arXiv preprint arXiv:2408.03892 (2024). https://doi.org/10.48550/arXiv.2408.03892
19. Yu, K., Chen, Z., Dong, W.: A predictive runtime verification framework for cyber-physical systems. In: 2014 IEEE Eighth International Conference on Software Security and Reliability-Companion, pp. 223–227. IEEE (2014). https://doi.org/10.1109/SERE-C.2014.43
20. Zhang, Z., Lyu, D., Arcaini, P., Ma, L., Hasuo, I., Zhao, J.: Effective hybrid system falsification using monte carlo tree search guided by qb-robustness. In: Interna-

tional Conference on Computer Aided Verification, pp. 595–618. Springer, Heidelberg (2021). https://doi.org/10.1007/978-3-030-81685-8_29

21. Zhu, H., Xiong, Z., Magill, S., Jagannathan, S.: An inductive synthesis framework for verifiable reinforcement learning. In: Proceedings of the 40th ACM SIGPLAN Conference on Programming Language Design and Implementation, PLDI '19, pp. 686–701. ACM (2019). https://doi.org/10.1145/3314221.3314638

Formalizing Requirements into Dafny Specifications with LLMs

Yi-Han Lu[1,2], Xue-Yang Zhu[2(✉)], Wenhui Zhang[2], and Rongjie Yan[2]

[1] Hangzhou Institute for Advanced Study, University of Chinese Academy of Sciences, Hangzhou, China

[2] Key Laboratory of System Software, Institute of Software, Chinese Academy of Sciences, Beijing, China

zxy@ios.ac.cn

Abstract. Software bugs often arise from inconsistencies between software requirements documented in natural language and their code implementations. Formal verification is a proven technique for solving this problem by formalizing requirements into specifications. However, specifications are notoriously difficult to write correctly. Consequently, automating the formalization of natural language requirements has attracted growing interest, especially after the advent of large language models (LLMs). This paper investigates the capability and potential of LLMs to formalize task requirements into Dafny specifications. We propose and evaluate three progressively enhanced prompting strategies—Basic Prompting, Syntax-Augmented Prompting, and Semantics-Augmented Prompting—to assess LLMs' capability of generating Dafny specifications. Additionally, we develop an evaluation method to assess specification correctness, applicable both with and without ground truth. Experiments are carried out across three LLMs (GPT-4, DeepSeek-V3, and DeepSeek-R1) on two datasets derived from MBPP, a benchmark consisting of basic Python programming problems. Results show that Semantics-Augmented Prompting effectively improves both syntactic and semantic correctness of LLM-generated Dafny specifications. To deepen our understanding of LLMs' formalization potential, we also conduct manual inspections and qualitative analysis, revealing the limitations of generating Dafny specifications with LLMs and bring up suggestions.

Keywords: Formal Specification · Large Language Models · Dafny

1 Introduction

Software bugs often arise from inconsistencies between software requirements described in informal natural language and formal code implementations [43,45]. Pre- and postconditions, as formal specifications that provide mathematical and unambiguous descriptions of program constraints, enable the verification of the consistency between requirements and implementations. Preconditions define

É. André et al. (Eds.): ICFEM 2025, LNCS 16229, pp. 97–116, 2026.
https://doi.org/10.1007/978-981-95-4213-0_6

conditions that must hold before executing a procedure. Postconditions specify conditions that must be met after the execution [17]. Dafny is a programming language integrated with automated formal verification [23]. By formalizing requirements into Dafny specifications, the Dafny verifier can automatically check whether the program implementations satisfy the specifications. The validity of the verification results depends on whether the specifications accurately reflect the requirements. In this paper, we focus on requirements formalization.

Formalizing requirements is a highly challenging task due to the inherent ambiguity and vagueness of natural language. Traditionally, this process relies on manual efforts, which are time-consuming, labor-intensive, and prone to errors. Misu et al. [32] report that two experts spent approximately 220 h writing Dafny programs for 50 programming tasks, yet subsequent analysis by Sun et al. [42] reveals that at least 6 expert-written Dafny programs have incorrect specifications. Thus, automated solutions for formalizing requirements are gaining increasing attention. Existing automated approaches have attempted to integrate techniques such as named pattern matching [34, 43–45], text normalization [5], entity recognition [53], and natural language parsing [54] to analyze API documentation or code comments for specification generation. However, they typically rely on manually crafted rules and heuristics, which limits their applicability to semi-structured input scenarios.

Recent breakthroughs in large language models (LLMs) have created new opportunities for automated specification generation. LLMs have demonstrated exceptional capabilities in natural language processing [39], logical reasoning [10], and code generation [46]. Their natural language processing capabilities enable them to understand natural language requirements. Their logical reasoning capabilities allow them to infer the logic behind the requirements. Their code generation capabilities permit the generation of formal specifications. Collectively, these capabilities endow LLMs with significant potential for automated Dafny specification generation. However, despite this promise, two challenges remain in practical applications. First, as an uncommon language, Dafny may be significantly less frequent in the pre-training corpora of LLMs than mainstream languages, making LLMs prone to produce syntactic hallucinations [3, 30], let alone ensuring semantic correctness. Second, there is a lack of standardized methods for evaluating specifications, particularly in scenarios lacking ground truth, leaving the specification evaluation as an open question.

This paper investigates the capability and potential of LLMs to formalize task requirements into Dafny specifications. Specifically, we address the following research questions:

RQ1: What is the baseline capability of LLMs to formalize requirements into Dafny specifications?
RQ2: To what extent can incorporating syntactic and semantic demands into prompts enhance the correctness of LLM-generated Dafny specifications?
RQ3: What room for improvement remains in using LLMs to formalize requirements into Dafny specifications?

To address these research questions, we design a research framework consisting of Dafny specification generation and evaluation (Sect. 3). We propose three prompting strategies for specification generation (Sect. 4) and a specification evaluation framework (Sect. 5). For experiments, we select three state-of-the-art LLMs as evaluation subjects and construct datasets from MBPP [2], a benchmark consisting of basic Python programming problems (Sect. 6.1). We quantitatively analyze the impact of different prompting strategies on LLMs' capability of generating Dafny specifications (Sect. 6.2). We also perform a qualitative analysis to explore LLMs' formalization potential (Sect. 6.3). We summarize our analysis results to answer the research questions (Sect. 6.4). Finally, we discuss limitations and threats to validity (Sect. 7). All implementation scripts, datasets, and experimental outputs are publicly available at GitHub[1].

Our main contributions are as follows:

- We propose three progressively enhanced prompting strategies (Basic Prompting, Syntax-Augmented Prompting, and Semantics-Augmented Prompting) using simple in-context learning (ICL) method [13] to assess the capability of LLMs to formalize requirements into Dafny specifications.
- We develop an evaluation method to assess the syntactic and semantic correctness of Dafny specifications, which integrates equivalence checking applicable to ground-truth-provided scenarios and mutation testing applicable to test-case-provided scenarios.
- We construct two datasets (one with ground truth, and the other with only test cases) from MBPP [2], and carry experiments on three state-of-the-art LLMs (GPT-4, DeepSeek-V3, and DeepSeek-R1). Experimental results demonstrate that Semantics-Augmented Prompting effectively enhances both syntactic and semantic correctness of LLM-generated Dafny specifications.
- We find the limitations of generating Dafny specifications with LLMs for three specific types of tasks and bring up recommendations for further enhancing the correctness of LLM-generated Dafny specifications.

2 Preliminaries

2.1 Dafny

Dafny [23] is a programming language combining imperative programming with automated verification capabilities. Dafny supports standard programming constructs including classes, methods, and variables, with syntax similar to C# and Java. Given potential syntactic variations across different Dafny versions [11], we adopt Dafny 4.9.0 version to ensure research consistency and reproducibility. In Dafny, developers can define mathematical constraints on program behavior through specifications such as pre- and postconditions. The verifier then automatically verifies code compliance with these specifications. This process can not only replace dynamic testing with mathematical induction, but

[1] https://github.com/Gabriella-Luu/Dafny-pre-postconditions-Generation.

also detect boundary condition errors that traditional testing might miss, significantly enhancing the reliability of safety-critical systems, such as distributed systems [18] and Ethereum Virtual Machine [7].

Figure 1 shows a simple Dafny program that calculates the maximum of two positive integers. Line 1 defines the method *Max* with two integer parameters a and b, returning their maximum value m. Line 3 sets the precondition, requiring both a and b to be positive. Lines 5–6 specify the postconditions, stating that m should be greater than or equal to both a and b and be one of them. Lines 9–12 implement the logic to compute the maximum. During verification, preconditions narrow the input scope and postconditions guide the verifier to construct the mathematical induction path. The Dafny verifier automatically proves that m satisfies postconditions when inputs comply with preconditions. Implementation errors (e.g., erroneous assignment $m := b$ instead of $m := a$ in Line 10) can trigger verification failures by violating specifications.

```
1 : method Max(a: int, b: int) returns (m: int)
2 :   // preconditions
3 :   requires a > 0 && b > 0
4 :   // postconditions
5 :   ensures m >= a && m >= b
6 :   ensures m == a || m == b
7 : {
8 :   // body
9 :   if a > b {
10:     m := a;
11:   } else {
12:     m := b;
13:   }
14: }
```

Fig. 1. Example of a Dafny method

For more complex Dafny programs, such as those with loops or recursion, developers may need to use loop invariants or other constructs like function, predicate, and lemma to aid verification. A function defines a side-effect-free mathematical computation. A predicate is a special function returning a boolean value. A lemma is a stepping stone for proving a theorem.

2.2 In-Context Learning (ICL)

Prompt engineering has emerged as a key technique for enhancing LLMs' capabilities [38]. A prompt refers to textual instructions guiding LLMs to generate text or perform a specific task. A well-designed prompt can significantly enhance the quality, relevance, and accuracy of LLMs outputs. Effective prompt engineering involves various strategies. One foundational and critical approach is ICL [13], which involves providing LLMs with contextual information or specific examples within the prompt, enabling it to learn the task at hand. Few-shot is an important variant of ICL that substantially improves complex task handling through minimal demonstration examples [47]. There are more advanced and sophisticated techniques which can be integrated with ICL. These include Chain of Thought (CoT) [49], which enhances reasoning through explicit stepwise rationale generation, as well as Retrieval-Augmented Generation (RAG) [15], which integrates external knowledge retrieval. These techniques further refine prompts to improve LLMs performance.

3 Basic Idea of Our Work

This study aims to investigate the capability and potential of LLMs to formalize requirements into Dafny specifications. Specifically, we set two main goals: (1) enabling LLMs to formalize requirements into correct Dafny specifications, and (2) automatically evaluating the correctness of specifications. To achieve these goals, we design a research framework depicted in Fig. 2, which includes two parts: Dafny specification generation and evaluation. In the generation part, task requirements and their corresponding Dafny method signatures are embedded into pre-designed prompting templates to guide LLMs to generate Dafny specifications. The evaluation part focuses on evaluating the syntactic and semantics correctness of specifications, integrating equivalence checking for ground-truth-provided scenarios and mutation testing for test-case-provided scenarios.

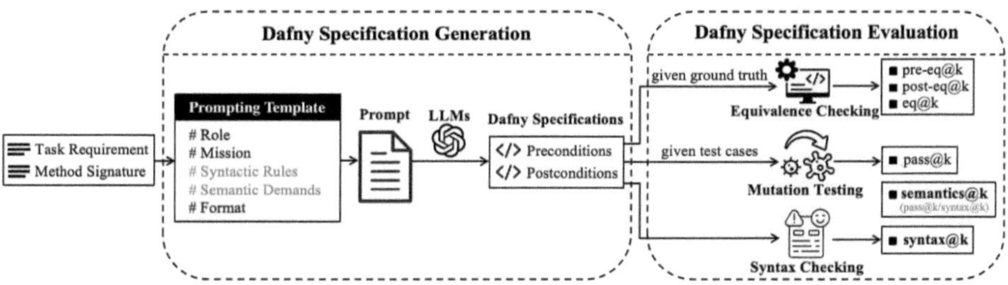

Fig. 2. Research framework

4 Dafny Specification Generation

To achieve better results with a concise method and process, we simply employ ICL method for prompt design and perform a single-round conversation with LLMs. To investigate the impact of different components within the prompts, we design three progressively enhanced prompting strategies: Basic Prompting, Syntax-Augmented Prompting, and Semantics-Augmented Prompting. The following describes the construction of the prompting templates, with complete templates available on GitHub[2].

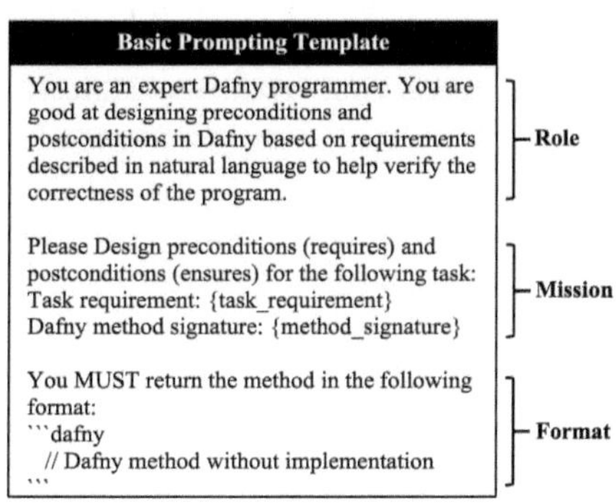

Fig. 3. Basic Prompting template

[2] https://github.com/Gabriella-Luu/Dafny-pre-postconditions-Generation/tree/main/spec-generation/Scripts/prompts.

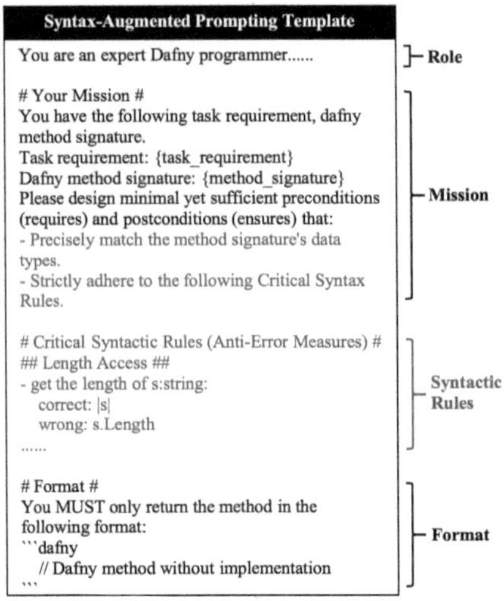

Fig. 4. Syntax-Augmented Prompting template

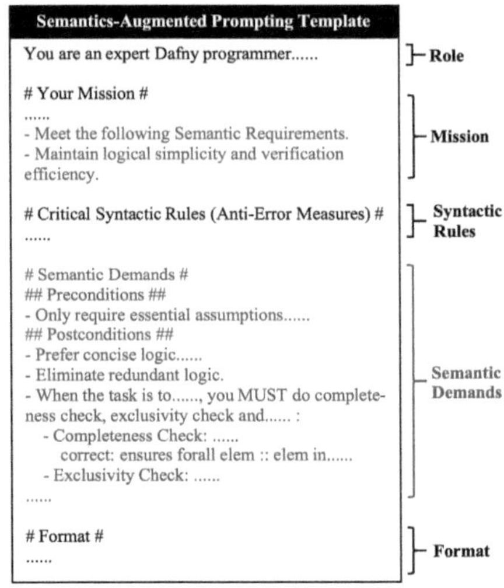

Fig. 5. Semantics-Augmented Prompting template

Basic Prompting: To evaluate LLMs' baseline capability in generating Dafny specifications and uncover inherent issues, we design a basic prompting template shown in Fig. 3. This template includes instructions on role [48], mission, and return format, without additional information.

Syntax-Augmented Prompting: Basic Prompting + Syntactic Rules. Our pilot study revealed that syntactic errors is the primary bottleneck limiting the correctness of LLM-generated Dafny specifications. We collected the recurrent syntactic error patterns and summarized critical syntactic rules that LLMs need to follow for generating Dafny specifications, such as using |s| for string length (not s.Length), enforcing explicit parentheses in logical implications, ensuring type consistency in expressions, and avoiding non-existent operators. Based on this, we design Syntax-Augmented Prompting to address syntactic challenges, whose template is shown in Fig. 4. This template is build upon Basic Prompting and incorporates critical syntactic rules using simple ICL method. We clearly categorize and structure the critical syntactic rules in the *Syntactic Rules* section of the template. To clarify the usage of these rules, we provide a concise usage instruction for each, normally followed with one correct and one incorrect examples.

Semantics-Augmented Prompting: Syntax-Augmented Prompting + Semantic Demands. Ensuring syntactic correctness alone is insufficient for generating correct Dafny specifications. We expect the generated specifications to correctly reflect the requirements. In our pilot study, we observed that LLM-generated Dafny specifications often suffer from semantic redundancy, logical complexity, and deficiency. Moreover, programming tasks exhibit type-specific semantic demands which are not explicitly required. For example, tasks that involve retrieving elements that meet certain conditions from the input parameters necessitate completeness, exclusivity, and uniqueness checks. Completeness check ensures all elements that meet the conditions are included in the return value; exclusivity check ensures all other elements are excluded; and uniqueness check ensures no duplicates are present in the return value unless explicitly permitted. These three checks provide effective constraints on the return value.

Here is an example that illustrates the necessary specifications for tasks that involve retrieving elements meeting certain conditions from input parameters, as shown in Fig. 6. For the task of finding shared elements from two given arrays, correct and complete specifications should include the following three checks. The completeness check ensures that all shared elements from the two arrays are included in the result. Without it, the method might miss some shared elements, leading to incomplete results. The exclusivity check ensures that only elements present in both arrays are included in the result. Without it, the result might contain elements that are not shared from the two arrays. The uniqueness check ensures that each element in the result appears only once, even if it appears multiple times in the input arrays. Without it, the result might contain duplicate elements, violating the requirement for a set-like result.

```
/*
"task_description": "Write a method in Dafny to find the shared elements from the given two array.",
"method_signature": "method sharedElements (arr1:array<int>, arr2:array<int>) returns (res: seq<int>)"
*/
method sharedElements (arr1: array<int>, arr2: array<int>) returns (res: seq<int>)
  requires true
  ensures forall elem :: (elem in arr1[..] && elem in arr2[..]) ==> elem in res // Completeness Check
  ensures forall elem :: elem in res ==> (elem in arr1[..] && elem in arr2[..]) // Exclusivity Check
  ensures forall i, j :: 0 <= i < j < |res| ==> res[i] != res[j] // Uniqueness Check
{
  // Method implementation goes here
}
```

Fig. 6. A concrete example of type-specific semantic demands

Based on these observations, we design Semantics-Augmented Prompting that addresses both syntactic and semantic issues. It's template is shown in Fig. 5. It extends Syntax-Augmented Prompting by incorporating semantic demands using simple ICL method. To facilitate LLMs' comprehension of type-specific semantic demands such as completeness, exclusivity, and uniqueness check, we provide examples of Dafny specification implementations following the explanation of each demand.

5 Dafny Specification Evaluation

Evaluating Dafny specifications is challenging, particularly in the absence of ground truth, as there exists no standardized method or metric. One direct method is to generate a complete Dafny program including specifications and code implementations, then check if the program can pass the verification [32]. However, the success of the verification does not guarantee the correctness of the specifications. Specifications containing logical flaws aligned with faulty implementations can still pass the verification. On the other hand, correct specifications paired with defective implementations may fail the verification. Moreover, postconditions that are overly weak may erroneously validate incorrect implementations by accepting broader return value ranges. Thus, better evaluation methods are in need. We develop an evaluation framework considering two evaluation scenarios: one with ground truth and another with test cases.

5.1 Ground-Truth-Based Evaluation

When ground truth is available, we directly check the equivalence between the specifications and the ground truth. Based on the method proposed by Sum et al. [42], we formalize equivalence as a lemma and use the Dafny verifier to prove the lemma. The specifications are regarded as equivalent to the ground truth if the lemma pass the verification. We define three different equivalence metrics: precondition equivalence rate (*pre-eq@k*), postcondition equivalence rate (*post-eq@k*), and specification equivalence rate (*eq@k*). These metrics represent the probabilities that at least one of the top k-generated samples for a task passes the respective equivalence checking.

The Dafny code templates for these equivalence checking are shown in Fig. 7. The predicates *pre_original* and *pre_gen* represent the ground-truth and generated preconditions, respectively. The predicates *post_original* and *post_gen* represent the ground-truth and generated postconditions. Equivalence of preconditions is verified via the lemma *pre-eq*, as shown in Fig. 7(a). For postcondition equivalence checking, both *post_original* and *post_gen* use *pre_original* as their preconditions, and the equivalence is verified via the lemma *post-eq*, as shown in Fig. 7(b). For specification equivalence, the lemma *post-eq* is used to verify equivalence between the ground-truth specifications and paired generated pre- and postconditions, as shown in Fig. 7(c).

5.2 Test-Case-Based Evaluation

It's not common for tasks to provide ground truth, as it's impractical to manually write specifications for a large number of tasks. Therefore, we consider the scenario where test cases are provided for tasks. We adopt the symbolic mutation testing method [22] to automate specification evaluation, and improve the method to support a broader range of data types for input and output. For each test case, we generate five mutated outputs using strategies such as flipping booleans, randomly adding or subtracting values to integers and floats, randomly replacing or appending a character to strings, and inserting or deleting an element at a randomly chosen index for arrays and sequences. Specifications pass the mutation testing if they can (1) validate all input-output pairs in test cases (accuracy) and (2) reject all incorrect input-output pairs mutated from

```
predicate pre_original(input: T, output: T)
{
  (precondition_1) && (precondition_2) && ...
}
predicate pre_gen(input: T, output: T)
{
  (precondition_1) && (precondition_2) && ...
}
lemma pre_eq(input: T, output: T)
  ensures pre_original(intput, output) <==>
          pre_gen(input, output)
{}
```

a. Precondition equivalence checking template

```
predicate pre_original(input: T, output: T)
{
  (precondition_1) && (precondition_2) && ...
}
predicate post_original(input: T, output: T)
  requires pre_original(intput, output)
{
  (postcondition_1) && (postcondition_2) && ...
}
predicate post_gen(input: T, output: T)
  requires pre_original(intput, output)
{
  (postcondition_1) && (postcondition_2) && ...
}
lemma post_eq(input: T, output: T)
  requires pre_original(intput, output)
  ensures post_original(intput, output) <==>
          post_gen(input, output)
{}
```

b. Postcondition equivalence checking template

```
predicate pre_original(input: T, output: T)
{
  (precondition_1) && (precondition_2) && ...
}
predicate pre_gen(input: T, output: T)
{
  (precondition_1) && (precondition_2) && ...
}
predicate post_original(input: T, output: T)
  requires pre_original(intput, output)
{
  (postcondition_1) && (postcondition_2) && ...
}
predicate post_gen(input: T, output: T)
  requires pre_gen(intput, output)
{
  (postcondition_1) && (postcondition_2) && ...
}
lemma post_eq(input: T, output: T)
  requires pre_original(intput, output)
  requires pre_gen(intput, output)
  ensures post_original(intput, output) <==>
          post_gen(input, output)
{}
```

c. Specification equivalence checking template

Fig. 7. Equivalence checking templates

test cases (completeness). Figure 8(a) shows the code for a test case with input 5 and correct output 10. Verification should pass if the specifications are accurate. Figure 8(b) shows the code with a mutated output of 11. Verification should fail if the specifications are complete. We denote the mutation testing pass rate as *pass@k*, which is the probability that at least one of the top k-generated samples for a task passes the mutation testing.

```
// Verification passes with accurate specifications.
method add5(n:int) returns (res:int)
  requires true
  ensures res == n + 5
{
  var v0 := 5;
  assume {:axiom} n == v0;
  res := 10; // original output
}
```

a. Accuracy testing with original output

```
// Verification fails with complete specifications.
method add5(n:int) returns (res:int)
  requires true
  ensures res == n + 5
{
  var v0 := 5;
  assume {:axiom} n == v0;
  res := 11; // mutated output
}
```

b. Completeness testing with mutated output

Fig. 8. Examples of mutation testing

To further refine the specification evaluation, we separately evaluate syntactic and semantic correctness. Syntactic correctness is evaluated by identifying compilation error messages and is measured using the *syntax@k* metric, which represents the probability that at least one of the top k-generated samples for a task is syntactically correct. Semantic correctness is evaluated only for specifications that are syntactically correct. Specifications are considered both syntactically and semantically correct if they pass the specification equivalence checking or mutation testing. Considering the wider applicability of mutation testing, we define *semantics@k* as *pass@k/syntax@k* to indicate the semantics correctness, which is the conditional probability that, among the top k-generated samples that are syntactically correct, at least one is also semantically correct.

6 Experimental Evaluation

This section details the experimental setup, followed by quantitative analysis and qualitative analysis of the results. Through the experiments, we aim to answer the following questions:

Q1: What is the baseline capability of LLMs in generating Dafny specifications?
Q2: What is the impact of Syntax-Augmented Prompting on the correctness of LLM-generated Dafny specifications?
Q3: What is the impact of Semantics-Augmented Prompting on the correctness of LLM-generated Dafny specifications?
Q4: What room for improvement remains in Dafny specifications generation with LLMs?
Q5: What differences exist among evaluation metrics?

6.1 Experimental Setup

LLM Selection. This study selects GPT-4, DeepSeek-V3, and DeepSeek-R1 as experimental subjects. GPT-4 excels in NLP and code generation tasks [1]. DeepSeek-V3 is a cost-effective model optimized for instruction tracing and reasoning [26], while DeepSeek-R1 leverages CoT for complex tasks [16]. By experimenting with multiple LLMs, we aim to evaluate the general capability and systematic limitations of our proposed specification generation strategies. For temperature parameter configuration, our pilot experiments on GPT-4 showed that a setting of 0.5 can balance output diversity and determinism, yielding optimal results. For DeepSeek models, we adhere to the official recommendation for code and math related tasks by setting temperature to 0 [12].

Evaluation Datasets. While no universal dataset exists for formalizing requirements into Dafny specifications, the work of Misu et al. [32] is highly relevant. They created the MBPP-DFY-228 dataset by adjusting the 228 Python program generation tasks in the sanitized MBPP dataset [2] to Dafny program generation tasks, forming a foundation for our work. We further divide MBPP-DFY-228 into two groups and filter the tasks to obtain MBPP-DFY-26 and MBPP-DFY-97.

MBPP-DFY-26 provides ground truth. In MBPP-DFY-228, 50 tasks have specifications and implementation code manually written by experts, which can be regarded as having ground-truth specifications. From the 50 tasks, we exclude 7 tasks with problematic ground truth detected through mutation testing, 15 tasks technically unsupported by equivalence checking, and 2 tasks with unclear requirements. Finally, 26 validated tasks constitute the MBPP-DFY-26 dataset. Besides ground truth, MBPP-DFY-26 also provides test cases.

MBPP-DFY-97 provides only test cases. Theoretically, all 228 tasks can serve as an evaluation dataset with test cases. However, to compare our specification generation method with the Dynamic Few-shot Prompting proposed by Misu et al. [32], we start with 164 tasks for which GPT-4 successfully generated verified Dafny code using Dynamic Few-shot Prompting. We exclude 50 tasks with manual written solutions, 9 tasks with unclear requirements, and 8 tasks technically unsupported by mutation testing, finalizing 97 tasks as MBPP-DFY-97 dataset.

6.2 Quantitative Analysis

We have the three LLMs (GPT-4, DeepSeek-V3, and DeepSeek-R1) generate Dafny specifications under three prompting strategies (Basic, Syntax-Augmented, and Semantics-Augmented) on MBPP-DFY-26 and MBPP-DFY-97 datasets. For tasks in MBPP-DFY-26, we perform three sampling rounds per task, while adopting five rounds for tasks in MBPP-DFY-97. All generated specifications undergo mutation testing and syntax checking, with additional equivalence checking applied to specifications generated from MBPP-DFY-26. Table 1 summarizes the experimental results on MBPP-DFY-26, presenting three equivalence rates (*pre-eq@k*, *post-eq@k*, and *eq@k*), mutation testing pass rate (*pass@k*), and syntactic correctness rate (*syntax@k*), where $k \in \{1, 2, 3\}$. Table 2 summarizes the results on MBPP-DFY-97, focusing on *pass@k*, *syntax@k*, and *semantics@k*, where $k \in \{1, 3, 5\}$. Additionally, we also evaluate the specifications of Dafny programs generated for tasks in MBPP-DFY-97 via Dynamic Few-Shot Prompting using GPT-4[3] and show their results in the last row of Table 2. In this section, we perform quantitative analysis on the experimental results to answer Q1-Q3.

Q1: Baseline capability. As shown in Table 2, under Basic Prompting, the syntax@5 across LLMs reaches a minimum of 73.20%, indicating their capability to generate syntactically correct specifications for nearly 3/4 of tasks, which means LLMs have good baseline performance in syntactic correctness. Furthermore, the minimum value of *semantics@5* is 78.41%, indicating that when LLM-generated Dafny specifications achieve syntactic correctness, they are also highly likely to be semantically correct. Among the considered LLMs, GPT-4 has the lowest baseline performance in terms of both syntax and semantics, while DeepSeek-R1 performs the best.

Q2: Impact of Syntax-Augmented Prompting. Table 2 shows GPT-4 exhibits respective improvements of 26.81% and 23.71% in *syntax@1* and *syntax@5* under Syntax-Augmented Prompting compared to those under Basic Prompting, while DeepSeek-R1 achieves 15.46% and 6.19% respectively. Both LLMs attain approximately 97% in *syntax@5*. GPT-4's significant improvement can be attributed to its weaker baseline capability, leaving substantial room for enhancement. Although DeepSeek-V3 has an intermediate baseline capability, it exhibits lower sensitivity to Syntax-Augmented Prompting, achieving

[3] https://github.com/Mondego/dafny-synthesis/tree/master/MBPP-DFY-153/src.

Table 1. Experimental results on MBPP-DFY-26

Prompts	GPT-4 (temp=0.5)						DeepSeek-V3 (temp=0)						DeepSeek-R1 (temp=0)					
		pre-eq @k	*post-eq @k*	*eq @k*	*pass @k*	*syntax @k*		*pre-eq @k*	*post-eq @k*	*eq @k*	*pass @k*	*syntax @k*		*pre-eq @k*	*post-eq @k*	*eq @k*	*pass @k*	*syntax @k*
Basic	***k=1***	38.46%	53.85%	50.00%	50.00%	61.54%	***k=1***	61.54%	80.77%	73.08%	80.77%	80.77%	***k=1***	69.23%	84.62%	80.77%	80.77%	84.62%
	k=2	57.69%	65.38%	61.54%	61.54%	73.08%	***k=2***	69.23%	84.62%	76.92%	84.62%	84.62%	***k=2***	76.92%	92.31%	88.46%	88.46%	88.46%
	k=3	61.54%	65.38%	61.54%	61.54%	80.77%	***k=3***	69.23%	88.46%	80.77%	84.62%	84.62%	***k=3***	**76.92%**	**92.31%**	**88.46%**	**88.46%**	**92.31%**
Syntax-Augmented	***k=1***	53.85%	76.92%	80.77%	80.77%	92.31%	***k=1***	76.92%	84.62%	80.77%	84.62%	88.46%	***k=1***	73.08%	88.46%	88.46%	96.15%	100.00%
	k=2	84.62%	88.46%	88.46%	88.46%	100.00%	***k=2***	84.62%	84.62%	84.62%	88.46%	88.46%	***k=2***	80.77%	92.31%	92.31%	96.15%	100.00%
	k=3	**84.62%**	88.46%	88.46%	88.46%	**100.00%**	***k=3***	**84.62%**	84.62%	84.62%	88.46%	88.46%	***k=3***	80.77%	**96.15%**	**96.15%**	**100.00%**	**100.00%**
Semantics-Augmented	***k=1***	65.38%	88.46%	84.62%	84.62%	92.31%	***k=1***	76.92%	88.46%	88.46%	92.31%	92.31%	***k=1***	73.08%	92.31%	92.31%	92.31%	96.15%
	k=2	69.23%	88.46%	84.62%	84.62%	92.31%	***k=2***	76.92%	88.46%	88.46%	92.31%	92.31%	***k=2***	73.08%	92.31%	92.31%	96.15%	100.00%
	k=3	69.23%	**96.15%**	**92.31%**	92.31%	96.15%	***k=3***	76.92%	88.46%	88.46%	92.31%	92.31%	***k=3***	**80.77%**	92.31%	**92.31%**	**96.15%**	**100.00%**

Table 2. Experimental results on MBPP-DFY-97

Prompts	GPT-4 (temp=0.5)				DeepSeek-V3 (temp=0)				DeepSeek-R1 (temp=0)			
		pass@k	*syntax@k*	*semantics@k*		*pass@k*	*syntax@k*	*semantics@k*		*pass@k*	*syntax@k*	*semantics@k*
Basic	***k=1***	43.30%	57.73%	75.00%	***k=1***	58.76%	72.16%	81.43%	***k=1***	65.98%	75.26%	87.67%
	k=3	54.64%	71.13%	76.81%	***k=3***	63.92%	78.35%	81.58%	***k=3***	77.32%	89.69%	86.21%
	k=5	57.73%	73.20%	78.87%	***k=5***	63.92%	78.35%	81.58%	***k=5***	**80.41%**	**91.75%**	**87.64%**
Syntax-Augmented	***k=1***	62.89%	84.54%	74.39%	***k=1***	70.10%	86.60%	80.95%	***k=1***	73.20%	90.72%	80.68%
	k=3	75.26%	96.91%	77.66%	***k=3***	71.13%	90.72%	78.41%	***k=3***	82.47%	96.91%	85.11%
	k=5	78.35%	96.91%	80.85%	***k=5***	71.13%	90.72%	78.41%	***k=5***	**84.54%**	**97.94%**	**86.32%**
Semantics-Augmented	***k=1***	76.29%	90.72%	84.09%	***k=1***	75.26%	87.63%	85.88%	***k=1***	76.29%	91.75%	83.15%
	k=3	85.57%	96.91%	88.30%	***k=3***	79.38%	90.72%	87.50%	***k=3***	86.60%	96.91%	89.36%
	k=5	**87.63%**	**97.94%**	**89.47%**	***k=5***	79.38%	90.72%	87.50%	***k=5***	86.60%	96.91%	89.36%
Dynamic Few-Shot [32]		75.26%	100.00%	75.26%								

only 90.72% in *syntax@5*. These results demonstrate that Syntax-Augmented Prompting effectively elevates the syntactic correctness of LLM-generated Dafny specifications to high levels. This conclusion is further supported by the data in Table 1.

The 23.71% increase in *syntax@5* for GPT-4 under Syntax-Augmented Prompting compared to that under Basic Prompting is accompanied by a 20.61% rise in *pass@5*. This indicates that enhancing syntactic correctness significantly improves the correctness of the specifications. We can also draw a conclusion that for MBPP-DFY-97, syntactic errors constitute the primary constraint on the correctness of LLM-generated specifications, and semantic issues further limit the correctness subsequently. Therefore, optimizing LLM-generated Dafny specifications should prioritize improving syntactic correctness then enhance semantic correctness, which includes both semantic accuracy and completeness.

Q3: Impact of Semantics-Augmented Prompting. The data in Table 2 demonstrate that for all LLMs, the *semantics@5* under Semantics-Augmented Prompting surpass those under Basic Prompting and Syntax-Augmented

Prompting. Both GPT-4 and DeepSeek-R1 attain *semantics@5* of approximately 89.4% under Semantics-Augmented Prompting, with GPT-4 showing the most pronounced improvements—10.60% and 8.52% increases compared to Basic Prompting and Syntax-Augmented Prompting, respectively. Furthermore, *syntax@5* under Semantics-Augmented Prompting is roughly the same as those under Syntax-Augmented Prompting across all LLMs, indicating that incorporating semantic demands does not compromise syntactic correctness. Additionally, *pass@5* under Semantics-Augmented Prompting are the highest among three prompting strategies, exemplified by GPT-4's 29.90% and 9.28% improvements over Basic Prompting and Syntax-Augmented Prompting, respectively. These results collectively suggest that Semantics-Augmented Prompting enables LLMs to generate Dafny specifications with enhanced semantic correctness and completeness, meanwhile maintaining high syntactic correctness.

To demonstrate the effectiveness of our method more comprehensively, we conduct a comparative analysis with Dynamic Few-Shot Prompting. Since MBPP-DFY-97 is built from tasks for which this method successfully generates verified Dafny programs, the specifications achieve 100% syntactic correctness. Moreover, their 5-round sampling stops once a verified Dafny program is generated, making it impossible to describe their results using metrics like *pass@k* which are based on k-round sampling. Here, we compare their mutation testing pass rate with our method's *pass@5*. As shown in Table 2, their mutation testing pass rate under Dynamic Few-Shot Prompting is only 75.26%, which is 3.09% and 12.37% lower than GPT-4's *pass@5* under Syntax-Augmented Prompting and Semantics-Augmented Prompting, respectively. This indicates that our proposed method enable LLMs to generate better Dafny specifications than Dynamic Few-Shot Prompting. Additionally, Dynamic Few-Shot Prompting employs a more complex approach than ours. It uses CoT and requires two-round conversations with LLMs. Each round incorporates lengthy few-shot examples retrieved through RAG, resulting in extended context lengths that increase both time and computational costs. Our Semantics-Augmented Prompting employs only simple ICL method and requires just a single-round conversation, achieving shorter context lengths and faster execution. correctness, our proposed method outperforms Dynamic Few-Shot Prompting in both effectiveness and efficiency.

6.3 Qualitative Analysis

To gain deeper insights into the room for improvement in these generated specifications, we conduct manual inspections of erroneous specifications. In this section, we answer Q4-Q5 based on the qualitative analysis.

Q4: Room for Improvement. First, we investigate whether adding syntactic and semantic demands to prompts might negatively impact Dafny specification generation. We observe that, in most cases, tasks passed under Basic Prompting are a subset of those passed under Syntax-Augmented Prompting, which are in turn a subset of those passed under Semantics-Augmented Prompting. This indicates that incorporating syntactic and semantic information can progressively improve specification correctness in general. However, there are exceptions as well. Detailed review attributes these failures primarily to semantic inconsistencies, suggesting that syntactic rules incorporation may slightly disrupt semantic correctness. This may stem from the increasing prompt length and complexity [24, 28]. Nevertheless, such interference is partially mitigated when explicit semantic demands are incorporated alongside syntactic rules in prompts.

Next, we summarize the errors in specifications generated under Semantics-Augmented Prompting, as the errors indicate the room for improvements. Besides syntactic issues caused by the omission of syntactic rules in prompts, we observe three specific programming task types for which LLMs consistently fail to generate high-correctness Dafny specifications:

Tasks Requiring In-place Modification of Input Parameters. Even if not explicitly mentioned in the requirements, such tasks implicitly require that the return value strictly preserves the order and count of unmodified elements from the original input parameters. LLMs consistently fail to generate postconditions that enforce this constraint. For example, *task_id_18* in MBPP-DFY-97 requires "*removing characters from the first string which are present in the second string*". LLMs persistently fail to generate postconditions constraining the return value to strictly preserve the order and count of the unmodified characters in the first string. Consequently, invalid outputs, such as "*bac*" or "*aabc*", are allowed to pass verification when the correct output should be "*abc*".

Tasks Involving Summing Elements Without Existing Formulas. When no direct mathematical formula exists for a summation problem, helper functions are always necessary. For example, *task_id_126* in MBPP-DFY-97 requires "*finding the sum of common divisors of two given numbers*". For such a complex summation task, it is difficult to find a math formula or other concise specifications that can avoid direct summation calculations. Thus, it's necessary to use helper functions to assist the specifications in performing the calculations. However, our pilot experiments reveal that LLMs tend to misuse helper functions and fail to generate correct implementation code for them, degrading the overall correctness of the generated specifications. Thus, Semantics-Augmented Prompting restricts specifications from calling helper functions, though limiting them to handle summation tasks.

Tasks Involving Complex Mathematical Problems. LLMs often struggle to find correct mathematical formulas for complex computations. For example, *task_id_770* in MBPP-DFY-97 asks to "*Write a method in Dafny to find the sum of fourth power of first n odd natural numbers.*" There exists a math formula for calculating this, but it is long and complex. Among our considered LLMs, only DeepSeek-R1 can come up with it. This deficiency may stem from the inherent limitations of LLMs or insufficient activation of mathematical capabilities through our prompting.

Q5: Differences Among Evaluation Metrics. Table 1 shows *pre-eq@k* is usually lower than *eq@k*, mainly due to imprecise task requirements causing LLMs to hypothesize input ranges in preconditions. Even if generated preconditions differ from ground truth, specifications can remain equivalent when pre- and postconditions match. Conversely, *post-eq@k* may exceed *eq@k* when there is a mismatch between generated pre- and postconditions. While equivalence checking and mutation testing both reflect specification correctness, practical divergence arises from mutation testing's reliance on test case coverage and equivalence checking's limitation in recognizing multiple valid solutions beyond the ground truth. Therefore, neither method alone is fully reliable, though both provide valuable insights.

6.4 Summary

Summarizing our answers to Q1–Q5, we now address the research questions.

Answer to RQ1. Experimental results show that LLMs demonstrate good baseline capabilities in generating Dafny specifications that are both syntactically and semantically correct, yet notable optimization potential remains. Comparatively, DeepSeek-R1 has the strongest baseline capability, while GPT-4 has the weakest.

Answer to RQ2. Incorporating syntactic and semantic demands into prompts using the ICL method (Semantics-Augmented Prompting) proves effective in enhancing both syntactic and semantic correctness of LLM-generated Dafny specifications, especially for GPT-4. Semantics-Augmented Prompting is also time-efficient and cost-effective.

Answer to RQ3. Besides syntactical issues due to the omission of syntactic rules in prompts, LLMs still struggle with three types of tasks under Semantics-Augmented Prompting: (1) tasks requiring in-place modification of input parameters, (2) tasks involving summing elements without existing formulas, and (3) tasks involving complex mathematical problems. We recommend that future research (1) identifies the implicit requirements in certain task types, (2) enables LLMs to generate necessary helper functions correctly, and (3) elicits and harnesses the potential mathematical capabilities of LLMs.

7 Discussion

Limitations. Our Semantics-Augmented Prompting strategy currently only covers the specific semantic demands of a single task category, as we have only summarized task types with implicit semantic demands from existing datasets and have not covered a broader range of tasks. Future work could enhance generalizability by extending data collection and identifying task types across a broader range. Additionally, technical limitations in our specification evaluation methods hinder the verification for certain tasks, thus limiting the evaluation scope. Optimizing the evaluation methods remains a focus for future work.

Threats to Validity. Internal validity is impacted by our evaluation methods: (1) Equivalence checking assumes high-quality ground truth specifications and acknowledges potential multiplicity of valid solutions. (2) The effectiveness of mutation testing critically depends on the quality of the test cases and the chosen mutation strategy. External validity is affected by our dataset: coverage is reduced as we excluded some tasks from the original MBPP-DFY-228 dataset. Construct validity faces a limitation from the Dafny verifier itself: its lack of complete soundness [20] means cases may occur where correct and complete specifications cannot be formally verified.

8 Related Work

LLMs for Specification Generation. The automated generation of formal specifications is a core challenge in software engineering and formal methods. With the rise of LLMs, increasing research is exploring their use for this purpose. Specification generation broadly fall into two categories: code-based specification generation and requirement-driven specification generation.

Code-based specification generation focuses on deriving formal specifications from implementation code to support verification. Recent studies have extensively focused on loop invariant generation. Kamath et al. [21] use LLMs to generate candidate loop invariants, then check and prune them with symbolic tools. Chakraborty et al. [8] introduce a ranking mechanism to prioritize relevant invariants to reduce verifier invocations. Pascoal et al. [35] develop an automatic loop invariants generation plugin for Visual Studio Code. Besides loop invariants, Mugnier et al. [33] highlight the importance of assertions. Other works aim to generate various specification types simultaneously. Wen et al. [50] use LLMs to generate candidate specifications, including loop invariants and pre- and postconditions, then use verification tools to assess their correctness and completeness. Ma et al. [29] combine conversational LLM interactions with mutation testing to generate invariants and postconditions.

Our study concentrates on requirement-driven specification generation, mapping user requirements directly to formal specifications to ensure implementation-requirement consistency. Some studies explore translating temporally or sequentially related constraints in natural language into Linear Temporal Logic (LTL) formulas. For instance, Cosler et al. [9] improve LLM-based LTL translation through user-guided refinement. While Xu et al. [51] embed guidance into prompts to reduce human interaction. Diverging from LTL-oriented research, we focus on translating natural language programming requirements into pre- and postconditions. Some studies use LLMs to generate postconditions for various purposes. Yu et al. [52] find LLM-generated postconditions can detect erroneous test cases. Cai et al. [6] use LLM-generated pre- and postconditions to verify code correctness. Our focus is solely on specification generation. While Endres et al. [14] and He et al. [19] investigate generating postconditions for conventional languages like Python, we target Dafny specifications due to Dafny's advanced verification support. Closest to our study, Baldonado et al. [4] employ RAG method for Dafny pre- and postconditions generation. But they experiment only on a simple and small-scale dataset and do not provide open-source code for reproduction and comparison.

Specification Evaluation. When ground truth is available, specifications can be directly compared to it using tools [4,27,42], or assessed via text similarity [36]. Our approach uses Dafny lemmas to verify the equivalence between specifications and ground truth. In scenarios lacking ground truth, specification evaluation becomes challenging, with existing studies adopting diverse methodologies. Sun et al. [42] propose leveraging LLMs to inversely generate natural language requirements from specifications, subsequently evaluating semantic equivalence between reconstructed and original requirements. However, this depends on LLMs outputs which are uncertain. The confidence metric proposed by Baldonado et al. [4] associate specification credibility with LLMs output distribution concentration, yet fails to precisely reflect the specification correctness. Endres et al. [14] and He et al. [19] assess assertion correctness and completeness by mutating provided implementation code and testing if assertions pass correct code and fail mutated code. Lahiri et al. [22] extend mutation testing with symbolic testing to eliminate reliance on implementation code, mutating test case outputs instead. Our mutation testing method is built on this work with further improvements to enhance evaluation precision and scalability.

LLMs for Dafny. Recent research has explored the application of LLMs for Dafny. Several studies leverage LLMs to generate complete Dafny programs containing pre- and postconditions, invariants, and implementation code, aiming to enhance the verification success rate [31,32]. Li et al. [25] further investigate whether compiling Dafny programs into target languages improves LLM-generated code quality. Other efforts focus on generating loop invariants [40], assertions [8,37], or lemmas [41] for Dafny programs when verification fails due to missing steps. In contrast, our work centers on leveraging LLMs to formalize natural language requirements into pre- and postconditions in Dafny.

9 Conclusion

We design three progressively enhanced prompting strategies—Basic Prompting, Syntax-Augmented Prompting, and Semantics-Augmented Prompting for Dafny specification generation with LLMs and propose an evaluation method applicable both with and without ground truth. We conduct experiments on MBPP-DFY-26 and MBPP-DFY-97 datasets, and select GPT-4, DeepSeek-V3, and DeepSeek-R1 as experimental subjects. Experimental results show that Semantics-Augmented Prompting effectively improves both syntactic and semantic correctness of LLM-generated Dafny specifications, outperforming Dynamic Few-Shot Prompting [32] in semantic correctness. Furthermore, we summarize the room for improvement remaining in generating Dafny specifications with LLMs for three specific types of tasks and bring up suggestions.

References

1. Achiam, J., et al.: GPT-4 technical report. arXiv preprint arXiv:2303.08774 (2023)
2. Austin, J., et al.: Program synthesis with large language models. arXiv preprint arXiv:2108.07732 (2021)
3. Azaria, A., Mitchell, T.: The internal state of an LLM knows when it's lying. arXiv preprint arXiv:2304.13734 (2023)
4. Baldonado, J.M.: Semantic performance-analysis of LLM-based autoformalization. University of Buenos Aires (2024)
5. Blasi, A., et al.: Translating code comments to procedure specifications. In: Proceedings of the 27th ACM SIGSOFT International Symposium on Software Testing and Analysis, pp. 242–253 (2018)
6. Cai, Y., et al.: Towards large language model aided program refinement. arXiv preprint arXiv:2406.18616 (2024)
7. Cassez, F., Fuller, J., Ghale, M.K., Pearce, D.J., Quiles, H.M.: Formal and executable semantics of the ethereum virtual machine in dafny. In: International Symposium on Formal Methods, pp. 571–583. Springer (2023)
8. Chakraborty, S., et al.: Ranking LLM-generated loop invariants for program verification. arXiv preprint arXiv:2310.09342 (2023)
9. Cosler, M., Hahn, C., Mendoza, D., Schmitt, F., Trippel, C.: nl2spec: interactively translating unstructured natural language to temporal logics with large language models. In: International Conference on Computer Aided Verification, pp. 383–396. Springer (2023)
10. Creswell, A., Shanahan, M., Higgins, I.: Selection-inference: exploiting large language models for interpretable logical reasoning. arXiv preprint arXiv:2205.09712 (2022)
11. Dafny-lang: Release_notes. https://github.com/dafny-lang/dafny/blob/master/RELEASE_NOTES.md. Accessed 10 June 2025
12. DeepSeek: The temperature parameter. https://api-docs.deepseek.com/quick_start/parameter_settings. Accessed 10 June 2025
13. Dong, Q., et al.: A survey on in-context learning. arXiv preprint arXiv:2301.00234 (2022)
14. Endres, M., Fakhoury, S., Chakraborty, S., Lahiri, S.K.: Can large language models transform natural language intent into formal method postconditions? Proc. ACM Softw. Eng. **1**(FSE), 1889–1912 (2024)
15. Gao, Y., et al.: Retrieval-augmented generation for large language models: a survey. arXiv preprint arXiv:2312.10997 **2**(1) (2023)
16. Guo, D., et al.: Deepseek-r1: incentivizing reasoning capability in LLMs via reinforcement learning. arXiv preprint arXiv:2501.12948 (2025)
17. Hatcliff, J., Leavens, G.T., Leino, K.R.M., Müller, P., Parkinson, M.: Behavioral interface specification languages. ACM Comput. Surv. (CSUR) **44**(3), 1–58 (2012)
18. Hawblitzel, C., et al.: Ironfleet: proving practical distributed systems correct. In: Proceedings of the 25th Symposium on Operating Systems Principles, pp. 1–17 (2015)
19. He, F., Zhai, J., Pan, M.: Beyond code generation: assessing code LLM maturity with postconditions. arXiv preprint arXiv:2407.14118 (2024)
20. Irfan, A., Porncharoenwase, S., Rakamarić, Z., Rungta, N., Torlak, E.: Testing dafny (experience paper). In: Proceedings of the 31st ACM SIGSOFT International Symposium on Software Testing and Analysis, pp. 556–567 (2022)

21. Kamath, A., et al.: Finding inductive loop invariants using large language models. arXiv preprint arXiv:2311.07948 (2023)
22. Lahiri, S.K.: Evaluating LLM-driven user-intent formalization for verification-aware languages. arXiv preprint arXiv:2406.09757 (2024)
23. Leino, K.R.M.: Dafny: an automatic program verifier for functional correctness. In: International Conference on Logic for Programming Artificial Intelligence and Reasoning, pp. 348–370. Springer (2010)
24. Li, T., Zhang, G., Do, Q.D., Yue, X., Chen, W.: Long-context LLMs struggle with long in-context learning. arXiv preprint arXiv:2404.02060 (2024)
25. Li, Y.C., Zetzsche, S., Somayyajula, S.: Dafny as verification-aware intermediate language for code generation. arXiv preprint arXiv:2501.06283 (2025)
26. Liu, A., et al.: Deepseek-v3 technical report. arXiv preprint arXiv:2412.19437 (2024)
27. Liu, J.X., et al.: Lang2ltl: translating natural language commands to temporal specification with large language models. In: Workshop on Language and Robotics at CoRL 2022 (2022)
28. Liu, N.F., et al.: Lost in the middle: how language models use long contexts. arXiv preprint arXiv:2307.03172 (2023)
29. Ma, L., Liu, S., Li, Y., Xie, X., Bu, L.: Specgen: automated generation of formal program specifications via large language models. arXiv preprint arXiv:2401.08807 (2024)
30. McKenna, N., Li, T., Cheng, L., Hosseini, M.J., Johnson, M., Steedman, M.: Sources of hallucination by large language models on inference tasks. arXiv preprint arXiv:2305.14552 (2023)
31. Mirchev, M., Costea, A., Singh, A.K., Roychoudhury, A.: Assured automatic programming via large language models. arXiv preprint arXiv:2410.18494 (2024)
32. Misu, M.R.H., Lopes, C.V., Ma, I., Noble, J.: Towards AI-assisted synthesis of verified dafny methods. Proc. ACM Softw. Eng. **1**(FSE), 812–835 (2024)
33. Mugnier, E., Anaya Gonzalez, E., Jhala, R., Polikarpova, N., Zhou, Y.: Laurel: generating dafny assertions using large language models. arXiv e-prints pp. arXiv–2405 (2024)
34. Pandita, R., Xiao, X., Zhong, H., Xie, T., Oney, S., Paradkar, A.: Inferring method specifications from natural language API descriptions. In: 2012 34th International Conference on Software Engineering (ICSE), pp. 815–825. IEEE (2012)
35. Pascoal Faria, J., Trigo, E., Abreu, R.: Automatic generation of loop invariants in dafny with large language models. In: International Conference on Fundamentals of Software Engineering, pp. 138–154. Springer (2025)
36. Pei, K., Bieber, D., Shi, K., Sutton, C., Yin, P.: Can large language models reason about program invariants? In: International Conference on Machine Learning, pp. 27496–27520. PMLR (2023)
37. Poesia, G., Loughridge, C., Amin, N.: Dafny-annotator: AI-assisted verification of dafny programs. arXiv preprint arXiv:2411.15143 (2024)
38. Sahoo, P., Singh, A.K., Saha, S., Jain, V., Mondal, S., Chadha, A.: A systematic survey of prompt engineering in large language models: Techniques and applications. arXiv preprint arXiv:2402.07927 (2024)
39. Shanahan, M., McDonell, K., Reynolds, L.: Role play with large language models. Nature **623**(7987), 493–498 (2023)
40. Shefer, A., Engel, I., Alekseev, S., Berezun, D., Verbitskaia, E., Podkopaev, A.: Can LLMs enable verification in mainstream programming? arXiv preprint arXiv:2503.14183 (2025)

41. Silva, Á.F., Mendes, A., Ferreira, J.F.: Leveraging large language models to boost dafny's developers productivity. In: Proceedings of the 2024 IEEE/ACM 12th International Conference on Formal Methods in Software Engineering (FormaliSE), pp. 138–142 (2024)
42. Sun, C., Sheng, Y., Padon, O., Barrett, C.: Clover: closed-loop verifiable code generation. In: International Symposium on AI Verification, pp. 134–155. Springer (2024)
43. Tan, L., Yuan, D., Krishna, G., Zhou, Y.: /* icomment: bugs or bad comments?*. In: Proceedings of Twenty-First ACM SIGOPS Symposium on Operating Systems Principles, pp. 145–158 (2007)
44. Tan, L., Zhou, Y., Padioleau, Y.: Acomment: mining annotations from comments and code to detect interrupt related concurrency bugs. In: Proceedings of the 33rd International Conference on Software Engineering, pp. 11–20 (2011)
45. Tan, S.H., Marinov, D., Tan, L., Leavens, G.T.: @ tcomment: testing javadoc comments to detect comment-code inconsistencies. In: 2012 IEEE Fifth International Conference on Software Testing, Verification and Validation, pp. 260–269. IEEE (2012)
46. Wang, J., Chen, Y.: A review on code generation with LLMs: application and evaluation. In: 2023 IEEE International Conference on Medical Artificial Intelligence (MedAI), pp. 284–289. IEEE (2023)
47. Wang, Y., Yao, Q., Kwok, J.T., Ni, L.M.: Generalizing from a few examples: a survey on few-shot learning. ACM Comput. Surv. (CSUR) **53**(3), 1–34 (2020)
48. Wang, Z.M., et al.: Rolellm: benchmarking, eliciting, and enhancing role-playing abilities of large language models. arXiv preprint arXiv:2310.00746 (2023)
49. Wei, J., et al.: Chain-of-thought prompting elicits reasoning in large language models. Adv. Neural. Inf. Process. Syst. **35**, 24824–24837 (2022)
50. Wen, C., et al.: Enchanting program specification synthesis by large language models using static analysis and program verification. In: International Conference on Computer Aided Verification, pp. 302–328. Springer (2024)
51. Xu, Y., Feng, J., Miao, W.: Learning from failures: translation of natural language requirements into linear temporal logic with large language models. In: 2024 IEEE 24th International Conference on Software Quality, Reliability and Security (QRS), pp. 204–215. IEEE (2024)
52. Yu, H., et al.: Decon: detecting incorrect assertions via postconditions generated by a large language model. arXiv preprint arXiv:2501.02901 (2025)
53. Zhong, H., Zhang, L., Xie, T., Mei, H.: Inferring resource specifications from natural language API documentation. In: 2009 IEEE/ACM International Conference on Automated Software Engineering, pp. 307–318. IEEE (2009)
54. Zhou, Y., Gu, R., Chen, T., Huang, Z., Panichella, S., Gall, H.: Analyzing APIs documentation and code to detect directive defects. In: 2017 IEEE/ACM 39th International Conference on Software Engineering (ICSE), pp. 27–37. IEEE (2017)

Detecting Vector Container Errors in C++ Programs via Abstract Interpretation

Siyu Liu, Liqian Chen(✉), Guangsheng Fan, Banghu Yin, Chun Huang, and Ji Wang

College of Computer Science and Technology, National University of Defense Technology, Changsha, China
{liusiyu23a,lqchen,guangshengfan,bhyin,chunhuang,wj}@nudt.edu.cn

Abstract. The vector container in the C++ Standard Template Library (STL) is widely adopted due to its flexibility and efficiency, but its element access and iterator operations lack boundary checks, potentially leading to memory safety issues such as buffer overflows and iterator invalidation. Existing static analysis tools demonstrate limited effectiveness in detecting these issues due to insufficient consideration of the characteristics of C++ vector containers, such as the combined usage of iterators with vectors and vector memory allocation mechanisms. To address these issues, this paper proposes an abstract interpretation-based defection approach that formally tracks vector size and iterator states, and identifies illegal operations. We have implemented our method as a tool named IKOS4VecErr (on top of IKOS) and evaluated it on hand-crafted benchmarks and five well-known open-source projects. Experimental results show that our tool performs much better than mainstream static analysis tools (including IKOS, CSA, Infer, and Cppcheck) in detection capability, which demonstrates the effectiveness of our work in identifying C++ vector-related defects. On hand-crafted benchmarks, IKOS4VecErr successfully identifies 503 out of 505 defects while the best of the compared tools can only identifies 435 defects. On real-world open-source projects, we discovered 16 previously undetected vector-related errors (while the best of the compared tools discovered 4 defects).

Keywords: Abstract Interpretation · Static Analysis · C++ STL Vector · Memory Safety · Abstract Domain

1 Introduction

C++ is widely used in critical technological domains due to its high performance and flexibility. The C++ Standard Template Library (STL) provides standardized implementations of fundamental data structures [1,2]. However, when using the standard template library, programmers may misuse it [3,4]. Among STL containers, the vector is one of the most commonly used containers. This paper focuses on two critical categories of vector-related errors, i.e., Vector Element Access Bugs (VEAB) and Vector Invalid Iterator Bugs (VIIB). Based on our

É. André et al. (Eds.): ICFEM 2025, LNCS 16229, pp. 117–133, 2026.
https://doi.org/10.1007/978-981-95-4213-0_7

empirical analysis of commits to the GitHub repository between 2014 and 2024 (as illustrated in Fig. 1), we observe that reports concerning iterator errors and sequence container errors consistently maintain high frequency.

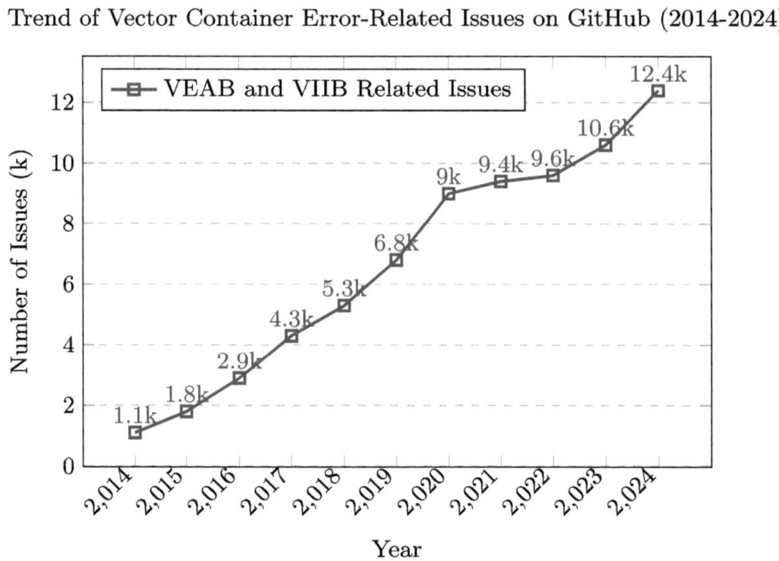

Fig. 1. Statistics of Vector Element Access Bugs (VEAB) and Vector Invalid Iterator Bugs (VIIB) related issues on GitHub from 2014 to 2024.

Mainstream static analysis tools for C++ code, such as IKOS (Inference Kernel for Open Static Analyzers) [5], CSA (Clang Static Analyzer) [6], Infer (Inference Engine for Real-time Analysis) [7], and Cppcheck [8], demonstrate poor performance in detecting VEAB/VIIB errors due to their lack of modeling for the interaction between vector and iterator states, as well as insufficient attention to vector memory allocation mechanisms. For instance, when detecting iterator out-of-bounds access, these tools fail to effectively track the valid range of iterator access due to the absence of joint modeling between iterators and vector objects, leading to missed detections of iterator boundary violations. Furthermore, when using iterators, the lack of attention to vector memory allocation mechanisms may result in incorrect judgments of iterator validity, causing missed detections of iterator invalidation errors.

To address these issues, we propose an abstract interpretation-based approach for detecting vector container errors. Abstract interpretation is a mathematical approximation-based program analysis theory that systematically models program semantics through abstraction to derive or verify program properties [9]. Our approach combines interval [10] and points-to abstract domains to automatically infer vector container behaviors and iterator states. Specifically, the interval abstract domain is used to infer container sizes and iterator offsets, while the points-to abstract domain tracks iterator base addresses and their relationships with containers. This approach enables systematic detection of five error scenarios: index out-of-bounds access, iterator out-of-bounds access, memory reallocation invalidation, illegal position iterators, and cross-container iterators.

We have implemented our method as a tool named IKOS4VecErr based on IKOS [5]. We evaluated our tool on two benchmark sets: a hand-crafted benchmark consisting of 505 test cases covering all five error scenarios, and five real-world open-source C++ projects with extensive vector usage. We compared IKOS4VecErr with four mainstream static analysis tools: IKOS, Clang Static Analyzer (CSA), Infer, and Cppcheck. Experimental results show that IKOS4VecErr significantly outperforms these existing tools, achieving a detection rate of 99.6% (503 out of 505) on the hand-crafted benchmark, while the best of the compared tools detected 88.1%. On real-world open-source projects, IKOS4VecErr discovered 16 previously undetected vector-related errors (while the best of the compared tools discovered 4) that were consolidated into 6 typical defects and reported to the project maintainers.

The rest of the paper is organized as follows. Section 2 introduces the abstract interpretation theory and vector containers. Section 3 presents motivating examples of vector-related errors. Section 4 describes our abstract interpretation-based approach. Section 5 presents our prototype implementation together with experimental results. Section 6 discusses some related work before Sect. 7 concludes.

2 Background

In this section, we introduce the abstract interpretation theory used in our work, along with the structure of vector containers and their memory allocation mechanisms. This background knowledge is essential for understanding our approach to detecting vector-related errors.

2.1 Abstract Interpretation Theory

Abstract interpretation [11] is a fundamental theory in static program analysis that constructs abstract domains to conservatively approximate concrete program semantics while ensuring reliability and computational efficiency. The theory establishes mathematical relationships between concrete and abstract domains through Galois connections [12], where the abstraction function α maps concrete states to their best abstract representations and the concretization function γ maps abstract elements back to corresponding concrete states, satisfying $\alpha(c) \sqsubseteq a \Leftrightarrow c \subseteq \gamma(a)$ to ensure reliable over-approximation of all program behaviors. In practice, the interval domain approximates scalar variables as $[l, u]$ ranges supporting operations like join ($[1,3] \sqcup [5,7] = [1,7]$) and meet ($[1,7] \sqcap [3,5] = [3,5]$) for analyzing array bounds and loop invariants, while the points-to domain models memory locations through abstract addresses (e.g., malloc_1) and points-to relations (e.g., $p \mapsto \{x, y\}$) with offset analysis for pointer arithmetic.

2.2 Memory Allocation Strategy of C++ Vector

The C++ STL `vector` implementation uses three critical iterators (`begin`, `end`, and `capacity`) to manage its memory layout, where `begin` marks the start of elements, `end` indicates the current size, and `capacity` represents the allocated memory boundary, maintaining `capacity` $\geq$ `end`. As illustrated in Fig. 2, when a vector needs to grow beyond its capacity, it employs an exponential growth strategy (typically 1.5 or 2) and performs reallocation through three steps: allocating new memory, copying elements, and releasing the old memory block. This reallocation process invalidates all existing iterators as they point to deallocated memory, which can lead to undefined behavior if used after reallocation. Therefore, careful tracking of iterator validity is crucial when performing vector operations that might trigger reallocation.

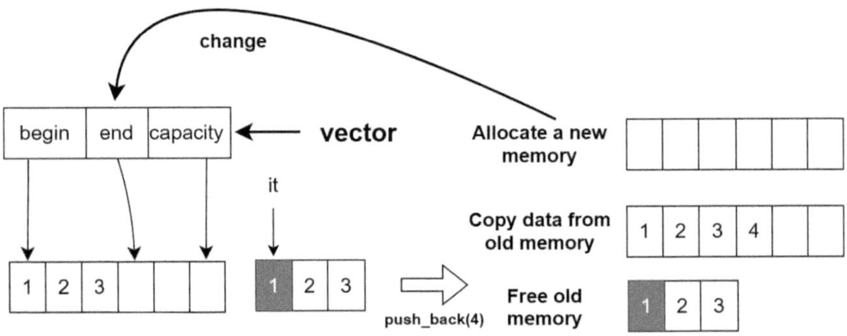

Fig. 2. Vector iterator operations and memory reallocation effects.

3 Motivating Examples

This section presents a comprehensive analysis of vector container errors through carefully crafted examples. We demonstrate five typical error scenarios that commonly occur in C++ vector operations, including both Vector Element Access Bugs (VEAB) and Vector Invalid Iterator Bugs (VIIB). These examples illustrate the challenges in detecting such errors and highlight the limitations of existing static analysis tools.

3.1 Error Scenarios in Vector Operations

Figure 3 demonstrates five typical error scenarios in vector containers, including Vector Element Access Bugs (VEAB) and Vector Invalid Iterator Bugs (VIIB). The example function `errorinVEAB_VIIB` illustrates the following error scenarios:

```
void errorinVEAB_VIIB(int a) {
    std::vector<int> v1({1,2});
    std::vector<int> v2({1,2,3});
    std::vector<int> v3({1,2,3,4});
    int b = 0;
    if (a == 1) {
        b = v1[3];//VEAB: Index out-of-bounds access
    } else if (a == 2) {
        auto it = v1.begin();
        it--;
        b = *(it);//VEAB: Iterator out-of-bounds access
    } else if(a == 3){
        auto it2 = v1.begin();
        v1.push_back(2);//This may cause reallocation
        b = *it2;//VIIB: Memory reallocation invalidation
    } else if(a == 4){
        auto pos1 = v1.begin() + 2;
        auto pos2 = v1.begin();
        //VIIB: Illegal position iterator
        v1.erase(pos1, pos2);
    }else{
        auto pos1 = v1.begin();
        auto pos2 = v2.end();
        //VIIB: Cross-container iterator
        v1.insert(v1.begin(), pos1,pos2);
    }
    return;
}
```

Fig. 3. Example code demonstrating five scenarios of vector-related errors.

Index Out-of-Bounds Error (a==1 branch): When parameter a is 1, the code attempts to access the fourth element of vector v1 (v1[3]), but vector v1 only contains 2 elements. This access will cause a Vector Element Access Bug (VEAB), specifically an out-of-bounds access where the index exceeds the vector's size.

Iterator Out-of-bounds Error (a==2 branch): When a is 2, the code obtains the v1.begin() iterator and then decrements it with the – operator. Since this makes the iterator point to a position before the first element of the vector, dereferencing it constitutes a typical iterator out-of-bounds error (VEAB).

Memory Reallocation Iterator Invalidation (a==3 branch): When a equals 3, the code first acquires the v1.begin() iterator, then potentially triggers a memory reallocation through the push_back operation. At this point, the original it2 iterator has been invalidated, and continuing to dereference it will cause a Vector Invalid Iterator Bug (VIIB) related to memory reallocation invalidation.

Illegal Position Iterator Error (a==4 branch): When a is 4, the code attempts to erase a range with iterators in reverse order: pos1 (v1.begin() + 2) as the first parameter and pos2 (v1.begin()) as the second parameter. Since the range's first iterator has a greater offset than its last iterator, this violates the requirement that first <= last for range operations, constituting a Vector Invalid Iterator Bug (VIIB) related to illegal position iterators.

Cross-Container Iterator Error (else branch): For other values of a, the code attempts to insert a range of elements into v1 using iterators from different containers: pos1 from v1 and pos2 from v2. This cross-container use of iterators in a range operation will trigger a Vector Invalid Iterator Bug (VIIB) related to cross-container iterators.

3.2 Limitations of Existing Tools

We evaluated five error scenarios using mainstream static analysis tools (IKOS, CSA, Infer, and CppCheck). As shown in Table 1, CppCheck's pattern-matching approach, while effective for certain error scenarios, analyzes all branches regardless of execution conditions, leading to both false positives and missed detections. Other tools (IKOS, CSA, and Infer) show limited effectiveness due to insufficient modeling of vector-iterator relationships. IKOS4VecErr addresses these limitations through integrated abstract domains, successfully detecting all test cases.

Table 1. Detection Results of Different Tools on Example Code

Tool	a = 1	a = 2	a = 3	a = 4	a = 5
IKOS4VecErr	✓	✓	✓	✓	✓
IKOS	×	×	×	×	×
CppCheck	✓	×	✓	×	×
Infer	×	×	✓	×	×
CSA	×	×	×	×	×

4 Methodology

4.1 Analysis Framework

This framework combines interval abstract domain for numerical calculations and points-to abstract domain for memory modeling to track container sizes and iterator states. It focuses on detecting five error scenarios: index out-of-bounds access, iterator out-of-bounds access, iterator invalidation due to memory reallocation, illegal position iterator usage, and cross-container iterator misuse.

The analysis workflow consists of the following three layers (Fig. 4):

Frontend Transformation Layer: Transformation of C++ source code into LLVM IR intermediate representation using the Clang compiler, followed by conversion of LLVM IR into Abstract Representation (AR) based on the IKOS analysis framework. This layer establishes intermediate representation models incorporating container operation semantics at the AR level.

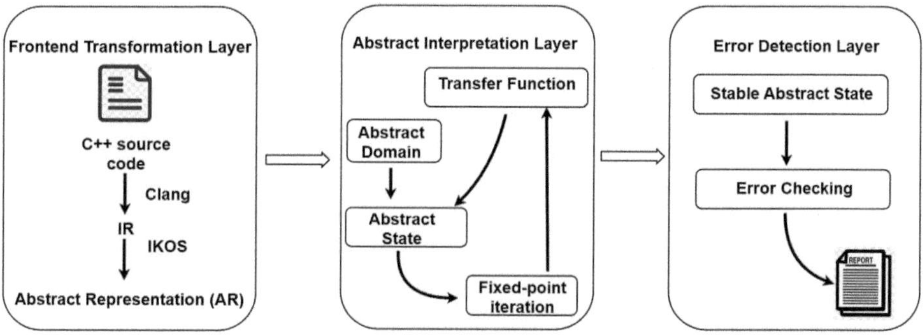

Fig. 4. The workflow of our abstract interpretation-based vector analysis framework.

Abstract Interpretation Layer: Extension of IKOS's existing numerical abstract domains, introducing the Interval Domain to model vector container size changes while enhancing the Points-to Domain to precisely track iterator states. This layer designs new transfer functions to handle vector-specific operations.

Error Detection Layer: Definition of detection predicates for five error scenarios in abstract states, with continuous error monitoring during fixed-point computation and generation of diagnostic reports.

4.2 Abstraction of Vector Containers and Iterators

To detect VEAB and VIIB errors, the model must precisely track both the size evolution of vector containers and the positional relationships between iterators and their corresponding containers. Our formal model combines interval abstraction and points-to abstraction domains to systematically track vector container states and iterator validity. Let $\mathbb{D}_p$ denote the points-to abstract domain and $\mathbb{D}_i$ the interval abstract domain.

Symbolic Notations. In our formal model, $\mathbb{A}_v$ represents the set of vector container addresses in $\mathbb{D}_p$, while $\mathbb{A}_i$ denotes the set of iterator base addresses in $\mathbb{D}_p$. The interval abstraction of container size is defined as $I_v = [size_{\min}, size_{\max}]$, and the interval abstraction of iterator offset is given by $I_i = [\mathit{offset}_{\text{low}}, \mathit{offset}_{\text{high}}]$.

Abstract Representation of Vector Containers and Iterators. Our formal model utilizes the following symbolic notations to represent the abstract states of vector containers and iterators. The abstraction is performed in two domains: the interval domain for size and offset tracking, and the points-to domain for address relationships.

Interval Domain Abstraction. In the interval domain $\mathbb{D}_i$, we perform abstraction for both vector container sizes and iterator offsets. For a vector container, its size is abstracted as an interval $I_v = [size_{\text{min}}, size_{\text{max}}]$, where $size_{\text{min}}$ and $size_{\text{max}}$ represent the minimum and maximum possible sizes of the container. Similarly, for an iterator, its offset relative to the base address is abstracted as $I_i = [offset_{\text{low}}, offset_{\text{high}}]$, capturing the range of possible positions the iterator can point to.

Points-to Domain Abstraction. In the points-to domain $\mathbb{D}_p$, we establish two key sets of addresses and their relationships. Let $\mathbb{A}_v$ denote the set of all vector container addresses, where $a_v \in \mathbb{A}_v$ represents an individual container address. Let $\mathbb{A}_i$ represent the complete iterator address space, where $a_i \in \mathbb{A}_i$ denotes a concrete iterator base address. The abstraction of iterator base addresses is performed using points-to abstraction, where each iterator is represented as a set of possible base addresses in the points-to domain.

We define two points-to relations to capture the relationships between these addresses:

- $P_v : \mathbb{A}_v \rightarrow 2^{\mathbb{A}_i}$ establishes a points-to relation from each vector container address to the set of iterator base addresses that may point to its elements. This relation is constructed by dereferencing vector addresses and projecting the resulting iterator abstract values.
- $P_i : \mathbb{A}_i \rightarrow \mathbb{A}_v$ establishes a points-to relation from each iterator base address to its unique originating container address. This injective relation ensures unambiguous container reference for iterator validity checks.

Based on these two abstract domains, we formally define the abstraction models for vector containers and iterators through joint abstractions.

Vector Container Abstraction: Each vector instance is modeled as a pair $\langle a_v, I_v \rangle \in \mathbb{A}_v \times \mathbb{D}_i$, where a_v denotes the container's address in points-to domain $\mathbb{D}_p$ and $I_v = [size_{\text{min}}, size_{\text{max}}]$ represents the interval abstraction of container size maintained in interval domain $\mathbb{D}_i$.

Iterator Abstraction: Each iterator is modeled as a pair $\langle d_p, I_i \rangle \in \mathbb{D}_p \times \mathbb{D}_i$, where $d_p \in \mathbb{D}_p$ denotes the points-to abstract domain state representing possible base addresses (a subset of $\mathbb{A}_i$) in iterator space, and $I_i = [offset_{\text{low}}, offset_{\text{high}}]$ captures the interval abstraction of iterator offset relative to possible base addresses.

For example, in Fig. 3, the vector 'v1(1, 0)' is abstracted as $\langle a_{v1}, [8, 8] \rangle$, and its iterator 'v1.begin()' as $\langle \{a_{i1}\}, [0, 0] \rangle$, with $P_v(a_{v1}) = \{a_{i1}\}$ and $P_i(a_{i1}) = a_{v1}$.

This abstraction allows us to track the relationship between iterators and their containers, which is crucial for detecting cross-container iterator usage errors.

4.3 Transfer Functions for Iterator Operations and Vector Methods in Abstract Domains

This section defines the abstract semantics of vector operations through transfer functions that map abstract states to new abstract states. We categorize

STL vector and iterator operations into three and five basic operation types respectively, based on their effects on container state and iterator validity. In the following tables, we use the symbol ⊞ to denote interval addition operation, which computes the sum of two intervals by adding their respective bounds: $[a, b] \boxplus [c, d] = [a + c, b + d]$. As shown in Table 2 and Table 3, we list the main categories of methods in vector and iterator operations that belong to these basic operations.

Table 2. Basic Operations of Iterators

Operation Type	Representative Operations
Initialization	begin(), end(), cbegin(), cend(), rbegin(), rend()
Copy	= (assignment operator)
Movement	it+n, it-n, it++, it--, advance(it, n), next(it, n), prev(it, n)

Table 3. Basic Operations of Vector Containers

Operation Type	Representative Operations
Construction	vector<T>(ptr,ptr+n), vector<T>(n), vector<T>(n, val), vector<T>(first, last), vector<T>({a,b,c}), vector<T>()
Resize	resize(n), resize(n, val), assign(n, val), assign(first, last), assign(il)
Change	push_back(val), emplace_back(args...), insert(pos, val), insert(pos, n, val), insert(pos, first, last), erase(pos), erase(first, last), pop_back(), clear()
Copy	= (assignment operator), operator=
Swap	swap(other), std::swap(v1, v2)

Table 4 presents the transfer functions for iterator operations, while Table 5 shows the transfer functions for the five basic vector container operations.

For each basic operation type shown in Tables 4 and 5, we illustrate their effects on abstract states using concrete examples.

For iterator operations, *Initialization* occurs when executing 'it = v1.begin()' where $v1 = \langle a_{v1}, [8, 8] \rangle$; the iterator state becomes $\langle \{a_{i1}\}, [0, 0] \rangle$, where a_{i1} is the base address of the iterator and $[0, 0]$ represents its offset from the beginning. In the *Copy* operation, for 'auto it2 = it1' where $it1 = \langle \{a_{i1}\}, [4, 4] \rangle$, the new iterator $it2$ inherits the same state $\langle \{a_{i1}\}, [4,4] \rangle$. During *Movement*, when executing 'it++' on an iterator with state $\langle \{a_{i1}\}, [0,0] \rangle$, the new state becomes $\langle \{a_{i1}\}, [4,4] \rangle$ (assuming 4-byte int elements).

For vector container operations, the *Construction* example shows that for 'std::vector<int> v1(1, 0)', the initial state is $\langle a_{v1}, [8,8] \rangle$, representing a vector with 2 elements (8 bytes total). In the *Resize* operation, when executing 'v1.resize(3)' on a vector with state $\langle a_{v1}, [8,8] \rangle$, the new state becomes $\langle a_{v1}, [12,12] \rangle$. For *Change* operations, 'v1.push_back(2)' on a vector with state $\langle a_{v1}, [8,8] \rangle$ results in the new state $\langle a_{v1}, [12,12] \rangle$. During *Copy*, when executing 'v2 = v1' where $v1 = \langle a_{v1}, [8,8] \rangle$, the new vector $v2$ gets state $\langle a_{v2}, [8,8] \rangle$. Finally, for *Swap* operations, 'swap(v1, v2)' where $v1 = \langle a_{v1}, [8,8] \rangle$ and $v2 = \langle a_{v2}, [12,12] \rangle$ results in states $v1 = \langle a_{v1}, [12,12] \rangle$ and $v2 = \langle a_{v2}, [8,8] \rangle$.

Table 4. Transfer Functions for Iterator Operations

Operation Type	Expression	Transfer Function
Initialization	Initialization(it_1, v_1, I_{pos})	$\dfrac{it_1 = \bot}{it_1 = \langle P_v(v_1.a_v), I_{pos} \rangle}$ $\forall a_i \in P_v(v_1.a_v) : P_i(a_i) = v_1.a_v$
Copy	Copy(it_1, it_2)	$\dfrac{it_1 = \langle d_p, I_i \rangle}{it_1 = \langle it2.d_p, it2.I_i \rangle}$
Movement	Movement(it_1, I_{mov})	$\dfrac{it_1 = \langle d_p, I_i \rangle}{it_1 = \langle d_p, I_i \boxplus I_{mov} \rangle}$

Table 5. Transfer Functions for Vector Container Operations

Operation Type	Expression	Transfer Function
Construction	Construct(v_1, I_{con})	$\dfrac{v_1 = \bot}{v_1 = \langle a_v, I_{con} \rangle}$
Resize	Resize(v_1, I_{res})	$\dfrac{v_1 = \langle a_v, I_v \rangle}{v_1 = \langle a_v, I_{res} \rangle}$
Change	Change(v_1, I_{change})	$\dfrac{v_1 = \langle a_v, I_v \rangle}{v_1 = \langle a_v, I_v \boxplus I_{change} \rangle}$
Copy	Copy(v_1, v_2)	$\dfrac{v_1 = \langle a_{v1}, I_{v1} \rangle, v_2 = \langle a_{v2}, I_{v2} \rangle}{v_1 = \langle a_{v1}, I_{v2} \rangle}$
Swap	Swap(v_1, v_2)	$\dfrac{v_1 = \langle a_{v1}, I_{v1} \rangle, v_2 = \langle a_{v2}, I_{v2} \rangle}{v_1 = \langle a_{v1}, I_{v2} \rangle, v_2 = \langle a_{v2}, I_{v1} \rangle}$ $\forall a_i \in P_v(v_1.a_v) : P_i(a_i) = v_2.a_v$ $\forall a_j \in P_v(v_2.a_v) : P_i(a_j) = v_1.a_v$

These examples demonstrate how the abstract states evolve through different operations while maintaining the consistency between vector containers and their iterators. The interval domain tracks size and offset changes, while the points-to domain maintains the relationships between containers and iterators. This dual-domain approach ensures precise analysis of both vector bounds and iterator validity across different execution paths.

4.4 Checking VEAB and VIIB Bugs

Based on the abstract models established earlier, we designed five error detection rules for the two scenarios of VEAB errors and three scenarios of VIIB errors. These rules continuously monitor container and iterator states along execution paths, reporting violations when detected.

Vector Element Access Bugs (VEAB) primarily occur when accessing vector elements through index operations or iterator dereferencing. These errors can be triggered by both direct index access (using operator[] or at()) and iterator-based element access.

Index Out-of-Bounds Detection. For index-based access (e.g., `v[i]`), the analyzer compares the container size abstraction $I_v = [size_{\min}, size_{\max}]$ with the index abstraction $I_i = [i_{\min}, i_{\max}]$. The analyzer reports an error when $\neg(I_i \prec I_v)$ (index interval is not strictly less than size interval) or when $I_i \prec [0, 0]$ (index interval is strictly negative). This detection mechanism identifies index out-of-bounds errors as demonstrated in line 7 of Fig. 3, where `b = v1[3]` attempts to access the fourth element of vector v1, which only contains 2 elements.

Iterator Out-of-Bounds Detection. For iterator dereferencing (e.g., `*it`), the analyzer compares the iterator's offset abstraction $I_i = [\mathit{offset}_{\text{low}}, \mathit{offset}_{\text{high}}]$ against the container size. The analysis handles iterators potentially associated with multiple containers by retrieving and joining size abstractions across all possible containers. Let $I_v = [size_{\min}, size_{\max}]$ denote the joined size interval. The analyzer reports an error when $\neg(I_i \prec I_v)$ (iterator offset interval is not strictly less than container size interval) or when $I_i \prec [0, 0]$ (iterator offset is strictly negative). This approach effectively detects iterator boundary violations as shown in line 10 of Fig. 3, where `b = *(it)` attempts to dereference an iterator that points before the first element of vector v1 after the decrement operation.

Vector Invalid Iterator Bugs (VIIB). When dereferencing iterators or using iterators as parameters in STL methods, Vector Invalid Iterator Bugs (VIIB) may occur.

Memory Reallocation Invalidation Detection. For memory reallocation invalidation, the analyzer verifies iterator validity through the combination of two points-to relations (P_i and P_v) integrated with iterator modeling properties. Given an iterator with base address set $\{a_i\} \subseteq \mathbb{A}_i$, the analyzer applies the points-to relation P_i to obtain the vector address $a_v = P_i(a_i)$ for each $a_i \in \{a_i\}$, creating groups where each group contains base addresses mapping to the same vector address (let $\{a_i^g\}$ denote the base address set for group g). For each group with vector address a_v, the analyzer applies the points-to relation P_v to obtain the current valid iterator base address set $\{a_i'\}$ for that vector.

The analyzer then compares each group's base address set $\{a_i^g\}$ with the derived set $\{a_i'\}$ through projection operations, classifying as valid when $\{a_i^g\} = \{a_i'\}$ (iterators remain valid), invalid when $\{a_i^g\} \cap \{a_i'\} = \emptyset$ (all iterators invalidated), or partially valid when $\{a_i^g\} \neq \{a_i'\}$ and $\{a_i^g\} \cap \{a_i'\} \neq \emptyset$. The final result combines all groups: safe when all groups are valid, error when all groups are invalid, and warning in all other cases. This detection mechanism effectively identifies invalidated iterators after memory reallocation operations, as demonstrated in line 14 of Fig. 3, where `*it2` dereferencing after `push_back` operation causes iterator invalidation. Figure 5 shows the detection process where iterator base addresses are divided into two groups with different validity states.

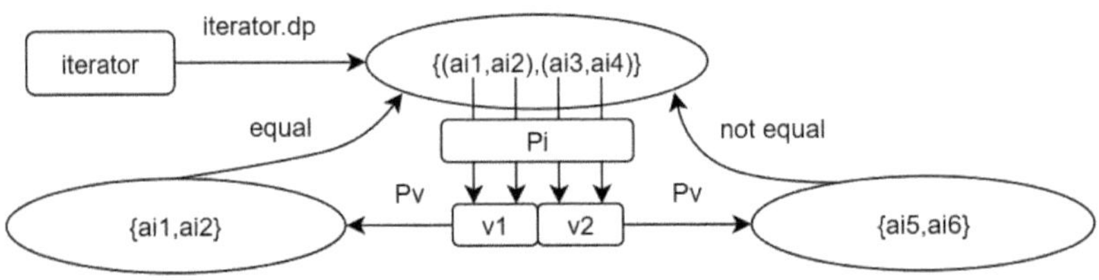

Fig. 5. Memory reallocation invalidation detection with iterator base addresses grouped by their target vectors.

Illegal Position Iterator Detection. For operations requiring valid iterator positions (e.g., `insert`, `erase`), the analyzer verifies position validity through interval domain comparisons. Given a vector container with size interval $I_v = [size_{\text{min}}, size_{\text{max}}]$ and iterator offset interval $I_i = [offset_{\text{low}}, offset_{\text{high}}]$, the analyzer performs interval comparisons:

For single-iterator operations, the analyzer compares the iterator offset interval I_i against the vector's size interval I_v and reports an error when $\neg(I_i \prec I_v)$ (iterator offset is not strictly less than container size) or when $I_i \prec [0, 0]$ (iterator offset is strictly negative).

For range operations (e.g., `insert(pos, first, last)`), the analyzer performs two interval comparisons: it first checks that the position iterator offset interval I_{pos} satisfies $I_{pos} \prec I_v$ (position is within bounds), then verifies that $I_{first} \preceq I_{last}$ (first iterator comes before last iterator in the range). An error is reported if either condition is violated.

This mechanism detects illegal iterator positions as shown in line 19 of Fig. 3, where `v1.erase(pos1, pos2)` attempts to erase with iterators in reverse order.

Cross-Container Iterator Detection. For operations requiring iterators from the same container, the analyzer must verify container consistency. Given an operation on container v with iterator parameters, the analyzer first maps each iterator base address a_i to its container address using the points-to relation $P_i(a_i)$ and then forms the set $\{a_v\}$ of all possible container addresses that these iterators might originate from. After obtaining the container address sets, the analyzer determines whether a cross-container usage error exists by examining the relationship between these sets.

When the method requires iterators to be from the same container but their container address sets are disjoint, a cross-container error is detected. This approach effectively identifies cross-container iterator misuse as demonstrated in line 24 of Fig. 3, where `v1.insert(v1.begin(), pos1, pos2)` incorrectly uses iterators with different container origins—the container address set for `pos1` differs from that of `pos2`, as they point to different vectors (`v1` and `v2` respectively), violating the requirement that range iterators must come from the same container.

5 Evaluation

To evaluate the effectiveness of our model and its ability to detect VEAB/VIIB errors, we conducted two sets of experiments to address the following research questions:

Research Question 1 (RQ1): Can IKOS4VecErr accurately detect the five error scenarios in hand-crafted benchmark tests?

Research Question 2 (RQ2): How effective is IKOS4VecErr in detecting actual VEAB/VIIB errors in open-source projects?

Research Question 3 (RQ3): How does IKOS4VecErr compare to the original IKOS in terms of time consumption and performance overhead?

To assess the effectiveness of IKOS4VecErr, we applied it to both hand-crafted benchmarks and five open-source C++ projects. We then compared the results with those of other state-of-the-art static analysis tools to evaluate IKOS4VecErr's capability in detecting VEAB/VIIB errors. These comparisons are discussed in Sects. 5.2 and 5.3.

5.1 Setup of Experiments

Environment and Tools: All experiments were conducted on a Linux server equipped with Intel®Core^{TM}i7-14700F CPU at 2.10GHz, with 28 threads and 64GB of memory. We compared IKOS4VecErr with four state-of-the-art tools in their latest versions: IKOS static analyzer version 3.5, Clang Static Analyzer (CSA) version 18, CppCheck version 2.14.0, and Infer version 1.2.0.

Benchmark Composition: Our benchmarking approach consisted of two distinct test sets: hand-crafted code snippets (Benchmark HM) and open-source C++ projects (Benchmark OP).

Hand-crafted Benchmark (HM): We designed code snippets, each containing exactly one error that could potentially lead to VEAB or VIIB errors. These snippets were categorized into five major groups corresponding to the five error scenarios described in Sect. 2.2.

Open-source Project Benchmark (OP): We selected five popular open-source C++ projects that extensively utilize std::vector containers for evaluation.

5.2 Research Question 1 (RQ1): Results on Hand-Crafted Benchmarks

Table 6. Detection Performance of Various Tools on Hand-crafted Benchmarks

Tool	TP	FP	FN	Precision (%)	Recall (%)	F1 (%)
IKOS4VecErr	503	0	2	100.0%	99.6%	99.8%
IKOS	7	3	495	70.0%	1.4%	2.7%
CppCheck	435	11	59	97.5%	88.1%	92.5%
Infer	78	0	427	100.0%	15.4%	26.7%
CSA	0	0	505	-	0.0%	0.0%

To evaluate the accuracy of IKOS4VecErr in detecting VEAB/VIIB errors, we compared its performance against four other tools on the hand-crafted benchmark (HM). Our test suite consists of 505 test cases covering five different error scenarios: Vector Access Overflow (170 cases), Iterator Out-of-bounds (100 cases), Iterator Memory Invalidation (65 cases), Iterator Location Out-of-bounds (60 cases), and Iterator Target Error (50 cases). The distribution reflects real-world error frequencies, with more test cases allocated to commonly occurring error scenarios.

We evaluated the performance of each tool using standard metrics: True Positives (TP), False Positives (FP), False Negatives (FN), as well as commonly used evaluation metrics including Precision, Recall, and F1-score. Table 6 presents the comprehensive evaluation results.

Table 6 shows IKOS4VecErr achieves 503/505 true positives (99.6

5.3 Research Question 2 (RQ2): Results on Open-Source Projects

Table 7. Details of Selected Open-source Projects

Project Name	Commit Hash	LOC (K)	Stars (k)
C-Plus-Plus-Project	77b9fs9	36	31.8
Algo_Ds_Notes	b0c11a2	72	2.3
algorithms_and_data_structures	60f95da	23	6
cp-notebook	292c614	71	2.6
cosmos	47fc66f8	44.8	13.7

Table 8. Detection Results on Open-source Projects (True Positives/Total Reports)

Project Name	IKOS4VecErr	IKOS	Cppcheck	Infer	CSA
C-plus-plus	10/39	2/2	1/12	0/0	0/0
Algo_Ds_Notes	0/3	0/0	3/3	0/0	0/0
algorithms_and_data_structures	0/0	0/0	0/0	0/0	0/0
cp-notebook	6/6	0/3	0/0	0/0	0/0
cosmos	0/6	0/3	0/0	0/0	0/0
Total	**16/54**	**2/8**	**4/15**	**0/0**	**0/0**

For the Open-source Project Benchmark (OP), we selected five popular open-source C++ projects that extensively utilize std::vector containers. The details of the selected projects are presented in Table 7, where the Vector-related LOC (K) column indicates the lines of code specifically in files containing vector containers.

Table 8 presents the detection results across all projects, with X/Y indicating X manually confirmed true positives out of Y total reports. IKOS4VecErr identified a total of 16 true positive reports across all projects, significantly outperforming IKOS (2) and Cppcheck (4), while both Infer and CSA failed to detect any vector-related issues. Based on careful analysis of these 16 true positive reports, we extracted 6 unique defects by categorizing them according to their root causes. We submitted these 6 categorized defect reports to the project maintainers for resolution, as detailed in Table 9. The observed false positives stem from abstract interpretation limitations: precision loss during widening operations, and necessarily conservative handling of global variables in our static analysis implementation.

Table 9. Submitted Bug Reports to Open-source Projects

Project Name	C-Plus-Plus-Project				cp-notebook
Issue ID	#2937	#2938	#2939	#2952	#34 #35

5.4 Research Question 3 (RQ3): Performance Comparison

Table 10. Time Consumption Comparison Between IKOS4VecErr and Original IKOS

Project Name	IKOS4VecErr	IKOS	Overhead
C-plus-plus-Project	280.365	285.758	−1.89%
Algo_Ds_Notes	39.352	43.804	−10.16%
algorithms_and_data_structures	68.451	67.489	1.42%
cosmos	364.856	322.326	13.19%
cp-notebook	824.539	892.300	−7.59%
HM	246.851	271.999	−9.25%
Average(in seconds)	**315.513**	**322.335**	**-2.12%**

IKOS4VecErr performs VEAB/VIIB checks before IKOS's analysis, which helps avoid redundant analysis steps. This approach leads to performance improvements in several projects (Table 10).

The experimental results show an average performance improvement of 2.12% across all benchmarks, with notable gains in projects with extensive vector usage (e.g., −10.16% for Algo_Ds_Notes, −7.59% for cp-notebook) and acceptable overhead in others (e.g., +13.19% for cosmos), demonstrating that our enhanced detection capability comes with minimal performance impact.

6 Related Work

Vector container usage can be analyzed through both static and dynamic analysis techniques. In static analysis, Li et al. [13] proposed modeling container-iterator relationships, but their variable-based approach lacks precision when handling value ranges, often defaulting to uncertain states in complex scenarios. D'evai et al. [14] and Pataki et al. [15] explored formal verification methods for STL containers, with Pataki [16] introducing iterator position representation for container size validation. However, these methods focus primarily on individual properties of containers or iterators, overlooking their dynamic interactions.

For STL method verification, different strategies have been explored. Dynamic analysis approaches, as implemented by Pataki et al. [17], employ runtime memory monitoring which effectively captures errors but incurs significant performance overhead. Static pattern matching methods, exemplified by CppCheck [8], can detect VEAB and VIIB errors but suffer from control flow insensitivity, generating warnings regardless of execution feasibility. Horváth et al. [18] proposed extending STL iterator traits for error detection, but their approach focuses solely on iterator properties without considering container states.

IKOS4VecErr advances beyond these approaches by combining interval and points-to abstract domains specifically for vector containers, enabling precise modeling of both container size evolution and iterator validity while maintaining path sensitivity.

7 Conclusion and Future Work

This paper presents an abstract interpretation-based approach for detecting vector container errors in C++ programs. By combining interval and points-to abstract domains, our approach accurately tracks vector capacity and iterator states, enabling the detection of five major error scenarios. Experimental results show that our implementation IKOS4VecErr outperforms existing tools, achieving an average detection rate of over 99% on hand-crafted benchmarks. Future work will focus on extending the analysis to support other STL containers, supporting newer C++ standards, optimizing performance, and integrating with developer tools to further enhance C++ memory safety.

Acknowledgments. This work is supported by the National Key R&D Program of China (No. 2022YFA1005101) and the National Natural Science Foundation of China (No. 62032024).

References

1. Prechelt, L.: Technical opinion: comparing Java vs. C/C++ efficiency differences to interpersonal differences. Commun. ACM **42**(10), 109–112 (1999)
2. Josuttis, N.M.: The C++ Standard Library: A Tutorial and Reference. Addison-Wesley (2012)
3. Babati, B., Pataki, N.: Static analysis of functors' mathematical properties in C++ source code. In: AIP Conference Proceedings, vol. 2116. AIP Publishing (2019)
4. Horváth, G., Pataki, N.: Clang matchers for verified usage of the C++ standard template library. Annales Mathematicae et Informaticae **44**, 99–109 (2015)
5. Online. Inference Kernel for Open Static Analyzers — github.com. https://github.com/NASA-SW-VnV/ikos
6. Online. Clang Static Analyzer — clang-analyzer.llvm.org. https://clang-analyzer.llvm.org
7. Online. Infer Static Analyzer | Infer | Infer — fbinfer.com. https://fbinfer.com
8. Online. Cppcheck - A tool for static C/C++ code analysis — cppcheck.sourceforge.io. https://cppcheck.sourceforge.io/
9. Chen, L., Fan, G., Yin, B., Wang, J.: Research progress on abstract interpretation and its application. J. Comput. Res. Dev. **60**(2), 227–247 (2023)
10. Cousot, P., Cousot, R.: Static determination of dynamic properties of programs. In: Proceedings of the 2nd International Symposium on Programming, Paris, France. Dunod, pp. 106–130 (1976)
11. Cousot, P.: Abstract interpretation. ACM Comput. Surv. (CSUR) **28**(2), 324–328 (1996)
12. Erné, M., Koslowski, J., Melton, A., et al.: A primer on Galois connections. Ann. N. Y. Acad. Sci. **704**(1), 103–125 (1993)
13. Li, Z., Ma, X., Hu, M., et al.: Detecting element accessing bugs in C++ sequence containers. In: ASE, pp. 883–894 (2024)
14. Dévai, G., Pataki, N.: A tool for formally specifying the C++ standard template library. In: Annales Universitatis Scientiarum Budapestinensis de Rolando Eötvös Nominatae, Sectio Computatorica, vol. 31, pp. 147–166 (2009)
15. Pataki, N.: C++ standard template library by ranges. In: Proceedings of the 8th International Conference on Applied Informatics (ICAI 2010), vol. 2, pp. 367–374 (2010)
16. Pataki, N.: Safe iterator framework for the C++ standard template library. Acta Electrotechnica et Informatica **12**(1), 17 (2012)
17. Pataki, N., Szűgyi, Z., Dévai, G.: Measuring the overhead of c++ standard template library safe variants. Electron. Notes Theor. Comput. Sci. **264**(5), 71–83 (2011)
18. Horváth, G., Páter-Részeg, A., Pataki, N.: Detecting misusages of the C++ standard template library. In: Proceedings of the 10th International Conference on Applied Informatics (ICAI 2017), pp. 129–136 (2017)

BCCIC3: Batch Clause Construction Enhanced Generalization in IC3

Yi Chen, Xinyi Gong, Liangze Yin(✉), Ji Wang, and Ting Wang

College of Computer Science and Technology, National University of Defense Technology, Changsha, China
{chenyi23c,gongxinyi,wangji,wangting}@nudt.edu.cn, yinliangze@163.com

Abstract. Model checking has emerged as a crucial formal verification technique for ensuring the correctness of safety-critical systems. Among its various approaches, the IC3 algorithm represents an important advancement in symbolic model checking, but its efficiency is limited by the computational cost of constraint solver invocations during clause generalization phases, where each generalization process typically yields only a single inductive clause despite the substantial solving effort required. We present a new approach that improves how IC3 explores invariant spaces through batch clause construction and incremental solving. Traditional IC3 implementations sequentially test literals for removal, requiring multiple expensive solver calls yet producing only a single generalized clause per iteration. Our framework introduces an alternative approach: instead of focusing on which literals to remove, we construct and verify multiple potential generalization candidates simultaneously. This combinatorial verification methodology enables the discovery of multiple inductive clauses from a single counterexample, expanding the invariant space covered in each solver invocation. Our approach examines intermediate results from verification steps and reuses this information to derive multiple valid clause generalizations in a single solver invocation. This methodology constrains the search space of the verification problem and influences the verification path, yielding more compact and precise invariants that improve the overall verification process. Through formal analysis, we establish the soundness of our approach and show how it enhances abstract state representation. Experimental evaluation across 1349 benchmarks from the FMCAD08 suite shows our method (BCCIC3) achieves a 21.21% reduction in overall verification time compared to state-of-the-art IC3 implementations. The techniques presented advance property-directed reachability algorithms with applications in hardware verification, software model checking, and cyber-physical system verification.

Keywords: IC3 Algorithm · Model Checking · Generalization

É. André et al. (Eds.): ICFEM 2025, LNCS 16229, pp. 134–151, 2026.
https://doi.org/10.1007/978-981-95-4213-0_8

1 Introduction

1.1 The Evolution of Formal Verification

The increasing complexity of safety-critical systems across domains—from microprocessor designs and communication protocols to autonomous vehicles and medical devices—has elevated the importance of formal verification as an essential technology for ensuring system correctness. Unlike testing, which can only reveal the presence of errors but not their absence, formal verification provides mathematical guarantees about system behavior under all possible conditions. Among formal verification techniques, model checking has proven to be a powerful approach for automatically verifying finite-state systems against temporal logic specifications [25].

Traditional model checking methods, however, have long struggled with the state explosion problem—where the number of states grows exponentially with the number of system variables. Early approaches using Binary Decision Diagrams (BDDs) proved effective for certain classes of systems but often failed to scale for complex real-world applications. Bounded Model Checking (BMC) offered partial solutions by limiting verification to execution traces of bounded length, but could not provide complete verification guarantees.

1.2 The IC3/PDR Paradigm

The introduction of IC3 (Incremental Construction of Inductive Clauses for Indubitable Correctness) by Bradley in 2011 [1], later renamed as Property Directed Reachability (PDR), marked a revolutionary advancement in symbolic model checking. The algorithm's distinctive characteristic is its ability to incrementally construct inductive invariants specifically tailored to proving the desired property, rather than computing the complete reachable state space. This property-directed approach allows IC3 to focus computational resources on regions of the state space that are relevant to the verification task.

As IC3 operates by maintaining a sequence of formula frames $F_0, F_1, \ldots, F_k$, where each F_i overapproximates the states reachable in i steps from the initial states. The algorithm iteratively refines these frames through two complementary processes: (1) identifying and blocking states that could lead to property violations, and (2) propagating learned clauses forward when they become inductively invariant. This incremental refinement continues until either a property violation is discovered or an inductive strengthening of the property is constructed.

1.3 The IC3 Bottleneck

Despite its revolutionary impact on formal verification, IC3 still faces significant performance challenges when handling complex systems. The algorithm's performance is limited by its heavy reliance on constraint solver invocations, particularly during the clause generalization phase. These solver calls dominate the computational workload, consuming up to 70% of the total verification time in typical applications [8].

The core inefficiency stems from IC3's approach to clause generation and refinement. When IC3 encounters a state that could potentially violate the safety property, it must derive a clause that blocks this state while generalizing to exclude as many other unreachable states as possible. The traditional approach processes one literal at a time, testing each for potential removal from the clause. For a clause with n literals, this process may require $O(n^2)$ solver invocations in the worst case, as each candidate removal must be validated through separate initiation and consecution checks.

Several approaches have attempted to address these limitations. Hassan et al. [13] introduced complementary "up" and "down" generalization directions to explore different regions of the clause space. Gurfinkel and Ivrii [6] proposed "pushing" techniques to maximize the effectiveness of derived clauses. While these methods improved IC3 efficiency, they still fundamentally operate within the sequential, single-result paradigm, leaving significant room for further optimization.

1.4 Our Contribution

In this paper, we present a novel approach to IC3 that addresses its core inefficiency by fundamentally reorienting the clause generalization process. Our key contributions include:

1. **Batch Clause Construction**: We introduce a combinatorial verification framework that evaluates multiple potential generalizations within a single solver invocation, enabling the discovery of diverse inductive clauses from a single counterexample. This approach significantly expands the invariant space covered in each iteration.
2. **Model-Based Inference**: We develop efficient inference mechanisms that leverage models from individual literal checks to predict the validity of combined literal combinations, reducing solver invocations by exploiting logical dependencies between verification conditions.
3. **Experimental Validation**: We provide comprehensive benchmarking across diverse verification tasks, demonstrating that our approach achieves significant performance improvements over state-of-the-art IC3 implementations, with particularly pronounced gains for complex transition systems with large state spaces. Experimental evaluation across 1349 benchmarks from the FMCAD08 suite shows our method (BCCIC3) achieves a 21.21% reduction in overall verification time compared to state-of-the-art IC3 implementations.

Our batch clause construction technique represents a fundamental shift in how IC3 explores the invariant space. By strategically combining literal checks and reusing intermediate results, we extract more information from each solver call, substantially reducing verification time while improving the quality of discovered invariants.

The remainder of this paper is organized as follows: Sect. 2 introduces the necessary background and formal notation. Section 3 details our enhanced generalization technique and its implementation. Section 4 presents experimental results and comparative analysis, while Sect. 5 discusses related work. Finally, Sect. 6 concludes with a summary of contributions and directions for future research.

2 Preliminaries

This section introduces the notation and concepts used throughout the paper.

2.1 Formal Logic and Notation

We work within the standard first-order logic framework. Let φ, ψ, I, T, P denote formulas, x, y denote variables, and X, Y, $\bar{X}$ denote sets of variables. Unless otherwise specified, we focus on quantifier-free formulas, where 0-arity predicates are treated as Boolean variables and 0-arity uninterpreted functions as theory variables.

A *literal* is either an *atom* (a propositional variable or its negation) or its negation. A *clause* is a disjunction of literals, while a *cube* is a conjunction of literals. For a cube $s = l_1 \wedge \ldots \wedge l_n$, we denote its negation $\neg s$ as the clause $\neg l_1 \vee \ldots \vee \neg l_n$, and vice versa. A formula is in conjunctive normal form (CNF) if it is a conjunction of clauses, and in disjunctive normal form (DNF) if it is a disjunction of cubes.

For each variable x, we assume a corresponding primed version x' exists. If X is a set of variables, then X' denotes the set obtained by replacing each variable with its primed version, i.e., $X' = \{x' \mid x \in X\}$. Given a formula φ, φ' represents the formula obtained by adding a prime to each variable in φ. For a theory T, we write $\varphi \models_T \psi$ (or simply $\varphi \models \psi$) to denote that formula ψ is a logical consequence of φ in theory T.

2.2 Transition Systems

A *transition system* $\mathcal{S}$ is formally defined as a tuple $\mathcal{S} = (X, I, T, P)$, where:

- $X = \{x_1, x_2, \ldots, x_n\}$ is a set of state variables that define the state space $\mathcal{X} = 2^X$.
- $I(X)$ is a formula representing the initial states.
- $T(X, X')$ is a transition relation formula, where X' denotes next-state variables. A pair (s, s') satisfies T if and only if there exists a transition from state s to state s'.
- $P(X)$ is a safety property to be verified.

A state of $\mathcal{S}$ is an assignment to the variables X. We use lowercase letters s to denote concrete states, and uppercase letters S to denote sets of states. A path of $\mathcal{S}$ is a finite sequence $s_0, s_1, \ldots, s_k$ of states such that $s_0 \models I$ and for all i, $0 \leq i < k$, $(s_i, s'_{i+1}) \models T$.

The verification problem, denoted by $\mathcal{S} \models P$, is to determine whether for all paths $s_0, s_1, \ldots, s_k$ of $\mathcal{S}$, for all i, $0 \leq i \leq k$, $s_i \models P$. Its dual is the reachability problem, which seeks to find a path $s_0, s_1, \ldots, s_k$ of $\mathcal{S}$ such that $s_k \models \neg P$.

The set of reachable states, denoted by $Reach(\mathcal{S})$, comprises all states that can be reached from initial states through a finite number of transitions. A system satisfies a safety property P if and only if $Reach(\mathcal{S}) \subseteq P$.

2.3 Inductive Invariants

Inductive invariants are fundamental to formal verification. A state formula $F(X)$ is an *inductive invariant* if and only if:

- $I(X) \models F(X)$ (initiation condition)
- $F(X) \wedge T(X, X') \models F(X')$ (consecution condition)

A weaker notion is that of relative inductive invariants: given a formula $\phi(X)$, $F(X)$ is inductive relative to ϕ if and only if:

- $I(X) \models F(X)$ (initiation condition)
- $\phi(X) \wedge F(X) \wedge T(X, X') \models F(X')$ (relative consecution)

If $F(X) \models P(X)$, then the inductive invariant F is sufficient to prove that property P holds for system $\mathcal{S}$. The challenge in formal verification lies in discovering appropriate inductive invariants that establish the desired safety properties.

2.4 IC3 Algorithm Framework

IC3 [1] works by maintaining a sequence of overapproximations $F_0, F_1, \ldots, F_k$ to sets of states reachable within i steps, where F_k is the frontier. Each F_i is a conjunction of the safety property P with an initially empty set of clauses, with the following invariants:

- $F_0 = I$ (the first frame is exactly the initial state set)
- For all $0 \leq i < k$, $F_i \Rightarrow F_{i+1}$ (the frame sequence is monotonically decreasing)
- For all $0 \leq i < k$, $F_i \wedge T \Rightarrow F'_{i+1}$ (adjacent frames satisfy relative inductiveness)
- All frames imply the safety property: $F_i \Rightarrow P$, for all $0 \leq i \leq k$

The algorithm operates through these complementary phases that iteratively refine these frames:

Blocking Phase: For each $k > 0$, IC3 refines the F_i's for $i \leq k$ to prove inductiveness of P relative to F_k. This refinement is property-driven: a counterexample to inductiveness (CTI)—a state s where $F_k(s)$ holds but has a $\neg P$-successor—triggers IC3 to derive a clause to block it. When encountering a CTI, IC3 explores its (transitive) predecessors to derive supporting strengthening clauses until the original CTI can be addressed. This exploration is guided by a priority queue of pairs (s, i), where each pair represents the obligation to prove state s unreachable for at least $i+1$ steps. Obligations are processed in lowest-index-first order, ensuring termination.

Generalization: When IC3 successfully addresses a CTI by finding a clause $c \subseteq \neg s$ that is inductive relative to some F_j (where $j \leq i$), it doesn't merely exclude the single state s. Instead, it applies induction to generalize the clause, allowing it to exclude many more states simultaneously. This generalized clause is then added to all frames F_i for $i \leq k$. Furthermore, if $j < k$, IC3 adds the obligation $(s, j+1)$ to the queue, allowing the early discovery of mutually inductive clauses and the detection of deep counterexamples even with small values of k. As shown in Fig. 1, the figure illustrates that during CTI processing, the inductive generalization of clauses aims to exclude a broader set of states. However, As shown in Fig. 2, if an unsafe path exists for state s, the algorithm reverses the generalization process to propagate initial values, thereby investigating the presence of potential counterexamples.

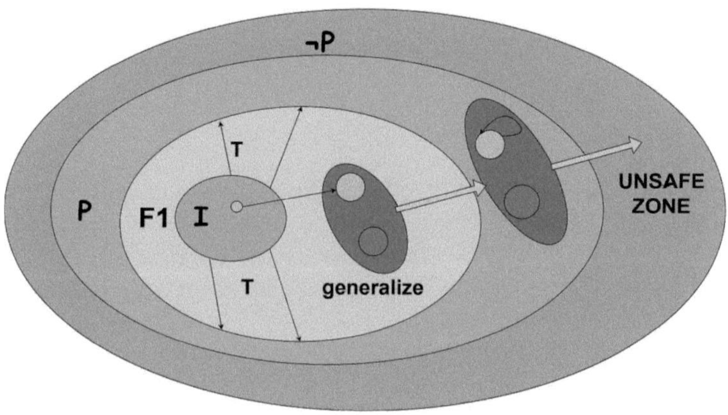

Fig. 1. Generalization

Propagation Phase: When no CTIs remain for F_k, IC3 checks each clause of each F_i to determine if it can be propagated forward—that is, if it has become inductive relative to F_i since its creation due to subsequent strengthening of F_i. During this process, IC3 determines whether any F_i has become an inductive strengthening of the property, in which case the property is proven to hold. If not, it increments k, creates a new frontier F_k, and "bootstraps" it with all clauses that are inductive relative to F_{k-1}.

This process continues until either IC3 finds an inductive strengthening of the property (verification success) or discovers a counterexample by following a sequence of CTIs back to an initial state (verification failure). The algorithm's efficiency stems from its focus on critical proof obligations and its ability to generalize from concrete counterexamples to broader invariants.

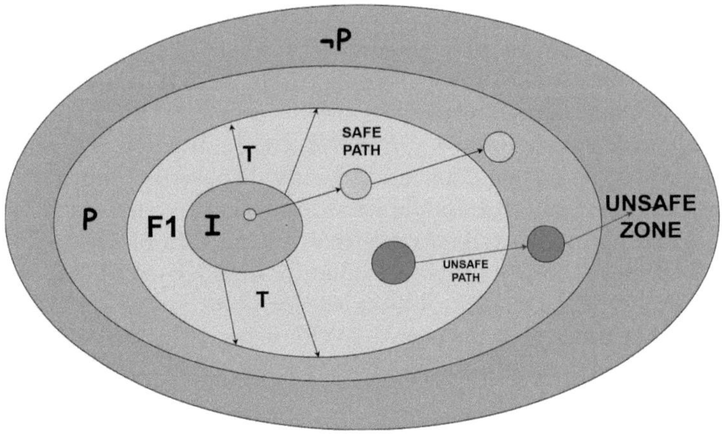

Fig. 2. Origin path

2.5 Generalization

In the original implementation of IC3, clause generalization employs a procedure called Minimal Inductive Clause (MIC), which systematically attempts to drop literals from a clause while maintaining its inductiveness. This procedure transforms concrete counterexamples into abstract invariants that exclude large regions of the state space.

The MIC procedure iteratively tests each literal for removal, while the *down* procedure validates if the resulting clause remains inductive. For each iteration, the solver determines whether the negated cube includes initial states, is inductive relative to F_i, or has predecessor states. When a predecessor is found, the cube is refined by taking common literals, gradually expanding the represented state set until finding an inductive subclause or determining none exists.

This approach can be optimized with the complementary *up* procedure [13], which strengthens clauses by adding literals. However, a significant limitation persists: for a cube with many literals, the algorithm requires multiple expensive solver calls yet produces only a single generalized result. Our analysis shows that a single generalization computation could yield multiple valid generalizations, identifying additional CTIs and expanding the set of unreachable states. We propose a combinatorial verification approach that enables discovering multiple valid invariants within a single solver invocation, significantly reducing verification time while maintaining soundness guarantees.

Algorithm 1. IC3 generalization procedure

```
procedure MIC(q: cube ref, i: level)
    for each literal l in q do
        q̂ := q \ l
        if down(q̂, i) then
            q := q̂
        end if
    end for
end procedure
procedure DOWN(q: cube ref, i: level)
    while true do
        if I ⇏ ¬q then
            return false
        end if
        if F_i ∧ ¬q ∧ T ⇒ ¬q' then
            return true
        end if
        with (F_i ∧ ¬q)-state s:
            q := q ⊔ s
    end while
end procedure
```

3 Enhanced Generalization Through Batch Clause Construction

Based on our analysis of the IC3 algorithm and its generalization process described earlier, traditional IC3 implementations must frequently perform generalization operations during both blocking and propagation phases. However, this approach suffers from a significant computational bottleneck: each generalization of a candidate clause requires substantial computation yet yields only a single generalized result. Our key insight reverses this conventional approach—instead of sequentially testing literals for removal, we construct potential generalization candidates and verify whether they satisfy the required properties. This enables us to obtain multiple valid generalized clauses within a single generalization process. This batch processing approach simultaneously identifies multiple unreachable state sets, more effectively constrains the search space, and optimizes the verification path by constructing shorter, more precise clauses for verification. By reducing the computational complexity of individual verification steps, we significantly decrease overall verification difficulty and time consumption.

Below, we detail our proposed batch clause construction methodology:

3.1 Formal Framework for Batch Generalization

Definition 1 (Literal Inductiveness Properties). *Given a transition system* $\mathcal{S} = (X, I, T, P)$ *and a literal* l *in a clause* $C = l_1 \vee l_2 \vee \ldots \vee l_n$*, we define two key properties:*

1. ***Initial Inductiveness:*** *A literal l is initially inductive if $I \models l$.*
2. ***Consecution Inductiveness:*** *A literal l is consecutively inductive relative to frame F_k if $F_k \wedge \neg l \wedge T \models l'$, where l' is the primed version of l.*

If a literal satisfies both inductiveness properties, it can be used to strengthen the invariant and provide a more concise representation of the unreachable state space.

Definition 2 (Literal Classification Sets). *During the batch generalization process, literals from a candidate clause $C = l_1 \vee l_2 \vee \ldots \vee l_n$ are classified into three sets:*

1. ***Keep Set*** *K: Literals that must be retained in the generalized clause.*
2. ***Head Set*** *H: Literals that satisfy initial inductiveness but fail consecution inductiveness.*
3. ***Drop Set*** *D: Literals that are candidates for removal, where $H \subseteq D$.*

Our batch generalization approach operates in two phases: individual literal analysis followed by combinatorial verification of literal subsets.

Phase 1: Individual Literal Analysis. For each literal l_i in clause $C = l_1 \vee l_2 \vee \ldots \vee l_n$, we perform two verification checks:

1 **Initial State Check**:

$$\text{Check satisfiability of } I \wedge \neg l_i \tag{1}$$

2 **Inductive Step Verification**:

$$\text{Check satisfiability of } P \wedge F_k \wedge T \wedge l_i \wedge \neg l_i' \tag{2}$$

During verification, each literal is dynamically classified based on its properties:

- For each literal l_i in clause C, we first perform an initial inductiveness check to determine if $I \wedge \neg l_i$ is UNSAT.
- If this initial check is UNSAT (meaning l_i is initially inductive), we then perform a consecution check to determine if $P \wedge F_k \wedge T \wedge l_i \wedge \neg l_i'$ is UNSAT.
- If both the initial and consecution checks are UNSAT, the literal satisfies both inductiveness properties and is placed in the Keep Set K.
- If the initial check is UNSAT but the consecution check is SAT, the literal satisfies initial inductiveness but fails consecution. In this case, we add l_i to both the Head Set H and the Drop Set D, and cache its satisfying model for later optimization.
- If the initial check is SAT, the literal fails initial inductiveness and is directly added to the Drop Set D as a candidate for removal.

Lemma 1 (Keep Set Invariant). *Any clause formed by a subset of literals from the Keep Set K maintains the invariant properties of the original clause with respect to F_k. This follows directly from the definition of the Keep Set.*

Phase 2: Combinatorial Verification. After classifying all literals, we perform combinatorial verification on pairs of literals from the Drop Set to identify additional valid generalizations.

Definition 3 (Combinatorial Verification Conditions). *For a subset of literals $\{l_i, l_j\} \subseteq D$, we define two verification conditions:*

1. ***Composite Initial Check:***

$$\textit{Check satisfiability of } I \wedge (\neg l_i \wedge \neg l_j) \tag{3}$$

2. ***Augmented Inductive Verification:***

$$\textit{Check satisfiability of } P \wedge F_k \wedge T \wedge (l_i \wedge l_j) \wedge (\neg l_i' \wedge \neg l_j') \tag{4}$$

Lemma 2 (Head Set Optimization). *If $l_i \in H$, then for any $l_j \in D$, the Composite Initial Check $I \wedge (\neg l_i \vee \neg l_j)$ is automatically UNSAT, as $I \wedge \neg l_i$ is already UNSAT.*

Lemma 3 (Model Reuse). *For literals $l_i, l_j \in H$ with cached models M_i and M_j from their individual inductive verification checks, if either $M_i \models \neg l_j'$ or $M_j \models \neg l_i'$, then the Augmented Inductive Verification for $\{l_i, l_j\}$ is UNSAT without requiring a new solver call.*

Theorem 1 (Batch Generalization Soundness). *Any clause formed by retaining all literals in the Keep Set K and excluding a subset of literals from the Drop Set D that passes combinatorial verification forms a valid inductive generalization of the original clause.*

The combinatorial verification process significantly expands the generalization potential by allowing multiple different valid generalizations to be discovered in a single solver invocation. Furthermore, the use of cached models from individual checks enables many verification conditions to be resolved through logical inference rather than expensive solver calls.

3.2 Implementation Details: Model Caching

To efficiently implement the batch generalization approach, we employ an optimized model caching system and incremental solving strategies:

Definition 4 (Model Cache Structure). *The model cache is implemented as a hash table $\mathcal{H}$ where:*

- *Keys are formula signatures derived from $P \wedge F_k \wedge T \wedge l_i \wedge \neg l_i'$*
- *Values are pairs $\langle Model_i, Result_i \rangle$ where $Model_i$ is the satisfying assignment and $Result_i \in \{SAT, UNSAT\}$*

The cache supports $\mathcal{O}(1)$ lookup operations for previously computed results.

Algorithm 2 illustrates our novel batch generalization algorithm with integrated model caching. This approach systematically explores multiple generalization trajectories concurrently while efficiently reusing intermediate computation results through our caching mechanism. The combinatorial verification strategy not only yields more comprehensive and precise generalizations but also substantially reduces the overall verification complexity. Our empirical evaluation confirms that this approach achieves considerable performance improvements over conventional sequential IC3 generalization techniques, particularly for complex transition systems with large state spaces.

Algorithm 2. BCCIC3

```
procedure BatchGeneralize(C, F_k)
    K ← ∅, H ← ∅, D ← ∅, G ← ∅, ℋ ← ∅        ▷ initialize sets and cache        ▷ Phase 1: Individual Literal Analysis
    for each literal l_i in C do
        if I ∧ ¬l_i ⊨ ⊥ then                                ▷ check initial inductiveness
            if P ∧ F_k ∧ T ∧ l_i ∧ ¬l'_i ⊨ ⊥ then             ▷ check consecution
                K ← K ∪ {l_i}                                 ▷ add to keep set
            else
                M_i ← model of P ∧ F_k ∧ T ∧ l_i ∧ ¬l'_i; ℋ[l_i] ← ⟨M_i, SAT⟩
                H ← H ∪ {l_i}; D ← D ∪ {l_i}                  ▷ add to head and drop sets
            end if
        else
            D ← D ∪ {l_i}                                     ▷ add to drop set
        end if
    end for                                   ▷ Phase 2: Combinatorial Verification
    for each pair {l_i, l_j} ⊆ D do
        if l_i ∈ H or l_j ∈ H then
            initialCheck ← UNSAT
        else
            initialCheck ← Check(I ∧ (¬l_i ∨ ¬l_j))
        end if
        if initialCheck ⊨ ⊥ then
            if l_i ∈ H and l_j ∈ H then
                Retrieve M_i, M_j from cache;
                if M_i ⊨ ¬l'_j or M_j ⊨ ¬l'_i then
                    inductiveCheck ← UNSAT
                else
                    inductiveCheck ← Check(P ∧ F_k ∧ T ∧ (l_i ∨ l_j) ∧ (¬l'_i ∨ ¬l'_j))
                end if
            else
                inductiveCheck ← Check(P ∧ F_k ∧ T ∧ (l_i ∨ l_j) ∧ (¬l'_i ∨ ¬l'_j))
            end if
            if inductiveCheck ⊨ ⊥ then
                G ← G ∪ {C \ {l_i, l_j}}
            end if
        end if
    end for
    return G                                  ▷ return set of generalized clauses
end procedure
```

Optimization Techniques

1. **Incremental Solver Context**: We maintain a persistent SMT solver context across verification queries, preserving the solver state and learned clauses between related checks. This eliminates costly solver reinitialization, particularly beneficial when verifying multiple literal combinations from the same clause.

2. **Model-Based Inference**: When verifying combinatorial conditions for literals $l_i, l_j \in H$, we leverage cached models to perform inference:

$$\text{If } M_i \models \neg l'_j, \text{ then } P \wedge F_k \wedge T \wedge (l_i \vee l_j) \wedge (\neg l'_i \vee \neg l'_j) \text{ is UNSAT} \quad (5)$$

This inference significantly reduces the number of solver calls required during verification.
3. **Formula Signature Compression**: To minimize hash table memory overhead, we employ bitvector compression for formula signatures, substantially reducing storage requirements while maintaining collision resistance.
4. **Temporal Coherence Management**: The cache implements version-aware invalidation based on frame indices, automatically clearing entries when frames are refined or propagated to maintain correctness.

Performance Optimization. Our implementation utilizes an LRU (Least Recently Used) replacement strategy for the model cache, prioritizing retention of frequently accessed entries. Empirical evaluation shows this approach achieves substantially higher hit rates compared to naive implementations, particularly effective in verification tasks with repetitive structural patterns.

4 Experiment

4.1 Benchmark and Experimental Setup

We evaluated our approach using the FMCAD08 benchmark suite, a standard collection for assessing formal verification tools. All experiments were conducted on an Intel Core i7-12700H (2.30GHz) with 32GB RAM running Ubuntu 22.04 LTS. Our implementation (BCCIC3) was compared against the standard IC3 algorithm in KIND2 [2], with a timeout limit of 500 s per benchmark. The cases in the FMCAD08 subset are primarily written in the Lustre language, a synchronous data flow language particularly suitable for describing reactive systems and natively supported by the KIND2 tool. Each benchmark typically includes model files describing system behavior, property files defining assertions to be verified, and expected results indicating property correctness. The FMCAD08 benchmark suite is an important component of KIND2-benchmarks and can be accessed through the KIND2 GitHub repository at https://github.com/kind2-mc/kind2-benchmarks/tree/master/FMCAD08.

Our evaluation was conducted in two phases. In the first phase, we selected 148 representative models from the FMCAD08 subset to validate our approach. In the second phase, we expanded our analysis to all 1349 examples in the FMCAD08 benchmark suite to verify consistent performance gains. It is worth noting that our baseline is the standard IC3 implementation in KIND2, highlighting the fundamental advantages of our approach.

To assess performance, we primarily measured verification time (total wall-clock time required to complete verification), memory usage, solver call count, and generalization efficiency (number of inductive clauses generated per generalization phase). A timeout limit of 500 s was imposed for each benchmark.

We compared our proposed method against the standard IC3 implementation in KIND2.

Experimental results were systematically collected and summarized in a spreadsheet, recording each tool's performance on every benchmark instance. The data includes model name, property, verification time, memory usage, solver call count, and result status. For each metric, we report both aggregate statistics and detailed per-instance results. All experimental materials, including code, scripts, and benchmark configurations, are available upon request.

4.2 Performance Analysis

Table 1. Performance Comparison on Representative Models (Total Time)

Category	Models	IC3(s)	BCCIC3(s)	Impr.%	$\Delta Time(s)$
Real_Int	21	337.90	284.42	15.83	53.48
Int	66	460.05	364.96	20.67	95.09
Int32	61	1626.85	1238.29	23.88	388.56
Total	148	2424.80	1887.67	22.15	537.13

Table 1 presents the results of our initial evaluation of 148 representative benchmark models. The data reveals a correlation between problem complexity and improvement efficacy. The Int32 category, despite comprising fewer models than the Int category (61 versus 66), required significantly more execution time with the standard IC3 implementation (1626.85 s compared to 460.05 s), indicating substantially higher computational complexity. Notably, our approach demonstrates varying efficacy across different problem categories: the Real_Int category shows a 15.83% improvement, while the Int and Int32 categories exhibit more substantial gains of 20.67% and 23.88% respectively. This progressive enhancement aligns with our theoretical foundation, as batch clause construction offers greater optimization opportunities when processing complex state spaces with numerous interrelated variables. In the computationally intensive Int32 category, our method reduced execution time by 388.56 s, constituting approximately 72% of the total time savings across all test cases. Overall, the 22.15% improvement across all selected benchmarks represents a significant enhancement in verification efficiency, particularly considering that IC3 is already highly optimized in standard implementations.

As shown in Table 2, our comprehensive evaluation across all 1349 models from the FMCAD08 benchmark suite confirms the effectiveness of our approach with an overall execution time reduction of 21.21%. The results reveal interesting performance variations across different model categories. The FuncChain models, although representing only a small fraction of the test cases (7 models), demonstrated the most dramatic improvement at 57.03%, suggesting our

Table 2. Performance Comparison on 1349 FMCAD08 Models (Total Time)

Category	Models	IC3(s)	BCCIC3(s)	Impr.%	$\Delta Time(s)$
FuncChain	7	227.67	97.83	57.03	129.84
Int32	587	5395.19	4330.03	19.74	1065.16
Int	730	1636.39	1290.65	21.13	345.74
Bool	25	1.25	1.83	−46.24	−0.58
Total	1349	7260.50	5720.34	21.21	1540.16

batch clause construction approach is particularly effective for certain specialized verification tasks. The Int and Int32 categories, which comprise the majority of the benchmark (730 and 587 models respectively), showed consistent performance improvements of 21.13% and 19.74%, indicating robust gains across diverse problem complexities. One notable exception was observed in the Bool category, where our approach experienced a slight performance degradation (-46.24 To provide a more comprehensive analysis of our approach, we conducted a detailed examination of algorithm performance across all 1349 benchmark instances. Figure 3 presents the execution time comparison between the standard IC3 algorithm and our BCCIC3 approach. Each data point represents an individual verification task, with the diagonal dashed line indicating equivalent performance. Points below this line demonstrate cases where BCCIC3 outperforms IC3, while the color gradient indicates the absolute time improvement in seconds.

4.3 Performance Visualization

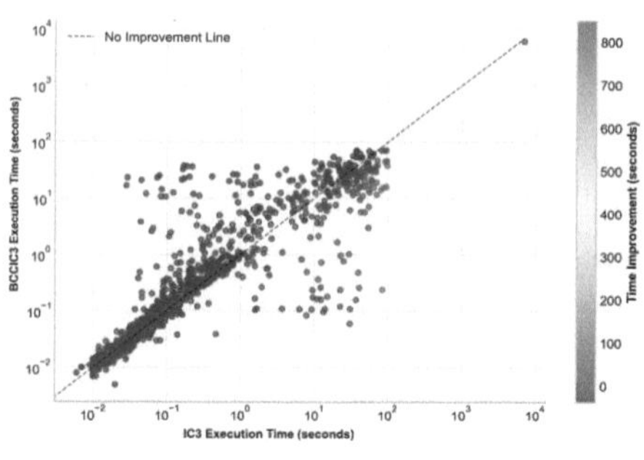

Fig. 3. Execution time comparison between IC3 and BCCIC3 across 1349 verification tasks. Points below the diagonal line represent improved performance.

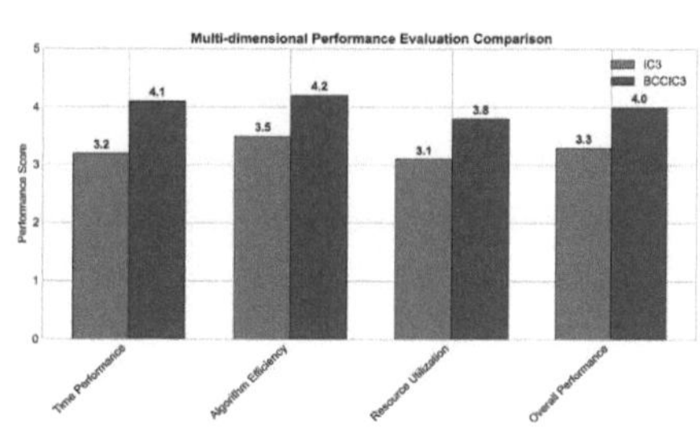

Fig. 4. Multi-dimensional performance evaluation comparing IC3 and BCCIC3 across four key metrics on a 5-point scale.

Figure 3 visualizes the execution time comparison between standard IC3 and BCCIC3. Approximately 57.2% of verification tasks showed improvement, with greater benefits observed as problem complexity increased. The improvement was most pronounced for tasks requiring 1–100 s with standard IC3, confirming that batch processing yields greater benefits for complex state spaces where redundant solver invocations are more common.

Figure 4 presents a multi-dimensional evaluation of our approach. Time performance improved from 3.2 to 4.1 (28.1% increase), while algorithm efficiency showed the most substantial enhancement, increasing from 3.5 to 4.2. This metric specifically measures solver invocation optimization—critical given that solver calls constitute approximately 70% of IC3's computational workload. Resource utilization improved from 3.1 to 3.8, reflecting more efficient memory management and reduced computational overhead through our combinatorial verification approach. The overall performance score increased from 3.3 to 4.0, closely aligning with the 21.21% reduction in total execution time.

These results confirm that our batch clause construction and incremental solving approach significantly enhances IC3 performance, particularly for complex verification tasks. By enabling the discovery of multiple inductive clauses from a single solver invocation, our method substantially reduces the computational overhead of the verification process while maintaining or improving the quality of discovered invariants.

5 Related Work

Model checking has evolved significantly since its inception, progressing from explicit state enumeration techniques [25] to more scalable symbolic approaches. Early explicit techniques, while conceptually straightforward, suffered from state explosion limitations and have been largely superseded by symbolic methods utilizing BDDs and, more efficiently, SAT solvers. Indeed, SAT-based model checking is now widely recognized as the most promising automatic verification approach for industrial applications [24].

State-of-the-art SAT-based model checking techniques include Bounded Model Checking (BMC) [24], Interpolation-based Model Checking (IMC) [16], IC3/PDR [1], and Counterexample-Guided Abstraction Refinement (CEGAR) [17]. BMC was the first approach to reduce model checking to SAT, where each query with a k-unrolling system answers whether a counterexample of length k exists. While effective at finding bugs, BMC struggles with correctness proofs for complex systems [5]. IMC builds upon BMC by maintaining an over-approximate state sequence refined using interpolants from unsatisfiable SAT queries, but both approaches face scalability challenges as formula sizes increase exponentially.

IC3/PDR represents a significant advancement by unrolling the system at most once, substantially reducing the computational burden of individual SAT queries. It computes Minimal Inductive Clauses (MICs) to refine an incremental over-approximate sequence, demonstrating particular strength in proving correctness. Recent years have seen numerous extensions to IC3/PDR. Hassan et al. [13] introduced complementary generalization techniques that explore different regions of the clause space more efficiently. Gurfinkel and Ivrii [6] developed "pushing" techniques to propagate clauses to higher frames earlier, while Vizel et al. [5] created hybrid approaches combining IC3 with interpolation-based methods.

More recent innovations include AVY/KAVY [18], which integrate IC3 with interpolation, and QUIP [19], which enhances quantifier handling. IC3-INN [20] leverages neural networks to guide the search process. Significant efforts have also focused on combining abstractions with IC3/PDR, as demonstrated in [21] and [15].

The Complementary Approximate Reachability (CAR) algorithm [22] represents another recent innovation that maintains both over- and under-approximate sequences for correctness proofs and bug finding, respectively. Unlike IC3/PDR, CAR's over-approximate sequence need not be incremental, following traditional reachability analysis approaches. This flexibility allows for easier integration of various heuristics, such as intersection and rotation strategies [20], which have demonstrated performance improvements. While CAR excels at bug finding, it generally underperforms IC3/PDR in proving correctness.

Parallel implementations have emerged as another promising direction. Berryhill et al. [14] explored learning support sets in IC3 that can be parallelized, while Marescotti et al. [23] developed a GPU-accelerated version of IC3.

Our work takes a different approach by focusing on the efficiency of individual solver invocations. Rather than parallelizing the algorithm or developing hybrid techniques, we fundamentally reorient the clause generalization process to extract multiple valid invariants from a single solver invocation. This batch clause construction technique represents a novel optimization that addresses the core inefficiency in IC3's generalization phase, where substantial solver effort typically yields only a single inductive clause. By enabling the discovery of multiple inductive clauses simultaneously, our approach significantly improves verification performance for complex systems while maintaining the theoretical strengths of IC3.

6 Conclusion

In this paper, we presented BCCIC3, a novel approach that enhances the IC3 algorithm through batch clause construction and incremental solving techniques. We identified a fundamental inefficiency in traditional IC3 implementations—the sequential nature of clause generalization that yields only a single inductive clause despite substantial solver effort—and developed a combinatorial verification framework that constructs and verifies multiple potential generalizations simultaneously. Our approach leverages efficient model caching and inference mechanisms to derive multiple valid clause generalizations within a single solver invocation, while maintaining theoretical soundness as demonstrated through comprehensive experimental evaluation. The results show that BCCIC3 achieves a 21.21% overall reduction in verification time across 1349 benchmark models, with gains of up to 57.03% for specialized verification tasks, effectively addressing the computational bottleneck in IC3's generalization phase. Looking forward, our work opens several promising research directions, including parallel clause generation for multi-core architectures, context-aware caching strategies, abstraction-guided prioritization of generalization candidates, and adaptation to other formal verification algorithms. By enabling more efficient exploration of invariant spaces, our approach brings formal verification closer to practical application in complex systems where traditional approaches face scalability challenges.

References

1. Bradley, A.R.: SAT-based model checking without unrolling. In: Verification, Model Checking, and Abstract Interpretation (VMCAI), pp. 70–87 (2011)
2. Champion, A., Mebsout, A., Sticksel, C., Tinelli, C.: The KIND2 model checker. In: Computer Aided Verification (CAV), pp. 510–517 (2016)
3. Bradley, A.R.: Understanding IC3. In: Theory and Applications of Satisfiability Testing (SAT), pp. 1–14 (2012)
4. Een, N., Mishchenko, A., Brayton, R.: Efficient implementation of property directed reachability. In: Formal Methods in Computer-Aided Design (FMCAD), pp. 125–134 (2011)
5. Vizel, Y., Gurfinkel, A., Malik, S.: Fast interpolating BMC. In: Computer Aided Verification (CAV), pp. 641–657 (2015)
6. Gurfinkel, A., Ivrii, A.: Pushing to the top. In: Formal Methods in Computer-Aided Design (FMCAD), pp. 65–72 (2015)
7. Welp, T., Kuehlmann, A.: QF BV model checking with property directed reachability. In: Design, Automation & Test in Europe (DATE), pp. 791–796 (2013)
8. Chockler, H., Ivrii, A., Matsliah, A., Moran, S., Nevo, Z.: Incremental formal verification of hardware. In: Formal Methods in Computer-Aided Design (FMCAD), pp. 135–143 (2011)
9. Komuravelli, A., Gurfinkel, A., Chaki, S.: SMT-based model checking for recursive programs. In: Biere, A., Bloem, R. (eds.) CAV 2014. LNCS, vol. 8559, pp. 17–34. Springer, Cham (2014). https://doi.org/10.1007/978-3-319-08867-9_2
10. Cimatti, A., Griggio, A., Mover, S., Tonetta, S.: IC3 modulo theories via implicit predicate abstraction. In: Ábrahám, E., Havelund, K. (eds.) TACAS 2014. LNCS, vol. 8413, pp. 46–61. Springer, Heidelberg (2014). https://doi.org/10.1007/978-3-642-54862-8_4
11. Hoder, K., Bjørner, N.: Generalized property directed reachability. In: Theory and Applications of Satisfiability Testing (SAT), pp. 157–171 (2012)
12. Vizel, Y., Gurfinkel, A.: Interpolating property directed reachability. In: Computer Aided Verification (CAV), pp. 260–276 (2014)
13. Hassan, Z., Bradley, A.R., Somenzi, F.: Better generalization in IC3. In: Formal Methods in Computer-Aided Design (FMCAD), pp. 157–164 (2013)
14. Berryhill, R., Veneris, A.: Leveraging support sets for IC3 learning. In: Formal Methods in Computer-Aided Design (FMCAD), pp. 135–142 (2017)
15. Goel, A., Sakallah, K.: Model checking of verilog RTL using IC3 with syntax-guided abstraction. In: Badger, J.M., Rozier, K.Y. (eds.) NFM 2019. LNCS, vol. 11460, pp. 166–185. Springer, Cham (2019). https://doi.org/10.1007/978-3-030-20652-9_11
16. McMillan, K.L.: Interpolation and SAT-based model checking. In: Computer Aided Verification (CAV), pp. 1–13 (2003)

17. Clarke, E., Grumberg, O., Jha, S., Lu, Y., Veith, H.: Counterexample-guided abstraction refinement for symbolic model checking. J. ACM **50**(5), 752–794 (2003)
18. Vizel, Y., Weissenbacher, G., Malik, S.: Lazy abstraction with interpolants for arrays. In: Logic for Programming, Artificial Intelligence and Reasoning (LPAR), pp. 167–185 (2017)
19. Blicha, M., Hyvärinen, A.E.J., Kofroň, J., Sharygina, N.: Decomposing farkas interpolants. In: Vojnar, T., Zhang, L. (eds.) TACAS 2019. LNCS, vol. 11427, pp. 3–20. Springer, Cham (2019). https://doi.org/10.1007/978-3-030-17462-0_1
20. Zhang, H., Gupta, A., Malik, S.: Verification acceleration with deep learning. In: Design Automation Conference (DAC), pp. 1–6 (2018)
21. Cimatti, A., Griggio, A., Mover, S., Tonetta, S.: Infinite-state invariant checking with IC3 and predicate abstraction. Formal Methods Syst. Des. **49**(3), 190–218 (2016)
22. Jovanović, D., Dutertre, B.: Property-directed k-induction. In: Formal Methods in Computer-Aided Design (FMCAD), pp. 85–92 (2016)
23. Marescotti, M., Hyvärinen, A.E.J., Sharygina, N.: SMTS: distributed, visualized constraint solving. In: Logic for Programming, Artificial Intelligence and Reasoning (LPAR), pp. 534–542 (2017)
24. Brayton, R., Mishchenko, A.: ABC: an academic industrial-strength verification tool. In: Computer Aided Verification (CAV), pp. 24–40 (2010)
25. Clarke, E.M., Henzinger, T.A., Veith, H., Bloem, R.: Handbook of Model Checking. Springer, Cham (2018)

MetaLogic: Robustness Evaluation of Text-to-Image Models via Logically Equivalent Prompts

Yifan Shen(✉), Yangyang Shu, Hye-young Paik, and Yulei Sui

University of New South Wales, Sydney, Australia
yifan.shen3@student.unsw.edu.au, {yangyang.shu,h.paik,y.sui}@unsw.edu.au

Abstract. Recent advances in text-to-image (T2I) models, especially diffusion-based architectures, have significantly improved the visual quality of generated images. However, these models continue to struggle with a critical limitation: maintaining semantic consistency when input prompts undergo minor linguistic variations. Despite being logically equivalent, such prompt pairs often yield misaligned or semantically inconsistent images, exposing a lack of robustness in reasoning and generalisation. To address this, we propose MetaLogic, a novel evaluation framework that detects T2I misalignment without relying on ground truth images. MetaLogic leverages metamorphic testing, generating image pairs from prompts that differ grammatically but are semantically identical. By directly comparing these image pairs, the framework identifies inconsistencies that signal failures in preserving the intended meaning, effectively diagnosing robustness issues in the model's logic understanding. Unlike existing evaluation methods that compare a generated image to a single prompt, MetaLogic evaluates semantic equivalence between paired images, offering a scalable, ground-truth-free approach to identifying alignment failures. It categorises these alignment errors (e.g., entity omission, duplication, positional misalignment) and surfaces counterexamples that can be used for model debugging and refinement. We evaluate MetaLogic across multiple state-of-the-art T2I models and reveal consistent robustness failures across a range of logical constructs. We find that even the SOTA text-to-image models like Flux.dev and DALLE-3 demonstrate a 59% and 71% misalignment rate, respectively. Our results show that MetaLogic is not only efficient and scalable, but also effective in uncovering fine-grained logical inconsistencies that are overlooked by existing evaluation metrics.

Keywords: Metamorphic testing · Image generation evaluation · Semantic misalignment · Robustness evaluation

1 Introduction

Text-to-image (T2I) generation has made remarkable strides in recent years, largely due to innovations in generative architectures such as diffusion mod-

É. André et al. (Eds.): ICFEM 2025, LNCS 16229, pp. 152–171, 2026.
https://doi.org/10.1007/978-981-95-4213-0_9

els (e.g., Imagen, GLIDE, DALLE-2) [16,18,19]. These models now produce high-quality and visually coherent outputs and have found applications across creative industries, education, healthcare, and architectural design. However, despite improvements in image fidelity, a critical limitation remains: **the semantic alignment between the generated image and the intended meaning of the input prompt.** In particular, these models often struggle to preserve logical consistency when semantically equivalent but syntactically different prompts are used.

This shortcoming reveals a fundamental issue of **robustness**, a reliable T2I model should generate semantically consistent images even when minor, logically equivalent variations are made to the input text. Yet, even state-of-the-art models frequently produce divergent outputs for prompts that differ only in phrasing but express the same logical content. For example, given the prompts "a cat next to a dog, with an apple" and "a dog next to a cat, with an apple," some models omit entities or alter the spatial relationships, revealing poor generalisation under minimal semantic perturbations.

In parallel, logic has also been applied on the generation side. For instance, Sueyoshi et al. [22] introduces Predicate Diffusion, which incorporates predicate logic constraints into diffusion models to improve prompt-image alignment. While complementary to our aims, such methods focus on logic-guided generation rather than evaluation.

Traditional evaluation methods, such as CLIPScore [17] or VQA-based frameworks (e.g., TIFA [10]), rely on comparing a generated image to its original text prompt, treating the text as a proxy ground truth. These methods are often computationally expensive, susceptible to biases, and fail to adequately assess fine-grained logical consistency. Moreover, they do not scale efficiently to large datasets and are not designed to evaluate robustness under semantically equivalent prompt variations.

To address these limitations, we introduce MetaLogic, a novel framework that shifts the evaluation paradigm from text-image alignment to **text-to-image pairwise robustness**. Rather than comparing a single image to its corresponding prompt, MetaLogic's novelty lies in using pairs of logically equivalent prompts to generate two images and comparing them directly. If the model is logically consistent and robust, these image pairs should be semantically identical. Misalignments between the generated image pair, despite semantic equivalence in their prompts, serve as counterexamples that highlight the model's failure to maintain logical consistency and robustness. These inconsistencies were observed across 1600 images generated by state-of-the-art models such as DALLE-3 [2] and Flux.dev [12], and they become increasingly pronounced as the logical complexity of prompts grows, posing significant challenges for users who expect consistent and reliable outputs.

Through extensive experiments, we show that MetaLogic not only detects misalignments due to robustness issues but also systematically categorises logical errors, including entity omission, duplication, and spatial misplacement, providing valuable insights for debugging and improving generative models. Unlike traditional approaches, MetaLogic enables scalable, oracle-free evaluation while emphasising the core requirement of robust semantic preservation under linguistic perturbation.

Our framework draws inspiration from predicate logic equivalence and metamorphic testing, a software testing methodology designed for systems without a reliable oracle. By using logically equivalent prompts as metamorphic relations, we circumvent the need for external ground truth and enable efficient, scalable evaluation of text-to-image robustness. These comparisons reveal fine-grained logical inconsistencies across a wide range of logic categories, including commutativity, associativity, distributivity, and DeMorgan transformations.

We summarise the main contributions of this work as follows:

- Robustness-oriented evaluation via counterexample generation: We propose a novel method to evaluate the robustness of text-to-image (T2I) models by measuring the semantic consistency of image pairs generated from logically equivalent prompts. Our approach systematically identifies and categorises inconsistencies as counterexamples, providing concrete evidence of model errors and enabling deeper analysis of failure modes.
- Ground truth-free detection of alignment errors: Our metamorphic testing approach avoids reliance on external labels by treating one generated image as the oracle for another, enabling scalable and efficient evaluation.
- Comprehensive analysis of state-of-the-art models: We apply our framework to two leading T2I models, Flux.dev and DALLE-3, evaluating their robustness across five categories of logical equivalence; Associative, Commutative, DeMorgan, Distributive, and Complement. The analysis is based on three semantic criteria: object presence, spatial positioning, and entity count, providing a multifaceted view of model performance under logical perturbations.

2 Preliminaries

In this section, we discuss the necessary preliminary knowledge and prior work, highlight their differences from ours, and then present our approach and methodology in detail.

Zero-Shot Image Classifiers. CLIP (Contrastive LanguageâĂŞImage Pretraining) [17] is a widely used benchmark for text-image alignment, trained on millions of image-text pairs to learn a joint embedding space where related images and texts are nearby. CLIPScore measures alignment via cosine similarity between embeddings. As a zero-shot classifier, CLIP works without ground truth labels, offering flexibility across tasks. However, it struggles with fine-grained semantics, logical reasoning, and complex prompts [1]. Consequently, in the context of this work, which focuses on detecting subtle logical inconsistencies, CLIP is used only as a coarse-grained baseline, not as a reliable measure for logic-sensitive evaluation.

VQA-Based Alignment Evaluation. The TIFA framework [10] evaluates text-image alignment using Vision Question Answering (VQA) models. An LLM generates question-answer pairs from the text prompt, and a VQA model answers these questions based on the image; alignment is measured by comparing the answers. However, generating QA pairs and VQA answers for each image is computationally intensive and limits scalability. Similarly, Singh et al. [21] propose Decompositional-Alignment-Score, where an LLM decomposes the prompt into factual assertions evaluated by a VQA model. While improving interpretability, it faces the same scalability challenges as TIFA.

Object-Based Evaluation. Object detection-based frameworks evaluate text-image alignment by comparing generated images against structured ground truth from standardised templates, as seen in TIAM [9] and GenEval [8]. While more computationally efficient than VQA-based methods, their reliance on templates and detectable entities limits flexibility with open-ended prompts. GenEval further categorises prompts into tasks (e.g., object recognition, counting, colour, spatial relations), enabling fine-grained diagnostics and identifying specific model failures for targeted improvements.

Logic-Based Evaluation. Recent work has integrated logical reasoning into AI evaluation. LogicAsker [23] tests LLMs using logic-based challenges (e.g., propositional logic, quantifiers, conditionals), with correctness judged against ground truth answers. In contrast, our MetaLogic framework removes the need for ground truth by applying metamorphic testing: it generates logically equivalent prompts in different forms, and misalignments between the resulting images indicate failures in logical consistency. This approach is well-suited for T2I models, where ground truth is often missing. Unlike LogicAsker's textual focus, our MetaLogic enables robust, oracle-free evaluation of logical consistency.

Metamorphic Testing. MetaLogic is grounded in predicate-logic-based metamorphic testing, a technique used when a reliable output oracle is unavailable [4,5,20]. Instead of verifying individual outputs, it evaluates the consistency between outputs by leveraging known input-output relationships, called metamorphic relations. For example, since $\sin(x) = \sin(\pi - x)$, a program claiming to compute $\sin(x)$ can be tested by comparing these outputs without needing exact ground truth. Similarly, MetaLogic tests T2I models by generating logically equivalent prompts and checking for alignment in the resulting images, revealing failures when consistency breaks.

Reasoning Capabilities in AI Models. A fundamental component of understanding logic is a high level of reasoning capabilities [3]. High-level reasoning is a core step in the gradual evolution of deep learning models, evident from the release of modern reasoning models, a progression from early large language models [11]. A recent study by [14] puts into question the robustness of mathematical reasoning in modern large language models. They observed that by introducing additional clauses, irrelevant to the process of reaching the final answer, a significant performance drop occurred across all state-of-the-art models. The observed fragility of current LLMs makes one question their relevance to other models in close proximity, such as text-to-image.

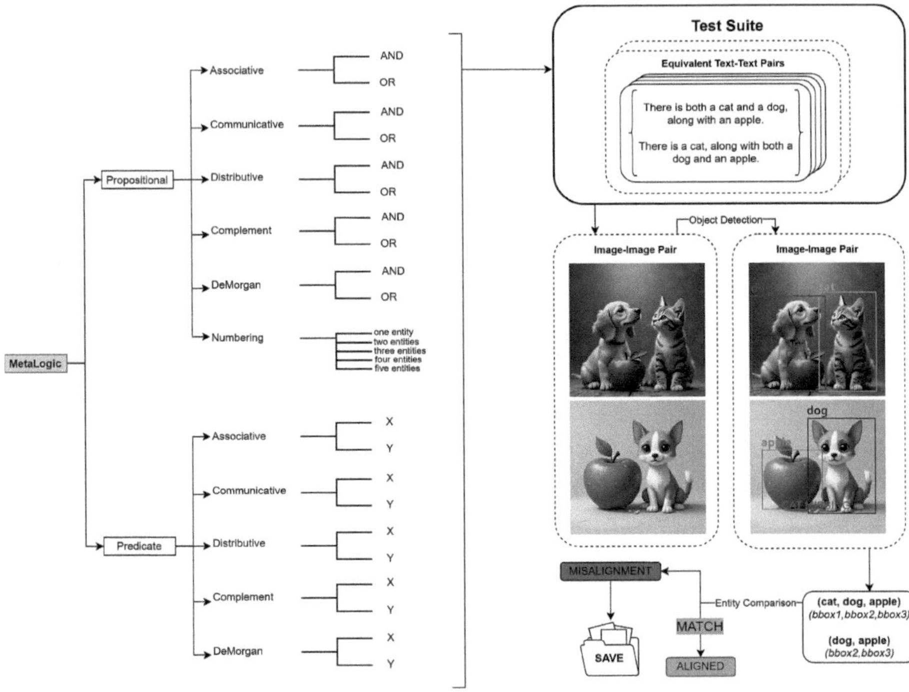

Fig. 1. Outline of MetaLogic framework which is split into two main sections. The left tree diagram shows the breakdown of all logic prompt categories and how they relate to each other. The right side outlines the misalignment detection process where we compare two images, generated from equivalent text pairs. Any detected inconsistencies are logged and saved as a counterexample.

3 Our Approach

We introduce a new framework in Fig. 1 to quickly and precisely identify text-image misalignment due to model robustness issues and procure effective counterexamples for model improvement. With speed and efficiency at the forefront, we present a methodology based on comparing image-image pairs instead of text-image pairs seen in existing methods. To facilitate the image-image comparison, we employ logic equivalence laws in each text-text pair. Hence, the text pairs for each image pair would be grammatically different but semantically equivalent. A fully robust T2I model would perfectly translate the semantic equivalence in each text pair into semantically identical image pairs. Therefore, inconsistencies between image pairs infer the existence of a text-image misalignment in either text-image pair.

First, we determine the compatible logic equivalence laws to apply to our set of prompt pairs. We then generate multiple prompt pairs based on the previously determined equivalence laws. Lastly, we generate images from each logically equivalent prompt pair and compare the image-image pairs. Inconsistencies between image-image pairs are noted as text-image misalignment and taken as counterexample data for future model improvements (See Fig. 1).

3.1 Logic Equivalence Laws

The metamorphic relationship found in trigonometry can be applied to the realm of natural language in the form of logically equivalent sentence pairs. Logical equivalence can be defined as when two statements have the same semantic meaning but are written in different forms.

Table 1. Logic equivalence law categories used with their respective mathematical notation, prompt transformation condition and natural language example.

Law	Logical Equivalence	Prompt Transformation	Prompt Example
Commutative	$P \wedge Q \Leftrightarrow Q \wedge P$	Reordering entities	There is a cat and a dog ⇔ There is a dog and a cat
	$P \vee Q \Leftrightarrow Q \vee P$	Reordering entities	There is a cat or a dog ⇔ There is a dog or a cat
Associative	$(P \wedge Q) \wedge R \Leftrightarrow P \wedge (Q \wedge R)$	Shifting semantic pairing	There is both a cat and a dog, along with an apple ⇔ There is a cat, along with both a dog and an apple
	$(P \vee Q) \vee R \Leftrightarrow P \vee (Q \vee R)$	Shifting semantic pairing	There is either a cat or a dog, otherwise there is an apple ⇔ There is a cat, otherwise there is a dog or an apple
Distributive	$P \wedge (Q \vee R) \Leftrightarrow (P \wedge Q) \vee (P \wedge R)$	Sharing entity across group	There is a cat with either a dog or an apple ⇔ There is a cat with a dog or a cat with an apple
	$P \vee (Q \wedge R) \Leftrightarrow (P \vee Q) \wedge (P \vee R)$	Sharing entity across group	There is a cat or there is a dog and an apple ⇔ There is a cat or a dog or there is a cat or an apple
Complement	$\neg(\neg P) \Leftrightarrow P$	Double negatives	It is not true that there is not a cat ⇔ There is a cat
DeMorgan	$\neg(P \wedge Q) \Leftrightarrow \neg P \vee \neg Q$	Sharing negation and sign flip	There isn't a cat and a dog ⇔ There isn't a cat or there isn't a dog
DeMorgan	$\neg(P \vee Q) \Leftrightarrow \neg P \wedge \neg Q$	Sharing negation and sign flip	There isn't a cat or a dog ⇔ There isn't a cat and there isn't a dog

Propositional Logic Law Selection. The framework required a large suite of test cases to analyse in order to test a given T2I model. Luckily, logical equivalence is categorised into discrete laws that behave differently from each other. We list all the logic law categories considered in Table 1. Early on, a problem with the initial method theory was found that involved disjunctive (OR) statements. An OR statement allowed for either subject to correctly exist in a generated image and be considered correct. However, with our image comparison framework, if even two correct outcomes were to exist for each prompt in a pair, a hypothetically infallible model would still show "errors" half of the time. Multiple expected outcomes break the underlying principle of metamorphic testing, and forcibly implementing them would be outside our current scope. We came up with a workaround to overcome this problem, outlined in the following section. Additionally, the Idempotent law was removed due to oversimplification and lack of characteristics to scale efficiently. The final chosen logic equivalence law categories were *Commutative, Associative, Distributive, Complement, and DeMorgan* (See Table 1).

The "Disjunctive" Problem. As stated previously, a significant challenge in applying metamorphic testing to OR statements emerged early in our methodology development. Disjunctive (OR) statements inherently allow for multiple valid interpretations if a prompt states "There is a cat or a dog", both an image containing only a cat or an image containing only a dog would be considered correct. Multiple valid outcomes fundamentally conflicts with the metamorphic testing principle, which requires consistent outputs for equivalent inputs. To address this limitation while still including disjunctive logic in our evaluation, we developed a workaround: embedding conjunctive (AND) statements within disjunctive (OR) statements. For example, instead of simply testing "There is a cat or a dog" against "There is a dog or a cat", we test "There is [(a cat and a dog)] or [(a dog and a cat)]" against "There is [(a dog and a cat)] or [(a cat and a dog)]" (See Table 2). This approach ensures that both sides of the OR statement contain identical conjunctive expressions that differ only in grammatical structure but maintain semantic equivalence. By structuring OR statements this way, we preserve the metamorphic relationship while still evaluating the model's handling of disjunctive logic. This technique allowed us to expand our testing scope to include all major logical operations while maintaining the validity of our comparison methodology.

Combination Prompting. To vertically scale the three chosen logic laws, we increase the number of unique prompts without increasing length. We do this by creating a list of entities and creating unique combinations of text prompt pairs guided by each logic category.

Our implementation of combination prompting is similar to techniques such as dynamic prompting found in recent literature [15,25,26]. While these methods may differ in terminology, they share a common objective: to expand the test space by systematically generating prompt variations from a common baseline.

Table 2. The baseline standard prompt pair templates used in the test suite.

Law	Prompt pair template (e = entity)
Commutative (AND)	There is **(e1)** and **(e2)** ⇔ There is **(e2)** and **(e1)**
Commutative (OR)	There is **[(e1) and (e2)]** or **[(e2) and (e1)]** ⇔ There is **[(e2) and (e1)]** or **[(e1) and (e2)]**
Associative (AND)	There is both **[(e1) and (e2)]**, along with **(e3)** ⇔ There is **(e1)**, along with both **[(e2) and (e3)]**
Associative (OR)	There is either **[(e1) and (e2) and (e3)]** or **[(e1) and (e3) and (e2)]** ,otherwise there is **[(e2) and (e1) and (e3)]** ⇔
	There is **[(e1) and (e2) and (e3)]**, otherwise there is **[(e1) and (e3) and (e2)]** or **[(e2) and (e1) and (e3)]**
Distributive (AND)	There is **(e1)** with either both **[(e2) and (e3)]** or both **[(e3) and (e2)]** ⇔
	There is **(e1)** with both **[(e2) and (e3)]** or **(e1)** with both **[(e3) and (e2)]**
Distributive (OR)	There is either **[(e1), (e2) and (e3)]** or both **[(e1), (e3) and (e2)]** and **[(e2), (e3) and (e1)]** ⇔
	There is either **[(e1), (e2) and (e3)]** or **[(e1),(e3) and (e2)]**, and there is either **[(e1), (e2) and (e3)]** or **[(e2), (e3) and (e1)]**

Since we are testing how well any given T2I model understands logical nuances in natural language, the scope of entities is not of great concern. We seek failure by misunderstanding logic, not by mistaking the likeness of an exotic object or animal. Hence, we refer to the common entities that appear in the widely used MS COCO data set [13]. The entities chosen were a cat, a dog, an apple, a banana and a cow. As MS COCO is commonly used as training data and an evaluation tool, we determined that sharing similar object prompting would benefit our methodology.

Predicate Logic. Due to a number of logic equivalence laws being incompatible with metamorphic testing, further variability was required to extend the scope that our framework tested on T2I models. Up to this point, only propositional logic was used, so in an effort to increase variety, positional predicates were introduced. This not only increased our testing scope but also added positional understanding as an additional criteria in which we assess T2I models.

Numbering Prompts. To evaluate the models' ability to handle multiple instances of the same entity, we developed "numbering prompts" using a core set of four entities: cat, dog, apple, and banana. These prompts explicitly specified multiple occurrences of entities (e.g., "There are two cats and a dog" ⇔ "There is a dog and two cats"). We based these prompts on conjunctive commutative logic due to its simplicity, ensuring that the equivalence relationship remained

Table 3. The baseline positional prompt pair templates used in the test suite.

Law	Prompt pair template (e = entity)
Commutative (X)	There is **(e1) on the right** and **(e2) on the left** ⇔ There is **(e2) on the left** and **(e1) on the right**
Commutative (Y)	There is **(e1) on the bottom** and **(e2) on top** ⇔ There is **(e2) on top** and **(e1) on the bottom**
Associative (X)	There is both **[(e1) on the right and (e2) on the left]**, along with **(e3) in the middle** ⇔
	There is **(e1) on the right**, along with both (**[(e2) on the left and (e3) in the middle]**
Associative (Y)	There is both **[(e1) on the bottom and (e2) on top]**, along with **(e3) in the middle** ⇔
	There is **(e1) on the bottom**, along with both **[(e2) on top and (e3) in the middle]**
Distributive (X)	There is **(e1) on the right** with either both **[(e2) on left and (e3) in the middle]** or both
	[(e3) in the middle and (e2) on the left] ⇔ **There is (e1) on the right with both [(e2) on the left and (e3) in the middle]**
	or **(e1) on the right** with both **[(e3) in the middle and (e2) on the left]**
Distributive (Y)	There is **(e1) on the bottom** with either both **[(e2) on top and (e3) in the middle]** or both
	[(e3) in the middle and (e2) on top] ⇔ **There is (e1) on the bottom with both [(e2) on top and (e3) in the middle]**
	or **(e1) on the bottom** with both **[(e3) in the middle and (e2) on top]**

straightforward and consistent. This approach allowed us to test whether T2I models could maintain proper entity counts while handling basic logical relationships, providing insights into how these models process quantitative information alongside qualitative descriptions. For each entity, we created prompt pairs specifying one through five instances, allowing us to track alignment rates as entity counts increased.

3.2 Prompt Pair Generation

The generation of logic prompt pairs were divided into the five chosen equivalence laws, Associative, Commutative, Complement, Distributive and DeMorgan. These sections were then further subdivided into conjunctive (AND), disjunctive (OR), horizontal (X-axis) and vertical (Y-axis) positioning, resulting in 20 categories (See Fig. 2). The numbering prompts also span across four entities and 10 numbers, totalling 40 categories. Overall, we have 60 categories, hence 60 equivalent prompt pair templates to evaluate any text-to-image model (See Tables 2, 3, 4 and 5)

Table 4. The baseline negation prompt pair templates used in the test suite.

Law	Prompt pair template (e = entity)
Complement (AND)	There is **(e1)** and **(e2)**. ⇔ It is not the case that there is not **(e1)** and **(e2)**.
Complement (OR)	There is **(e1) and (e2)]** or **[(e2)** and (e1)] ⇔ It is not the case that there is not **[(e1) and (e2)]** or **[(e2) and (e1)]**.
Complement (X)	There is **[(e1) on the right]** and **[(e2) on the left]** ⇔ It is not the case that there is not **[(e1) on the right]** and **[(e2) on the left]**
Complement (Y)	There is **[(e1) on the bottom]** and **[(e2) on top]** ⇔ It is not the case that there is not **[(e1) on the bottom]** and **[(e2) on top]**
DeMorgan (AND)	It is not the case that there is **[no (e1) and no (e2)]** and **[no (e2) and no (e1)]** ⇔
	There isn't **[no (e1) and no (e2)]** or there isn't **[no (e2) and no (e1)]**
DeMorgan (OR)	It is not the case that there is **[no (e1) and no (e2)]** or **[no (e2) and no (e1)]** ⇔
	There isn't **[no (e1) and no (e2)]** and there isn't **[no (e2) and no (e1)]**
DeMorgan (X)	It is not the case that there is **[no (e1) on the right and no (e2) on the left]** and **[no (e2) on the left and no (e1) on the right]** ⇔
	There isn't **[no (e1) on the right and no (e2) on the left]** or there isn't **[no (e2) on the left and no (e1) on the right]**
DeMorgan (Y)	It is not the case that there is **[no (e1) on the bottom and no (e2) on top]** and **[no (e2) on top and no (e1) on the bottom]** ⇔
	There isn't **[no (e1) on the bottom and no (e2) on top]** or there isn't **[no (e2) on top and no (e1) on the bottom]**

Table 5. The baseline number prompt pair templates used in the test suite.

Law	Prompt pair template (e = entity)
Numbering (1)	There is a **(e1)** and *one* **(e2)** ⇔ There is *one* **(e1)** and a **(e2)**
Numbering (2)	There is a **(e1)** and *two* **(e2)** ⇔ There is *two* **(e1)** and a **(e2)**
Numbering (3)	There is a **(e1)** and *three* **(e2)** ⇔ There is *three* **(e1)** and a **(e2)**
Numbering (4)	There is a **(e1)** and *four* **(e2)** ⇔ There is *four* **(e1)** and a **(e2)**
Numbering (5)	There is a **(e1)** and *five* **(e2)** ⇔ There is *five* **(e1)** and a **(e2)**
Numbering (6)	There is a **(e1)** and *six* **(e2)** ⇔ There is *six* **(e1)** and a **(e2)**
Numbering (7)	There is a **(e1)** and *seven* **(e2)** ⇔ There is *seven* **(e1)** and a **(e2)**
Numbering (8)	There is a **(e1)** and *eight* **(e2)** ⇔ There is *eight* **(e1)** and a **(e2)**
Numbering (9)	There is a **(e1)** and *nine* **(e2)** ⇔ There is *nine* **(e1)** and a **(e2)**
Numbering (10)	There is a **(e1)** and *ten* **(e2)** ⇔ There is *ten* **(e1)** and a **(e2)**

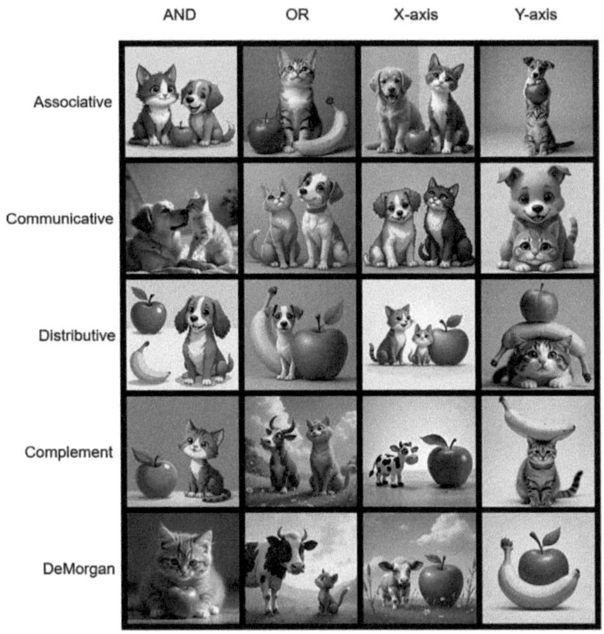

Fig. 2. Illustrative example of variations in logic equivalence law categories.

Object-Focused Prompts. Object-focused prompts otherwise known as prompt pairs with unspecified positioning acts as the standard and baseline for more complex prompts. The five categories of logic equivalence laws were converted into prompt templates that retain the same semantic equivalence but in the form of natural language. Each logic category is split into AND/OR sections which each hold a different template, totalling 16 templates for object-focused prompting (See Table 2). A Python script was written for each equivalence law to generate all possible combinations of prompt pairs using the chosen list of entities.

Position-Focused Prompts. As stated previously, to increase the scope of testing, we incorporated positional information into the prompt pairs. By leveraging the bounding box output of object-detection models, we are also able to compare the relative position of any given entity in an image (See Table 3).

Numbering-Focused Prompts. To test the numbering capabilities of text-to-image models, we modified the simplest prompt template, Commutative (AND), seen in Table 2 and introduced a number from 1–10 to one of the two entities present in the prompt. This allows us to isolate the models capabilities in both ascending entity counts as well as potential differences between types of entities. See Table 5 for all prompt templates used in the numbering category.

3.3 Image Pair Comparison

This section will outline the methodology taken to evaluate the image pair generated from the test suite. Our approach leverages the principle that semantically equivalent prompts produce semantically equivalent images, thereby allowing each generated image pair to serve as validation for each other. Therefore, the choice of image comparison to evaluate semantic equivalence is crucial in determining the overall efficacy of the framework.

Object-detection vs VQA vs VLM. As outlined in Sect. 1, the current literature highlights two dominant approaches for image evaluation: methods based on Visual Question Answering (VQA) models and those using Object Detection models. A third alternative, Vision-Language Models (VLMs), was also considered. However, our approach is orthogonal to object detection, and any detection method can be selected as the method for semantic image comparison due to its ability to produce consistent and quantifiable output.

Unlike VQA and VLMs, which generate rich but qualitative natural language descriptions, object detection yields structured outputs in the form of labelled objects and bounding boxes. This structured representation enables reliable and repeatable comparisons between images, which is important for quickly evaluating semantic alignment. The variability and subjectivity in language-based inferences from VQA and VLMs make them less suitable for tasks that require consistent, measurable comparison [27]. Hence, object detection provides a more efficient, robust and interpretable way for our semantic image comparison.

Position-Less Image Pair Assessment. From position-unspecified prompts, we define semantic equivalence in an image pair as two images that contain the same entity labels, as well as having an equal number of total entities. Using Florence-2's object detection output, we create an entity matrix containing all labels and respective instances present within both images in the pair. The two corresponding matrices are compared with each other, noting any detected inconsistencies to represent the presence of text-image misalignment in either pair of text-image groups.

Position Pair Assessment. Following on from comparing entities, we evaluate the spatial consistency of matching entities between image pairs. By taking the bounding box outputs provided by Florence-2, we calculate the centroid for every entity and take it as the reference point for determining relative positions from one another. These calculations are done on the x or y axis, depending on whether the initial prompt pair specified vertical or horizontal positional predicates.

Object-Detection Accuracy. Since our evaluation relies on object detection, we examined the reliability of Florence-2 by randomly sampling misaligned pairs flagged by the framework. To validate accuracy, we manually inspected random samples of 10 pairs of misaligned images in all categories. Florence-2 demonstrated around a 90% success rate in flagging genuine misaligned image pairs. Although not a full benchmark, these checks suggest that Florence-2 provides sufficiently reliable outcomes for our diagnostic purposes.

4 Experiments

In this section, we will discuss our experimental setup, and showcase the effectiveness of our approach with experimental results. The goal of these experiments is to evaluate the effectiveness of our methodology at exposing flaws in semantic robustness in SOTA models like DALLE-3 and Flux.dev.

4.1 Experimental Setup

To evaluate the effectiveness of our proposed framework, MetaLogic, we apply it to two state-of-the-art text-to-image (T2I) models representing both open-source and proprietary systems: Flux.dev [12] and DALLE-3 [2], respectively.

Model Setup. For both Flux.dev and DALLE-3, the images were generated through the API using a Python script in the VSCode IDE. DALLE-3 naturally expands on the initial prompt given as a means of adding detail and complexity to the final image. In our case, we want to avoid this situation as much as possible to avoid introducing unwanted variables that can sway our embedded semantic equivalence. We follow the DALLE-3 documentation provided by OpenAI to prevent any prompt alterations by including the phrase "**I NEED to test how the tool works with extremely simple prompts. DO NOT add any detail, just use it AS-IS:**" as a prefix to all input prompts. This prompt control technique has also been adopted in prior work to reduce generation bias [6,7].

Flux, regarded as one of the most advanced open-source T2I models, is available in two variants: Schnell, optimised for fast generation, and Dev, designed for higher image quality at the cost of speed. For our experiments, we selected the Flux.dev version to avoid trade-offs in image fidelity.

We generate 1600 images across both models from the 800 logic prompt pairs in the test suite. The prompts pairs consist of five logic law categories (Associative, Commutative, Distributive, Complement, DeMorgan) across 4 modifiers (AND, OR, X, Y). Additionally, the numbering category spans across 4 entities (cat, dog, apple, banana) up to a count of 10.

For the object detection, Florence-2, the base, non-fine-tuned version was used as it demonstrated the highest degree of accuracy at labelling entities from manual inspection of generated image pair samples [24]. The model was loaded in Python script through the Hugging Face transformer library.

4.2 Effectiveness of MetaLogic

Our experimental evaluation shows that MetaLogic effectively identifies logical misalignment in text-to-image generation, with detection rates varying significantly between different logical categories and their subsequent variations (See Fig. 3).

Overall, MetaLogic detected logical inconsistencies in 65% of generated image pairs. Performance varied substantially across logical categories, with the highest misalignment detection rates occurring in the Distributive category, followed by Associative, DeMorgan, Complement, and Commutative. This trend of increasing misalignment rates runs adjacent to the categories in order of logical complexity. This suggests that the models struggle with prompts involving complex logical structures where entities are distributed across different groups and clauses.

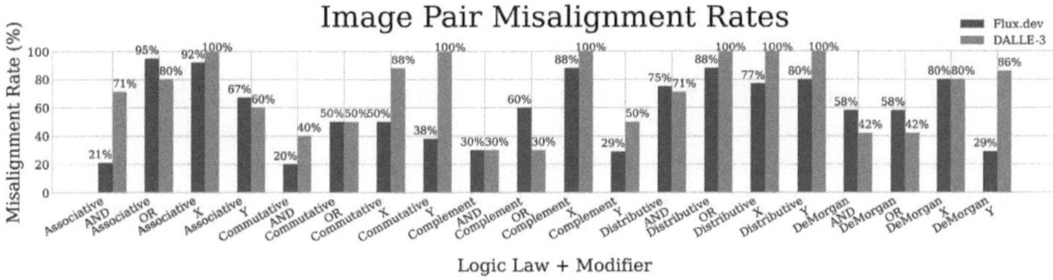

Fig. 3. The misalignment rates of all 5 logic law categories (Associative, Commutative, Distributive, Complement, DeMorgan) across all 4 modifiers (AND, OR, X, Y) for both Flux.dev and DALLE-3.

A clear pattern emerged when comparing AND versus OR variants across all logical categories. AND-based prompts resulted in 45.8% misalignment rate overall, while OR-based prompts showed significantly higher inconsistency at 65.3%. This difference suggests that the model struggles more with disjunctive logic than conjunctive logic. We likely attribute this to the grammatically complex nature of the Associative(OR) and Distributive(OR) prompts required to sustain consistent semantic equivalence (See Table 2).

The addition of positional constraints had significant effects on the overall misalignment rate. Standard conjunctive (AND) prompts without positional information showed only a 21% misalignment rate in Flux.dev, while prompts with explicit positional information (both horizontal and vertical) showed a substantial increase to 63% on average for vertical, up to 85% for horizontal position prompts. Surprisingly, the X modifier performed much worse than Y where you would expect them to be similar. Nevertheless, it's evident that current SOTA image models still struggle with consistent positional understanding.

Overall Flux.dev performed significantly better than DALLE-3, demonstrating an average misalignment rate of 59% whilst DALLE-3 performed significantly worse at 71%. There were some standout differences in some categories, namely Associative(AND), Commutative(Y), and DeMorgan(Y). DALLE-3 was observed to prefer generating multiple of an entity when only prompted for one, as well as significant misunderstanding in vertical positional prompts.

4.3 Common Misalignment Errors

By performing a manual inspection of the saved misalignment image pairs, we are able to identify distinct categories of misalignments detected by MetaLogic. We classified these errors into five main types: (1) X-Axis misposition, (2) Y-axis misposition, (3) Entity duplication, (4) Optical character, and (5) Entity omission (See Fig. 4). This classification provides insight into the specific challenges text-to-image models face when interpreting logical relationships.

Both entity duplication and entity omission were identified in almost all logic categories and variations. This is likely a result of failure in logic reasoning that manifests as failure to generate a specific object or mistakenly doubling up on a singular entity.

As expected, the spatial mispositioning of entities across both horizontal and vertical axis appeared only in image pairs generated from X and Y variants of prompt pairs. This result was already anticipated as those were the only prompts that incorporated positional information within its semantic equivalence. However, additional information within the prompts had little to no impact on the average misalignment rate compared to its baseline. We believe a proportion of the images seeding at inference are weaker in understanding both conjunctive and positional semantics, resulting in a similar failure rate for both categories.

The most unexpected error type we observed was Optical Character Generation, where the model resorted to generating text explanations within the image rather than properly representing the logical relationship visually. This occurred predominantly with long and complex prompts such as Associative (OR) and Distributive (OR), which contained embedded Commutative logic to maintain a singular semantic equivalence. Both models consistently struggled to understand the underlying logic within the prompt and fell back on simply generating parts, or all of the initial prompt within the image. As shown in Fig. 4, when faced with these complex logical structures, the model occasionally generated explanatory text or diagrams within the image, effectively "giving up" on pure visual representation in favour of textual explanation. This suggests a fallback mechanism when the model's visual generation capabilities are unable to handle complex logical operations.

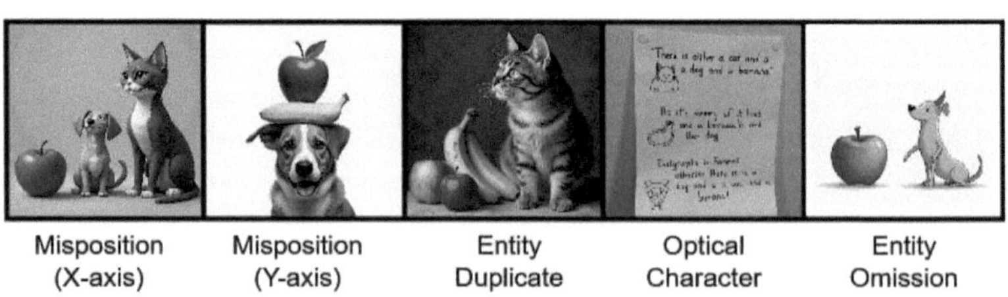

Fig. 4. Examples of misalignment errors categorised under 5 labels: X-Misposition, Y-Misposition, Entity Duplication, Optical Character and Entity Omission.

4.4 Numbering Entities

Figure 5 illustrates a clear trend, as the number of entities in a prompt increases, misalignment rates increase across both models. Prompts with a single entity maintain low misalignment (10%), but performance declines steeply beyond two entities. By the time prompts include seven or more entities, alignment often drops below 30% on average.

It was also observed in misalignment output directory that the trajectory of this decline varies by entity type. While "cat", "dog", and "apple" show relatively stable degradation, "banana" exhibits a significantly sharper increase in misalignment, even at lower counts. This may stem from its typical representation in training data, where bananas appear in bunches rather than individually. Such visual-semantic biases likely interfere with logical interpretation, underscoring that model errors arise not only from prompt complexity but also from mismatches between learned visual associations and logical intent.

5 Discussion

Our findings reveal fundamental gaps in how current text-to-image models process logical relationships. The consistent pattern of increasing misalignment rates as logical complexity increases from simple commutative to complex distributive relationships, suggests that these models lack robust logical reasoning capabilities despite their impressive visual generation abilities.

The high failure rates with OR statements (75% misalignment versus 46% for AND statements) indicate that disjunctive logic presents a particular challenge. This may stem from the inherent ambiguity in training data, where multiple valid visual interpretations exist for prompts containing "or" relationships. Model architectures may benefit from explicit training on logical equivalence relationships, potentially through contrastive learning approaches that minimise differences between outputs from logically equivalent prompts. The unexpected emergence of text generation within images when faced with complex logic (observed in 8% of cases) represents a fascinating fallback mechanism. This suggests that when the model's visual generation capabilities cannot adequately represent the logical relationship, it defaults to its text generation capabilities, essentially "explaining" rather than "showing" the relationship. This insight could inform hybrid approaches that leverage both visual and textual representation for complex prompts.

The identification of logical reasoning gaps in text-to-image models has implications beyond technical improvement. As these models increasingly serve as interfaces between human intent and visual creation, logical consistency becomes crucial for applications in education, design, and communication. Misalignments in logical understanding could lead to miscommunication or even potentially harmful outputs in sensitive contexts. By providing a method to systematically identify and categorise these misalignments, MetaLogic contributes to the broader goal of making generative AI systems more reliable, predictable, and

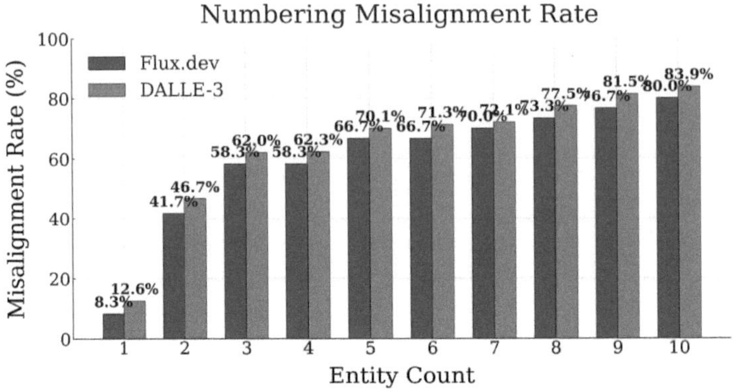

Fig. 5. The misalignment rate for varying entity counts from 1 to 10 of (cat, dog, apple, banana) using Flux.dev and DALLE-3.

aligned with human intent. The counterexamples generated through our approach not only highlight current limitations but also provide concrete materials for improving model transparency and user understanding of these systems' capabilities and limitations.

6 Limitations

The core innovation of MetaLogic, eliminating the need for external ground truth through semantically equivalent prompt pairs inherently creates specific limitations in evaluation scope. While our approach successfully identifies misalignment without requiring a predetermined ground truth, it fundamentally assumes that logically equivalent prompts should produce semantically identical images. This assumption breaks down in two key scenarios:

- First, prompts containing disjunctive statements (OR) pose a theoretical challenge, since multiple distinct visual outputs can all be valid. For example, "There is a cat or a dog" could yield either only a cat or only a dog, making differences between logically equivalent prompts ambiguous rather than reveal true misalignments. To address this, we introduced workarounds using embedded Commutative equivalence, though symptoms of this solution are apparent in the misalignment rates found in the Distributive category where these unwarranted complexities potentially skewed the final results as theoretically, AND and OR prompts require similar levels of logical reasoning to understand.
- Second, our approach cannot evaluate true negation. Statements like "There is no cat" have theoretically infinite correct visual representations, as any scene without a cat would be valid. Since there is no single expected visual output for negation statements, the semantic equivalence comparison mechanism breaks down entirely. The assumption that semantic equivalence in prompts

should produce visual consistency in outputs does not hold when the space of valid outputs is unbounded. Our approach circumvents this by applying a double negative to return the prompt back to a singular correct output, but still falls short of true negation statements.
- Lastly, our framework remains dependent on strong object-detection capabilities. Whilst Florence-2 demonstrates strong performances from our manual checks, occasional inaccuracies can still influence results. This reliance highlights the need for complementary validation strategies or future benchmarks that can assess detection accuracy on generated images.

These limitations highlight an important trade-off in our reference-free approach: by eliminating the need for external ground truth, we necessarily constrain our evaluation scope to logical relationships that produce well-defined, consistent visual expectations across equivalent prompts. Future work will explore hybrid approaches that maintain MetaLogic's efficiency while addressing these edge cases.

7 Conclusion

In this paper, we present MetaLogic, a framework for evaluating text-to-image model robustness via metamorphic testing with logically equivalent prompts. Unlike conventional reference-based methods, MetaLogic compares image pairs from grammatically different but semantically equivalent prompts, enabling scalable, ground truth-free robustness assessment. Experiments on state-of-the-art models (Flux.dev, DALLE-3) reveal significant robustness failures under minor logic-preserving variations. Misalignment rates increase with logical complexity: Distributive (86%), Associative (73%), DeMorgan (59%), Complement (52%), and Commutative (54%), with a stark contrast between conjunctive and disjunctive forms (45% vs. 62%). Common errors include entity omission, duplication, positional shifts, and unexpected text generation. These counterexamples offer actionable insights for model improvement with lower computational cost than existing evaluations. As T2I models are adopted in real-world applications, MetaLogic provides a principled and efficient robustness evaluation, advancing logically consistent and trustworthy generative systems.

References

1. Ahmadi, S., Agrawal, A.: An examination of the robustness of reference-free image captioning evaluation metrics. arXiv preprint arXiv:2305.14998 (2023)
2. Betker, J., et al.: Improving image generation with better captions. **2**(3), 8 (2023). https://cdn.openai.com/papers/dall-e-3.pdf
3. Bronkhorst, H., Roorda, G., Suhre, C., Goedhart, M.: Logical reasoning in formal and everyday reasoning tasks. Int. J. Sci. Math. Educ. **18**, 1673–1694 (2020). https://doi.org/10.1007/s10763-019-10039-8
4. Chen, T.Y., Cheung, S.C., Yiu, S.M.: Metamorphic testing: a new approach for generating next test cases (2020). https://arxiv.org/abs/2002.12543

5. Chen, T.Y., et al.: Metamorphic testing: A review of challenges and opportunities. ACM Comput. Surv. **51**(1) (2018). https://doi.org/10.1145/3143561
6. Conwell, C., Tawiah-Quashie, R., Ullman, T.: Relations, negations, and numbers: looking for logic in generative text-to-image models. arXiv preprint arXiv:2411.17066 (2024)
7. Fu, X., He, M., Lu, Y., Wang, W.Y., Roth, D.: Commonsense-T2I challenge: can text-to-image generation models understand commonsense? arXiv preprint arXiv:2406.07546 (2024)
8. Ghosh, D., Hajishirzi, H., Schmidt, L.: GenEval: an object-focused framework for evaluating text-to-image alignment. Adv. Neural. Inf. Process. Syst. **36** (2024)
9. Grimal, P., Le Borgne, H., Ferret, O., Tourille, J.: TIAM-a metric for evaluating alignment in text-to-image generation. In: Proceedings of the IEEE/CVF Winter Conference on Applications of Computer Vision, pp. 2890–2899 (2024). https://doi.org/10.1109/wacv57701.2024.00287
10. Hu, Y., et al.: TIFA: accurate and interpretable text-to-image faithfulness evaluation with question answering. In: Proceedings of the IEEE/CVF International Conference on Computer Vision, pp. 20406–20417 (2023). https://doi.org/10.1109/iccv51070.2023.01866
11. Huang, J., Chang, K.C.C.: Towards reasoning in large language models: a survey. arXiv preprint arXiv:2212.10403 (2022)
12. Labs, B.F.: Flux (2024). https://github.com/black-forest-labs/flux
13. Lin, T.-Y., et al.: Microsoft COCO: common objects in context. In: Fleet, D., Pajdla, T., Schiele, B., Tuytelaars, T. (eds.) ECCV 2014. LNCS, vol. 8693, pp. 740–755. Springer, Cham (2014). https://doi.org/10.1007/978-3-319-10602-1_48
14. Mirzadeh, I., Alizadeh, K., Shahrokhi, H., Tuzel, O., Bengio, S., Farajtabar, M.: GSM-symbolic: understanding the limitations of mathematical reasoning in large language models. arXiv preprint arXiv:2410.05229 (2024)
15. Mo, W., Zhang, T., Bai, Y., Su, B., Wen, J.R., Yang, Q.: Dynamic prompt optimizing for text-to-image generation. In: Proceedings of the IEEE/CVF Conference on Computer Vision and Pattern Recognition (CVPR), pp. 26627–26636 (2024). https://doi.org/10.1109/CVPR52733.2024.02514
16. Nichol, A., et al.: GLIDE: towards photorealistic image generation and editing with text-guided diffusion models. In: International Conference on Machine Learning (2021). https://api.semanticscholar.org/CorpusID:245335086
17. Radford, A., et al.: Learning transferable visual models from natural language supervision. In: International Conference on Machine Learning, pp. 8748–8763. PMLR (2021). https://arxiv.org/abs/2103.00020
18. Ramesh, A., Dhariwal, P., Nichol, A., Chu, C., Chen, M.: Hierarchical text-conditional image generation with CLIP latents. arXiv preprint arXiv:2204.06125, vol. 1, no. 2, p. 3 (2022)
19. Saharia, C., et al.: Photorealistic text-to-image diffusion models with deep language understanding. ArXiv abs/2205.11487 (2022). https://api.semanticscholar.org/CorpusID:248986576
20. Segura, S., Towey, D., Zhou, Z.Q., Chen, T.Y.: Metamorphic testing: testing the untestable. IEEE Softw. **37**(3), 46–53 (2020). https://doi.org/10.1109/MS.2018.2875968
21. Singh, J., Zheng, L.: Divide, evaluate, and refine: Evaluating and improving text-to-image alignment with iterative VQA feedback. Adv. Neural. Inf. Process. Syst. **36**, 70799–70811 (2023)

22. Sueyoshi, K., Matsubara, T.: Predicated diffusion: predicate logic-based attention guidance for text-to-image diffusion models. In: Proceedings of the IEEE/CVF Conference on Computer Vision and Pattern Recognition, pp. 8651–8660 (2024). https://doi.org/10.1109/cvpr52733.2024.00826
23. Wan, Y., et al.: LogicAsker: evaluating and improving the logical reasoning ability of large language models. pp. 2124–2155 (2024). https://doi.org/10.18653/v1/2024.emnlp-main.128
24. Xiao, B., et al.: Florence-2: advancing a unified representation for a variety of vision tasks. In: Proceedings of the IEEE/CVF Conference on Computer Vision and Pattern Recognition, pp. 4818–4829 (2024). https://doi.org/10.1109/cvpr52733.2024.00461
25. Xu, L., Bu, X., Tian, X.: Dynamic prompt-driven zero-shot relation extraction. IEEE/ACM Trans. Audio Speech Lang. Process. **32**, 2900–2912 (2024). https://doi.org/10.1109/TASLP.2024.3402063
26. Yang, F., Yang, S., Butt, M.A., van de Weijer, J., et al.: Dynamic prompt learning: addressing cross-attention leakage for text-based image editing. Adv. Neural Inf. Process. Syst. 36, 26291–26303 (2023). https://doi.org/10.48550/arXiv.2309.15664 https://doi.org/10.48550/arXiv.2309.15664 https://doi.org/10.48550/arXiv.2309.15664
27. Yuan, Y., Wang, S., Jiang, M., Chen, T.Y.: Perception matters: detecting perception failures of VQA models using metamorphic testing. In: Proceedings of the IEEE/CVF Conference on Computer Vision and Pattern Recognition (CVPR), pp. 16908–16917 (2021). https://doi.org/10.1109/cvpr46437.2021.01663

Formal Construction of Threat Detections from Attack Trees

Dumitru-Bogdan Prelipcean[1,2,3(✉)], Cătălin Dima[1], and Daniele Varacca[1]

[1] LACL, Université Paris-Est Créteil, Créteil, France
{dima,daniele.varacca}@u-pec.fr
[2] Bitdefender, Iaşi, Romania
bprelipcean@bitdefender.com
[3] Alexandru Ioan Cuza University, Iaşi, Romania

Abstract. Writing threat detection signatures directly from informal reports is error-prone and may omit critical details. Attack trees provide a rigorous model for specifying complex threats, but bridging the gap between attack trees and implementable detection logic requires a formal methodology. In this paper, we present a correct-by-construction approach for generating threat detections from attack trees. We formalize the trace semantics of attack trees, defining precisely the sets of event traces corresponding to successful attacks. We also provide a formal semantics for the Generic Threat Detection Language (GTDL), a simplified fragment of a production detection language used in a commercial security product (Bitdefender (https://www.bitdefender.com)), focusing on detection logic essential for practical deployment. We then give a structural translation from attack trees to GTDL, encoding sequencing, choice, and parallelism directly at the level of event traces. We prove that this translation is sound: every event trace detected by the GTDL signature corresponds to a valid attack trace permitted by the original attack tree semantics, and vice versa. By aligning high-level threat models with executable detection logic in operational security products, our results enable the automated synthesis of provably correct and robust detection signatures for real-world environments.

1 Introduction

Threat detection in real-world systems relies on rules or signatures written in dedicated detection languages. These signatures are often derived from informal natural language reports or ad-hoc threat models, which makes them susceptible to errors, omissions, and semantic inconsistencies. Inaccurate or incomplete detection signatures can lead to missed attacks or false positives, undermining the effectiveness of security monitoring.

Attack trees have emerged as a principled method for modeling complex security threats, capturing alternative attack paths, sequences of actions, and dependencies in a rigorous, compositional way. However, deploying these models in operational settings requires translating the attack tree into executable detection logic that can be evaluated by detection engines over event traces.

É. André et al. (Eds.): ICFEM 2025, LNCS 16229, pp. 172–188, 2026.
https://doi.org/10.1007/978-981-95-4213-0_10

The *Generic Threat Detection Language* (GTDL) formalized in this work is a subset of a proprietary detection language developed and used in production by Bitdefender for creating security detection signatures. As such, the theoretical results and translation methodology we present have immediate real-world applicability: they provide a sound, semantics-preserving bridge from high-level attack models to detection logic deployed in operational security products.

In this paper, we address the following research problem: *How can we construct correct, implementable threat detection signatures from attack trees, ensuring that the detection logic precisely and completely captures the behaviors specified by the tree?* In other words, assuming that an attack tree has been constructed in a way which ensures its correctness with respect to some attack scenarios, automatically generate a GTDL script whose semantics is aligned with the attack tree semantics. Note that we do not address the problem of verifying attack trees against specifications describing desirable properties, which can be delegated e.g. to approaches like [5,7,21] and the tools proposed therein.

We formalize both attack tree semantics and the semantics of the GTDL detection engine using traces, and show how to translate attack trees into GTDL signatures such that the resulting signature detects a trace if and only if there exists a subtrace of the trace which is generated by the attack tree.

The paper is structured as follows: The introduction outlines the motivation and the challenges of translating attack tree models into reliable operational detection logic, highlighting the risks of informal signature construction. The related work section surveys prior research in attack modeling, formal methods for security, and existing detection languages, emphasizing the persistent gap between formal threat models and practical deployment. We then present the formal preliminaries, establishing the semantics of attack trees and defining key concepts such as traces and event sequences. Next, we introduce the Generic Threat Detection Language (GTDL), describing its syntax and execution semantics as used in real-world security products. Our core methodology section details the correct-by-construction translation from attack trees to GTDL detection signatures, including the formal translation rules and proof of correctness. This is followed by an extensive examples section, where we illustrate our approach through concrete case studies and comparative analyses, demonstrating both the limitations of informal detection logic and the benefits of our formal methodology. The paper concludes with a summary of contributions and a discussion of potential avenues for future work.

2 Related Work

Attack trees were introduced by Schneier [18] as a way to model security threats in a hierarchical, goal-oriented manner. The root of the tree represents the attacker's ultimate objective, while internal nodes represent subgoals that can be combined either through alternative choices or joint requirements. Leaves correspond to atomic attacker actions, typically observable events such as exploiting a vulnerability, sending a phishing email, or using stolen credentials.

Formally, attack trees provide a *compositional* framework:

- **OR-nodes** capture alternative strategies, where achieving any child suffices.
- **AND-nodes** capture conjunctive requirements, where all children must be satisfied, but the order of execution does not matter.
- **SAND-nodes** (Sequential AND, introduced in [14]) enforce an ordering among child actions, expressing multi-step causal chains.

Because of their clarity and modularity, attack trees have become a widely adopted methodology in both academia and industry. They are now used not only for qualitative reasoning about attack feasibility but also for quantitative analyses such as likelihood estimation, cost/benefit evaluation, and automated synthesis of attack paths [21]. Standards bodies (e.g., ETSI, ISO/SAE 21434 for automotive security) recommend attack tree modeling as part of structured risk assessment, while operational security teams use them to communicate and reason about adversary tactics in complex enterprise infrastructures.

In this work, we use attack trees not just as high-level models but as formal specifications that can be translated into executable threat detection logic, thus bridging the gap between abstract reasoning and concrete, deployable security signatures.

Formal methods have been extensively applied to security protocol verification, with Ryan et al. [17] establishing foundational approaches using process algebras like CSP. In intrusion detection systems (IDS), Pouzol et al. [15] developed formal specifications for detection rules, while Vigna and Kemmerer [20] proposed NetSTAT for network-based detection using formal modeling techniques. Bryans et al. [8] developed formal template-based methods for automated attack tree generation, but focusing on model generation rather than operational translation.

Recent surveys [13] highlight persistent challenges in bridging formal security models with practical detection systems, noting that most deployed systems rely on ad-hoc rules rather than formally verified logic. Our work extends this area by establishing formal semantics for both attack trees and detection languages, enabling provably correct translations with operational deployment guarantees.

Security complexity has driven development of specialized detection languages. Snort [16] established rule-based network intrusion detection patterns, while Sigma [19] provides vendor-neutral signature formats for SIEM platforms and YARA [22] enables malware pattern matching. However, these practical DSLs typically lack formal foundations for reasoning about detection correctness.

A persistent challenge in security research is the gap between theoretical models with strong guarantees and practical implementations lacking formal foundations. This is particularly acute in threat detection, where operational systems rely on manual rules or machine learning without formal guarantees. While tools like SPIN [12] and NuSMV [2] enable exhaustive analysis of system models, they remain underutilized in threat-detection engineering. The CADP toolbox (Construction and Analysis of Distributed Processes) [1,11] offers rich support for compositional verification, equivalence checking, and model checking based on process algebra—but its application to intrusion detection or automated generation of detection signatures is limited. Similarly, cryptographic protocol analyzers like ProVerif [3] focus on symbolic security properties and have seen little use in IDS rule synthesis. These gaps emphasize the novelty and practical importance of our correct-by-construction methodology, which leverages formal semantics directly to derive operational detection logic.

3 Preliminaries

Throughout the paper, for a finite set of symbols Σ, Σ^* denotes the set of finite sequences of symbols in Σ. We will refer to such sequences as *traces*. The *length* of a trace $u = a_1 \dots a_n$ is n. ϵ is the empty trace, and uv denotes concatenation.

Given two traces u_1, u_2, we say that u_1 is a *subtrace of* u_2 and denote $u_1 \sqsubseteq u_2$ whenever $u_1 = a_1 \dots a_n$ and $u_2 = v_0 a_1 \dots v_{n-1} a_n v_n$ for some (possibly empty) traces $v_i \in \Sigma^*$ $(0 \leq i \leq n)$

The *shuffle* operation on two traces is defined as follows:

$$u \sqcup\!\sqcup v = \{u_1 v_1 \dots u_n v_n \mid u = u_1 \dots u_n,\ v = v_1 \dots v_n,\ u_i, v_i \in \Sigma^*,\ i = 1, \dots, n\}$$

$\sqcup\!\sqcup$ is extended to sets of traces as usual. Later we will need the following folklore property about shuffle:

Lemma 1. *Let u, v, w be traces. Let $w \in u \sqcup\!\sqcup v$ Then $w' \sqsubseteq w$ if and only if there exist $u' \sqsubseteq u$ and $v' \sqsubseteq v$ such that $w' \in u' \sqcup\!\sqcup v'$.*

3.1 Attack Trees and Event Traces

Attack trees provide a hierarchical and compositional model of complex multistep attacks. To enable formal reasoning and translation into detection signatures, we provide a rigorous semantic foundation. We present the *Trace semantics*, which describes the set of event sequences (traces) corresponding to successful attacks.

Let Σ be a finite set of atomic actions (security-relevant events). The syntax of action-based attack trees with standard operators is defined inductively as follows:

$$A ::= nil \mid a \mid OR(A_1, A_2) \mid AND(A_1, A_2) \mid SAND(A_1, A_2)$$

where:

- nil denotes the empty (no-op) attack,
- $a \in \Sigma$ is an atomic action,
- $OR(A_1, A_2)$ denotes disjunction (at least one of A_1 or A_2),
- $AND(A_1, A_2)$ is the (unordered) conjunction (both A_1 and A_2 must be achieved in any order),
- $SAND(A_1, A_2)$ is sequential (ordered) conjunction (first A_1, then A_2).

Definition 1 (Trace Semantics of Attack Trees with Standard Operators). *Let $\mathcal{T} : AT(\Sigma) \to 2^{\Sigma^*}$ map each attack tree to its set of traces:*

$$\begin{aligned}
\mathcal{T}(nil) &= \{\epsilon\} \\
\mathcal{T}(a) &= \{a\} \\
\mathcal{T}(OR(A_1, A_2)) &= \mathcal{T}(A_1) \cup \mathcal{T}(A_2) \\
\mathcal{T}(SAND(A_1, A_2)) &= \{uv \mid u \in \mathcal{T}(A_1),\ v \in \mathcal{T}(A_2)\} \\
\mathcal{T}(AND(A_1, A_2)) &= \mathcal{T}(A_1) \sqcup \mathcal{T}(A_2)
\end{aligned}$$

By precisely characterizing traces, subtraces, and the combinatorial effects of choice, sequence, and parallelism we lay the groundwork for a compositional treatment of attack trees. This trace-based semantics not only supports the formal analysis of attack models but also serves as the basis for the semantics-preserving translation of attack trees into executable detection logic, as developed in the subsequent sections.

4 GTDL Syntax and Semantics

The Generic Threat Detection Language (GTDL) used in this work is a simplified fragment derived from an operational detection language deployed in real-world environments at Bitdefender. The original operational language supports a wide range of features, including event correlation, state tracking, and integration with various system sensors and analytics modules.

For the purposes of this research, GTDL has been distilled to focus on the core aspects of detection logic, abstracting away auxiliary language features that do not impact the semantic correctness of attack detection. This simplified fragment retains the essential constructs needed to encode detection signatures corresponding to attack trees, such as boolean variables, conditional assignments, and plugin calls for event observation. By working with a precise yet expressive subset, we are able to formally analyze the translation from attack trees to executable signatures, while ensuring that the resulting logic is representative of detection rules deployed in practical, operational security products.

The detection process follows a structured workflow to identify and respond to potential threats. It begins with the **sensors** layer, which captures system events such as process executions, file modifications, and network activities, relaying this data to the appropriate **plugins**. These plugins process the raw event data, extract relevant security indicators, and submit the processed information to the **evaluation engine**. The evaluation engine then applies **detection rules** defined in GTDL signatures, leveraging both real-time data and historical state tracking. When the specified conditions in a **detection signature** (script) are met, the system flags the corresponding threat, triggering response actions such as alerting security teams or initiating automated mitigation measures.

The detection language syntax is:

$$
\begin{aligned}
\mathit{sig} &::= \mathit{block} \\
\mathit{block} &::= \mathit{assign} \mid \textbf{IF}\ \mathit{cond}\ \textbf{THEN}\ \mathit{block} \\
\mathit{assign} &::= x := e; \mid x := e;\ \ \mathit{assign} \\
\mathit{cond} &::= \mathit{cond}\ \mathit{boolop}\ \mathit{cond} \mid \textbf{true} \mid \textbf{false} \mid e \\
\mathit{boolop} &::= \textbf{AND} \mid \textbf{OR} \mid == \mid <> \\
e &::= x \mid \textbf{true} \mid \textbf{false} \mid \texttt{inPluginCall("a")}
\end{aligned}
$$

where x is a boolean variable in a set Var, a is an event in the set of events Σ and `inPluginCall` is a call to an API module which is triggered when the current event maps the argument.

To enable real-time threat detection based on attack trees, GTDL detection signatures are continuously evaluated over an input stream of system events. This is formalized by a synchronous operational model where all signatures evolve in parallel and share the same event stream input.

Global Evaluation Semantics. Let Σ be the set of observable atomic actions (events), shared by both the attack trees and the detection engine. Let $u = a_1 a_2 \ldots a_n$ be a sequence of events (a trace), with $a_t \in \Sigma$ the event observed at time step t.

A *GTDL script* is a tuple $\mathcal{S} = (S_1, \ldots, S_k, x)$ where S_i are GTDL signatures and x a variable that we call the *detection variable*. We require that the set of variables which are updated by two different signatures S_i and S_j is disjoint (though different signatures can read the same variables). The set of GTDL scripts is denoted $\mathcal{G}$.

Given a GTDL script S, a configuration of S is a mapping from variables to truth values, $\sigma : Var \longrightarrow \{true, false\}$. The set of configurations of a GTDL script S is denoted $\mathcal{C}(S)$.

At the beginning of a detection, all variables are initialized to **false**, hence the initial configuration is $\sigma^{(0)}(x) = false$ for all $x \in Var$. Then, at each time step t, the detection engine:

- Feeds the current event a_t to all plugin calls.
- Executes each signature S_j using the shared state $\sigma^{(t)}$.
- Produces an updated global state $\sigma^{(t+1)}$ based on the effect of all assignments across signatures.

We define this global transition as $\sigma^{(t)} \xrightarrow{a_t} \sigma^{(t+1)}$, where $a_t \in \Sigma$.

While signatures are generally evaluated in parallel, in the translation of sequential composition ($SAND$) we impose an execution order by guarding the right-hand subtree with the variable of the left-hand subtree. Thus, strict parallelism does not hold in this case. In a script $(S_1, \ldots, S_k, x)$, the signatures are executed one after the other (starting from S_1), following the standard rules of imperative languages. The only special rule is the evaluation of the "plugins".

Plugin Evaluation. Each occurrence of `inPluginCall("a")` is interpreted as a predicate that evaluates to **true** at instant u if and only if $a_t = a$ for some $t < u$.

It provides the mechanism by which the current event a_t is inspected by the signature logic. An assignment is evaluated as:

$$[\text{Assign}] \qquad (x := \texttt{inPluginCall("a")}, \sigma^{(t)}) \rightarrow \sigma^{(t)}[x \mapsto (a_t = a)]$$

Execution Trace. The overall detection process results in a sequence:

$$\sigma^{(0)} \xrightarrow{a_1} \sigma^{(1)} \xrightarrow{a_2} \cdots \xrightarrow{a_n} \sigma^{(n)}$$

with $\sigma^{(0)}(x) = \textbf{false}$ for all x.

Detection Outcome. A script comes with a special boolean variable x, that defines the output of the detection.

Definition 2 (Detection). *Let $\mathcal{S} = (S_1, \ldots, S_k\, x)$ be a GTDL script. Let $u = a_1 \ldots a_n$ be a finite event trace. Let $\sigma^{(n)}$ be the final global state after evaluating $\mathcal{S}$ on u. Then $\mathcal{S}$* detects *u if $\sigma^{(n)}(x) = \textbf{true}$.*

Definition 3 (Monotonicity of Variables). *A GTDL signature is said to be* monotone *if, for every execution run*

$$\sigma^{(0)} \xrightarrow{a_1} \sigma^{(1)} \xrightarrow{a_2} \cdots,$$

*and for every variable x, whenever $\sigma^{(t)}(x) = \textbf{true}$ for some step t, then $\sigma^{(t')}(x) = \textbf{true}$ for all $t' \geq t$. That is, once a detection variable becomes **true**, it never reverts to **false**.*

Remark. Not all GTDL signatures are necessarily monotone in general (e.g., if the language admits assignments that reset variables to **false** or state updates that revoke progress).

Also note that some events may not change the state. This is intended: it simply means that some events do not contribute to a given detection.

Summary.

- The detection engine evaluates all GTDL signatures in parallel, at each time step, consuming events from the system log u, where each $a_t \in \Sigma$.
- Each GTDL rule matches against the current event (using *inPluginCall* predicates) and its internal state to determine if detection conditions are met.
- This process is directly aligned with the trace semantics of attack trees, enabling rigorous reasoning about detection correctness.

5 Detection Construction from Attack Trees

The systematic construction of operational detections from action-based attack trees is grounded in formal semantics. This ensures that complex threat scenarios are rigorously captured and faithfully translated into executable detection logic. By unifying attack tree analysis, translation to GTDL, and formal proof of correctness, our methodology bridges the gap between high-level threat modeling and robust, practical detection mechanisms.

Attack-Tree Correctness versus Translation Correctness. Our contribution is orthogonal to the problem of constructing or validating attack trees. In particular, frameworks such as Is My Attack Tree Correct? by Audinot, Pinchinat, and Kordy [5] provide a formal means to check whether a given attack tree is consistent with a system modeled as a transition system . Similarly, Guided Design of Attack Trees [6] offers system-based tool support to assist security experts in constructing well-founded, trace-grounded attack trees. In contrast, our focus is on the **semantics-preserving translation** of an already correct attack tree into GTDL detection logic. We assume the tree accurately models the threat scenarios (as validated by the aforementioned tools), and we guarantee that the translation yields detection logic that faithfully preserves the attack tree's semantics.

5.1 Detection Construction Methodology

Our approach to building GTDL detection logic from attack trees proceeds via a compositional, semantics-preserving translation. Given an attack tree defined over a set of observable atomic actions, we first analyze the tree's structure to identify its constituent nodes and the operators governing their relationships—namely, OR, AND, and $SAND$. Each leaf node is mapped to a concrete, observable system event, ensuring that every atomic action corresponds to a real-world indicator of compromise that can be monitored by the detection engine. For each such event, we generate a GTDL primitive by introducing a boolean variable assignment using the `inPluginCall` predicate, which directly encodes the observation of the event in the input stream.

Internal nodes representing composite behavior are translated according to their semantics: OR nodes are encoded as logical disjunctions, assigning the parent variable to the OR of their children's detection variables; AND nodes are represented as conjunctions, capturing unordered satisfaction of multiple subgoals; and $SAND$ nodes, which express ordered (sequential) conjunction, are encoded by conditioning the detection logic of each subsequent stage on the satisfaction of the prior stage's detection variable—typically realized by wrapping the translation of each subtree in an `IF` block. This process enforces that the detection logic precisely mirrors the compositional and temporal structure of the original attack tree, including proper enforcement of ordering constraints where required.

Throughout the translation, each subtree is associated with a unique detection variable that records the satisfaction of the corresponding attack subgoal along the input trace. The root node's detection variable serves as the final predicate for the GTDL script, signaling successful detection of the modeled attack pattern. This correct-by-construction methodology guarantees that every event trace admitted by the attack tree semantics is recognized by the GTDL signature,

5.2 From Attack Trees to GTDL

We are now ready to define the translation of attack trees into GTDL scripts. Let $A \in AT(\Sigma)$ be an attack tree. The translation function $\phi : AT(\Sigma) \to \mathcal{G}$ produces a GTDL script for each attack tree $A \in AT(\Sigma)$:

$$\phi(A) = (S_1, \ldots, S_k, x_A)$$

with the intended meaning that x_A evaluates to **true** at the end of the detection run on trace u if and only if a subtrace u' of u is generated by A. The translation is defined inductively as follows.

1. **Base case:** For $A = a$, generate the GTDL signature:

$$S \triangleq x_A := \texttt{inPluginCall("a");}$$

   Then

$$\phi(A) = (S, x_A).$$

2. **Choice:** For $A = OR(A_1, A_2)$, assuming $\phi(A_1) = (S_1^1, \ldots, S_1^{k_1}, x_{A_1})$ and $\phi(A_2) = (S_2^1, \ldots, S_2^{k_2}, x_{A_2})$ have been generated, define the signature:

$$S \triangleq x_A := x_{A_1} \textbf{ OR } x_{A_2};$$

   where x_A is a new variable, disjoint from the variables used in $\phi(A_i)$, $i = 1, 2$. Then:

$$\phi(A) := (S_1^1, \ldots, S_1^{k_1}, S_2^1, \ldots, S_2^{k_2}, S, x_A)$$

3. **Parallel composition:** For $A = AND(A_1, A_2)$, with the same notations as above for $\phi(A_i)$, we generate the signature:

$$S \triangleq x_A := x_{A_1} \textbf{ AND } x_{A_2};$$

   with the same considerations about x_A as in the previous case. Then:

$$\phi(A) := (S_1^1, \ldots, S_1^{k_1}, S_2^1, \ldots, S_2^{k_2}, S, x_A)$$

4. **Synchronized sequence:** For $A = SAND(A_1, A_2)$ and the same notations for $\phi(A_i)$, first, for each signature $S_2^i \in \phi(A_2)$, define the following modified signature:

$$\overline{S_2^i} = \textbf{if } x_{A_1} \textbf{ THEN } S_2^i$$

   Then, the signature associated to $SAND(A_1, A_2)$ is:

$$\phi(A) := (\overline{S_2^1}, \ldots, \overline{S_2^{k_2}}, S_1^1, \ldots, S_1^{k_1}, x_{A_2})$$

   Hence the detection flag is the same as in $\phi(A_2)$.

In the context of the last point, we will also denote $\overline{\phi(A_2)} = (\overline{S_2^1}, \ldots, \overline{S_2^{k_2}})$. Note that this is not really a script since the detection variable is missing. Then we can rephrase the definition of $\phi(SAND(A_1, A_2))$ as

$$\phi(SAND(A_1, A_2)) = (\overline{\phi(A_2)}, \phi(A_1), x_{A_2})$$

where the comma is used as juxtaposition of lists of signatures.

Note also that the order of evaluating the signatures in the GTDL script $\phi(SAND(A_1, A_2))$ is: first evaluate $\overline{\phi(A_2)}$, then $\phi(A_1)$.

6 Correctness of the Translation

Our main theorem states that traces described by an attack tree A are precisely those detected by the GTDL translation $\phi(A)$.

The following lemma ensures that, under certain conditions, GTDL scripts generated by Φ from attack trees satisfy the monotonicity property.

Lemma 2. *Let A be an attack tree with distinct actions on its leaves. Then all variables in the GTDL script $\phi(A)$ are monotone: if $\sigma^{(t)}(x) = \textbf{true}$ at some step t, then $\sigma^{(t')}(x) = \textbf{true}$ for all $t' \geq t$.*

Proof. By induction on A. Base case: for a leaf a, $x_a :=$ `inPluginCall("a")` is set to **true** when a occurs and never reset. Inductive step: for OR and AND, the new variable is a monotone Boolean combination of monotone variables. For $SAND$, assignments from $\phi(A_2)$ are guarded by x_{A_1}, which is monotone by induction, so $\phi(A_2)$ evolves monotonically once enabled. No rule in $\phi(A)$ assigns **false**, hence all variables are monotone.

Theorem 1. *Let $A \in AT(\Sigma)$ be an attack tree. Let $u = a_1 \dots a_n$ be a finite event trace. Then $\phi(A)$ detects u if and only if there exists a subtrace $u' \sqsubseteq u$ such that $u' \in \mathcal{T}(A)$.*

Proof. We proceed by structural induction on A.

The Base Case: $A = a$, hence $\mathcal{T}(A) = \{a\}$, and:

$$\phi(A) = (v_A := \texttt{inPluginCall("a");}x_A).$$

For any trace u not containing a, clearly $\sigma^{(i)}(x_A) = \textbf{false}$ for any $i \leq |E|$. Assume now u contains a, let $u = u_1 a u_2$ with u_1 not containing a, and let $k_1 = |u_1|$ (the length of u_1). Then $\sigma^{(i)}(x_A) = \textbf{false}$ for any $i < k_1$ and $\sigma^{(k_1)}(x_A) =$ (`inPluginCall("a")`) $= \textbf{true}$. Subsequently, due to the monotonicity property, $\sigma^{(i)}(x_A) = \textbf{true}$ for any $i > k_1$. so $\sigma^{(|u|)}(x_A) = \textbf{true}$. This concludes the base case.

The Case of Choice Nodes: Take $A = OR(A_1, A_2)$, hence $\mathcal{T}(A) = \mathcal{T}(A_1) \cup \mathcal{T}(A_2)$. Assume also the property holds for A_1 and A_2 and take a trace u.

Assume first that there exists $u' \sqsubseteq u$ with $u \in \mathcal{T}(A)$. If $u' \in \mathcal{T}(A_1)$, by the induction hypothesis we get that $\phi(A_1)$ detects u. It then follows that x_{A_1} holds true at the end of u, which clearly implies that x_A also holds true at the end of u, which proves one implication.

For the reverse implication, assume $\phi(A)$ detects u, which implies that either x_{A_1} or x_{A_2} hold true. Then the induction hypothesis can be applied to get that there exists $u' \sqsubseteq u$ with $u' \in \mathcal{T}(A_1) \cup \mathcal{T}(A_2)$, and we're done.

The Case of Parallel Composition: Take $A = AND(A_1, A_2)$, hence $\mathcal{T}(P) = \mathcal{T}(P_1) \sqcup\!\sqcup \mathcal{T}(P_2)$.

Take a trace u such that there exists a subtrace $u' \sqsubseteq u$ with $u' \in \mathcal{T}(A_1) \sqcup\!\sqcup \mathcal{T}(A_2)$. This implies that there exists $u_1' \in \mathcal{T}(A_1)$ and $u_2' \in \mathcal{T}(A_2)$ with $u' \in u_1' \sqcup\!\sqcup u_2'$. Using the assumption that A_1 utilizes disjoint symbols from A_2 and Lemma

1, we get that u_1' and u_2' are subtraces of U. Using the induction hypothesis, we get that $\phi(A_1)$ detects u_1' and $\phi(A_2)$ detects u_2'. Since the variable valuations in $\phi(A)$ are monotone, this also implies that both x_{A_1} and x_{A_2} hold true at the end of u. But then the last signature in $\phi(A)$ will also evaluate x_A to true at the end of u, that is, $\phi(A)$ detects u.

Conversely, assume $\phi(A)$ detects some trace u, which clearly implies that $x_{A_1} = x_{A_2}$ hold true at the end of u. By the induction hypothesis we get that there exists $u_1 \in \mathcal{T}(A_1)$ and $u_2 \in \mathcal{T}(A_2)$, both subtraces of u. Now, using again the hypothesis on the disjointness of the events in $\mathcal{T}(A_1)$ from the events in $\mathcal{T}(A_2)$ and Lemma 1 (reverse implication), we obtain that $u_1 \sqcup\!\sqcup\, u_2$ has a nonempty intersection with the set of subtraces of u. This can be shown by identifying the position within u of each event occurring in each u_i, and showing that these positions are distinct.

The Case of Sequential Composition: $A = SAND(A_1, A_2)$.

Take a trace u for which we have a subtrace $u' \in T(SAND(A_1, A_2))$. This implies that there exist u_1, u_2 traces with $u = u_1 \cdot u_2$, $u_i' \sqsubseteq u_i$ and $u_i' \in T(A_i)$. Recall also that $\phi(A) = (\overline{\phi(A_2)}, \phi(A_1), x_{A_2})$. Since each signature in $\overline{\phi(A_2)}$ starts with **if** x_{A_1} **THEN**..., they are never executed along u_1.

On the other hand, by the induction hypothesis, $\phi(A_1)$ detects u_1. This also means that x_{A_1} holds true when the GTDL script $\phi(A)$ parses u_1. Using the monotonicity of variable valuations, this implies that x_{A_1} remains true along u_2, hence the effect of the $\overline{\phi(A_2)}$ part of the script is the same as the effect of the script $\phi(A_2)$ on u_2. By the induction hypothesis, $\phi(A_2)$ detects u_2, hence it follows that v_{A_2} holds true at the end of $u_1 \cdot u_2$.

For the reverse implication, take a trace u which is detected by $\phi(A)$. As x_{A_2} can only be set by the $\overline{(A_2)}$ part and each signature in this part is guarded by **if** x_{A_1} **THEN**..., there must exist a moment when x_{A_1} becomes true. Hence u can be decomposed into $u = u_1 \cdot u_2$. It then follows that $\phi(A_1)$ detects u_1 and $\phi(A_2)$ detects u_2, which clearly implies the desired outcome.

Note that monotonicity does not imply that we must keep unboundedly many copies of variables. Each syntactic occurrence of an action is assigned its own detection variable, and once set to true it persists for the remainder of the trace. Thus the number of variables is bounded by the size of the attack tree, independent of trace length.

The correctness proof, as presented, assumes for simplicity that every atomic action appearing in the attack tree is distinct, i.e., no action label occurs more than once in any tree. This assumption ensures that subtraces corresponding to different subgoals can be uniquely mapped to occurrences in the event trace, simplifying the induction and reasoning about the shuffle and sequencing operators. In practical scenarios, however, it is often necessary to model repeated actions or the same event label appearing in multiple locations within the tree. The formal translation and proof can be extended to accommodate such cases by introducing a separate detection variable for each syntactic occurrence of an action in the tree, together with suitable indexing or positional constraints to ensure that each instance is satisfied by a distinct occurrence in the trace and that ordering is preserved where required. Thus, the distinctness assumption is not a fundamental limitation, but rather a notational convenience; with this additional bookkeeping, the soundness and completeness guarantees of our translation remain valid even when actions are repeated within the attack tree.

7 Implementation: AT2GTDL

Building upon the structural translation ϕ from attack trees to GTDL in the previous section, we have developed **AT2GTDL**[1], a practical tool that implements the correct-by-construction synthesis of detection signatures. The tool is designed to ensure that every GTDL rule it emits corresponds precisely to the semantics-preserving translation defined in the formal development, thereby guaranteeing that the behaviors recognized by the generated signatures are weakly trace equivalent to those described by the original attack tree.

Implementation of the Structural Translation. AT2GTDL automates the inductive translation described in this section. Each attack tree is specified in YAML using the compositional syntax of atomic actions, choice (OR), parallel composition (AND), and sequential composition ($SAND$). The tool parses this specification and recursively constructs detection rules as follows:

- **Atomic Actions:** For every leaf node a, the tool creates a detection rule that sets the corresponding flag upon observing the atomic event, as prescribed by the base case of $\phi(a)$.
- **Choice (OR) and Parallel (AND):** For internal nodes, the tool generates Boolean detection logic that combines the flags of child nodes using logical OR or AND, exactly as defined by the translation rules for $\phi(OR(A_1, A_2))$ and $\phi(AND(A_1, A_2))$.
- **Sequential ($SAND$):** For every sequential composition $SAND(A_1, A_2)$, the tool modifies the detection rules for the right-hand subtree to be guarded by the detection variable of the left subtree, faithfully realizing the construction of $\phi(SAND(A_1, A_2))$ and preserving ordered detection as required by the trace semantics.

The output signatures produced by AT2GTDL are not ad-hoc or handcrafted; they are the direct image of the inductively defined, sound translation function ϕ developed and proven as above. The final detection variable generated by the tool serves as a precise implementation of the detection predicate proved correct by Theorem 1, ensuring that an event trace is accepted by the GTDL script if and only if it corresponds to a subtrace recognized by the original attack tree.

For each node in the attack tree, the tool emits a `[DETECTION]` block in GTDL, with metadata including the detection name (corresponding to the node's

[1] https://at2gtdl.vercel.app.

unique identifier) and its structural role. Crucially, AT2GTDL appends a `FINAL` detection signature at the end of each output, which monitors the detection variable of the attack tree's root and triggers a centralized alert upon successful recognition of the modeled threat. This ensures that downstream systems or analysts can act upon a single, explicit indicator of detection, fully aligned with the semantics of the modeled attack.

Input/Output Consistency with the Formal Model. The tool enforces a strict correspondence between input and output domains: the input YAML format is parsed and normalized to match the abstract syntax of $AT(\Sigma)$ in the formalism, and the output GTDL is structured according to the operational semantics specified for detection engines in Sect. 4. The translation mechanism is thus a faithful, executable realization of the theoretical construction, bringing the guarantees of formal verification directly into the signature synthesis workflow.

Summary. In summary, AT2GTDL embodies the practical outcome of our formal approach: it translates attack trees into detection logic in a manner that is provably correct, transparent, and readily deployable. Every signature and detection variable produced can be traced back to a step in the formal inductive construction, and the soundness of the translation is preserved end-to-end. This robust connection between theory and implementation ensures that security analysts can model complex threats at a high level, confident that the resulting detection logic will precisely and completely capture the intended behaviors.

8 Use-Cases and Discussion

The challenge of translating high-level threat scenarios into correct and effective detection logic is not merely theoretical. In our experience deploying threat detections for real-world enterprise environments, we repeatedly observed that informal, intuition-driven approaches to building GTDL detection rules often led to missed attacks (false negatives) or spurious alerts (false positives). The following examples, inspired by both public threat reports and our own operational history, illustrate these pitfalls and motivate the need for formal, semantics-driven construction.

Attack Scenario. Our team was tasked with detecting sophisticated lateral movement and privilege escalation activity such as those documented in APT29 (Cozy Bear) [9], and observed in advanced red teaming exercises [10], often involve chained actions:

1. **Route A (Multi-step Progression):** The attacker first compromises a workstation via an exploit (`ExploitWorkstation`), such as exploiting a vulnerable browser or document reader (MITRE ATT&CK technique T1203 [4]). After gaining initial access, the attacker dumps credentials from memory (`DumpCreds`, e.g., using Mimikatz, ATT&CK T1003). With these credentials,

the attacker performs remote authentication (`RemoteAuth`) to a more valuable server using protocols like RDP or SMB (T1021). All actions must occur in this sequence for successful escalation.

2. **Route B (Direct Account Compromise):** Alternatively, the attacker may phish or otherwise compromise a privileged account directly (`DirectPrivAccount`), then immediately authenticate remotely to the server (`RemoteAuth`).

This scenario reflects common enterprise kill-chains where each stage is crucial for the next, and sequence enforcement is essential for accurate detection [4,9,10].

In early iterations, we observed that analysts often built detection logic using only conjunctions and disjunctions, aiming to capture "all the relevant activities." A typical rule is represented in the left side of Fig. 2.

Operational Impact: During live deployments, this logic produced both false positives and false negatives.

- *False positives*: Alerts fired even if the three events were unrelated or distributed across users and time windows, since no ordering or linkage was enforced.
- *False negatives*: Attackers who performed actions in close sequence, but with delays or interleaving benign events, often went undetected, as the logic was not sensitive to temporal or causal structure.

Over-approximate rules, while easy to implement, fail to capture the nuanced behavior of real attacks, resulting in unreliable coverage and analyst fatigue.

To model the threat more precisely, we described the scenario with the attack tree displayed in Fig. 1, using `SAND` (read the figure from left to right) for ordered conjunction and `OR` for alternative routes.

Here, the `SAND` operator captures the required strict sequencing for Route A (exploit → dump credentials → remote auth), while the `OR` allows for the alternative, direct privilege compromise route.

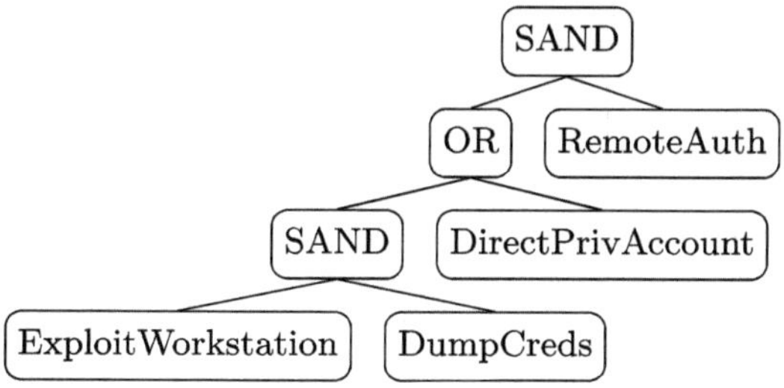

Fig. 1. Attack tree for the privilege escalation scenario (two alternative routes).

In the next phase, analysts sought to more accurately translate the attack tree structure into GTDL logic. Naturally, they mapped each `SAND` in the tree to a sequence of nested `IF` statements in the detection code:

```
// Informal rule (ignores order)
x_exploit :=
    inPluginCall("ExploitWorkstation");
x_dump    :=
    inPluginCall("DumpCreds");
x_direct  :=
    inPluginCall("DirectPrivAccount");
x_remote  :=
    inPluginCall("RemoteAuth");

x_detect := (x_exploit AND x_dump
    AND x_remote)
        OR (x_direct AND x_remote);
```

```
// Generated script from attack tree
x_exploit :=
    inPluginCall("ExploitWorkstation");
IF x_exploit THEN
    x_dump :=
        inPluginCall("DumpCreds");
    IF x_dump THEN
        x_remote1 :=
            inPluginCall("RemoteAuth");

x_direct :=
    inPluginCall("DirectPrivAccount");
IF x_direct THEN
    x_remote2 :=
        inPluginCall("RemoteAuth");

x_detect := x_remote1 OR x_remote2;
```

Fig. 2. Comparison of a naive GTDL script (left), which ignores ordering, and the generated script from our translation (right), which enforces correct sequencing

Operational Impact: While this construction intuitively enforced ordering, we observed if variables were evaluated per event and did not persist across steps the following happens:

- *Missed attacks (FN)*: When attack steps were separated by gaps or interleaved with benign activity, the detection logic failed to "remember" previous stages. This resulted in valid multi-stage attacks going undetected.
- *Multi-user ambiguity*: In environments with multiple simultaneous user sessions, context-free variables led to confusion and either missed alerts or noisy matches.

Example Trace (Missed): `ExploitWorkstation` → (benign) → `DumpCreds` → `RemoteAuth`

The alert failed to trigger because the variable for the first step was not retained across events.

Discussion. Modeling attack chains using nested IFs (SAND) without persistent state is fragile and error-prone. Valid attacks were missed in production because the logic could not handle time gaps or real-world event noise.

As seen also in practice a key property of our formal semantics is monotonicity: once a partial match to an attack pattern is observed, it cannot be invalidated by future events. This reflects the intuition that progress toward an attack goal accumulates over time, even in the presence of noise or benign interleaving. Monotonic semantics ensure that intermediate detection state is preserved across event streams, enabling reliable recognition of long or temporally fragmented attack sequences. Crucially, this avoids the brittleness of event-scoped logic, where detection variables may be reset or overwritten, leading to missed alerts.

These contrasting experiences highlight why formal semantics are indispensable for building trustworthy detection logic. Informal or ad hoc rule writing cannot reliably capture complex attack behavior in dynamic, real-world environments. Our operational journey strongly motivated the formal methodology presented in this paper.

9 Conclusion

We have presented a correct-by-construction methodology for translating attack trees into executable detection logic in the Generic Threat Detection Language (GTDL). Our contribution lies not in the syntactic encoding of tree operators but in the formal semantics and correctness guarantees: every detection triggered by the GTDL signature corresponds to a valid realization of the original attack model. This avoids the pitfalls of ad hoc or informal rule writing, which often fail under interleaving events, benign noise, or repeated actions.

Although the translation rules for atomic actions, choice, parallelism, and sequential composition are syntactically simple, they provide a scalable and compositional framework that applies to arbitrarily complex attack trees. Our approach is therefore broadly applicable, from targeted APT scenarios to ransomware kill-chains and supply-chain compromises. The automated synthesis implemented in our AT2GTDL tool demonstrates that these results are not purely theoretical but can be directly deployed in operational security products.

There are several promising directions for future research. One avenue is to extend our methodology by expressing attack trees as terms in a suitable process algebra. This would allow us to leverage existing algebraic tools for reasoning about concurrency, synchronization, and refinement in attack scenarios, potentially yielding more general and compositional frameworks for threat modeling. Furthermore, such an approach opens the possibility of developing a general methodology for constructing detection logic from models specified in a wide range of formal languages. Ultimately, this could enable a unified and language-agnostic theory of semantics-preserving detection synthesis, advancing both the automation and the correctness guarantees of security engineering.

References

1. CADP: Construction and Analysis of Distributed Processes. https://cadp.inria.fr/. Concurrency toolbox with process-algebraic modeling and verification
2. Nusmv. http://nusmv.fbk.eu/. Symbolic model checker for CTL/LTL verification
3. Proverif. https://prosecco.gforge.inria.fr/personal/bblanche/proverif/. Automated cryptographic protocol verifier
4. MITRE ATT&CK matrix (2025). https://attack.mitre.org/matrices/enterprise/
5. Audinot, M., Pinchinat, S., Kordy, B.: Is my attack tree correct? In: Foley, S.N., Gollmann, D., Snekkenes, E. (eds.) ESORICS 2017, Part I. LNCS, vol. 10492, pp. 83–102. Springer, Cham (2017). https://doi.org/10.1007/978-3-319-66402-6_7

6. Audinot, M., Pinchinat, S., Kordy, B.: Guided design of attack trees: a system-based approach. In: 31st IEEE Computer Security Foundations Symposium, CSF 2018, Oxford, United Kingdom, 9–12 July 2018, pp. 61–75. IEEE Computer Society (2018). https://doi.org/10.1109/CSF.2018.00012
7. Brihaye, T., Pinchinat, S., Terefenko, A.: Adversarial formal semantics of attack trees and related problems. **370**, 162–177 (2022). https://doi.org/10.4204/EPTCS.370.11
8. Bryans, J.W., Liew, L.S., Nguyen, H.N., Sabaliauskaite, G., Shaikh, S.A.: Formal template-based generation of attack-defence trees for automated security analysis. Inf. **14**(9), 481 (2023). https://doi.org/10.3390/INFO14090481
9. FireEye: APT29: the dukes cozy bear (2017). https://www.fireeye.com/blog/threat-research/2017/05/apt29_targeted_attacks.html
10. FireEye: Red team operations: real-world adversary simulation (2017). https://www.fireeye.com/current-threats/anatomy-of-a-red-team-attack.html
11. Garavel, H., Lang, F., Mateescu, R., Serwe, W.: CADP 2011: a toolbox for the construction and analysis of distributed processes. Int. J. Softw. Tools Technol. Transf. **15**(2), 89–107 (2013). https://doi.org/10.1007/s10009-012-0244-z
12. Holzmann, G.J.: The SPIN model checker. IEEE Trans. Software Eng. **23**(5), 279–295 (1997). https://doi.org/10.1109/32.588521
13. Khraisat, A., Gondal, I., Vamplew, P., Kamruzzaman, J.: Survey of intrusion detection systems: techniques, datasets and challenges. Cybersecur. **2**(1), 20 (2019). https://doi.org/10.1186/S42400-019-0038-7
14. Kordy, B., Mauw, S., Radomirović, S., Schweitzer, P.: Attack-defense trees. J. Log. Comput. **24**(1), 55–87 (2014). https://doi.org/10.1093/logcom/exs029
15. Pouzol, J., Ducassé, M.: Formal specification of intrusion signatures and detection rules. In: 15th IEEE Computer Security Foundations Workshop (CSFW-15 2002), Cape Breton, Canada. IEEE Computer Society (2002). https://doi.org/10.1109/CSFW.2002.1021807
16. Roesch, M.: Snort: lightweight intrusion detection for networks. Lisa **99**(1), 229–238 (1999)
17. Ryan, P., Schneider, S., Goldsmith, M., Lowe, G., Roscoe, B.: The Modelling and Analysis of Security Protocols: The CSP Approach. Addison-Wesley (2000)
18. Schneier, B.: Attack trees. Dr. Dobb's J. **24**(12), 21–29 (1999). https://www.schneier.com/academic/archives/1999/12/attack_trees.html
19. Sigma Community: Sigma: Generic and open signature format for siem systems (2024). https://sigmahq.io/. Accessed 01 June 2025
20. Vigna, G., Kemmerer, R.A.: NetSTAT: a network-based intrusion detection approach. In: Proceedings of the 14th Annual Computer Security Application Conference, pp. 25–34. IEEE (1998)
21. Widel, W., Audinot, M., Fila, B., Pinchinat, S.: Beyond 2014: formal methods for attack tree-based security modeling. ACM Comput. Surv. **52**(4), 75:1–75:36 (2019). https://doi.org/10.1145/3331524
22. YARA Project: Yara: The pattern matching swiss knife (2024). https://yara.readthedocs.io/. Accessed 01 June 2025

A Test-Driven Approach for Refining Use Case Specifications of Software Requirements with LLMs

Haibo Li(✉), Lixiao Zheng, and Qihang Cai

College of Computer Science and Technology, Huaqiao University, Xiamen 361021, China
{lihaibo,zhenglx}@hqu.edu.cn, 24014083004@stu.hqu.edu.cn

Abstract. Requirements described in natural language often require manual organization to align with specifications for test case generation. Similarly, when test cases are modified or enhanced, corresponding updates to the requirements must be performed manually to maintain consistency across design and development. UML use case specifications use textual descriptions to define scenarios and behaviors that achieve user goals. However, existing practices heavily rely on manual efforts to create and maintain use case specifications, leading to inefficiencies and potential inconsistencies. To address these issues, we propose a test-driven approach to further refine UML use case specifications, leveraging large language models (LLMs) to facilitate the synchronization of natural language requirements, UML specifications, and test cases. We introduce a structured format that enables LLMs to transform ambiguous natural language requirements into precise use case specifications compliant with UML, from which test cases can be automatically generated. Conversely, modifications to test cases are propagated back to update the corresponding use cases, ensuring bidirectional consistency. This iterative feedback loop continuously refines use case specifications, enhancing their accuracy and alignment with evolving requirements. Experimental evaluation on two real-world software projects demonstrates the practical application of our approach.

Keywords: software requirement · specification · UML · use case · test case · LLM

1 Introduction

Automatically generating test cases from software requirements is an important task in software engineering [1]. Acceptance testing is a critical phase for ensuring that the software system, as a whole, meets its functional requirements and business objectives, and for determining its readiness for delivery [2]. Effective acceptance testing requires well-defined test criteria, which help test engineers understand what to test and how to conduct tests. However, such criteria depend on clear user requirements. Natural language, with its inherent ambiguities, often introduces interpretational biases when describing requirements, making it impractical to directly derive test cases from such descriptions.

É. André et al. (Eds.): ICFEM 2025, LNCS 16229, pp. 189–208, 2026.
https://doi.org/10.1007/978-981-95-4213-0_11

Existing manual methods—including the Given/When/Then structure, rule-based criteria, and scenario-based approaches—are still widely used but are labor-intensive and prone to inconsistencies.

To address these issues, researchers have turned to software requirements modeling techniques [3, 4] such as Unified Modeling Language (UML). UML use case modeling combines visual diagrams with detailed textual specifications, offering a comprehensive view of requirements. Use case specifications, in particular, include a main success scenario and alternative/exception paths. Despite their strengths, the descriptions of use case specifications are only guided at the principle level, including the use of simple logic and freedom from design-oriented interactions. The means of describing them remains natural language. This gap underscores the need for better ways to bridge requirements engineering and acceptance testing.

Recent advancements in large language models (LLMs) offer promising opportunities to address these weaknesses in requirements engineering [5, 6]. LLMs, known for their ability to process and generate human-like text, can be fine-tuned through iterative prompting to perform complex reasoning tasks [7]. For example, researchers have explored using LLMs to generate acceptance criteria directly from user stories [8]. While these efforts are promising, providing a comprehensive solution for requirements characterization and testing as a whole remains a challenge. Moreover, most existing studies use LLMs only for natural language processing, limiting their ability to tackle the deeper structural and semantic challenges of defining test cases [9].

To address these challenges, we propose a test-driven approach leveraging LLMs. This approach systematically formalizes and iteratively refines UML textual use case specifications through automated test generation and validation. We present a structured format that formalizes the description of both basic and alternative/exception within use case specifications. This structured representation enables the automatic generation of comprehensive test cases, ensuring full-coverage testing for specific requirements. Furthermore, LLMs assist in identifying and resolving missing or ambiguous elements by generating extended use cases. These extensions are then seamlessly integrated back into the refined requirements. Although UML use case modeling serves as the illustrative framework in this study, the core methodology is adaptable to other requirements modeling techniques.

By combining normalization techniques, test-driven development principles, and the reasoning capabilities of LLMs, this paper aims to provide a practical framework for enhancing the accuracy and completeness of software requirements while bridging the gap between use case specifications and acceptance testing. This approach not only improves the quality of test cases but also simplifies the construction of requirements, ultimately contributing to more robust and reliable software development. The primary contributions of this work are as follows:

1) Use Case Specification Structure: We propose a structure that formalizes the use case specification and supports the automatic generation of test cases that serve as full-coverage test scenarios for the specified requirements. This structure is designed to be understandable by LLMs, enabling effective utilization of their capabilities.
2) Feedback-Enabled Refining Framework: Our framework establishes a feedback loop between use case specification and generated test cases. Extended test cases, identified

and created with the help of LLMs as part of the test scenarios, are incorporated back into the requirements. This creates a closed-loop process that improves both requirements and testing outcomes.

The remainder of this paper is organized as follows: Sect. 2 reviews related work. Section 3 analyzes use case-based software requirements, test cases, and their mappings. Section 4 outlines our proposed framework for software requirements refinement and the specification structure. Section 5 details the evaluation results. Finally, Sect. 6 offers concluding remarks.

2 Related Work

The application of LLMs in software engineering has garnered significant attention in recent years [6, 7, 10, 11]. Models like OpenAI's GPT-4 have demonstrated remarkable capabilities in understanding and generating natural language, paving the way for automation and improvement in traditionally labor-intensive software requirements engineering (SRE) tasks [5, 6]. Accurate processing and analysis of software is critical to the success of any software project, and LLMs offer a promising avenue for addressing longstanding challenges in this domain.

Recent studies highlight the potential of LLMs to enhance several SRE processes. These include requirements model extraction [12–14], classification [15], ambiguity detection [16, 17], and refinement. For example, Fantechi et al. [18] showed that ChatGPT can detect inconsistencies in requirements with an accuracy comparable to human experts. Krishna et al. [19] demonstrated the ability of LLMs to automate the generation of software requirements specifications (SRS), significantly improving productivity and reducing development time. Lubos et al. [9] investigated how LLMs can refine requirements following ISO 29148 standards, thereby improving quality and standardization. Similarly, Ren et al. [20] proposed a framework for using LLMs to generate goal models from user reviews, enabling developers to identify additional requirements. Bertram et al. [21] leveraged NLP techniques to enhance the consistency of requirements specifications through LLM-based automation, while Hasso et al. [22] demonstrated that dynamic question generation using LLMs can improve precision and completeness. Luitel et al. [23] further investigated how BERT can identify incomplete natural language requirements by integrating contextual and machine learning-based analysis. Moreover, complementary approaches utilizing LLMs to analyze requirements consistency and detect incompleteness have shown their potential to simplify requirements analysis [24].

In parallel, the standardization of requirements to improve quality and consistency has become an important area of focus. Yang et al. [25] proposed automating the generation of prototypes from formal requirements models for validation. Other studies introduced template structures for normalizing or semi-formalizing requirements to address inconsistencies and ambiguities [16, 26]. Some approaches used LLMs to extract semantic relationships from requirements to enhance consistency analysis [14], while others transformed vague user requirements into structured data that can be mapped to application services [15]. Although the idea of structured requirements has been explored for years, their practical adoption has been limited due to challenges in implementation and integration.

Another closely related domain examines the mapping of software requirements to test cases to ensure traceability and comprehensive testing [27]. Generating test cases directly from requirements has been shown to improve coverage and traceability, but it remains underexplored in SRE and software engineering due to the complexity of handling ambiguous natural language requirements. Mustafa et al. [1] highlighted this challenge, emphasizing the barriers created by incomplete and vague requirements. To address the problem, Jiao et al. [28] developed a framework for parallel test case generation using Natural Language Processing (NLP), while Wang et al. [29] proposed a method to automatically generate acceptance test cases directly from use case specifications. These efforts significantly reduce manual effort while improving test coverage. Alternative methods, such as leveraging mutation testing to generate test cases [30] or using tools designed for safety-critical systems to extract clear, unambiguous requirements for test generation [2], have also been explored. Kiyoshi et al. [31] advanced automated test case generation using topic modeling to match similar requirement specifications, reducing training sample requirements and enhancing accuracy.

Despite these advancements, notable limitations remain. Existing studies have primarily focused on high-level requirements, while paying insufficient attention to ensuring consistency between use cases and test cases in terms of the more specific low-level requirements.

3 Requirement Specification and Test Case Analysis

3.1 Software Requirement Description in Use Case

High-level requirements typically describe the overall goals, core functions, business value, and scope boundaries of a system. For example, "the system should allow registered users to purchase goods online". In contrast, low-level requirements elaborate on specific functional points, behaviors, rules, constraints, and acceptance criteria necessary to fulfill high-level requirements. For example, "users must log in before they can add goods to the shopping cart". One of the core activities in requirement analysis is to gradually refine and decompose high-level requirements into low-level ones.

Use case modeling refers to the process of describing the functional requirements of a system using use cases. A use case model mainly consists of two components: use case diagram and use case specification. Among them, the use case specification contains both business goals and macro-oriented business steps, as well as business rules and interactions rules that are gradually refined to low-level details. It carries a complete requirement chain from high-level goals to low-level details. The acceptance criteria implied in the process steps can be directly transformed into test cases. Therefore, the use case specification is crucial for software acceptance testing.

A use case specification contains a detailed description of a use case and usually conforms to a template [32]. A use case consists of a basic flow of events, which describes the scenario in which the use case can be successfully executed; alternative flows, which represent optional steps within the use case—typically triggered by specific conditions and branching off from the basic flow; and exception flows, which outline steps for handling potential conditions that would prevent the use case from succeeding. For example, a use case for handling telephone orders from buyers can be described, as shown in Fig. 1.

Use Case ID	01
Intent	Company handles phone orders of buyers
Role	order clerk
Pre-conditions	
Post-conditions	buyer completes payment.
Basic Flow	
1. Buyer calls in with a purchase request. 2. Company captures buyer's name, address, requested goods, etc. 3. Company gives buyer information on goods, prices, delivery dates, etc. 4. Buyer pays for order. 5. Company creates order, ships order to buyer. 6. Company ships invoice to buyer. 7. Buyer pays invoice.	
Alternative Flow(s):	
3a. Company is out of one of the ordered items: 3a1. Renegotiate order. 4a. Buyer pays directly with credit card: 4a1. Take payment by credit card (use case 44) 7a. Buyer returns goods: 7a1. Handle returned goods (use case 105)	
Exception Flow(s):	
4a. User payment fails 4a1. The system prompts the user to change the payment method.	

Fig. 1. An example of textual use case template

3.2 Mapping Between Use Case Specifications and Test Cases

There is a mapping relationship between use case specifications and test cases, analyzed primarily from software engineering principles.

In classical software engineering, which follows a top-down development approach (such as the traditional V-model and its variants like double or triple V-models [33]), acceptance testing has a special role: it directly validates alignment with use case specifications, ensuring the software meets user expectations and business needs. This makes it a critical check to decide if the software is ready for delivery.

In agile development, the relationship evolves dynamically. Use case specifications are often simplified into user stories, with acceptance criteria embedded within them. Here, acceptance tests are co-created by developers, testers, and stakeholders (e.g., via Behavior-Driven Development) and act as living documentation. They not only verify compliance with the evolving use case details but also drive development increments, with test cases refining and clarifying use case specifications iteratively.

Test scenarios, derived from use case flows (basic and alternative), ensure requirement coverage, with mapping rules facilitating systematic translation from flows to test cases.

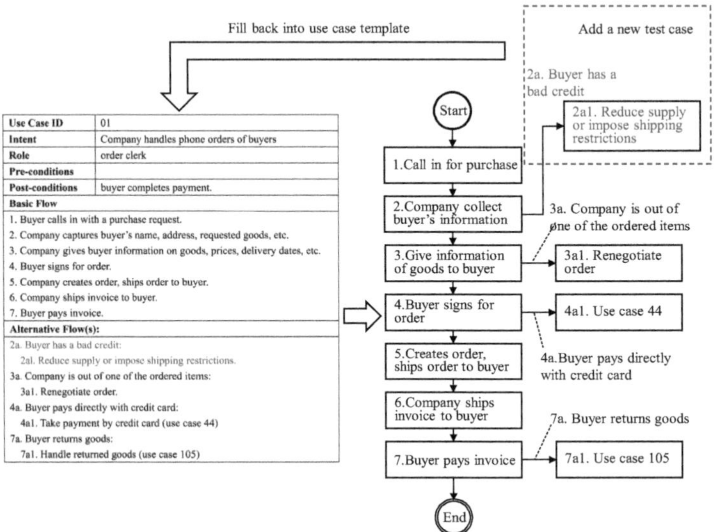

(a) Use case template (b) Test cases

Fig. 2. An example of mapping between a use case and the test cases

The process for generating test cases from use case specifications can be outlined as follows:

1) Begin with the basic flow.
2) Extend the basic flow with individual alternative steps that branch from it, ensuring each step in the alternative flows is used at least once and leads to the use case's conclusion.

The basic flow, as shown in Fig. 2(a), can generate a test case, while the basic flow combined with an alternative step can produce a new test case. Test cases generated from this process might include: 1) the basic flow, 2) the basic flow with alternative step 3a1, 3) the basic flow with alternative step 4a1, and 4) the basic flow with alternative step 7a1, as shown in Fig. 2(b). If additional test cases, such as step 2a1, are required, they can also be directly mapped to specific use case flows.

4 The Refinement Framework

4.1 An Overview

To support full-coverage business scenarios essential for system or acceptance testing, this paper proposes a framework for refining use case specifications, as illustrated in Fig. 3. The framework adopts a predefined structure which guides LLMs to translate natural language requirements into structured UML use case specifications. These structured use case specifications can then be directly used to generate test cases based on mapping rules, which help test engineers grasp accurate and comprehensive business scenarios. To normalize this process, each step of both basic and alternative flows within use case specifications is described using a structured format. This ensures the requirements are suitable not only for automated test generation but also for other software engineering tasks, such as identifying class diagrams in object-oriented design.

Additionally, when new test cases are generated by the LLMs, the newly added alternative steps can be filled back into the textual use case specifications according to this structure. LLMs can enhance user requirements by introducing extended use cases, providing further refinement for requirements engineers.

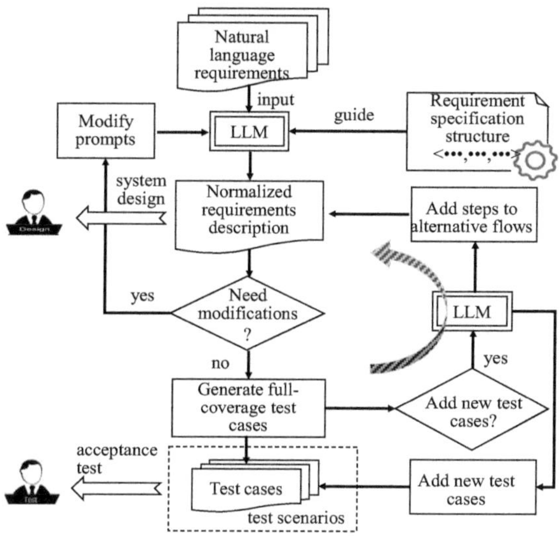

Fig. 3. The test-driven refinement framework

4.2 Requirement Specifications Structure

The UML use case template is too "coarse-grained". If test cases are to be automatically generated from natural language requirements, the natural language still needs to be further structured. This is very important for generating test cases (which require machine-readable requirements) and facilitating object-oriented design (which requires clear identification of actors and affected business objects). For this purpose, we set up a structured text format for natural language requirements, where each sentence follows the format below:

$$< Pre - conditions\left[Previous\ Step\right], actor, action, business\ objects, [toactor], [Post - conditions] > \quad (1)$$

This structure uses angle brackets to enclose the requirement's core description. The element "*Pre-conditions*" specifies prerequisites, which may also be interpreted as preceding steps. "*Business object*" denotes a real-world entity (e.g., order, invoice) impacted by the "actor" (the entity initiating the action). "*Post-conditions*" define the conditions that must be held after successful execution. For example, the natural language requirement "*Buyer creates order, Company ships order to the buyer.*" can be expressed as the structured format < *Buyer*, *creates*, *order* > and < *if buyer creates order, Company*, *ships*, *order*, *to buyer* >.

This standardized structure ensures requirements are both machine-readable and human-understandable, facilitating automated processing by LLMs. If other use cases need to be executed in alternative flows, the requirement specification structure can be simplified to the following form:

$$< Pre - conditions \left[Previous\ Step\right],\ use\ case\ ID > \tag{2}$$

For example, the natural language requirement "*buyer returns goods, handling returned goods.*" can be expressed as "*if buyer returns goods, use case 105*", because handling returned goods is a separate use case.

4.3 Refining Requirement Using LLMs

Integrating LLMs into this framework is critical for refining requirements. This process involves systematically transforming raw, natural language requirements into structured descriptions, generating UML use case specifications, and creating high-quality test cases. Furthermore, an iterative feedback mechanism makes it possible to refine the use case specifications and improve subsequent outputs. Below, the components of the proposed approach are outlined in detail.

1) Structured Use Case Specifications

The first step in our framework is converting raw natural language requirements into the structured format. Contextual knowledge relevant to software requirements, including the elements of the specified structure (e.g., pre-conditions, actor, action, post-conditions, etc.) is provided to LLMs to ensure they fully understand the task. LLMs are guided with the following prompt:

> "*Given the following unstructured software requirement described in natural language, structuring it according to the predefined requirements pattern. Ensure each sentence follows the <Pre-conditions, actor, action, business objects, to actor, Post-conditions> pattern and includes pre-conditions, post-conditions, and exceptions (if any). Present the structured requirement in a clear and concise format.*"

Once structured, the requirements are further processed to generate UML use case specifications. Using this prompt:

> "*Based on the following structured requirement, create a UML use case specification that includes intent, role, preconditions, post-conditions, and basic/alternative flows. Ensure the description is clear and comprehensive.*"

The output provides well-structured, detailed use case specifications that are optimized for accuracy and readability. These specifications can be further refined based on new requirements or feedback from testing phases, ensuring they meet the precise needs of various stakeholders.

2) Automatic Test Case Generation

To generate test cases from the UML use case specifications, we leverage LLMs with targeted prompt:

> "*Given the UML use case: [insert UML use case template here], generate a set of test cases that cover both the basic and alternative flows. Each test case should detail the test data, steps, and expected results with clarity and precision.*"

This ensures that the generated test cases comprehensively cover both intended functionality and edge cases derived from alternative flows. Additional refinement can be introduced by specifying the desired test case format or including examples of well-formed test cases to guide the LLM's output.

3) Iterative Refinement of Requirements Based on Test Case Reviews

Test case reviews help find flaws in original requirements, such as gaps, ambiguities or inconsistencies. These flaws are then fixed to improve test scenarios and requirement specifications. For example, uncovering unconsidered exceptions may lead to new requirements, while mismatches between requirements and test cases prompt revisions to align them. This iterative feedback keeps requirements in step with evolving system understanding. LLMs can aid this review via prompts:

- Identifying Gaps and Inconsistencies

> "*Analyze the following test cases to check if there are any contradictions within the test steps, if any steps are missing, or if the expected results are not clearly defined.*"

- Suggesting Additional Test Cases

> "*Based on the following test cases, suggest additional test cases that would provide more comprehensive coverage of the functionality being tested, such as edge cases, boundary conditions, or error handling.*"

- Discovering Implicit Requirements

> "*Analyze the following test cases and identify underlying assumptions about the system's behavior that may not be explicitly documented in the requirements.*"

Feedback from these analyses is then used to refine the requirements further. For example: "*Based on the feedback from the test case review: [insert feedback], refine the following requirement: [insert requirement]. Ensure that the refined requirement addresses the identified issues*". Additional constraints, such as ensuring the refined requirement aligns with SMART principles (Specific, Measurable, Achievable, Relevant, and Time-bound), can also be incorporated. Iterative refinement not only improves the quality of requirements but also enhances the LLM's accuracy in subsequent tasks as it learns from prior feedback.

This closed-loop process integrates LLMs to streamline requirement refinement and test case generation, ensuring that requirements evolve iteratively while maintaining alignment with testing efforts. By automating these processes, the framework reduces ambiguity and enhances the precision of software requirements, enabling systems or acceptance testing in full-coverage test scenarios for the specified requirements.

5 Evaluation

5.1 Set up

To evaluate our proposed approach, we selected software requirements from the PURE dataset [34], a publicly accessible repository of natural language requirements documents sourced from various online platforms. We identified two specific projects from the dataset based on following selection criterion: their documentations contain detailed natural language descriptions of software functionalities, providing rich semantic material for use case extraction. The details of these two projects are as follows.

1) KeePass password management system is a lightweight application designed to address the challenge of securely managing and storing passwords. Its primary function is to maintain a secure, encrypted database where users can store passwords, usernames, email accounts, and related information, all protected by a master password.
2) GAMMA-J Web Store is an online E-commerce system designed to allow new online store owners a quick and easy means to setup and perform sales and other core business over the internet. Its primary function is to manage customer accounts, manage customers' shopping carts and confirm orders, manage online store inventory, and so on.

Since the PURE dataset also includes non-functional details such as implementation and technical aspects, we filtered the data, extracting only functional requirements to be used as input for structuring in our framework. To better validate our approach, we also extended natural language description for some of the requirements when necessary.

GPT-4, a LLM developed by OpenAI, was selected for this experiment due to its ability to process and generate human-level text. The experimental process adopted a "human-in-the-loop" approach, where human reviewers and the language model collaborated iteratively. Key steps in the process included structuring natural language requirements, transforming natural languages into structured use case specification, generating test cases, reviewing test cases, and refining use cases based on feedback. Supplemental project information, such as scope and an overview of the KeePass system or Web Store system, were also provided to the LLM to help it generate more accurate and relevant outputs during the iterative process.

Our experimental evaluation[1] consists of two parts. First, as a demonstration example, one of the authors created use cases for the KeePass requirements by following our

[1] Data available at https://github.com/HQU-CaiQihang/data.

proposed method. Second, for comparative analysis, we conducted a study to evaluate the performance of two groups of requirements engineers in analyzing requirements for all the functional descriptions of the Web Store system.

5.2 Example on KeePass

Below, we outline each step following our approach using an example extracted from the KeePass requirements document. One of the natural language requirements in KeePass describes a feature for opening an existing database. The original description is stated as follows:

> "*When choosing to open a database a user is transferred to his documents where he navigates to find the database he wants. When the database is found, the master password is wanted so that the database will be unlocked. Once this is done the user is free to access his data. The user can view, modify, add, or delete the data if he has the proper permissions. The user also can perform backup and recovery operations on the data. If the user closes the database, the system returns to the navigation interface of the document.*"

The refinement follows three key steps:

1) Natural Language Structuring

The original natural language requirement is structured into a unified format as described in Sect. 4.2. The LLM-generated description (with minor manual refinements) is presented in Table 1.

Table 1. The structured requirement description

No.	The Structured Natural Language Requirement
1	*<[User initiates database opening process], User, navigates, database>*
2	*<[User navigates to database], System, prompts for, master password>*
3	*<[System prompts for master password], User, enters, master password>*
4	*<[User enters master password],System, verifies, master password>*
5	*<[Password is correct], System, unlocks, database>*
6	*<[Password is incorrect], System, displays, error message>*
7	*<[System unlocks database], User, accesses, database content>*
8	*<[User has the proper permissions], User, view/modify/add/delete, data>*
9	*<[User has the proper permissions], User, performs, backup and recovery operations>*
10	*<[User closes database], System, returns, navigation interface of the document>*

In addition, Deepseek is chosen as a baseline LLM, and one version of the generated structured requirement descriptions is shown in Table 2. Through comparison, this version strictly complies with the original requirement descriptions. The capability of LLMs largely depends on prompt engineering, and various LLM products are also constantly evolving. In the future, requirement descriptions can be organized through more complex structures.

Table 2. The structured requirement description by Deepseek

No.	The Structured Natural Language Requirement
1	*<[User chooses to open a database], User, Navigates through documents, Database>*
2	*<[Database is found], User, Enters, Master password>*
3	*<[Database is unlocked], User, Accesses, Data>*
4	*<[Database is unlocked + user has permissions], User, Views, modifies, adds, or deletes, Data>*
5	*<[Database is unlocked], User, Performs backup/recovery operations, Data>*
6	*<[User finishes data interactions], User, Closes database, Database>*
7	*<[Database is closed, System], Returns to, Navigation interface>*

2) Use Case Template Transformation

Since the structured requirements align with the use case specification format, the transformation process requires only minimal adjustments. The structured requirements are easily adapted into a UML use case template using either a manual process or the LLM. The resulting use case includes eight steps in the basic flow and four steps in alternative flows (steps 3a1, 4a1, 6a1, and 6b1). Figure 4 shows a detailed view of the basic and alternative flows.

Use Case ID	03
Intent	User accesses database content
Role	End users/Desktop
Pre-conditions	
Post-conditions	
Basic Flow	
1. User opens KeePass and selects "Open Database" operation. 2. System prompts for master password. 3. User enters master password. 4. System verifies master password. 5. System unlocks database. 6. User access his data: views, modifies, adds, or deletes the data, or perform backup and recovery operations on the data. 7. User closes database. 8. System returns to the main window.	
Alternative Flow(s):	
1a. User selects a type of folder non suitable for database. 1a1. System displays "file not found" message. 1b. There are too much databases in the system. 1b1. System provides a database search function. 3a. The system checks user has no permissions to access the database. 3a1. The system displays error message and access is denied. 3a2. User resets the master password. 4a. System verifies master password and password is incorrect. 4a1. System displays error message. 6a. User forgets to save modification. 6a1. The system saves user modifications in real time. 6b. User operations are inactive for long periods of time. 6b1. System automatically locks the database and the master password to be entered again for continued access.	Additional steps

Fig. 4. The flows in the use case template of KeePass example

3) Test Case Review and Iterative Refinement.

The generated test cases, as shown in Table 3, are then reviewed by test engineers or by LLM. In our experiments, we tasked GPT-4 with reviewing the generated test cases, and the missing test cases are proposed, as shown in Table 4.

Table 3. The flows in the use case specifications generating test cases

No.	The Flows in the Use Case that Generate Test Cases
1	Basic flow
2	Basic flow + step 3a1 in alternative flow
3	Basic flow + step 4a1 in alternative flow
4	Basic flow + step 6a1 in alternative flow
5	Basic flow + step 6b1 in alternative flow

Table 4. The added test cases and flows in use case specification

No.	Test Cases	Flows in Use Case	Supplemental Functionality Requirement
1	*"If User selects a type of folder non suitable for database, System displays "file not found" message."*	Basic flow + step 1a1 in alternative flow	Database navigates functionality: *"When User selects a type of folder non suitable for database, the system displays "file not found" message."*
2	*"User can search the database if it is difficult to find."*	Basic flow + step 1b1 in alternative flow	Database search functionality: *"System provides a database search mechanism if there are too many databases in the navigation page, so that the user can easily find the database he wants."*
3	*"user resets password if forgotten."*	Basic flow + step 3a2 in alternative flow	Password reset functionality: *"System provides a password reset mechanism such that the user is able to successfully reset the master password and regain access to the database."*

Its feedback includes suggestions for improvements and additional flows in use case specification. Using this feedback, the functional requirements are refined further by adding a new feature, as shown in Table 4. The corresponding steps are 1a1, 1b1, and 3a2, as shown in Fig. 4.

We compared other test case generation tools, such as TestSonic. The test cases generated by these tools with AI functions are comparable to the method in this paper in terms of quantity and quality, but they cannot feed back to the original requirements. Those without AI functions are basically unable to expand and supplement test cases from the original requirement descriptions.

This iterative process of interaction with LLM continues until the requirement description sufficiently meets the needs of all stakeholders. Each iteration improves the clarity and completeness of the requirements while identifying and addressing potential gaps in test coverage.

5.3 Comparison Analysis

5.3.1 Effectiveness Comparison

We conducted a comparative study to evaluate the performance of two groups of requirements engineers in analyzing software requirements and developing test cases for all the functional descriptions of Web Store. Each group consists of three engineers, differentiated by their level of experience: junior (1–2 years), mid-level (3–5 years), and senior (6–8 years). One group utilizes the LLM GPT-4 following our approach, while the other serves as a baseline by performing tasks manually without the test-driven approach or LLM assistance, that is, the traditional manual method of analyzing requirements. The study focuses on assessing two aspects: the effectiveness and efficiency of the approaches.

Table 5 summarizes the results of use case specifications for Web Store created by engineers of different experience levels of each group. The first row shows the use case specifications in the original Web Store document. The results show that the number of basic flows in the use case specifications remains consistent regardless of the use of LLM. Both groups identified fewer use cases than the dataset due to redundant use cases in the raw requirement. LLM assistance significantly increased alternative flow identification, particularly for mid-level and junior engineers. Senior engineers exhibited inherent proficiency in detecting edge cases, resulting in more comprehensive and accurate requirement specifications.

These findings highlight the value of LLM in augmenting human analytical capabilities, particularly in identifying exceptional cases and uncovering hidden requirements. Additionally, senior engineers display an inherent strength in identifying exceptional scenarios, resulting in more comprehensive specifications.

We evaluated the quality of the use case specifications according to the following four characteristics defined in ISO 29148 [35].

1) Complete: All information needed to understand the requirement is included in the description (completeness).
2) Correct: The need is accurately represented in the requirement (consistency).
3) Unambiguous: The requirement is clearly stated, understandable, and allows only one interpretation (accuracy).
4) Verifiable: The requirement is formulated in a way that its fulfillment can be proven or, in the best case, measured (testability).

Table 5. Use case specification results for Web Store.

Mode	Level	Number of		
		Use Cases	Basic Flows	Alternative Flows
Original	–	26	26	14
Our approach	Junior	20	20	36
	Mid-level	20	20	42
	Senior	20	20	32
Baseline manually	Junior	20	20	33
	Mid-level	21	20	14
	Senior	20	20	26

The specifications were reviewed and scored by five independent experts, three from academic institutions and two from industry, and each with more than 10 years of experience in requirements engineering. The experts evaluated the specifications using a scale of 1 to 10 for each criterion.

Table 6. Quality of use case specification for Web Strore

Mode	Level	Completeness	Consistency	Accuracy	Testability
Original	–	6.1	6.7	5.8	7.1
Our approach	Junior	7.8	8.2	8.5	6.8
	Mid-level	8.9	8.8	9.1	8.3
	Senior	9.5	9.1	9.6	9.5
Baseline manually	Junior	5.2	6.3	5.4	6.7
	Mid-level	6.4	7.7	6.8	8.1
	Senior	8.4	8.9	8.6	9.4

As shown in Table 6, LLM-assisted use cases consistently outperform manual efforts across all quality dimensions. By structuring the raw requirements, the LLM facilitates the identification of both basic and alternative flows while also reducing ambiguities and incorrectness, thereby improving the accuracy and consistency of the specifications. Moreover, adopting a test-driven approach to iteratively enhance the use case specifications effectively improves their completeness and testability.

To further evaluate our approach, we compared three use case specifications for Web Store: 1) the original use case specification from the PURE dataset, 2) for benchmarking validation, without LLM assistance, a manually created specification developed by an expert-level engineer with over 15 years of experience reverse-engineered the functional requirements by analyzing the requirement documentation, and 3) the specifications generated by three engineers, junior, mid-level, and senior engineers using our test-driven LLM approach. Removing the 6 duplicate use cases, there are 20 available use case templates in Web Store. The reverse-engineered requirement specification developed by the expert-level engineer served as the ground truth for evaluating precision and recall across the three specifications, calculated using the following two formulas:

$$precision = \frac{\#flows\ matching\ the\ ground\ truth}{\#total\ flows\ in\ the\ specification} \tag{3}$$

$$recall = \frac{\#flows\ matching\ the\ ground\ truth}{\#total\ flows\ in\ the\ ground\ truth} \tag{4}$$

The evaluation was conducted by the two experts to assess alignment and discrepancies between the use case flows (basic and alternative flows) in each specification and the ground truth. The experts made their judgments independently and then cross-validated their assessments. The results of this comparison are summarized in Table 7. We analyze the results as follows.

Table 7. Comparison of different use case specifications for Web Store

Use Case Specifications	Precision	Recall
Original	44.82%	33.33%
Junior	50.77%	76.92%
Mid-level	52.63%	84.62%
Senior	65.38%	87.18%

1) Original use case specifications achieved a precision rate of 44.82% and a recall rate of 33.33%, indicating suboptimal performance where over half of identified cases were irrelevant and two-thirds of relevant cases were missed.
2) The specifications obtained following our approach achieved higher precision compared to the original specification. Notably, engineers leveraging LLM achieved a higher recall rate than precision. This demonstrates that our test-driven, LLM-assisted approach helped identify most additional alternative flows, which allows for a broader scenario coverage despite potential trade-offs in precision.

5.3.2 Efficiency Comparison

To assess efficiency, we measured the time taken by both groups to complete each functional requirement specification for Web Store. For the group using our approach, we also recorded the number of times participants refined their LLM prompts and refined the use case specifications. In the baseline manual group, the total time spent in constructing the use case specifications was recorded. The results are shown in Table 8.

Table 8. Efforts saved by using our approach.

Level	Refine Times	Overall Time consumed(min)			Satisfaction
		Our approach	*Baseline manually*	*Speed up*	
Junior	11	63	645	10x	high
Mid-level	9	38	313	8x	high
Senior	7	30	156	5x	high

The analysis shows that the use of our approach results in a significant 5–10 fold increase in productivity compared to manual approaches. The reduction in manual effort allows participants to complete their tasks significantly faster. Moreover, the group reports high satisfaction with the test-driven approach facilitated by LLM. Junior engineer requires more time and need timely adjustments compared to their mid-level and senior counterparts, highlighting the need for additional training in the use of the LLM and software requirements engineering fundamentals.

6 Conclusion

This paper explores the UML use case specification of software requirements and the mapping rules between use case specifications and test cases. We present a test-driven approach that employs LLMs to bridge the gap between natural language and structured descriptions. Our findings demonstrate that LLMs effectively identify and transform requirements into the proposed structure, enabling the partial or full generation of use case specifications and test cases. Our case study on KeePass evaluated this approach with requirements engineers of varying experience levels. The case study on Web Store demonstrated improvements in both the efficiency and effectiveness of requirements analysis. Specifically, the test-driven and LLM-enhanced method facilitated the identification of additional alternative flows and produced more structured, accurate, and testable requirements.

Future research will aim to further enrich requirements documentation to generate higher quality test cases by incorporating inputs from business process models developed during the design phase. Additionally, we plan to explore alternative perspectives to further refine and optimize software requirements.

Acknowledgments. This work is supported by the Fundamental Research Funds for the Central Universities (No. ZQN-1010), Fujian Province Science and Technology Plan, China (No. 2019H0017).

References

1. Mustafa, A., et al.: Automated test case generation from requirements: a systematic literature review. Comput. Mater. Contin. **67**(2), 1819–1833 (2021). https://doi.org/10.32604/cmc.2021.014391
2. Moitra, A., et al.: Automating requirements analysis and test case generation. Requir. Eng. **24**(3), 341–364 (2019). https://doi.org/10.1007/s00766-019-00316-x
3. Necula, S.C., Dumitriu, F., Greavu-Şerban, V.: A systematic literature review on using natural language processing in software requirements engineering. Electron. **13**(11) (2024). https://doi.org/10.3390/electronics13112055
4. Ayenew, H., Wagaw, M.: Software test case generation using natural language processing (NLP): a systematic literature review. Artif. Intell. Evol. 1–10 (2024). https://doi.org/10.37256/aie.5120243220
5. Arora, C., Grundy, J., Abdelrazek, M.: Advancing requirements engineering through generative AI: assessing the role of LLMs. Gener. AI Eff. Softw. Dev. 129–148 (2024). https://doi.org/10.1007/978-3-031-55642-5_6
6. Vogelsang, A.: From specifications to prompts: on the future of generative large language models in requirements engineering. IEEE Softw. **41**(5), 9–13 (2024). https://doi.org/10.1109/MS.2024.3410712
7. Wei, J., et al.: Chain-of-thought prompting elicits reasoning in large language models. Adv. Neural. Inf. Process. Syst. **35**, 24824–24837 (2022)
8. Li, Y., Keung, J., Yang, Z., Ma, X., Zhang, J., Liu, S.: SimAC: simulating agile collaboration to generate acceptance criteria in user story elaboration. Autom. Softw. Eng. **31**(2) (2024). https://doi.org/10.1007/s10515-024-00448-7

9. Lubos, S., et al.: Leveraging LLMs for the quality assurance of software requirements. In: Proceedings of the IEEE International Conference on Requirement Engineering, pp. 389–397 (2024). https://doi.org/10.1109/RE59067.2024.00046
10. Norheim, J.J., Rebentisch, E., Xiao, D., Draeger, L., Kerbrat, A., De Weck, O.L.: Challenges in applying large language models to requirements engineering tasks. Des. Sci. **10** (2024). https://doi.org/10.1017/dsj.2024.8
11. Borg, M., Borg, M.: Requirements engineering and large language models: insights from a panel. IEEE Softw. **41**(2), 6–10 (2024). https://doi.org/10.1109/MS.2023.3339934
12. Siddeshwar, V., Alwidian, S., Makrehchi, M.: Goal model extraction from user stories using large language models, pp. 269–276 (2024). https://doi.org/10.1007/978-3-031-70245-7_19
13. Arulmohan, S., Meurs, M.J., Mosser, S.: Extracting domain models from textual requirements in the era of large language models. In: Proceedings - 2023 ACM/IEEE International Conference on Model Driven Engineering Languages and Systems Companion, Model 2023, pp. 580–587 (2023). https://doi.org/10.1109/MODELS-C59198.2023.00096
14. Feng, N., et al.: Normative requirements operationalization with large language models. In: Proceedings of the IEEE International Conference on Requirement Engineering, pp. 129–141 (2024). https://doi.org/10.1109/RE59067.2024.00022
15. Ruixiang, L., Qiujun, D., Xianhui, L., Chenglin, Z., Weidong, Z.: Requirement-service mapping technology in the industrial application field based on large language models. Appl. Intell. **55**(1) (2025). https://doi.org/10.1007/s10489-024-05969-y
16. Tikayat Ray, A., Cole, B.F., Pinon Fischer, O.J., Bhat, A.P., White, R.T., Mavris, D.N.: Agile methodology for the standardization of engineering requirements using large language models. Systems **11**(7) (2023). https://doi.org/10.3390/systems11070352
17. Ezzini, S., Abualhaija, S., Arora, C., Sabetzadeh, M.: Automated handling of anaphoric ambiguity in requirements: a multi-solution study. In: Proceedings - International Conference on Software Engineering, vol. 2022-May, pp. 187–199 (2022). https://doi.org/10.1145/3510003.3510157
18. Fantechi, A., Gnesi, S., Passaro, L., Semini, L.: Inconsistency detection in natural language requirements using ChatGPT: a preliminary evaluation. In: Proceedings of the IEEE International Conference on Requirements Engineering, vol. 2023-Septe, pp. 335–340 (2023). https://doi.org/10.1109/RE57278.2023.00045
19. Krishna, M., Gaur, B., Verma, A., Jalote, P.: Using LLMs in software requirements specifications: an empirical evaluation. In: Proceedings of the IEEE International Conference on Requirements Engineering, pp. 475–483 (2024). https://doi.org/10.1109/RE59067.2024.00056
20. Ren, S., Nakagawa, H., Tsuchiya, T.: Combining prompts with examples to enhance LLM-based requirement elicitation, pp. 1376–1381 (2024). https://doi.org/10.1109/compsac61105.2024.00181
21. Bertram, V., Kausch, H., Kusmenko, E., Nqiri, H., Rumpe, B.,Venhoff, C.: Leveraging natural language processing for a consistency checking toolchain of automotive requirements. In: Proceedings of the IEEE International Conference on Requirements Engineering, vol. 2023-Septe, pp. 212–222 (2023). https://doi.org/10.1109/RE57278.2023.00029
22. Hasso, H., Fischer-Starcke, B., Geppert, H.: Quest-RE QUestion generation and exploration STrategy for requirements engineering. In: Proceedings - 32nd IEEE International Requirements Engineering Conference Workshops, REW 2024, pp. 3–11 (2024). https://doi.org/10.1109/REW61692.2024.00006
23. Luitel, D., Hassani, S., Sabetzadeh, M.: Improving requirements completeness: automated assistance through large language models. Requir. Eng. **29**(1), 73–95 (2024). https://doi.org/10.1007/s00766-024-00416-3

24. Uygun, Y., Momodu, V.: Local large language models to simplify requirement engineering documents in the automotive industry. Prod. Manuf. Res. **12**(1) (2024). https://doi.org/10.1080/21693277.2024.2375296
25. Yang, Y., Li, X., Ke, W., Liu, Z.: Automated prototype generation from formal requirements model. IEEE Trans. Reliab. **69**(2), 632–656 (2020). https://doi.org/10.1109/TR.2019.2934348
26. Norheim, J.J., Rebentisch, E.: Structuring natural language requirements with large language models. In: Proc. - 32nd IEEE International Requirements Engineering Conference Workshops, REW 2024, pp. 68–71 (2024). https://doi.org/10.1109/REW61692.2024.00013
27. Li, Y., Liu, P., Wang, H., Chu, J., Wong, W.E.: Evaluating large language models for software testing. Comput. Stand. Interfaces 93 (2025). https://doi.org/10.1016/j.csi.2024.103942
28. Jiao, Y., Wang, J., Li, R., Wang, F.-Y., Zhao, H., Xiong, G.: Intelligent generation of test cases for a parallel testing system: a case study on railway systems. IEEE Intell. Transp. Syst. Mag. 2–13 (2024). https://doi.org/10.1109/mits.2024.3435828
29. Wang, C., Pastore, F., Goknil, A., Briand, L.C.: Automatic generation of acceptance test cases from use case specifications: an NLP-based approach. IEEE Trans. Softw. Eng. **48**(2), 585–616 (2022). https://doi.org/10.1109/TSE.2020.2998503
30. Dakhel, A.M., Nikanjam, A., Majdinasab, V., Khomh, F., Desmarais, M.C.: Effective test generation using pre-trained Large Language Models and mutation testing. Inf. Softw. Technol. **171** (2024). https://doi.org/10.1016/j.infsof.2024.107468
31. Ueda, K., Shikama, R., Shimizu, Y.: Automatic test cases generation with selection of training data for various system specifications. In: Proceedings of the IEEE International Conference on Computer Communication and the Internet, ICCCI, no. 2024, pp. 1–6 (2024). https://doi.org/10.1109/ICCCI62159.2024.10674503
32. Mai, P.X., Goknil, A., Shar, L.K., Pastore, F., Briand, L.C., Shaame, S.: Modeling security and privacy requirements: a use case-driven approach. Inf. Softw. Technol. **100**, 165–182 (2018). https://doi.org/10.1016/j.infsof.2018.04.007
33. Han, Y., Lee, D.H., Choi, B., Hinchey, M., In, H.P.: Value-driven V-model: from requirements analysis to acceptance testing. IEICE Trans. Inf. Syst. **E99D**(7), 1776–1785 (2016). https://doi.org/10.1587/transinf.2015EDP7451
34. Ferrari, A., Spagnolo, G.O., Gnesi, S.: PURE: a dataset of public requirements documents. In: Proceedings - 2017 IEEE 25th International Requirement Engineering Conference, RE 2017, pp. 502–505 (2017). https://doi.org/10.1109/RE.2017.29
35. ISO/IEC/IEEE15288. INTERNATIONAL STANDARD ISO/IEC/IEEE Systems and software engineering. Int. Stand. ISO/IEC/IEEE 42010, vol. First edit, pp. 1–104 (2018). https://ieeexplore.ieee.org/servlet/opac?punumber=8559684

ZK-ProVer: Proving Programming Verification in Non-interactive Zero-Knowledge Proofs

Haoyu Wei, Jingyu Ke, Ruibang Liu, and Guoqiang Li(✉)

School of Computer Science, Shanghai Jiao Tong University, Shanghai, China
{haoyuwei,Windocotber,628628,li.g}@sjtu.edu.cn

Abstract. *Program verification* ensures software correctness through formal methods but incurs substantial computational overhead. It typically encodes program execution into formulas that are verified using a SAT solver and its extensions. However, this process exposes sensitive program details and requires redundant computations when multiple parties need to verify correctness. To overcome these limitations, zero-knowledge proofs (ZKPs) generate compact, reusable proofs with fast verification times, while provably hiding the program's internal logic. We propose a two-phase zero-knowledge protocol that hides program implementation details throughout verification. In Phase I, a zero-knowledge virtual machine (zkVM) is employed, which adopts HyperPlonk as the underlying protocol. This zkVM enables the encoding of programs into Boolean Satisfiability (SAT) formulas, while strictly avoiding the disclosure of the programs' semantic information. Phase II employs the encoding of resolution proofs for UNSAT instances and circuits for satisfying assignment verification for SAT instances through PLONKish circuits. Evaluation on the Boolector benchmark demonstrates that our method achieves verification time that is efficient and is independent of clause width for UNSAT instances and formula size for SAT instances. The resulting ZKPs enable efficient verification of program properties while providing strong end-to-end privacy guarantees.

Keywords: program verification · zero-knowledge proofs · SAT · PLONKish · zkVM

1 Introduction

Program verification, the process of formally proving that software satisfies its specifications, has become increasingly critical for safety-critical systems in domains such as finance, autonomous vehicles, and smart contracts [1–3]. Various program verification techniques have been developed. *Symbolic execution* [4] explores all possible execution paths by treating inputs as symbolic values. *Bounded model checking* [5] verifies properties within a finite number of execution steps by unrolling loops and recursive calls up to a specified bound.

É. André et al. (Eds.): ICFEM 2025, LNCS 16229, pp. 209–227, 2026.
https://doi.org/10.1007/978-981-95-4213-0_12

Invariant generation [6] automatically discovers loop invariants and function preconditions/postconditions. Generally speaking, some of these techniques reduce program verification to satisfiability modulo theories (SMT) over the bit-vector theory, and rely on the bit-blasting technique to further transform the problem into low-level SAT instances. For the resulting SAT formula, if it is satisfiable, the underlying SAT solver produces a satisfying assignment under which the formula evaluates to true; otherwise, it generates a resolution proof certifying that no such assignment exists.

In practice, this verification workflow faces two critical challenges. First, proving the correctness of verification typically requires disclosing both the program and its corresponding SAT formula along with the proof, thereby revealing concrete implementation details and posing potential intellectual property risks. Second, independent re-verification by multiple parties incurs redundant computational costs while demanding blind trust undermines the credibility of verification. For instance, a fintech company seeking to prove to regulators that its trading algorithm satisfies specific properties would need to expose the SAT formula and the program itself, creating an unacceptable trade-off between transparency and confidentiality.

ZKPs enable proving the validity of statements [7] without revealing program information, SAT formula solutions (for satisfiable instances), or resolution proofs (for unsatisfiable instances) while offering computational efficiency through one-time proof generation and lightweight verification. This unique combination of privacy preservation and computational efficiency makes ZKPs ideally suited to address the dual challenges of protecting proprietary program information while enabling efficient third-party verification.

We present a novel two-phase protocol that leverages recent advances in zkVM [8] and PLONKish circuits [9] to construct ZKPs, addressing the challenges of privacy-preserving program verification and reducing redundant computation. Phase I enhances zkVM with a custom HyperPlonk [10] protocol to transform public program properties and private program implementation into SAT formulas, thereby avoiding the exposure of code segments. Phase II utilizes PLONKish-based arithmetic circuits to verify SAT results. We construct PLONKish circuits for both SAT and UNSAT cases - encoding resolution proofs for unsatisfiable instances and verifying satisfying assignments for satisfiable ones, both concealing the SAT formula throughout the verification process. Phases are cryptographically linked through polynomial commitments to the SAT formula, ensuring consistency of the formula representation between phases. Evaluation demonstrates the remarkable efficiency of our protocol: Phase I achieves a three-fold performance improvement over native zkVM through our HyperPlonk protocol implementation; in Phase II, the Boolector benchmark evaluation shows that for UNSAT cases, verification time is independent of clause width; for SAT cases with valid assignments, verification is independent of formula size, making it practical for selective property disclosure while protecting intellectual property. The main contributions of this paper are:

- A zkVM-based approach enhanced with HyperPlonk protocol that achieves three-fold performance improvement for proving correct private SAT encoding while maintaining program privacy.
- A novel PLONKish arithmetic circuit design with two approaches: encoding resolution proofs for UNSAT instances to achieve verification time independent of clause width, and efficient satisfying assignment verification for SAT instances to achieve verification time independent of formula size, both generating efficiently verifiable privacy-preserving proofs.
- Experimental evaluation demonstrating the practicality of our approach on real-world program verification benchmarks.

Paper Organization. The remainder of this paper is organized as follows: Sect. 2 reviews the foundational technical principles and results underpinning our work. Section 3 introduces an overview of our two-phase protocol. Section 4 provides a detailed technical exposition of our protocol and optimizations; Sect. 5 describes the implementation and empirical evaluation of our protocol. Section 6 introduces the related work, and Sect. 7 concludes the paper.

2 Preliminaries

2.1 Zero-Knowledge Proofs (ZKPs)

A Zero-Knowledge Proof (ZKP) is a cryptographic protocol involving two parties: a *Prover* and a *Verifier*. The goal of a ZKP is for the prover to convince the verifier that a statement (or computation) is correct, without revealing any additional information about the witness or computation itself. In other words, the verifier learns only whether the statement is valid and nothing else.

Formally, let L be a language and R_L be the corresponding relation such that $(x, w) \in R_L$ if and only if $x \in L$ and w is a valid witness for x. A pair (P, V) of probabilistic polynomial-time algorithms is called a zero-knowledge proof system for L if the following three conditions hold [11]:

Completeness. For all $(x, w) \in R_L$, an honest prover P can produce a proof $\pi = P(x, w)$ that convinces an honest verifier V with probability 1 (or at least $1 - \text{negl}(\lambda)$), i.e.,

$$\Pr[V(x, \pi) = 1] = 1.$$

Soundness. For all $x \notin L$ and for any (possibly malicious) prover P^*, the probability that P^* convinces the verifier to accept is negligible in the security parameter λ:

$$\Pr[V(x, P^*(x, w)) = 1] \leq \text{negl}(\lambda).$$

Zero-Knowledge. There exists a probabilistic polynomial-time simulator S such that for all $(x, w) \in R_L$, the verifier's view of the interaction with the prover is computationally indistinguishable from the output of $S(x)$:

$$\{V(x, P(x, w))\} \approx_c \{S(x)\}.$$

This guarantees that the verifier learns nothing beyond the validity of $x \in L$.

Here, x is called the *public input*, w is the *private witness* (kept secret from the verifier), and $\pi = P(x, w)$ is the *proof.*

These properties ensures that ZKPs provide a secure, and privacy-preserving method for verifying computations without exposing sensitive information. ZKPs can be categorized into interactive and non-interactive protocols [12]. Non-interactive ZKPs compress the entire proof into a single message π, eliminating the need for multiple rounds of communication between prover and verifier. This enables efficient verification by multiple parties without repeated proof generation.

Zero-Knowledge Succinct Non-Interactive Argument of Knowledge (zkSNARK) extends ZKPs with succinctness and non-interactivity, making it particularly suitable for verifying complex computations while preserving privacy [13]. The proof size remains constant regardless of the computation complexity [14], and verification requires no interaction between the prover and the verifier.

The core insight of zkSNARK is transforming computations into polynomial constraints over a finite field $\mathbb{F}$ with prime order p. Let $\mathcal{C}$ be a computation and w be its witness. The computation is encoded as a system of polynomial equations:

$$\mathcal{C}(x, w) = 0 \iff \{q_i(x, w) = 0\}_{i=1}^{m}$$

where q_i is a constraint polynomial over $\mathbb{F}_p$.

To construct zkSNARK proofs, the computation must undergo *arithmetization*, which transforms program semantics into polynomial constraint systems. PLONKish provides a flexible arithmetization framework by modeling computation as a structured matrix $M \in \mathbb{F}^{n \times m}$ where n is the number of rows and m is the number of columns. Each column in the matrix belongs to one of three types: *advice* columns (containing private witness data), *fixed* columns (containing public constants), or *instance* columns (containing public inputs). Each column corresponds to a polynomial obtained through Lagrange interpolation over the column values. The framework enables proving that the filled values satisfy specific constraints through four types of polynomial relations:

Gate Constraints. For each gate type g, define polynomial relation $P_g : \mathbb{F}^k \to \mathbb{F}$ where k is the number of columns involved. At row i, the constraint enforces: $P_g(M_{i,c_1}, M_{i,c_2}, \ldots, M_{i,c_k}) = 0$ where $c_1, c_2, \ldots, c_k$ are the relevant column indices.

Permutation Constraints. Define permutation $\sigma : [n] \times [m] \to [n] \times [m]$ that maps cell positions. For any (i, j) in the domain: $M_{i,j} = M_{\sigma(i,j)}$ This enforces equality between cells at positions (i, j) and $\sigma(i, j)$.

Lookup Constraints. Given a predefined lookup table $L = \{l_1, l_2, \ldots, l_t\} \subseteq \mathbb{F}$, for a specified column c and rows in the lookup region $R \subseteq [n]$: $\forall i \in R, \quad M_{i,c} \in L$ This ensures all values in column c within the lookup region are elements of the lookup table L.

Shuffle Constraints. For columns a and b in M viewed as element sets, we require set equality: a and b must contain the same elements with identical multiplicities, irrespective of ordering.

Building upon these zkSNARK foundations, zkVM such as ZKWASM [15] provides an abstraction layer that automatically transforms program execution into bytecode runtime execution traces and establishes universal circuit constraints on the runtime specification, thereby achieving a general-purpose zero-knowledge circuit construction scheme without manual circuit design.

2.2 Program Verification

Program verification formally proves that software satisfies its specifications, ensuring correctness properties. Let P denote a program, ϕ a specification property, we use $P \models \phi$ to denote program P satisfies property ϕ. In SAT-based verification, the problem is reduced to Boolean satisfiability. The reduction constructs a formula ψ such that ψ is satisfiable if and only if P violates ϕ. This enables leveraging highly optimized SAT solvers for automated verification. Common SAT-based approaches include bounded model checking with a bound of n and symbolic execution with a path set Π.

Particularly, programs P are first transformed into Static Single Assignment (SSA) form P_{SSA} for SAT encoding. Then for bounded verification with bound n, states $s_0, s_1, ..., s_n \in \mathcal{S}$, and initial condition predicate I, the verification condition $VC(P_{SSA}, \phi, n)$ is given by:

$$VC(P_{SSA}, \phi, n) = I(s_0) \wedge \bigwedge_{i=0}^{n-1} \tau(s_i, s_{i+1}) \wedge \neg\phi(s_n)$$

Here, $\tau : \mathcal{S} \times \mathcal{S} \to \{0, 1\}$ is the transition relation. The program satisfies ϕ within bound n if and only if $VC(P_{SSA}, \phi, n)$ is unsatisfiable.

Then the encoding function $\mathcal{E}$ maps program constructs to Boolean formulas. For an m-bit variable v, bit-vector $b^v = \{b_0^v, b_1^v, ..., b_{m-1}^v\}$ with $b_i^v \in \{0, 1\}$, the encoding is $\mathcal{E}(v) = b^v$. For arithmetic operation op and Boolean circuit C_{op}, $\mathcal{E}(v_1 \ op \ v_2) = C_{op}(b^{v_1}, b^{v_2})$. For path $\pi = \{c_1, c_2, ..., c_k\}$ with conditions c_i, $\mathcal{E}(\pi) = \bigwedge_{i=1}^{k} \mathcal{E}(c_i)$. Finally, a SAT solver determines the encoded formula $\psi = \mathcal{E}(VC(P_{SSA}, \phi, n))$'s satisfiability. That means, if ψ is satisfiable, the satisfying assignment provides a concrete counterexample demonstrating the violation of property ϕ; otherwise, the program satisfies the property within the bounded scope n.

2.3 ZK Proof Systems for UNSAT/SAT

The Boolean Satisfiability Problem (SAT) determines whether a given Boolean formula has an assignment that makes it evaluate to true. Let $X = \{x_1, x_2, \ldots, x_m\}$ be the set of Boolean variables. A literal l_{it} is either a variable x_j (positive literal) or its negation $\neg x_j$ (negative literal) for some $x_j \in X$. Let $F^* = \{f_1^*, f_2^*, \ldots, f_n^*\}$ be a Boolean formula where each f_i^* is a clause consisting of a disjunction of literals over variables in X.

Unsatisfiability (UNSAT): Let $D^* = \{d_1^*, d_2^*, \ldots, d_k^*\}$ be a sequence of derived clauses, $T^* = \{t_1^*, t_2^*, \ldots, t_{2k}^*\}$ be a trace of clauses used in resolution, and pivot_i

be the variable on which resolution is performed at step i. For an unsatisfiable formula F^*, a resolution proof demonstrates that no satisfying assignment exists. To verify an UNSAT result, the following relations must be satisfied: (1) Each d_i^* is either in F^* or derived by resolving two parent clauses from $T^* \subseteq \{F^* \cup D^*\}$ that contain pivot_i and $\neg\text{pivot}_i$ respectively (2) The derived clause d_i^* contains all literals from both parent clauses except pivot_i and $\neg\text{pivot}_i$ (3) The trace length equals the derivation length: $|T^*| = 2|D^*|$ (4) The final clause is empty: $d_k^* = \perp$ which means no variable exists in this clause.

Satisfiability (SAT): Let $\alpha : X \rightarrow \{0, 1\}$ be an assignment that maps each variable to a Boolean value. For a satisfiable formula F^*, the proof is a satisfying assignment α such that $F^*(\alpha) = 1$. To verify a SAT result, the following relations must be satisfied: (1) For each $x_i \in X$, $\alpha(x_i)$ is uniquely defined as either 0 or 1 (2) For each clause $f_i^* \in F^*$, at least one literal evaluates to true under α, i.e., $\exists l_{it} \in f_i^*$ such that: If $l_{it} = x_j$, then $\alpha(x_j) = 1$, If $l_{it} = \neg x_j$, then $\alpha(x_j) = 0$.

These two proof types—satisfying assignments for SAT instances and resolution proofs for UNSAT instances—provide complete verification of SAT solver outputs, enabling formal reasoning about the satisfiability of Boolean formulas.

3 Overviews

Unlike traditional program verification, which directly analyzes program code and generates proof artifacts (such as verification conditions or proof obligations), our protocol operates on encrypted representations. We prove that a specific property of a private program has been verified by generating cryptographic proofs for two components: (1) the constraints encoding the program-to-SAT transformation, and (2) the satisfiability determination through either resolution proofs (UNSAT) or satisfying assignments (SAT). These proofs ensure that the program's property has been validated while protecting all internal details. The protocol's soundness guarantees that only correct verification can produce valid proofs.

3.1 Two-Phase Zero-Knowledge Protocol for Program Verification

As shown in Fig. 1, consider a scenario where we wish to verify that a program p satisfies a specific property ϕ, but without exposing the program itself. Our privacy-preserving protocol achieves this in two phases.

Phase I: Program to SAT Formula Transformation Verification. In Phase I, the prover demonstrates that a SAT formula is correctly derived from the hidden program. The prover provides the program's specification ϕ as public input, while keeping both the source code and its corresponding SAT formula $\mathcal{F}_{SAT}$ private.

To achieve verifiable transformation, we implement the program-to-SAT conversion logic in a high-level language, which is then compiled into zkSNARK

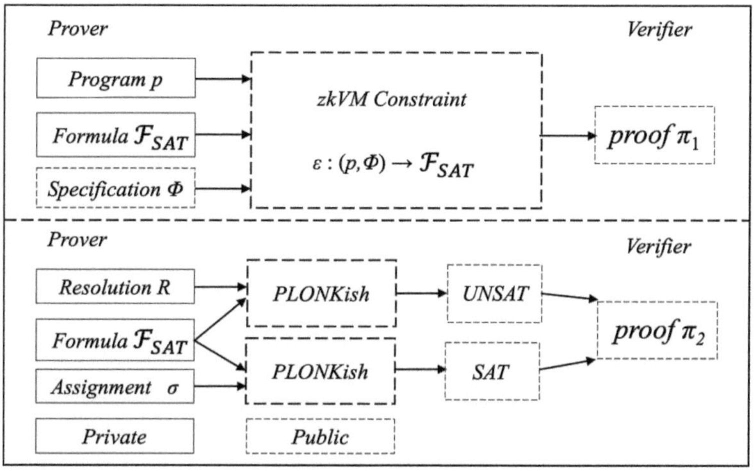

Fig. 1. zkVM and Plonkish-based Verification Pipeline

circuits through zkVM. This allows the prover to generate a proof π_1 that certifies the SAT formula was honestly derived from the program, without revealing either the program or the formula. The zkVM ensures the transformation follows the correct semantics while maintaining complete privacy of the program's internal logic.

Phase II: UNSAT/SAT Verification. In Phase II, the prover demonstrates the satisfiability status of the SAT formula from Phase I while maintaining its privacy. The verification approach depends on whether the formula is satisfiable or unsatisfiable.

For the *UNSAT case*, we encode the resolution proof verification using PLONKish circuits. The prover constructs a resolution proof by representing clauses as column polynomials and establishing resolution relationships between them. Through polynomial constraints in PLONKish, we verify that each resolution step follows valid inference rules, ultimately deriving the empty clause. This allows the prover to generate proof π_2 that certifies the formula is unsatisfiable without revealing the formula or resolution steps. For the *SAT case*, the prover demonstrates the existence of a satisfying assignment. Using PLONKish circuits, we encode constraints that verify the assignment satisfies all clauses. The prover generates proof π_2 certifying that such an assignment exists without revealing the assignment values.

In both cases, the verifier only learns the satisfiability result and can verify the proofs π_1 and π_2. The protocol ensures complete privacy of the program's internal logic, the SAT formula, and any intermediate computations, while still allowing the verifier to confirm that the program satisfies the required property ϕ.

3.2 Protocol Security Through Commitment Binding

The security of our protocol relies on the soundness of both underlying proof systems. As established in Sect. 2.1, the zkVM provides computational integrity guarantees, while the PLONKish system ensures arithmetic circuit satisfiability.

To ensure consistency between phases, we enforce a binding constraint through polynomial commitments. Specifically, we introduce a commitment constraint com_{SAT} that cryptographically binds the SAT formula used across both phases, ensuring the prover cannot use different formulas while keeping the formula itself as private input in Phase II. This binding property is crucial for maintaining protocol soundness across the two-phase composition. The protocol carefully controls information disclosure at each stage. The composed proof (π_1, π_2) convinces the verifier that (1) some valid program-to-SAT encoding was performed according to the public specification, and (2) the encoded formula has the claimed satisfiability status, all without revealing the program structure or verification details. The zero-knowledge property ensures that the verifier learns nothing beyond the validity of these claims, achieving our goal of privacy-preserving program verification.

4 ZK-Verifiable Encoding Framework

This section instantiates our abstract protocol with concrete constraint systems. We detail the zkVM transformation that converts programs into SAT formula while preserving privacy. For Phase II, we present PLONKish modeling approaches for both SAT result types and introduce two novel techniques: an encoding method for resolution proof checking that compresses each clause into a single finite field element, achieving verification complexity independent of clause width, and an assignment validation approach that constructs two matrices to store variable assignments, achieving verification complexity independent of formula length through exclusivity constraints. These innovations enable efficient verification optimized for each satisfiability case.

4.1 Program-to-Formula Transformation

Following the SAT-based verification approach defined in Subsect. 2.2, the encoding function $\mathcal{E}$ transforms the verification condition $VC(P_{SSA}, \phi, n)$ into SAT formula. The output is a SAT formula F that encodes the verification information. We implement the encoding function $\mathcal{E} : P_{SSA} \rightarrow \mathcal{F}_{SAT}$ in a high-level language and compile it into bytecode for execution within zkVM, enable privacy-preserving transformation. The zkVM takes three inputs: private program P, private SAT formula F, and public property specification ϕ.

The zkVM constraints enforce that $F = \mathcal{E}(P, \phi)$, ensuring the SAT formula is correctly derived from the program and property through the standard SSA-to-SAT transformation. The bytecode execution proves that the private program and its corresponding SAT formula are genuinely generated through our encoding function with specification ϕ. This includes bit-vector encoding of variables,

Boolean circuit representation of operations, and path condition constraints. The computation produces commitment com_{SAT} that cryptographically binds to F without revealing the program logic or formula structure. This design achieves privacy-preserving program-to-SAT transformation where the verifier only observes the property specification and proof of correct encoding, while both the program and resulting SAT formula remain completely private.

4.2 Constraints of Resolution Proof for UNSAT

First, let us define the variables and constraints for the zero-knowledge resolution framework of the protocol. Recall that PLONKish provides a matrix $M \in \mathbb{F}^{n \times m}$ with three column types (advice, fixed, instance) and three constraint mechanisms. We encode literals l_{it} from Sect. 2.3 as field elements: let $\ell \in \mathbb{F}$ denote an encoded literal where $\ell > 0$ represents variable x_j and $\ell < 0$ represents negation $\neg x_j$. A clause c is defined as a set of encoded literals $c = \{\ell_1, \ell_2, \ldots, \ell_k\}$ where each $\ell_i \in \mathbb{F}$. We use f to denote a c in original formula, d to denote a derived c from resolution, and t to denote any c in the combined set. We construct the formula with incrementing indices $i^* \in \mathbb{F}$. The original formula is $F = \{(i^*, f_i) \mid i^* = 1, 2, \ldots, |F|\}$. The derived clause set from resolution is $D = \{(i^*, d_i) \mid i^* = |F| + 1 \ldots |F| + |D|\}$. The combined clause set is $T = F \cup D = \{(i^*, t_i) \mid i^* = 1, 2, \ldots, |F| + |D|\}$ containing all clauses with their indices. Let W denote the maximum number of literals across all clauses in T. For UNSAT verification, the resolution relations between clauses must be validated through the constraint system.

Matrix Construction Process. We fill each clause from F (original formula), D (derived clauses from resolution), and T (trace of parent clauses used in derivation) into the PLONKish matrix M, where each clause is represented as a separate advice column.

The main challenge is constructing the constraint that $T \subseteq \{F \cup D\}$. While PLONKish provides powerful lookup functionality to build subset constraints between columns and enable fast lookups, in our case, the resolution steps $|T|$ can reach thousands, making multiple lookups impact system performance. Additionally, since PLONKish constraint systems have fixed column-to-column relationships that do not change based on input data, we cannot specify that t_i should lookup to a specific clause in F or D. To address this, we introduce challenge values. The challenge values are defined as $\tilde{\chi} = \{\chi_0, \ldots, \chi_W\} \subseteq \mathbb{F}$ provided by the verifier and regenerated for each verification. Thus, a clause can be transformed into a single field element through element-wise multiplication with challenge values:

$$Encode(clause, \tilde{\chi}) = i^* \cdot \chi_0 + \sum_{j=1}^{|c|} \chi_j \cdot \ell_j$$

Here, i^* is the clause index, and for each clause the subscript j runs from 1 to $|W|$ where ℓ_j denotes the j-th variable in that clause. Consequently, a sequence of clauses can be encoded into a single column in PLONKish. Therefore, in the constraint system we construct two lookup tables: L_1 represents the column filled with F and D encoded through element-wise multiplication with challenge values, and L_2 represents the column filled with T encoded through the same challenge values encoding for each verification. This technique essentially constructs a hash function within the PLONKish system, enabling our implementation to elegantly solve the challenge of lookups between matrices.

Another challenge is the merge constraint for pivot variables between t_{2i-1} and t_{2i}. To address this, we introduce a new matrix T' in M, where each column is an advice column. Each column in T' is almost identical to T, except that the pivot variable is swapped with the second variable (after i^*) in each column. The purpose of introducing this matrix is to ensure that pivot variables are not randomly distributed across t_{2i} and t_{2i-1} to address the aforementioned challenge.

Finally, we create two instance columns I_{ns1} and I_{ns2}, each filled with only one element in a single row: $|W|$ and $|T|$ respectively. Additionally, we add one fixed column F_{ix} containing only the empty result $\perp$, represented as the zero element in the finite field. The construction process of M is described in Algorithm 1. We treat T, D, F, and T' as input data to construct M, while I_{ns1}, I_{ns2}, and F_{ix} are built into the matrix as they vary with input data. The lookup tables L_1 and L_2 are generated with different values for each verification after the constraint system is established.

Constraint Establishment Process. With the arithmetization matrix defined, we need to enforce the relationships defined in Sect. 2.3. Due to our challenge encoding technique, clauses of any length are encoded into single field elements, and formulas become L_1 and L_2. Thus, our first constraint is $C_1 : L_2 \xrightarrow{\text{lookup}} L_1$. We introduce additional T'. As defined previously, we implement a shuffle algorithm in the PLONKish backend using lookup and permutation, which enforces that one column is a shuffle of another. This gives us the second constraint $C_2 : T' \xrightarrow{\text{shuffle}} T$. Additionally, we enforce that t'_{2i} and t'_{2i-1}, after removing the first element i^* and second element (pivot), lookup to D_i without its first element i^*: $C_3 : (t'_{2i}, t'_{2i-1})_{-i^*,-\text{pivot}} \xrightarrow{\text{lookup}} (D_i)_{-i^*}$. We define constraint C_4 where the second elements of columns t'_{2i} and t'_{2i-1} sum to zero: $C_4 : t'_{2i}[2] + t'_{2i-1}[2] = 0$. Finally, we add constraints $C_5 : 2|D| = |T|$ and $D_{|D|} = 0_{\mathbb{F}}$, implemented through gate constraints.

Theorem 1. *Given a valid resolution proof (F, D, T, T') for an unsatisfiable formula F, our PLONKish-based protocol accepts the proof with probability 1, while revealing nothing about F.*

Proof. Correctness follows from constraints C_1-C_5: C_1 ensures valid resolution rules, C_3 verifies empty clause derivation, C_4 enforces correct pivot selection, and C_2/C_5 maintain trace consistency. These constraints fully capture resolution proof semantics. The ZKP system guarantees completeness (honest provers can

Algorithm 1. PLONKish Matrix Construction for UNSAT Verification

Require: SAT formula F, derived clauses D, trace T, max clause width W
Step 1: Initialize Advice Columns
for each clause $c \in F \cup D \cup T$ **do**
  Add c as advice column to matrix M
end for
Step 2: Challenge Values Encoding
Receive challenge values $\chi = \chi_0, \chi_1, \ldots, \chi_W \in \mathbb{F}$
for each clause $c \in F \cup D$ **do**
  $L_1 \leftarrow L_1 \cup i^* \cdot \chi_0 + \sum_{j=1}^{|c|} \chi_j \cdot l_{it_j}$
end for
for each clause $t \in T$ **do**
  $L_2 \leftarrow L_2 \cup i^* \cdot \chi_0 + \sum_{j=1}^{|t|} \chi_j \cdot l_{it_j}$
end for
Step 3: Create Shuffled Trace Matrix
for $i = 1$ to $|T|/2$ **do**
  Extract pivot from t_{2i-1} and t_{2i}
  Add shuffled t'_{2i-1} and t'_{2i} to T'
end for
Step 4: Add Instance Fixed Columns
Create I_{ns1} of width $|W|$, Create I_{ns2} of width $|T|$
Create F_{ix} as zero-filled column in $\mathbb{F}$
Add empty clause
return Matrix M

construct valid matrix M), soundness (forgery bounded by $W/|\mathbb{F}|$ via Schwartz-Zippel), and zero-knowledge (clauses hidden in advice columns, challenge encoding with random $\tilde{\chi}$ masks values). Thus, our protocol correctly verifies UNSAT while revealing only proof validity.

4.3 Constraints of SAT Proof

We present a novel encoding scheme for zero-knowledge SAT result verification that transforms satisfying assignments into privacy-preserving constraint systems, instantiating the framework from Sect. 2.3. First, let us define the variables and constraints for the zk sat assignment framework of the protocol. For SAT verification, we use the satisfying assignment $\alpha : X \to \{0, 1\}$ where $X = \{x_1, \ldots, x_m\}$ is the set of Boolean variables, as defined in Sect. 2.3. To verify SAT results, the relation between F and assignment α remains unchanged. Same as Sect. 4.2, we encode literals l_{it} as field elements ℓ.

Algorithm 2. PLONKish Modeling for SAT Verification

Require: SAT formula F^*, assignment $\alpha : X \to \{0,1\}$, row count L_m

Part 1: Matrix Construction
for each clause $f_i \in F^*$ **do**
  Add f_i as advice column to M
end for
Initialize M_1, M_2 with L_m rows (advice columns)
for each variable $x_i \in X$ **do**
  $(j,k) \leftarrow (\lfloor i/L_m \rfloor, i \bmod L_m)$; $M_1[j,k] \leftarrow 1 - \alpha(x_i)$; $M_2[j,k] \leftarrow \alpha(x_i)$
end for ▷ Construct M_f to encode assignment α
for each ℓ at (i,t) in F^* **do**
  $M_f[i,t] \leftarrow \begin{cases} 1 & \text{if } (\ell < 0 \land \alpha(x_{|\ell|}) = 0) \lor (\ell > 0 \land \alpha(x_{|\ell|}) = 1) \\ 0 & \text{otherwise} \end{cases}$
end for
Create $L_1 \leftarrow \{1\}$ (instance column)
Part 2: Constraints
Add gate constraint: $M_1[i,j] + M_2[i,j] = 1$ for all (i,j) ▷ C_1
Add lookup constraint: $M_f \xrightarrow{\text{lookup}} L_1$ ▷ C_2

Matrix Construction Process. First, we fill each clause from F^* into the PLONKish matrix M, where each clause is represented as a separate advice column. Our main challenge is ensuring the uniqueness of variable assignments. To address this challenge, we construct two matrices to store variable assignments.

We create two matrices $M_1, M_2 \subseteq M$ in PLONKish, where all columns are advice columns and both matrices have fixed row count L_m determined by the prover. M_1 represents the assignment matrix for variables assigned 0, while M_2 represents the assignment matrix for variables assigned 1. Variable values are filled based on their positions. Since variables are mapped to field elements, we can determine their position in the matrix as:

$$\text{position}(j,k) = (\lfloor |\ell|/L_m \rfloor, \ell \bmod L_m)$$

We introduce maps variable assignment α to two matrices, giving us the ability to construct constraints for unique assignments, while the fixed row length prevents impact on circuit size. Then, we create a matrix M_f with the same dimensions as F^*, where all columns are instance columns, containing field elements 0 or 1. The construction of M_f encodes the assignment α. For each literal ℓ in F^*: if ℓ is negative, we fill position (i,t) in M_f with field element 1 when $x_{|\ell|} = 0$, and 0 otherwise. When ℓ is positive, it is exactly the opposite. This construction enables us to verify the constraint defined previously that each clause $f_i \in F^*$ has at least one literal evaluating to true. Finally, we construct a lookup table L_1 containing only one element: the field element 1. Both L_1 and M_f consist of instance columns.

Constraint Establishment Process. With the arithmetization matrix M constructed, we need to enforce the relationships defined in Sect. 2.3. We establish two types of constraints. First, we define gate constraint C_1: for each row and corresponding position in M_1 and M_2, the sum must equal 1: $C_1 : M_1[i,j] + M_2[i,j] = 1$ for all valid positions. This constraint ensures the uniqueness of variable assignments. Second, we define lookup constraint C_2: each column in M_f must lookup to L_1: $C_2 : M_f \xrightarrow{\text{lookup}} L_1$. This ensures that each clause $f_i \in F^*$ has at least one literal evaluating to true. Algorithm 2 shows our modeling process.

Theorem 2. *Given a valid satisfying assignment for a SAT formula F, our PLONKish-based protocol accepts the assignment with probability 1, while revealing nothing about F or the assignment values.*

Proof. Correctness follows from constraints C_1-C_2: C_1 ensures unique boolean assignments via $M_1[i,j] + M_2[i,j] = 1$, while C_2 verifies clause satisfaction through lookups to L_1. These constraints fully capture SAT verification semantics. The ZKPs system guarantees completeness (honest provers can construct valid matrices), soundness (forgery probability negligible in $|\mathbb{F}|$), and zero-knowledge (assignments remain in advice columns M_1, M_2 while instance columns only reveal satisfaction patterns). Thus, our protocol correctly verifies SAT while preserving complete privacy.

5 Experimental Evaluation

We evaluate our privacy-preserving program verification protocol through comprehensive experiments that measure execution time, proof sizes, and scalability across various constraint implementations. The evaluation analyzes (1) program to SAT formula transformation time comparing native zkVM with our HyperPlonk-enhanced protocol, (2) UNSAT resolution proof verification comparing zkVM and PLONKish implementations, (3) SAT assignment verification performance, and (4) zero-knowledge resolution proof size in our protocol.

All experiments were conducted on AMD EPYC 7402 processors with 32 GB of RAM. Following recent advances in zero-knowledge proof systems. In Phase I program-to-SAT formula transformation, we replace the native proof protocol with HyperPlonk in zkVM. This optimization significantly reduces proof generation time for program transformation, establishing an efficient foundation for the entire protocol. For complex computational tasks like UNSAT resolution proof verification, zkVM approaches such as ZKWASM [15] face significant performance limitations due to the overhead of translating intricate logical operations into WebAssembly bytecode and subsequent constraint compilation. Our implementation primarily utilizes Halo2 [16], which provides direct constraint system construction through its PLONKish framework with efficient polynomial commitments and lookup arguments. This approach enables optimized circuit construction specifically tailored for resolution proof verification, avoiding the compilation overhead inherent in general-purpose zkVM systems.

We utilize the publicly available Boolector benchmark suite [17], selecting test cases with SAT formula sizes ranging from 100 to 10,000 clauses and UNSAT resolution proof lengths from 20 to 2450 steps. To validate clause-width independence, we construct test cases with varying clause widths by adjusting the width parameter on the same datasets. All experimental results represent the average of ten independent runs to ensure reliability. The experiments demonstrate that our Halo2-based implementation achieves the design goals: UNSAT verification time remains independent of clause width through our challenge values encoding, while SAT assignment verification maintains constant time complexity regardless of formula size due to our assignment matrix construction.

5.1 Program-to-Formula Performance Characteristics

We evaluate the program-to-formula transformation performance comparing native ZKWASM with our HyperPlonk-enhanced implementation, as shown in Table 1. Our approach replaces ZKWASM's native proof system protocol with HyperPlonk, which features linear-time prover complexity and high-degree custom gates. This architectural modification optimizes polynomial commitment schemes and reduces the computational overhead of constraint generation, resulting in approximately 3× performance improvement over the baseline ZKWASM implementation. The implementation supports Boolean operations (AND, OR, NOT, XOR), conditional expressions (ITE), logical relations (implies, equals), and assertions. To ensure correctness, we add require statements verifying that the generated SAT formula correctly encodes the input SSA program.

Table 1. Performance Comparison between ZKWASM and Our Approach

Program Type	SSA Nodes	Variables	Clauses	Verify Time	
				ZKWASM	Ours
Boolean assignments	23	26	91	1.23 s	0.41 s
AND/OR operations	34	47	203	2.45 s	0.78 s
XOR/NOT operations	27	41	175	2.23 s	0.71 s
ITE expressions	38	73	285	2.87 s	0.92 s
Nested ITE (depth 3)	64	127	498	4.87 s	1.56 s
Implies chains	43	103	403	4.25 s	1.36 s
Mixed Boolean logic	89	231	960	8.05 s	2.58 s
Complex assertions	126	256	1,065	7.93 s	2.54 s
Large-scale programs	2,537	2,719	11,248	27.40 s	8.77 s

Results demonstrate efficient transformation with linear scaling. ITE expressions generate 4 clauses each, while basic Boolean operations produce 2–4 clauses.

The require checks add minimal overhead while ensuring transformation correctness. Our approach scales effectively from small programs (20 variables) to large-scale applications (12K variables). All test cases complete within reasonable time bounds, confirming practical feasibility for ZKWASM-based verification across diverse program sizes.

5.2 Verification Time and Proof Size Analysis for ZK UNSAT Cases

Table 2 presents the verification time comparison between ZKWASM and Halo2 for Phase II. ZKWASM directly encodes computation into circuit constraints, while Halo2 expresses formula relationships through specialized polynomials. The key difference: ZKWASM's step-by-step modeling leads to larger circuits, while Halo2's direct constraint modeling achieves compact circuits. Experiments show that for resolution lengths from 20 to 2450 clauses, ZKWASM requires 1.2–81 s while Halo2 only needs 35–2800ms.

Table 2. ZK Resolution Proof Verification Time: Halo2 vs ZKWASM Benchmark

Resolution Len	Clause Width	Halo2		ZKWASM	
		Circuit Size	Verify Time	Circuit Size	Verify Time
20	5	2^6	34.47ms	2^{18}	1.20 s
274	34	2^9	412.46ms	2^{19}	8.33 s
1034	84	2^{11}	1501.44ms	2^{21}	42.54 s
1511	98	2^{11}	1598.96ms	2^{21}	43.78 s
2450	142	2^{12}	2804.03ms	2^{22}	81.90 s

Our key contribution is achieving verification time independent of clause width. To construct the dataset, we increase the maximum clause width on fixed-length resolution by padding zero literals to clause tails in the PLONK-ish system. Table 3 demonstrates this property for Halo2 UNSAT verification. Unlike traditional SAT checking that examines each literal in wide clauses, our challenge technique in Sect. 4.2 maps each clause to a hash value. This is particularly valuable for arithmetic circuit verification containing wide clauses, with experimental results confirming our theoretical analysis.

ZKPs maintain compact sizes determined by the cryptographic scheme. Table 4 compares proof sizes between ZKWASM and Halo2 for UNSAT formulas. Halo2 consistently produces smaller proofs due to efficient polynomial commitments and specialized circuits eliminating VM overhead. Proof sizes remain practical for large formulas, ensuring efficient transmission and storage.

5.3 Verification Time for ZK SAT Assignment Cases

Our assignment matrix struct achieves verification time independence from formula size through controlled circuit construction. Matrix width depends only

Table 3. Clause Width-Independent Verification for UNSAT Cases Using Halo2

Benchmark 1			Benchmark 2		
Formula Len	Clause Width	Verify Time	Formula Len	Clause Width	Verify Time
1034	80	1.493 s	2450	80	2.83 s
1034	150	1.527 s	2450	150	2.85 s
1034	200	1.482 s	2450	200	2.80 s
1034	400	1.513 s	2450	400	2.91 s

Table 4. UNSAT Case Proof Size Comparison Between ZKWASM and Halo2

Resolution Len	Clause Width	Proof Size	
		ZKWASM	Halo2
20	5	9.216MB	32.50KB
274	34	210.04MB	90.60KB
1034	84	415.46MB	154.09KB
1511	98	506.80MB	411.43KB
2450	142	1344.38MB	1219.73KB

on maximum clause width, not formula size. Since Halo2's circuit size is determined by row count, our circuit remains fixed. We configure 240 rows for the each matrix, plus 10 hidden rows in Halo2, totaling $2^8 = 256$ rows. To construct the dataset, we fix clause width across SAT formulas of varying lengths. As shown in Table 4, Halo2's verification time depends on circuit scale, this fixed-size design ensures constant verification complexity. Results confirm SAT assignment verification time remains formula-size independent (Table 5).

Table 5. ZK SAT Assignment Verification Time

Formula Size	Clause Width	Verify Time	Circuit Size
498	50	378.64ms	2^8
1065	50	395.27ms	2^8
4372	50	417.88ms	2^8

6 Related Work

The combination of program verification and ZKPs is an emerging research direction. Pinocchio pioneered verifiable computation, converting arbitrary computations into verifiable proofs [18]. Giraffe extended this idea to data-parallel computations [19]. The Pepper project [20] reduced computational costs by over 20 orders of magnitude, making verifiable computation practically feasible. These works laid the foundation for general-purpose ZKPs for computation.

In the formal verification of SAT solvers, Zhang and Malik [21] introduced foundational methods for generating verifiable resolution proofs using independent checkers. DRAT-trim standardized the proof format for SAT solvers [22], enabling efficient verification of solver outputs. Recent advances have explored zero-knowledge verification of SAT formula and privacy-preserving SAT solving in multi-party environments, though these remain largely theoretical.

The development of zkVM has opened new possibilities for program verification. TinyRAM proved the correctness of C program execution [23], demonstrating that general-purpose programming languages could be efficiently verified using zero-knowledge techniques. Modern zkVM implementations have expanded these capabilities to support complex program executions across various architectures. Cairo provides a dedicated programming language for integrity proofs [24], introducing novel concepts for accelerating operations within zero-knowledge contexts.

In the area of program analysis using ZKPs, Luo et al. [25] proposed an interactive and high-performance zero-knowledge protocol for UNSAT proof verification. Compared to our system, which achieves a fully automated toolchain for zero-knowledge verification from programs to SAT formulas in a non-interactive manner, their protocol remains interactive and does not encompass the full verification pipeline. Additionally, their work [26] on zero-knowledge SMT solving supports Boolean logic, equality with uninterpreted functions and so on, but does not handle the bit-vector theory. As a result, encoding general-purpose programs under their framework still incurs nontrivial additional overhead. Separately, Fang et al. [27] developed zero-knowledge static program analysis techniques that enable verification of program properties without revealing sensitive implementation details. Our work builds upon these foundations and proposes a two-phase zero-knowledge protocol specifically for SAT-based program verification, achieving efficient privacy-preserving verification through innovative encoding techniques.

7 Conclusion

In our work, comprehensive approach that maintains complete privacy throughout the entire verification pipeline—from program implementation to SAT formula generation and final verification. This end-to-end privacy-preserving pipeline allows developers to prove program properties to third parties without exposing proprietary implementation details, addressing the fundamental trade-off between verification transparency and intellectual property protection.

For UNSAT instances, we successfully applied challenge values encoding that compresses arbitrary-width clauses into single field elements, achieving verification time independent of clause width. For SAT instances, our assignment matrix construction enables verification time independent of formula size through fixed-size matrix operations. This scalability breakthrough makes the

ZK-ProVer pipeline practical for real-world program verification scenarios with complex formula.

Acknowledgment. The authors wish to thank Dr. Ning Luo, whose excellent talk provided inspiration for this research. This research is supported by the Special Project on Key Technologies in Blockchain, Shanghai Science and Technology Innovation Action Plan, with grant No. 24BC3200200.

References

1. Rao, A., Wang, Y.: Formal verification of autonomous vehicles: bridging the gap between model-based design and model checking. SAE Int. J. Adv. Curr. Pract. Mob. **6**(2), 814–826 (2024). https://doi.org/10.4271/2023-01-0116. https://www.sae.org/publications/technical-papers/content/2023-01-0116/
2. Zhang, Y., Wen, S., Xu, C.: Blockchain-based certificate verification system using smart contracts. Int. J. Adv. Comput. Sci. Appl. **9**(8), 166–171 (2018). https://doi.org/10.14569/IJACSA.2018.090822
3. Sarswat, S., Singh, A.K.: Formally verified trades in financial markets. In: Lin, S.-W., Hou, Z., Mahony, B. (eds.) ICFEM 2020. LNCS, vol. 12531, pp. 217–232. Springer, Cham (2020). https://doi.org/10.1007/978-3-030-63406-3_13
4. King, J.C.: Symbolic execution and program testing. Commun. ACM **19**(7), 385–394 (1976)
5. Biere, A., et al.: Symbolic model checking using SAT procedures instead of BDDs. In: Proceedings of the 36th Annual Design Automation Conference, pp. 317–320. ACM (1999). https://doi.org/10.1145/309847.309942
6. Leino, K.R.M.: Automating induction with an SMT solver. In: Kuncak, V., Rybalchenko, A. (eds.) VMCAI 2012. LNCS, vol. 7148, pp. 315–331. Springer, Heidelberg (2012). https://doi.org/10.1007/978-3-642-27940-9_21
7. Goldreich, O., Micali, S., Wigderson, A.: Proofs that yield nothing but their validity or all languages in NP have zero-knowledge proof systems. J. ACM **38**(3), 690–728 (1991). https://doi.org/10.1145/116825.116852
8. Dokchitser, T., Bulkin, A.: Zero knowledge virtual machine step by step. Cryptology ePrint Archive, Paper 2023/1032 (2023). https://eprint.iacr.org/2023/1032
9. Gabizon, A., Williamson, Z.J., Ciobotaru, O.: PLONK: permutations over lagrange-bases for oecumenical noninteractive arguments of knowledge. Cryptology ePrint Archive, Paper 2019/953 (2019). https://eprint.iacr.org/2019/953
10. Chen, B., et al.: HyperPlonk: plonk with linear-time prover and high- degree custom gates (2022). ePrint: 2022/1355 (IACR Cryptology)
11. Garimella, K.K., Conway, D.: Zero-knowledge proofs and privacy: a technical look at privacy. In: Lacity, M.C., Coon, L. (eds.) Human Privacy in Virtual and Physical Worlds. TWG, pp. 157–179. Palgrave Macmillan, Cham (2024). https://doi.org/10.1007/978-3-031-51063-2_8
12. Guo, J., et al.: Efficient and secure EMR storage and sharing scheme based on hyperledger fabric and IPFS. Appl. Sci. **14**(12), 5005 (2024)
13. Gennaro, R., Gentry, C., Parno, B., Raykova, M.: Quadratic span programs and succinct NIZKs without PCPs. In: Johansson, T., Nguyen, P.Q. (eds.) EUROCRYPT 2013. LNCS, vol. 7881, pp. 626–645. Springer, Heidelberg (2013). https://doi.org/10.1007/978-3-642-38348-9_37

14. Polytope Research. Verkle Trees (2025). https://research.polytope.technology/verkle-trees. Accessed 14 June 2025
15. Gao, S., Li, G., Fu, H.: ZKWASM: a ZKSNARKWASM emulator. IEEE Trans. Serv. Comput. **17**(6), 4508–4521 (2024). https://doi.org/10.1109/TSC.2024.3422798
16. Bowe, S., Grigg, J., Hopwood, D.: Recursive proof composition without a trusted setup. Cryptology ePrint Archive, Paper 2019/1021 (2019). https://eprint.iacr.org/2019/1021
17. Brummayer, R., Biere, A.: Boolector: an efficient SMT solver for bit-vectors and arrays. In: Kowalewski, S., Philippou, A. (eds.) TACAS 2009. LNCS, vol. 5505, pp. 174–177. Springer, Heidelberg (2009). https://doi.org/10.1007/978-3-642-00768-2_16
18. Parno, B., et al.: Pinocchio: nearly practical verifiable computation. In: Proceedings of the IEEE Symposium on Security and Privacy. Best Paper Award, pp. 238–252. IEEE (2013). https://eprint.iacr.org/2013/279.pdf
19. Wahby, R.S., et al.: Full accounting for verifiable outsourcing. In: Proceedings of the ACM SIGSAC Conference on Computer and Communications Security (CCS), pp. 2071–2086. ACM (2017). https://eprint.iacr.org/2017/242.pdf
20. Setty, S.T.V., et al.: Making argument systems for outsourced computation practical (sometimes). In: Proceedings of the Network and Distributed System Security Symposium (NDSS). The Internet Society (2012)
21. Zhang, L., Malik, S.: Validating SAT solvers using an independent resolution-based checker: practical implementations and other applications. In: Proceedings of the Design, Automation and Test in Europe Conference (DATE), pp. 10880–10885. IEEE (2003). https://www.princeton.edu/~chaff/publication/DATE2003_validating_sat_solver.pdf
22. Wetzler, N., Heule, M.J.H., Hunt, W.A.: DRAT-trim: efficient checking and trimming using expressive clausal proofs. In: Sinz, C., Egly, U. (eds.) SAT 2014. LNCS, vol. 8561, pp. 422–429. Springer, Cham (2014). https://doi.org/10.1007/978-3-319-09284-3_31
23. Ben-Sasson, E., Chiesa, A., Genkin, D., Tromer, E., Virza, M.: SNARKs for C: verifying program executions succinctly and in zero knowledge. In: Canetti, R., Garay, J.A. (eds.) CRYPTO 2013. LNCS, vol. 8043, pp. 90–108. Springer, Heidelberg (2013). https://doi.org/10.1007/978-3-642-40084-1_6
24. StarkWare. Cairo – a Turing-complete STARK-friendly CPU architecture. Technical Report. StarkWare technical documentation (2021). https://eprint.iacr.org/2021/1063
25. Luo, N., et al.: Proving UNSAT in zero knowledge. In: Proceedings of the 2022 ACM SIGSAC Conference on Computer and Communications Security (CCS), pp. 2203–2217. ACM (2022). https://doi.org/10.1145/3548606.3559373
26. Luick, D., et al.: ZKSMT: a VM for proving SMT theorems in zero knowledge. In: 33rd USENIX Security Symposium (USENIX Security 2024), pp. 3837–3845 (2024)
27. Fang, Z., et al.: Zero knowledge static program analysis. In: Proceedings of the 2021 ACM SIGSAC Conference on Computer and Communications Security (CCS), pp. 2271–2288. ACM (2021). https://david.darais.com/assets/papers/zk-sa/zk-sa.pdf

Synthesizing Loops from Linear Ranking Functions

Rui-Juan Jing[1], Yaru Yuan[1], Yuxing Cai[2,3], Yi Li[2,3], and Changbo Chen[2,3](✉)

[1] School of Mathematical Sciences, Jiangsu University, Zhenjiang, China
rjing@ujs.edu.cn, yryuan@stmail.ujs.edu.cn

[2] Chongqing Institute of Green and Intelligent Technology, Chinese Academy of Sciences, Chongqing, China
{caiyuxing,liyi,chenchangbo}@cigit.ac.cn

[3] Chongqing School, University of Chinese Academy of Sciences, Chongqing, China

Abstract. Synthesizing ranking functions is a typical technique for proving loop termination. In this work, we propose an approach to handle the backward, or the reverse, problem. That is, one constructs loops such that a given linear function is a ranking function for these loops. To achieve this, we firstly demonstrate by experiments the necessity to introduce parameters to increase the success ratio. We then formulate this problem as a proper existential quantifier elimination (or parametric system solving) problem, and propose two efficient methods to handle it. We have implemented our methods and demonstrated their effectiveness by extensive experiments.

Keywords: Quantifier elimination · Parametric system solving · Linear ranking function · Loop termination · Loop synthesis

1 Introduction

Proving termination of a program [6] is an important research topic in program verification [21]. To prove that a loop terminates, one main technique is to synthesize ranking functions from loops [2, 19]. We call synthesizing a ranking function from a loop a forward problem. In this work, we are interested in the backward, or the reverse, problem. That is, given a ranking function f, we would like to find loops such that f is a ranking function for them.

Although there have been many work addressing the forward problem, we do not find relevant work focusing on the reverse problem for loop termination analysis. In a broader sense, this problem falls in the category of reverse/backward generation of data. That is, given labels or properties to be predicted, one generates the corresponding examples. There are at least two important reasons

This work is supported by the National Key Research Project of China under Grant No. 2023YFA1009402, the National Natural Science Foundation of China under Grant No. 12101267 and Chongqing Talents Plan Youth Top-Notch Project (2021000263).

É. André et al. (Eds.): ICFEM 2025, LNCS 16229, pp. 228–246, 2026.
https://doi.org/10.1007/978-981-95-4213-0_13

to synthesize data in this way: solely relying on forward data generation may lead to imbalanced data and inverse data generation can help balance the number of examples in different classes; forward data generation may be expensive and backward data generation may be more cost-effective. A successful combination of forward and backward data generation can significantly improve the performance of machine learning models in many tasks, such as learning symbolic integration [18], learning to compute Gröbner bases [16], learning to prove geometry theorems [24], etc.

This work is also motivated by the recent works on synthesizing loops from program invariants [14,15]. Given a polynomial invariant p, the work [14] computes polynomial constraints defining all the loops having the invariant p. Along this line of research, the work [15] goes further to construct linear loops. Note that there is a wide research on program synthesis [13], whose goal is to synthesize programs satisfying both syntax and semantic requirements. The goal in this research is bit different, which is to synthesize loops satisfying a given property, namely any constructed loop makes a given function satisfy the conditions of ranking functions. Our method also deviates from another wide research community that leverages the generative models, such as the generative adversarial networks [10] or diffusion models [12], for synthesizing data [1]. One main difference is that we employ symbolic computation techniques to synthesize examples such that a given function is a precise label of the example.

In this paper, we focus on synthesizing linear simple while programs [19] from a given linear function f such that f is a ranking function for all these loops. A necessary and sufficient condition for such program to have a given linear ranking functions has been established in [19], that is Eq. (2) in Sect. 2. Intuitively, if both the loop and a linear function are given, such condition is hard to be met. This intuition is justified by intensive experiments, which reveals the necessity to have some free parameters to increase the success ratio of synthesizing loops. We formulate this naturally as a real quantifier elimination (QE) problem, for which many methods exist [9]. The system for this particular application is in some sense weakly nonlinear, in the sense that the nonlinearity in the input only arises for the product of two different variables. For such systems, we find that the virtual term substitution method [23,25,26] implemented in the REDLOG package [8] is more effective than the method of cylindrical algebraic decomposition [5], widely implemented in Maple [4], Mathematica [22], Z3 [7], etc. This particular structure also enables us to propose a special precondition method to help REDLOG on hard problems, and a dedicated partial quantifier elimination approach. We remark that, if one is only interested in synthesizing only one loop from a given ranking function, one could formulate this problem as a satisfiability problem, for which more efficient methods based on SMT exist [7]. The (partial) QE-based approach has the advantage of providing a class of (even infinitely many) loops having the same linear ranking function. To summarize, the main contribution of our work is three-fold:

- We cast the loop synthesis problem to a proper quantifier elimination problem and highlight the importance to introduce free parameters.

- We propose a simple effective precondition method for general quantifier elimination approaches.
- We propose a dedicated partial quantifier elimination approach and demonstrate its effectiveness on synthesizing loops.

2 Loop Termination and Ranking Function

In this section, we firstly recall the existing forward procedure on computing linear ranking functions for a given linear simple loop. Then we show how to formulate the backward problem on synthesizing loops from given ranking functions as an existential quantifier elimination problem.

2.1 Linear Ranking Function of Linear Simple Loop

Throughout this paper, we consider a loop $L \triangleq (\mathbf{x}, \mathbf{x}', G(\mathbf{x}), U(\mathbf{x}, \mathbf{x}'))$, where $\mathbf{x} = x_1, \ldots, x_n$ and $\mathbf{x}' = x_1', \ldots, x_n'$ are respectively the set of variables before and after the execution of an iteration, G is the loop guard defined by a conjunction of finitely many linear inequalities of the form $\alpha_1 x_1 + \cdots + \alpha_n x_n \leq \alpha_0$, and U is the loop body described by a conjunction of finitely many linear inequalities of the form $a_1' x_1' + \cdots + a_n' x_n' \leq a_1 x_1 + \cdots + a_n x_n + a_0$. Here, all the constants and variables take values from the real number field $\mathbb{R}$. Such a loop is called a *linear arithmetic simple while* program in [19]. For the linear loop program L defined above, we could write $G(\mathbf{x}) \wedge U(\mathbf{x}, \mathbf{x}')$ in a more compact form

$$A\mathbf{x} + C\mathbf{x}' \leq \mathbf{b}, \tag{1}$$

where $A_{m \times n}$ and $C_{m \times n}$ are matrices and $\mathbf{b}$ is a vector of size m. Denote by p the number of constraints in G, implying that the first p rows of C are 0.

Definition 1. *Given a linear loop program L, $r(\mathbf{x})$ is its ranking function if the following two conditions are both satisfied:*

- $\exists r_0 \in \mathbb{R}$ *such that* $\forall \mathbf{x}, \mathbf{x}', G(\mathbf{x}) \wedge U(\mathbf{x}, \mathbf{x}') \implies r(\mathbf{x}) \geq r_0$,
- $\exists \delta \in \mathbb{R}, \delta > 0,$ *such that* $\forall \mathbf{x}, \mathbf{x}', G(\mathbf{x}) \wedge U(\mathbf{x}, \mathbf{x}') \implies r(\mathbf{x}) - r(\mathbf{x}') \geq \delta$.

Theorem 1 ([19]). *Assume that Eq. (1) has solutions in $\mathbb{R}^{2n}$. Then L has a linear ranking function if and only if the following system*

$$\{\lambda \geq 0, \lambda' \geq 0, \lambda C = 0, (\lambda - \lambda')A = 0, \lambda'(A + C) = 0, \lambda' \mathbf{b} < 0\} \tag{2}$$

has solutions in $\mathbb{R}^{2m}$. Moreover, when Eq. (2) has solutions, $r(\mathbf{x}) = (\lambda' C)\mathbf{x}$ is a ranking function.

2.2 Loop Synthesis from a Given Linear Ranking Function

Assume that Eq. (1) has solutions in $\mathbb{R}^{2n}$. By Theorem 1, a linear function $r(\mathbf{x}) = \mathbf{ax}$ is a ranking function if the following system has a solution:

$$\{\lambda \geq 0, \lambda' \geq 0, \lambda C = 0, (\lambda - \lambda')A = 0, \lambda'(A+C) = 0, \lambda'\mathbf{b} < 0, \mathbf{a} - \lambda' C = 0\}. \quad (3)$$

Note that, if Eq. (1) has no solutions in $\mathbb{R}^{2n}$, no matter Eq. (3) has solutions or not, the loop must terminate. Indeed, if Eq. (1) has no solutions, the loop trivially terminates. Thus, in the rest of this section, we focus on the following quantifier elimination problem:

$$\exists \lambda, \lambda', \lambda \geq 0, \lambda' \geq 0, \lambda C = 0, (\lambda - \lambda')A = 0, \lambda'(A+C) = 0, \lambda'\mathbf{b} < 0, \mathbf{a} - \lambda' C = 0. \quad (4)$$

Here, the goal is to eliminate λ and λ' and to find conditions on the elements of A, C and $\mathbf{b}$. In practice, some elements of A, C and $\mathbf{b}$ might be known. We could also set some elements to fixed values to reduce the complexity. Note that there is an equivalent problem to Eq. (4) by simple substitution:

$$\exists \lambda, \lambda', \lambda \geq 0, \lambda' \geq 0, \lambda C = 0, \lambda A + \mathbf{a} = 0, \lambda' A + \mathbf{a} = 0, \lambda' C - \mathbf{a} = 0, \lambda'\mathbf{b} < 0. \quad (5)$$

3 Algorithm

In this section, we focus on solving the quantifier elimination problem presented in Eq. (5). That is, we need to eliminate the variables λ and λ' and get a quantifier free formula involving only the variables $\mathbf{a}$. Solving such a QE problem can also be viewed as a parametric polynomial system solving problem. That is, we treat λ and λ' as unknowns and $\mathbf{a}$ as parameters. The goal is to find conditions on the parameters for this system to have real solutions. In the rest of this paper, we mainly state our algorithms in the view of parametric system solving.

To facilitate the discussion, we introduce the following notation. Let $A = (a_{ij})$ and $C = (c_{ij})$ denote two matrices of size $m \times n$. Define $\lambda = [\mu_1, \ldots, \mu_m]$ and $\lambda' = [\nu_1, \ldots, \nu_m]$ as two row vectors of dimension m. Let $\mathbf{b} = [b_1, \ldots, b_m]^T$ be a column vector of dimension m, and let $\mathbf{a} = [a_1, \ldots, a_n]$ be a row vector of dimension n. Equation (5) can be equivalently decomposed into the following two systems, based on the partitioning of the variables.

$$\lambda A + \mathbf{a} = 0, \lambda C = 0, \lambda \geq 0. \quad (6)$$

$$\lambda' A + \mathbf{a} = 0, \lambda' C = \mathbf{a}, \lambda' \geq 0, \lambda'\mathbf{b} < 0. \quad (7)$$

Our objective is to identify parameter assignments such that both Eq. (5) and Eq. (1) admit solutions simultaneously. From Fig. 1 in Sect. 4.2, we observe that when parameters are instantiated with randomly chosen values, the probability that both systems have solutions at the same time is very low. Moreover, we find that the success rate of Eq. (5) is significantly lower than that of Eq. (1). To improve the likelihood of finding solutions, we adopt a hybrid approach: we fix some parameters while assigning random values to the others. Before presenting the algorithms to solve the parametric system, we provide the following remarks:

Remark 1. From Eq. (6) and Eq. (7), it is evident that the subsystems are decoupled w.r.t. the variables λ and λ'. The equations in Eq. (6) and (7) share the same coefficient matrix. Although they differ in the constants in some of the equations, their solution sets exhibit structural similarity.

Remark 2. For a given integer n, we use $[n]$ to denote the list $[1, 2, \ldots, n]$. For a given matrix P and integers i, j, we use $P_{i,j}$ to denote the (i, j)-th element in P, $P_{i,:}$ and $P_{:,j}$ to denote the i-th row and j-th column of P, respectively. Given two index sets ind_1 and ind_2, the notation P_{ind_1,ind_2} refers to the submatrix consisting of all entries $P_{i,j}$ with $i \in ind_1$ and $j \in ind_2$. Given an expression f and a substitution sol, we write $\mathsf{eval}(f, \mathsf{sol})$ to denote the evaluation of f under the substitution sol. When f is a list of expressions, $\mathsf{eval}(f, \mathsf{sol})$ denotes the element-wise evaluation. We denote by $\mathsf{den}(f)$ the denominator of an expression f. We use $\text{Append}(L_1, L_2)$ to denote the list obtained by appending L_2 to L_1.

3.1 The Main Idea

In this paper, we present two approaches for solving parametric linear systems. Both approaches rely on solving parametric systems of linear equations as a preprocessing step. To handle this, we introduce a "parametric Gaussian elimination" method in Sect. 3.2, which extends the standard technique already implemented in many software systems. Our approach allows reordering the variables in a specific way and selecting the variables to eliminate, tailored to the structure of the problem. This flexible control supports a variety of use cases and downstream tasks. After solving the parametric equation system, we obtain: (*i*) a parametric solution set; (*ii*) a condition set on the parameters. We then substitute the solution into the remaining inequality system. The core problem reduces to determining whether the resulting parametric inequality system, under the additional parameter conditions, is satisfiable.

The first approach performs preprocessing by eliminating linear variables in the inequalities using FourierMotzkin elimination, implemented in MAPLE. Once the strong linear variables (variables having numeric coefficients in all constraints) are eliminated, the resulting simpler system is passed to REDLOG for quantifier elimination and satisfiability checking. Experimental results in Sect. 4 show that this preprocessing step can significantly improve the effectiveness of REDLOG on certain problem instances. However, this method has limitations. There remain many cases where both the preprocessing step and REDLOG fail to solve the system. Furthermore, we hit some problems when handling parametric problems with REDLOG. Firstly, in some cases involving unsatisfiable constraints, although REDLOG completes the quantifier elimination step, the resulting formula lacks a consistency check. Secondly, we observe that REDLOG may output a long formula even the formula is equivalent to be "true".

To address the limitations of the first method, we propose a second approach that solves the parametric system directly. The method proceeds as follows: (1) solve the system of parametric equations using the technique described in

Sect. 3.2; (2) use a heuristic detection method (Sect. 3.4) to check satisfiability; (3) use a generic detection method (Sect. 3.5) to check satisfiability.

If the heuristic method succeeds, it returns a set of parameter conditions under which the system is satisfiable. This method is fast and performs well when solutions exist. However, it may fail in certain cases—either by missing a solution or being unable to confirm satisfiability. To balance completeness and efficiency, we introduce a generic detection method in Sect. 3.5, based on polyhedral computation theory. When the heuristic method fails, the generic detection method is applied as a fallback. It guarantees a definitive answer: true, along with the parameter conditions ensuring satisfiability, or false, certifying that the system is unsatisfiable generically (for almost all parameter values).

3.2 Parametric Gauss Elimination

In this section, we introduce a parametric Gauss elimination procedure that aims to eliminate as many linear variables as possible from a system of equations with parametric coefficients. For simplicity, we denote the parametric linear system to be solved as $P\mathbf{x} = \mathbf{q}$, where P is an $m \times n$ parametric matrix, $\mathbf{q}$ is an m-dimensional parametric vector, and $\mathbf{x}$ is an n-dimensional vector of unknowns.

A direct approach to solve such a system is to treat all variables in $\mathbf{x}$ equally and apply Gaussian elimination. The main difference of our approach is that it attempts to solve a subset of the variables given in a specified order $\overline{\mathbf{x}}$. The list $\overline{\mathbf{x}}$ can be a reordering or a sublist of $\mathbf{x}$. The method is outlined in Algorithm 1. This algorithm is designed to solve a parametric linear system $P\mathbf{x} = \mathbf{q}$, where the first ℓ variables in $\mathbf{x}$ are targeted for elimination. The algorithm returns a list of solutions sol and a list of parameter conditions con. Lines 1–4 compute the row-reduced echelon form of submatrix $P_{:,[\ell]}$ and the transformation matrix U, determines the rank r and column pivot indices, and initializes the solution and condition lists. Lines 5–9 check consistency for rows from $r+1$ to m, returning no solution if a nonzero constant contradiction is found, or adding parameter-containing equations to the condition list. Line 11 builds the solution set. Line 12 adds all non-zero parameter denominators from the solutions to the condition list. Line 13 returns the condition lists.

Definition 2 (Reduced Row-Echelon Form [17]**).** *A matrix is in* reduced row-echelon form *if*

1. *All nonzero rows are above any rows of zeros.*
2. *Each leading entry of a row is in a column to the right of the leading entries of any rows above it.*
3. *Each leading entry of a row is equal to 1.*
4. *All entries in a column above and below a leading entry are zero.*

To determine the order of variables, given a system of linear equations with parametric coefficients, we classify variables in $\mathbf{x}$ into the following three types:

1. **Strong linear variables (slv)**: variables with numerical coefficients in *all* equations;

Algorithm 1: Solve Parametric Linear Equation System (SolvePLE)

Input: A parametric linear system $P\mathbf{x} = \mathbf{q}$; a variable order $\mathbf{x}$; an integer ℓ, indicating that the first ℓ variables in $\mathbf{x}$ are targeted for elimination.

Output: A list of solutions sol and a list of parameter conditions con.

1 Compute the row-reduced echelon form (rref) $\mathsf{rref}(P_{:,[\ell]})$ of the submatrix $P_{:,[\ell]}$, and the associated transformation matrix U such that $\mathsf{rref}(P_{:,[\ell]}) = UP_{:,[\ell]}$.
2 Let r be the number of non-zero rows in $\mathsf{rref}(P_{:,[\ell]})$ (i.e., the rank).
3 Let $\bar{P} = UP$, $\bar{\mathbf{q}} = U\mathbf{q}$, and let `pivots` $= [i_1, i_2, \ldots, i_r]$ be the column pivot indices.
4 Initialize sol = [], con = [].
5 **for** $i = r + 1$ **to** m **do**
6   **if** $\sum_{k=\ell+1}^{n} \bar{P}_{i,k}x_k - \bar{\mathbf{q}}_i$ *is a known nonzero constant* **then return** ([], []) ;
7   **if** *the expression contains parameters* **then**
8   Append the equation to con: $\sum_{k=\ell+1}^{n} \bar{P}_{i,k}x_k - \bar{\mathbf{q}}_i = 0$.
9   **end**
10 **end**
11 sol $= \bigcup_{j=1}^{r} \{x_{i_j} = -\sum_{k=i_j+1}^{n} \bar{P}_{j,k}x_k + \bar{\mathbf{q}}_j\}$.
12 Append to con all parametric denominators of sol not equal to zero.
13 **return** (sol, con).

2. **Weak linear variables (wlv)**: variables with numerical coefficients in *some* equations and parametric ones in others;
3. **Parametric coefficient linear variables (pclv)**: variables that have parametric coefficients in *all* equations.

For any system $P\mathbf{x} = \mathbf{q}$, we can reorder the variable list $\mathbf{x}$ by grouping it as [slv, wlv, pclv]. Let ℓ be the total number of variables of types slv and wlv. Then a lazy strategy is to apply SolvePLE($P\mathbf{x} = \mathbf{q}, \mathbf{x}, \ell$), which attempts to eliminate only the slv and wlv variables. The main advantage of this lazy approach is that the resulting solutions avoid parameters in their denominators with high probability, making the conditions more tractable. Therefore, Line 12 in Algorithm 1 is often not necessary.

Correspondingly, we consider the non-lazy method, which attempts to solve all possible variables in $\mathbf{x}$, including those with parametric coefficients. Specifically, we invoke SolvePLE($P\mathbf{x} = \mathbf{q}, \mathbf{x}, n$), to solve for as many variables in $\mathbf{x}$ as possible. In this setting, Line 12 of Algorithm 1 becomes effective, since the solutions may involve nontrivial conditions on the parameters due to division. However, this approach may lose certain solution branches. For instance, consider the equation $\{-c_{11}\mu_5 + \frac{7}{8}c_{12}\mu_5 = 0\}$, which will appear in Example 1. Calling SolvePLE($\{-c_{11}\mu_5 + \frac{7}{8}c_{12}\mu_5 = 0\}, [\mu_5]$, 1) returns a single solution branch: $branch_1 = [\mu_5 = 0], [-8c_{11} + 7c_{12} \neq 0]$. Nevertheless, there exists an additional solution branch corresponding to the case when the coefficient of μ_5 vanishes: $branch_2 = [\mathsf{true}], [-8c_{11} + 7c_{12} = 0]$. Here [true] means that μ_5 can take any values. This illustrates that solving equations involving parametric coefficients directly may miss degenerate cases where a parameter-dependent coefficient becomes zero, leading to multiple solution branches.

Example 1. Given the linear ranking function: $r(\mathbf{x}) = \mathbf{ax} = -7x_1 - 8x_2$, we aim to construct loop programs in the following form:

$$\begin{aligned}\mathsf{while}\ &\{a_{11}x_1 + a_{12}x_2 \le b_{11}, 2x_1 + 3x_2 \le -9, 8x_1 - x_2 \le -5, -9x_1 + 7x_2 \le -2\}\\ &\{-9x_1 + 7x_2 + c_{11}x_1' + c_{12}x_2' \le -9, -x_1 - 9x_2 + 7x_1' + 8x_2' \le -4\}.\end{aligned}$$

To achieve this, we need to solve the following system with parameters $a_{11}, a_{12}, c_{11}, c_{12}, b_{11}$:

$$sys := \begin{cases} a_{11}\mu_1 + 2\mu_2 + 8\mu_3 - 9\mu_4 - 9\mu_5 - \mu_6 = 7 \\ a_{12}\mu_1 + 3\mu_2 - \mu_3 + 7\mu_4 + 7\mu_5 - 9\mu_6 = 8 \\ c_{11}\mu_5 + 7\mu_6 = 0, c_{12}\mu_5 + 8\mu_6 = 0 \\ \mu_1, \mu_2, \mu_3, \mu_4, \mu_5, \mu_6 \ge 0 \\ a_{11}\nu_1 + 2\nu_2 + 8\nu_3 - 9\nu_4 - 9\nu_5 - \nu_6 = 7 \\ a_{12}\nu_1 + 3\nu_2 - \nu_3 + 7\nu_4 + 7\nu_5 - 9\nu_6 = 8 \\ c_{11}\nu_5 + 7\nu_6 = -7, c_{12}\nu_5 + 8\nu_6 = -8 \\ b_{11}\nu_1 - 9\nu_2 - 5\nu_3 - 2\nu_4 - 9\nu_5 - 4\nu_6 < 0 \\ \nu_1, \nu_2, \nu_3, \nu_4, \nu_5, \nu_6 \ge 0 \end{cases} \tag{8}$$

The strong linear variables are $\mu_2, \mu_3, \mu_4, \mu_6, \nu_2, \nu_3, \nu_4, \nu_6$, the weak linear variables are μ_5 and ν_5, and the parametric linear variables are μ_1 and ν_1. We reorder the variables as: $\mathsf{vars} = [\mu_2, \mu_3, \mu_4, \mu_6, \nu_2, \nu_3, \nu_4, \nu_6, \mu_5, \nu_5, \mu_1, \nu_1]$. Our goal is to solve as many of the strong and weak linear variables as possible using the eight given equations. To do this, we invoke: $\mathsf{SolvePLE}(\mathsf{sys}, \mathsf{vars}, 8)$, which returns:

$$\begin{cases} \mu_2 = \left(-\frac{1}{26}a_{11} - \frac{4}{13}a_{12}\right)\mu_1 - \frac{47}{26}\mu_4 + \left(-\frac{47}{26} - \frac{73}{208}c_{12}\right)\mu_5 - \frac{71}{26} \\ \mu_3 = \left(-\frac{3}{26}a_{11} + \frac{1}{13}a_{12}\right)\mu_1 + \frac{41}{26}\mu_4 + \left(\frac{41}{26} + \frac{15}{208}c_{12}\right)\mu_5 + \frac{5}{26} \\ \nu_2 = \left(-\frac{1}{26}a_{11} - \frac{4}{13}a_{12}\right)\nu_1 - \frac{47}{26}\nu_4 + \left(-\frac{47}{26} - \frac{73}{208}c_{12}\right)\nu_5 - \frac{1}{13} \\ \nu_3 = \left(-\frac{3}{26}a_{11} + \frac{1}{13}a_{12}\right)\nu_1 + \frac{41}{26}\nu_4 + \left(\frac{41}{26} + \frac{15}{208}c_{12}\right)\nu_5 + \frac{10}{13} \\ \mu_6 = -\frac{c_{12}\mu_5}{8}, \nu_6 = -\frac{c_{12}\nu_5}{8} - 1 \end{cases} \tag{9}$$

and two remaining equations not fully simplified to $0 = 0$:

$$\{-c_{11}\mu_5 + \frac{7}{8}c_{12}\mu_5 = 0, -c_{11}\nu_5 + \frac{7}{8}c_{12}\nu_5 = 0\}. \tag{10}$$

Solving the additional conditions in Eq. (10) leads to two possible solution branches, namely $-8c_{11} + 7c_{12} \neq 0$ and $-8c_{11} + 7c_{12} = 0$. The first branch corresponds to the generic case. In the following examples, to simplify the presentation, we focus instead on the degenerate case:

$$\mathsf{extra\_sys} = [-8c_{11} + 7c_{12} = 0]. \tag{11}$$

We now evaluate the solutions obtained in Eq. (9) against the remaining inequalities, including the parameter conditions described in Eq. (10). The resulting reduced system we need to analyze is as follows:

$$\begin{cases} -\mu_1 \leq 0, \quad -\mu_4 \leq 0, \quad -\mu_5 \leq 0, \quad \dfrac{c_{12}\mu_5}{8} \leq 0, \\ \left(\dfrac{1}{26}a_{11} + \dfrac{4}{13}a_{12}\right)\mu_1 + \dfrac{47}{26}\mu_4 + \left(\dfrac{47}{26} + \dfrac{73}{208}c_{12}\right)\mu_5 \leq \dfrac{71}{26}, \\ \left(\dfrac{3}{26}a_{11} - \dfrac{1}{13}a_{12}\right)\mu_1 - \dfrac{41}{26}\mu_4 - \left(\dfrac{41}{26} + \dfrac{15}{208}c_{12}\right)\mu_5 \leq \dfrac{5}{26}, \\ -\nu_1 \leq 0, \quad -\nu_4 \leq 0, \quad -\nu_5 \leq 0, \quad \dfrac{c_{12}\nu_5}{8} \leq -1, \\ \left(\dfrac{1}{26}a_{11} + \dfrac{4}{13}a_{12}\right)\nu_1 + \dfrac{47}{26}\nu_4 + \left(\dfrac{47}{26} + \dfrac{73}{208}c_{12}\right)\nu_5 \leq -\dfrac{1}{13}, \\ \left(\dfrac{3}{26}a_{11} - \dfrac{1}{13}a_{12}\right)\nu_1 - \dfrac{41}{26}\nu_4 - \left(\dfrac{41}{26} + \dfrac{15}{208}c_{12}\right)\nu_5 \leq \dfrac{10}{13}, \\ \left(b_{11} + \dfrac{12}{13}a_{11} + \dfrac{31}{13}a_{12}\right)\nu_1 + \dfrac{83}{13}\nu_4 + \left(\dfrac{343}{104}c_{12} - \dfrac{8}{13}\right)\nu_5 < -\dfrac{11}{13} \end{cases} \tag{12}$$

In the following, we present two approaches to solve the system given in Eq. (12), under the additional condition specified in Eq. (11).

3.3 Preprocessing the Parametric System

In this section, we present a preprocessing method for handling the input parametric system, with the goal to eliminate as many linear variables as possible.

We begin by applying the SolvePLE procedure introduced in Algorithm 1 to eliminate the strong and weak linear variables. After substituting the resulting solutions into the remaining system, we are left with a reduced set of inequalities that may still contain eliminable variables—including some of the original strong or weak variables that could not be eliminated previously.

To further reduce the system, we consider the use of the FourierMotzkin Elimination (FME) method, as implemented by the command RegularChains:-SemiAlgebraicSetTools:-LinearSolve in Maple. Although FME can theoretically handle parametric variables, it becomes computationally expensive in practice when applied to general parametric systems. Some existing works, such as [20] and [11], apply FME to parametric systems; however, these are typically limited to systems with specific structural restrictions. In our setting, the parametric coefficients may appear arbitrarily within the system, which makes direct FME impractical. A naive application of FME, eliminating variables one by one, leads to exponential growth in the size of intermediate expressions.

To mitigate this issue, we apply a symbolic abstraction strategy briefly mentioned in [3]: we introduce fresh variables to replace all expressions involving parametric coefficients, thereby transforming the parametric system into one with rational (constant) coefficients. This transformation enables more efficient elimination using FME. In particular, FME can then eliminate all strong linear variables, and potentially some weak or parametric linear variables.

Example 2. In Eq. (12), the strong linear variables are μ_4 and ν_4. Thus, we can project them out using FME. After applying the preprocessing procedure, the resulting system becomes:

$$\begin{cases} -\mu_1 \le 0, -\mu_5 \le 0, -\nu_1 \le 0, -\nu_5 \le 0, c_{12}\mu_5 \le 0, c_{12}\nu_5 \le -8 \\ \frac{7}{8}c_{12}\nu_5 - c_{11}\nu_5 = 0, \frac{7}{8}c_{12}\mu_5 - c_{11}\mu_5 = 0 \\ \left(a_{11} + \frac{9}{7}a_{12}\right)\mu_1 + \frac{11}{7}c_{12}\mu_5 \le \frac{121}{7}, (a_{11} + 8a_{12})\mu_1 + \left(\frac{73}{8}c_{12} + 47\right)\mu_5 \le 71 \\ \left(a_{11} + \frac{9}{7}a_{12}\right)\nu_1 + \frac{11}{7}c_{12}\nu_5 \le \frac{33}{7}, (a_{11} + 8a_{12})\nu_1 + \left(\frac{73}{8}c_{12} + 47\right)\nu_5 \le -2 \\ \left(a_{11} + \frac{13}{12}b_{11} + \frac{31}{12}a_{12}\right)\nu_1 + \left(\frac{343}{96}c_{12} - \frac{2}{3}\right)\nu_5 < -\frac{11}{12} \\ \left(a_{11} + \frac{41}{57}b_{11} + \frac{85}{57}a_{12}\right)\nu_1 + \left(\frac{493}{228}c_{12} - \frac{287}{57}\right)\nu_5 < \frac{31}{19} \end{cases} \tag{13}$$

3.4 Heuristic Detection for Parametric Linear Inequality Systems

In this section, we provide a heuristic detection method for checking the satisfiability of parametric linear inequality systems.

We denote the system as $E\mathbf{x} \le \mathbf{f}$, where E is an $m \times n$ matrix with parametric entries and $\mathbf{f}$ is a parametric m-vector. A key observation is that if all coefficients of a variable x_i are negative, then the corresponding constraints are trivially satisfiable. This requirement, however, is often too restrictive. To relax the condition, we collect the row indices of negative coefficients with respect to the ordered variables $x_1, x_2, \ldots, x_n$, where the index set for variable x_i is restricted to the zero coefficient indices of the preceding variables $x_1, \ldots, x_{i-1}$. This procedure is carried out in Lines 2–9 of Algorithm 2. If the index set obtained in this way covers all m rows, then the system is guaranteed to be consistent. Note that in the system described by Eq. (5), the coefficient matrices for the variables μ_i and ν_i are identical, except for the final strict inequality involving ν_i. Thus, the system resulting after solving the strong and weak linear variables retains this symmetry, except for one strict inequality related to ν_i. Since Algorithm 2 depends only on the coefficient matrix of the inequality system, we can ignore the μ_i-related inequalities during the detection.

Algorithm 2: Quick Check Satisfiability of Parametric Linear Inequality System (QuickCheckSatPLI)

Input: A parametric linear inequality system $E\mathbf{x} \leq \mathbf{f}$, and a set of additional conditions extra_sys.

Output: Either `[true, sol]`, where `sol` is a set of parameter conditions under which the system is satisfiable, or `FAILED`.

1 **Initialize**: Let `con` := `extra_sys`, and `ind` := $\emptyset$.
2 **for** $i = 1$ **to** n **do**
3   Let `ind_i` be the set of row indices (not in `ind`) where $E[k, i] \neq 0$:

$$\texttt{ind\_i} := \{k \mid E[k,i] \neq 0,\ 1 \leq k \leq m,\ k \notin \texttt{ind}\}.$$

4   **if** *the system* $\{E[k, i] < 0 \mid k \in$ *`ind_i`*$\}$ *is unsatisfiable* **then**
5   **continue**
6   **else**
7   `con` := `con` $\cup$ $\{E[k, i] < 0 \mid k \in$ `ind_i`$\}$; `ind` := `ind` $\cup$ `ind_i`.
8   **end**
9 **end**
10 **if** *`ind`* $\neq \{1, \ldots, m\}$ **then return** *`FAILED`*;
11 **Solve**: Let `sol` := `solve(con)`;
12 **if** *`sol` is not empty* **then return** *`[true, sol]`* ;
13 **return** *`FAILED`*

Example 3. Consider the extra conditions in Eq. (11) and the system in Eq. (12). The coefficient matrix E and constant vector $\mathbf{f}$ involving ν_1, ν_4, and ν_5 become:

$$E = \begin{bmatrix} -1 & 0 & 0 \\ 0 & -1 & 0 \\ 0 & 0 & -1 \\ 0 & 0 & \frac{c_{12}}{8} \\ \frac{a_{11}+8a_{12}}{26} & \frac{47}{26} & \frac{376+73c_{12}}{208} \\ \frac{3a_{11}-2a_{12}}{26} & -\frac{41}{26} & -\frac{328+15c_{12}}{208} \\ b_{11} + \frac{12a_{11}+31a_{12}}{13} & \frac{83}{13} & \frac{343c_{12}-64}{104} \end{bmatrix}, \quad \mathbf{f} = \begin{bmatrix} 0 \\ 0 \\ 0 \\ -1 \\ -\frac{1}{13} \\ \frac{10}{13} \\ -\frac{11}{13} \end{bmatrix}.$$

The set of parameter constraints collected during the for-loop (Lines 2–9) is: $\texttt{con} = \{-8c_{11}+7c_{12} = 0, \frac{a_{11}+8a_{12}}{26} < 0, \frac{3a_{11}-2a_{12}}{26} < 0, b_{11} + \frac{12a_{11}+31a_{12}}{13} < 0, \frac{c_{12}}{8} < 0\}$. Solving con yields two possible solutions: $\texttt{sol}_1 = \{c_{11} - \frac{7}{8}c_{12} = 0, a_{11} - \frac{2}{3}a_{12} < 0, a_{12} \leq 0, b_{11} + \frac{12a_{11}+31a_{12}}{13} < 0, c_{12} < 0\}$, and $\texttt{sol}_2 = \{c_{11} - \frac{7}{8}c_{12} = 0, a_{11} + 8a_{12} < 0, -a_{12} < 0, b_{11} + \frac{12a_{11}+31a_{12}}{13} < 0, c_{12} < 0\}$. Hence, Algorithm 2 returns `true`, along with the corresponding parameter constraints. From $\texttt{sol}_1$, we can extract a concrete instance such as: $a_{11} = -1, a_{12} = -1, b_{11} = 0, c_{11} = -\frac{7}{8}, c_{12} = -1$, which ensures that the original system in Eq. (8) has a solution. Therefore, we find the while program: while $\{-x_1 - x_2 \leq 0, 2x_1 + 3x_2 \leq -9, 8x_1 - x_2 \leq -5, -9x_1 + 7x_2 \leq -2\}$ $\{-9x_1 + 7x_2 - \frac{7}{8}x_1' - x_2' \leq -9, -x_1 - 9x_2 + 7x_1' + 8x_2' \leq -4\}$.

3.5 Detecting Parametric Vertices of a Polyhedron

In this section, we describe a method for determining the satisfiability of a parametric linear inequality system by searching for *parametric vertices* of the corresponding polyhedron.

Given a linear inequality system $E\mathbf{x} \leq \mathbf{f}$, the set of solutions defines a polyhedron when the system is consistent. Thus, the system is satisfiable if and only if the corresponding polyhedron has a nonempty feasible region, i.e., it contains at least one face. Here, a *face* refers to any geometric subset of the polyhedron, ranging in dimension from 0 to n, where n is the number of variables in $\mathbf{x}$. In the non-degenerate case, the minimal face has dimension zero and is referred to as a *vertex*. In general, we assume that if the system is consistent, then it contains at least one vertex.

To detect a vertex, we select n inequalities from $E\mathbf{x} \leq \mathbf{f}$ and convert them into equalities, forming a system of n parametric linear equations. Solving this system may yield: (*i*) no solution (in which case the selected inequalities do not define a vertex); (*ii*) or a parametric solution, along with a corresponding set of parameter conditions. We then substitute the solution into the remaining inequalities to obtain a reduced inequality system. If the reduced system, together with the parameter conditions, admits a solution, then the candidate point is a valid parametric vertex of the original polyhedron. Algorithm 3 summarizes this process for parametric vertex detection.

Algorithm 3: VertexDetection

Input: A parametric inequality system $E\mathbf{x} \leq \mathbf{f}$ and additional constraints extra_sys.

Output: Either `[v, con]`, where v is a parametric vertex under condition `con`, or `[]` if no vertices are found.

Let *IndSet* be all possible combinations of n elements from $\{1, \ldots, m\}$;
for *ind in IndSet* **do**
  sol, con $\leftarrow$ SolvePLE($E_{\texttt{ind},:} \cdot \mathbf{x} = \mathbf{f}_{\texttt{ind}}, \mathbf{x}, n$);
  if *sol contains fewer than n elements* **then continue** ;
  $\overline{\texttt{ind}} \leftarrow [m] \setminus \texttt{ind}$;
  con $\leftarrow$ con $\cup$ extra_sys; con $\leftarrow$ con $\cup$ eval($E[\overline{\texttt{ind}}, :] \cdot \mathbf{x} \leq \mathbf{f}[\overline{\texttt{ind}}]$, sol);
  if *solve(con) is not empty* **then return** *[sol, con]* ;
end
return *[]*

We continue with the system in Eq. (12), together with the parameter conditions in Eq. (11), to illustrate Algorithm 3. Unlike the heuristic detection method, finding a vertex for the inequalities related to ν_i does not imply the same for those related to μ_i. Therefore, we must analyze each subsystem separately. Let sys_μ and sys_ν denote the subsystems in Eq. (12) corresponding to the variables μ_i and ν_i, respectively. Choosing the index set $\texttt{ind} = [1, 2, 5]$, we observe that both subsystems admit parametric vertices. For sys_μ, the parametric vertex is $[\mu_1 = 0,\ \mu_4 = 0,\ \mu_5 = \frac{568}{73c_{12}+376}]$, under the parameter condition $\mathsf{con}_1 = \{-\frac{376}{73} \le c_{12} \le 0, \quad c_{11} = \frac{7c_{12}}{8}\}$. Similarly, for sys_ν, the parametric vertex is $[\nu_1 = 0,\ \nu_4 = 0,\ \nu_5 = -\frac{16}{73c_{12}+376}]$, under the condition $\mathsf{con}_2 = \{-\frac{376}{71} \le c_{12} < -\frac{376}{73}, \quad c_{11} = \frac{7c_{12}}{8}\}$. Combining these two conditions, we obtain $\mathsf{con} = \mathsf{con}_1 \cup \mathsf{con}_2 = \{-\frac{376}{71} \le c_{12} < -\frac{376}{73}, \quad c_{11} = \frac{7c_{12}}{8}\}$, which defines a region in the parameter space where the system is satisfiable. From this, we can extract specific parameter values: $a_{11} = 0, a_{12} = 0, b_{11} = 0, c_{11} = -\frac{329}{71}, c_{12} = -\frac{376}{71}$, which guarantee that the original system in Eq. (8) has a solution. Therefore, we find the while program: while $\{2x_1+3x_2 \le -9, 8x_1-x_2 \le -5, -9x_1+7x_2 \le -2\}$ $\{-9x_1 + 7x_2 - \frac{329}{71}x_1' - \frac{376}{71}x_2' \le -9, -x_1 - 9x_2 + 7x_1' + 8x_2' \le -4\}$.

3.6 The Main Algorithm for Solving Parametric Linear Systems

In this section, we present the main algorithm for solving parametric linear systems. For all benchmark instances considered in this paper, the variables to be eliminated are either of type μ_i or ν_i. Moreover, the constraints involving these two types of variables are given separately.

In Algorithm 4, the variables and constraints are partitioned: (i) ineqs_μ and ineqs_ν denote the subsets of inequality constraints involving the variables μ and ν, respectively; (i) similarly, $\mathsf{con\_eqs}_\mu$ and $\mathsf{con\_eqs}_\nu$ represent the corresponding parameter conditions obtained after solving the linear equations. The algorithm proceeds in three main phases: 1) Solve the parametric linear equations using parametric Gaussian elimination. If the system has no solution, return `false`. 2) Evaluate the inequality system under the obtained solution and check satisfiability of the ν-subsystem using a fast heuristic. 3) If the heuristic fails, invoke vertex detection for both the μ and ν subsystems. If both admit vertices under consistent parameter conditions, return satisfiability; otherwise, return `false`.

4 Experimentation

All experiments were conducted on a machine equipped with an Intel® Xeon® Platinum 8272CL CPU @ 2.60 GHz. The preprocessing procedure, heuristic detection, vertex detection, and the main algorithm for solving parametric linear systems were implemented in MAPLE 2024. REDLOG, bundled with REDUCE (CSL, revision 7107), was used for comparative experiments. Additionally, Z3 (version 4.15.1, 64-bit) was employed to get the satisfiable ratios.

4.1 Setting of Dimensions and Parameters

We generate two types of benchmarks for Eq. (5): totally random benchmarks and parametric benchmarks. By *totally random*, we mean that all entries in the matrices A, C and the vectors $\mathbf{b}$ and $\mathbf{a}$ are randomly chosen integer values. All the integer values in $A, C, \mathbf{a}$ are in the range $[-9, 9]$ while the values in $\mathbf{b}$

Algorithm 4: SolveParametricLinearSystem

```
Input: A parametric system {Px = q, Ex ≤ f}.
Output: [true, con] if the system is satisfiable under condition con;
        otherwise, false.
sol, con_eqs ← SolvePLE(Px = q, x, ℓ) ;   // x is ordered by types [slv,
   wlv, plv]; ℓ is the number of slv/wlv variables
if sol = ∅ then return false ;
ineqs ← eval(Ex ≤ f, sol);
Split ineqs and con_eqs into ineqs_μ, ineqs_ν and con_eqs_μ, con_eqs_ν;
res ← QuickCheckSatPLI(ineqs_ν, con_eqs_ν);
if res ≠ FAILED then return res ;
(sol_μ, con_μ) ← VertexDetection(ineqs_μ, con_eqs_μ);
if sol_μ = ∅ then return false ;
(sol_ν, con_ν) ← VertexDetection(ineqs_ν, con_eqs_ν);
if sol_ν = ∅ then return false ;
if con_μ ∪ con_ν admits a solution then return [true, con] ;
return false
```

are in the range $[-9, 0)$. Totally random benchmarks are generated based on combinations of the parameters n, m, and p, where:

$$n \in \{2,3,4,5\}, m \in \{2n, 3n, 4n\}, p \in \{1,2,4,8\} \text{ and } m \geq n + p.$$

This results in a total of 39 valid combinations of the triple (m, n, p). Each dataset is named using the format m($m)n($n)p($p), where $m, $n and $p represent the concrete values used. For example, the dataset m4n2p1 corresponds to $m = 4$, $n = 2$, and $p = 1$. In this case, A and C are 4×2 matrices. The first row of C is set to zero, $\mathbf{b}$ is a 4-dimensional column vector, and $\mathbf{a}$ is a 2-dimensional row vector. We first randomly generate 10 vectors $\mathbf{a}$. For each $\mathbf{a}$, we generate one dataset for the triple (m, n, p), which contains 100 randomly generated benchmark instances. In each instance, the matrices A and C and the vector $\mathbf{b}$ are randomly generated, while the vector $\mathbf{a}$ is fixed and shared across all 100 benchmarks in the same dataset.

To increase the likelihood of satisfiability in the totally random benchmarks, we introduce parametric variations by selectively placing parameters in the system. Given a specified number of parameters $k \in \{1,2,4,8\}$, the k parameters are randomly distributed among A, C, and $\mathbf{b}$. For the parametric cases, we generate one fixed vector $\mathbf{a}$ for each triple (m, n, p). Since there are four choices for k, we obtain a total of $39 \times 4 = 156$ datasets for each placement strategy. Each dataset contains 100 randomly generated benchmark instances.

4.2 Experimental Results on Benchmarks Without Parameters

Our objective is to find matrices A, C, and a vector $\mathbf{b}$ such that, for a fixed vector $\mathbf{a}$, both Eq. (5) and Eq. (1) are simultaneously satisfiable. Equation (1) and Eq. (5) are referred respectively as the *original system* and the *generated system*.

Figure 1 presents the satisfiable ratios for the generated system, the original system, and the proportion of instances where both systems are simultaneously satisfiable—denoted by the legends "generated", "original", and "common", respectively. It can be observed that the original system generally exhibits a higher satisfiability probability than the generated one. Among the 39 datasets, there are 27 for which the satisfiable ratio is below 50% in the generated system, whereas only 12 datasets fall below this threshold in the original system. Moreover, the probability that both systems are simultaneously satisfiable is low.

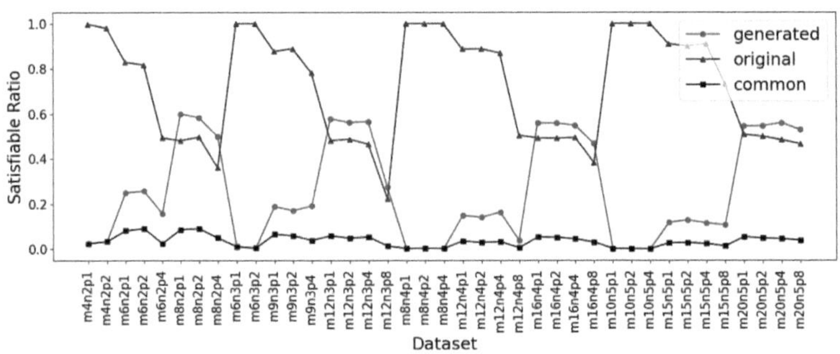

Fig. 1. Satisfiable ratio on random benchmarks without parameters.

4.3 Experimental Results for Parametric Benchmarks

In this section, all reported metrics are averaged over 100 instances in each dataset folder. Figure 2 shows the satisfiable ratio for each dataset folder under different numbers of parameters. It is evident that as the number of parameters k increases, the satisfiable ratio also tends to increase. Comparing Fig. 2 with Fig. 1, we observe that introducing parameters significantly improves the satisfiable ratio. For fixed values of n and p, increasing the number of inequalities m also leads to higher satisfiable ratios. These observations suggest that the satisfiable ratio can be improved by increasing both the values of k and m.

In this paper, we proposed two methods for solving parametric linear systems: the use of REDLOG with a preprocessing step (denoted as pre+redlog), and the SolveParametricLinearSystem procedure (denoted as SPLS), introduced in Algorithm 4. We evaluate these methods on the parametric benchmarks and compare their performance against that of REDLOG alone. The time limit for solving a single instance is set to 100 s for both REDLOG and SPLS. For pre+redlog, the total time limit is 200 s—100 s for preprocessing and 100 s for the subsequent REDLOG execution. Although the total allotted time is technically higher than that of the other two methods, this setup is still fair for two reasons. First, if the

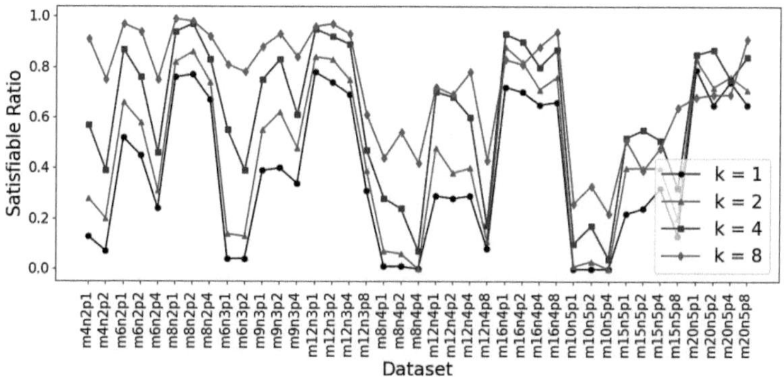

Fig. 2. Ratio of satisfiable instances on parametric benchmarks.

preprocessing step times out, REDLOG will not be launched. Second, as demonstrated in Fig. 3, the average time consumed by pre+redlog never exceeds 100 s on any dataset. For the unsolved instances, the time is counted as 100 s when computing the average time.

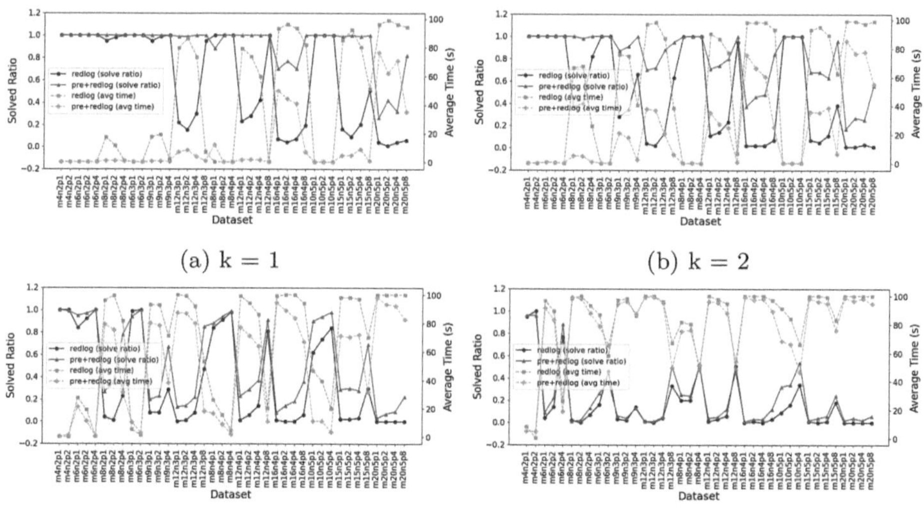

(a) k = 1

(b) k = 2

(c) k = 4

(d) k = 8

Fig. 3. Solved ratio and average time on parametric benchmarks.

Figure 3 presents the proportion of instances solved by REDLOG and pre+redlog, as well as the average time spent on each dataset. As shown, the average solving time for pre+redlog never exceeds 100 s. We observe a significant decline in the solved ratio as the number of parameters increases, accompanied by an increase in average solving time. The pre+redlog approach is highly effective when the system contains 1 or 2 parameters, and it still provides noticeable improvements for cases with 4 or 8 parameters, albeit to a lesser extent. These results demonstrate that the preprocessing step greatly enhances the performance of solving parametric linear systems.

Based on the performance of REDLOG, we selected 108 datasets which are regarded as "hard" due to a high proportion of timeouts during solving. They are sorted in descending order based on the ratio of instances solved by REDLOG. Figure 4 compares the performance of three solving approaches. We observe that SPLS outperforms REDLOG on more than half of the datasets. The pre+redlog method achieves the best overall performance on easier instances. However, as the difficulty of the benchmarks increases, SPLS tends to perform more favorably than pre+redlog, demonstrating its robustness in more challenging scenarios.

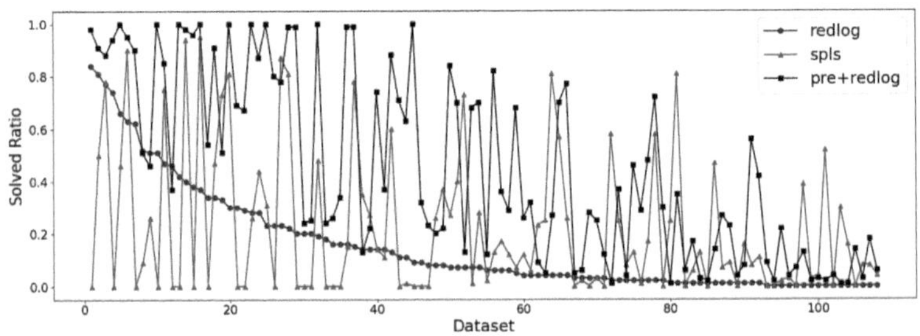

Fig. 4. Solved ratio of instances on hard parametric benchmarks.

5 Conclusion

In this work, we proposed a method to synthesize linear simple loops from any given linear ranking functions. We observed that one key to increase the success ratio of synthesis is to introduce certain amount of free parameters, which reduces the synthesis problem to solving a weakly nonlinear parametric system. We proposed two efficient methods for solving such systems. Both approaches firstly employ a parametric Gauss elimination procedure to solve the equational constraints and simply the input system. Then the first method leverages Fourier-Motzkin elimination to precondition the simplified system and then calls a general quantifier elimination method. The other is to utilize the structure of such systems to combine a heuristic detection method based solely on the signs of coefficients of variables and a generic method relying on detecting vertices of parametric polyhedrons. We have demonstrated the effectiveness of the proposed methods by comparing it with quantifier elimination procedures specialized for handling weakly nonlinear systems implemented in the REDLOG system. One possible application of current work is to utilize the synthesized loops to help learning the generation of linear ranking functions. We plan to investigate such an application in a future work.

References

1. Bauer, A., et al.: Comprehensive exploration of synthetic data generation: a survey (2024)
2. Bradley, A.R., Manna, Z., Sipma, H.B.: The polyranking principle. In: Caires, L., Italiano, G.F., Monteiro, L., Palamidessi, C., Yung, M. (eds.) ICALP 2005. LNCS, vol. 3580, pp. 1349–1361. Springer, Heidelberg (2005). https://doi.org/10.1007/11523468_109
3. Chen, C., Chen, X., Keita, A., Moreno Maza, M., Xie, N.: Metafork: a compilation framework for concurrency models targeting hardware accelerators and its application to the generation of parametric CUDA kernels. In: Proceedings of 25th Annual International Conference on Computer Science and Software Engineering, CASCON 2015, Markham, Ontario, Canada, 2–4 November 2015, pp. 70–79. IBM/ACM (2015)
4. Chen, C., Moreno Maza, M.: Quantifier elimination by cylindrical algebraic decomposition based on regular chains. J. Symb. Comput. **75**, 74–93 (2016)
5. Collins, G.E.: Quantifier elimination for real closed fields by cylindrical algebraic decompostion. In: Brakhage, H. (ed.) GI-Fachtagung 1975. LNCS, vol. 33, pp. 134–183. Springer, Heidelberg (1975). https://doi.org/10.1007/3-540-07407-4_17
6. Colón, M.A., Sipma, H.B.: Practical methods for proving program termination. In: Brinksma, E., Larsen, K.G. (eds.) CAV 2002. LNCS, vol. 2404, pp. 442–454. Springer, Heidelberg (2002). https://doi.org/10.1007/3-540-45657-0_36
7. de Moura, L., Bjørner, N.: Z3: an efficient SMT solver. In: Ramakrishnan, C.R., Rehof, J. (eds.) TACAS 2008. LNCS, vol. 4963, pp. 337–340. Springer, Heidelberg (2008). https://doi.org/10.1007/978-3-540-78800-3_24
8. Dolzmann, A., Sturm, T.: Redlog: computer algebra meets computer logic. ACM SIGSAM Bull. **31**(2), 2–9 (1997)
9. England, M.: Recent developments in real quantifier elimination and cylindrical algebraic decomposition (extended abstract of invited talk). In: Boulier, F., Mou, C., Sadykov, T.M., Vorozhtsov, E.V. (eds.) CASC 2024. LNCS, vol. 14938, pp. 1–10. Springer, Cham (2024). https://doi.org/10.1007/978-3-031-69070-9_1
10. Goodfellow, I., et al.: Generative adversarial networks. Commun. ACM **63**(11), 139–144 (2020)
11. Größlinger, A., Griebl, M., Lengauer, C.: Quantifier elimination in automatic loop parallelization. J. Symb. Comput. **41**(11), 1206–1221 (2006)
12. Ho, J., Jain, A., Abbeel, P.: Denoising diffusion probabilistic models. Adv. Neural. Inf. Process. Syst. **33**, 6840–6851 (2020)
13. Hozzová, P., Kovács, L., Norman, C., Voronkov, A.: Program synthesis in saturation. In: Pientka, B., Tinelli, C. (eds.) CADE 2023. LNCS, vol. 14132, pp. 307–324. Springer, Cham (2023). https://doi.org/10.1007/978-3-031-38499-8_18
14. Humenberger, A., Amrollahi, D., Bjørner, N., Kovács, L.: Algebra-based reasoning for loop synthesis. Form. Asp. Comput. **34**(1) (2022)
15. Kenison, G., Kovács, L., Varonka, A.: From polynomial invariants to linear loops. In: Proceedings of the 2023 International Symposium on Symbolic and Algebraic Computation, ISSAC 2023, Tromsø, Norway, 24–27 July 2023, pp. 398–406. ACM (2023)
16. Kera, H., Ishihara, Y., Kambe, Y., Vaccon, T., Yokoyama, K.: Learning to compute gröbner bases. In: Advances in Neural Information Processing Systems, vol. 37, pp. 33141–33187. Curran Associates, Inc. (2024)
17. Kuttler, K., Farah, I.: A first course in linear algebra. Lyryx Alberta (2017)

18. Lample, G., Charton, F.: Deep learning for symbolic mathematics. In: International Conference on Learning Representations (2020)
19. Podelski, A., Rybalchenko, A.: A complete method for the synthesis of linear ranking functions. In: Steffen, B., Levi, G. (eds.) VMCAI 2004. LNCS, vol. 2937, pp. 239–251. Springer, Heidelberg (2004). https://doi.org/10.1007/978-3-540-24622-0_20
20. Renganarayanan, L., Kim, D., Strout, M.M., Rajopadhye, S.: Parameterized loop tiling. ACM Trans. Program. Lang. Syst. (TOPLAS) **34**(1), 1–41 (2012)
21. Sieber, K.: The Foundations of Program Verification. Springer, Cham (2013)
22. Strzeboński, A.W.: Cylindrical algebraic decomposition using validated numerics. J. Symb. Comput. **41**(9), 1021–1038 (2006)
23. Sturm, T.: Thirty years of virtual substitution: foundations, techniques, applications. In: Proceedings of the 2018 ACM International Symposium on Symbolic and Algebraic Computation, pp. 11–16 (2018)
24. Trinh, T.H., Wu, Y., Le, Q.V., He, H., Luong, T.: Solving olympiad geometry without human demonstrations. Nature **625**(7995), 476–482 (2024)
25. Weispfenning, V.: The complexity of linear problems in fields. J. Symb. Comput. **5**(1–2), 3–27 (1988)
26. Weispfenning, V.: Quantifier elimination for real algebra–the quadratic case and beyond. Appl. Algebra Eng. Commun. Comput. **8**, 85–101 (1997)

Modeling and Verifying Concurrent Reactive Systems Using Separation Logic

Huan Sun[1], David Sanán[2], Jun Sun[3], and Wenhai Wang[1(✉)]

[1] Zhejiang University, Hangzhou, China
Wenhai.Wang@zju.edu.cn
[2] Singapore Institute of Technology, Singapore, Singapore
[3] Singapore Management University, Singapore, Singapore

Abstract. Reactive systems depend on a well-defined set of event handlers to continuously respond to environmental stimuli. In concurrent environments, interactions between these handlers introduce additional complexities, such as hardware interrupts in preemptive systems and inter-handler communication in multicore architectures. Existing techniques for concurrency in imperative languages often face challenges in modeling potentially unbounded sequences of handler invocations and accurately capturing the event context—both of which are essential for effective reasoning about concurrent reactive systems.

In this paper, we present ReCore, a fully mechanized framework for modeling and verifying shared resources in concurrent reactive systems. Building upon PiCore, an event-based language that naturally represents unbounded handler invocation sequences and precisely tracks event context, we develop a separation logic-based reasoning framework tailored for concurrent reactive system correctness verification. Our ReCore framework is implemented in Isabelle/HOL and validated through a non-trivial case study involving the concurrent stack mechanism in Zephyr's IPC module, demonstrating its practical effectiveness.

1 Introduction

At a high level, a reactive system [4] can be viewed as a non-terminating loop that continuously receives inputs from the environment and dispatches the appropriate event handlers in response. In a concurrent setting, a concurrent reactive system (CRS) is formed by the parallel composition of multiple reactive systems. Many real-world systems fall into this category, including operating systems [33], communication protocols [32], and distributed control systems [10,24]. Given that many CRSs are safety- or security-critical, rigorous methods for verifying their correctness are essential. However, verifying CRSs is inherently challenging due to the need to reason about an unbounded number of interactions with the environment and to analyze interference between concurrently executing components.

While recent research has made significant strides in the field of shared-memory concurrency verification [6,14,15,18,20,22,25,26,31]. Most existing

É. André et al. (Eds.): ICFEM 2025, LNCS 16229, pp. 247–265, 2026.
https://doi.org/10.1007/978-981-95-4213-0_14

approaches are designed for imperative languages. Adapting these methodologies for modeling and verifying CRSs is far from straightforward. The complexity stems from several factors. Firstly, in a CRS, the environment continuously selects which event handler to trigger non-deterministically, along with the associated arguments for the triggering event. Although it might be tempting to simulate a reactive system using a simple "while{true}" loop program that reads data from the environment and invokes relevant handlers in the loop body [5], such an approach introduces unnecessary modeling intricacies. To make matters worse, certain CRS verification tasks necessitate the recording of system-level information (e,g., which event has occurred or which event handler is executed within the specific reactive system). For instance, when verifying the noninterference based on state-based automation models [27,28], it becomes significant to utilize this information to define the domain of actions.

Arguably, the fundamental reason for the above problems is the mixture of system behaviors and program behaviors. Jones et al. [21] mention that employing "actions" [8] or "events" [3] can offer an extremely neat framework for modeling systems. Some previous works, such as Event-B [19] and PiCore [35] have introduced event-based languages that embrace this concept in concurrent settings, utilizing rely-guarantee style reasoning. However, the event-based language in these works cannot be applied to separation logic reasoning as it treats the entire state as shared without reflecting the ownership of resources.

In this paper, we present ReCore, an extension of PiCore that integrates resource ownership to enable reasoning based on Concurrent Separation Logic (CSL) [25]. While the original PiCore system employs rely-guarantee reasoning for verifying CRSs, ReCore adopts CSL to avoid the complexity of specifying and proving interference between components. This shift significantly reduces the proof burden. To support CSL, we extend the existing event-based language with a resource structure that manages ownership in event-based systems. As a result, our framework enables compositional reasoning over shared resources using CSL.

To evaluate the effectiveness of our framework, we use ReCore to model and verify the concurrent stack module of the real-world operating system Zephyr [1]. ReCore enables precise modeling of system-level behavior while leveraging existing frameworks for imperative languages to encapsulate program-level behavior. The separation logic reasoning framework we adopt simplifies verification by avoiding the complexity of specifying and reasoning about interference between components, as required in rely-guarantee approaches. Instead, it focuses on preserving invariants over shared resources, thereby streamlining the verification process.

Our contributions are summarized as follows:

1. We introduce an event-based language ReCore to model resource ownership in event-based systems.
2. We demonstrate how our event-based language enables the formalization of noninterference properties for CRSs.

3. We develop a proof system for ReCore based on CSL and establish its soundness.
4. We validate our framework through a case study on the concurrent stack mechanism in Zephyr's IPC module. The entire development is fully mechanized in Isabelle/HOL, comprising approximately 5,700 lines of code, and is publicly available at [2].

2 Modeling and Verification of CRS: An Overview

2.1 An Illustrative Example

```
struct msgs {
  top, max :: nat;
  stack :: msg list;
  mutex l;}
struct kernel_state {
  cid :: tid;
  t_msg :: tid  → msgs}
msg recv(){
  msgs q = t_msg(cid);
  msg m = Null;
  lock(q->l)
  if (q->top > 0)
    msg m = q->stack[top-1];
    q->top --;
    unlock(q->l);
    return m}
int send(tid id, msg m){
  if check(cid, id, policy)
    msgs q = t_msg(id);
    lock(q->l)
    if (q->top >= q->max)
      return -1
    else
      q->stack[top] = m;
      q->top ++;
    unlock(q->l)
  else
  return 0}
```

Fig. 1. IPC Mechanism in multicore OS.

Figure 1 shows a simplified IPC module used in the multicore OS Zephyr. The message stack is a shared data structure consisting of a list of messages *stack*, where *top* indicates the index of the most recently inserted element, and *max* defines the stack's capacity. Since this stack is accessed by multiple threads, a mutex l is used to manage access, ensuring that only one thread can access the queue at a time. The kernel state comprises three elements: *cid* represents the thread ID of the currently executing thread, *t_msg* is a mapping from thread IDs to message stacks, representing the message buffer of each thread. The kernel provides two system calls: send(id, m) tries to send the message m to the thread id. Before pushing the message into the buffer of thread id, the system call checks the security policy to ensure that the information transfer from the calling thread to id is permitted. recv() pops a message from the calling thread's message stack.

Applications—potentially running on different CPUs—constantly invoke the send and recv system calls to communicate. The OS continuously evaluates the trigger conditions for each system call (e.g., whether a thread is scheduled), and non-deterministically selects a triggered call to execute.

Certain verification tasks, such as noninterference [27,28], require reasoning beyond state properties. Specifically, they necessitate tracking system-level information to identify which module or thread is responsible for each step. In the context of the IPC mechanism, noninterference ensures that communication between threads adheres to a specified security policy—for example, preventing high-security data from leaking to low-security users. This requires that every atomic step preserve state indistinguishability unless the policy explicitly permits a change in another thread's observable state.

Consequently, verifying such properties requires tracking the agent performing each action. For example, when the system pushes a message into the stack by executing the command $q \rightarrow stack[size] = m$, we must determine which CPU performs the command and which thread on that CPU is executing to determine which thread is responsible for its execution.

Existing frameworks designed for imperative languages can be used to model CRSs by the parallel composition of reactive systems, where each reactive system is simulated by a while(true) loop with a loop body executing corresponding event handlers (e.g. [5]). However, to account for environmental nondeterminism and to select the appropriate event handler along with its arguments, an auxiliary case structure must be embedded within the loop body. This increases the proof burden, especially in systems with numerous events and parameters. Furthermore, verifying properties that depend on more than just the program state—such as noninterference—requires additional auxiliary state and proof rules to capture system-level information, further complicating the model and making verification more cumbersome.

2.2 Event-Based Language

The main cause of the problems associated with modeling CRSs is the mixing of the system and program behavior. PiCore addresses this issue by providing an event-based language that decouples the handler program from the system behaviors. A system call is modeled by a guarded event **EVENT** Send [Tid t, Msg m] @ κ **WHEN** $cid = t$ **THEN** C which determines the parameters of the system call (Tid t, Msg m), where it executes (i.e., on CPU κ), conditions (e.g., $cid = t$) that trigger the system call, with an imperative program (C) as its body. A parallel component (e.g., a single CPU) is modeled as an event system that continuously evaluates the guards of the events from its event set for which their associated guard condition holds in the current state. One event is non-deterministically selected to be triggered, and its body is executed. After the event finishes, the evaluation of guards starts again, looking for the next event to be executed. The CRSs are modeled as a parallel composition of event systems. To determine which module performs a specific step, PiCore's semantics use labels to record which event system performs the single command, and event context to record which event is currently executed in an event system, which enables verification of noninterference [36].

However, rely-guarantee style reasoning requires explicitly specifying, and then ruling out, the possibility of interference between different systems. Besides, since PiCore views the entire program state as shared, one needs to specify the environmental updates and system progress for all variables, including irrelevant state space and local variables.

3 The ReCore Language

The main challenge with using PiCore for CSL-style reasoning is that it treats the entire state as shared, without reflecting the ownership of resources. Our ReCore overcomes this limitation by redefining the syntax and semantics of PiCore to keep track of shared resources declared by the system.

The abstract syntax of and operational semantics of ReCore are shown in Fig. 2 and Fig. 3, respectively. We use the language provided by [9] to model the behavior of the handler program. **Skip** is the symbol of program termination. $x := [E]$ and $[E] := [E']$ reads and writes the heap at the location E, respectively. Here x is a variable and E is an expression. In the separation logic view, the entire state is separated into local variables and shared resources. **local** v **in** C declares a local variable v. **with** r **when** B **do** C **od** represents *a conditional critical region* (CCR). In our setting, r represents the identifier of the shared resource, which is mapped to concrete memory when reading or writing its value. A thread can possess the shared resource r when r is available and the guard B is true. Then it executes its body C in isolation from other CCRs requiring the same resource. Commands including memory allocation, de-allocation, sequential composition, conditional, and loops, are regular.

Event handlers are modeled as events. The syntax for events is divided into basic events **Event** α, representing an untriggered event, and inner events $\lfloor C \rfloor$, representing a triggered event, i.e., the event is under execution. **Event** α is a tuple $g \times C$ where g is the trigger condition and C is the handler program of the event. Whenever g holds in the current state, a basic event **Event** α is triggered and then transitions into an inner event $\lfloor C \rfloor$, and its handler program begins to execute.

The behavior of a parallel component is modeled by an event system, which can be either an event sequence or an event set as shown in Fig. 2. An event set continually evaluates the trigger conditions of the events within its set, selecting one event non-deterministically if the current state satisfies its trigger condition. The selected event's handler program is then executed. Upon completion (represented as $\perp$), the evaluation of guards resumes to identify the next event for execution. An event sequence models the sequential execution of events. It can serve as an intermediate representation of event system execution or be used to model the initialization of the system.

To facilitate CSL-style reasoning, we introduce an extra variable rs to keep track of shared resources declared by the CRS. rs is a distinct list of resource identifiers that represents the shared resources and is not part of the state but rather contextual information added to the specification. This enables us to determine during the verification which systems have access to shared resources at any given time, ensuring that these resources are not accessed simultaneously

Program:

C ::= **Skip** | $x := E$ | $x := [E]$ | $[E_1] := [E_2]$

| $x :=$ **alloc**(E) | **dispose**(E) | $C_1; C_2$

| **if** B **then** C_1 **else** C_2 **fi** | **local** v **in** C

| **with** r **when** B **do** C **od** | **While** B **do** C **od**

Event:

$\mathcal{E}$ ::= **Event** α *(Basic Event)*

| $\lfloor C \rfloor$ *(Inner Event)*

Event System:

$\mathcal{S} ::= \{\mathcal{E}_0, \ ..., \ \mathcal{E}_n\}$ *(Event Set)*

| $\mathcal{E} \oplus \mathcal{S}$ *(Event Sequence)*

Parallel Event System:

$\mathcal{PS} ::= \langle rs, [\mathcal{S}_0, \ ..., \ \mathcal{S}_n] \rangle$

(Stack) $\sigma \in \Sigma ::= \text{Var} \rightharpoonup \mathtt{N}$ (Heap) $h \in H ::= \mathtt{N} \rightharpoonup \mathtt{N}$ (State) $s \in S ::= (\sigma, h)$

(Resource) $rs ::= \text{Id list}$ (EvtCtx) $x ::= \mathcal{S} \mapsto \mathcal{E}$ (Action) $t ::= C \mid \mathcal{E}$

Fig. 2. Abstract Syntax of ReCore

by multiple parallel components. A CRS is thus modeled as the parallel event system which is a list of event systems, where each event system is identifiable by a list index ($\mathcal{PS}!\kappa$ means the κth element of $\mathcal{PS}$) and equipped with an extra parameter rs to represent resources shared between all event systems.

The operational semantics of ReCore is defined as a labeled configuration transitions $(\#_1, s_1, x_1) \xrightarrow{\delta} (\#_2, s_2, x_2)$. A configuration c is defined as $(\#, s, x)$ where # stands for either a program, an event, an event system, or a parallel event system, We use $\sharp_{\mathsf{c}}$, s_{c}, and x_{c} to represent the three components of a configuration c respectively; s represents the system state; and $x : \mathcal{K} \rightarrow \mathcal{E}$ is an event context, indicating which event is currently executed in an event system. The transition label $\delta = t@\kappa$ signifies the specific action taking place in that transition. $t ::= C \mid \mathcal{E}$ represents action type, where c is a program action representing an atomic step of the handler program, and $\mathcal{E}$ represents the occurrence of event $\mathcal{E}$. $@\kappa$ means that the action δ occurs in event system κ. The event context is updated when a new event occurs (BasicEvt rule), while program execution won't change the event context (AnonyEvt rule). A configuration can move from one stage to another or abort, which occurs due to an execution fault such as data racing (two event systems access the same resource simultaneously) or accessing unallocated memory. Here, the function *locked* $\mathcal{S}$ returns a set of shared resources locked by (through executing **with** r **when** B **do** C **od**) the event system $\mathcal{S}$ and the functions $access(\mathcal{S}, s)$ and $writes(\mathcal{S}, s)$ return the set of heap locations accessed or modified by $\mathcal{S}$ respectively. The formal definition of these auxiliary functions can be found in [2].

4 Formalizing Noninterference for Concurrent Systems

This section shows how ReCore specifies noninterference for CRSs. The standard way to model and verify the noninterference [27,28] is to model the system as

$$\text{[InnerEvt]}\ \frac{(C,s)\longrightarrow(C',s')}{(\lfloor C\rfloor,s,x)\xrightarrow{C@\kappa}(\lfloor C'\rfloor,s',x)}\qquad \text{[BasicEvt]}\ \frac{C=body(\alpha)\quad s\in guard(\alpha)\quad x'=x(\kappa\mapsto\textbf{Event }\alpha)}{(\textbf{Event }\alpha,s,x)\xrightarrow{\textbf{Event }\alpha@\kappa}(\lfloor C\rfloor,s,x')}$$

$$\text{[EvtA]}\ \frac{(C,s)\longrightarrow\textbf{abort}}{(\lfloor C\rfloor,s,x)\longrightarrow\textbf{abort}}\qquad \text{[EvtSet]}\ \frac{\exists i\leq n\quad(\mathcal{E}_i,s,x)\xrightarrow{\mathcal{E}_i@\kappa}(\mathcal{E}'_i,s',x')}{(\{\mathcal{E}_0,\ ...,\ \mathcal{E}_n\},s,x)\xrightarrow{\mathcal{E}_i@\kappa}(\mathcal{E}'_i\oplus\{\mathcal{E}_0,\ ...,\ \mathcal{E}_n\},s',x')}$$

$$\text{[EvtSeq1]}\ \frac{\mathcal{E}'\neq\perp\quad(\mathcal{E},s,x)\xrightarrow{C@\kappa}(\mathcal{E}',s',x)}{(\mathcal{E}\oplus\mathcal{S},s,x)\xrightarrow{C@\kappa}(\mathcal{E}'\oplus\mathcal{S},s',x)}\qquad \text{[EvtSeq2]}\ \frac{\mathcal{E}'=\perp\quad(\mathcal{E},s,x)\xrightarrow{C@\kappa}(\mathcal{E}',s',x)}{(\mathcal{E}\oplus\mathcal{S},s,x)\xrightarrow{C@\kappa}(\mathcal{S},s,x)}$$

$$\text{[EvtSeqA]}\ \frac{(\mathcal{E},s,x)\longrightarrow\textbf{abort}}{(\mathcal{E}\oplus\mathcal{S},s,x)\longrightarrow\textbf{abort}}\qquad \text{[EvtSetA]}\ \frac{\exists i\leq n.\quad(\mathcal{E}_i,s,x)\longrightarrow\textbf{abort}}{(\{\mathcal{E}_0,\ ...,\ \mathcal{E}_n\},s,x)\longrightarrow\textbf{abort}}$$

$$\text{[EvtParA]}\ \frac{\exists\kappa<\textbf{length }\mathcal{PS}.\quad(\mathcal{PS}!\kappa,s,x)\longrightarrow\textbf{abort}}{(\langle rs,\mathcal{PS}\rangle,s,x)\longrightarrow\textbf{abort}}\qquad \text{[RaceA]}\ \frac{\begin{array}{c}\exists i,j<\textbf{length }\mathcal{PS}\quad i\neq j\\ \textbf{accesses}(\mathcal{PS}!i,\sigma)\cap\textbf{writes}(\mathcal{PS}!j,\sigma)\neq\emptyset\end{array}}{(\langle rs,\mathcal{PS}\rangle,s,x)\longrightarrow\textbf{abort}}$$

$$\text{[Par]}\ \frac{\begin{array}{l}\exists\kappa<\textbf{length }\mathcal{PS}.\quad(\mathcal{PS}!\kappa,s,x)\xrightarrow{t@\kappa}(\mathcal{S}',s',x')\quad\mathcal{PS}'=\mathcal{PS}(\kappa:=\mathcal{S}')\\ \forall j<\textbf{length }\mathcal{PS}.\ i\neq j\longrightarrow\textbf{locked }\mathcal{S}'\ \cap\ \textbf{locked }(\mathcal{PS}!j)=\emptyset\end{array}}{(\langle rs,\mathcal{PS}\rangle,s,x)\xrightarrow{t@\kappa}(\langle rs,\mathcal{PS}'\rangle,s',x')}$$

Fig. 3. Operational Semantics for ReCore.

a state machine and prove that every step within the system maintains state indistinguishability unless explicitly permitted by the security policy.

To define noninterference for CRSs, we first model the CRS as a state machine $\mathcal{M}=\langle\mathcal{C},A,step,\mathsf{c}_0\rangle$, where $\mathcal{C}$ is the set of parallel event system configurations, A is the set of actions, $step:A\rightarrow\mathcal{P}(\mathcal{C}\times\mathcal{C})$ is the transition function, and c_0 is the initial configuration.

We define the event domain function $dome:\mathcal{E}\times S\rightarrow\mathcal{D}$, which maps an event with a state to a corresponding domain (e.g., a thread or the scheduler in our example). A state-dependent *dome* function is necessary for reasoning about many systems in which the domain of a handler program depends on the currently running thread or process [23,29,34]. For the example shown in Fig. 1, the domain of the send or recv event is determined by the variable *cid*, which is state-dependent.

We define an action as a tuple $\langle\delta,ev,d\rangle$, where δ is a transition label that encodes the action type and identifies which event system acts, ev specifies which event being executed acts, and d records the domain of the action. Given an action a, we refer to its components as δ_a, ev_a and d_a, respectively. An action is either the occurrence of a new event or an atomic step of a triggered event, where the event of action is determined by the event context. We encode these requirements as constraints on the event context and transition label, ensuring it complies with the domain of the action.

$$
\begin{aligned}
step(a) = \{(\mathsf{c}, \mathsf{c}') \mid \mathsf{c} \xrightarrow{\delta_a} \mathsf{c}' \wedge ((\delta_a = ev_a @\kappa \wedge dome(s_\mathsf{c}, ev_a) = d_a) \vee \\
(\delta_a = C@\kappa \wedge ev_a = x_\mathsf{c}(\kappa) \wedge dome(s_\mathsf{c}, ev_a) = d_a))\}
\end{aligned}
$$

Specifically, the function $step(a)$ returns all possible pairs of configurations resulting from the execution of action a. The transition label between two configurations must match δ_a. If the action represents the occurrence of a new event ev_a, then the domain of that event must equate to d_a. Alternatively, if the action corresponds to a program action, the event of that action ev_a should match the event context, and the domain of ev_a must equate to d_a.

The permitted information flow within the system is specified by the information flow configuration $\texttt{Info} = \langle \mathcal{D}, \rightsquigarrow, dom, \sim \rangle$, where $\mathcal{D}$ is the set of domains, $\rightsquigarrow \subseteq \mathcal{D} \times \mathcal{D}$ is the security relation defined on $\mathcal{D}$, the function $dom : A \rightarrow \mathcal{D}$ maps actions to domains, here the function dom is defined as $dom(a) = d_a$. The observational equivalence relation $\sim \subseteq \mathcal{D} \times H \times H$ describes the set of heaps appearing indistinguishable to a given domain. We extend the equivalence relation to state $s_1 \overset{d}{\sim} s_2$ to denote $(d, h_1, h_2) \in \sim$ where h_1 and h_2 are heap components of s_1 and s_2, respectively.

The standard proof technique of intransitive noninterference is by proving a set of unwinding conditions [23,27–29,34] that examine individual actions on the system. Given a system $\mathcal{M} = \langle \mathcal{C}, A, step, \mathsf{c}_0 \rangle$ and its associated information flow configuration $\texttt{Info} = \langle \mathcal{D}, \rightsquigarrow, dom, \sim \rangle$, the local respect (LR) condition requires that an action a executed in a configuration c can affect the state indistinguishability of only those domains to which the domain executing a is permitted to send information:

Definition 1 (Local Respect).

$$
LR(\mathcal{M}, \texttt{Info}) \triangleq \forall a\ d\ \mathsf{c}\ \mathsf{c}'.\ (\mathsf{c}, \mathsf{c}') \in step(a) \longrightarrow dom(a) \not\rightsquigarrow d \longrightarrow s_\mathsf{c} \overset{d}{\sim} s_{\mathsf{c}'}
$$

Intuitively, the SC condition requires that executing an action on two states preserves equivalence for all domains if those states are equivalent from the perspective of the action's domain:

Definition 2 (Step Consistent).

$$
\begin{aligned}
&SC(\mathcal{M}, \texttt{Info}) \triangleq \forall a\ d\ \mathtt{c1}\ \mathtt{c2}\ \mathtt{c1}'\ \mathtt{c2}'.\ (\mathtt{c1}, \mathtt{c1}') \in step(a) \longrightarrow (\mathtt{c2}, \mathtt{c2}') \in step(a) \longrightarrow \\
&s_{\mathtt{c1}} \overset{d}{\sim} s_{\mathtt{c2}} \longrightarrow ((dom(a) \rightsquigarrow d) \longrightarrow (s_{\mathtt{c1}} \overset{dom(a)}{\sim} s_{\mathtt{c2}})) \longrightarrow s_{\mathtt{c1}'} \overset{d}{\sim} s_{\mathtt{c2}'}
\end{aligned}
$$

Noninterference can be derived from unwinding conditions defined above. We omit the formal definition of noninterference due to page limit, and readers can refer to the appendix for a detailed definition:

Theorem 1 (Unwinding Theorem of Noninterference).

$$
SC(\mathcal{M}, \texttt{Info}) \wedge LR(\mathcal{M}, \texttt{Info}) \longrightarrow NI(\mathcal{M}, \texttt{Info})
$$

5 CSL Framework for ReCore

With ReCore, we develop a CSL-based proof framework in this section to deal with systems with light environmental interference.

5.1 CSL Specification

The CSL specification for ReCore is denoted as $\mathcal{I} \models \{P\}\#\{Q\}$, where P and Q are precondition and postcondition, and $\mathcal{I}$ is the resource invariant, a mapping from shared resource to booleans. It implies that if the system # (which can be an imperative program, an event, an event system, or the parallel event system) starts with the state that satisfies the precondition P can be safely executed until termination while satisfying the postcondition Q. Besides, it requires the resource invariant $\mathcal{I}$ to be preserved throughout the execution. To define safe execution given a configuration, we introduce an auxiliary proposition $\mathbf{safe}_n^{\square}(\#, \sigma, h, \mathcal{I}, Q)$ similar to [30]. The $\square$ can be either P, e, es, or pes, representing the proposition for the imperative program, event, event system, and parallel event system, respectively. The proposition $\mathbf{safe}_n^{\square}(\#, \sigma, h, \mathcal{I}, Q)$ holds when the system # with stack σ, local heap h, resource invariant $\mathcal{I}$, and postcondition Q can be safely executed for up to n steps.

Definition 5.1. *(n-step safety)* $\boldsymbol{safe}_0^{\square}(\#, \sigma, h, \mathcal{I}, Q)$ *always holds* $\boldsymbol{safe}_{n+1}^{\square}(\#, \sigma, h, \mathcal{I}, Q)$ *holds if and only if all the following propositions hold:*

(i) If $\# = \bot$, *then* $(\sigma,\ h) \models Q$; *and*
(ii) for all h_F, x, *if* $h \uplus h_F$ *is well defined , then* $(\#, (\sigma, h \uplus h_F), x) \not\rightarrow$ ***abort****; and*
(iii) $\boldsymbol{access}(\#, \sigma) \subseteq h$;
(iv) for all $h_J,\ h_F,\ \mathcal{E}',\ \sigma', h', x, x', \delta$, *if* $(\sigma,\ h_J) \models \circledast_{r \in locked(\#') \setminus locked(\#)} \mathcal{I}(r)$, *and* $(\#,\ (\sigma,\ h \uplus h_J \uplus h_F), x) \xrightarrow{\delta} (\#',\ (\sigma',\ h'), x')$, *then there exists* h'' *and* h'_J *such that* $h' =\ h'' \uplus h'_J \uplus h_F$ *and* $(\sigma',\ h'_J) \models \circledast_{r \in locked(\#) \setminus locked(\#')} \mathcal{I}(r)$ *and* $\boldsymbol{safe}_n^{\square}(\#', \sigma', h', \mathcal{I}, Q)$.

We divide the whole heap into three parts while defining configuration safety. h represents event-local memory that no other events are permitted to modify. h_J stands for the memory of the shared resources, which may be accessed by different events due to ownership transfer, and must adhere to the resource invariant. h_F stands for irrelevant memory. Any configuration is safe for zero steps. For $n+1$ steps, (i) it must satisfy the postcondition if it is a terminal configuration (i.e., the body of the event is **Skip**), (ii) does not abort (iii) and only accesses memory within the heap h, (iv) after one step execution, re-establish the resource invariant and the transited configuration is safe for n steps. Here the separating conjunction operator $P * Q$ represents the union of two disjoint heaps that satisfies assertion P and Q respectively, and $\circledast_{r \in \alpha}$ represents the union of the set of disjoint heaps H such that for all r in α there exists a h in H satisfying $\mathcal{I}(r)$.

$$\frac{\mathcal{I} \vdash \{P \wedge guard(\alpha)\}body(\alpha)\{Q\}}{\mathcal{I} \vdash \{P\}\textbf{Event } \alpha\{Q\}}\ [\text{BasicEvt}] \qquad \frac{P \subseteq P' \quad Q' \subseteq Q \quad \mathcal{I} \vdash \{P'\}\#\{Q'\}}{\mathcal{I} \vdash \{P\}\#\{Q\}}\ [\text{Conseq}]$$

$$\frac{\mathcal{I} \vdash \{P\}C\{Q\}}{\mathcal{I} \vdash \{P\}\lfloor C \rfloor\{Q\}}\ [\text{InnerEvt}] \qquad \frac{\mathcal{I} \vdash \{P\}\mathcal{E}\{R\} \quad \mathcal{I} \vdash \{R\}\mathcal{S}\{Q\}}{\mathcal{I} \vdash \{P\}\mathcal{E} \oplus \mathcal{S}\{Q\}}\ [\text{EvtSeq}]$$

$$\frac{\mathcal{I} \vdash \{P\}\#\{Q\} \quad \textbf{fv}(R) \cap \textbf{writes}(\#) = \emptyset}{\mathcal{I} \vdash \{P * R\}\#\{Q * R\}}\ [\text{Frame}]$$

$$\frac{\forall i \leq n.\ \mathcal{I} \vdash \{P_i\}\mathcal{E}_i\{Q_i\} \quad \forall i,j \leq n.\ Q_i \subseteq P_j \quad \forall i \leq n.\ Q_i \subseteq Q \quad \forall i \leq n.\ P \subseteq P_i}{\mathcal{I} \vdash \{P\}\{\mathcal{E}_0,\ ...,\ \mathcal{E}_n\}\{Q\}}\ [\text{EvtSet}]$$

$$\frac{\forall i < \textbf{length } \mathcal{PS}.\ \mathcal{I}(rs \overset{*}{:=} J) \vdash \{P_i\}\mathcal{PS}!i\{Q_i\} \quad \forall i,j < \textbf{length } \mathcal{PS}.\ i \neq j \rightarrow \textbf{fv}(P_i, r\mathcal{S}_i, Q_i) \cap \textbf{writes}(r\mathcal{S}_j) = \emptyset}{\mathcal{I} \vdash \{P_0 * ... * P_{(\textbf{length } \mathcal{PS})-1} * J\}\langle rs, \mathcal{PS}\rangle\{Q_0 * ... * Q_{(\textbf{length } \mathcal{PS})-1} * J\}}\ [\text{Par}]$$

Fig. 4. Separation Logic Proof Rules for ReCore

The validity of the specification is defined according to the above definition. It states that the system # is valid if the initial state satisfies the precondition P, then it can be safely executed for any number of steps:

Definition 5.2. *(validity)* $\mathcal{I} \models \{P\}\#\{Q\}$ *if and only if for all* n, σ, h, *if* $(\sigma, h) \models P$ *then* $\textbf{\textit{safe}}_n^{\square}(\#, \sigma, h, \mathcal{I}, Q)$.

5.2 CSL Proof Rules

Figure 4 illustrates the CSL proof rules for ReCore. $\mathcal{I}(rs \overset{*}{:=} J)$ is an abbreviation for updating the resource invariant for all resources in rs. It associates each shared resource in list rs with a new resource invariant and ensures that $\circledast_{r \in set(rs)} \mathcal{I}(rs \overset{*}{:=} J)$ satisfies the J.

The InnerEvt rule and BasicEvt rule are used to verify events. The inner program of the event is simply a wrapper for its handler program. Consequently, if the handler program C satisfies the CSL specification, so does the event $\lfloor C \rfloor$. If the body of a basic event satisfies the CSL specification with the conjunction of guard and precondition, the CSL specification for that event is satisfied.

The EvtSeq rule and EvtSet rule are used to verify the validity of event systems. The EvtSeq rule is similar to the sequential rule in Hoare Logic, as the postcondition of event $\mathcal{E}$ is the precondition of the successor event system $\mathcal{S}$. We need to prove four premises as indicated in EvtSet rule to show that an event set satisfies the CSL specification. (i) Each event needs to satisfy its CSL specification. (ii) Each event's postcondition must imply its precondition since the event set behaves identically after the event terminates. (iii) The overall postcondition must include the postcondition of each event, and (iv) the overall precondition must imply the precondition of each event.

The Par rule is the parallel composition rule for ReCore. To prevent interference with local proof, we have to ensure that free variables of the event system specification cannot be modified by others except itself. The precondition and postcondition of the parallel event system should be the separating conjunction of the precondition and postcondition of the individual event system, respectively. Besides, if we have a heap fragment that satisfies J, we can pass it as a resource invariant to all event systems within the parallel event system. So that every event system can access the heap fragment, but must obey the resource invariant during execution.

The Frame rule allows us to ignore the irrelevant memory when verifying events, event systems, and parallel event systems, and the assertion R for that memory is unchanged in the postcondition. Here the function **fv** returns free variables. The Conseq rule can be used to strengthen the precondition and weaken the postcondition for events, event systems, and parallel event systems. We prove the soundness of all proof rules presented above, and details can be found in the Isabelle implementation [2].

6 Case Study

In this section, we apply the above-introduced proving framework to the verification of Zephyr's concurrent stack mechanism. Zephyr [1] is an open-sourced real-time operating system for connected, resource-constrained, and embedded devices supporting multiple architectures. Zephyr uses concurrent stacks as one of the IPC mechanisms used to exchange data between different processes.

6.1 Concurrent Stack in Zephyr

```
struct k_stack {
   _wait_q_t wait_q;
   struct k_spinlock lock;
   stack_data_t *base, *next, *top;
   u8_t flags;
}
```

Fig. 5. The data Structure of stack

The data structure of the stack is shown in Fig. 5. *wait_q* is a linked list that stores the blocked thread requests data from the stack. *lock* is used for the synchronization of the stack between different threads. The pointers *base*, *next*, and *top* point to the bottom of the stack buffer, the next available cell, and the top of the stack buffer, respectively. Initially, *wait_q* is empty, and the pointer *next* points to the bottom of the buffer.

Figure 6 presents a set of assertions designed to describe the data structures within our system. The assertion $s \mapsto [x_0, \cdots, x_n]$ represents a contiguous heap fragment that stores the values of an array. The data buffer of the stack is defined by *stack_buf*. It can be viewed as an array, with the pointer b pointing to the array's head and the pointer t pointing to the next memory location of the array's tail. *thread_node* defines the structure of threads, which is pointed to by the pointer p. In this case study, we only consider the relevant structure fields:

$$s \mapsto [x_0, \cdots, x_n] = (s \mapsto x_0) * ... * (s + n \mapsto x_n)$$

$$stack\_buf(b,t,xs) = \begin{cases} b = t & if\ xs\ =\ [\,] \\ (b \mapsto x) * stack\_buf(b+1,t,xs) & if\ xs\ =\ x\#xs \end{cases}$$

$$thread\_node(p,t) = \begin{cases} False \wedge emp & if\ p\ =\ \text{NULL} \\ p \mapsto [thd\_st\ t, thd\_next\ t, thd\_data\ t] & otherwise \end{cases}$$

$$thread\_slseg(h,t,ts) = \begin{cases} h = t & if\ ts\ =\ [\,] \\ Fasle \wedge emp & if\ h\ =\ \text{NULL} \\ * \begin{cases} thread\_node(h,x) \\ thread\_slseg(thd\_next\ x,t,xs) \end{cases} & if\ xs\ =\ x\#xs \end{cases}$$

$$thread\_sl(t,ts) = thread\_slseg(t, \text{NULL}, ts)$$

Fig. 6. Assertions of Data Structure.

state, next pointer, and swapped data of the thread. We enforce the constraint that pointer p must not be NULL. The assertions *thread_slseg* and *thread_sl* are employed to define linked lists of threads. The *thread_slseg* assertion defines a fragment of a linked list which has three parameters: h and t representing pointers to the head and tail elements of the linked list, and t indicating the list of threads contained within it. The linked list *thread_sl* simply mandates that the tail pointer points to NULL.

Zephyr provides two kernel services *k_stack_push* and *k_stack_pop*, for pushing data to the stack and popping data from the stack, respectively. When a thread invokes service *k_stack_push*, Zephyr checks whether the stack is full first. If it is, the service just returns an error message. Otherwise, it then checks whether threads are waiting for data. In that case, a thread is removed from the wait queue, and the pushed data is transmitted to that thread directly. Otherwise, the data is pushed into the stack buffer. The tricky point here is that we don't need to check the wait queue when the stack is full, since the stack is full implies that no threads are waiting for data. When a thread invokes service *k_stack_pop*, Zephyr first checks whether the stack is empty. If so, it either returns an error message or appends the thread to the wait queue, depending on the parameter timeout. If not, it retrieves data from the stack and transmits it to the thread.

6.2 Modeling Concurrent Stack in Zephyr

Figure 7 shows the big picture of modeling the operating system. A kernel service is modeled as an 'event', which contains a handler name serving as the unique identifier for the service, a trigger condition that determines when the service is triggered and what parameter a service will receive, and a handler program that will be executed when the service is triggered. A single reactive system, which in our model of operating systems, the scheduler or the thread, is modeled as an 'event system'. In addition to the regular heap and stack, the event system applies an 'event context' which connects the event system to the event handler that is currently in execution. When an event is triggered within the

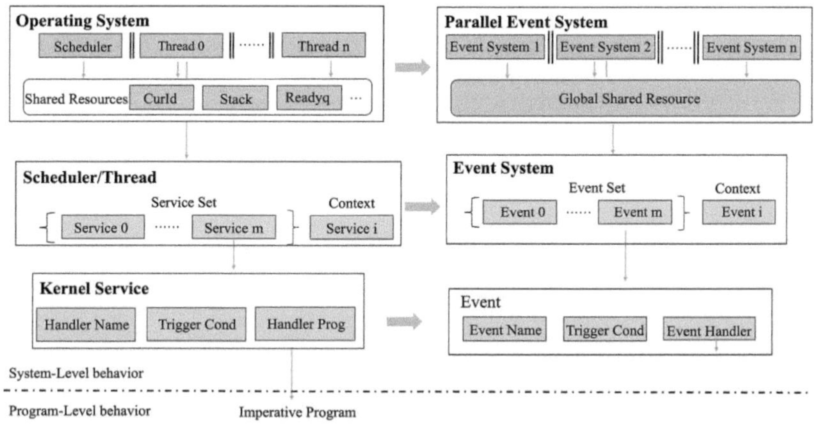

Fig. 7. Using Event-based Language to Model the Operating System.

event system, the event context updates to reflect that event. The entire operating system is modeled as a parallel event system, achieved through the parallel composition of multiple event systems. We consider three shared resources for the stack model: the concurrent stack *Stack*, the ready queue *Readyq*, and the thread that is being scheduled *Cur*.

The case study includes three events: $(t \neq \text{NULL}, stack\_push\ t\ d)$, $(t \neq \text{NULL}, stack\_pop\ t\ time)$, $(True, scheduler)$, representing *k_stack_push* service, *k_stack_pop* service and schedule service, respectively. The *k_stack_push* service and *k_stack_pop* service receive three parameters, t denoting the invoking thread, which will be used for thread context preemption, d representing the data to be pushed into the stack, and *time* representing the waiting time. We impose the constraint that the thread must not be NULL, as indicated by the trigger condition. Given that our scenario focuses on a single stack, there is no necessity to pass the stack's address as a parameter to the service.

Figure 8 defines the formal specification for the kernel service stack push. In the C code, the statement *return* stops the execution of the program and returns control to the calling function. In our specification, we use an auxiliary parameter *end* to control the execution flow of the kernel service (Lines 2, 34–38). Before executing the stack operation, the required information of the stack structure is assigned to local variables (Lines 4–6). Then it checks whether the stack buffer is full (Line 7). If it is, it returns an error message (Lines 8–9). Otherwise, it checks whether some threads are waiting for data (Line 13). If there are waiting threads, the heading thread is removed from the wait queue, and the pushed data is transmitted to that thread directly (Lines 16–17, 24–29). If there are not, the data is pushed into the stack buffer (Lines 20–21). The execution of the kernel service invoked by a thread can be stopped by the scheduler to be resumed later. This behavior is modeled using a global shared *cur*, which is a heap cell $a\_cur \mapsto t$, indicating thread t is currently scheduled and is being executed. The

```
// local variable declaration ...
t ▶ end = 0;
with Stack when True do
  t ▶ stack := [a_stack] ;
  t ▶ next := [stack -> next] ;
  t ▶ top := [stack -> top] ;
  if next = top then
    t ▶ ret := ENOMEN;
    t ▶ end := 1
  else
    t ▶ (
    first := [stack -> wait];
    if first = NULL THEN
      Skip
    else
      waitq := [first -> next];
      [stack -> wait] := waitq
    fi);
    if first = NULL then
      t ▶ [next] := data;
      t ▶ [stack -> next] := next
          + 1
    else
      t ▶ (
      [first -> state] := READY;
      [first -> data] := date;
      with Readyq when True do
        ready := [a_readyq];
        first := ready;
        [a_readyq] := first
      od)
    fi
  fi
od
if end = 0 then
  t ▶ ret := 0
else
  Skip
fi
```

Fig. 8. Formal Specification for Stack Push Service.

kernel service will be executed only when t is scheduled. This is accomplished by employing the expression $t \blacktriangleright p$ in Fig. 9. It uses a test and set (TAS) mechanism to ensure that thread t can be progressed only if it is scheduled.

```
t ▶ p ≡
flag := 0;
while flag = 0 do
  with Cur when True do
    cur := [a_cur];
    if cur = t then
      flag := 1; p
    else Skip fi
  od
od
```

Fig. 9. Context Preemption

The scheduler $\mathcal{S}_{sched}$, which is represented as an event system $\{scheduler\}$, removes a thread from the ready queue and executes its services. The thread $\mathcal{S}_{t_i}$, which is represented as event system $\{pop(t_i, time), push(t_i, d_{push})\}$), will invoke stack pop/push service consistently. We consider three global shared resources in the concurrent stack module: *Stack*, *Readyq*, and *Cur*, which represent the concurrent stack, the ready queue, and the currently running thread, respectively. The entire operating system is modeled as the parallel event system $([Stack, Readyq, Cur], [\mathcal{S}_{sched}, \mathcal{S}_{t_0}, ..., \mathcal{S}_{t_n}])$

6.3 Verification and Evaluation

Our goal is to prove the preservation of resource invariant throughout the system execution. Figure 10 defines the resource invariant of the shared resources in our system. *inv_stack* defines the invariant for the stack. It has a heap cell that records the address of the stack and a block of heaps for the stack regulated by *is_stack*. *is_stack* defines that a stack should (i) have a block of memory

$$
\begin{aligned}
&inv\_stack = \exists s\ base\ next\ top\ wait\ buf\ ts.\\
&(a\_stack \mapsto s) * is\_stack(base, next, top, wait, buf, ts)\\
&is\_stack(base, next, top, wait, ds, ts) =\\
&\quad * \begin{cases} s \mapsto [base, next, top, wait] \\ stack\_buf(base, top, ds) \\ thread\_sl(r, ts) \wedge all\_blocked(ts) \end{cases} \wedge \begin{cases} base < top \\ base \le next \le top \\ wait \neq \text{NULL} \implies base = next \end{cases}\\
&inv\_readyq = \exists r\ ts.\ (a\_readyq \mapsto r) * thread\_sl(r, ts) \wedge all\_ready(ts)\\
&inv\_cur = \exists p\ r\ t.\ (a\_cur \mapsto p) * thread\_node(r, t) \wedge is\_running(t)
\end{aligned}
$$

Fig. 10. Definition of Resource Invariant.

that records the information of stack structure (ii) and have a stack buffer used to store data (iii) and have a wait queue which is a linked list of threads and the states of those threads have to be BLOCKED (iv) and the stack buffer should be non-empty (v) and the pointer *next* has to be between pointer *base* and *top* and (vi) it is impossible that stack buffer has data to offer while some threads are waiting for data simultaneously. *inv_readyq* defines the invariant for the ready queue. It has a heap cell that records the address of the ready queue and a linked list of threads with all threads' state READY. *inv_cur* defines the invariant over the currently executing thread *cur*, as a heap cell that records the address of the tcb of the currently running thread and a thread whose state must be RUNNING.

The operating system begins with a state where the heap satisfies all resource invariants $inv\_stack * inv\_readyq * inv\_cur$. Then we apply the rule PAR to break down the verification of the parallel event system into individual proofs of each event system. During this step, the heap fragment is passed as resource invariants to inner event systems, resulting in each shared resource in rs is attached with the corresponding resource invariant, represented as $\mathcal{I}(Stack := inv\_stack, Readyq := inv\_readyq, Cur := inv\_cur)$. Subsequently, as all event systems are event sets, we further apply rule EVTSET to each event system to decompose the proof of event systems into the proof of specific events.

We then employ rule BASICEVT to decompose the proof of events into the proof of handler programs. Finally, we use the rules for imperative programs to prove the handler program. The key point is that when successfully occupying the resource, the program gets the heap fragments regulated by the resource invariant, while before releasing the resource, the resource invariant must be rebuilt. We can abstract away irrelevant heap using the rule FRAME, e.g., when verifying the operation on the ready queue, we can ignore the heap that stores the data structure of the stack.

The proving system and case study have been implemented in Isabelle/HOL (publicly available in [2]). All specifications and proof scripts have been verified with ≈ 5700 lines of specification and proof scripts.

7 Related Work

Concurrency Verification. A vast body of work addresses the verification of concurrent systems, including Owicki-Gries [26], rely-guarantee [20], separation logic [6,14,15,22,25,31], and refinement [18]. However, these frameworks are designed for imperative languages and need extra effort to model and verify the continuous and non-deterministic execution of handler services and parameter passing in the setting of CRS.

Furthermore, our framework possesses the capability to capture system-level information, such as which event handler is executed on a specific reactive system. This feature becomes particularly significant when addressing certain verification tasks, like state-based automation models for noninterference [27,28]. For noninterference properties, the transition function in automata not only considers how states transition but also the actions that occur during these transitions. In our framework, actions can be defined as records that include the reactive system, the event context, and the executing command using our event-based language. Most existing frameworks designed for imperative programs may require supplementary structures or auxiliary variables to record this information. In contrast, our framework introduces the concepts of 'event context' and 'transition labels', providing a neat way to specify and verify these properties within concurrent settings.

Reactive Systems. The refinement of reactive systems [7], followed by Event-B [3], offers a refinement-based verification approach for reactive systems. However, it lacks concurrency support. An extension of Event-B for concurrency [19] introduces a rely-guarantee style reasoning framework for imperative languages, but not for Event-B itself. Other works [13,16,17,17] study event-based systems, but the semantics differ from ours as the event is triggered by the imperative program in other events, whereas in our context, events are triggered by the environment. The UNITY framework provided an early foundation for reasoning about concurrent reactive systems by explicitly incorporating the rely/guarantee paradigm for compositional verification [11,12]. PiCore [35] introduces an event-based language similar to ours and a corresponding rely-guarantee reasoning framework. It has been applied to verify real-world OS memory management modules [33]. However, the event-based language in PiCore cannot be applied to CSL-style reasoning as it treats the entire state as shared without reflecting the ownership of resources. Consequently, it necessitates complicated proofs that rely on explicitly specifying, and then ruling out, the possibility of interference between different systems.

8 Conclusion and Future Work

In this work, we introduce a new event-based language that can deal with resource ownership for modeling CRSs. We provide a reasoning framework based on CSL to enable verification for the newly developed semantics. We integrate a reasoning framework for an imperative program and use it to verify the correctness of the concurrent stack mechanism of Zephyr's IPC module. All the specification and proof of our reasoning framework is implemented using Isabelle/HOL. For future work, first and foremost, we aspire to design novel proof techniques for the noninterference of state-based automation models. Next, we can incorporate techniques such as RGSep [31] to deal with fine-grained systems. Finally, more proof tactics can be provided to lighten the proof burden.

Acknowledgement. This work was supported by the Fundamental Research Funds for the Central Universities (Grant No. 2025ZFJH02) and Zhejiang University Fellowship for Graduate International Research and Exchange.

A The Definition of Noninterference

A purged trace is a sequence of system actions from which all actions related to high-security domains have been removed. To construct a purged trace, we must identify which actions the policy permits to influence a given domain, and consequently, should be retained in the trace. We use the function $sources(as, d)$ to identify the set of domains that are allowed to transfer information to the domain d over the action trace as, either directly or indirectly through other intermediate actions in the trace.

$$\begin{cases} sources([\,], d) = \{d\} \\ sources(a\#as, d) = \begin{array}{l} sources(as, d) \cup \{w.\ w = dom(a)\ \wedge \\ (\exists v.\ (w \rightsquigarrow v) \wedge v \in sources(as, d))\} \end{array} \end{cases}$$

Then we use function $ipurge(as, d)$ to obtain the purged trace that retains the actions whose domain is identified by the function $sources$.

$$\begin{cases} ipurge([\,], d) = [\,] \\ ipurge(a\#as, d) = \begin{array}{l} \textbf{if } d_a \in sources(a\#as, d) \textbf{ then } a\#ipurge(as, d) \\ \textbf{else } \ ipurge(as, d) \end{array} \end{cases}$$

Given a system $\mathcal{M} = \langle \mathcal{C}, A, step, \mathtt{c}_0 \rangle$ and its information flow configuration $\mathtt{Info} = \langle \mathcal{D}, \rightsquigarrow, dom, \sim \rangle$, intransitive noninterference is formally defined as:

$$\mathrm{NI}(\mathcal{M}, \mathtt{Info}) \triangleq \forall as, d.\ run(\mathtt{c}_0, as) \overset{d}{\simeq} run(\mathtt{c}_0, ipurge(as, d))$$

where

$$\mathcal{C}_1 \overset{d}{\simeq} \mathcal{C}_2 \triangleq \forall \mathtt{c1} \in \mathcal{C}_1, \mathtt{c2} \in \mathcal{C}_2.\ s_{\mathtt{c1}} \overset{d}{\sim} s_{\mathtt{c2}}$$

References

1. The zephyr project. https://www.zephyrproject.org/
2. The recore project (2025). https://github.com/SunHuan321/ReCore
3. Abrial, J.R., Hallerstede, S.: Refinement, decomposition, and instantiation of discrete models: application to event-b. Fund. Inform. **77**(1–2), 1–28 (2007)
4. Aceto, L., Ingólfsdóttir, A., Larsen, K.G., Srba, J.: Reactive Systems: Modelling, Specification and Verification. Cambridge University Press (2007)
5. Andronick, J., Lewis, C., Morgan, C.: Controlled owicki-gries concurrency: reasoning about the preemptible echronos embedded operating system. arXiv preprint arXiv:1511.04170 (2015)
6. Appel, A.W.: Program Logics for Certified Compilers. Cambridge University Press (2014)
7. Back, R.J.R., Sere, K.: Superposition refinement of reactive systems. Formal Aspects Comput. **8**(3), 324–346 (1996). https://doi.org/10.1007/BF01214918
8. Back, R.J.R., Sere, K.: Stepwise refinement of action systems. In: van de Snepscheut, J.L.A. (ed.) MPC 1989. LNCS, vol. 375, pp. 115–138. Springer, Heidelberg (1989). https://doi.org/10.1007/3-540-51305-1_7
9. Brookes, S.: A semantics for concurrent separation logic. Theor. Comput. Sci. **375**(1–3), 227–270 (2007)
10. Chavoya, A., Sanchez, A., Lano, K.: Formal implementation of procedural controllers for event-driven sequential systems in chemical processes. Comput. Chem. Eng. **24**(2–7), 297–302 (2000)
11. Collette, P.: Application of the composition principle to unity-like specifications. In: Gaudel, M.-C., Jouannaud, J.-P. (eds.) CAAP 1993. LNCS, vol. 668, pp. 230–242. Springer, Heidelberg (1993). https://doi.org/10.1007/3-540-56610-4_67
12. Collette, P.: Composition of assumption-commitment specifications in a unity style. Sci. Comput. Program. **23**(2–3), 107–125 (1994)
13. Dingel, J., Garlan, D., Jha, S., Notkin, D.: Towards a formal treatment of implicit invocation. Citeseer (1997)
14. Dinsdale-Young, T., Dodds, M., Gardner, P., Parkinson, M.J., Vafeiadis, V.: Concurrent abstract predicates. In: D'Hondt, T. (ed.) ECOOP 2010. LNCS, vol. 6183, pp. 504–528. Springer, Heidelberg (2010). https://doi.org/10.1007/978-3-642-14107-2_24
15. Feng, X.: Local rely-guarantee reasoning. In: Proceedings of the 36th annual ACM SIGPLAN-SIGACT Symposium on Principles of Programming Languages, pp. 315–327 (2009)
16. Fenkam, P., Gall, H., Jazayeri, M.: Composing specifications of event based applications. In: Pezzè, M. (ed.) FASE 2003. LNCS, vol. 2621, pp. 67–86. Springer, Heidelberg (2003). https://doi.org/10.1007/3-540-36578-8_6
17. Fenkam, P., Gall, H., Jazayeri, M.: Constructing deadlock free event-based applications: a rely/guarantee approach. In: Araki, K., Gnesi, S., Mandrioli, D. (eds.) FME 2003. LNCS, vol. 2805, pp. 636–657. Springer, Heidelberg (2003). https://doi.org/10.1007/978-3-540-45236-2_35
18. Gu, R., et al.: Deep specifications and certified abstraction layers. ACM SIGPLAN Not. **50**(1), 595–608 (2015)
19. Hoang, T.S., Abrial, J.-R.: Event-B decomposition for parallel programs. In: Frappier, M., Glässer, U., Khurshid, S., Laleau, R., Reeves, S. (eds.) ABZ 2010. LNCS, vol. 5977, pp. 319–333. Springer, Heidelberg (2010). https://doi.org/10.1007/978-3-642-11811-1_24

20. Jones, C.B.: Tentative steps toward a development method for interfering programs. ACM Trans. Program. Lang. Syst. (TOPLAS) **5**(4), 596–619 (1983)
21. Jones, C.B., Hayes, I.J., Colvin, R.J.: Balancing expressiveness in formal approaches to concurrency. Formal Aspects Comput. **27**, 475–497 (2015)
22. Jung, R., Krebbers, R., Jourdan, J.H., Bizjak, A., Birkedal, L., Dreyer, D.: Iris from the ground up: a modular foundation for higher-order concurrent separation logic. J. Funct. Program. **28**, e20 (2018)
23. Klein, G., et al.: Comprehensive formal verification of an OS microkernel. ACM Trans. Comput. Syst. (TOCS) **32**(1), 1–70 (2014)
24. Lano, K., Sanchez, A.: Design of reactive control systems for event-driven operations. In: Fitzgerald, J., Jones, C.B., Lucas, P. (eds.) FME 1997. LNCS, vol. 1313, pp. 142–161. Springer, Heidelberg (1997). https://doi.org/10.1007/3-540-63533-5_8
25. O'hearn, P.W.: Resources, concurrency, and local reasoning. Theor. Comput. Sci. **375**(1), 271–307 (2007)
26. Owicki, S., Gries, D.: An axiomatic proof technique for parallel programs I. Acta Informatica **6**(4), 319–340 (1976)
27. Rushby, J.: Noninterference, transitivity, and channel-control security policies. Technical report, SRI International, Computer Science Laboratory (1992)
28. Rushby, J.M.: Design and verification of secure systems. ACM SIGOPS Oper. Syst. Rev. **15**(5), 12–21 (1981)
29. Sigurbjarnarson, H., Nelson, L., Castro-Karney, B., Bornholt, J., Torlak, E., Wang, X.: Nickel: a framework for design and verification of information flow control systems. In: 13th USENIX Symposium on Operating Systems Design and Implementation (OSDI 2018), pp. 287–305 (2018)
30. Vafeiadis, V.: Concurrent separation logic and operational semantics. Electron. Notes Theor. Comput. Sci. **276**, 335–351 (2011)
31. Vafeiadis, V., Parkinson, M.: A marriage of rely/guarantee and separation logic. In: Caires, L., Vasconcelos, V.T. (eds.) CONCUR 2007. LNCS, vol. 4703, pp. 256–271. Springer, Heidelberg (2007). https://doi.org/10.1007/978-3-540-74407-8_18
32. Xu, W., Zhao, Y., Ma, D., Zhang, Y., Xiao, Q.: Rely-guarantee reasoning about messaging system for autonomous vehicles. In: 2020 International Symposium on Theoretical Aspects of Software Engineering (TASE), pp. 89–96. IEEE (2020)
33. Zhao, Y., Sanán, D.: Rely-guarantee reasoning about concurrent memory management in zephyr RTOS. In: Dillig, I., Tasiran, S. (eds.) CAV 2019. LNCS, vol. 11562, pp. 515–533. Springer, Cham (2019). https://doi.org/10.1007/978-3-030-25543-5_29
34. Zhao, Y., Sanán, D., Zhang, F., Liu, Y.: Reasoning about information flow security of separation kernels with channel-based communication. In: Chechik, M., Raskin, J.-F. (eds.) TACAS 2016. LNCS, vol. 9636, pp. 791–810. Springer, Heidelberg (2016). https://doi.org/10.1007/978-3-662-49674-9_50
35. Zhao, Y., Sanán, D., Zhang, F., Liu, Y.: A parametric rely-guarantee reasoning framework for concurrent reactive systems. In: ter Beek, M.H., McIver, A., Oliveira, J.N. (eds.) FM 2019. LNCS, vol. 11800, pp. 161–178. Springer, Cham (2019). https://doi.org/10.1007/978-3-030-30942-8_11
36. Zhao, Y., Sanan, D., Zhang, F., Liu, Y.: Event-based compositional reasoning of information-flow security for concurrent systems. arXiv preprint arXiv:2309.09141 (2023)

Formal Modeling and Verification of Blockchain Consensus Protocols: A Case Study on ChainMaker

Minfan Xu[1], Shuo Zhou[1], Xian Xu[1(✉)], and Huan Long[2(✉)]

[1] East China University of Science and Technology, Shanghai, China
{y80230055,y80230051}@mail.ecust.edu.cn, xuxian@ecust.edu.cn

[2] Shanghai Jiaotong University, Shanghai, China
longhuan@sjtu.edu.cn

Abstract. This study conducts a rigorous investigation into the inherent limitations of existing blockchain consensus protocols, particularly with respect to security, scalability, and resilience against adversarial behaviors. A critical gap in current designs is the lack of formal verification to ensure protocol correctness under various operating conditions. Centered on the ChainMaker platform, this work develops a formal model of its consensus mechanism and employs model checking techniques to verify essential protocol properties. The proposed methodology integrates CSP# for formal modeling, Linear Temporal Logic (LTL) for property specification, and the Process Analysis Toolkit (PAT) for exhaustive verification under both normal execution and timeout scenarios. The experimental evaluation reports quantitative metrics such as verification time and state space size, accompanied by a detailed analysis of key attributes including liveness, safety, and fault tolerance. The primary contributions of this work are threefolds: (1) we construct complete formal models of the TBFT and HotStuff consensus protocols using CSP#, capturing core message interactions and state transitions; (2) we specify and verify key correctness properties—including safety, liveness, and delay attack resilience—using LTL and the PAT model checker; (3) we uncover a critical vulnerability in TBFT, where the proposer identity in a proposal cannot be authenticated by verifiers, enabling potential consensus manipulation. We address this flaw by introducing proposer identity consistency checks, significantly improving protocol security.

Keywords: Blockchain Consensus · Formal Methods · CSP# · Liveness · Safety Verification

1 Introduction

Background and Motivation. With the rapid adoption of blockchain technology in areas like finance, supply chains, and digital identity, increasing attention

M. Xu and S. Zhou—Are Co-first Authors.

É. André et al. (Eds.): ICFEM 2025, LNCS 16229, pp. 266–284, 2026.
https://doi.org/10.1007/978-981-95-4213-0_15

is being paid to the security and reliability of its core architecture. At the heart of blockchain systems are consensus protocols, which enable decentralized coordination and data consistency without a central authority. Consensus protocols ensure that all nodes in a decentralized network agree on the validity and order of transactions. This mechanism maintains network-wide data consistency, providing all nodes with a uniform blockchain view and identical transaction histories. They also safeguard the system against attacks via transaction uniqueness and finality. Consensus protocols allow independent nodes to operate under shared rules without a trusted authority, using strict verification and block generation to prevent manipulation and attacks.

However, as application scenarios become more complex and security demands rise, hidden flaws, boundary conditions once overlooked in traditional protocol design, and inefficiencies of traditional analysis methods have gradually emerged. Considering representative consensus protocols, such as Proof of Work (PoW), Proof of Stake (PoS) [14], and Byzantine Fault Tolerance (BFT) [11], exhibit various limitations in terms of security, liveness, scalability, and formal verifiability. PoW protocols, exemplified by Bitcoin [3], demand intensive computational resources, leading to substantial energy consumption and environmental concerns [8]. As mining difficulty increases, computational power concentrates in large mining pools, which compromises decentralization. Moreover, network liveness can be impaired if the hash rate drops significantly, resulting in slower block production [17]. PoS protocols, on the other hand, often exacerbate wealth concentration, as nodes with more tokens gain disproportionate influence over block generation. This dynamic not only challenges decentralization, but also poses security risks if a malicious entity acquires a majority stake. Moreover, many PoS-based systems lack formal verification, leaving their correctness properties underexplored. BFT protocols, while providing strong safety guarantees, are typically designed for small, permissioned networks and struggle to scale due to significant communication overhead. In large decentralized environments, they experience degraded performance, increased latency, and reduced throughput. Additionally, adverse conditions like network partitions can compromise their liveness. While BFT protocols are theoretically mature, practical implementations often lack formal verification, making them vulnerable to subtle design flaws and unverified assumptions. Compared to traditional methods such as simulation and empirical testing, formal verification [5] employs mathematical logic and models to rigorously specify and reason about protocol behavior, thereby enabling comprehensive proofs of critical properties such as safety, liveness, and consistency. Naturally, formal verification plays a crucial role in the design and analysis of blockchain consensus protocols, particularly in safety and security-critical contexts.

ChainMaker [7] is widely used in finance, government, and other key sectors in China, with its consensus mechanism serving as the foundation for system performance and security. Flaws or unverified assumptions in this mechanism could cause service outages, data inconsistencies, or security breaches. However, no prior work has fully verified the consensus logic. This study addresses that gap by rigorously proving its correctness under realistic adversarial conditions.

This work conducts a systematic formal verification of the consensus protocol in a real blockchain, the ChainMaker, including complete protocol modeling, security property verification, and vulnerability detection. In comparison to the previous work, we introduce a formal verification approach based on CSP#, which is particularly suitable for capturing concurrent interactions and verifying temporal properties. To the best of our knowledge, this is the first verification of TBFT (Tendermint Byzantine Fault Tolerance) [6] and HotStuff [21] using CSP# and the first to rigorously analyze their behavior under delay-based adversarial conditions within a model-checking framework. Unlike previous studies, this work focuses on modern consensus mechanisms and leverages a verification framework capable of capturing both protocol logic and adversarial dynamics, offering new insights into ensuring the correctness of blockchain protocols.

Related Work. Consensus protocols are mainly categorized into two groups based on their fault tolerance capabilities: Crash Fault Tolerant (CFT) protocols and Byzantine Fault Tolerant (BFT) protocols. CFT protocols manage benign failures, such as component crashes and communication link failures, with representative algorithms including variants of Paxos and the Raft protocol. Here, we summarize the relevant research in this field along with some discussions.

Bokor [2] optimizes model checking of fault-tolerant protocols via Quorum Transitions, consolidating multi-message operations and refining partial order reduction, which reduces state space complexity and achieves 92% memory and 85% time savings in MP-Basset when verifying Paxos, storage, and BFT protocols. Woos [20] conducts the first formal verification of Raft with Coq, proving linearizability through 90 invariants and generating executable OCaml code, offering a systematic verification methodology. DiGiacomo-Castillo [9] models Bitcoin's PoW with UPPAAL, showing improved chain quality but higher common-prefix failure under selfish mining. Li [13] formalizes CBC Casper in Coq, proving safety and non-triviality, while Rashid [16] uses SPIN to verify Ethereum 2.0 beacon chain attestation and finalization via PROMELA and LTL. Afzaal [1] applies PAT to verify Ethereum beacon chain initialization and checkpoint finalization with CSP# and LTL, analyzing time, state access, and memory. For BFT derivatives, Duan [10] formalizes BFT in SDL and verifies them in Telelogic Tau, while Tholoniat [19] applies ByMC to Red Belly Blockchain, uncovering vulnerabilities and proving safety and termination. Yoo [22] validates Stellar's quorum configuration with UPPAAL, and Thin [18] formalizes Tendermint in CSP# with PAT, proving deadlock-freedom but noting censorship risks. Braithwaite [4] uses TLA+ and TLAPS to verify Tendermint's safety and termination, analyzing timeout, latency, and block rates, while Jehl [12] highlights the inherent complexity of TLA+ safety proofs in view- and tree-based models.

Table 1 summarizes recent advances in the formal verification of consensus protocols. It categorizes mainstream protocols based on their verification properties, specification languages, and corresponding verification tools, highlighting the diversity of techniques and objectives in the verification landscape.

Table 1. Formal verification of consensus protocols

Protocol Type	Verification Properties	Specification Language	Verification Tool
Paxos	Consistency, Validity, Termination	Quorum Transitions	MP-Basset
Raft	State machine, Election Safety	Coq proof assistant	Verdi + OCaml
PoW	DNS/Sybil Resistance, Double-Spending Prevention	BIP	SBIP
Bitcoin PoW	Chain Growth, Chain Quality, Common Prefix	Timed Automata	UPPAAL
Casper	Safety, Non-Triviality	Coq proof assistant	Coq proof assistant
Beacon Chain	Safety	PROMELA	SPIN
BFT	Consistency, Justification, Termination, Selfish Mining Resistance	Threshold Automata	ByMC
Improved BFT	Deadlock/Livelock Freedom, State Ambiguity Prevention, Bounded Collision Risk	SDL	Telelogic Tau
PBFT	Safety, Fault Tolerance Upper Bound	PROMELA	SPIN
HotStuff	Safety	Ivy/TLA+	Ivy/TLAPS
Tendermint	Deadlock Freedom	CSP#,LTL	PAT
Tendermint	Termination, Synchronization	TLA+	TLAPS
STBC	Safety, Fault Tolerance	CSP#,LTL	PAT
TBC	Liveness, Consistency	CSP#,LTL	PAT

Contribution. The main contributions of this paper are threefolds:

- We create formal CSP# models of the TBFT and HotStuff consensus protocols, accurately capturing their message interactions and state transitions.
- We define key correctness properties—safety, liveness, and resilience to delay attacks—using Linear Temporal Logic (LTL). These properties are formally verified with the Process Analysis Toolkit (PAT), showing that both protocols meet the required correctness and robustness guarantees.
- Our verification reveals a critical vulnerability in the TBFT protocol: while the proposal explicitly specifies the proposer's identity, the verifier cannot confirm if this identity matches the actual proposer. This flaw can be exploited by malicious actors, enabling transaction reordering, exclusion, or invalid consensus. To mitigate this, we propose enhancing the proposal validation process with identity consistency checks, strengthening the protocol's security and robustness.

Organization. The structure of this paper is as follows: Sect. 2 provides an overview of key concepts related to consensus protocols and verification settings. Section 3 explains the formal modeling methodology in detail. Section 4 showcases the experimental validation and comparative analysis. Finally, Sect. 5 concludes the paper with closing remarks and directions for future research.

2 Preliminary

2.1 The Consensus Protocol

To meet the varying requirements of blockchain applications in terms of performance, security, and decentralization, a diverse range of consensus mechanisms has been developed. These protocols feature distinct designs, fault tolerance,

Table 2. Comparison of mainstream consensus protocols

Category	Examples	Features
PoX	PoW PoS PoA	PoW offers high security and decentralization but consumes much energy. PoS is more efficient and eco-friendly, fitting scalable systems. PoA(Proof of Authority) trades decentralization for speed, suitable for permissioned blockchains.
BFT	TBFT HotStuff	BFT ensures consistency with up to 1/3 faulty nodes. TBFT suffers from high message complexity ($\mathcal{O}(n^2)$), while HotStuff improves scalability via linear view change, making it better for medium-scale permissioned systems.
Hybrid	PoET DPoS	PoET(Proof of Elapsed Time) reduces energy use via trusted hardware. DPoS(Delegated Proof of Stake) improves throughput using elected delegates. Both face trade-offs in trust, decentralization, and governance transparency.

and comm costs, suiting varied blockchain environments. For clarity, we group mainstream consensus protocols into three categories, summarized in Table 2.

Among the listed consensus protocols, our work focuses on TBFT and HotStuff. Next, we introduce each of them concisely.

Firstly, TBFT is one of the primary consensus algorithms employed by ChainMaker. TBFT is a Byzantine fault-tolerant consensus algorithm that ensures secure system operation when the number of Byzantine nodes is less than one-third of the total. The TBFT consensus algorithm builds upon the Tendermint algorithm, inheriting its core characteristics while introducing several optimizations and enhancements. For more details about TBFT, one can refer to [24].

Here we only highlight the phases that are key to our verification. The TBFT consensus protocol consists of several phases: *NewHeight*, *NewRound*, *Propose*, *Prevote*, *Precommit*, and *Commit*, of which the core three-phases are:

- Propose Phase. The leader node creates and broadcasts a proposal to all replicas. All nodes initiate a timer at this stage. Two timeout scenarios may occur: (a) the leader fails to create a proposal within the timeout period, or (b) replicas fail to receive the proposal before timeout expiration. In either case, nodes cast an empty vote. Upon receiving a valid proposal or upon timeout, nodes generate either a *prevote* for the proposal or an empty *prevote*, subsequently advancing to the second phase.
- Prevote Phase. Nodes collect *prevote* messages from the first phase. Each node must gather $\lfloor 2n/3 \rfloor + 1$ *prevotes* for the same proposal (where *prevotes* may include empty votes generated during timeout). During collection, if $\lfloor 2n/3 \rfloor + 1$ arbitrary votes are received (potentially for different proposals or empty votes), nodes activate the second-phase timer. Upon collecting suffi-

cient *prevotes* or upon timeout, nodes generate *precommit* votes to enter the third phase.
- Precommit Phase. Nodes aggregate *precommit* votes from the second phase. Mirroring the second phase's logic, this stage requires $\lfloor 2n/3 \rfloor + 1$ *precommits* for the same proposal. If $\lfloor 2n/3 \rfloor + 1$ arbitrary *precommits* are received, the third-phase timer activates. Successful collection of sufficient *precommits* or timeout expiration triggers transition to the *Commit* phase.

Secondly, HotStuff is a modern Byzantine Fault Tolerant (BFT) consensus protocol introduced by VMware Research in 2018, specifically designed for blockchain systems. It forms the consensus foundation for several blockchain projects, including Facebook's Diem (formerly Libra). HotStuff stands out for its simple and efficient design, utilizing a three-phase commit mechanism—Prepare → Pre-Commit → Commit → Decide—that replaces the complexity of traditional PBFT, enabling smoother state transitions. By leveraging signature aggregation (such as threshold signatures), HotStuff reduces communication overhead to linear complexity, significantly improving scalability. Additionally, it enables flexible leader rotation to boost fault tolerance and responsiveness, with its modular architecture facilitating optimizations like pipelining. HotStuff begins with the leader proposing a block (Propose), followed by replicas validating with Prepare responses. Upon collecting more than $2f + 1$ Prepare votes, the leader generates a Quorum Certificate (QC) and broadcasts a Pre-Commit message. The same process repeats for the Commit phase, and once a QC is formed at this stage, the Decide phase is reached, finalizing the block for execution. Throughout each phase, the key operation is gathering votes from at least $2f + 1$ nodes to form a valid QC, ensuring consensus can be reached even with up to f Byzantine nodes (in a system with $n = 3f + 1$ nodes).

2.2 The Modeling Language CSP#

Within the PAT framework, CSP# extends classical CSP with a compact yet extensible syntax for modeling, simulating, and verifying modern concurrent and real-time systems. It supports global definitions (e.g., `#define N 5;` for constants, `x = 0;` for variables) and arrays for shared state representation. Syntactic sugar enables parameterized channels and channel arrays, offering concise modeling of homogeneous communication structures. Core constructs include inert and terminating states, event-prefixing, channel-based communication, logical branching, sequential composition, and multiple forms of parallel composition.

The RTS module complements the above constructs by integrating runtime channel-status queries, such as `cfull`, `cempty`, `ccount`, `csize`, and `cpeek`, invoked via `call(...)` and seamlessly embedded into event prefixes. In this way, RTS enables dynamic inspection of buffer states during execution. For example, `c[i]!i → Sender(i)` defines a sender process that transmits an index $i \in \{0, 1\}$ via an asynchronous channel, while a receiver can nondeterministically read from multiple channels using `c[0]?x → process(x) [] c[1]?x → process(x)`. This example illustrates CSP#'s capabilities for channel arrays, event synchronization, and non-deterministic external choice. When combined with RTS queries, e.g., `call(ccount, c)` that queries the number of messages that transmit via c, it demonstrates how runtime conditions control process behavior. Furthermore, RTS supports stateful timed CSP, dense-time model checking, and clock-zone abstraction. This support ensures the verification of schedulability, deadlock freedom, and LTL properties, while providing formal guarantees for behaviors such as deadlines, periodic events, and timeouts. These syntax extensions offer significant expressive power in a concise form, achieving a balance between modeling clarity, operational control, and verification efficiency. The complete syntax specification of CSP# is available in the Process Analysis Toolkit (PAT) [15].

2.3 Model Checking on Security Properties

In general, model checking is a highly automated technique that systematically explores the entire state space to determine whether the system satisfies given temporal logic specifications and generates counterexamples for debugging if violations are found. Owing to its automation and exhaustive nature, model checking has become the most widely adopted method for practical protocol verification.

In our work, we adopt a combined approach using CSP# and LTL for modeling and property specification. CSP# is a process-algebra-based modeling language that accurately captures the concurrent interactions and synchronizations between processes, effectively modeling system behavior. LTL, on the other hand, employs temporal operators like "globally" and "eventually" to formally define critical properties such as safety and liveness. These two are semantically complementary: CSP# models how the system behaves, while LTL constrains what the system must satisfy. Furthermore, the Process Analysis Toolkit (PAT) used in this study offers notable advantages in both verification efficiency and diagnostic capability. PAT supports native modeling of distributed concurrency, employs on-the-fly model checking with state space compression, and provides interactive simulation and counterexample visualization, significantly enhancing the verifiability and interpretability of the consensus protocol. It is widely used in blockchain verification [23]. For the purposes of this work, two of the key security properties of the TBFT protocol that we will explore are as follows:

Safety. Once a block is confirmed on the blockchain, all honest nodes must agree on it, and no conflicting versions of the block can appear. In other words, the system prevents forks or double-spending, and all participants see a consistent and immutable transaction history. This ensures that the results of transactions are *final* and cannot be reversed.

Liveness. As long as a sufficient number of honest nodes keep operating, the blockchain can continue processing new transactions and generating new blocks. It guarantees that user-submitted transactions will eventually be included in the blockchain, and will not be ignored indefinitely due to protocol stagnation. Liveness ensures the *availability* and *progress* of the system.

3 Formal Verification of the ChainMaker Consensus Protocol

This section provides the explanation of the processes and algorithms involved in verifying the TBFT and HotStuff protocols, serving as the basis for automated security verification in the following section. To facilitate exposition, the presented code incorporates pseudocode notations for explanatory purposes. Due to space constraints, we present three core parts of the CSP# modeling of TBFT, i.e., initialization, simulating corrupt and propose. The complete modeling code of TBFT and HotStuff can be found at the GitHub repository at: https://github.com/iclive/conseCheck.

3.1 TBFT Modeling

Figure 1 presents a simplified flowchart of the TBFT consensus algorithm, which serves as the basis for the subsequent modeling.

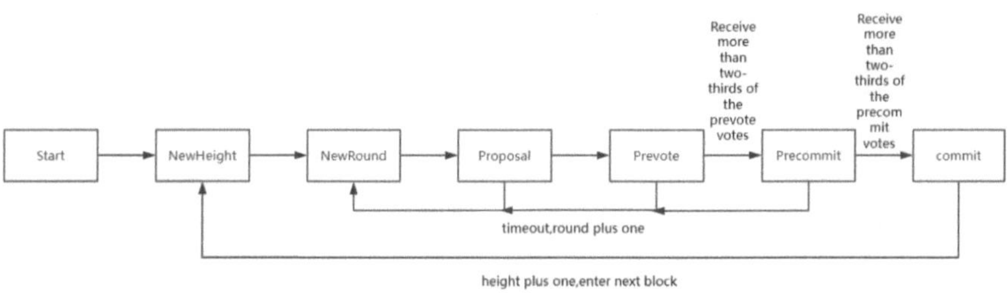

Fig. 1. Flowchart of TBFT algorithm process.

TBFT Protocol Process Modeling

1. **Initialization**. As shown in Algorithm 1, this process begins by creating a container to hold all consensus nodes, and instantiating each node with default parameters according to the total number of participating nodes. Once all nodes are created and added to the consensus group, initial timeout values are assigned to prepare for the first consensus round. The system then processes the genesis block to bootstrap the consensus mechanism, while simultaneously starting network listeners for message handling. Finally, the consensus height is incremented by one, and the block's voting status is reset, marking the completion of the initialization phase.
2. **New Height**. This phase marks the start of a new consensus level, indicating that the previous `batchMsg` has been committed and the next level initiated.

Algorithm 1. Initialization

```
function InitConsensus
    nodes ← new ConsensusNodes()  ▷ Initialize container for all consensus nodes
    for i ← 0 to N − 1 do
        node ← new ConsensusNode(1, i, 0, 0, N, 0, 0)  ▷ Create a node with initial parameters
        nodes.addConsensusNode(node)  ▷ Add node to the global node list
        nodeTimeout[i] ← consensusTimeout  ▷ Set initial timeout for each node
    end for
    → Skip deadline[0]  ▷ Trigger timeout handling for the first round
end function
function StartConsensus(nodeId, gb)
    ProcessBlock(nodeId, nodes.getByKey(nodeId), gb)  ▷ Begin consensus using the genesis block
    || StartListener(nodeId)  ▷ Start network listener for message handling
end function
function ProcessBlock(nodeId, node, block)
    node.processBlock(block)  ▷ Store or validate incoming block at the node
    → Skip deadline[0]  ▷ Trigger timeout for this block height
    NewHeight(nodeId, node, block.getHeight() + 1)  ▷ Advance to next block height in consensus
end function
```

3. **New Round**. Following the `NewHeight` stage, the protocol enters the `New Round` stage, starting from round 0. TBFT may require multiple rounds due to timeouts in the three-phase process (Propose–Prevote–Precommit), where empty votes can be generated. If, during the commit phase, fewer than $\lfloor 2N/3 \rfloor + 1$ `precommit` votes are collected for the same proposal, the round ends without consensus. In this case, the protocol increments the round number ($round \leftarrow round+1$) and re-enters the `NewRound` stage, before proceeding to the `Propose` stage for another attempt.
4. **Simulating Corrupt**.
Following the `NewRound` stage, the protocol enters the `Mock Corrupt` stage as shown in Algorithm 2. This stage can simulate various delay attacks against different nodes depending on the testing environment, in order to evaluate the protocol's resilience to such attacks. The specific scenarios are detailed in Sect. 4.1, and by default, no delay attacks are sent in this stage.
5. **Propose**. As shown in Algorithm 3, during the initial phase of the consensus protocol, the primary node is elected according to the predetermined leader selection algorithm, which subsequently formulates and broadcasts a `proposal` to all secondary nodes, immediately triggering the transition to the *prevote* phase. Upon reception of the `proposal`, each secondary node undergoes a verification process to validate both the proposal content and associated metadata before proceeding to the *prevote* phase. Crucially, all participating nodes initialize a first-phase timer during the *Propose* stage; should any node fail to receive a valid `proposal` within the specified timeout

Algorithm 2. Simulating Corrupt

```
function MockCorrupt(nodeId, node, height, round)
    Corrupt(nodeId, height, round, node.getLastProposer())  ▷ Send delay instructions to target nodes
    || Corrupted(nodeId, node, height, round)              ▷ Simulate receiving delay info
    deadline[0]
    ProposeBlock(nodeId, node, height, round, node.getLastProposer())
end function
function Corrupt(nodeId, h, r, lp)
    if attackCase = CorruptProposerLowerTimeout then
        SendCorruptToProposer(nodeId, corruptLowerTimeout, h, r, lp)
    else if attackCase = CorruptProposerAndValidatorLowerTimeout then
        SendCorruptToProposerAndValidator(nodeId, corruptLowerTimeout, h, r, lp)
    else if attackCase = CorruptValidatorLowerTimeout then
        SendCorruptToValidator(nodeId, corruptLowerTimeout, h, r, lp)
    else if attackCase = CorruptProposerHigherTimeout then
        SendCorruptToProposer(nodeId, corruptHigherTimeout, h, r, lp)
    else if attackCase = CorruptProposerAndValidatorHigherTimeout then
        SendCorruptToProposerAndValidator(nodeId, corruptHigherTimeout, h, r, lp)
    else if attackCase = CorruptValidatorHigherTimeout then
        SendCorruptToValidator(nodeId, corruptHigherTimeout, h, r, lp)
    else
        SendCorruptToNone(nodeId)
    end if
    within[0]                      ▷ Corruption action bounded within current round
end function
function SendCorruptToNone(nodeId)
    corruptChannel[nodeId]!defaultConnTime → Skip  ▷ No delay; default communication time = 1 unit
end function
function SendCorruptToProposer(nodeId, delay, h, r, lp)
    if nodeId = call(NextProposer, lp, h, r, N) then
        corruptChannel[nodeId]!delay → Skip
    else
        corruptChannel[nodeId]!defaultConnTime → Skip
    end if                         ▷ Delay only for current proposer
end function
function SendCorruptToProposerAndValidator(nodeId, delay, h, r, lp)
    if nodeId = call(NextProposer, lp, h, r, N) ∨
      nodeId = (call(NextProposer, lp, h, r, N) + 1) mod N then
        corruptChannel[nodeId]!delay → Skip
    else
        corruptChannel[nodeId]!defaultConnTime → Skip
    end if                         ▷ Delay for proposer and one validator
end function
function SendCorruptToValidator(nodeId, delay, h, r, lp)
    if nodeId = (call(NextProposer, lp, h, r, N) + 1) mod N then
        corruptChannel[nodeId]!delay → Skip
    else
        corruptChannel[nodeId]!defaultConnTime → Skip
    end if                         ▷ Delay only for one validator
end function
function Corrupted(nodeId, node, height, round)
    corruptChannel[nodeId]?delay → saveDelayTime
    node.setDelayTime(height, round, delay)
    → Skip                         ▷ Node records the received delay time
end function
```

Algorithm 3 Propose

```
function ProposeBlock(nodeId, node, height, round, lastProposer)
    node.setStep(Step_PROPOSE)                    ▷ Set node's consensus step to PROPOSE
    if node.needGenProposal(height, round, (attackCase = DisguiseProposer ∨ DisguiseProposer2)) = 1 then
        GenerateProposal(node, nodeId, height, round)       ▷ Only proposer or attacker generates the proposal
    else
        Skip
    end if
    deadline[0]
    atomic
    if attackCase = DisguiseProposer ∧ node.isDisguiser(height, round) = 1 then
        (WaitProposal(nodeId) ||
            SendMessage(nodeId, proposals.getProposal(nodeId, height, round),
                defaultConnTime, (nodeId + 1)%N) ||
            Prevote(nodeId, node, height, round))       ▷ Simulate behavior of a disguised malicious proposer
    else
        (WaitProposal(nodeId) ||
            BroadcastMessage(nodeId, proposals.getProposal(nodeId, height, round),
                node.getDelayTime(height, round)) ||
            Prevote(nodeId, node, height, round))       ▷ Normal proposer broadcasts proposal and enters prevote
    end if
end function
function GenerateProposal(node, nodeId, height, round)
    proposal ← node.generateProposal()                  ▷ Node generates a block proposal
    proposals.addProposal(nodeId, height, round, proposal)    ▷ Proposal is stored for later access
    → Skip
end function
function WaitProposal(nodeId)
    atomic
    receivedProposalCh[nodeId]?ps → procProposal        ▷ Wait for proposal reception via channel
    do
    a ← 0
    → enterPrevoteCh[nodeId]!1 → Skip
    timeout[nodeTimeout[nodeId]] → enterPrevoteCh[nodeId]!0 → Skip within[0]    ▷ Enter prevote step on message or timeout
end function
```

period, the protocol mandates an automatic state transition to the *prevote* phase while generating a null vote in accordance with the Byzantine fault-tolerant consensus specifications.

6. **Prevote**. At the start of the *Prevote* phase, each node issues a `prevote` based on the received `proposal`, or a null vote if no valid proposal is available due to network faults or timeouts. Nodes then aggregate `prevote` votes under two termination conditions: (1) once $\lfloor 2N/3 \rfloor + 1$ votes (including its own) are collected, the phase-two timer is activated; if no proposal gathers $\lfloor 2N/3 \rfloor + 1$

matching votes before expiration, the protocol advances to *precommit*; (2) immediate transition to *precommit* occurs if $\lfloor 2N/3 \rfloor + 1$ identical votes are received for a proposal, including null votes. Importantly, the timer starts only when the $\lfloor 2N/3 \rfloor + 1$ threshold is reached, irrespective of vote consistency.

7. **Precommit**. Transition from *Prevote* to *Precommit* occurs either on timeout or after $\lfloor \frac{2N}{3} \rfloor + 1$ `prevote` votes. Nodes with $\lfloor \frac{2N}{3} \rfloor$ matching `prevote` votes then broadcast `precommit` votes. As in *Prevote*, a timer is triggered once any $\lfloor \frac{2N}{3} \rfloor + 1$ `precommit` votes are received. If no proposal collects $\lfloor \frac{2N}{3} \rfloor + 1$ identical votes before expiration, the system still advances to *Commit*; otherwise, immediate transition occurs upon reaching this quorum, ensuring timely progress or termination under partial synchrony.
8. **Commit**. The *Commit* phase is the final stage of the consensus protocol. Nodes check two conditions: (1) receipt of at least $\lfloor \frac{2N}{3} \rfloor + 1$ `precommit` votes for the current round, and (2) prior receipt of the corresponding `proposal`. If both hold, the `batchMsg` in the `proposal` is committed and the system moves to the *NewHeight* phase, advancing the blockchain height. Otherwise—due to either insufficient `precommit` votes or a missing `proposal`—the protocol enters the *NewRound* phase, starting a new round with updated parameters while keeping the current height.

3.2 HotStuff Modeling

Figure 2 presents a simplified flowchart of the HotStuff consensus algorithm, which serves as the basis for the subsequent modeling. Although HotStuff and TBFT exhibit certain similarities in their stage-based protocol frameworks, their core mechanisms and the detailed designs of their communication workflows differ significantly. As a result, the modeling code designed for the stages of one protocol cannot be directly applied to the corresponding stages of the other. Therefore, we conducted independent modeling for each protocol.

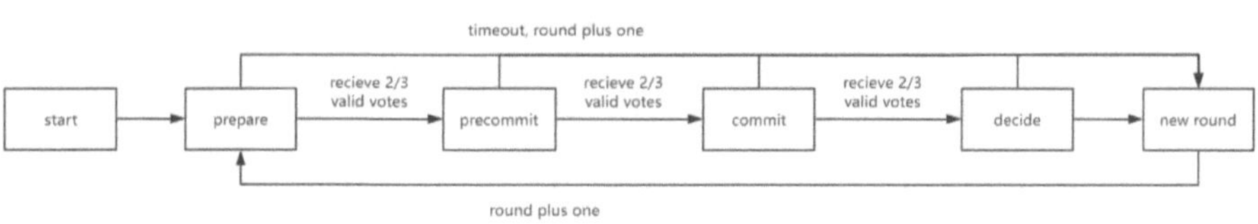

Fig. 2. Flowchart of HotStuff algorithm process.

HotStuff Protocol Process and Modeling

1. **New Round**. Algorithm NewRound is a CSP model of `NextRound()` function in the HotStuff consensus protocol. When the round is less than `R`, the function starts a new round by incrementing the round, updating the leader, and calculating a new `leaf` value. Then, it triggers the `BlockChain()` function to handle blockchain-related operations. If the round is greater than or equal to `R`, it simply skips the current operation.

2. **Prepare**. Algorithm prepareLeader and Algorithm prepareRep model the Prepare phase of the HotStuff protocol. The leader of the current round first creates and broadcasts a new block proposal, which is received by the replica nodes. Each replica verifies the validity of the proposal and, if valid, generates a vote. The leader then collects votes from a quorum of replicas ($2f+1$), and once the threshold is met, proceeds to the next phase.
3. **Precommit**. Algorithm precommitLeader is a CSP model for the `precommit` phase in the HotStuff protocol. In the `PrecommitLeader(i)` function, the leader node selects a block with the minimum support from the corresponding `prevote` votes and sets it as a proposal. Leaders broadcast proposals and await responses; non-leaders store received proposals in `proposalList`.
   In the `PrecommitRep(i)` function, nodes perform different actions based on whether they are the leader. Leader node processes votes and update counts. When the vote count reaches 3, the `voteCounter` is reset. Non-leader nodes store leader votes in the precommitVote list. These votes will be used to determine if the system should proceed to the next phase.
4. **Commit**. Algorithm commitLeader is a CSP model for the `commit` phase in the HotStuff protocol. In the `CommitLeader(i)` function, the leader node selects the block with the minimum support from the corresponding `precommit` votes and sets it as a proposal. Leaders broadcast proposals and await responses; non-leaders store them in `proposalList`.
   In the `CommitRep(i)` function, nodes perform different actions based on whether they are the leader. Leader node processes votes and reset voteCounter when the count reaches 3. Non-leader nodes receive and store votes from the leader. These votes are added to the corresponding `precommitVote` list, and the votes will be used to determine whether the system should proceed to the next phase.
5. **Decide**. Algorithm decideLeader is a CSP model for the `decide` phase in the HotStuff protocol. In the `DecideLeader(i)` function, the leader node selects the least-supported precommit block as its proposal. The leader broadcasts the proposal and awaits responses; non-leaders receive it into `proposalList`.
   In the `DecideRep(i)` function, nodes perform decision operations. When the leader receives a proposal, it checks if the block in the proposal is valid by comparing its hash with the block hash in the quorum certificate (QC). If the block's hash matches the QC and the block is valid, the node adds it to its blockchain. Then, the node skips the current operation and proceeds. Non-leader nodes perform similar operations using the leader's ID.

4 Automatic Verification and Analysis

Experimental Environment. Our formal verification of the protocol is performed on an Intel CPU @ with 16 GB of memory, running Windows 11 home and PAT version 3.5.1. The experimental configuration mainly includes the following constants and global variables:Constant: Number of nodes (default is 4), target consensus height (set at 2), voting type (distinguishing between Prevote and Precommit), message type (distinguishing between Proposal, Prevote and Precommit), consensus steps, delay attack time (divided into two cases: greater than and less than the timeout time), attack scenario; Global variable: Node list, genesis block, the latest proposal put forward by each node, the latest prevote vote generated by each node, the latest precommit vote generated by each node, the current simulated attack scenario, the interaction channel between the attacker and the node (used for sending network delay information), network channel Timeout array (used to record the timeout time of the latest round of consensus for each node).

4.1 Verification of Security Properties

We have automatically verified two key security properties across several protocol variants. The following provides some details.

- **Protocol variants**. The formal specification of the proposed consensus protocol is rigorously verified using the PAT model checker under both normal and Byzantine conditions. We systematically examined six distinct protocol variants: (1) normal consensus simulation process, (2) delayed PROPOSER nodes exclusively (with delays below system timeout thresholds), (3) fewer than f delayed VALIDATOR nodes (sub-timeout delays), (4) concurrent delays affecting both PROPOSER and fewer than $f-1$ VALIDATOR nodes (sub-timeout conditions), (5) exclusively delayed PROPOSER nodes (exceeding system timeout thresholds), (6) fewer than f delayed VALIDATOR nodes (super-timeout conditions), and (7) concurrent delays impacting both PROPOSER and fewer than $f-1$ VALIDATOR nodes (super-timeout scenarios), thereby comprehensively evaluating the protocol's resilience across various network perturbation conditions.

```
Consensus() = InitConsensus();
(|||i:{0..N-1}@StartConsensus(i, genesisBlock));
ConsensusOnlyProposerCorruptL() = InitConsensus();
SetCorruptcase(CorruptProposerLowerTimeout);
(|||i:{0..N-1}@StartConsensus(i, genesisBlock));
ConsensusOnlyValidatorCorruptL() = ...
ConsensusProposerAndOneValidatorCorruptL() = ...
ConsensusOnlyValidatorCorruptH() = ...
ConsensusProposerAndOneValidatorCorruptH() = ...
```

- **LTL specification of properties:** We formalize two critical properties using LTL to verify the protocol's correctness. The first property, *reachTargetHeight*, checks whether at least $\lfloor \frac{2N}{3} \rfloor + 1$ consensus nodes have reached the target height, representing protocol consistency. The second property, *HasTimeout*, examines the absence or presence of timeout conditions, encoded as 0 for no timeout and 1 for timeout occurrence, thereby characterizing liveness guarantees. These properties respectively embody the fundamental consensus requirements of agreement and termination. We then use the PAT model checker to verify these properties across all protocol variants under diverse network conditions and fault assumptions, formally proving the protocol's safety and liveness in both normal and Byzantine failure scenarios.

```
#define target (nodes.reachTargetHeight(TARGET) == 1 );
#define HasTimeout (nodes.hasTimeout() == 0);
#assert Consensus() reaches target;
#assert ConsensusOnlyProposerCorruptH() reaches target;
...
```

4.2 Identifying and Fixing Protocol Vulnerabilities

Our verification of the CSP# models reveals failed safety properties. After analyzing ChainMaker's source code, we confirms the issue is not caused by modeling inaccuracies. We subsequently reconstruct a 4-node ChainMaker environment to reproduce the vulnerability. Table 3 presents an analysis of two adversarial scenarios and their associated attack objectives along with the corresponding difficulty levels. In the first scenario, involving a single malicious node, several types of disruptive behaviors are considered. The malicious node may reorder transactions within a proposal (CASE 1), which has a moderate likelihood of occurrence. It may also drop certain transactions, leading to their exclusion from the block (CASE 2), though this is relatively unlikely due to the limited influence a single node can exert across multiple consensus rounds. Similarly, the node may propose invalid consensus blocks devoid of valid transactions (CASE 3), which also has a moderate probability but is constrained by the same limitation. Additionally, the node may intentionally cause timeouts to trigger a round change (CASE 4), which has been observed in formal models such as CSP but has not been successfully reproduced in real-world test environments. In the second scenario, which combines a single malicious node with a network delay attack targeting the proposer, the likelihood and effectiveness of the aforementioned attacks are significantly amplified. The delay in communication enables the malicious proposal to be accepted more easily, making transaction reordering (CASE 1), transaction dropping (CASE 2), and invalid consensus (CASE 3) all highly feasible. The timeout-induced round change (CASE 4) remains a theoretical outcome observed in models but not yet manifested in empirical deployments. These findings highlight that while a single malicious node alone may pose limited threat, the introduction of network-layer adversarial conditions—particularly those affecting proposers—can drastically increase the success rate and impact of consensus-level attacks, underscoring the importance of robust network protection mechanisms in practical blockchain systems.

Table 3. Vulnerability hazard

Attack Scenario	Objective	Attack Difficulty
Single Malicious Node	CASE 1: Change transaction order	Likely to occur
	CASE 2: Delete transactions, causing them to be discarded	Low probability
	CASE 3: Perform invalid consensus	Likely to occur
	CASE 4: Cause timeout, resulting in next-round trigger	Occurs only in CSP model
Single Malicious Node & Network Delay Attack on Proposer Node	CASE 1: Change transaction order	Very likely to occur
	CASE 2: Delete transactions, causing them to be discarded	Very likely to occur
	CASE 3: Perform invalid consensus	Very likely to occur
	CASE 4: Cause timeout, resulting in next-round trigger	Occurs only in CSP model

Through an analysis of the source code, it was determined that the vulnerability originates from a defect in the authentication mechanism of TBFT. Specifically, while proposals are required to include the identity identifier of the proposer, the verification process does not ensure that this identifier corresponds to the actual identity of the block generator. This oversight allows attackers to circumvent the verification process by using forged identifiers. To address this issue, the vulnerability has been resolved by incorporating a validation step to verify the actual identity of the proposer during the proposal verification process.

The discovery and repair of the above-mentioned vulnerabilities demonstrate the advantages of formal verification, which can abstract and simplify the actual system and highlight the verification of the core process. Model validation traverses all states and can cover scenarios that cannot be tested in actual tests. It can achieve process execution sequence control and customized test scenarios.

4.3 Result and Analysis

As illustrated in Fig. 3, the state graph is generated as an intermediate outcome of executing the modeling code. This graph provides a formal representation of the protocol's runtime behavior, capturing state transitions and interactions between components during the execution of the modeled consensus mechanism.

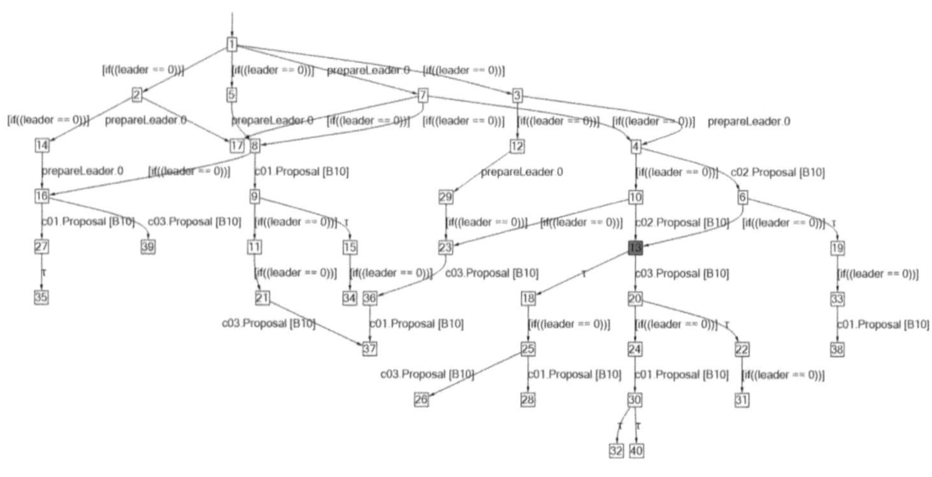

Fig. 3. A fraction of the experimental process.

Subsequently, based on the security attribute definitions of the above consensus protocol, we obtained the verification results as shown in Table 4 through PAT verification and analyzed to draw the following conclusions:

- The consensus protocol guarantees agreement and liveness by reaching consensus within a finite amount of time.

- Under the condition that network delay attacks have a latency below the timeout threshold, the consensus protocol can ultimately achieve consensus—ensuring both safety and liveness—regardless of whether the attacks target proposer nodes, verifier nodes, or both, as long as no more than f nodes are compromised.
- If network delay attacks cause latency to exceed the timeout threshold, the consensus protocol will fail to reach consensus, even if no more than f nodes are compromised, and will instead move to the next round.

Table 4. Verification results for safety and liveness properties of ChainMaker protocols

Assertions	reaches-target	hasTimeout
#assert Consensus()	T	F
#assert ConsensusOnlyProposerCorruptH()	F	T
#assert ConsensusOnlyValidatorCorruptH()	F	T
#assert ConsensusProposerAndOneValidatorCorruptH()	F	T
#assert ConsensusOnlyProposerCorruptL()	T	F
#assert ConsensusOnlyValidatorCorruptL()	T	F
#assert ConsensusProposerAndOneValidatorCorruptL()	F	F

5 Conclusion

Blockchain technology is widely recognized both domestically and internationally for its key attributes, including decentralization, distribution, tamper resistance, and immutability. However, the security verification of blockchain-based consensus protocols encounters substantial challenges. In complex, large-scale systems, it is impractical to exhaustively simulate all possible scenarios, making it difficult to ensure absolute correctness.

To address these limitations, this work leverages formal methods, which utilize rigorously defined, mathematics-based models for the design of critical systems. Specifically, we employ model checking techniques to represent real-world problems using expressive logical properties, perform exhaustive state-space exploration, and conduct formal verification. We applied these techniques to formally verify the TBFT and HotStuff consensus protocols on the ChainMaker platform. To ensure protocol security, we modeled the protocols using CSP# (Communicating Sequential Processes) and specified their safety and liveness properties using Linear-time Temporal Logic (LTL). The security verification process is carried out using the PAT (Process Analysis Toolkit) framework. In our experiments, we first validated the inherent correctness of the protocol design. For network modeling, we systematically analyzed various behavioral scenarios involving both primary and backup nodes under timeout and non-timeout conditions. Experiments show timeouts do not compromise security highlighting the protocol's robust resilience against timeout attacks—and ensure the consensus mechanism upholds safety and liveness properties. Our work further validates and enhances the security and reliability of ChainMaker.

For future work, we plan to continue modeling and analyzing additional attack vectors that could compromise the security of consensus protocols, including common Sybil attacks. Furthermore, we aim to investigate advanced model-checking techniques to improve the efficiency of security verification.

Acknowledgment. The work is supported by Shanghai "Science and Technology Innovation Action Plan" (24BC3200300, 24BC3200500). We sincerely thank the anonymous reviewers for their constructive comments and valuable suggestions.

References

1. Afzaal, H., Imran, M., Janjua, M.U., Gochhayat, S.P.: Formal modeling and verification of a blockchain-based crowdsourcing consensus protocol. IEEE Access **10**, 8163–8183 (2022). https://doi.org/10.1109/ACCESS.2022.3141982
2. Bokor, P., Kinder, J., Serafini, M., Suri, N.: Efficient model checking of fault-tolerant distributed protocols. In: 2011 IEEE/IFIP 41st International Conference on Dependable Systems & Networks (DSN), pp. 73–84. IEEE (2011). https://doi.org/10.1109/DSN.2011.5958208
3. Bonneau, J., Miller, A., Clark, J., Narayanan, A., Kroll, J.A., Felten, E.W.: SoK: research perspectives and challenges for bitcoin and cryptocurrencies. In: 2015 IEEE Symposium on Security and Privacy, pp. 104–121 (2015). https://doi.org/10.1109/SP.2015.14
4. Braithwaite, S., et al.: Formal specification and model checking of the tendermint blockchain synchronization protocol (short paper). In: 2nd Workshop on Formal Methods for Blockchains (FMBC 2020), pp. 10–1. Schloss Dagstuhl–Leibniz-Zentrum für Informatik (2020). https://doi.org/10.1007/978-3-030-61362-4_27
5. Brunese, L., Mercaldo, F., Reginelli, A., Santone, A.: A blockchain based proposal for protecting healthcare systems through formal methods. Procedia Comput. Sci. **159**, 1787–1794 (2019). https://doi.org/10.1016/j.procs.2019.09.350. knowledge-Based and Intelligent Information & Engineering Systems: Proceedings of the 23rd International Conference KES2019
6. Buchman, E., Kwon, J., Milosevic, Z.: The latest gossip on BFT consensus. CoRR **abs/1807.04938** (2018). https://doi.org/10.48550/arXiv.1807.04938
7. Chainmaker homepage (2025). https://chainmaker.org.cn/home
8. de Vries, A.: Bitcoin's growing energy problem. Joule **2**(5), 801–805 (2018). https://doi.org/10.1016/j.joule.2018.04.016
9. DiGiacomo-Castillo, M., Liang, Y., Pal, A., Mitchell, J.C.: Model checking bitcoin and other proof-of-work consensus protocols. In: 2020 IEEE International Conference on Blockchain (blockchain), pp. 351–358. IEEE (2020). https://doi.org/10.1109/ICBC48266.2020.9169468
10. Duan, Z., Mao, H., Chen, Z., Bai, X., Hu, K., Talpin, J.P.: Formal modeling and verification of blockchain system. In: Proceedings of the 10th International Conference on Computer Modeling and Simulation, pp. 231–235 (2018). https://doi.org/10.1145/3177457.3177485

11. Gramoli, V.: From blockchain consensus back to byzantine consensus. Futur. Gener. Comput. Syst. **107**, 760–769 (2020). https://doi.org/10.1016/j.future.2017.09.023
12. Jehl, L.: Formal verification of HotStuff. In: Peters, K., Willemse, T.A.C. (eds.) FORTE 2021. LNCS, vol. 12719, pp. 197–204. Springer, Cham (2021). https://doi.org/10.1007/978-3-030-78089-0_13
13. Li, E., Serbănută, T., Diaconescu, D., Zamfir, V., Rosu, G.: Formalizing correct-by-construction casper in coq. In: 2020 IEEE International Conference on Blockchain and Cryptocurrency (ICBC), pp. 1–3. IEEE (2020). https://doi.org/10.1109/ICBC48266.2020.9169468
14. Nguyen, T., Kim, K.: A survey about consensus algorithms used in blockchain. J. Inf. Process. Syst. **14**, 101–128 (2018). https://doi.org/10.3745/JIPS.01.0024
15. PAT: Process analysis toolkit homepage (2025). https://www.comp.nus.edu.sg/~pat/OnlineHelp/index.html
16. Rashid, M., Rasool, I., Zafar, N.A., Afzaal, H.: Formal modeling and verification of justification and finalization of checkpoints in ethereum 2.0 beacon chain. In: 2024 IEEE 1st Karachi Section Humanitarian Technology Conference (KHI-HTC), pp. 1–6. IEEE (2024). https://doi.org/10.1109/KHI-HTC60760.2024.10481930
17. Sompolinsky, Y., Zohar, A.: Secure high-rate transaction processing in bitcoin. In: Böhme, R., Okamoto, T. (eds.) FC 2015. LNCS, vol. 8975, pp. 507–527. Springer, Heidelberg (2015). https://doi.org/10.1007/978-3-662-47854-7_32
18. Thin, W.Y.M.M., Dong, N., Bai, G., Dong, J.S.: Formal analysis of a proof-of-stake blockchain. In: 2018 23rd International Conference on Engineering of Complex Computer Systems (ICECCS), pp. 197–200. IEEE (2018). https://doi.org/10.1109/ICECCS2018.2018.00031
19. Tholoniat, P., Gramoli, V.: Formal verification of blockchain byzantine fault tolerance. In: Handbook on Blockchain, pp. 389–412. Springer (2022). https://doi.org/10.1007/978-3-031-07535-3_12
20. Woos, D., Wilcox, J.R., Anton, S., Tatlock, Z., Ernst, M.D., Anderson, T.: Planning for change in a formal verification of the raft consensus protocol. In: Proceedings of the 5th ACM SIGPLAN Conference on Certified Programs and Proofs, pp. 154–165 (2016). https://doi.org/10.1145/2854065.2854081
21. Yin, M., Malkhi, D., Reiter, M.K., Golan-Gueta, G., Abraham, I.: Hotstuff: BFT consensus with linearity and responsiveness. In: Robinson, P., Ellen, F. (eds.) Proceedings of the 2019 ACM Symposium on Principles of Distributed Computing, PODC 2019, Toronto, ON, Canada, July 29 - August 2, 2019, pp. 347–356. ACM (2019). https://doi.org/10.1145/3293611.3331591
22. Yoo, J., Jung, Y., Shin, D., Bae, M., Jee, E.: Formal modeling and verification of a federated byzantine agreement algorithm for blockchain platforms. In: 2019 IEEE International Workshop on Blockchain Oriented Software Engineering (IWBOSE), pp. 11–21. IEEE (2019). https://doi.org/10.1109/IWBOSE.2019.8666514
23. Yu, Y., Dong, N., Hou, Z., Song Dong, J.: Model checking concurrency in smart contracts with a case study of safe remote purchase. In: International Conference on Formal Engineering Methods, pp. 391–407. Springer, Cham (2024). https://doi.org/10.1007/978-981-96-0617-7_22
24. Zhang, G., et al.: Reaching consensus in the byzantine empire: a comprehensive review of BFT consensus algorithms. ACM Comput. Surv. **56**(5), 1–41 (2024). https://doi.org/10.1145/3636553

A Unified Method to Efficiently Verify Opacity of Discrete-Timed Automata

Julian Klein[1(✉)], Kuize Zhang[2], and Sabine Glesner[1]

[1] Software and Embedded Systems Engineering, TU Berlin, Berlin, Germany
{j.klein,sabine.glesner}@tu-berlin.de

[2] Department of Mathematics and Statistics, Xi'an Jiaotong University, Xi'an, China
kuize.zhang@xjtu.edu.cn

Abstract. Opacity is a powerful confidentiality property which guarantees that secret information of a system cannot be inferred from its observable behavior. To account for timing attacks, opacity has been extended to continuous-time systems, but the verification problem was proven to be generally undecidable. As a result, multiple recent works study the opacity verification problem of discrete-timed automata. The advantage of a discrete time setting is that it can discretize any timed automaton as a discrete-state system, where opacity can be verified. However, such verification methods usually rely on separating time steps into distinct hybrid states. This results in state explosion and limited scalability for real-world problems.

In this paper, we present a new, more efficient verification method for opacity in a discrete time setting that avoids the state explosion problem. Our verification method groups multiple time steps to intervals, instead of evaluating each time step individually. We define four timed opacity notions and show that our method is capable of verifying all of them in a unified manner. We analyze the efficiency of our method on a case study of a wireless sensor network and randomized systems.

Keywords: Opacity · Timed Opacity · Timed Automata

1 Introduction

As IT systems grow rapidly in size, complexity, and interconnectedness, so do the risks associated with cyber threats that can lead to catastrophic data breaches. To guarantee confidentiality in real-world systems, rigorous verification is required. Opacity is a powerful confidentiality property that can provide safety guarantees in such systems. Opacity holds if an external intruder cannot deduce secret information by observing a system. In recent years, opacity has been extensively studied in the context of discrete event systems [9,17]. Due to the growing prominence of time attacks, opacity has been extended to timed models, such as timed automata (TA).

Franck Cassez first adapted opacity to TA and proved the verification problem to be undecidable [8]. To overcome this undecidability, two general kinds

É. André et al. (Eds.): ICFEM 2025, LNCS 16229, pp. 285–304, 2026.
https://doi.org/10.1007/978-981-95-4213-0_16

of restrictions have been considered in the literature. One method is to heavily restrict the class of considered TA to a decidable subclass, where timed opacity can be verified [3,4,19,20,23]. However, such a decidable subclass might not be expressive enough to model a real-world system. A second method is to consider weaker opacity notions, which can be verified on general TA [2,4,5]. However, a weaker opacity notion provides less confidentiality guarantees and might not satisfy safety requirements. Both methods therefore lack practical applicability.

Recently, a third approach has been explored, by imposing restrictions on the time domain [10,12,14,15,21]. Here, the usually continuous time domain ($\mathbb{R}$) is restricted to a discrete time domain ($\mathbb{N}$). The assumption is that a discrete time model is sufficient to represent the threat model with regards to the intruder. The advantage is that verification of opacity on TA in a discrete time setting is always possible without any further restrictions [12]. In a discrete time model, the progression of time can be treated as a sequence of discrete time steps. Existing methods use this idea and separate single time steps into distinct hybrid-states, which are then evaluated individually. While this method makes opacity verification possible, the number of states quickly explodes as each possible time step is stored in an individual state. This limited scalability makes verification infeasible in practice.

In this paper, we address this lack with a new, more efficient verification method. The key idea is to group several time steps into intervals, which are evaluated at once, instead of evaluating every time step individually. We call our verification method the *timed concurrent composition* (TCC), as it is an adaptation of the concurrent composition [22] to a timed setting.

We consider four timed opacity notions: *initial-location* timed opacity (`ILTO`), *current-location* timed opacity (`CLTO`), *infinite-step* timed opacity (`ISTO`), and *K-step* timed opacity (`KSTO`) in the discrete time model. We show that all four opacity notions can be verified using the TCC as a single verification structure.

The remainder of this paper is structured as follows. Section 2 reviews related works. Section 3 provides relevant definitions and notation, which we use throughout this paper. In Sect. 4, we define the four timed opacity notions, which we consider in this paper. In Sect. 5, we provide a formal definition of the TCC and explain how the TCC can be used to verify all four timed opacity notions. Finally, in Sect. 6, we analyze the efficiency of our method and Sect. 7 concludes this paper.

2 Related Work

The verification of timed opacity is generally undecidable [8]. To overcome this undecidability and derive a decidable problem, multiple restrictions have been considered in the literature. These restrictions can be roughly classified in three main categories: restrictions on the *class* of considered TA, restricted *opacity notions*, and restrictions on the *time domain*, which we review in the following.

There have been several works proving that opacity can be verified for subclasses of TA [3,4,19,20,23]. The considered subclasses must be very specific, as opacity verification is already undecidable for any TA with more than one clock [4], or a single clock and unobservable transitions [3,4]. Decidability results therefore mainly exist for real-time automata (RTA), which are equipped with a single clock, which is reset on every transition [19,20,23]. Due to the strict restriction on the structure of the TA, only specific systems can be addressed.

Multiple works also consider restricted notions of timed opacity [2,4–6]. The key idea is that intruders might have limited access to a system in certain scenarios. This is formalized by restricting the observability [4,6], or setting bounds on time or secrecy [2,5]. Such restricted opacity notions have been shown to be verifiable for subclasses, general TA, and sometimes even parametric TA [5,6]. However, as only restricted opacity can be verified, the safety level is lower. As a result, only specific safety guarantees can be provided.

There also exist multiple works, proving that opacity can be verified in the discrete time setting on general TA [3,4,12]. Intuitively, a discrete time setting means that there is a finite accuracy to measure time. This restriction simplifies the passing of time to a sequence of discrete time steps, making opacity verifiable with methods, similar to verification methods for untimed discrete event systems [12]. The common method is to represent the discrete time steps in distinct hybrid-states, which are then evaluated individually [12,14,15,21]. This leads to a large number of states for TA with many distinguishable time steps. Such methods therefore have a limited scalability for real-world systems. In this paper, we address this scalability problem with a more efficient verification method.

3 Preliminaries

In this section, we provide required formalisms and definitions that we use throughout the paper. First, we define labeled transition systems (LTS) and timed automata (TA) as our system model in Sect. 3.1. Then, in Sect. 3.2, we explain our partially observable system model and how it represents opacity problems. For general notation, we denote the empty word by ϵ, a sequence of two symbols σ_1, σ_2 by $\sigma_1\sigma_2$, and a sequence of $k \in \mathbb{N}$ symbols by σ^k. An interval $I = [a, b]$ is the set of all $i \in \mathbb{N}$ with $a \leq i \leq b$ and $a, b \in \mathbb{N}$. Let $L(I) := a$ and $R(I) := b$ and let $I - k := \{L(I) - k, \dots, R(I) - k\} \cap \mathbb{N}$ for $k \in \mathbb{N}$. The set of all intervals is denoted by $\mathcal{I}$. For a given set S, $\mathcal{P}(S)$ is the power set of S.

3.1 System Model

In this paper, we consider TA in the discrete time setting, which is an abstraction of TA in the commonly used dense time setting. The key difference is that the discrete time setting assumes a smallest time step τ, representing a single time unit. Any longer time span τ^t is then a sequence of $t \in \mathbb{N}$ time steps. A timed event sequence is $w = \tau^{t_0}e_1\tau^{t_1} \dots \tau^{t_{n-1}}e_n\tau^{t_n}$, where all $t_j \in \mathbb{N}$ and each e_i is a discrete event at time $\sum_{k=0}^{i-1} t_k$ for $i \in [1, n], j \in [0, n]$. We use timed event sequences to model the behavior of LTS, which are defined as follows.

Definition 1 (Labeled Transition System). *A labeled transition system is a 3-tuple $\mathcal{G} = (S, \Sigma, \rightarrow)$, where*

- *S is a set of states,*
- *$\Sigma = E \cup \{\tau\}$ is an alphabet of discrete events E and the time step τ, and*
- *$\rightarrow \subseteq S \times \Sigma \times S$ is a transition relation.*

We write $s_1 \xrightarrow{\sigma} s_2$ for $(s_1, \sigma, s_2) \in \rightarrow$. A run of $\mathcal{G}$ is a sequence of transitions $\pi = s_0 \xrightarrow{\sigma_1} \ldots \xrightarrow{\sigma_n} s_n$, with $n \in \mathbb{N}$ and $(s_{i-1}, \sigma_i, s_i) \in \rightarrow$ for all $i \in [1, n]$. We also write $\pi = s_0 \xrightarrow{w} s_n$, where $w = \sigma_1 \ldots \sigma_n$. Since $w \in (E \cup \{\tau\})^*$, we can rewrite w as $w = \tau^{t_0} e_1 \tau^{t_1} \ldots \tau^{t_{n-1}} e_n \tau^{t_n}$, with $t_j \in \mathbb{N}$ and $e_i \in E$, for all $i \in [1, n], j \in [0, n]$. Let $\mathcal{S} : \Sigma^* \rightarrow \mathbb{N}$ be a function to count the events of w with $\mathcal{S}\left(\tau^{t_0} e_1 \tau^{t_1} \ldots \tau^{t_{n-1}} e_n \tau^{t_n}\right) = n$. Let $\Pi\left(\mathcal{G}\right)$ be the set of all runs over $\mathcal{G}$. We write $S_1 \xrightarrow{w} S_2 \subseteq \Pi(\mathcal{G})$ if $S_1, S_2 \subseteq S$ and $\forall s_2 \in S_2 \exists s_1 \in S_1$: $s_1 \xrightarrow{w} s_2 \in \Pi(\mathcal{G})$.

In the following, we will use LTS to define the behavior, of several classes of automata. We use discrete-timed automata (TA) [1] as our system model. We only consider TA with a single clock, as the discrete time setting allows TA with multiple clocks to always be transformable to equivalent TA with a single clock, though in exponential runtime [12]. We abstract this transformation as a preprocessing step and consider TA with a single clock to simplify the formalisms throughout this paper.

Definition 2 (Timed Automata). *A timed automaton (TA) with a single discrete clock c is a 4-tuple $\mathcal{A} = (L, L_0, E, \Delta_{\mathcal{A}})$, where*

- *L is a finite set of locations,*
- *$L_0 \subseteq L$ is a finite set of initial locations,*
- *E is a finite alphabet of discrete events,*
- *$\Delta_{\mathcal{A}} \subseteq L \times E \times \Gamma \times \{\top, \bot\} \times L$ is a finite set of transitions.*

The set of all possible guards Γ over c is defined by the grammar $\gamma ::= c = k \mid c \leq k \mid c \geq k \mid c < k \mid c > k \mid \gamma_1 \wedge \gamma_2$ with $k \in \mathbb{N}, \gamma_1, \gamma_2 \in \Gamma$. If c satisfies γ, we write $c \models \gamma$. We denote $\mathcal{M}_{\mathcal{A}}$ to be the largest constant in all guards of $\mathcal{A}$. A state of $\mathcal{A}$ is a pair $\langle \ell, t \rangle \in L \times \mathbb{N}$ where $\ell \in L$ is a location and $t \in \mathbb{N}$ is a time instant that represents the value of c. A transition $(\ell, e, \gamma, \lambda, \ell') \in \Delta_{\mathcal{A}}$ is possible on the occurrence of event e in a state $\langle \ell, t \rangle$ if $t \models \gamma$. The new active state is $\langle \ell', f_\lambda(t) \rangle$, where $f_\lambda(t)$ is the new, modified time instant with $f_\lambda(t) = 0$ if $\lambda = \top$ and $f_\lambda(t) = t$ if $\lambda = \bot$. Let $\overline{\delta}$ be the set of all such transitions $\langle \ell, t \rangle \xrightarrow{e} \langle \ell', t' \rangle$. Elapsing time in a state is modeled by an increased clock value, i.e. $\langle \ell, t \rangle \xrightarrow{\tau} \langle \ell, t+1 \rangle$. Let $\overline{\delta_\tau}$ be the set of all such transitions. Then, $\overline{\mathcal{A}} = (L \times \mathbb{N}, E \cup \{\tau\}, \overline{\delta} \cup \overline{\delta_\tau})$ is the induced LTS of $\mathcal{A}$. Time can elapse unbounded and from any state $\langle \ell, t \rangle$ the state $\langle \ell, t+k \rangle$ is reachable for any $k \in \mathbb{N}$, even if there is no transition in $\langle \ell, t+k \rangle$.

To restrict the infinite state space of TA to an equivalent, finite subset of states, we use the region abstraction [1], adapted to the discrete-time setting [12].

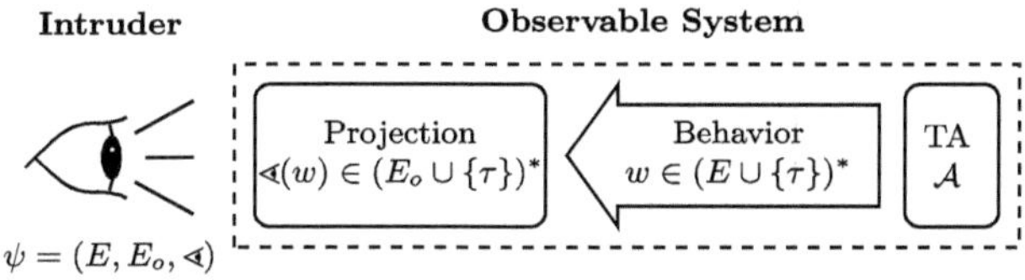

Fig. 1. Partially observable system model [11].

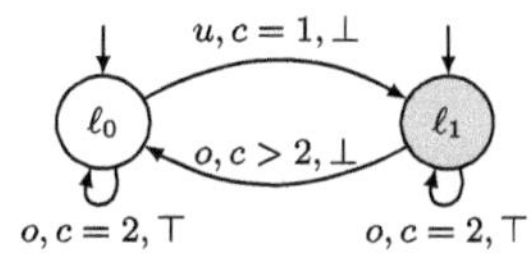

Fig. 2. Example TA $\mathcal{A}_E$.

Definition 3 (Region Abstraction). *Given a TA* $\mathcal{A} = (L, L_0, E, \Delta_\mathcal{A})$*, the region abstraction* $\alpha : \mathbb{N} \to [0, \mathcal{M}_\mathcal{A} + 1]$ *is a function with* $\alpha(t) = \mathcal{M}_\mathcal{A} + 1$ *if* $t > \mathcal{M}_\mathcal{A}$ *and* $\alpha(t) = t$ *if* $t \leq \mathcal{M}_\mathcal{A}$*. For a state* $\langle \ell, t \rangle \in L \times \mathbb{N}$*, we also write* $\alpha(\langle \ell, t \rangle) = \langle \ell, \alpha(t) \rangle$*.*

3.2 Partial Observability

In the opacity framework, an intruder tries to deduce secret information from observations of a system. These observations might only represent part of the internal events of the system, as some events are *unobservable*. To model a partially observable system, we define an intruder with a projection function.

Definition 4 (Intruder). *Given a TA* $\mathcal{A} = (L, L_0, E, \Delta_\mathcal{A})$*, an intruder is a 3-tuple* $\psi = (E, E_o, \lessdot)$*, where* $E_o \subseteq E$ *is the observable alphabet and* $\lessdot : E \cup \{\tau\} \to E_o \cup \{\tau\}$ *is the projection function. Let* $\lessdot(\sigma) = \sigma$ *if* $\sigma \in E_o \cup \{\tau\}$ *and* $\lessdot(\sigma) = \epsilon$ *otherwise. We extend* $\lessdot : (E \cup \{\tau\})^* \to (E_o \cup \{\tau\})^*$ *recursively with* $\lessdot(\sigma w) = \lessdot(\sigma)\lessdot(w)$*, for* $\sigma \in E \cup \{\tau\}$ *and* $w \in (E \cup \{\tau\})^*$*.*

We visualize the partially observable system model in Fig. 1. The projection function $\lessdot$ refines the word w to the observable word $\lessdot(w)$. Note that τ is always observable, as the intruder can measure the elapsing of a single time unit without further observations. If $\lessdot(w) = \epsilon$, then $w \in (E \backslash E_o)^*$ and no time has elapsed. Given the observable word $\lessdot(w)$ and knowledge of the structure of the TA, the intruder tries to deduce which states are active. Such a set of possible active states is called a current-state estimate (CSE) [11]. Using a CSE, further secret information might be deducible by the intruder.

Definition 5 (Current-State Estimate). *Given a TA* $\mathcal{A} = (L, L_0, E, \Delta_\mathcal{A})$*, a CSE* $\theta = \{\langle \ell_1, t_1 \rangle, \ldots, \langle \ell_n, t_n \rangle\} \in \mathcal{P}(L \times \mathbb{N})$ *is a set of states. Let* $\oplus$ *be the modified addition for CSE and natural numbers with* $\theta \oplus k = \{\langle \ell_1, t_1 + k \rangle, \ldots, \langle \ell_n, t_n + k \rangle\}$ *for* $k \in \mathbb{N}$*. Given a CSE* θ *and a projection function* $\lessdot$*, we define the unobservable reach as* $\mathscr{R}_\epsilon^\lessdot(\theta) = \{\langle \ell', t' \rangle \mid \langle \ell, t \rangle \xrightarrow{w} \langle \ell', t' \rangle \in \Pi(\overline{\mathcal{A}}), \langle \ell, t \rangle \in \theta, \lessdot(w) = \epsilon\}$*. We also write* $\alpha(\theta) = \{\alpha(\langle \ell, t \rangle) \mid \langle \ell, t \rangle \in \theta\}$ *to denote the abstracted states of a CSE.*

Example 1. An example TA $\mathcal{A}_E = (\{\ell_0, \ell_1\}, \{\ell_0, \ell_1\}, \{o, u\}, \Delta_\mathcal{A})$ is depicted in Fig. 2. Each transition $(\ell, \sigma, \gamma, \lambda, \ell') \in \Delta_\mathcal{A}$ is depicted by $\ell \xrightarrow{\sigma, \gamma, \lambda} \ell'$. An example of a run is $\pi = \langle \ell_0, 0 \rangle \xrightarrow{\tau u} \langle \ell_1, 1 \rangle \xrightarrow{\tau \tau o} \langle \ell_0, 3 \rangle \in \Pi(\overline{\mathcal{A}_E})$. Suppose we have an intruder $\psi_E = (\{u, o\}, \{o\}, \lessdot)$. We assume that u is unobservable to ψ_E, so

$\triangleleft(o) = o$ and $\triangleleft(u) = \epsilon$. The observed word of π would be $\triangleleft(\tau u \tau^2 o) = \tau^3 o$. Since $\mathcal{A}_E$ has two initial locations ℓ_0 and ℓ_1, the intruder cannot be sure in which location the run started. Initially, the CSE is therefore $\theta = \{\langle \ell_0, 0\rangle, \langle \ell_1, 0\rangle\}$. After observing τ^3, the CSE is $\theta' = \theta \oplus 3 = \{\langle \ell_0, 3\rangle, \langle \ell_1, 3\rangle\}$. After observing o, the intruder can deduce that only $\langle \ell_0, 3\rangle$ can be active, as only $(\ell_1, o, c > 2, \bot, \ell_0)$ is enabled for $c = 3$, resulting in the CSE $\theta'' = \{\langle \ell_0, 3\rangle\}$.

4 Notions of Timed Opacity

In this section, we define four timed opacity notions. These timed opacity notions are adaptations of opacity notions, which have mainly been studied in untimed systems [7] and in part also for subclasses of timed automata (TA) [3]. We adapt these notions to the discrete time setting as follows.

Definition 6 (Timed Opacity). *Given a TA $\mathcal{A} = (L, L_0, E, \Delta_\mathcal{A})$, a set of secret locations $L_S \subseteq L$, and an intruder $\psi = (E, E_o, \triangleleft)$, we define four timed opacity notions as follows.*

***Definition 6.1* (ILTO).** *Initial-location timed opacity (ILTO.) holds in $\mathcal{A}$ with respect to ψ and L_S if for all runs $\pi \in \Pi(\overline{\mathcal{A}})$, there exists a run $\overline{\pi} \in \Pi(\overline{\mathcal{A}})$, where $\pi = \langle \ell_0, 0\rangle \xrightarrow{w} \langle \ell_1, t_1\rangle$ and $\overline{\pi} = \langle \overline{\ell_0}, 0\rangle \xrightarrow{\overline{w}} \langle \overline{\ell_1}, \overline{t_1}\rangle$, $\ell_0 \in L_0 \cap L_S, \overline{\ell_0} \in L_0 \backslash L_S$, such that $\triangleleft(w) = \triangleleft(\overline{w})$.*

***Definition 6.2* (CLTO).** *Current-location timed opacity (CLTO) holds in $\mathcal{A}$ with respect to ψ and L_S if for all runs $\pi \in \Pi(\overline{\mathcal{A}})$, there exists a run $\overline{\pi} \in \Pi(\overline{\mathcal{A}})$, where $\pi = \langle \ell_0, 0\rangle \xrightarrow{w} \langle \ell_1, t_1\rangle$ and $\overline{\pi} = \langle \overline{\ell_0}, 0\rangle \xrightarrow{\overline{w}} \langle \overline{\ell_1}, \overline{t_1}\rangle$, $\ell_0, \overline{\ell_0} \in L_0, \ell_1 \in L_S, \overline{\ell_1} \in L \backslash L_S$, such that $\triangleleft(w) = \triangleleft(\overline{w})$.*

***Definition 6.3* (ISTO).** *Infinite-step timed opacity (ISTO) holds in $\mathcal{A}$ with respect to ψ and L_S if for all runs $\pi \in \Pi(\overline{\mathcal{A}})$, there exists a run $\overline{\pi} \in \Pi(\overline{\mathcal{A}})$, where $\pi = \langle \ell_0, 0\rangle \xrightarrow{w_1} \langle \ell_1, t_1\rangle \xrightarrow{w_2} \langle \ell_2, t_2\rangle$ and $\overline{\pi} = \langle \overline{\ell_0}, 0\rangle \xrightarrow{\overline{w_1}} \langle \overline{\ell_1}, \overline{t_1}\rangle \xrightarrow{\overline{w_2}} \langle \overline{\ell_2}, \overline{t_2}\rangle$, $\ell_0, \overline{\ell_0} \in L_0, \ell_1 \in L_S, \overline{\ell_1} \in L \backslash L_S$, such that $\triangleleft(w_1) = \triangleleft(\overline{w_1})$ and $\triangleleft(w_2) = \triangleleft(\overline{w_2})$.*

***Definition 6.4* (KSTO).** *K-step timed opacity (KSTO) holds for a value $K \in \mathbb{N}$ in $\mathcal{A}$ with respect to ψ and L_S if for all runs $\pi \in \Pi(\overline{\mathcal{A}})$, there exists a run $\overline{\pi} \in \Pi(\overline{\mathcal{A}})$, where $\pi = \langle \ell_0, 0\rangle \xrightarrow{w_1} \langle \ell_1, t_1\rangle \xrightarrow{w_2} \langle \ell_2, t_2\rangle$ and $\overline{\pi} = \langle \overline{\ell_0}, 0\rangle \xrightarrow{\overline{w_1}} \langle \overline{\ell_1}, \overline{t_1}\rangle \xrightarrow{\overline{w_2}} \langle \overline{\ell_2}, \overline{t_2}\rangle$, $\ell_0, \overline{\ell_0} \in L_0, \ell_1 \in L_S, \overline{\ell_1} \in L \backslash L_S$ and $\mathcal{S}(\triangleleft(w_2)) \leq K$, such that $\triangleleft(w_1) = \triangleleft(\overline{w_1})$ and $\triangleleft(w_2) = \triangleleft(\overline{w_2})$.*

In order to encode secret information, we consider a set of secret locations. Secret information is leaked if the intruder can infer that a secret location is, or was, active, depending on the opacity notion. ILTO holds if for any run, an intruder cannot decide, whether the run started in a secret location. Similarly, CLTO holds if for any run, an intruder cannot decide, whether the run reached a secret location. ISTO holds if for any run, an intruder cannot decide, whether a past location was secret. Finally, KSTO holds if for any run, an intruder cannot decide, whether a secret location was active within the last K observed events.

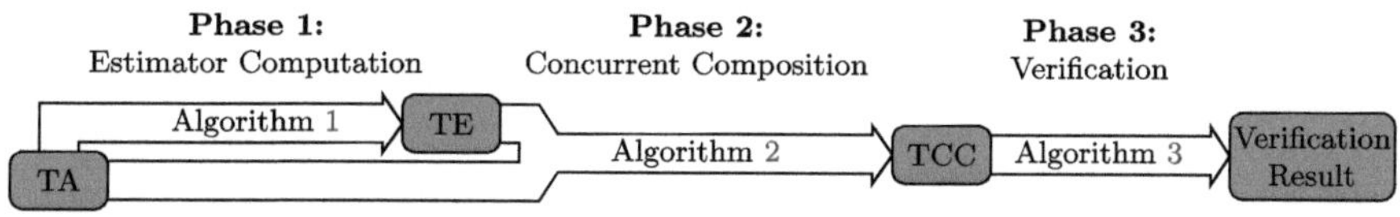

Fig. 3. Proposed unified verification method for timed opacity based on the TCC.

Example 2. Consider $\mathcal{A}_E$ in Fig. 2 and assume ℓ_1 is a secret location. Since u is unobservable, all runs within the first two time units look identical to ψ_E. The first o-transition for $c > 2$ reveals that ℓ_1 was active before. However, ℓ_1 could have also been entered via the u-transition, meaning that it is not clear, whether ℓ_1 was indeed the initial location. ILTO therefore holds in $\mathcal{A}_E$. Similarly, CLTO also holds in $\mathcal{A}_E$, as all observable behavior is equivalent in both locations. The only observable difference is the o-transition for $c > 2$ revealing that now the non-secret location ℓ_0 is currently active. Finally, ISTO does not hold in $\mathcal{A}_E$, since the o-transition for $c > 2$ reveals that ℓ_1 was previously active. Likewise, KSTO does not hold for any $\mathtt{K} > 0$ in $\mathcal{A}_E$.

5 Timed Concurrent Composition Verification Method

In this section, we present a verification method for all opacity notions, defined in Sect. 4. Our method combines two key aspects: *efficiency* and *uniformity*. Our method is *efficient* as it is based on grouping equivalent time steps into intervals, which are evaluated at once. We thereby avoid the evaluation of single time steps, which leads to computational blow up in related methods [12,15]. Our method is *uniform* as it can be used to verify all opacity notions, defined in Sect. 4. Related works only present verification methods for a single timed opacity notion [2,5,6,23]. An overview of our method is depicted in Fig. 3 and consists of three phases:

1. In the first phase, we derive a *threshold estimator* (TE) [11] from the given timed automaton (TA). A TE is a state estimator of a given TA and can provide a current state estimate (CSE) for any given input [11]. We consider a modified notion of TE, which we explain in detail in Sect. 5.1.
2. In the second phase, we compute the *timed concurrent composition* (TCC) of the input TA and its TE. The TCC is an adaptation of the concurrent composition (CC) [22], which is a composition of standard untimed finite automata (FA). We provide a formal definition of the TCC in Sect. 5.2 and an efficient computation method in Sect. 5.3.
3. In the third phase, we verify the desired opacity notion, by checking reachability properties on the TCC. We explain this process in Sect. 5.4 for all timed opacity notions, defined in Sect. 4.

5.1 Threshold Estimators

TE are a class of state estimators for TA [11]. We consider an adapted notion of TE, which slightly differs from [11] and is defined in the following.

Definition 7 (Threshold Estimator). *Given a TA $\mathcal{A} = (L, L_0, E, \Delta_{\mathcal{A}})$ and an intruder $\psi = (E, E_o, \lhd)$, a threshold estimator (TE) is a 5-tuple $\mathscr{E} = (K, \kappa_0, E_o, \delta^{\tau}_{\mathscr{E}}, \Delta_{\mathscr{E}})$, where*

- $K = \{\alpha(\kappa) \mid \kappa \in \mathcal{P}(L \times \mathbb{N}) \wedge \exists \langle \ell, t \rangle \in \kappa : t = 0\} \cup \{\emptyset\}$ *is the finite set of locations,*
- $\kappa_0 = \mathscr{R}^{\lhd}_{\epsilon}(\{\langle \ell_0, 0\rangle \mid \ell_0 \in L_0\})$ *is the initial location,*
- $\delta^{\tau}_{\mathscr{E}} : K \times \mathbb{N} \to K \times \mathbb{N}$ *is the delay transition function,*
- $\Delta_{\mathscr{E}} \subseteq K \times E_o \times \mathcal{I} \times \{\top, \bot\} \times K$ *is the finite set of transitions.*

Each location $\kappa \in K$ is a CSE of $\mathcal{A}$. A super state $\langle \kappa, t\rangle$ in $\mathscr{E}$ consists of a location $\kappa \in K$ at a time instant $t \in \mathbb{N}$ and represents the CSE $\kappa \oplus t$. Since there is at least one $\langle \ell, 0\rangle \in \kappa$, each CSE $\theta \in \mathcal{P}(L \times \mathbb{N})$ is represented by a unique location $\kappa \in K$ at a unique time instant $t \in \mathbb{N}$ with $\theta = \kappa \oplus t$. $\delta^{\tau}_{\mathscr{E}}$ represents state changes that are caused by passing time steps with $\delta^{\tau}_{\mathscr{E}}(\langle \kappa, t\rangle) = \langle \kappa', t'\rangle$ such that $\kappa' \oplus t' = \alpha(\mathscr{R}^{\lhd}_{\epsilon}(\kappa \oplus t))$. $\Delta_{\mathscr{E}} = \Delta^{\top} \cup \Delta^{\bot} \cup \Delta^{\emptyset}$ represents transitions of timed observations and is defined as follows.

$$\Delta^{\top} = \{(\kappa_1, e, I, \top, \kappa_2) \mid \forall t \in I : \exists w \in E^*_{\tau} : \kappa_1 \xrightarrow{w} \kappa_2 \subseteq \Pi(\overline{\mathcal{A}}) \wedge \lhd(w) = \tau^t e\},$$

$$\Delta^{\bot} = \{(\kappa_1, e, I, \bot, \kappa_2) \mid \forall t \in I : \nexists (\kappa_1, e, I', \top, \kappa_2') \in \Delta^{\top} : t \in I' \wedge \exists w \in E^*_{\tau} : \kappa_1 \xrightarrow{w} \kappa_2 \oplus t \subseteq \Pi(\overline{\mathcal{A}}) \wedge \lhd(w) = \tau^t e\},$$

where $E_{\tau} = E \cup \{\tau\}$. $\Delta^{\top}$ represents transitions, where at least one clock is reset in $\mathcal{A}$. $\Delta^{\bot}$ represents all transitions that cannot be represented by $\Delta^{\top}$ (highlighted in red), i.e. transitions where no clock is reset in $\mathcal{A}$. Note that this distinction is not required if all intervals I of the transitions are singletons. However, $\Delta^{\bot}$ reduces the total number of required transitions by enabling the use of longer intervals [11]. In the case of $\Delta^{\bot}$, we consider transitions at time instant $t \in I$ that end in $\kappa_2 \oplus t$ (highlighted in blue), meaning the old clock values are preserved. For more information on the distinction between $\Delta^{\top}$ and $\Delta^{\bot}$, we refer to [11]. Finally, for all $\kappa \in K, e \in E, I \in \mathcal{I}$, if there is no $(\kappa_1, e, I', \lambda, \kappa_2) \in \Delta^{\top} \cup \Delta^{\bot}$ with $I' \cap I \neq \emptyset$, there is $(\kappa, e, I, \top, \emptyset)$ in $\Delta^{\emptyset}$ where $\emptyset$ is the empty CSE.

Let $\langle \kappa, t\rangle$ be a state in $\mathscr{E}$. The progression of time is represented by a transition $\langle \kappa, t\rangle \xrightarrow{\tau} \delta^{\tau}_{\mathscr{E}}(\langle \kappa, t+1\rangle)$. Let $\overline{\delta_{\tau}}$ be the set of all such transitions. A transition of an event $\langle \kappa, t\rangle \xrightarrow{e} \langle \kappa', f_{\lambda}(t)\rangle$ can happen if $(\kappa, e, I, \lambda, \kappa') \in \Delta_{\mathscr{E}}$ and $t \in I$. Let $\overline{\delta}$ be the set of all such transitions. Then, $\overline{\mathscr{E}} = \left(K \times \mathbb{N}, E_o \cup \{\tau\}, \overline{\delta} \cup \overline{\delta_{\tau}}\right)$ is the induced LTS of $\mathscr{E}$.

Example 3. Consider the example TA $\mathcal{A}_E$ in Fig. 2. Let $\mathscr{E}_E$ be the TE of $\mathcal{A}_E$. Figure 4 depicts a part of $\mathscr{E}_E$. We depict a transition $(\kappa, e, I, \lambda, \kappa') \in \Delta_{\mathscr{E}}$ by $\kappa \xrightarrow{e,I,\lambda} \kappa'$ and each τ-transition $\delta^{\tau}_{\mathscr{E}}(\langle \kappa, t\rangle) = \langle \kappa', t'\rangle$ by $\kappa \xrightarrow{\tau:t \to t'} \kappa'$. We omit τ-transitions where $\delta^{\tau}_{\mathscr{E}}(\langle \kappa, t\rangle) = \langle \kappa, t\rangle$. Consider $\kappa_0 = \{\langle \ell_0, 0\rangle, \langle \ell_1, 0\rangle\}$. Both ℓ_0

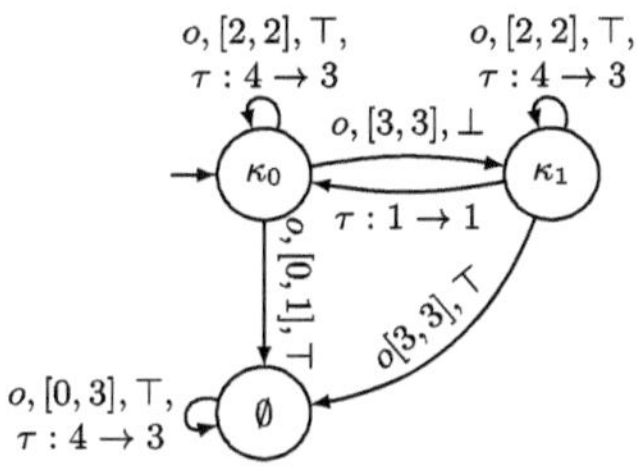

Fig. 4. Part of $\mathscr{E}_E$.

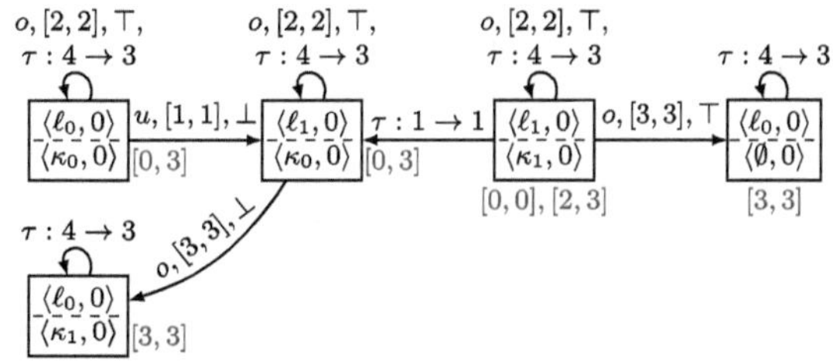

Fig. 5. Part of the TCC $\mathcal{C}_E$ of $\mathcal{A}_E$ and $\mathscr{E}_E$.

and ℓ_1 have an observable o-transition for the interval $[2, 2]$, resetting the clock. We therefore have a transition $(\kappa_0, o, [2, 2], \top, \kappa_0) \in \Delta_{\mathscr{E}}$. The u-transition in ℓ_0 is neglected, as u is unobservable and does not extend the CSE. ℓ_1 has a second o-transition for $c > 2$, leading to ℓ_0 and not resetting the clock. Since $\alpha(\langle \ell_1, k\rangle) = \langle \ell_1, 3\rangle$ for all $k \geq 4$, we only consider the interval $[0, 3]$. We thus get the transition $(\kappa_0, o, [3, 3], \perp, \kappa_1) \in \Delta_{\mathscr{E}}$ and enter a new CSE $\kappa_1 = \{\langle \ell_0, 0\rangle\}$, which we evaluate the same way. Considering the delay transitions, we have $\delta_{\mathscr{E}}^{\tau}(\langle \kappa_1, 1\rangle) = \langle \kappa_0, 1\rangle$, $\delta_{\mathscr{E}}^{\tau}(\langle \kappa_1, 4\rangle) = \langle \kappa_1, 3\rangle$, and $\delta_{\mathscr{E}}^{\tau}(\langle \kappa_0, 4\rangle) = \langle \kappa_0, 3\rangle$.

Intuitively, a TE is a state estimator (also called observer [22]) of a TA. Our Definition 7 slightly differs from the original definition of TE in [11]. The key difference is that $\kappa \oplus t = \alpha(\mathscr{R}_{\epsilon}^{\triangleleft}(\kappa \oplus t))$ holds for all $\kappa \in K, t \in \mathbb{N}$, before $\delta_{\mathscr{E}}^{\tau}$ changes the state. We use this fact later in Theorem 1. Having defined TE, we have the following result.

Lemma 1. *Given a TA* $\mathcal{A} = (L, L_0, E, \Delta_{\mathcal{A}})$ *and an intruder* $\psi = (E, E_o, \triangleleft)$, *let* $\mathscr{E} = (K, \kappa_0, E_o, \delta_{\mathscr{E}}^{\tau}, \Delta_{\mathscr{E}})$ *be the derived TE from* $\mathcal{A}$ *with respect to* ψ. *For all* $\langle \kappa_1, t_1\rangle, \langle \kappa_2, t_2\rangle \in K \times \mathbb{N}$ *and* $w \in (E \cup \{\tau\})^*$, *we have*

$$\kappa_1 \oplus t_1 \xrightarrow{w} \kappa_2 \oplus t_2 \subseteq \Pi(\overline{\mathcal{A}}) \Leftrightarrow \langle \kappa_1, t_1\rangle \xrightarrow{\triangleleft(w)} \langle \kappa_2, t_2\rangle \in \Pi(\overline{\mathscr{E}}).$$

Lemma 1 follows from Definition 7. We provide a detailed proof of Lemma 1 in our artifact [13]. Intuitively, Lemma 1 states that a TE accumulates all estimates of an intruder for given observable words.

Algorithm 1 computes the reachable part of a TE $\mathscr{E} = (K, \kappa_0, E_o, \delta_{\mathscr{E}}^{\tau}, \Delta_{\mathscr{E}})$ with respect to a TA $\mathcal{A}$ and an intruder ψ from a given set of states $\mathscr{U} \subseteq K \times \mathbb{N}$. Initially, we extract a state $\langle \kappa, t\rangle$ from $\mathscr{U}$ to be evaluated (Line 2). We then compute the smallest time instant η that requires a transition to a new state and set $\delta_{\mathscr{E}}^{\tau}$ accordingly (Lines 3 and 4). Any time instant $T > \eta$ is now not relevant for $\langle \kappa, t\rangle$ and is therefore not evaluated. In Line 5, we mark the interval $[t, \eta]$ as visited in κ, as this range is evaluated in the following. In Lines 6–8, we evaluate the actual behavior of κ in the interval $[t, \eta - 1]$ with respect to observable transitions. We do this exactly as in Algorithm 1 in [11]. We add all newly discovered reachable states to $\mathscr{U}$ and repeat the loop. The worst case complexity of Algorithm 1 is the same as in [11] with $\mathcal{O}(2^{|L|\cdot\mathcal{M}_{\mathcal{A}}}\cdot|E|\cdot|L|\cdot\mathcal{M}_{\mathcal{A}}\cdot|\Delta|)$. For further information on the worst case complexity, we refer to [11].

Algorithm 1: Compute reachable part in $\mathscr{E}$ from $\mathscr{U}$.

Input: TA $\mathcal{A} = (L, L_0, E, \Delta_{\mathcal{A}})$, intruder $\psi = (E, E_o, \sphericalangle)$, initial set $\mathscr{U}$
Output: Reachable part of the TE $\mathscr{E}$ for all $\langle \kappa, t\rangle \in \mathscr{U}$

while *$\mathscr{U}$ is not empty* **do**
  $\langle \kappa, t\rangle \leftarrow$ extract an element from $\mathscr{U}$ and add κ to K
  compute the smallest $\eta \in \mathbb{N}$ s. t. $\kappa \oplus t \oplus \eta \neq \alpha(\mathscr{R}^{\sphericalangle}_{\epsilon}(\kappa \oplus t \oplus \eta))$
  set $\delta^{\mathcal{T}}_{\mathscr{E}}(\langle \kappa, t+\eta\rangle) = \langle \kappa', t'\rangle$ with $\kappa' \oplus t' = \alpha(\mathscr{R}^{\sphericalangle}_{\epsilon}(\kappa \oplus t \oplus \eta))$
  mark $[t, \eta]$ as visited in κ, add $\langle \kappa', t'\rangle$ to $\mathscr{U}$ if t' was not visited in κ' before
  foreach $e \in E_o$ **do**
    compute all $(\kappa, e, I, \lambda, \kappa'') \in \Delta_{\mathscr{E}}$ with η as in Algorithm 1 in [11]
    add $\langle \kappa'', f_\lambda(t)\rangle$ to $\mathscr{U}$ if $\langle \kappa'', f_\lambda(t)\rangle$ was not visited before

---

5.2 Timed Concurrent Composition

Having defined TE in the previous section, we now provide a formal definition of the timed concurrent composition (TCC) on TA and TE as follows.

Definition 8 (Timed Concurrent Composition). *Given a TA $\mathcal{A} = (L, L_0, E, \Delta_{\mathcal{A}})$ and an intruder $\psi = (E, E_o, \sphericalangle)$, let $\mathscr{E} = (K, \kappa_0, E_o, \delta^{\mathcal{T}}_{\mathscr{E}}, \Delta_{\mathscr{E}})$ be the TE of $\mathcal{A}$ with respect to ψ. The timed concurrent composition (TCC) of $\mathcal{A}$ and $\mathscr{E}$ is a tuple $\mathcal{C} = (Y, E, \delta^{\mathcal{T}}_{\mathcal{C}}, \Delta_{\mathcal{C}})$, where*

- $Y = \{(\langle \breve{\ell}, \breve{t}\rangle, \langle \hat{\kappa}, \hat{t}\rangle) \in (L \times \mathbb{N}) \times (K \times \mathbb{N}) \mid (\breve{t} = 0 \vee \hat{t} = 0) \wedge \breve{t} \leq \mathcal{M}_{\mathcal{A}} + 1 \wedge \hat{t} \leq \mathcal{M}_{\mathcal{A}} + 1\}$ *is the finite set of locations,*
- $\delta^{\mathcal{T}}_{\mathcal{C}} : Y \times \mathbb{N} \to Y \times \mathbb{N}$ *is the delay transition function,*
- $\Delta_{\mathcal{C}} \subseteq Y \times E \times \mathcal{I} \times \{\top, \bot\} \times Y$ *is the finite set of transitions.*

Each location $y \in Y$ is a pair of states $\langle \breve{\ell}, \breve{t}\rangle \in L \times \mathbb{N}$ in $\mathcal{A}$ and $\langle \hat{\kappa}, \hat{t}\rangle \in K \times \mathbb{N}$ in $\mathscr{E}$. A state $\langle y, t\rangle$ consists of a location $y \in Y$ at a time instant $t \in \mathbb{N}$ and represents the states $\langle \breve{\ell}, \breve{t} + t\rangle$ and $\langle \hat{\kappa}, \hat{t} + t\rangle$. Since $\breve{t} = 0 \vee \hat{t} = 0$ holds, any pair $(\langle \breve{\ell}, \breve{t}'\rangle, \langle \hat{\ell}, \hat{t}'\rangle)$ is represented by a unique state $\langle((\langle \breve{\ell}, \breve{t}\rangle, \langle \hat{\kappa}, \hat{t}\rangle), t\rangle$ with $\breve{t}' = \breve{t} + t$ and $\hat{t}' = \hat{t} + t$. Since $\breve{t} \leq \mathcal{M}_{\mathcal{A}} + 1 \wedge \hat{t} \leq \mathcal{M}_{\mathcal{A}} + 1$, Y is a finite set.

$\delta^{\mathcal{T}}_{\mathcal{C}}$ represents state changes caused by passing time steps. For all $y_1, y_2 \in Y$, with $y_j = (\langle \breve{\ell}_j, \breve{t}_j\rangle, \langle \hat{\kappa}_j, \hat{t}_j\rangle)$ and $j \in \{1, 2\}$, we set $\delta^{\mathcal{T}}_{\mathcal{C}}(\langle y_1, t_1\rangle) = \langle y_2, t_2\rangle$ if

$$\begin{aligned} \alpha(\langle \breve{\ell}_1, \breve{t}_1 + t_1\rangle) &= \langle \breve{\ell}_2, \breve{t}_2 + t_2\rangle, \\ \delta^{\mathcal{T}}_{\mathcal{C}}(\langle \hat{\kappa}_1, \hat{t}_1 + t_1\rangle) &= \langle \hat{\kappa}_2, \hat{t}_2 + t_2\rangle, \end{aligned} \tag{1}$$

for all $t_1, t_2 \in \mathbb{N}$. To represent event transitions, we set $(y_1, e, I, \lambda, y_2) \in \Delta_{\mathcal{C}}$ if for all $t \in I$ we have $\delta^{\mathcal{T}}_{\mathcal{C}}(\langle y_1, t\rangle) = \langle y_1, t\rangle$, and there exist

$$\begin{aligned} \langle \breve{\ell}_1, \breve{t}_1\rangle &\xrightarrow{\tau^t e} \langle \breve{\ell}_2, \breve{t}_2 + f_\lambda(t)\rangle \in \Pi\left(\overline{\mathcal{A}}\right), \\ \langle \hat{\kappa}_1, \hat{t}_1\rangle &\xrightarrow{\sphericalangle(\tau^t e)} \langle \hat{\kappa}_2, \hat{t}_2 + f_\lambda(t)\rangle \in \Pi\left(\overline{\mathscr{E}}\right), \end{aligned} \tag{2}$$

where $f_\top(t) = 0$ *and* $f_\bot(t) = t$.

Let $\langle y, t\rangle$ *be a state in* $\mathcal{C}$. *The progression of time is represented by a transition* $\langle y, t\rangle \xrightarrow{\tau} \delta^{\tau}_{\mathcal{C}}(\langle y, t+1\rangle)$. *Let* $\overline{\delta_\tau}$ *be the set of all such transitions. A transition* $\langle y, t\rangle \xrightarrow{e} \langle y', f_\lambda(t)\rangle$ *can happen if* $(y, e, I, \lambda, y') \in \Delta_{\mathcal{C}}$ *and* $t \in I$. *Let* $\overline{\delta}$ *be the set of all such transitions.* $\overline{\mathcal{C}} = (Y \times \mathbb{N}, E \cup \{\tau\}, \overline{\delta} \cup \overline{\delta_\tau})$ *is the induced LTS of* $\mathcal{C}$.

We show an example of a TCC in Sect. 5.3 and provide an algorithmic method to compute it. Having defined the TCC, we have the following result.

Lemma 2. *Given a TA* $\mathcal{A} = (L, L_0, E, \Delta_{\mathcal{A}})$, *and an intruder* $\psi = (E, E_o, \sphericalangle)$. *Let* $\mathscr{E} = (K, \kappa_0, E_o, \delta^{\tau}_{\mathscr{E}}, \Delta_{\mathscr{E}})$ *be the TE of* $\mathcal{A}$ *with respect to* ψ *and let* $\mathcal{C} = (Y, E, \delta^{\tau}_{\mathcal{C}}, \Delta_{\mathcal{C}})$ *be the TCC of* $\mathcal{A}$ *and* $\mathscr{E}$. *For all* $\langle y_1, t_1\rangle, \langle y_2, t_2\rangle \in Y \times \mathbb{N}$ *and* $w \in (E \cup \{\tau\})^*$ *with* $y_j = (\langle \breve{\ell}_j, \breve{t}_j\rangle, \langle \hat{\kappa}_j, \hat{t}_j\rangle)$ *and* $j \in \{1, 2\}$, *we have*

$$\langle y_1, t_1\rangle \xrightarrow{w} \langle y_2, t_2\rangle \in \Pi(\overline{\mathcal{C}}) \Leftrightarrow \langle \breve{\ell}_1, \breve{t}_1 + t_1\rangle \xrightarrow{w} \langle \breve{\ell}_2, \breve{t}_2 + t_2\rangle \in \Pi(\overline{\mathcal{A}}) \wedge$$
$$\langle \hat{\kappa}_1, \hat{t}_1 + t_1\rangle \xrightarrow{\sphericalangle(w)} \langle \hat{\kappa}_2, \hat{t}_2 + t_2\rangle \in \Pi(\overline{\mathscr{E}}).$$

Lemma 2 follows from Lemma 1 and Definition 8. We provide a detailed proof of Lemma 2 in our artifact [13]. Intuitively, Lemma 2 states that the TCC accumulates all estimates of the intruder for all possible paths in the given TA.

5.3 Computing the Timed Concurrent Composition

We now provide an algorithmic method to compute the TCC of a given TA and TE. To compute the TCC efficiently we group multiple time steps into intervals. These intervals are then evaluated at once. We thereby avoid the evaluation of single time steps, increasing the efficiency of our method. In the following, we identify cases where this is possible.

Most of the time, it is not necessary to compute the whole TCC to verify opacity. We therefore also compute only the reachable part of the TCC from a given set $\mathscr{U} \subseteq Y \times \mathbb{N}$ of states. Let $\mathcal{A} = (L, L_0, E, \Delta_{\mathcal{A}})$ be a TA and let $\mathscr{E} = (K, \kappa_0, E_o, \delta^{\tau}_{\mathscr{E}}, \Delta_{\mathscr{E}})$ be the TE of $\mathcal{A}$ with respect to an intruder $\psi = (E, E_o, \sphericalangle)$. Fix some $\langle y_1, t\rangle \in \mathscr{U}$ with $y_1 = (\langle \breve{\ell}_1, \breve{t}_1\rangle, \langle \hat{\kappa}_1, \hat{t}_1\rangle)$ and let $\eta \in \mathbb{N}$ be the smallest time instant such that

$$\hat{\kappa} \oplus \hat{t}_1 \oplus \eta \neq \alpha(\mathscr{R}^{\sphericalangle}_{\epsilon}(\kappa \oplus \hat{t}_1 \oplus \eta)). \quad (3)$$

Intuitively, η is the next time instant, where $\delta^{\tau}_{\mathscr{E}}$, and thus $\delta^{\tau}_{\mathcal{C}}$, will change state. We therefore only need to compute all transitions for y_1 that can happen within the interval $[t, \eta - 1]$. Fix some $e \in E$ and some $(\breve{\ell}_1, e, \breve{\gamma}, \breve{\lambda}, \breve{\ell}_2) \in \Delta_{\mathcal{A}}$. Let $\mathcal{I}_{\breve{\gamma}}$ be the set of the largest intervals that enable $\breve{\gamma}$ with $\mathcal{I}_{\breve{\gamma}} = \{[a, b] \cap [t, \eta - 1] \mid \forall t' \in [a, b] : \breve{t}_1 + t' \models \breve{\gamma}, a - 1 \not\models \breve{\gamma}, b + 1 \not\models \breve{\gamma}\}$. Fix some $\hat{I} \in \mathcal{I}_{\breve{\gamma}}$. Now, we find all transitions within $\hat{I}$ of $\mathscr{E}$. Consider $\langle \hat{\kappa}_1, \hat{t}_1\rangle$. We define a set of sub intervals of $\hat{I}$

in which the same transitions of $\mathscr{E}$ are enabled, with

$$f(\langle\hat{\kappa}_1, \hat{t}_1\rangle, \hat{I}) = \begin{cases} \{(\hat{I}, (\hat{\kappa}_1, e, \hat{I}, \perp, \hat{\kappa}_1))\} \text{ if } \lessdot(e) = \epsilon, \text{ and otherwise,} \\ \{(\tilde{I}, \tilde{\delta}) \mid \tilde{\delta} = (\hat{\kappa}_1, e, \hat{I}, \hat{\lambda}, \hat{\kappa}_2) \in \Delta_{\mathscr{E}}, \tilde{I} = \hat{I} \cap (\hat{I} - \hat{t}_1)\}. \end{cases} \tag{4}$$

By Definition 7, the intervals $\tilde{I}$ in $(\tilde{I}, \tilde{\delta}) \in f(\langle\hat{\kappa}_1, \hat{t}_1\rangle, \hat{I})$ form a partition of $\hat{I}$, since $\mathscr{E}$ is deterministic. Fix $(\tilde{I}, (\hat{\kappa}_1, e, \hat{I}, \hat{\lambda}, \hat{\kappa}_2)) \in f(\langle\hat{\kappa}_1, \hat{t}_1\rangle, \hat{I})$. We now identify cases, in which we can group multiple time steps in a single transition. This is possible if all time steps $t \in \tilde{I}$ lead to the same $y_2 = (\langle\breve{\ell}_2, \breve{t}_2\rangle, \langle\hat{\kappa}_2, \hat{t}_2\rangle)$.

Case 1: $\breve{\lambda} = \hat{\lambda} = \top$. Clearly, $\langle\breve{\ell}_1, \breve{t}_1\rangle \xrightarrow{\tau^t e} \langle\breve{\ell}_2, 0\rangle \in \Pi(\overline{\mathcal{A}})$ and $\langle\hat{\kappa}_1, \hat{t}_1\rangle \xrightarrow{\tau^t e} \langle\hat{\kappa}_2, 0\rangle \in \Pi(\overline{\mathscr{E}})$, for all $t \in \tilde{I}$. In this case, we can express all transitions in $\tilde{I}$ by a single transition $(y_1, e, \tilde{I}, \top, y_2)$, with $y_2 = (\langle\breve{\ell}_2, 0\rangle, \langle\hat{\kappa}_2, 0\rangle)$.

Case 2: $\breve{\lambda} = \hat{\lambda} = \perp$. Now, $\langle\breve{\ell}_1, \breve{t}_1\rangle \xrightarrow{\tau^t e} \langle\breve{\ell}_2, \breve{t}_1 + t\rangle \in \Pi(\overline{\mathcal{A}})$ and $\langle\hat{\kappa}_1, \hat{t}_1\rangle \xrightarrow{\tau^t e} \langle\hat{\kappa}_2, \hat{t}_1 + t\rangle \in \Pi(\overline{\mathscr{E}})$, for all $t \in \tilde{I}$. Here, we can express all transitions in $\tilde{I}$ by a single transition $(y_1, e, \tilde{I}, \perp, y_2)$, with $y_2 = (\langle\breve{\ell}_2, \breve{t}_1\rangle, \langle\hat{\kappa}_2, \hat{t}_1\rangle)$.

Case 3: If the first two cases do not hold, different time steps in $\tilde{I}$ might lead to different y_2. In this case, we compute single time step transitions for each $t \in \tilde{I}$ with $(y_1, e, [t, t], \top, y_2)$ and $y_2 = (\langle\breve{\ell}_2, f_{\breve{\lambda}}(\breve{t}_1 + t)\rangle, \langle\hat{\kappa}_2, f_{\hat{\lambda}}(\hat{t}_2 + t)\rangle)$.

Algorithm 2: Compute reachable part of the TCC from $\mathscr{U}$.

Input: TA $\mathcal{A} = (L, L_0, E, \Delta_{\mathcal{A}})$, TE $\mathscr{E} = (K, \kappa_0, E_o, \delta_{\mathscr{E}}^{\tau}, \Delta_{\mathscr{E}})$, initial set $\mathscr{U}$
Output: Reachable part of the TCC $\mathcal{C}$ from all $\langle y, t\rangle \in \mathscr{U}$

1: **while** $\mathscr{U}$ *is not empty* **do**
2: $\quad \langle y, t\rangle = \langle(\langle\breve{\ell}, \breve{t}\rangle, \langle\hat{\kappa}, \hat{t}\rangle), t\rangle \leftarrow$ extract an element from $\mathscr{U}$
3: $\quad$ extend $\mathscr{E}$ for $\langle\hat{\kappa}, \hat{t} + t\rangle$, if necessary, using Algorithm 1
4: $\quad$ compute η and set $\delta_{\mathcal{C}}^{\tau}(\langle y, \eta\rangle) = \langle y', t'\rangle$ according to Definition 8
5: $\quad$ mark $[t, \eta]$ as visited in y, add $\langle y', t'\rangle$ to $\mathscr{U}$ if t' was not visited in y' before
6: $\quad$ **foreach** $(\breve{\ell}, e, \breve{\gamma}, \breve{\lambda}, \breve{\ell}') \in \Delta_{\mathcal{A}}$ **do**
7: $\quad\quad$ compute $\mathcal{I}_{\breve{\gamma}}$ and all $f(\langle\hat{\kappa}, \hat{t}\rangle, \hat{I})$ as in Eq. 4
8: $\quad\quad$ **foreach** $\hat{I} \in \mathcal{I}_{\breve{\gamma}}$ *and* $(\tilde{I}, (\hat{\kappa}, e, \hat{I}, \hat{\lambda}, \hat{\kappa}')) \in f(\langle\hat{\kappa}, \hat{t}\rangle, \hat{I})$ **do**
9: $\quad\quad\quad$ **if** $\breve{\lambda} = \hat{\lambda} = \top$ **then**
10: $\quad\quad\quad\quad$ compute all $(y_1, e, \tilde{I}, \top, y_2)$ as in **Case 1**
11: $\quad\quad\quad$ **else if** $\breve{\lambda} = \hat{\lambda} = \perp$ **then**
12: $\quad\quad\quad\quad$ compute all $(y_1, e, \tilde{I}, \perp, y_2)$ as in **Case 2**
13: $\quad\quad\quad$ **else**
14: $\quad\quad\quad\quad$ compute all $(y_1, e, [t, t], \top, y_2)$ for $t \in \tilde{I}$ as in **Case 3**
15: $\quad$ add all $\langle y_2, f_{\lambda}(t)\rangle$ to $\mathscr{U}$ if $f_{\lambda}(t)$ was not visited in y_2 before

---

Algorithm 2 derives the reachable part of the TCC from a given set of locations $\mathscr{U}$. Initially, we extract a location $y = (\langle\breve{\ell}, \breve{t}\rangle, \langle\hat{\kappa}, \hat{t}\rangle)$ from $\mathscr{U}$ which is evaluated in the following (Line 2). First, we check if all reachable locations of $\hat{\kappa}$ are already computed and extend $\mathscr{E}$ if necessary (Line 3). This ensures that we only compute the required parts of $\mathscr{E}$. Then we compute η according to Eq. 3 and set $\delta_{\mathcal{C}}^{\mathcal{T}}$ according to Definition 8 (Line 4). We then mark the interval $[t, \eta]$ as visited in y, as this range is evaluated in the following (Line 5). Finally, we compute all transitions within $[t, \eta - 1]$ (Lines 6–15), as described in the above case distinction. At most $|\Delta_{\mathcal{A}}| \cdot \mathcal{M}_{\mathcal{A}}$ transitions can be computed in each iteration of the main loop. At most, there can be $|L| \cdot |K| \cdot \mathcal{M}_{\mathcal{A}}^2$ locations in the TCC, where $|K|$ is at most $2^{|L| \cdot \mathcal{M}_{\mathcal{A}}}$. The worst case complexity of Algorithm 2 is therefore $\mathcal{O}(2^{|L| \cdot \mathcal{M}_{\mathcal{A}}} \cdot |L| \cdot |\Delta_{\mathcal{A}}| \cdot \mathcal{M}_{\mathcal{A}}^3)$.

Example 4. Consider our example TA $\mathcal{A}_E$, depicted in Fig. 2, and part of its TE $\mathscr{E}_E$, depicted in Fig. 4. Figure 5 depicts part of the TCC $\mathcal{C}_E$ of $\mathcal{A}_E$ and $\mathscr{E}_E$. Consider location $y = (\langle \ell_1, 0 \rangle, \langle \kappa_1, 0 \rangle)$ and assume we want to compute the reachable part of $\mathcal{C}$ from $\langle y, 0 \rangle$. According to Definition 8, we have $\eta = 1$ and $\delta_{\mathcal{C}}^{\mathcal{T}}(\langle y, 1 \rangle) = \langle y', 1 \rangle$ with $y' = (\langle \ell_1, 0 \rangle, \langle \kappa_0, 0 \rangle)$. The evaluated interval is $[0, 0]$ and no transitions can happen. We depict the visited intervals in red below each $y \in Y$. Now assume we want to compute the reachable part of $\mathcal{C}$ from $\langle y, 2 \rangle$. According to Definition 8, we now have $\eta' = 4$ and $\delta_{\mathcal{C}}^{\mathcal{T}}(\langle y, 4 \rangle) = \langle y, 3 \rangle$. Furthermore, we have $\langle \ell_1, 2 \rangle \xrightarrow{o} \langle \ell_1, 0 \rangle \in \Pi(\overline{\mathcal{A}_E})$ and $\langle \kappa_1, 2 \rangle \xrightarrow{o} \langle \kappa_1, 0 \rangle \in \Pi(\overline{\mathscr{E}_E})$. We thus get the transition $(y, o, [2, 2], \top, y)$ (see Case 1). Moreover, we have $\langle \ell_1, 3 \rangle \xrightarrow{o} \langle \ell_0, 3 \rangle \in \Pi(\overline{\mathcal{A}_E})$and $\langle \kappa_1, 3 \rangle \xrightarrow{o} \langle \emptyset, 0 \rangle \in \Pi(\overline{\mathscr{E}_E})$. We thus get the transition $(y, o, [3, 3], \top, y'')$, where $y'' = (\langle \ell_0, 0 \rangle, \langle \emptyset, 0 \rangle)$ (see Case 3).

5.4 Unified Verification of Timed Opacity

Having defined the TCC in the previous section, we have the following result.

Theorem 1. *Given a TA $\mathcal{A} = (L, L_0, E, \Delta_{\mathcal{A}})$, a set of secret locations $L_S \subseteq L$, and an intruder $\psi = (E, E_o, \lessdot)$, let $\mathscr{E} = (K, \kappa_0, E_o, \delta_{\mathscr{E}}^{\mathcal{T}}, \Delta_{\mathscr{E}})$ be the TE of $\mathcal{A}$ with respect to ψ, and let $\mathcal{C} = (Y, E, \delta_{\mathcal{C}}^{\mathcal{T}}, \Delta_{\mathcal{C}})$ be the TCC of $\mathcal{A}$ and $\mathscr{E}$. We define*

$$
\begin{aligned}
\mathscr{U}_{\texttt{ILTO}} =& \{\langle((\langle\breve{\ell}, 0\rangle, \langle\hat{\kappa}, 0\rangle), 0\rangle \mid \breve{\ell} \in L_0 \cap L_S, \hat{\kappa} = \mathscr{R}_{\epsilon}^{\lessdot}(\{\langle \ell_0, 0\rangle \mid \ell_0 \in L_0 \backslash L_S\})\},\\
\mathscr{U}_{\texttt{CLTO}} =& \{\langle((\langle\breve{\ell}, 0\rangle, \langle\hat{\kappa}, 0\rangle), 0\rangle \mid \breve{\ell} \in L_0, \hat{\kappa} = \kappa_0\},\\
\mathscr{U}_{\texttt{ISTO}} =& \{\langle((\langle\breve{\ell}, \breve{t}\rangle, \langle\hat{\kappa}, \hat{t}\rangle), t\rangle \mid \exists \langle y_1, 0\rangle \xrightarrow{w} \langle y_2, t\rangle \in \Pi(\overline{\mathcal{C}}),\\
& \langle y_1, 0\rangle \in \mathscr{U}_{\texttt{CLTO}}, y_2 = ((\langle\breve{\ell}, \breve{t}\rangle, \langle\hat{\kappa}', \hat{t}\rangle), \breve{\ell} \in L_S, \hat{\kappa} = \mathscr{R}_{\epsilon}^{\lessdot}(\hat{\kappa}' \backslash (L_S \times \mathbb{N}))\}.
\end{aligned}
$$

Theorem 1.1. *`ILTO` holds with respect to L_S and ψ iff $L_0 \nsubseteq L_S$ and*

$$(\forall \langle y, t\rangle \in \mathscr{U}_{\texttt{ILTO}})(\forall \langle y, t\rangle \xrightarrow{w} \langle((\langle\breve{\ell}, \breve{t}\rangle, \langle\hat{\kappa}, \hat{t}\rangle), T\rangle \in \Pi(\overline{\mathcal{C}}))[\hat{\kappa} \neq \emptyset].$$

Theorem 1.2. *`CLTO` holds with respect to L_S and ψ iff*

$$(\forall \langle y, t\rangle \in \mathscr{U}_{\texttt{CLTO}})(\forall \langle y, t\rangle \xrightarrow{w} \langle((\langle\breve{\ell}, \breve{t}\rangle, \langle\hat{\kappa}, \hat{t}\rangle), T\rangle \in \Pi(\overline{\mathcal{C}}))[\hat{\kappa} \backslash (L_S \times \mathbb{N}) \neq \emptyset].$$

Theorem 1.3. *$\mathtt{ISTO}$ holds with respect to L_S and ψ iff $\mathtt{CLTO}$ holds and*

$$(\forall\langle y,t\rangle \in \mathscr{U}_{ISTO})(\forall\langle y,t\rangle \xrightarrow{w} \langle((\langle\breve{\ell},\breve{t}\rangle,\langle\hat{\kappa},\hat{t}\rangle),T\rangle \in \Pi(\overline{\mathcal{C}}))[\hat{\kappa}\neq\emptyset].$$

Theorem 1.4. *$\mathtt{KSTO}$ holds with respect to L_S,ψ, and $\mathtt{K}\in\mathbb{N}$ iff $\mathtt{CLTO}$ holds and*

$$(\forall\langle y,t\rangle \in \mathscr{U}_{ISTO})(\forall\langle y,t\rangle \xrightarrow{w} \langle((\langle\breve{\ell},\breve{t}\rangle,\langle\hat{\kappa},\hat{t}\rangle),T\rangle \in \Pi(\overline{\mathcal{C}}))[\hat{\kappa}\neq\emptyset \wedge \mathcal{S}(\triangleleft(w))\leq \mathtt{K}].$$

Theorem 1 follows from Definition 8 and Lemma 2. We provide a detailed proof of Theorem 1 in our artifact [13]. Intuitively, Theorem 1 states that the TCC can be used as the verification structure to verify all timed opacity notions, defined in Sect. 4. In particular, we state reachability criteria on the TCC that hold if and only if the corresponding opacity notion holds for the given TA.

Example 5. Figure 5 depicts parts of the TCC $\mathcal{C}_E$ of $\mathcal{A}_E$ and $\mathscr{E}_E$. We first compute

$$\begin{aligned}
\mathscr{U}_{\mathtt{ILTO}} &= \{\langle((\langle\ell_1,0\rangle,\langle\kappa_1,0\rangle),0\rangle\},\\
\mathscr{U}_{\mathtt{CLTO}} &= \{\langle((\langle\ell_0,0\rangle,\langle\kappa_0,0\rangle),0\rangle,\langle((\langle\ell_1,0\rangle,\langle\kappa_0,0\rangle),0\rangle\},\\
\mathscr{U}_{\mathtt{ISTO}} &= \{\langle((\langle\ell_1,0\rangle,\langle\kappa_1,0\rangle),t\rangle \mid t\in\{0,2,3\}\}\cup\{\langle((\langle\ell_1,0\rangle,\langle\kappa_0,0\rangle),1\rangle\}.
\end{aligned}$$

Consider the reachable part of $\mathscr{U}_{\mathtt{CLTO}}$. For all reachable locations $\langle\ell,\kappa\rangle$ from $\mathscr{U}_{\mathtt{CLTO}}$, we have $\kappa\backslash(\{\ell_1\}\times\mathbb{N})\neq\emptyset$. By Theorem 1.2, CLTO therefore holds in $\mathcal{A}_E$. Consider the reachable part of $\mathscr{U}_{\mathtt{ILTO}}$. There is no reachable location with $\emptyset$. By Theorem 1.1 , ILTO therefore holds in $\mathcal{A}_E$. Consider the reachable part of $\mathscr{U}_{\mathtt{ISTO}}$. There exists the reachable location $y=(\langle\ell_0,0\rangle,\langle\emptyset,0\rangle)$. By Theorem 1.3, ISTO therefore does not hold in $\mathcal{A}_E$. As y is reachable by a single transition from $\langle((\langle\ell_1,0\rangle,\langle\kappa_1,0\rangle),3\rangle\in\mathscr{U}_{\mathtt{ISTO}}$, KSTO does not hold for any $\mathtt{K}>0$ by Theorem 1.4.

Using Theorem 1, Algorithm 3 verifies $\mathtt{NOTION}\in\{\mathtt{ILTO},\mathtt{CLTO},\mathtt{ISTO},\mathtt{KSTO}\}$ on a given TA $\mathcal{A}$ with respect to an intruder ψ and a set of secret states L_S. If our goal is to verify ILTO (Line 1), we first compute $\mathscr{U}_{\mathtt{ILTO}}$ (Line 2) and check Theorem 1.1 on the reachable part of $\mathscr{U}_{\mathtt{ILTO}}$ in the TCC of $\mathcal{A}$ and its TE $\mathscr{E}$ with respect to the intruder (Line 3). If $\mathtt{NOTION}\neq\mathtt{ILTO}$, we compute $\mathscr{U}_{\mathtt{CLTO}}$ since $\mathscr{U}_{\mathtt{CLTO}}$ is required to verify any other timed opacity notion. If our goal is to verify CLTO (Line 6), we check Theorem 1.2 on the reachable part of $\mathscr{U}_{\mathtt{CLTO}}$ in the TCC of $\mathcal{A}$ and its TE $\mathscr{E}$ with respect to the intruder (Line 7). If our goal is to verify ISTO or KSTO, we compute $\mathscr{U}_{\mathtt{ISTO}}$ from the reachable part from $\mathscr{U}_{\mathtt{CLTO}}$ in the TCC (Line 9). Now, if our goal is to verify ISTO, we check Theorem 1.3 on the reachable part of $\mathscr{U}_{\mathtt{ISTO}}$ in the TCC (Line 11) and if our goal is to verify KSTO, we check Theorem 1.4 on the reachable part of $\mathscr{U}_{\mathtt{ISTO}}$ in the TCC (Line 13).

Throughout Algorithm 3 we always only compute the required parts of the TE and the TCC to minimize computational costs. However, in the worst case, we need to compute the whole TE and then the whole TCC. Algorithm 3 therefore has the same worst case complexity as Algorithm 2.

Algorithm 3: Verification of Timed Opacity.

Input: TA $\mathcal{A}$, secret states L_S, intruder ψ, timed opacity notion `NOTION`
Output: Verification result

if *NOTION* = *ILTO* **then**
  compute $\mathscr{U}_{\text{ILTO}}$
  check Theorem 1.1 on $\mathscr{U}_{\text{ILTO}}$ in the TCC using Algorithm 2
else
  compute $\mathscr{U}_{\text{CLTO}}$
  if *NOTION* = *CLTO* **then**
    check Theorem 1.2 on $\mathscr{U}_{\text{CLTO}}$ in the TCC using Algorithm 2
  else
    compute $\mathscr{U}_{\text{ISTO}}$ from $\mathscr{U}_{\text{CLTO}}$ using Algorithm 2
    if *NOTION* = *ISTO* **then**
      check Theorem 1.3 on $\mathscr{U}_{\text{ISTO}}$ in the TCC using Algorithm 2
    else
      check Theorem 1.4 on $\mathscr{U}_{\text{ISTO}}$ in the TCC using Algorithm 2

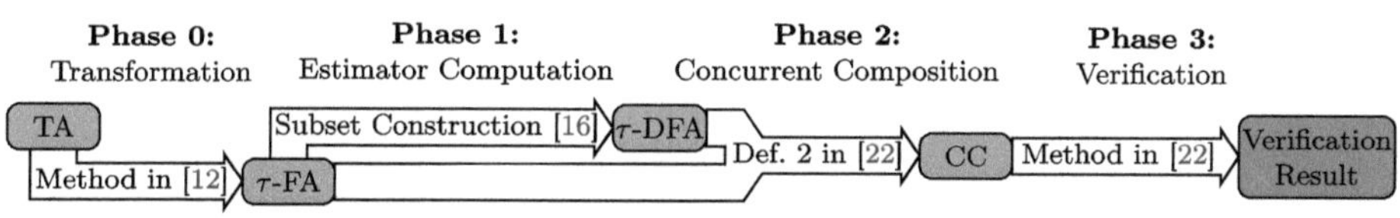

Fig. 6. Verification method based on finite tick automata.

6 Evaluation

In this section, we analyze the efficiency of our presented method and illustrate how it can be used to formulate and verify several safety constraints in real-world applications. To assess the efficiency of our method, we use a baseline algorithm, which we explain in Sect. 6.1. To illustrate the applicability of our method we define a class of confidentiality-problems for agents in sensor networks, which we explain in Sect. 6.2. We consider a case study of such a system, as well as randomized experiments, which we present in Sect. 6.3. We have implemented our method as a fully documented open source software prototype [13] that we use in all our experiments.

6.1 Baseline Method

A key factor in the efficiency of our verification method is the grouping of multiple time steps into intervals, which are then evaluated at once. We thereby avoid the computational blow-up caused by evaluating every time step, as in other methods [12]. To assess this gain in efficiency, we base our baseline method on [12], as depicted in Fig. 6. It is similar to our presented method in Sect. 5 but relies on evaluating every time step individually. Initially, the input TA is transformed to an equivalent finite tick automaton (τ-FA). τ-FA are standard

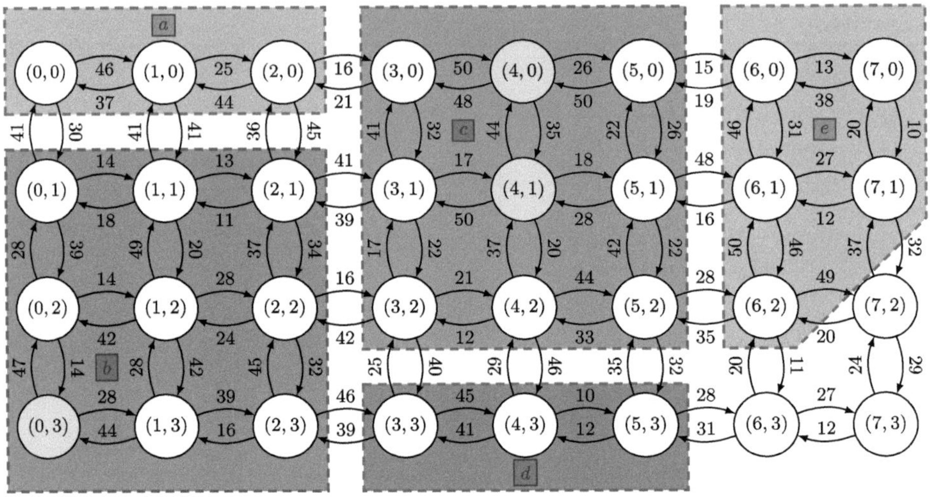

Fig. 7. The wireless sensor network considered in the case study.

finite automata (FA) that enumerate every discrete time value in distinct hybrid states that are connected by τ-transitions to represent time steps [12]. We then employ FA-based methods from the literature for every phase in our three-phase method (see Sect. 5). We use the subset construction [16] to derive a state estimator (Phase 1) and the standard concurrent composition [22] (Phase 2) to obtain a verification result (Phase 3). As the adaptation of these methods is straight forward, we omit it here. We provide a detailed explanation and prove correctness for all four timed opacity notions from Sect. 4 in our artifact [13]. Note that the baseline method is also *unified* in the sense that we can use it to verify all timed opacity notions, defined in Sect. 4. However, the key downside is that τ-FA enumerate every time step in distinct hybrid states, which significantly limits scalability. In the following, we measure this difference in *efficiency*.

6.2 Tracking of Agents in Sensor Networks

We consider a class of systems that model wireless sensor networks (WSN) that try to track the movements of an agent in an area. The area is a two dimensional $n \times m$ grid. The agent can be at a location (x, y) and move to any vertically or horizontally neighbouring location (x', y'). A set of sensor nodes S is deployed to track the movements of the agent. A sensor node $z \in S$ covers a set of locations Z, sending a signal z if the agent enters a location $(x, y) \in Z$. This kind of problem was originally proposed in [18] and modelled using untimed finite automata. We extend this model by introducing time constraints, making it more realistic. Each transition has a minimum delay $d((x, y), (x', y')) \in \mathbb{N}$. The time it takes the agent to move from (x, y) to (x', y'), can then be any value $t \geq d((x, y), (x', y'))$. We assume that the agent can start in any location at the border of the grid.

Table 1. Verification times for timed opacity notions on the case study.

	ILTO	✗	CLTO	✓	ISTO	✗	KSTO (K $\geq$ 1)	✗
CC	3 min 6.66 s		1 min 48.23 s		3 min 6.25 s		3 min 8.67 s	
TCC	35.41 s	**-81%**	29.76 s	**-72%**	43.20 s	**-76%**	35.58 s	**-81%**

We consider the sensor network to be the intruder $\psi = (S \cup \{\varepsilon\}, S, \lessdot)$. We check if the intruder can deduce whether the agent is currently in a secret location (CLTO), started in a secret location (ILTO), or was previously (within K $\in \mathbb{N}$ observations) in a secret location ISTO (KSTO).

6.3 Experiments

To assess the efficiency of our method, we have implemented a software prototype [13] that can be used to reproduce all presented results. We have used this prototype on an Intel Core i5-10600K CPU in all our experiments. Our experiments are twofold. We first consider a concrete case study. Afterwards, we consider randomized systems of several sizes. We average the computation times to compare the efficiency of our presented method and the baseline method.

Our case study is a 8×4 grid, depicted in Fig. 7. Each transition from a location (x, y) to a neighbouring location (x', y') is labelled with its minimum delay $d((x, y), (x', y'))$. The secret locations are $(4, 0), (4, 1)$, and $(0, 3)$. The five sensor nodes $S = \{a, b, c, d, e\}$ are depicted with their ranges in the respective colors. The locations $(7, 2), (6, 3)$, and $(7, 3)$ are not covered by any sensor node.

We represent this system as a TA and use our software prototype to verify the timed opacity. We have measured and averaged the computation times across 10 runs for each opacity notion. The results are listed in Table 1. CLTO holds, while ILTO, ISTO and KSTO do not hold for any K > 0. The verification times of the presented method (TCC) are significantly reduced for all considered opacity notions, compared to the baseline, ranging from 72% to 81%. Our proposed method thus provides a significant speed up in verifying all considered opacity notions on the case study.

To gain better understanding of the scalability of the presented method, we also analyze the computation times of our software prototype on randomized systems. We test $n \times m$ grids in several sizes. In each system, we have n sensors at random positions and a randomized range r, drawn from a uniform distribution of $[\frac{n}{2}, n]$. The minimum delay of each transition is drawn from a normal distribution with a mean $\mu = 10$ and a standard deviation $\sigma = 1$. We verify ILTO, CLTO, ISTO, and KSTO for K $\in \{1, 2, 3\}$ on 100 generated systems for each size $n \times m \in \{2 \times 2, 3 \times 2, 3 \times 3, 4 \times 3, 4 \times 4\}$ using both verification methods. Figure 8 depicts the results, averaged over the 100 generated systems. The results for our presented method are depicted in red and our baseline method is depicted in blue. Our presented method (TCC) outperforms the baseline method for every opacity notion and every grid size $n \times m$. Moreover, the improvements get more

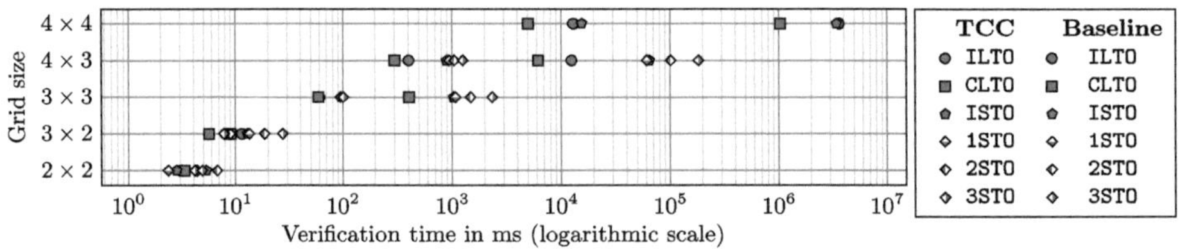

Fig. 8. Verification time comparison on randomized grids of several sizes.

significant with larger grid sizes and indicate significantly improved scalability for larger systems.

7 Conclusion

In this paper, we have addressed the problem of verifying opacity of discrete-timed automata without further restrictions. We have defined *initial-location* timed opacity (ILTO), *current-location* timed opacity (CLTO), *infinite-step* timed opacity (ISTO), and *K-step* timed opacity (KSTO) in the discrete time model. Furthermore, we have defined the *timed* concurrent composition (TCC) on timed automata and threshold estimators. We have proven that the TCC can be used as the single verification structure to verify all four considered timed opacity notions. Finally, we have implemented our method as an open source software prototype [13] and analyzed the efficiency on a case study and randomized systems. Our results show significantly reduced computation times in all experiments, compared to our baseline method.

Our definition of the TCC enables several exciting possibilities for future work. We plan to consider strong timed opacity notions and develop a TCC-based verification method. Furthermore, we plan to develop an opacity enforcement method based on the TCC. Finally, we will explore TCC-based timed opacity verification methods in settings with multiple intruders.

References

1. Alur, R., Dill, D.: The theory of timed automata. Theor. Comput. Sci. 183–235 (1992). https://doi.org/10.1016/0304-3975(94)90010-8
2. Ammar, I., El Touati, Y., Yeddes, M., Mullins, J.: Bounded opacity for timed systems. J. Inf. Secur. Appl. (2021). https://doi.org/10.1016/j.jisa.2021.102926
3. An, J., Gao, Q., Wang, L., Zhan, N., Hasuo, I.: The opacity of timed automata. In: Proceedings of the 2024 26th International Symposium on Formal Methods (FM). FM 2024, pp. 620–637. Springer, Cham (2025). https://doi.org/10.1007/978-3-031-71162-6_32
4. André, É., Dépernet, S., Lefaucheux, E.: The bright side of timed opacity. In: Proceedings of the 2024 25th International Conference on Formal Engineering Methods (ICFEM). ICFEM 2024, pp. 51–69. Springer, Cham (2024). https://doi.org/10.1007/978-981-96-0617-7_4

5. André, É., Lefaucheux, E., Marinho, D.: Expiring opacity problems in parametric timed automata. In: Proceedings of the 2023 27th International Conference on Engineering of Complex Computer Systems (ICECCS). ICECCS 2023, pp. 89–98. IEEE (2023). https://doi.org/10.1109/ICECCS59891.2023.00020
6. André, E., Lime, D., Marinho, D., Sun, J.: Guaranteeing timed opacity using parametric timed model checking. ACM Trans. Softw. Eng. Methodol. 64–100 (2022). https://doi.org/10.1145/3502851
7. Balun, J., Masopust, T.: On transformations among opacity notions. In: Proceedings of the 2022 25th IEEE International Conference on Systems, Man, and Cybernetics (SMC). SMC 2022, pp. 3012–3017. IEEE (2022). https://doi.org/10.1109/SMC53654.2022.9945608
8. Cassez, F.: The dark side of timed opacity. In: Park, J.H., Chen, H.-H., Atiquzzaman, M., Lee, C., Kim, T., Yeo, S.-S. (eds.) ISA 2009. LNCS, vol. 5576, pp. 21–30. Springer, Heidelberg (2009). https://doi.org/10.1007/978-3-642-02617-1_3
9. Cassez, F., Dubreil, J., Marchand, H.: Dynamic observers for the synthesis of opaque systems. In: Liu, Z., Ravn, A.P. (eds.) ATVA 2009. LNCS, vol. 5799, pp. 352–367. Springer, Heidelberg (2009). https://doi.org/10.1007/978-3-642-04761-9_26
10. Deng, W., Qiu, D., Yang, J.: New insights into the decidability of opacity in timed automata. arXiv preprint arXiv:2504.00625 (2025)
11. Klein, J., Kogel, P., Glesner, S.: Efficient state estimation of discrete-timed automata. In: Proceedings of the 2024 25th International Conference on Formal Engineering Methods (ICFEM). ICFEM 2024, pp. 85–105. Springer, Cham (2024). https://doi.org/10.1007/978-981-96-0617-7_6
12. Klein, J., Kogel, P., Glesner, S.: Verifying opacity of discrete-timed automata. In: Proceedings of the 2024 IEEE/ACM 12th International Conference on Formal Methods in Software Engineering (FormaliSE). FormaliSE 2024, pp. 55–65. Association for Computing Machinery (2024). https://doi.org/10.1145/3644033.3644376
13. Klein, J., Zhang, K., Glesner, S.: A unified method to efficiently verify opacity of discrete-timed automata - software prototype (2025). https://doi.org/10.5281/zenodo.16994338
14. Li, J., Lefebvre, D., Hadjicostis, C.N., Li, Z.: Observers for a class of timed automata based on elapsed time graphs. IEEE Trans. Autom. Control. 767–779 (2021). https://doi.org/10.1109/TAC.2021.3064542
15. Li, J., Lefebvre, D., Hadjicostis, C.N., Li, Z.: Verification of state-based timed opacity for constant-time labeled automata. IEEE Trans. Autom. Control, 503–509 (2025). https://doi.org/10.1109/TAC.2024.3432788
16. Noord, G.V.: Treatment of epsilon moves in subset construction. Comput. Linguist. 61–76 (2000). https://doi.org/10.1162/089120100561638
17. Saboori, A., Hadjicostis, C.N.: Notions of security and opacity in discrete event systems. In: Proceedings of the 2007 46th International Conference on Conference on Decision and Control (CDC). CDC 2007, pp. 5056–5061. IEEE (2007). https://doi.org/10.1109/CDC.2007.4434515
18. Saboori, A., Hadjicostis, C.N.: Verification of k-step opacity and analysis of its complexity. IEEE Trans. Autom. Sci. Eng. 549–559 (2011). https://doi.org/10.1109/TASE.2011.2106775
19. Wang, L., Zhan, N.: Decidability of the initial-state opacity of real-time automata. In: Jones, C., Wang, J., Zhan, N. (eds.) Symposium on Real-Time and Hybrid Systems. LNCS, vol. 11180, pp. 44–60. Springer, Cham (2018). https://doi.org/10.1007/978-3-030-01461-2_3

20. Wang, L., Zhan, N., An, J.: The opacity of real-time automata. IEEE Trans. Comput.-Aided Des. Integr. Circ. Syst. 2845–2856 (2018). https://doi.org/10.1109/TCAD.2018.2857363
21. Yin, X., Zamani, M., Liu, S.: On approximate opacity of cyber-physical systems. IEEE Trans. Autom. Control. 1630–1645 (2021). https://doi.org/10.1109/TAC.2020.2998733
22. Zhang, K.: A unified concurrent-composition method to state/event inference and concealment in labeled finite-state automata as discrete-event systems. Annu. Rev. Control. (2023). https://doi.org/10.1016/j.arcontrol.2023.100902
23. Zhang, K.: State-based opacity of labeled real-time automata. Theoret. Comput. Sci. (2024). https://doi.org/10.1016/j.tcs.2023.114373

Quantitative Verification for Temporal Properties of Massive Linear Systems

Qing Liu[1], Yuntao Li[1], Sung Woo Choi[1], Luan Viet Nguyen[2(✉)], and Hoang-Dung Tran[1]

[1] University of Florida, Gainesville, USA
{qliu1,yli17,sungwoo.choi,dungtran}@ufl.edu
[2] Department of Computer Science, University of Dayton, Dayton, USA
lnguyen1@udayton.edu

Abstract. The verification of linear systems has been extensively studied through reachability analysis to determine the set of states reachable from initial conditions. While traditional methods focus on qualitative safety checks, this work extends verification to *quantitative analysis* using probabilistic star sets (ProbStars), which incorporate Gaussian-distributed variables for probabilistic reachability. To handle large-scale linear systems, we use Krylov subspace methods (e.g., Arnoldi and Lanczos iterations), incorporating numerical simulation for efficiently approximating the exponential matrix to get simulation equivalent reachable sets. We also introduce a verification framework based on ProbStar Temporal Logic (ProbStarTL) for specifying and analyzing complex temporal properties. Experiments on benchmarks up to 10,000 dimensions show the scalability and effectiveness of our approach.

Keywords: Linear system · Formal verification · Temporal logic

1 Introduction

Verifying dynamic systems is crucial for ensuring the safety and reliability of engineered systems in fields like aerospace, automotive control, and signal processing. A key part of verification is *reachability analysis*, which identifies all states a system can reach from initial conditions. Broadly, existing reachability methods can be grouped into three categories. Reachable set methods compute exact or over-approximated sets of all states a system can reach, typically using symbolic constraint representations such as polytopes [2,15,30,58], zonotopes [4,26,28,34], star sets [12,13,53], or support functions [22,27,36,57]. Simulation-based methods perform a finite number of simulations of the system from a set of initial conditions and enlarge the resulting trajectories (reachable sets) to conservatively account for uncertainty [7–10,20,29]). SMT-based methods encode the reachability problem into formulas in first-order logic over the reals and solve them (exactly or approximately) using Satisfiability Modulo Theories (SMT)

É. André et al. (Eds.): ICFEM 2025, LNCS 16229, pp. 305–328, 2026.
https://doi.org/10.1007/978-981-95-4213-0_17

solvers [14,24,33,38,44]. However, these methods are primarily targeted at *qualitative verification*, providing a YES or NO answer regarding the verification problem of the system.

In this paper, we propose a framework for *quantitative verification* of large-scale, discrete-time, linear time invariant (LTI) systems with bounded time using a simulation-based reachability approach. Since uncertainties in initial states, sensing noise, or disturbances are often well approximated by Gaussian distributions, our approach leverages *probabilistic star* sets (ProbStars) [52], an extension of traditional star set representations that incorporates Gaussian distributed random variables and predicates. By doing so, our framework supports both *qualitative verification*, which answers the binary result, and *quantitative verification*, which computes the probability of satisfaction. This makes our approach more convenient and effective than existing methods, which often provide only qualitative verification. In addition, we extend our work to quantitatively verify the temporal behavior of linear systems using *ProbStar Temporal Logic* (ProbStarTL) [51], a formal language for expressing quantitative temporal properties. ProbStarTL is defined over a (bounded-time) *ProbStar Signal*, a sequence of probabilistic star reachable sets, which symbolically captures states satisfying an STL formula [19], enabling integrated analysis of safety, liveness, and other system behaviors through both qualitative and quantitative reasoning.

In the reachability analysis of discrete-time, LTI systems, constructing reachable sets requires evaluating matrix exponentials, which correspond to solving the underlying ordinary differential equation (ODE) at each discrete time step. While direct computation using Taylor series or Padé approximations [43] is feasible for small systems, these methods are impractical for large-scale systems due to prohibitive memory and time requirements. We address these challenges with a simulation-based reachability algorithm for large-scale linear systems. Our algorithm adopts some scalable methods, such as those used in the Hylaa tool [10], which uses initial and output space projection and Krylov subspace [3,45], such as Arnoldi and Lanczos iterations, for numerical simulations to efficiently approximate reachable sets and integrate with ProbStar representations. These methods significantly reduce the computational and memory overhead associated with matrix exponential calculations.

To verify the temporal behavior of a linear system, we develop a quantitative verification algorithm based on ProbStarTL that supports both exact and approximate verification. The process begins by computing an *Abstract Disjunctive Normal Form* (ADNF) of the specification, which encodes the temporal logic constraints over time. The ADNF is then transformed into a *Computable Disjunctive Normal Form* (CDNF) via the realization process on the ProbStar signal. Verification proceeds by checking the feasibility of the CDNF over the signal: if feasible, we can compute the exact probability based on the length of the CDNF; otherwise, we conclude that the probability of satisfaction is zero.

The proposed methods are implemented in *StarV* [50]. We evaluate our proposed framework on nine benchmark systems, each tested against three user-defined ProbStarTL specifications, including systems with up to 10,000 dimensions. The results highlight the efficacy, scalability, and practical applicability of our approach. The first specification for each benchmark corresponds to its original unsafe requirement. To assess effectiveness, we compare our method against Hylaa [7], a state-of-the-art tool for verifying discrete-time LTI systems, using the same reachability techniques described in [10]. While Hylaa provides only binary verification outcomes, our framework supports both quantitative and qualitative verification, and further extends to verify temporal properties across all specifications. Overall, the main contributions of this paper are:

- Proposing a simulation-based reachability method for efficiently constructing the reachable set of high-dimensional discrete-time LTI systems using Krylov subspaces and state-space projections in simulation.
- Leveraging ProbStar representation and ProbStarTL to analyze and verify complex temporal properties over ProbStar signals quantitatively.
- Demonstrating the scalability and effectiveness of the approach on nine large-scale benchmark systems.

2 Preliminaries

In this section, we present the foundational concepts of ProbStars [52] and ProbStar Temporal Logic [51], providing the essential background that supports our quantitative verification approach.

2.1 Probabilistic Star [52]

Definition 1. *(Probabilistic Star) A* ***probabilistic star*** *(or simply ProbStar) Θ is a tuple $\langle c, V, \mathcal{N}, P, l, u\rangle$ where $c \in \mathbb{R}^n$ is the* ***center****, $V = \{v_1, v_2, \cdots, v_m\}$ is a set of m vectors in $\mathbb{R}^n$ called* ***basis vectors****, $P : \mathbb{R}^m \to \{\top, \bot\}$ is a* ***predicate****, l and u are the* ***lower-bound*** *and* ***upper-bound*** *vectors of the predicate variables α, which are random variables of a Gaussian distribution $\mathcal{N}(\mu, \Sigma)$. The basis vectors are arranged to form the ProbStar's $n \times m$ basis matrix. The set of states represented by the ProbStar is given as:*

$$\begin{aligned} [\![\Theta]\!] = \{x \mid x = c + \Sigma_{i=1}^{m}(\alpha_i v_i),\ \alpha = [\alpha_1, \cdots, \alpha_m]^T \sim \mathcal{N}, \\ P(\alpha) \triangleq C\alpha \leq d,\ l[i] \leq \alpha_i \leq u[i]\}. \end{aligned} \tag{1}$$

We will refer to the tuple Θ and the set of states $[\![\Theta]\!]$ as Θ. In this work, we restricted predicates to be a conjunction of linear constraints, $P(\alpha) \triangleq C\alpha \leq d$ where, for p linear constraints, $C \in \mathbb{R}^{p \times m}$ and $d \in \mathbb{R}^{p \times 1}$. Based on the ProbStar definition, we now provide an example of a probabilistic star and define its probabilistic characteristics in the following.

Example 1 (ProbStar). Consider the following 1-dimensional discrete linear system $\mathcal{S} : x[t+1] = 3x[t] + 1$, where the system's initial state is $x(0) \in \mathcal{N}(0, 1)$. One can see that the set of initial states R_0 can be represented as a ProbStar as follows: $x(0) \in R_0 = \{x \in \mathbb{R}^1 |\ x = c + \alpha v = 0 + \alpha, \alpha \in \mathcal{N}(0, 1), P(\alpha) = \top, -\infty \leq \alpha \leq +\infty\}$. In this case, we have no constraints on the random predicate variable α, i.e., $P(\alpha) = \top$.

Definition 2. *(Probability) Given a ProbStar Θ, the* ***probability of the ProbStar***, $\mathbf{P}$, *is the probability of the predicate random variables $\alpha = [\alpha_1, \alpha_2, \ldots, \alpha_m]^T$ satisfying its constraints and bounds, i.e., $\mathbf{P}[\Theta] = \mathbf{P}[P(\alpha) \wedge l \leq \alpha \leq u,\ \alpha \sim \mathcal{N}]$. A ProbStar is an* ***empty set*** *if its probability is zero, i.e., $\mathbf{P}[\Theta] = 0$. The algorithm for probability computation can be found in [52] (Algorithm 1).*

2.2 ProbStar Temporal Logic (ProbStarTL) [51]

Definition 3. *(ProbStar Signal) Given a system $\mathcal{S}$, a maximum time T with step size h, and a Probstar set of initial conditions R_0. The* ***ProbStar signal*** *of $\mathcal{S}$ is a sequence of reachable ProbStar sets defined as: $\mathcal{R} = (R_0, R_1, R_2, \ldots, R_{\frac{T}{h}})$, that contains all possible trajectories of the system up to time T.*

Example 2 (ProbStar Signal). Following the Example 1 as we introudced in Sect. 2.1, the evolution of the system for four time steps creates a 4-steps ProbStar signal: $\mathcal{R} = (R_0, R_1, R_2, R_3, R_4)$, where: $R_0 = \alpha, R_1 = 3\alpha + 1, R_2 = 9\alpha + 4, R_3 = 27\alpha + 13$, and $R_4 = 81\alpha + 40$, $\alpha \in \mathcal{N}(0, 1)$.

Definition 4. *(DT-STL Syntax [19]) The discrete-time STL syntax is:*

$$\varphi := \mu_{p,q} \mid \neg\varphi \mid \varphi \wedge \varphi \mid \varphi \vee \varphi \mid \Box_I \varphi \mid \Diamond_I \varphi \mid \bigcirc \varphi,$$

where $\wedge$ and $\vee$ are the Boolean operators; $\Box_I$ and $\Diamond_I$ denote always and eventually temporal operator over a boounded time interval $I \subset \mathbb{N}$; $\bigcirc$ is the next time operator; and $\mu_{p,q}$ is an atomic predicate defined as a linear inequality constraint on state variable x at time t with parameter vectors p, q.

Notice that we do not consider the *until* operator ($\mathcal{U}$) in Definition 4. When the semantics are defined over discrete and bounded time, the until operator can be defined as a disjunction of a finite number of always and eventually operators, or using a finite number of compositions of the next operator.

Definition 5. *(DT-STL Semantics) Given a discrete-time signal $x : [0, T] \to \mathbb{R}^n$ and a DT-STL specification φ, the semantics are defined by:*

$$\begin{aligned}
(x,t) \models \mu_{p,q} \quad & \textit{iff} \quad p^T x(t) + q \geq 0, \\
(x,t) \models \neg\varphi \quad & \textit{iff} \quad (x,t) \not\models \varphi, \\
(x,t) \models \varphi_1 \wedge \varphi_2 \quad & \textit{iff} \quad (x,t) \models \varphi_1 \textit{ and } (x,t) \models \varphi_2, \\
(x,t) \models \varphi_1 \vee \varphi_2 \quad & \textit{iff} \quad (x,t) \models \varphi_1 \textit{ or } (x,t) \models \varphi_2, \\
(x,t) \models \bigcirc\varphi \quad & \textit{iff} \quad (x,t+h) \models \varphi, \\
(x,t) \models \Box_{[t_1,t_2]}\varphi \quad & \textit{iff} \quad \forall t' \in [t+t_1, t+t_2], \quad (x,t') \models \varphi, \\
(x,t) \models \Diamond_{[t_1,t_2]}\varphi \quad & \textit{iff} \quad \exists t' \in [t+t_1, t+t_2], \quad (x,t') \models \varphi,
\end{aligned}$$

where $\not\models$ stands for "does not satisfy".

To compute the probability of satisfaction on an STL formula, we introduce ProbStar temporal logic(ProbStarTL), interpreted over ProbStar signals and an STL formula. It operates as a function C that returns a propositional formula symbolically capturing all constraints under which the system state satisfies φ.

Definition 6. *(ProbStarTL [51]) Given a ProbStar signal $\mathcal{R} = (R_0, R_1, \ldots, R_{\frac{T}{h}})$ and a DT-STL formula φ in Negation Normal Form (NNF), the constraints over time that characterize the linear system state variable x that satisfy φ can be derived recursively based on the structure of the formula φ:*

$$\begin{aligned}
C(\mathcal{R}, t, \mu_{p,q}) &= [\![R_t]\!] \cap [\![\mu_{p,q}]\!] = [\![R_t]\!] \cap \{x \,|\, p^T x + q \geq 0\},\\
C(\mathcal{R}, t, \neg\mu_{p,q}) &= [\![R_t]\!] \cap \overline{[\![\mu_{p,q}]\!]} = [\![R_t]\!] \cap \{x \,|\, p^T x + q < 0\},\\
C(\mathcal{R}, t, \varphi_1 \wedge \varphi_2) &= C(\mathcal{R}, t, \varphi_1) \wedge C(\mathcal{R}, t, \varphi_2),\\
C(\mathcal{R}, t, \varphi_1 \vee \varphi_2) &= C(\mathcal{R}, t, \varphi_1) \vee C(\mathcal{R}, t, \varphi_2),\\
C(\mathcal{R}, t, \bigcirc\varphi) &= C(\mathcal{R}, t+h, \varphi),\\
C(\mathcal{R}, t, \Box_{[t_1,t_2]}\varphi) &= \wedge_{t'=t+t_1}^{t+t_2} C(\mathcal{R}, t', \varphi),\\
C(\mathcal{R}, t, \Diamond_{[t_1,t_2]}\varphi) &= \vee_{t'=t+t_1}^{t+t_2} C(\mathcal{R}, t', \varphi).
\end{aligned}$$

ProbStarTL Disjunctive Normal Form (DNF). Directly computing the probability $\mathbf{P}[C(\mathcal{R}, 0, \varphi)]$ is challenging due to arbitrarily nested conjunctions and disjunctions. To address this, we first transform the user-defined specification φ into an *abstract disjunctive normal form (ADNF)*, which symbolically encodes temporal logic constraints over time independent of the actual ProbStar signal $\mathcal{R}$. Then, we apply a *realization process* to convert this ADNF into *computable disjunctive normal form (CDNF)*, which involves the ProbStar signal on which the specification is reasoned. This transformation explicitly outlines the evolved constraints required for satisfaction. The DNF of a ProbStarTL i.e., $C(\mathcal{R}, 0, \varphi)$ is a disjunction of conjunction terms of form:

$$dnf(C(\mathcal{R}, 0, \varphi)) = \bigvee_i (\bigwedge_j \psi_{ij}), \tag{2}$$

where dnf denotes the function that translates any formula into its equivalent DNF, and each ψ_{ij} is some ProbStar $[\![R_{t_{ij}}]\!] \cap [\![\mu_{ij}]\!]$ or $[\![R_t]\!] \cap \overline{[\![\mu_{p,q}]\!]}$. The detailed derivation algorithm of the DNF can be found in [51] (Algorithm 4). Finally, we use the following lemma to show how ProbStarTL in the form of its DNF can be used to compute bounds of the satisfaction probability.

Lemma 1 (Probability of a ProbStarTL [51]). *Given a DT-STL φ and a ProbStar signal $\mathcal{R}$, let*

$$\varphi_{dnf} = dnf(C(\mathcal{R}, 0, \varphi)) = \bigvee_{i=0}^{n} \psi_i = \bigvee_{i=0}^{n} \bigwedge_{j=0}^{m_n} \psi_{ij}, \tag{3}$$

where ψ_{ij} correspond to ProbStars for some n, m_n. Then, the probability of satisfaction is

$$\mathbf{P}[\varphi_{dnf}] = \Sigma_{i=1}^{n}\mathbf{P}[\psi_i] + (-1)^1\Sigma_{i\neq j}\mathbf{P}[\psi_i \wedge \psi_j] + (-1)^2\Sigma_{i\neq j\neq k}\mathbf{P}[\psi_i \wedge \psi_j \wedge \psi_k] \\ + \cdots + (-1)^{n-1}\mathbf{P}[\psi_1 \wedge \psi_2 \cdots \wedge \psi_n] \tag{4}$$

and its estimated lower bound can be computed as:

$$\tilde{P}_l(\varphi_{dnf}) = \max\left(\mathbf{P}[\psi_1], \mathbf{P}[\psi_2], \ldots, \mathbf{P}[\psi_n]\right) \leq \mathbf{P}[\varphi_{dnf}]. \tag{5}$$

To illustrate DNF derivation and Lemma 1 for probability computation, we use the timed harmonic oscillator system as an example in the following.

Example 3 (DNF Derivation of Harmonic example). We define two temporal logic specifications with time bound π to verify the harmonic oscillator system:

$$\varphi_1 = \Diamond_{[0,4]}(\varphi_4), \quad \varphi_2 = \Box_{[1,2]}\left(\varphi_3 \vee \Diamond_{[2,3]}(\varphi_4)\right)$$

, where $\varphi_3 : x \leq 4$, and $\varphi_4 : x \geq 4$. In this example, we use φ_2, a more complex specification, to show how we get its *Disjunctive Normal Form (DNF).*

Automate ADNF Derivation. Figure 1 describes the automatic process to transform the specification φ_2 into an abstract disjunctive normal form φ_{ADNF}. In Fig. 1, *Scope 0* is the innermost scope, and *Scope 3* is the outermost scope of the specification φ_2. Scope 0 contains the (atomic) predicate φ_4, we expand φ_2's ADNF in this scope to $\varphi_{ADNF} = \varphi_4(0)$, where 0 means "$t = 0$". Then, we search outwardly to Scope 1, which contains the eventually temporal operator $\diamond_{[2,3]}$. We expand the ADNF with this operator and get the new ADNF as $\varphi_{ADNF} = \varphi_4(2) \vee \varphi_4(3)$. Note that the timing information has changed in this time from $t = 0$ to $t = \frac{\pi}{2}$ and $t = \frac{3\pi}{4}$. Continue moving outwardly to Scope 2, which contains the *OR* operator with predicate φ_3, we expand the ADNF to $\varphi_3(0)\vee\varphi_4(2)\vee\varphi_4(3)$. Finally, we move to Scope 3, the outermost scope containing the always temporal operator $\Box_{[1,2]}$. We expand this ADNF with this operator to get the final ADNF at Scope 4: $\varphi_{ADNF} = (\varphi_3(1) \vee \varphi_4(3) \vee \varphi_4(4)) \wedge (\varphi_3(2) \vee \varphi_4(4) \vee \varphi_4(5)))$. Since the final result for any expansion step needs to be in the abstract disjunctive normal form (Eq. 2), the final ADNF is as follows:

$$\begin{aligned} \varphi_{ADNF} = &(\varphi_3(1) \wedge \varphi_3(2)) \vee (\varphi_3(1) \wedge \varphi_4(4) \vee (\varphi_3(1) \wedge \varphi_4(5)) \\ &\vee(\varphi_4(3) \wedge \varphi_3(2)) \vee (\varphi_4(3) \wedge \varphi_4(4) \vee (\varphi_4(3) \wedge \varphi_4(5)) \\ &\vee(\varphi_4(4) \wedge \varphi_3(2)) \vee (\varphi_4(4) \wedge \varphi_4(4) \vee (\varphi_4(4) \wedge \varphi_4(5)). \end{aligned}$$

In our example, we only consider the satisfaction of the specification φ_2 on 4-steps ProbStar signal $\mathcal{R} = (R_0, R_1, R_2, R_3, R_4)$, i.e., $\varphi_3(5) = \bot$ (R_5 does not exist), thus $\varphi_3(1) \wedge \varphi_4(5) = \varphi_3(1) \wedge \bot = \bot$, $\varphi_4(3) \wedge \varphi_4(5) = \varphi_4(3) \wedge \bot = \bot$, $\varphi_4(4) \wedge \varphi_4(5) = \varphi_4(4) \wedge \bot = \bot$ ($\bot$ states for FALSE).

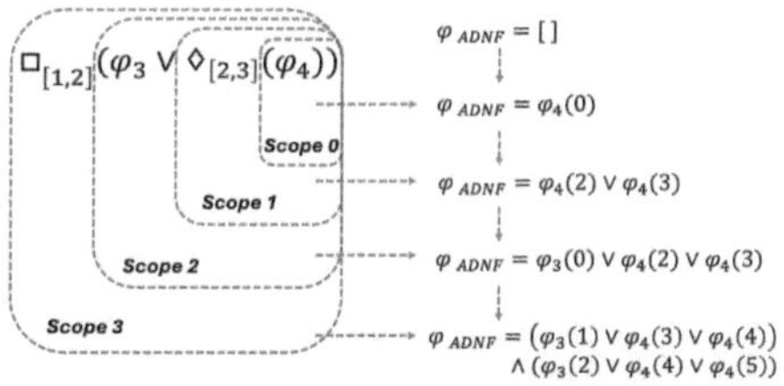

Fig. 1. Abstract disjunctive normal form derivation of harmonic example.

CDNF Derivation. The computable DNF of φ_2 is obtained by realizing its ADNF on the ProbStar signal. Mathematically, the CDNF of φ_2 is as follows:

$$\begin{aligned}\varphi_{CDNF} &= (\varphi_{ADNF})_{\mathcal{R}}\\ &= (\varphi_3(1)_{\mathcal{R}} \wedge \varphi_3(2)_{\mathcal{R}}) \vee (\varphi_3(1)_{\mathcal{R}} \wedge \varphi_4(4)_{\mathcal{R}})\\ &\vee (\varphi_4(3)_{\mathcal{R}} \wedge \varphi_3(2)_{\mathcal{R}}) \vee (\varphi_4(3)_{\mathcal{R}} \wedge \varphi_4(4)_{\mathcal{R}})\\ &\vee (\varphi_4(4)_{\mathcal{R}} \wedge \varphi_3(2)_{\mathcal{R}}) \vee (\varphi_4(4)_{\mathcal{R}} \wedge \varphi_4(4)_{\mathcal{R}}).\end{aligned}$$

Therefore, the CDNF of the specification φ_2 after realization is as follows:

$$\begin{aligned}&\varphi_2 = S_1 \vee S_2 \vee S_3 \vee S_4 \vee S_5 \vee S_6,\\ &S_1 = (\varphi_3(1) \wedge \varphi_3(2))_{\mathcal{R}}, S_2 = (\varphi_3(1) \wedge \varphi_4(4))_{\mathcal{R}}, S_3 = (\varphi_4(3) \wedge \varphi_3(2))_{\mathcal{R}},\\ &S_4 = (\varphi_4(3) \wedge \varphi_4(4))_{\mathcal{R}}, S_5 = (\varphi_4(4) \wedge \varphi_3(2))_{\mathcal{R}}, S_6 = (\varphi_4(4) \wedge \varphi_4(4))_{\mathcal{R}}.\end{aligned}$$

We can see that $S_1, S_2, S_3, S_4, S_5, S_6$ are ProbStar sets and are feasible on the ProbStar signal; the length of CDNF is 6. Thus, we use Lemma 1 to compute the probability of satisfaction on φ_2, which is to compute $\mathbf{P}(S_1 \vee S_2 \vee S_3 \vee S_4 \vee S_5 \vee S_6)$. In the exact verification, we enumerate all non-empty conjunctions of the six disjuncts in the CDNF and compute their probabilities,i.e. $\{\mathbf{P}(S_i), \mathbf{P}(S_i \wedge S_j), ..., \mathbf{P}(S_1 \wedge S_2 \wedge S_3 \wedge S_4 \wedge S_5 \wedge S_6) \mid 1 \leq i < j \leq 6\}$. This requires $2^6 - 1 = 63$ probability computations. The exact probability is then obtained using the inclusionâĂŞexclusion probability principle, which exactly accounts for overlaps between events. In contrast, the approximate verification requires only 6 computations to get an estimated lower bound, i.e., $\{\mathbf{P}(S_1), \mathbf{P}(S_2), \mathbf{P}(S_3), \mathbf{P}(S_4), \mathbf{P}(S_5), \mathbf{P}(S_6)\}$.

Remark. The verification complexity depends on the number of probability computations involved in the verification process. As shown in Lemma 1 and Example 3, the complexity of exact verification is $O(2^n)$, while for estimated verification is $O(n)$, which is computationally much cheaper, where n is the number of disjuncts in the CDNF formulas (the length of CDNF).

3 Problem Formulation

In this study, we focus on discrete-time, linear time-invariant (LTI) systems with piecewise-constant inputs, represented by the equation:

$$\dot{x}(t) = Ax(t) + Bu(t), \quad u(t) \in U \tag{6}$$

, where $x(t)$ is the state vector, $A \in \mathbb{R}^{n \times n}$ is the dynamics matrix, $B \in \mathbb{R}^{n \times m}$ is the input matrix, and $U \subseteq \mathbb{R}^m$ defines the set of possible inputs $u(t)$. All references to linear systems in this paper refer to such discrete-time LTI systems. We address two fundamental problems: *probabilistic reachability analysis* and *quantitative verification* of high-dimensional linear systems using ProbStarTL.

Problem 1. (Probabilistic Reachability) Given a linear system $\mathcal{L} : \dot{x}(t) = Ax(t) + Bu(t)$, an input ProbStar set $R_0 := \{x(0) \in \mathbb{R}^n \mid P(\alpha) \wedge\ l \leq \alpha \leq u,\ \alpha \sim \mathcal{N}\}$ with initial states $x(0)$, and a time bound T with step size h, the probabilistic reachability analysis of linear system is the process of getting the ProbStar signal $\mathcal{R}$ with corresponding probability.

Problem 2. (Quantitative Verification) Given a linear system $\mathcal{L} : \dot{x}(t) = Ax(t) + Bu(t)$, an input probabilistic set R_0, and a user-defined temporal specification φ, the quantitative verification of the linear system is to compute the probability of the ProbStar signal $\mathcal{R}$ satisfying temporal specification at some time t, which is to compute $\mathbf{P}[(x,t) \models \varphi \mid x(0) \in [\![R_0]\!]] = \mathbf{P}[C(\mathcal{R}, t, \varphi)]$.

4 Numerical Simulation Reachability Computation

Analyzing linear dynamical systems typically involves computing the matrix exponential e^{At}, which becomes intractable for high-dimensional systems due to exponential growth in computation and memory costs. To efficiently perform reachability analysis in such cases, we employ numerical simulation reachability methods from [10], which use Krylov subspaces and leverage initial and output spaces to efficiently handle e^{At} and incorporate the ProbStar framework introduced in Sect. 2.1 to represent output reachable sets. In what follows, we introduce a probabilistic reachability algorithm (Algorithm 1) [9] to generate a ProbStar signal, a sequence of simulation-equivalent ProbStar reachable sets.

4.1 Leveraging Initial and Output Space

Our approach significantly reduces the memory overhead of storing matrix exponentials by leveraging the initial and output space. Since the verification results are typically dependent on some critical system state variables, we define an *output space* $O \in \mathbb{R}^{o \times n}$ to project the matrix exponential from $e^{At} \in \mathbb{R}^{n \times n}$ to $Oe^{At} \in \mathbb{R}^{o \times n}$, effectively capturing only relevant variable dynamics.

Additionally, since some state variables may be correlated and have fixed values at the start, the initial conditions where the system evolves can be described in a much lower-dimensional *initial space* $I \in \mathbb{R}^{n \times i}$. Combining both projections, we can result in an $Oe^{At}I \in \mathbb{R}^{o \times i}$ exponential matrix. In our work, we use basis vectors V from the input ProbStar set R_0 to define the initial space I.

4.2 Using Krylov Subspace in Numerical Simulations

We also adopt the numerical simulation methods from [43] and incorporate with Krylov subspace [23,45] to avoid directly computing the reduced exponential matrix $Oe^{At}I$ for further time efficiency improvement.

The matrix exponential e^{At} can be computed column by column by utilizing the identity: $e^{At} = e^{At}E_{n\times n} = e^{At}(e_1 \mid e_2 \mid \ldots \mid e_n)$. We simulate each column up to the time bound T and repeat this for all columns to construct e^{At}. We employ each column of the initial space I instead of using each column of identity matrix E for simulation (lines 2 - 4), which is $e^{At}I = e^{At}(I_{*,1} \mid I_{*,2} \mid \cdots \mid I_{*,i})$, and then project the simulation result onto the output space O, resulting in $Oe^{At}I$. The number of simulations required equals the number of columns in I, enhancing efficiency over direct computations of $Oe^{At}I$. Moreover, when the dimension of output space O is significantly lower than the initial space, we can change to leverage the column of transposed output space O^T for simulation by utilizing the transposed dynamics A^T(lines 6 - 8), where $Oe^{At}I = \left((Oe^{At}I)^T\right)^T = \left(I^T(e^{At})^T O^T\right)^T = \left(I^T(e^{A^T t})O^T\right)^T$, which require only o simulations, one per column of O^T, thus significantly improving computational efficiency.

What's more, we use the Krylov subspace method to speed up computation in each simulation further. The Krylov subspace, denoted $K_k(A, v)$, is the span of the vectors generated by repeated multiplication of the matrix A with the vector v, up to $k-1$ iterations $K_k(A, v) = \text{span}\{v, Av, A^2v, \ldots, A^{k-1}v\}$. This method efficiently approximates $e^A v$ by projecting the n-dimensional dynamics A into a smaller k subspace using Arnoldi and Lanczos [10] iterative algorithm, where v is the initial state vector corresponding to each column of I or O^T in our work. Note that the Lanczos algorithm is specifically tailored for systems with symmetric dynamics, which is more time-efficient than the Arnoldi algorithm. The approximation equation is defined as $e^{At}v \approx \|v\| V_k e^{H_k t} e_1$, where V_k and H_k are generated by iterative algorithm, and V_k a sequence of orthonormal vectors spinning the subspace and H_k is an upper Hessenberg matrix that approximates A in the smaller subspace.

Algorithm 1. Quantitative Reachability of Linear System

Inputs: $R_0\langle c, V, \mathcal{N}, P, l, u\rangle$, dynamic matrix A, iteration count k, step size h, time bound T, iteration tolerance δ, error bound ϵ, output sapce $O^{o\times n}$

Outputs: $\mathcal{R}$ # probstar signal

```
1: procedure R = SIMREACHKRYLOV( R_0, A, k, h, T, δ, ε, O )
2:     if use each column of initial space for simulation then
3:         𝒱 = I = R_0.V
4:         P = O    # output space as projection mat
5:     else    # use transpose dynamics
6:         𝒱 = O^T
7:         P = I = R_0.V^T    # initial space as projection mat
8:         A = A^T
9:     Z = [ ]
10:    N = 𝒱.shape[1], steps = T/h]
11:    for i from 1 to N do
12:        v = 𝒱[*, i]    # using initial column vector
13:        V_k, H_k = Arnoldi(v, A, k, δ, ε, P) or    # two krylov iterative algorithms
14:        V_k, H_k = Lanczos(v, A, k, δ, ε, P)
15:        Z_i = simKrylov(h, steps, V_k, H_m)    # simulate and project e^{At}v
16:        Z.append(Z_i)
17:    R = [ ]
18:    R.append(R_0)
19:    for i from 1 to steps do
20:        V = [ ]
21:        for j from 1 to N do    # combine each vectors to form basis vectors
22:            V.append(Z[j][i, *])
23:        V = vstack(V)
24:        R_i = ⟨R_0.c, V, R_0.𝒩, R_0.P, R_0.l, R_0.u⟩
25:        p_i = estimateProbability(R_i) #    # algorithm 1 in [52]
26:        R.append((R_i, p_i))
27:    return R
```

What's more, the iterative algorithms employ a posteriori error bounds, as shown in [56] (Thorem 3.1), to compute an error bound of approximating $e^{At}v$, which ensures the approximation accuracy while keeping computational costs reasonable in determining the number of iterations k (lines 13–14) in iterative algroithms. Further, we use the function *simKrylov* to simulate $e^{At}v$ with up to $\frac{T}{h}$ steps, which returns a list of state vectors after N simulations (lines 15). We then use the list of resulting vectors to compose the basis vectors V (lines 19–23), which are used to define a ProbStar set for reachability analysis, encapsulating the reachability bounds of the system (line 24). After computing the probability of each ProbStar reachable set within its constraints, we finally get a sequence of ProbStar sets $\mathcal{R}$ with their corresponding probability (lines 25–26).

4.3 Reachability for Timed Harmonic Oscillator Example

In this part, we continue to use a timed harmonic oscillator example to demonstrate how a sequence of ProbStar reachable sets (ProbStar signal) is obtained through quantitative reachability, as detailed in Algorithm 1.

Example 4. The *timed harmonic oscillator* is defined by the system dynamics $\dot{x} = y, \dot{y} = -x$, which is a two-dimensional system. The initial condition are $x_0 \in [-6, -5]$, and $y_0 \in [0, 1]$. We transform the two-state variables system $x = (x, y)^T$ into a four-variable system $x = (x, y, u_1, u_2)^T$ where u_1, u_2 stand for system input and are kept constant at each time step. Thus, the system dynamics are now captured by the transformed linear time-invariant system $\dot{x} = Ax$, where A is a 4×4 matrix:

$$A = \begin{pmatrix} 0 & 1 & 1 & 0 \\ -1 & 0 & 0 & 1 \\ 0 & 0 & 0 & 0 \\ 0 & 0 & 0 & 0 \end{pmatrix}$$

To perform probabilistic reachability analysis of the harmonic example, we need to construct the initial ProbStar set $R_0 = \langle c, V, \mathcal{N}, P, lb, ub \rangle$ based on the initial condition of the system. The mean of the Gaussian distribution is computed as $\mu = (lb+ub)/2$, and standard deviation is determined as $\sigma = (ub-\mu)/a$, where $lb = (-1, -1, -1, -1), ub = (1, 1, 1, 1)$ are predicated lower and upper bound and a is a positive coefficient. When a increases, the probability of the inputs lying between their lower and upper bounds of interest increases as well. In this example, we choose $a = 3$.

Since the unsafe specification is defined as $x \geq 4$, we can define an output space matrix $O \in \mathbb{R}^{1 \times 4} = (1, 0, 0, 0)$ and projects the full exponential matrix onto the state variable x, yielding a reduced exponential matrix $Oe^{At} \in \mathbb{R}^{1 \times 4}$. Further, we project the initial state of the system onto an initial space using basis vectors $V \in \mathbb{R}^{4 \times 3}$of the input ProbStar set:

$$I = \begin{pmatrix} -5.5 & 0.5 & 0 \\ 0.5 & 0 & 0.5 \\ 0.5 & 0 & 0 \\ 0.5 & 0 & 0 \end{pmatrix}$$

, thereby the final reduced computation $Oe^{At}I \in \mathbb{R}^{1 \times 3}$ effectively lowers the matrix exponential from 4×4 form to a compact 1×3 form. Further, we leverage the columns of O^T, which uses only one simulation to save computation time. To approximate the system states, we employ the Arnoldi algorithm with a predefined iteration count $k = 2$, computing matrices V_k and H_k. Given a step size $h = \pi/4$ and a time bound $T = \pi$, the approximation is performed over four discrete-time steps, starting from $\frac{\pi}{4}$. Finally, we construct ProbStar basis vectors V and represent the simulation results as a ProbStar set at each discrete-time step after simulation. Then, we obtain a ProbStar signal $\mathcal{R} = [R_0, R_1, R_2, R_3, R_4]$ starting from initial time 0 with computed corresponding probabilities.

For better reachability visualization in an x-y plane, we extend the output space matrix to $O = [(1, 0, 0, 0), (0, 1, 0, 0)]$. The ProbStar signal with Gaussian distribution of the Harmonic example is shown in Fig. 2a, and we also provide the probability of the ProbStar signal reaching its unsafe condition in Fig. 2b.

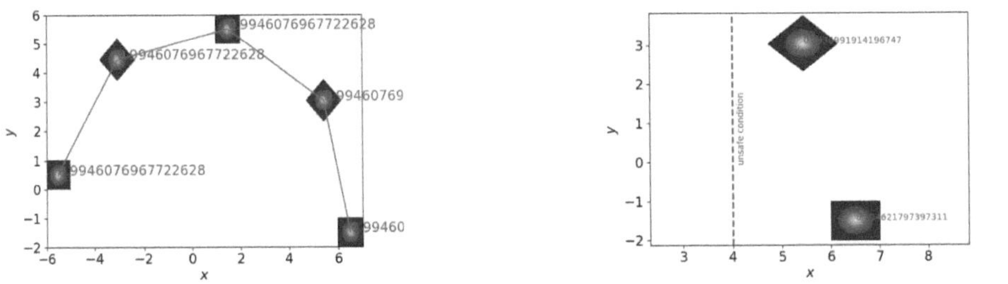

(a) ProbStar signal: $\mathcal{R}$

(b) ProbStar signal with satisfaction probability

Fig. 2. Computation of the ProbStar signal after five steps for the harmonic example, and the probability of satisfying the unsafe condition $x \geq 4$.

5 Quantitative Verification of Linear System

Building on the probabilistic representation of star sets introduced in Sect. 2.1, the ProbStarTL formalism defined in Sect. 2.2, and the reachability methods described in Sect. 4, we develop a quantitative verification approach for large-scale linear systems. Our method computes upper and lower bounds on the probability that the output ProbStar signal satisfies a given temporal specification expressed in ProbStarTL. In what follows, we detail the verification algorithm and demonstrate its application through timed harmonic oscillator examples.

5.1 Quantitative Verification Algorithm

In our work, we perform quantitative verification to evaluate the system's property, which can not only answer Yes/No in satisfying a property but also compute the probability of satisfaction with the property. We create user-defined ProbStar specifications using the proposed ProbStarTL to verify the temporal behavior of linear systems. The detailed steps of our quantitative verification process are outlined in Algorithm 2. The input of the algorithm is the user-defined temporal specification φ along with the input parameters to Algorithm 1. The outputs are the lower bound and upper bound probability of satisfaction, $p_{\min}$ and $p_{\max}$.

We initialize all verification results to empty (line 2). Using Algorithm 1, we get the ProbStar signal $\mathcal{R}$, a sequence of probabilistic reachable sets (line 3). And compute the probability of the initial ProbStar set (line 4) using Algorithm 1 in [52]. After getting the computable disjunctive normal form φ_{CDNF} of the user-defined specification φ (line 5) using Algorithm 4 in [51], we then proceed to compute the ProbStarTL specification probability. Finally, we check the φ_{CDNF} feasibility. Note that feasibility indicates that the specification may be satisfied by the ProbStar signal, whereas infeasibility means that the specification is not satisfied, i.e., the length of CDNF is zero, resulting in $p_{\min} = p_{\max} = 0$ (line 21). If feasible, we compute the satisfaction probability using Lemma 1. If the length of CDNF is fewer than 11, we compute the precise satisfaction probability (lines 7–13) using the exact verification method. Otherwise, we compute estimated lower and upper bounds by assuming that all disjuncts in CDNF are satisfied, then compute approximate lower and upper bounds for the satisfaction probability at a reduced computational cost (lines 15–19).

Algorithm 2. Quantitative Verification of Linear System using ProbstarTL

Inputs: R_0 $\langle c, V, \mathcal{N}, P, l, u\rangle$, A, k, h, T, δ, ϵ, $O^{o\times n}$, φ
 # φ is ProbStar temporal logic specification formula
Outputs: $p_{\min}$,$p_{\max}$
lower and upper bound probability of satisfaction

1: **procedure** $\mathcal{R}$ = QUNTIVERIFY(R_0, A, k, h, T, δ, ϵ, O,φ)
2: $\quad p_{\min} = [\,], p_{\max} = [\,], SAT = [\,]$
3: $\quad \mathcal{R} = simReachKrylov(R_0, A, k, h, T, \delta, \epsilon, O)$ # algorithm 1
4: $\quad p_0 = estimateProbability(R_0)$ # algorithm 1 in [52]
5: $\quad \varphi_{CDNF} = getDNF(\varphi, \mathcal{R})$ # algorithm 4 in [51]
6: $\quad$ **if** φ_{CDNF} is feasible **then** # compute probability using lemma 1
7: $\quad\quad$ **if** len(φ_{CDNF}) ≤ 11 **then** # exact verification method
8: $\quad\quad\quad$ **for** i from 1 to $length(\varphi_{CDNF})$ **do**
9: $\quad\quad\quad\quad comb = combinations(length(\varphi_{CDNF}, i)$ # list all combinations
10: $\quad\quad\quad\quad$ **for** j in list(comb) **do**
11: $\quad\quad\quad\quad\quad prob{+} = (-1)^{(i-1)} * getprobability(\varphi_{CDNF}(j)$
12: $\quad\quad\quad\quad p_{\max} = prob$
13: $\quad\quad\quad p_{\min} = p_{\max}$
14: $\quad\quad$ **else** # approximate verification method
15: $\quad\quad\quad$ **for** i from 1 to $length(\varphi_{CDNF})$ **do**
16: $\quad\quad\quad\quad prob = getProbability(\varphi_{CDNF}(i))$
17: $\quad\quad\quad\quad SAT.append(prob)$
18: $\quad\quad\quad p_{\min} = \max(SAT)$
19: $\quad\quad\quad p_{\max} = \max(p_{\min}, p_0)$
20: $\quad$ **else**
21: $\quad\quad p_{\min} = p_{\max} = 0$
22: $\quad$ **return** p_{min}, p_{max}

Remark. To manage verification complexity, we compute exact satisfaction probabilities only when the length of the CDNF is less than 11. This threshold is necessary to ensure computational tractability but is not the sole limiting factor, as additional challenges may arise from the complexity of the temporal properties themselves. In particular, specifications with intricate nested temporal operators or large predicate sets can further increase the size and complexity of the CDNF, potentially leading to memory exhaustion or longer verification times. For cases where exact computation becomes impractical, we perform an approximate method to estimate the probability bounds while avoiding excessive computational overhead.

Moreover, note that our verification method builds on a simulation-based reachability method, as used in prior work [8–10]. Without assuming that the simulator can reproduce the true trajectories to negligible error, there is no unconditional formal proof of soundness and completeness. Under this assumption, the reachable set is sound and complete with respect to the simulator's accuracy.

5.2 Verifying Timed Harmonic Oscillator Example

We get the ProbStar signal $\mathcal{R}$ through the proposed reachability approach using the reachability Algorithm 1, and we also create two temporal specifications in Example 3 for verification purposes. Thus, we can use the above quantitative verification Algorithm 2 to compute the probability of satisfaction of the output ProbStar signal on these two specifications.

Table 1. Verification results of Harmonic example.

model	φ	N_{adnf}	N_{cdnf}	$p_{\min}$	$p_{\max}$	t_r	t_c	t_v
Harmonic	φ_1	5	2	0.993713	0.993713	0.00396752	0.0294676	0.0334351
	φ_2	9	6	0.995154	0.995154	0.00396752	0.411774	0.415742

For the first specification, which is $\varphi_1 = \Diamond_{[0,4]}(x \geq 4)$, we want to compute the probability that the system is unsafe ($x \geq 4$)at some time between 0 and π. For the second specification, which is $\varphi_2 = \Box_{[1,2]}((x \leq 4) \vee \Diamond_{[2,3]}(x \geq 4))$, we want to compute the probability of the system always being safe at the time between $\frac{\pi}{4}$ to $\frac{\pi}{2}$ and eventually the system is unsafe within next 2 time steps.

Table 1 shows the verification result, where $p_{\min}$ and $p_{\max}$ represent the upper bound and lower bound probability of satisfaction on a specification; t_r, t_c, t_v stands for the reachability computation time, checking time, and total verification time, respectively. From the table, we observe that the system satisfies φ_1 with a high exact satisfaction probability of 0.993713 within 1 s, as its length of CDNF is 2. For φ_2, we also get a high exact satisfaction probability around 4 s, i.e., 0.995154, and the length of CDNF is 6, which is consistent with the calculated length of CDNF in Example 3.

6 Evaluation

6.1 Implementation

We implement our approach in a tool named ***StarV***[1] (Star-based Verification tool) using Python3. We use the built-in Botev method [11] in the Scipy package to compute the probability of a probabilistic star. Our experiment is done on a computer with the following configurations: Intel Core i7-10700 CPU, 31.1 GiB Memory, 64-bit Ubuntu 20.04.6 LTS OS.

[1] All experimental results are reproducible using StarV:https://github.com/V2A2/StarV.

Table 2. ProbStar temporal logic specification of all benchmarks.

	Specification (φ)
Motor	$\varphi_1 = \Diamond_{[0,200]}(y_1 \in [0.3, 0.4] \wedge y_2 \in [0.4, 0.6])$
	$\varphi_2 = \Box_{[10,15]}((y_1 \in [0.3, 0.4] \wedge y_2 \in [0.4, 0.6]) \vee \Diamond_{[10,15]}(y_1 \leq 0.3 \wedge y1 \geq 0.4 \wedge y_2 \leq 0.4 \wedge y_2 \geq 0.6))$
	$\varphi_3 = \Box_{[10,15]}(y_1 \geq 0.3 \vee y_1 \leq 0.4 \vee y_2 \geq 0.4 \vee y_2 \leq 0.6)$
Building	$\varphi_1 = \Diamond_{[0,200]}(y_1 \geq 0.004)$
	$\varphi_2 = \Box_{[0,200]}(y_1 \leq 0.004)$
	$\varphi_3 = \Diamond_{[10,15]}((y_1 \leq 0.004) \vee \Box_{[10,15]}(y_1 \geq 0.004))$
PDE	$\varphi_1 = \Diamond_{[0,200]}(y_1 \geq 10.75)$
	$\varphi_2 = \Box_{[0,200]}(y_1 \leq 10.75)$
	$\varphi_3 = \Diamond_{[0,20]}((y_1 \leq 10.75) \vee \Box_{[10,20]}(y_1 \geq 10.75))$
ISS	$\varphi_1 = \Diamond_{[0,200]}(y_1 \leq -0.0001 \vee y_1 \geq 0.0001)$
	$\varphi_2 = \Box_{[0,200]}(-0.0001 \leq y_1 \leq 0.0001)$
	$\varphi_3 = \Diamond_{[50,100]}((y_1 \geq -0.0001) \vee \Box_{[50,100]}(y_1 \leq -0.0001))$
Beam	$\varphi_1 = \Diamond_{[0,200]}(y_1 \geq 500)$
	$\varphi_2 = \Box_{[0,200]}(y_1 \leq 500)$
	$\varphi_3 = \Diamond_{[100,200]}((y_1 \leq 500) \vee \Box_{[100,200]}(y_1 \geq 500))$
MNA1	$\varphi_1 = \Diamond_{[0,200]}(y_1 \geq 0.2)$
	$\varphi_2 = \Box_{[0,200]}(y_1 \leq 0.2)$
	$\varphi_3 = \Diamond_{[150,195]}((y_1 \leq 0.2) \vee \Box_{[150,195]}(y_1 \geq 0.2))$
FOM	$\varphi_1 = \Diamond_{[0,200]}(y_1 \geq 7)$
	$\varphi_2 = \Box_{[0,200]}(y_1 \leq 7)$
	$\varphi_3 = \Diamond_{[50,100]}((y_1 \leq 7) \vee \Box_{[50,100]}(y_1 \geq 7))$
MNA5	$\varphi_1 = \Diamond_{[0,200]}(y_1 \geq 0.1 \vee y_2 \geq 0.15)$
	$\varphi_2 = \Box_{[0,200]}(y_1 \leq 0.1 \wedge y_1 \leq 0.15)$
	$\varphi_3 = \Diamond_{[100,200]}((y_1 \leq 0.1 \wedge y_1 \leq 0.15) \vee \Box_{[100,200]}(y_1 \geq 0.1 \vee y_2 \geq 0.15))$
Heat3D	$\varphi_1 = \Diamond_{[0,200]}(y_1 \geq 0.012)$
	$\varphi_2 = \Box_{[0,200]}(y_1 \leq 0.012)$
	$\varphi_3 = \Diamond_{[50,180]}((y_1 \leq 0.012) \vee \Box_{[50,180]}(y_1 \geq 0.012))$

We evaluate the proposed quantitative verification framework on nine large-scale linear system benchmarks, mostly from model order reduction examples in [54], with `Heat3D` adapted from a case study presented in [10]. To strengthen evaluation, we adjust the initial states and unsafe specifications of some selected models, ensuring that each model reaches its corresponding unsafe condition during its evolution. To verify the temporal properties, we create three temporal specifications for each model based on its unsafe conditions, incorporating different compositions of temporal operators, as shown in Table 2.

Furthermore, we consider a fixed time bound $T = 20$ with step size $h = 0.1$ ($steps = 200$) and select $a = 3$ to calculate the Gaussian distribution, ensuring consistency in the approach across different models. Each model contains constant input variables u_i at each discrete-time step. To capture the effect of these inputs, we augment system dynamics with additional columns, thereby transforming the system into a higher-dimensional system. For example, the `MNA5` model, initially with 10913 variables and 9 inputs, is now considered a 10922-

dimensional system, and this model is the highest dimensional model used in our work. Note that all input and output matrices are implemented in dense format.

6.2 Evaluation Analysis

We successfully verify the temporal properties of nine linear systems using ProbStarTL and compare our approach with Hylaa [7], using the same reachability methods [10]. While Hylaa is limited to qualitative verification of invariant properties, our method supports both qualitative and quantitative verification of temporal properties across diverse ProbStarTL specifications, including invariant, liveness, and nested temporal operators, such as events within a specific time interval or one condition eventually following another. The evaluation results are summarized in Table 3.

Probability Analysis on Specifications. In the `Building` model, for specification φ_1, we want to compute the probability of the system satisfying condition $y_1 \geq 0.004$ at some time step between 0 and 200. Table 3 shows that the probability of satisfaction on φ_1 is 0, implying that the system does not meet this specification. The result is consistent with Hylaa, which returns "No", indicating that the system does not reach the unsafe condition within the time bound. The specification φ_2 is the opposite of φ_1, which states that the system is always the case satisfying the condition $y_1 \leq 0.004$ from time step 0 to 200. We get an exact and high probability (0.96708) of satisfaction on φ_1. A more complex specification φ_3 indicates that eventually, between steps 10 and 15, there is the case that the system satisfies $y_1 \leq 0.004$ and may always reach the opposite case $y_1 \geq 0.004$ within the next five steps. The exact probability of satisfaction is 0.69487 for verification with φ_3.

In the `Beam` model, for verifying φ_1, the result shows that the probability of the system eventually reaching the condition $y_1 \geq 200$ within 0 to 200 steps lies between $p_{\text{min}} = 0.000634204$ and $p_{\text{max}} = 0.8759$. For the verification with opposite specification φ_2, we obtain an exact high probability (0.883983) of satisfaction, indicating that the system is very likely to always satisfy the condition $y_1 \leq 500$ from time step 0 to 200. When verifying the system on specification φ_3, we choose different step ranges for verification in specification φ_3. The verification result indicates that the system has a high probability (0.878191) of eventually satisfying the condition $y_1 \leq 500$ between steps 100 and 200, and will always reach the opposite condition $y_1 \geq 500$ within the next 100 steps.

Table 3. Verification results of all models compare with Hylaa, where p_{min} and p_{max} is the upper and lower bound probabilities of satisfaction; t_r, t_c and t_v are reachability time, checking time and total verification in seconds respectively.

	ProbStarTL						Hylaa	
model	φ	$p_{\min}$	$p_{\max}$	t_r	t_c	t_v	SAT	t_v
Motor	φ_1	1.39577e-11	0.989244	0.00980091	0.974593	0.984394	YES	0.005317
	φ_2	1.21007e-13	0.989244	0.00980091	0.0837743	0.0935752	-	-
	φ_3	0.989953	0.989953	0.00980091	23.3009	23.3107	-	-
Building	φ_1	0	0	0.0398626	0.49032	0.530183	NO	0.160578
	φ_2	0.968708	0.968708	0.0398626	9.56005	9.59992	-	-
	φ_3	0.69487	0.69487	0.0398626	65.041	65.0808	-	-
PDE	φ_1	0.000464905	0.944809	0.166748	5.25236	5.41911	YES	0.371748
	φ_2	0.944424	0.944424	0.166748	10.8728	11.0395	-	-
	φ_3	0.945636	0.945636	0.166748	2.03815	2.2049	-	-
ISS	φ_1	0.779119	0.779119	2.1172	333.022	335.139	YES	3.292322
	φ_2	0	0	2.1172	0.647329	2.76452	-	-
	φ_3	0.785919	0.785919	2.1172	263.735	265.852	-	-
Beam	φ_1	0.000634204	0.87593	2.53663	9.63472	12.1713	YES	4.475225
	φ_2	0.883983	0.883983	2.53663	14.4092	16.9458	-	-
	φ_3	0.878191	0.878191	2.53663	44.1315	46.6682	-	-
MNA1	φ_1	0.996313	0.996313	2.71408	0.227393	2.94148	YES	3.634282
	φ_2	0	0	2.71408	0.00620031	2.72029	-	-
	φ_3	0.998814	0.998814	2.71408	0.165903	2.87999	-	-
FOM	φ_1	0.00253155	0.871207	13.2172	53.7279	66.9451	YES	22.683661
	φ_2	0.869113	0.869113	13.2172	14.5056	27.7228	-	-
	φ_3	0.872215	0.872215	13.2172	56.8823	70.0994	-	-
MNA5	φ_1	0.97435	0.97435	51.2157	2.55923	53.7749	YES	4.217258
	φ_2	0	0	51.2157	0.0364957	51.2522	-	-
	φ_3	0.974305	0.974305	51.2157	1.62111	52.8368	-	-
Heat3D	φ_1	0.726053	0.726053	18.1401	885.643	903.783	YES	0.066165
	φ_2	0	0	18.1401	0.908379	19.0485	-	-
	φ_3	0.700407	0.700407	18.1401	194.691	212.831	-	-

In the `MNA5` model, we get a high probability (0.97435) of satisfaction on specification φ_1, while the probability of satisfaction on specification φ_2 is 0, which means the system is not always reaches the condition,i.e., $y_1 \leq 0.1 \wedge y_1 \leq 0.15$, between step 0 and 200. Moreover, when verifying a more complex temporal specification φ_3, the verification result indicates that the system has a high probability (0.878191) of satisfying φ_3.

In the `Heat3D` model, the task is to examine the temperature at the center point of a $1.0 \times 1.0 \times 1.0$ block, discretized into a $d \times d \times d$ grid, thereby configuring a d^3-dimensional linear state space system. In our work, we set $d = 20$, resulting in total system dimensions of 8000 with symmetric properties, which enable us to use more efficient Lanczos iteration in reachability analysis. For specification φ_1, the results show that the probability of the center point temperature will eventually exceed 0.012 at some time within the time bound is 0.726053. For verification on φ_2, we get 0 probability of satisfaction, meaning that the temperature will not always be larger than 0.012 within a time bound. In addition, for specification φ_3, the results show that we can get a probability of satisfaction on this specification, i.e., 0.700407.

Time Performance and Scalability Analysis. In our reachability computations, we use each column of the transposed output space for simulation across all models, typically requiring only one or two simulations. Thus, the reachability time t_r mainly depends on the model's dimensionality and complexity. As presented in Table 3, the reachability time increases progressively from the smallest (`Motor`) to the largest (`MNA5`) model.

The checking time (t_c) measures how long it takes to evaluate ProbStarTL probabilities. Analyzing the variations in checking times across specifications and models is complicated, as system complexity (state space dimension, etc.) and specification differences are involved. We therefore restrict our analysis to variations in t_c for different specifications on the same model, which isolates the effect of specification complexity from that of system complexity.

The complexity of computing the probability of ProbStarTL can be affected by the complexity of the specification, which directly influences the number of ProbStar probability computations required, thereby affecting the overall checking time. The complexity of the specification can be characterized by two factors: the length of the CDNF (i.e., the number of disjuncts) and its internal structure (i.e., the number of conjuncts inside each disjunct).

Based on our evaluation results, we observed that increased CDNF length tends to increase checking time within the same model. Table 4 summarizes the length of ADNF and CDNF for each model specification. For example, in `Motor` model, the order of CDNF length follows $|CDNF\varphi_2| < |CDNF\varphi_1| < |CDNF\varphi_3|$, which align with the order of checking time spent in each specification, where $t_c(\varphi_2) < t_c(\varphi_1) < t_c(\varphi_3)$. Similar observations apply to other models, such as the `Building`, `PDE`, `ISS`, `MNA1`, `MNA5`, and `Heat3D` model.

Table 4. Length of ADNF and CDNF of each specification.

	Motor			Building			PDE			ISS			Beam			MNA1			FOM			MNA5			Heat3D		
	φ_1	φ_2	φ_3	φ_1	φ_2	φ_3	φ_1	φ_2	φ_3	φ_1	φ_2	φ_3	φ_1	φ_2	φ_3	φ_1	φ_2	φ_3	φ_1	φ_2	φ_3	φ_1	φ_2	φ_3	φ_1	φ_2	φ_3
N_{adnf}	201	12	4096	201	1	22	201	1	42	402	1	102	201	1	202	201	1	92	201	1	102	402	1	202	201	1	262
N_{cdnf}	201	12	4096	0	1	11	200	1	42	402	0	102	201	1	102	45	0	6	191	1	102	95	0	54	201	1	131

However, even within the same model, a specification with much shorter CDNF does not always imply faster verification. For example, in the Beam benchmark, the length of CDNF for φ_3 is only half as long as that for φ_1, yet its checking time is higher. This is because each disjunct of φ_3 contains more conjuncts, whereas each disjunct of φ_1 is a single atomic predicate. A similar pattern holds in the FOM model. Thus, this shows that the internal structure of the CDNF also affects the complexity of the probability computations.

Overall, our approach can effectively provide both qualitative and quantitative verification of the temporal properties of all nine large-scale linear models using ProbStarTL. The length of CDNFs varies with model complexity, nesting of operators, and time intervals, all of which affect verification complexity. To the best of our knowledge, no existing technique supports quantitative temporal property verification of linear systems at this scale.

7 Related Work

Temporal Logic Verification. Verification of temporal logic properties is typically classified into runtime and static approaches. Runtime verification, often realized via monitoring [17,18,40,42], checks whether observed traces satisfy a property, either online or offline. Static verification assumes a system model and checks that all behaviors satisfy the specification [25,37,38,46,47]. Signal Temporal Logic (STL) [42] is widely used to express and verify temporal properties of real-valued signals from dynamic systems. In the static setting, [37] reduces bounded STL satisfiability to first-order logic over the reals, solved via SMT with a complete discretization. The method in [46] applies reachability analysis to produce discrete-time reachable sets for STL checking. Most existing methods focus on deterministic verification, whereas our approach performs quantitative verification in terms of reachability-based STL model checking.

Probabilistic Modeling and Verification. The verification of systems under uncertainty has been extensively explored in probabilistic model checking, where discrete- and continuous-time Markov models are analyzed against logics such as PCTL and CSL [6]. Mature tools like PRISM [35] and STORM [16] have enabled scalable verification, with recent work improving numerical robustness in floating-point computations [31]. Beyond discrete models, stochastic hybrid and continuous-state systems have been addressed through formal abstractions [49] and statistical model checking [1]. Recent advances target scalability for complex dynamics, e.g., PCA-DDReach [32] combines conformal inference with dimensionality reduction for high-dimensional analysis. In parallel, conformal prediction (CP) [5,21,48,55] has emerged as a distribution-free uncertainty quantification framework, recently applied to verification and control [39,41], offering calibrated confidence sets under mild assumptions for safety-critical systems. Our work differs in combining a scalable, simulation-based reachability method with a symbolic representation (ProbStars) and a quantitative temporal logic (ProbStarTL) to compute exact or bounded satisfaction probabilities for high-dimensional linear systems.

8 Conclusion

This paper presents a quantitative verification framework for analyzing and verifying the temporal logic behavior of discrete-time LTI systems using ProbStarTL. By integrating Probabilistic Stars with Krylov subspace methods, our approach efficiently computes probabilistic reachable sets, enabling both qualitative and quantitative verification. Implemented in StarV, our framework successfully verifies multiple temporal properties across large-scale benchmarks, including systems with up to 10,000 dimensions. The results demonstrate its scalability, efficiency, and potential for verifying complex safety and performance requirements in high-dimensional linear systems.

Acknowledgments. This work is supported by the National Science Foundation (NSF) under grants NSF-CAREER-2441334, NSF-SLES-2331937, and NSF-FMitF-2220418. Any opinions, findings, conclusions, or recommendations expressed in this publication are those of the authors and do not necessarily reflect the views of NSF.

References

1. Agha, G., Palmskog, K.: A survey of statistical model checking. ACM Trans. Model. Comput. Simul. (TOMACS) **28**(1), 1–39 (2018)
2. Althoff, M.: Reachability analysis of nonlinear systems using conservative polynomialization and non-convex sets. In: Proceedings of the 16th International Conference on Hybrid Systems: Computation and Control. HSCC 2013, pp. 173–182. Association for Computing Machinery, New York (2013). https://doi.org/10.1145/2461328.2461358
3. Althoff, M.: Reachability analysis of large linear systems with uncertain inputs in the krylov subspace. IEEE Trans. Autom. Control **65**(2), 477–492 (2020). https://doi.org/10.1109/TAC.2019.2906432
4. Althoff, M., Krogh, B.H.: Zonotope bundles for the efficient computation of reachable sets. In: 2011 50th IEEE Conference on Decision and Control and European Control Conference, pp. 6814–6821 (2011). https://doi.org/10.1109/CDC.2011.6160872
5. Angelopoulos, A.N., Bates, S., et al.: Conformal prediction: a gentle introduction. Found. Trends® Mach. Learn. **16**(4), 494–591 (2023)
6. Baier, C., Katoen, J.P.: Principles of Model Checking. MIT Press, Cambridge (2008)
7. Bak, S., Duggirala, P.S.: Hylaa: a tool for computing simulation-equivalent reachability for linear systems. In: Proceedings of the 20th International Conference on Hybrid Systems: Computation and Control, pp. 173–178 (2017)
8. Bak, S., Duggirala, P.S.: Rigorous simulation-based analysis of linear hybrid systems. In: Legay, A., Margaria, T. (eds.) TACAS 2017. LNCS, vol. 10205, pp. 555–572. Springer, Heidelberg (2017). https://doi.org/10.1007/978-3-662-54577-5_32
9. Bak, S., Duggirala, P.S.: Simulation-equivalent reachability of large linear systems with inputs. In: Majumdar, R., Kunčak, V. (eds.) CAV 2017. LNCS, vol. 10426, pp. 401–420. Springer, Cham (2017). https://doi.org/10.1007/978-3-319-63387-9_20

10. Bak, S., Tran, H.D., Johnson, T.T.: Numerical verification of affine systems with up to a billion dimensions. In: Proceedings of the 22nd ACM International Conference on Hybrid Systems: Computation and Control, pp. 23–32 (2019)
11. Botev, Z.I.: The normal law under linear restrictions: simulation and estimation via minimax tilting. J. R. Stat. Soc. Ser. B (Stat. Methodol.) **79**(1), 125–148 (2017)
12. Choi, S.W., Ivashchenko, M., Nguyen, L.V., Tran, H.D.: Reachability analysis of sigmoidal neural networks. ACM Trans. Embed. Comput. Syst. (2023). https://doi.org/10.1145/3627991. just Accepted
13. Choi, S.W., et al.: Reachability analysis of recurrent neural networks. Nonlinear Analysis: Hybrid Systems (2025)
14. Cimatti, A., Griggio, A., Mover, S., Tonetta, S.: HyComp: an SMT-based model checker for hybrid systems. In: Baier, C., Tinelli, C. (eds.) TACAS 2015. LNCS, vol. 9035, pp. 52–67. Springer, Heidelberg (2015). https://doi.org/10.1007/978-3-662-46681-0_4
15. Dang, T., Testylier, R.: Reachability analysis for polynomial dynamical systems using the Bernstein expansion. Reliab. Comput. **17**(2), 128–152 (2012)
16. Dehnert, C., Junges, S., Katoen, J.-P., Volk, M.: A Storm is coming: a modern probabilistic model checker. In: Majumdar, R., Kunčak, V. (eds.) CAV 2017. LNCS, vol. 10427, pp. 592–600. Springer, Cham (2017). https://doi.org/10.1007/978-3-319-63390-9_31
17. Deshmukh, J.V., Donzé, A., Ghosh, S., Jin, X., Juniwal, G., Seshia, S.A.: Robust online monitoring of signal temporal logic. Formal Methods Syst. Des. **51**(1), 5–30 (2017). https://doi.org/10.1007/s10703-017-0286-7
18. Donzé, A., Ferrère, T., Maler, O.: Efficient robust monitoring for STL. In: Sharygina, N., Veith, H. (eds.) CAV 2013. LNCS, vol. 8044, pp. 264–279. Springer, Heidelberg (2013). https://doi.org/10.1007/978-3-642-39799-8_19
19. Donzé, A., Maler, O.: Robust satisfaction of temporal logic over real-valued signals. In: Chatterjee, K., Henzinger, T.A. (eds.) FORMATS 2010. LNCS, vol. 6246, pp. 92–106. Springer, Heidelberg (2010). https://doi.org/10.1007/978-3-642-15297-9_9
20. Duggirala, P.S., Viswanathan, M.: Parsimonious, simulation based verification of linear systems. In: Chaudhuri, S., Farzan, A. (eds.) CAV 2016. LNCS, vol. 9779, pp. 477–494. Springer, Cham (2016). https://doi.org/10.1007/978-3-319-41528-4_26
21. Fontana, M., Zeni, G., Vantini, S.: Conformal prediction: a unified review of theory and new challenges. Bernoulli **29**(1), 1–23 (2023)
22. Frehse, G., Ray, R.: Flowpipe-guard intersection for reachability computations with support functions*. IFAC Proceedings Volumes **45**(9), 94–101 (2012). https://doi.org/10.3182/20120606-3-NL-3011.00053, https://www.sciencedirect.com/science/article/pii/S1474667015371809. 4th IFAC Conference on Analysis and Design of Hybrid Systems
23. Gallopoulos, E., Saad, Y.: Efficient solution of parabolic equations by Krylov approximation methods. SIAM J. Sci. Stat. Comput. **13**(5), 1236–1264 (1992)
24. Gao, S., Kong, S., Clarke, E.M.: Satisfiability modulo odes. In: 2013 Formal Methods in Computer-Aided Design, pp. 105–112 (2013). https://doi.org/10.1109/FMCAD.2013.6679398
25. Gao, Y., Abate, A., Jiang, F.J., Giacobbe, M., Xie, L., Johansson, K.H.: Temporal logic trees for model checking and control synthesis of uncertain discrete-time systems. IEEE Trans. Autom. Control **67**(10), 5071–5086 (2021)
26. Girard, A.: Reachability of uncertain linear systems using zonotopes. In: Morari, M., Thiele, L. (eds.) HSCC 2005. LNCS, vol. 3414, pp. 291–305. Springer, Heidelberg (2005). https://doi.org/10.1007/978-3-540-31954-2_19

27. Girard, A., Guernic, C.L.: Efficient reachability analysis for linear systems using support functions. IFAC Proceedings Volumes 41(2), 8966–8971 (2008). https://doi.org/10.3182/20080706-5-KR-1001.01514, https://www.sciencedirect.com/science/article/pii/S1474667016403939. 17th IFAC World Congress
28. Girard, A., Le Guernic, C.: Zonotope/hyperplane intersection for hybrid systems reachability analysis. In: Egerstedt, M., Mishra, B. (eds.) HSCC 2008. LNCS, vol. 4981, pp. 215–228. Springer, Heidelberg (2008). https://doi.org/10.1007/978-3-540-78929-1_16
29. Girard, A., Pappas, G.J.: Verification using simulation. In: Hespanha, J.P., Tiwari, A. (eds.) HSCC 2006. LNCS, vol. 3927, pp. 272–286. Springer, Heidelberg (2006). https://doi.org/10.1007/11730637_22
30. Han, Z., Krogh, B.H.: Reachability analysis of large-scale affine systems using low-dimensional polytopes. In: Hespanha, J.P., Tiwari, A. (eds.) HSCC 2006. LNCS, vol. 3927, pp. 287–301. Springer, Heidelberg (2006). https://doi.org/10.1007/11730637_23
31. Hartmanns, A.: Correct probabilistic model checking with floating-point arithmetic. In: TACAS 2022. LNCS, vol. 13244, pp. 41–59. Springer, Cham (2022). https://doi.org/10.1007/978-3-030-99527-0_3
32. Hashemi, N., Lindemann, L., Deshmukh, J.: Pca-ddreach: efficient statistical reachability analysis of stochastic dynamical systems via principal component analysis. arXiv preprint arXiv:2505.14935 (2025)
33. Katz, G., Barrett, C., Dill, D.L., Julian, K., Kochenderfer, M.J.: Reluplex: an efficient SMT solver for verifying deep neural networks. In: Majumdar, R., Kunčak, V. (eds.) CAV 2017. LNCS, vol. 10426, pp. 97–117. Springer, Cham (2017). https://doi.org/10.1007/978-3-319-63387-9_5
34. Kochdumper, N., Althoff, M.: Sparse polynomial zonotopes: a novel set representation for reachability analysis. IEEE Trans. Autom. Control **66**(9), 4043–4058 (2021). https://doi.org/10.1109/TAC.2020.3024348
35. Kwiatkowska, M., Norman, G., Parker, D.: PRISM 4.0: verification of probabilistic real-time systems. In: Gopalakrishnan, G., Qadeer, S. (eds.) CAV 2011. LNCS, vol. 6806, pp. 585–591. Springer, Heidelberg (2011). https://doi.org/10.1007/978-3-642-22110-1_47
36. Le Guernic, C., Girard, A.: Reachability analysis of linear systems using support functions. Nonlinear Anal. Hybrid Syst **4**(2), 250–262 (2010)
37. Lee, J., Yu, G., Bae, K.: Efficient SMT-based model checking for signal temporal logic. In: 2021 36th IEEE/ACM International Conference on Automated Software Engineering (ASE), pp. 343–354. IEEE (2021)
38. Lee, J., Yu, G., Bae, K.: SMT-based robust model checking for signal temporal logic. Sci. Comput. Program. **246**, 103332 (2025). https://doi.org/10.1016/j.scico.2025.103332, https://www.sciencedirect.com/science/article/pii/S0167642325000711
39. Lin, A., Bansal, S.: Verification of neural reachable tubes via scenario optimization and conformal prediction. In: 6th Annual Learning for Dynamics & Control Conference, pp. 719–731. PMLR (2024)
40. Lindemann, L., Qin, X., Deshmukh, J.V., Pappas, G.J.: Conformal prediction for stl runtime verification. In: Proceedings of the ACM/IEEE 14th International Conference on Cyber-Physical Systems (with CPS-IoT Week 2023), pp. 142–153 (2023)
41. Lindemann, L., Zhao, Y., Yu, X., Pappas, G.J., Deshmukh, J.V.: Formal verification and control with conformal prediction. arXiv preprint arXiv:2409.00536 (2024)

42. Maler, O., Nickovic, D.: Monitoring temporal properties of continuous signals. In: Lakhnech, Y., Yovine, S. (eds.) FORMATS/FTRTFT -2004. LNCS, vol. 3253, pp. 152–166. Springer, Heidelberg (2004). https://doi.org/10.1007/978-3-540-30206-3_12
43. Moler, C., Van Loan, C.: Nineteen dubious ways to compute the exponential of a matrix. SIAM Rev. **20**(4), 801–836 (1978)
44. Mufid, M.S., Adzkiya, D., Abate, A.: SMT-based reachability analysis of high dimensional interval max-plus linear systems. IEEE Trans. Autom. Control **67**(6), 2700–2714 (2022). https://doi.org/10.1109/TAC.2021.3090525
45. Niesen, J., Wright, W.M.: Algorithm 919: a krylov subspace algorithm for evaluating the ϕ-functions appearing in exponential integrators. ACM Trans. Math. Softw. (TOMS) **38**(3), 1–19 (2012)
46. Roehm, H., Oehlerking, J., Heinz, T., Althoff, M.: STL model checking of continuous and hybrid systems. In: Artho, C., Legay, A., Peled, D. (eds.) ATVA 2016. LNCS, vol. 9938, pp. 412–427. Springer, Cham (2016). https://doi.org/10.1007/978-3-319-46520-3_26
47. Rozier, K.Y.: Linear temporal logic symbolic model checking. Comput. Sci. Rev. **5**(2), 163–203 (2011). https://doi.org/10.1016/j.cosrev.2010.06.002, https://www.sciencedirect.com/science/article/pii/S1574013710000407
48. Shafer, G., Vovk, V.: A tutorial on conformal prediction. J. Mach. Learn. Res. **9**(3) (2008)
49. Soudjani, S.E.Z., Gevaerts, C., Abate, A.: FAUST^2: Formal Abstractions of Uncountable- STate STochastic Processes. In: Baier, C., Tinelli, C. (eds.) TACAS 2015. LNCS, vol. 9035, pp. 272–286. Springer, Heidelberg (2015). https://doi.org/10.1007/978-3-662-46681-0_23
50. Tran, H.D., Choi, S.W., Li, Y., Liu, Q., Okamoto, H., Hoxha, B., Fainekos, G.: Starv: a qualitative and quantitative verification tool for learning-enabled systems. In: International Conference on Computer Aided Verification, pp. 376–394. Springer, Cham (2025). https://doi.org/10.1007/978-3-031-98679-6_17
51. Tran, H.D., Choi, S., Li, Y., Okamoto, H., Hoxha, B., Fainekos, G.: Probstar temporal logic for verifying complex behaviors of learning-enabled systems. In: Proceedings of the 28th ACM International Conference on Hybrid Systems: Computation and Control (2025)
52. Tran, H.D., Choi, S., Okamoto, H., Hoxha, B., Fainekos, G., Prokhorov, D.: Quantitative verification for neural networks using probstars. In: Proceedings of the 26th ACM International Conference on Hybrid Systems: Computation and Control, pp. 1–12 (2023)
53. Tran, H.-D., et al.: Star-based reachability analysis of deep neural networks. In: ter Beek, M.H., McIver, A., Oliveira, J.N. (eds.) FM 2019. LNCS, vol. 11800, pp. 670–686. Springer, Cham (2019). https://doi.org/10.1007/978-3-030-30942-8_39
54. Tran, H.D., Nguyen, L.V., Johnson, T.T.: Large-scale linear systems from order-reduction (benchmark proposal). In: 3rd Applied Verification for Continuous and Hybrid Systems Workshop (ARCH), Vienna, Austria (2016)
55. Vovk, V., Gammerman, A., Shafer, G.: Algorithmic Learning in a Random World. Springer, Cham (2005)
56. Wang, H., Ye, Q.: Error bounds for the Krylov subspace methods for computations of matrix exponentials. SIAM J. Matrix Anal. Appl. **38**(1), 155–187 (2017)

57. Wetzlinger, M., Kochdumper, N., Bak, S., Althoff, M.: Fully-automated verification of linear systems using reachability analysis with support functions. In: Proceedings of the 26th ACM International Conference on Hybrid Systems: Computation and Control. HSCC 2023, Association for Computing Machinery, New York (2023). https://doi.org/10.1145/3575870.3587121
58. Xue, B., She, Z., Easwaran, A.: Under-approximating backward reachable sets by polytopes. In: Chaudhuri, S., Farzan, A. (eds.) CAV 2016. LNCS, vol. 9779, pp. 457–476. Springer, Cham (2016). https://doi.org/10.1007/978-3-319-41528-4_25

Avoiding Larger Conflict Regions in CDCL-Style Methods for Solving SMT-NRA

Xinpeng Ni(✉), Tianyi Ding(✉), and Bican Xia(✉)

School of Mathematical Sciences, Peking University, Beijing, China
{nxp,dingty}@stu.pku.edu.cn, xbc@math.pku.edu.cn

Abstract. A key step in CDCL-style search methods for Satisfiability Modulo the Theory of Nonlinear Real Arithmetic (SMT-NRA for short) is, given an unsat sample point, to find a conflict cell/region containing the point expressed by constructed lemmas. A larger conflict region typically reduces both backtracking frequency and computational time. Conventional techniques for constructing conflict regions are based on cylindrical algebraic decomposition (CAD), and have led to the development of *single-cell projection operators* [3,7,10]. In this paper, we propose a novel conflict region construction method that adaptively utilizes any existing single-cell projection operator. At each projection step, our approach may (i) remove more unnecessary algebraic operations (including resultant and discriminant computations) and (ii) detect more adjacent cells and merge them into a larger region. Case studies demonstrate that the new method produces larger conflict regions than conventional techniques.

Keywords: SMT-NRA · CDCL · CAD · Single-Cell Projection

1 Introduction

Satisfiability Modulo Theories (SMT) under the background theory of Nonlinear Real Arithmetic (NRA) aims to determine the satisfiability of first-order formulas with polynomial constraints. The first decision procedure for real-closed fields is established by Tarski [13], which takes SMT-NRA as a special case. Tarski's decision procedure has super-exponential complexity. Another complete decision procedure for quantifier elimination over the reals is the Cylindrical Algebraic Decomposition (CAD) [4] introduced by Collins, which has double exponential complexity. Due to efficiency, solving SMT-NRA problems typically does not employ CAD directly, but rather uses Conflict Driven Clause Learning (CDCL)-style search paradigms, such as Model Constructing Satisfiability Calculus (MCSAT) [5] and CDCL(T) [11]. When the search procedure finds a feasible sample point, the problem is determined to be satisfiable. Conversely, when encountering an unsat sample point, a lemma is learned (constructed), which is a formula describing the conflict cell/region containing the point. Each

É. André et al. (Eds.): ICFEM 2025, LNCS 16229, pp. 329–347, 2026.
https://doi.org/10.1007/978-981-95-4213-0_18

polynomial maintains a constant sign in this region. This region is then excluded in subsequent backtracking steps. Consequently, a larger conflict region generally leads to improved computational efficiency in the remaining search space.

The theory of mapping a sample point to a region is derived from CAD. In a step of CAD, each sample point is mapped to its corresponding sign-invariant cell (a connected region where all polynomials maintain constant signs) through successive applications of projection operators. In 2013, Brown proposed an algorithm for single-cell construction that only computes one cell containing a given sample point [3]. Brown's construction utilizes McCallum's projection operator [8], which projects a k-variable polynomial set to a $(k-1)$-variable polynomial set and obtains an interval indicating the cell's range on the k-th variable $(k \geq 1)$. Iteratively applying this projection to the polynomial set with a fixed variable ordering $x_n, x_{n-1} \ldots, x_1$, one obtains a cell containing the point in $\mathbb{R}^n$. McCallum's method projects polynomial sets to lower dimensions by collecting their coefficients, discriminants, and pairwise resultants. In 2020 and 2024, Li *et al.* [7] and Nalbach *et al.* [10] simplified McCallum's projection operator by strategically reducing redundant resultants. While retaining all coefficients and discriminants, both works proved that only the resultants between boundary polynomials (the nearest lower and upper bounding polynomials for the sample point) and other polynomials in the set are necessary. A smaller projected polynomial set defines fewer constraints, yielding a larger sign-invariant cell/region. In 2024, Nalbach *et al.* [9] proposed a projection method that merges adjacent cells by detecting irrelavent roots of resultants.

In this paper, we propose a novel projection method that may construct a larger sign-invariant cell that contains a given sample point. Unlike previous works, including [3,7,10], which focus on minimizing projection polynomial sets through projections on one level, our approach simultaneously projects on two levels and considers merging adjacent cells to obtain a larger cell. Although the recent work [9] also employed projection on two levels, our projection method detect "irrelavent" roots of both resultants and discriminants, which witness more adjacent cells that can be merged, resulting in a larger cell. While their cell merging technique relies on local delineability, our approach is based on the union and intersection of pre-cells (see Definition 7). Case studies demonstrate that our method produces larger cells than previous techniques.

The remainder of this paper is organized as follows. Section 2 introduces the notation and results of CAD and the sample-cell projection operators in [7,10]. Section 3 illustrates our motivation through an example. Section 4 presents our projection method through a main algorithm (Algorithm 2) and two subalgorithms (Algorithm 3 and 4) resolving subproblems. Section 5 presents case studies that demonstrate the effectiveness of our method. Finally, Sect. 6 concludes this paper.

2 Preliminaries

In this section, we introduce some basic concepts of CAD [1,2,4,6,8] and single-cell construction [3,7,9,10] that will be used in this paper. Although all the notation, definitions, and results are classic, we use some new notation for the convenience of introducing our method.

2.1 Notation

Denote by $\mathbb{R}, \mathbb{Q}$ and $\mathbb{Z}$ the set of real numbers, rational numbers, and integer numbers, respectively. Let $\boldsymbol{x} = (x_1, x_2, \ldots, x_n)$ be a vector of variables with a fixed *ordering* $x_1 \prec x_2 \prec \cdots \prec x_n$, and define $\boldsymbol{x}_{[k]} = (x_1, \ldots, x_k)$ for $1 \leq k \leq n$. Let $\mathbb{R}[\boldsymbol{x}], \mathbb{Q}[\boldsymbol{x}]$ and $\mathbb{Z}[\boldsymbol{x}]$ be the ring of polynomials in the variables $\boldsymbol{x}$ with coefficients in $\mathbb{R}, \mathbb{Q}$ and in $\mathbb{Z}$, respectively. For a sample point $\boldsymbol{s} = (s_1, s_2, \ldots, s_n) \in \mathbb{R}^n$, its first k entries are denoted by $\boldsymbol{s}_{[k]} = (s_1, \ldots, s_k)$ where $1 \leq k \leq n$.

For a polynomial $f \in \mathbb{Q}[\boldsymbol{x}]$ and a variable x_r, where $1 \leq r \leq n$, the polynomial can be expressed as $f = a_m x_r^m + a_{m-1} x_r^{m-1} + \cdots + a_0$, where $\{a_m, \ldots, a_0\} \subseteq \mathbb{Q}[x_1, \ldots, x_{r-1}, x_{r+1}, \ldots, x_n]$. The set of nonzero coefficients of f with respect to (w.r.t.) x_r is denoted by $\texttt{coeff}(f, x_r) = \{a_j | 0 \leq j \leq m \wedge a_j \not\equiv 0\}$; the *sample coefficients* [7] of f at $\boldsymbol{s}$ w.r.t. x_r is $\texttt{s\_coeff}(f, x_r, \boldsymbol{s}) = \{a_m, a_{m-1}, \ldots, a_j\}$ if $a_j(\boldsymbol{s}) \neq 0$ and $a_i(\boldsymbol{s}) = 0$ for all $i > j$; the discriminant of f w.r.t. x_r is denoted by $\texttt{disc}(f, x_r)$; and the resultant of f and g w.r.t. x_r is denoted by $\texttt{res}(f, g, x_r)$. The *level* of f, denoted as $\texttt{level}(f)$, is defined as k if x_k is the highest variable appearing in f.

The *order* of f at $\boldsymbol{s}$, denoted as $\texttt{order}_{\boldsymbol{s}}(f)$, is defined as the smallest non-negative integer d for which there exists a partial derivative of total degree d of f that does not vanish at $\boldsymbol{s}$. If all the partial derivatives of f vanish at $\boldsymbol{s}$, then it is defined to be ∞. The polynomial f is called *order-invariant* on $S \subseteq \mathbb{R}^n$ if $\texttt{order}_{\boldsymbol{s}_1}(f) = \texttt{order}_{\boldsymbol{s}_2}(f)$ for any $\boldsymbol{s}_1, \boldsymbol{s}_2 \in S$. Similarly, f is *degree-invariant* on S if the degree of f is the same at every point in S, and f is *sign-invariant* on S if the sign of f is the same at every point in S. For a set of polynomials F, denote by $\texttt{Factors}(F)$ the set of all irreducible factors of polynomials in F, and for any $\boldsymbol{s}_{[n-1]} \in \mathbb{R}^{n-1}$, let $\texttt{Isolate}(F, \boldsymbol{s}_{[n-1]})$ be the increasing sequence of distinct real roots of the equation $\prod_{f \in F} f(\boldsymbol{s}_{[n-1]}, x_n) = 0$.

If $f \in \mathbb{R}[\boldsymbol{x}]$ is a polynomial with $\texttt{level}(f) = k$ and the univariate equation $f(\boldsymbol{s}_{[k-1]}, x_k) = 0$ in x_k has $R(> 0)$ real roots counting multiplicities for a fixed $\boldsymbol{s}_{[k-1]} \in \mathbb{R}^{k-1}$, then $\texttt{Root}(f(\boldsymbol{s}_{[k-1]}, x_k), r)$ denotes the r-th smallest real root counting multiplicities of the equation for $1 \leq r \leq R$. If $f(\boldsymbol{s}_{[k-1]}, x_k)$ has no real roots or $r \notin [1, R]$, then $\texttt{Root}(f(\boldsymbol{s}_{[k-1]}, x_k), r)$ is undefined. So, the *real root function* $\texttt{Root}(f(\boldsymbol{x}_{[k-1]}, x_k), r) : S \to \mathbb{R}$ is a function that maps any $\boldsymbol{s}'_{[k-1]} \in S$ to $\texttt{Root}(f(\boldsymbol{s}'_{[k-1]}, x_k), r)$. For a real root function $\theta = \texttt{Root}(f(\boldsymbol{x}_{[k-1]}, x_k), r)$, $\texttt{Poly}(\theta)$ denotes f and $\theta(\boldsymbol{s}_{[k-1]})$ denotes $\texttt{Root}(f(\boldsymbol{s}_{[k-1]}, x_k), r)$.

Definition 1 (Root Symbolic Interval). [2,7,9] *Suppose $\theta_i : \mathbb{R}^{k-1} \to \mathbb{R}$ $(i = l, u)$ is a real root function* $\texttt{Root}(p_i(\boldsymbol{x}_{[k-1]}, x_k), r_i)$ *for some polynomial $p_i \in \mathbb{R}[\boldsymbol{x}_{[k]}]$ and positive integer r_i, or is identically equal to $\pm\infty$. If $\llbracket \in \{(, [\}$ and $\rrbracket \in \{),]\}$, then $\phi_k := \llbracket \theta_l, \theta_u \rrbracket$ is called a* root symbolic interval *on level k.*

Two root symbolic intervals $\phi_k^1 = \llbracket^1 \theta_{l_1}, \theta_{u_1} \rrbracket^1$ and $\phi_k^2 = \llbracket^2 \theta_{l_2}, \theta_{u_2} \rrbracket^2$ $(k > 1)$ are said to be *adjacent* if they share a common boundary function $\theta_{u_1} = \theta_{l_2}$, with their shared interval endpoints $]\!]^1$ and $[\![^2$ having complementary openness (one open, one closed). A sample point $\boldsymbol{s}_{[k-1]} \in \mathbb{R}^{k-1}$ is *consistent* with a root symbolic interval $\phi_k = [\![\theta_l, \theta_u]\!]$ on level k, if $\phi_k(\boldsymbol{s}_{[k-1]}) = [\![\theta_l(\boldsymbol{s}_{[k-1]}), \theta_u(\boldsymbol{s}_{[k-1]})]\!]$ is a well-defined nonempty interval. A set $S \subseteq \mathbb{R}^{k-1}$ is *consistent* with ϕ_k, if every point in S is consistent with ϕ_k.

Definition 2 (Cell). [2,7,9] *A* cell *is a finite-dimensional connected set generated by the following rules.*

(i) Every nonempty interval in $\mathbb{R}$ *with algebraic numbers or* $\pm\infty$ *as endpoints is a* cell*;*

(ii) If $C \subseteq \mathbb{R}^{k-1}$ $(k > 1)$ *is a* cell *and* ϕ_k *is a root symbolic interval on level* k *such that* C *is consistent with* ϕ_k*, then the connected set*

$$C \times \phi_k := \left\{ \boldsymbol{s}_{[k]} \in \mathbb{R}^k \,\middle|\, \boldsymbol{s}_{[k-1]} \in C,\ s_k \in \phi_k(\boldsymbol{s}_{[k-1]}) \right\}$$

is a cell.

Example 1. The set $(-1, 1) \times (x_1, x_1 + 1)$ is a cell because for all $x_1 \in (-1, 1)$, the interval $(x_1, x_1 + 1)$ is always nonempty. However, $(-1, 1) \times (x_1, 1 - x_1)$ is not a cell, as the interval $(x_1, 1 - x_1)$ is empty for $x_1 \in [\frac{1}{2}, 1)$. Similarly, if $f(x_1, x_2) = -x_1 + x_2^2$, then $(-1, 1) \times [\texttt{Root}(f(x_1, x_2), 1), +\infty)$ is not a cell because when $x_1 = -\frac{1}{2}$, the function $x_2^2 + \frac{1}{2} = 0$ does not have real roots.

2.2 CAD Projection Operator

The Cylindrical Algebraic Decomposition (CAD) method partitions $\mathbb{R}^n$ into finitely many cells such that a given set of polynomials $F = \{f_1, \ldots, f_r\}$ maintains sign invariance within each cell. Conventionally, McCallum's projection operator is employed in CAD to achieve this decomposition.

Definition 3 (McCallum's Projection Operator). [8] *Let* $F \subseteq \mathbb{Z}[\boldsymbol{x}]$ *be a set of polynomials. McCallum's Projection Operator* $\texttt{Proj}_M$ *projects* F *w.r.t.* x_n *to*

$$\mathop{\texttt{Proj}}_M(F) = \bigcup_{f \in F} \{\texttt{coeff}(f, x_n), \texttt{disc}(f, x_n)\} \cup \bigcup_{\substack{f,g \in F \\ f \neq g}} \{\texttt{res}(f, g, x_n)\}\,.$$

This operator maps a set of n-variate polynomials to a set of $(n-1)$-variate polynomials while preserving order invariance, a property stronger than sign invariance.

Definition 4 (Delineability). [4] *A k-variable polynomial* $f(\boldsymbol{x}_{[k]})$ *is said to be* delineable *on a connected set* $S \subseteq \mathbb{R}^{k-1}$ *if there exists finitely many continuous functions* $\theta_1, \ldots, \theta_r : S \to \mathbb{R}$ *where* $r \geq 0$ *such that*

(i) $\theta_1 < \cdots < \theta_r$*;*

(ii) for all $\boldsymbol{s}_{[k-1]} \in S$*, the set of real roots of the univariate polynomial* $f(\boldsymbol{s}_{[k-1]}, x_k)$ *is* $\{\theta_1(\boldsymbol{s}_{[k-1]}), \ldots, \theta_r(\boldsymbol{s}_{[k-1]})\}$*; and*

(iii) there exist positive integers $m_1, \ldots, m_r$ *such that for all* $\boldsymbol{s}_{[k-1]} \in S$ *and* $i = 1, \ldots, r$*, the multiplicity of the root* $\theta_i(\boldsymbol{s}_{[k-1]})$ *of* $f(\boldsymbol{s}_{[k-1]}, x_k)$ *is* m_i*.*

The following theorem proves the correctness of McCallum's projection operator.

Theorem 1. [8] *Let $f(\boldsymbol{x}_{[k]}) \in \mathbb{R}[\boldsymbol{x}_{[k]}]$ be a polynomial of positive degree, and $S \subseteq \mathbb{R}^{k-1}$ be a connected set, where $k \geq 2$. Suppose f is degree-invariant in S and does not vanish identically. If* $\mathtt{disc}(f, x_k)$ *is a nonzero polynomial and is order-invariant in S, then*

(i) f is delineable on S; and

(ii) f is order-invariant in each f-section over S.

2.3 Single-Cell Projection Operators

Different from CAD, which globally decomposes the entire space, single-cell construction focuses on the local cell that contains a given sample point, ensuring sign-invariance only within this cell. The projection operators proposed in [7,10] are designed for single-cell construction. These operators efficiently guide CDCL search by constructing conflict explanation clauses directly related to the sample point, avoiding redundant computations and accelerating conflict resolution.

We first introduce the concepts of sample interval and sample polynomial proposed in [7]. For a polynomial set $F \subseteq \mathbb{Z}[\boldsymbol{x}_{[n]}]$, and a sample point $\boldsymbol{s} \in \mathbb{R}^n$, the *sample interval* of F at $\boldsymbol{s}$ is $\mathtt{s\_interval}(F, x_n, \boldsymbol{s})$ (see Algorithm 1, it is a root symbolic interval containing $\boldsymbol{s}_{[n]}$, where the two boundary functions are w.r.t. $\boldsymbol{x}_{[n]}$ and depend on F); the *sample polynomial* of F at $\boldsymbol{s}$ is $\mathtt{s\_poly}(F, x_n, \boldsymbol{s}) = \{\mathtt{Poly}(g) \mid g \in \mathtt{s\_interval}(F, x_n, \boldsymbol{s})\}$.

Algorithm 1: $\mathtt{s\_interval}$

Input : a polynomial set $F \subseteq \mathbb{Z}[\boldsymbol{x}_{[n]}]$, a variable x_n, and a sample point $\boldsymbol{s} \in \mathbb{R}^n$
Output: a root symbolic interval ϕ such that $s_n \in \phi(\boldsymbol{s}_{[n-1]})$

Compute $\mathtt{Isolate}(F, \boldsymbol{s}_{[n-1]})$
if *there is no real root* **then return** $(-\infty, +\infty)$
suppose we get $\theta_1 < \cdots < \theta_m$ where θ_i is of the form $\mathtt{Root}(f_{j_i}(\boldsymbol{x}_{[n-1]}, x_n), r_i)$ for some $f_{j_i} \in F$ and $r_i > 0$
invList $\leftarrow [(-\infty, \theta_1), [\theta_1, \theta_1], (\theta_1, \theta_2), \ldots, (\theta_m, +\infty)]$
for ϕ *in invList* **do**
  if $s_n \in \phi(\boldsymbol{s}_{[n-1]})$ **then return** ϕ

Definition 5. [7,10] *Let $F \subseteq \mathbb{Z}[\boldsymbol{x}]$ be a set of polynomials, $\boldsymbol{s} \in \mathbb{R}^n$ a sample point and $[\![\theta_l, \theta_u]\!] = \mathtt{s\_interval}(F, x_n, \boldsymbol{s})$. Define*

$$\underset{L}{\mathtt{Proj}}(F, x_n, \boldsymbol{s}) = \bigcup_{f \in F} \{\mathtt{s\_coeff}(f, x_n, \boldsymbol{s}), \mathtt{disc}(f, x_n)\} \cup \bigcup_{\substack{f \in F, \\ g \in \mathtt{s\_poly}(F, \boldsymbol{s}), \\ f \neq g}} \{\mathtt{res}(f, g, x_n)\},$$

$$\begin{aligned}\underset{N}{\mathtt{Proj}}(F, x_n, \boldsymbol{s}) = & \bigcup_{f \in F} \{\mathtt{s\_coeff}(f, x_n, \boldsymbol{s}), \mathtt{disc}(f, x_n)\} \cup \{\mathtt{res}(\mathtt{Poly}(\theta_l), \mathtt{Poly}(\theta_u), x_n)\} \\ & \cup \left\{\mathtt{res}(p, \mathtt{Poly}(\theta_l), x_n) \mid p \in F,\ p(\boldsymbol{s}_{[n-1]}, \alpha) = 0 \textit{ for some } \alpha \leq \theta_l\right\} \\ & \cup \left\{\mathtt{res}(p, \mathtt{Poly}(\theta_u), x_n) \mid p \in F,\ p(\boldsymbol{s}_{[n-1]}, \alpha) = 0 \textit{ for some } \alpha \geq \theta_u\right\}.\end{aligned}$$

It is easy to see that $\texttt{Proj}_N$ presents a more algorithmic refinement, which may avoid more unnecessary resultant computations than $\texttt{Proj}_L$. The following theorem proves the correctness of the projection operators. The *squarefree basis* is a set of polynomials in $\mathbb{Z}[\boldsymbol{x}]$ that are of positive degree, primitive, squarefree and pairwise coprime.

Theorem 2. [7,10] *Let $F \subseteq \mathbb{Z}[\boldsymbol{x}_{[k]}]$ be a finite squarefree basis, $S \subseteq \mathbb{R}^{k-1}$ be a connected set and $\boldsymbol{s}_{[k]} \in \mathbb{R}^k$ be a sample point, where $k \geq 2$. If each polynomial in $\texttt{Proj}_L(F, x_k, \boldsymbol{s}_{[k]})$ ($\texttt{Proj}_N(F, x_k, \boldsymbol{s}_{[k]})$) is order-invariant in S, then each polynomial in F which does not vanish identically on S*

(i) is delineable on S; and

(ii) is order-invariant in $S \times \texttt{s\_interval}(F, x_k, \boldsymbol{s}_{[k]})$.

3 Motivation

In this section, we use a simple example to clarify the intuition of our work. Consider the SMT-NRA formula $\Phi := (f_1 < 0 \vee f_2 < 0) \wedge (f_3 > 0 \vee f_4 > 0)$, where the polynomials in $\mathbb{Z}[z, x, y]$ are

$$\begin{aligned} f_1(z,x,y) &= -8z + 2x + 3y^2, \\ f_2(z,x,y) &= 3z - 5 + x + 3(y-3)^2, \\ f_3(z,x,y) &= 5z + 2y, \\ f_4(z,x,y) &= 30 - x + 8y. \end{aligned} \tag{1}$$

The sample point $\boldsymbol{s} = (1, 1, -2)$ is not a model for Φ, and we aim to construct a conflict region containing $\boldsymbol{s}$ where $f_1, ..., f_4$ are sign-invariant.

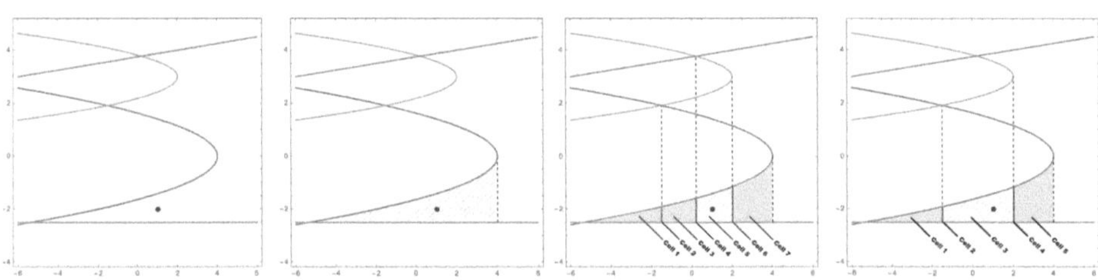

(a) The zero sets of f_1 (blue), f_2 (yellow), f_3 (green), and f_4 (red) are shown on the plane $z = 1$, with the sample point $\boldsymbol{s}$ marked by a dot.

(b) The largest cell (shaded area) containing $\boldsymbol{s}$ is the region above the green curve, below the blue curve and to the left of the dashed vertical line.

(c) McCallum's projection operator $\texttt{Proj}_M$ partitions the largest cell into seven distinct cells, one of which (shaded area) contains $\boldsymbol{s}$.

(d) $\texttt{Proj}_L$ and $\texttt{Proj}_N$ both partition the largest cell into five distinct cells, one of which (shaded area) contains $\boldsymbol{s}$.

Fig. 1. Conflict region construction for the polynomial set $\{f_1, f_2, f_3, f_4\}$ and the sample point $\boldsymbol{s} = (1, 1, -2)$ at the plane $z = 1$. The constructed cells are displayed in the (x, y)-plane (x: horizontal axis, y: vertical axis), with our method produces the largest cell, followed by $\texttt{Proj}_L$ and $\texttt{Proj}_N$ producing the medium cell, and McCallum's projection operator producing the smallest cell.

Given the fixed variable ordering $z \prec x \prec y$. The zero sets of $f_1, ..., f_4$ are shown on the plane $z = 1$ (see Fig. 1a). The cell obtained by McCallum's projection is shown in Fig. 1c while a larger cell obtained by $\texttt{Proj}_L$ or $\texttt{Proj}_N$ is shown in Fig. 1d. Our first observation is that the largest sign-invariant region (Fig. 1b) can be obtained by merging some adjacent cells. For this example, the largest cell (Fig. 1b) can be defined by

$$\mathcal{C} := \{(x, y) \in \mathbb{R}^2 \mid [\texttt{Root}(\texttt{res}(f_1, f_3, y)), 2) < x < \texttt{Root}(\texttt{disc}(f_1, y), 1)] \wedge [\texttt{Root}(f_3, 1) < y < \texttt{Root}(f_1, 1)]\}. \tag{2}$$

Our second observation is that some resultants during the projection process are unnecessary. Figure 2 shows the changes of graphs of $\texttt{Root}(\texttt{disc}(f_1, y), 1)$ and $\texttt{Root}(\texttt{disc}(f_2, y), 1)$ in the (x, y)-plane as z decreases from 1 to $\frac{7}{10}$. We observe that whether the two graphs intersect does not affect the validity of our constructed cell (see (2)). Thus, the resultant of these two discriminants is unnecessary. In contrast, both $\texttt{Proj}_L$ and $\texttt{Proj}_N$ compute this resultant.

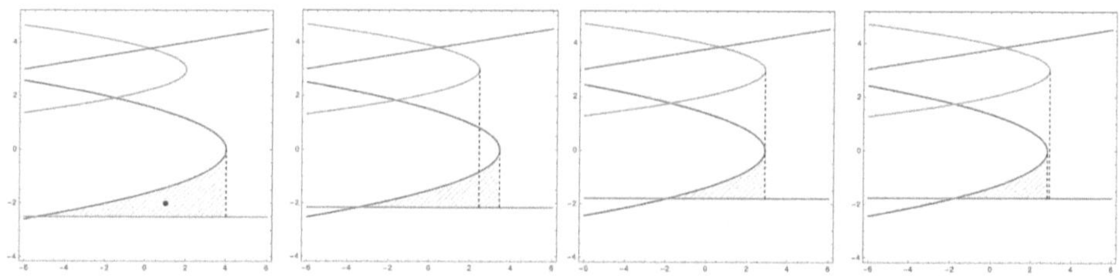

(a) The (x, y)-plane at $z = 1$.

(b) The (x, y)-plane at $z = \frac{6}{7}$.

(c) The (x, y)-plane at $z = \frac{5}{7}$.

(d) The (x, y)-plane at $z = \frac{7}{10}$.

Fig. 2. Dynamic geometric evolution of $\texttt{Root}(\texttt{disc}(f_1, y), 1)$ (dashed), $\texttt{Root}(\texttt{disc}(f_2, y), 1)$ (dashed) and the largest cell (shaded area) containing $\boldsymbol{s}$ in the (x, y)-plane (x: horizontal axis, y: vertical axis) as z decreases from 1 to $\frac{7}{10}$. The line $\texttt{Root}(\texttt{disc}(f_1, y), 1)$ is tangent to the zero set of f_1 (blue), and the line $\texttt{Root}(\texttt{disc}(f_2, y), 1)$ is tangent to the zero set of f_2 (yellow) for any fixed z. The dashed lines coincide at $z = \frac{5}{7}$, indicating a change in the ordering of root functions.

4 A New Projection Method

4.1 Pre-Cell

We use the notation `SingleCellProj` to refer to a fixed single-cell projection operator (*e.g.*, $\texttt{Proj}_L$ or $\texttt{Proj}_N$) and fix this choice henceforth.

Definition 6 (Single-Cell Construction). [7,10] *Given a polynomial set $P_n \subset \mathbb{R}[\boldsymbol{x}_{[n]}]$, and a sample point $\boldsymbol{s} \in \mathbb{R}^n$. The* single-cell construction *process using* `SingleCellProj` *proceeds as follows.*

$$\phi_n = \texttt{s\_interval}(P_n, x_n, \boldsymbol{s}_{[n]}), \qquad P_{n-1} = \texttt{SingleCellProj}(P_n, \boldsymbol{s}_{[n]}), \tag{3}$$

$$\phi_{n-1} = \texttt{s\_interval}(P_{n-1}, x_{n-1}, \boldsymbol{s}_{[n-1]}), \quad P_{n-2} = \texttt{SingleCellProj}(P_{n-1}, \boldsymbol{s}_{[n-1]}), \tag{4}$$

$$\ldots, \qquad\qquad \ldots,$$

$$\phi_1 = \texttt{s\_interval}(P_1, x_1, \boldsymbol{s}_{[1]}), \qquad P_0 = \texttt{SingleCellProj}(P_1, \boldsymbol{s}_{[1]}), \tag{5}$$

where the root symbolic interval ϕ_i *is on level* i $(i = 1, \ldots, n)$ *and the polynomial set* $P_j \subseteq \mathbb{R}[\boldsymbol{x}_{[j]}]$ $(j = 0, \ldots, n-1)$*. The constructed cell* $\phi_1 \times \cdots \times \phi_n$ *is denoted by* $\mathcal{C}(P_n, \boldsymbol{s}_{[n]})$*, which contains* $\boldsymbol{s}_{[n]}$ *and ensures sign invariance for all polynomials in* P_n*.*

Based on our observations in Sect. 3, our new method will insert some steps into single-cell construction for merging cells and detecting unnecessary resultants. The merging process involves unions and intersections of regions represented during intermediate steps of single-cell construction. We therefore introduce the term *pre-cell* to denote these intermediate regions.

Definition 7 (Pre-Cell). *A* pre-cell *is a finite dimensional connected set generated by the following rules.*

(i) For a polynomial set $P_k \subseteq \mathbb{R}[\boldsymbol{x}_{[k]}]$ *and a sample point* $\boldsymbol{s}_{[k]} \in \mathbb{R}^k$, $\mathcal{C}(P_k, \boldsymbol{s}_{[k]})$ *(see Definition 6) is a* (k, k)-proj pre-cell*;*

(ii) Let C *be a* (k, i)*-proj pre-cell and* ϕ_{i+1} *a root symbolic interval on level* $i + 1$*. If* C *is consistent with* ϕ_{i+1}*, then*

$$C \times \phi_{i+1} := \{\boldsymbol{s}_{[i+1]} \in \mathbb{R}^{i+1} \mid \boldsymbol{s}_{[i]} \in C, s_{i+1} \in \phi_{i+1}(\boldsymbol{s}_{[i]})\}$$

is a $(k, i + 1)$-proj pre-cell*, where* $i = k, k + 1, \ldots$*.*

Remark 1. Given a polynomial set $P_n \subset \mathbb{R}[\boldsymbol{x}_{[n]}]$ and a sample point $\boldsymbol{s} \in \mathbb{R}^n$, the followings are all pre-cells $\mathcal{C}(P_{n-1}, \boldsymbol{s}_{[n-1]}) \times \phi_n, \mathcal{C}(P_{n-2}, \boldsymbol{s}_{[n-2]}) \times \phi_{n-1} \times \phi_n, \ldots$. These pre-cells are all equal to the cell $\mathcal{C}(P_n, \boldsymbol{s}_{[n]}) := \phi_1 \times \cdots \times \phi_n$ but represent different intermediate computing results of single-cell construction.

Remark 2 (Single-Cell Construction via Pre-Cells). The single-cell construction process described in Definition 6 can be characterized in terms of pre-cells. Given a polynomial set $P_n \subset \mathbb{R}[\boldsymbol{x}_{[n]}]$ and a sample point $\boldsymbol{s} \in \mathbb{R}^n$. Suppose $\mathcal{C}$ is the target cell that we aim to determine its range (*i.e.*, root symbolic interval) on each level. In the following steps, we generate a sequence of pre-cells that are provably equal to $\mathcal{C}$.

Step 0. We initialize $\mathcal{C}$ with (n, n)-proj pre-cell $\mathcal{C}(P_n, \boldsymbol{s}_{[n]})$, which is just a notation now, and we have no other information about this cell except that polynomials in P_n maintain order-invariance in it, and $\boldsymbol{s}$ is in it.

Step 1. The first projection (via (3)) updates $\mathcal{C}$ with an $(n - 1, n)$-proj pre-cell $\mathcal{C}(P_{n-1}, \boldsymbol{s}_{[n-1]}) \times \phi_n$, establishing the cell's range for variable x_n.

Step 2. The second projection (via (4)) updates $\mathcal{C}$ with an $(n-2,n)$-proj pre-cell $\mathcal{C}(P_{n-2}, \boldsymbol{s}_{[n-2]}) \times \phi_{n-1} \times \phi_n$, establishing the cell's range for variables x_{n-1} and x_n.

......

Step $\boldsymbol{n}$. The n-th projection (via (5)) updates $\mathcal{C}$ with a $(0,n)$-proj pre-cell $\phi_1 \times \cdots \times \phi_n$, establishing the cell's range for variables $x_1, x_2, \ldots, x_n$.

Example 2. Using the motivating example from Sect. 3 with the polynomial set $P_3 = \{f_1, f_2, f_3, f_4\}$ (defined in (1)) and sample point $\boldsymbol{s}_{[3]} = (1,1,-2)$ under variable ordering $z \prec x \prec y$, we demonstrate the single-cell construction via pre-cells. We start with the pre-cell $\mathcal{C} = \mathcal{C}(P_3, (1,1,-2))$. If we take `SingleCellProj` as $\texttt{Proj}_N$, then by the projection on the first level (corresponding to y),

$$\mathcal{C} = \mathcal{C}(P_2, (1,1)) \times (\texttt{Root}(f_3, 1), \texttt{Root}(f_1, 1)),$$

where $P_2 = \texttt{SingleCellProj}(P_3, (1,1,-2))$, and $\mathcal{C}$ is in the state of Fig. 1d; by the projection on the second level (corresponding to x),

$$\begin{aligned}\mathcal{C} = \mathcal{C}(P_1, (1)) &\times (\texttt{Root}(\texttt{res}(f_1, f_2, y), 2), \texttt{Root}(\texttt{disc}(f_2, y), 1)) \\ &\times (\texttt{Root}(f_3(z,x,y), 1), \texttt{Root}(f_1(z,x,y), 1)),\end{aligned} \tag{6}$$

where $P_1 = \texttt{SingleCellProj}(P_2, (1,1))$; and by the projection on the third level (corresponding to z), we finally get

$$\begin{aligned}\mathcal{C} = (5/7, 25/17) &\times (\texttt{Root}(\texttt{res}(f_1, f_2, y), 2), \texttt{Root}(\texttt{disc}(f_2, y), 1)) \\ &\times (\texttt{Root}(f_3(z,x,y), 1), \texttt{Root}(f_1(z,x,y), 1)).\end{aligned}$$

Weaker polynomial constraints (*i.e.*, smaller polynomial sets) generate larger cells, and vice versa. This relationship is formally described by the following property.

Property 1. For polynomial sets $P^1, P^2 \subseteq \mathbb{R}[\boldsymbol{x}_{[n]}]$ and a sample point $\boldsymbol{s} \in \mathbb{R}^n$, if $P^1 \subseteq P^2$, then $\mathcal{C}(P^2, \boldsymbol{s}) \subseteq \mathcal{C}(P^1, \boldsymbol{s})$.

The next property shows that for any polynomial set, sample points taken from the same $(k-1,k)$-proj pre-cell generate identical pre-cells.

Property 2. Let $F \in \mathbb{R}[\boldsymbol{x}_{[k]}]$ be a set of polynomials on level k and $\boldsymbol{s}_{[k]} \in \mathbb{R}^k$ a sample point. If $\phi_k = \texttt{s\_interval}(F, \boldsymbol{s}_{[k]})$ and $P_{k-1} = \texttt{SingleCellProj}(F, \boldsymbol{s}_{[k]})$, then for any sample point $\boldsymbol{s}^*_{[k]} \in \mathcal{C}(P_{k-1}, \boldsymbol{s}_{[k-1]}) \times \phi_k$, $\texttt{s\_interval}(F, \boldsymbol{s}^*_{[k]}) = \phi_k$ and $\texttt{SingleCellProj}(F, \boldsymbol{s}^*_{[k]}) = P_{k-1}$.

Recall that in single-cell construction, after the projection of a polynomial set F with the sample point $\boldsymbol{s}_{[n]}$ on variables x_n and x_{n-1}, we obtain pre-cells with a common root symbolic interval ϕ_n and a common sample point $\boldsymbol{s}_{[n-2]}$. In order to merge some of these pre-cells to obtain a lager pre-cell containing $\boldsymbol{s}_{[n]}$, we consider the union and intersection operations of $(n-2,n-1)$-proj pre-cells

$$\begin{aligned} \mathcal{C}^1 &= \mathcal{C}(P_{n-2}^1, \boldsymbol{s}_{[n-2]}) \times \phi_{n-1}^1, \\ \mathcal{C}^2 &= \mathcal{C}(P_{n-2}^2, \boldsymbol{s}_{[n-2]}) \times \phi_{n-1}^2, \\ &\cdots \\ \mathcal{C}^m &= \mathcal{C}(P_{n-2}^m, \boldsymbol{s}_{[n-2]}) \times \phi_{n-1}^m. \end{aligned} \tag{7}$$

The union operation for pre-cells is only defined for pairs of adjacent pre-cells. Two pre-cells $\mathcal{C}^1$ and $\mathcal{C}^2$ are said to be *adjacent* if the root symbolic intervals ϕ_{n-1}^1 and ϕ_{n-1}^2 are adjacent.

Definition 8 (Union of Pre-Cells). *Suppose $\mathcal{C}^1$ and $\mathcal{C}^2$ are pre-cells in (7), where $\phi_{n-1}^1 = [\![^1\theta_1^1, \theta]\!]^1$ and $\phi_{n-1}^2 = [\![^2\theta, \theta_2^2]\!]^2$ are adjacent root symbolic intervals. The* union *of pre-cells $\mathcal{C}^1$ and $\mathcal{C}^2$ is defined as*

$$\mathcal{C}^1 \cup_c \mathcal{C}^2 := \mathcal{C}(P_{n-2}^1 \cup P_{n-2}^2, \boldsymbol{s}_{[n-2]}) \times \phi_{n-1},$$

where $\phi_{n-1} = \phi_{n-1}^1 \cup \phi_{n-1}^2 = [\![^1\theta_1^1, \theta_2^2]\!]^2$.

Theorem 3. *If $\mathcal{C}^1$ and $\mathcal{C}^2$ are pre-cells in (7), where ϕ_{n-1}^1 and ϕ_{n-1}^2 are adjacent root symbolic intervals, then $\mathcal{C}^1 \cup_c \mathcal{C}^2$ is an $(n-2, n-1)$-proj pre-cell contained in $\mathcal{C}^1 \cup \mathcal{C}^2$.*

Proof. It follows from Definition 8 that $\mathcal{C}^1 \cup_c \mathcal{C}^2$ is an $(n-2, n-1)$-proj pre-cell. For any $\boldsymbol{x}_{[n]} \in \mathcal{C}^1 \cup_c \mathcal{C}^2$, we have $\boldsymbol{x}_{[n-1]} \in \mathcal{C}(P_{n-1}^1 \cup P_{n-1}^2, \boldsymbol{s}_{[n-2]})$, and $x_n \in \phi_{n-1} = \phi_{n-1}^1 \cup \phi_{n-1}^2$. By Property 1, $\mathcal{C}(P_{n-1}^1 \cup P_{n-1}^2, \boldsymbol{s}_{[n-2]}) \subseteq \mathcal{C}(P_{n-1}^i, \boldsymbol{s}_{[n-2]})$, where $i = 1, 2$. So, if $x_n \in \phi_{n-1}^i$, then $\boldsymbol{x}_{[n]} \in \mathcal{C}^i$. Therefore, $\mathcal{C}^1 \cup_c \mathcal{C}^2 \subseteq \mathcal{C}^1 \cup \mathcal{C}^2$.

Example 3. Using the example from Sect. 3, we show the union of pre-cells from an intermediate step of our method, which are

$$\begin{aligned} \mathcal{C}^3 &= \mathcal{C}(P, (1, 1, -2), \boldsymbol{s}^3) = \mathcal{C}(P^3, (1)) \times (\texttt{Root}(\texttt{res}(f_1, f_2, y), 2), \texttt{Root}(\texttt{disc}(f_2, y), 1)), \\ \mathcal{C}^4 &= \mathcal{C}(P, (1, 1, -2), \boldsymbol{s}^4) = \mathcal{C}(P^4, (1)) \times [\texttt{Root}(\texttt{disc}(f_2, y), 1), \texttt{Root}(\texttt{disc}(f_2, y), 1)], \end{aligned}$$

where the pre-cell $\mathcal{C}^i$ and the sample point $\boldsymbol{s}^i$ $(1 \le i \le 5)$ are shown in Fig. 3a. Since the two pre-cells are adjacent, their union is well-defined, which is

$$\mathcal{C}^3 \cup_c \mathcal{C}^4 = \mathcal{C}(P^3 \cup P^4, (1)) \times (\texttt{Root}(\texttt{res}(f_1, f_2, y), 2), \texttt{Root}(\texttt{disc}(f_2, y), 1)].$$

When computing the union of pre-cells $\mathcal{C}^1, \ldots, \mathcal{C}^5$, we operate union on pairs of them from left to right, *i.e.*, $(((\mathcal{C}^1 \cup_c \mathcal{C}^2) \cup_c \mathcal{C}^3) \cup_c \mathcal{C}_4) \cup_c \mathcal{C}^5$, which results in

$$\mathcal{C}(P^1 \cup_c P^2 \cup_c \cdots \cup_c P^5, (1)) \times (\texttt{Root}(\texttt{res}(f_1, f_3, y), 1), \texttt{Root}(\texttt{disc}(f_1, y), 1)).$$

(a) The polynomials f_1, f_2, f_3, f_4 and sample points. (b) The bounary polynomials f_1, f_3, the non-boundary polynomial f_2 and sample points.

Fig. 3. The largest cell encompasses five adjacent pre-cells $\mathcal{C}^1, \ldots, \mathcal{C}^5$ (left to right) in the (x, y)-plane at $z = 1$, and their root symbolic intervals of variable x are $\phi_2^1 = (\texttt{Root}(\texttt{res}(f_1, f_3, y), 2), \texttt{Root}(\texttt{res}(f_1, f_2, y), 2))$, $\phi_2^2 = [\texttt{Root}(\texttt{res}(f_1, f_2, y), 2), \texttt{Root}(\texttt{res}(f_1, f_2, y), 2)]$, $\phi_2^3 = (\texttt{Root}(\texttt{res}(f_1, f_2, y), 2), \texttt{Root}(\texttt{disc}(f_2, y), 1))$, $\phi_2^4 = [\texttt{Root}(\texttt{disc}(f_2, y), 1), \texttt{Root}(\texttt{disc}(f_2, y), 1)]$ and $\phi_2^5 = (\texttt{Root}(\texttt{disc}(f_2, y), 1), \texttt{Root}(\texttt{disc}(f_1, y), 1))$, respectively. Each of the pre-cells contains a representative sample point $\boldsymbol{s}^1, \ldots, \boldsymbol{s}^5$ (blue dots, left to right).

Definition 9 (Intersection of Pre-Cells). *Suppose $\mathcal{C}^1, \mathcal{C}^2, \ldots, \mathcal{C}^m$ are pre-cells in* (7) *and $[\![^1\theta_l^1, \theta_u^1]\!]^1, \ldots, [\![^m\theta_l^m, \theta_u^m]\!]^m$ are root symbolic intervals. Denote by $F = \{\texttt{Poly}(\theta_l^i), \texttt{Poly}(\theta_u^i) \mid 1 \leq i \leq m\}$. The* intersection *of pre-cells $\mathcal{C}^1, \mathcal{C}^2, \ldots, \mathcal{C}^m$ is defined as*

$$\mathcal{C}^1 \cap_c \mathcal{C}^2 \cap_c \cdots \cap_c \mathcal{C}^m := \mathcal{C}(P_{n-2}^1 \cup \cdots \cup P_{n-2}^m \cup G, \boldsymbol{s}_{[n-2]}) \times [\![\theta_l, \theta_u]\!],$$

where the polynomial set

$$\begin{aligned} G = & \bigcup_{f \in F} \{\texttt{s\_coeff}(f, x_n, \boldsymbol{s}), \texttt{disc}(f, x_n)\} \\ & \cup \{\texttt{res}(\texttt{Poly}(\theta_l^i), \texttt{Poly}(\theta_l), x_n) \mid \theta_l^i \neq \theta_l, 1 \leq i \leq m\} \\ & \cup \{\texttt{res}(\texttt{Poly}(\theta_u^i), \texttt{Poly}(\theta_u), x_n) \mid \theta_u^i \neq \theta_u, 1 \leq i \leq m\} \end{aligned}$$

and the root symbolic interval $[\![\theta_l, \theta_u]\!]$ satisfies
(i) $\exists 1 \leq i \leq m, \theta_l = \theta_l^i$;
(ii) $\exists 1 \leq j \leq m, \theta_u = \theta_u^j$; *and*
(iii) $[\![(\theta_l(\boldsymbol{s}_{[k-2]}), \theta_u(\boldsymbol{s}_{[k-2]})]\!] = \bigcap_{i=1}^m [\![^i\theta_l^i(\boldsymbol{s}_{[k-2]}), \theta_u^i(\boldsymbol{s}_{[k-2]})]\!]^i$.

Theorem 4. *If $\mathcal{C}^1, \mathcal{C}^2, \ldots, \mathcal{C}^m$ are pre-cells in* (7)*, then $\mathcal{C}^1 \cap_c \mathcal{C}^2 \cap_c \cdots \cap_c \mathcal{C}^m$ is an $(n-2, n-1)$-proj pre-cell contained in $\mathcal{C}^1 \cap \mathcal{C}^2 \cap \cdots \cap \mathcal{C}^m$.*

Proof. By Property 1, $\mathcal{C}' := \mathcal{C}(P_{n-2}^1 \cup \cdots P_{n-2}^m \cup G, \boldsymbol{s}_{[n-2]}) \subseteq \mathcal{C}(G, \boldsymbol{s}_{[n-2]})$, thus $\mathcal{C}'$ is consistent with $[\![\theta_l, \theta_u]\!]$. From Definition 9, it follows that $\mathcal{C}^1 \cap_c \mathcal{C}^2 \cap_c \cdots \cap_c \mathcal{C}^m$ is an $(n-2, n-1)$-proj pre-cell. For each $1 \leq i \leq m$, Property 1 guarantees $\mathcal{C}' \subseteq \mathcal{C}(P_{n-2}^i, \boldsymbol{s}_{[n-2]})$, and in $\mathcal{C}(G, \boldsymbol{s}_{[n-2]})$, G is order-invariant, which ensures that $[\![\theta_l, \theta_u]\!] \subseteq [\![^i\theta_l^i, \theta_u^i]\!]^i$ always holds. Consequently, we have the inclusion $\mathcal{C}' \times [\![\theta_l, \theta_u]\!] \subseteq \mathcal{C}^i$, and thus $\mathcal{C}' \times [\![\theta_l, \theta_u]\!] \subseteq \mathcal{C}^1 \cap \cdots \cap \mathcal{C}^m$.

4.2 Main Algorithm

Our main algorithm for conflict region construction targets the following problem with the stated goal. Our projection method differs from conventional single-cell construction by simultaneously reducing two variables per projection operation.

Problem (P0): Given a (k,n)-proj pre-cell $\mathcal{C}(F_k, \boldsymbol{s}_{[k]}) \times \phi_{k+1} \times \cdots \times \phi_n$, where integers $2 \leq k \leq n$. Construct a $(k-2,n)$-proj pre-cell $\mathcal{C}^M := \mathcal{C}(F_{k-2}, \boldsymbol{s}_{[k-2]}) \times \phi_{k-1} \times \cdots \times \phi_n$ containing $\boldsymbol{s}_{[k]}$ such that all polynomials in F_k are order-invariant in $\mathcal{C}^M$.

Our goal is to compute a "maximal" pre-cell that solves problem P0. Here, "maximal" does not imply maximality in the n-dimensional space, but rather refers to a pre-cell that is maximal within its two-dimensional subspace when the first $k-2$ dimensions are fixed (*i.e.*, under the constraint $\boldsymbol{x}_{[k-2]} = \boldsymbol{s}_{[k-2]}$). To remove unnecessary algebraic operations, we introduce the concepts of boundary polynomial and non-boundary polynomial. For a polynomial set $\Theta \subseteq \mathbb{Z}[\boldsymbol{x}_{[k]}]$ and a sample point $\boldsymbol{s}_{[k]} \in \mathbb{R}^k$, if $[\![\theta_l, \theta_u]\!] = \texttt{s\_interval}(\Theta, x_k, \boldsymbol{s}_{[k]})$, then $\texttt{Poly}(\theta_l)$ and $\texttt{Poly}(\theta_u)$ are said to be *boundary polynomials*, other polynomials in Θ are said to be *non-boundary polynomials*.

Algorithm 2: BigCellProj

Input : a connected (k,n)-proj pre-cell $\mathcal{C}(F_k, \boldsymbol{s}_{[k]}) \times \phi_{k+1} \times \cdots \times \phi_n$, where $2 \leq k \leq n$
Output: a connected $(k-2,n)$-proj pre-cell $\mathcal{C}(F_{k-2}, \boldsymbol{s}_{[k-2]}) \times \phi_{k-1} \times \cdots \times \phi_n$ wherein every polynomial in F_k is order-invariant

1 $G \leftarrow \texttt{Factors}(F_k)$
2 $G_\perp \leftarrow G \cap \mathbb{R}[\boldsymbol{x}_{[k-1]}]$
3 $\mathcal{C}_\perp = \mathcal{C}(\texttt{SingleCellProj}(G_\perp), \boldsymbol{s}_{[k-1]}) \times \texttt{s\_interval}(G_\perp, \boldsymbol{s}_{[k-1]})$
4 $G \leftarrow G \setminus G_\perp$
5 $\phi_k := [\![\theta_l, \theta_u]\!] \leftarrow \texttt{s\_interval}(G, \boldsymbol{s}_{[k]})$
6 $\mathcal{C}^B \leftarrow \texttt{BoundaryProjector}(\phi_k, \boldsymbol{s}_{[k]})$
7 $i \leftarrow 0$
8 **for** $g \in G \setminus \{\texttt{Poly}(\theta_l), \texttt{Poly}(\theta_u)\}$ **do**
9     $i++$
10     $\mathcal{C}_i \leftarrow \texttt{NonBoundaryProjector}(\phi_k, g, \boldsymbol{s}_{[k]}, \mathcal{C}^B)$
11 $\mathcal{C}(F_{k-2}, \boldsymbol{s}_{[k-2]}) \times \phi_{k-1} \leftarrow \mathcal{C}_\perp \cap_c \mathcal{C}^B \cap_c \mathcal{C}_1 \cap_c \cdots \cap_c \mathcal{C}_m$
12 **return** $\mathcal{C}(F_{k-2}, \boldsymbol{s}_{[k-2]}) \times \phi_{k-1} \times \cdots \times \phi_n$

Algorithm 2 computes the target pre-cell $\mathcal{C}^M$ by the following steps. This procedure can be considered as two steps in Remark 2.

1. The factor polynomials of F_k on level $k-1$ are projected onto level $k-2$ using `SingleCellProj`, forming a $(k-2, k-1)$-proj pre-cell $\mathcal{C}_\perp$. In steps 2-4, we only need to consider factor polynomials of F_k not on level $k-1$.
2. The set of polynomials corresponding to real root functions of F_k is partitioned into boundary polynomials and non-boundary polynomials. Therefore, the problem is divided into a boundary polynomial subproblem (P1) and several non-boundary polynomial subproblems (P2's). The boundary polynomial subproblem involves all boundary polynomials, while the non-boundary polynomial subproblem involves the boundary polynomials and one non-boundary polynomial.

3. The boundary polynomial subproblem w.r.t. ϕ_k and $\boldsymbol{s}_{[k]}$ (described in Sect. 4.2) is solved by Algorithm 3, yielding a $(k-2, k-1)$-proj pre-cell $\mathcal{C}^B$.
4. For each non-boundary polynomial $g \in G := \texttt{Factors}(F_k)$, the non-boundary polynomial subproblem w.r.t. ϕ_k, g and $\boldsymbol{s}_{[k]}$ (described in Sect. 4.3) is solved by Algorithm 4, yielding a $(k-2, k-1)$-proj pre-cell $\mathcal{C}_i$ $(i = 1, 2, \dots, m)$.
5. The pre-cell $\mathcal{C}^M$ is constructed by merging pre-cells from all subproblems through the intersection operation $\mathcal{C}(F_{k-2}, \boldsymbol{s}_{[k-2]}) \times \phi_{k-1} := \mathcal{C}_\perp \cap_c \mathcal{C}^B \cap_c \mathcal{C}_1 \cap_c \cdots \cap_c \mathcal{C}_{|G|-2}$, and augmenting the result with the root symbolic intervals $\phi_k, \dots, \phi_n$. This forms the pre-cell $\mathcal{C}^M = \mathcal{C}(F_{k-2}, \boldsymbol{s}_{[k-2]}) \times \phi_{k-1} \times \cdots \times \phi_n$.

Boundary Polynomial Subproblem (P1): Given a root symbolic interval $\phi_k := [\![\theta_l, \theta_u]\!]$ on level k, and a sample point $\boldsymbol{s}_{[k]} \in \mathbb{R}^k$. Construct a $(k-2, k-1)$-proj pre-cell $\mathcal{C}^B$ containing $\boldsymbol{s}_{[k]}$ with the form $\mathcal{C}^B = \mathcal{C}(P, \boldsymbol{s}_{[k-2]}) \times \phi_{k-1}$, where $P \subseteq \mathbb{R}[\boldsymbol{x}_{[k-2]}]$ is a polynomial set, such that $\texttt{Poly}(\theta_l)$ and $\texttt{Poly}(\theta_u)$ are order-invariant in $\mathcal{C}^B \times \phi_k$.

Algorithm 3 solves P1 through the same steps as in Remark 2. In fact, the boundary polynomial subproblem is an intermediate step of a specific single-cell construction. Thus, the correctness of Algorithm 3 is clear.

Algorithm 3: BoundaryProjector

Input : a root symbolic interval $\phi_k := [\![\theta_l, \theta_u]\!]$ on level k, and a sample point $\boldsymbol{s}_{[k]} \in \mathbb{R}^k$
Output: a $(k-2, k-1)$-proj pre-cell $\mathcal{C}^B$ such that $\texttt{Poly}(\theta_l)$ and $\texttt{Poly}(\theta_u)$ are order-invariant in $\mathcal{C}^B \times \phi_k$

$p_1 \leftarrow \texttt{Poly}(\theta_l)$, $p_2 \leftarrow \texttt{Poly}(\theta_u)$
$G_1 \leftarrow \texttt{SingleCellProj}(\{\texttt{Poly}(\theta_l), \texttt{Poly}(\theta_u)\}, \boldsymbol{s}_{[k]})$
$G_2 \leftarrow \texttt{SingleCellProj}(G_1, \boldsymbol{s}_{[k-1]})$
$\mathcal{C}^B \leftarrow \mathcal{C}(G_2, \boldsymbol{s}_{[k-2]}) \times \texttt{s\_interval}(G_2, x_{k-1}, \boldsymbol{s}_{[k-1]})$
return $\mathcal{C}^B$

Example 4. Using the example from Sect. 3, the cell's root symbolic interval corresponding to y is $\phi_3 = (\texttt{Root}(f_3, 1), \texttt{Root}(f_1, 1))$, which implies f_1 and f_3 are boudary polynomials, while f_2 and f_4 are non-boundary polynomials. Therefore, our method divides the P0 for the input $\mathcal{C}(\{f_1, f_2, f_3, f_4\}, \boldsymbol{s})$ into three subproblems, which are (i) P1 for the input $(\phi_3, \boldsymbol{s})$ (suppose the answer to it is $\mathcal{C}^B$), (ii) P2 for the input $(\phi_3, f_2, \boldsymbol{s}, \mathcal{C}^B)$, and (iii) P2 for the input $(\phi_3, f_4, \boldsymbol{s}, \mathcal{C}^B)$.

4.3 Projection of Non-Boundary Polynomials

Non-Boundary Polynomial Subproblem (P2): Given a root symbolic interval $\phi_k := [\![\theta_l, \theta_u]\!]$ on level k, a polynomial g (distinct from $\texttt{Poly}(\theta_l)$ and $\texttt{Poly}(\theta_u)$), and a sample point $\boldsymbol{s}_{[k]} \in \mathbb{R}^k$. Suppose $\mathcal{C}^B$ is the $(k-2, k-1)$-proj pre-cell obtained from solving P1 for the input ϕ_k and $\boldsymbol{s}_{[k]}$. Construct a $(k-2, k-1)$-proj pre-cell $\mathcal{C}^N$ such that $\mathcal{C}^{BN} := (\mathcal{C}^B \cap \mathcal{C}^N) \times \phi_k$ is a set containing $\boldsymbol{s}_{[k]}$, and g, $\texttt{Poly}(\theta_l)$ and $\texttt{Poly}(\theta_u)$ are order-invariant in $\mathcal{C}^{BN}$.

Algorithm 4: NonBoundaryProjector

Input : a root symbolic interval $\phi_k = [\![\theta_l, \theta_u]\!]$ on level k, a polynomial $g \in \mathbb{R}[\boldsymbol{x}_{[k]}]$, and a sample point $\boldsymbol{s}_{[k]} \in \mathbb{R}^k$

Output: a $(k-2, k-1)$-proj pre-cell $\mathcal{C}$ such that g is order-invariant in the pre-cell $(\mathcal{C}^B \cap \mathcal{C}) \times \phi_k$, where $\mathcal{C}^B = \texttt{BoundaryProjector}(\phi_k, \boldsymbol{s}_{[k]})$

1 $p_1 \leftarrow \texttt{Poly}(\theta_l)$, $p_2 \leftarrow \texttt{Poly}(\theta_u)$
2 $P \leftarrow \texttt{FullCellProj}(\{p_1, p_2, g\}, \boldsymbol{s}_{[k]}) \setminus \texttt{SingleCellProj}(\{p_1, p_2\}, \boldsymbol{s}_{[k]})$
3 $sampleList \leftarrow \texttt{AdjacentCellSampler}(\{p_1, p_2, g\}, P, \boldsymbol{s}_{[k]}, \mathcal{C}^B \times \phi_k)$
4 **for** $\boldsymbol{s}^*_{[k]} \in sampleList$ **do**
5 $\quad G_1 \leftarrow \texttt{SingleCellProj}(\{g\}, \boldsymbol{s}^*_{[k]}) \setminus \texttt{SingleCellProj}(\{p_1, p_2\}, \boldsymbol{s}_{[k]})$
6 $\quad G_2 \leftarrow \texttt{SingleCellProj}(G_1, \boldsymbol{s}^*_{[k-1]})$
7 $\quad \mathcal{C}^* \leftarrow \mathcal{C}(G_2, \boldsymbol{s}_{[k-2]}) \times \texttt{s\_interval}(G_2, \boldsymbol{s}_{[k-1]})$
8 $\quad$ **if** $\mathcal{C}$ *is undefined* **then** $\mathcal{C} \leftarrow \mathcal{C}^*$
9 $\quad$ **else** $\mathcal{C} \leftarrow \mathcal{C} \cup_c \mathcal{C}^*$
10 **return** $\mathcal{C}$

Our goal is to compute a "maximal" pre-cell which is an answer to P2, where maximality follows the description in Sect. 4.2. The procedure in Algorithm 4 computes $\mathcal{C}^N$ through the following steps.

1. Detect mergeable adjacent cells and extract representative sample points (Sect. 4.4).
2. For each sample point, project the polynomial set $\{p_1, p_2, g\}$ (*i.e.*, the boundary polynomials with one non-boundary polynomial) at the first level, and remove duplicates from it that appear in the first-level projection of the boundary polynomial subproblem (Algorithm 3, line 3); and then project G_1 at the second level to obtain the polynomial set $G_2 \subseteq \mathbb{R}[\boldsymbol{x}_{[k-2]}]$, defining a pre-cell $\mathcal{C}^*$.
3. The set $\mathcal{C}^N$ is constructed by merging adjacent pre-cells $\mathcal{C}^*$'s through the union operation.

Example 5. Using the motivating example from Sect. 3, we consider the subproblem P2 for the input $(\phi_3, f_2, \boldsymbol{s}, \mathcal{C}^B \times \phi_3)$, where $\phi_3 = (\texttt{Root}(f_3, 1), \texttt{Root}(f_1, 1))$, see Fig. 3b. Suppose $\boldsymbol{s}^1, \ldots, \boldsymbol{s}^5$ (defined in Fig. 3a) are sample point from all adjacent cells detected by Algorithm 5. As a result, we obtain the cell $\mathcal{C}(P, (1)) \times (\texttt{Root}(\texttt{res}(f_1, f_3, y), 1),\ \texttt{Root}(\texttt{disc}(f_1, y), 1))$.

Theorem 5. *Let $\phi_k := [\![\theta_l, \theta_u]\!]$ be a root symbolic interval on level k, $g \in \mathbb{R}[\boldsymbol{x}_{[k]}]$ and $\boldsymbol{s}_{[k]} \in \mathbb{R}^k$ a sample point. Suppose $\mathcal{C}^B = \texttt{BoundaryProjector}(\phi_k, \boldsymbol{s}_{[k]})$, $\mathcal{C}^N = \texttt{NonBoundaryProjector}(\phi_k, g, \boldsymbol{s}_{[k]})$, and $C^{BN} = (\mathcal{C}^B \cap \mathcal{C}^N) \times \phi_k$, then*
(i) $\mathcal{C}^N$ is a $(k-2, k-1)$-proj pre-cell; and
(ii) $g, \texttt{Poly}(\theta_l)$ and $\texttt{Poly}(\theta_u)$ are order-invariant in set $\mathcal{C}^{BN}$.

Proof. We begin by proving that $\mathcal{C}^N$ is a $(k-2, k-1)$-proj pre-cell. The set $\mathcal{C}^*$ constructed in line 8 is an intermediate result of the first step of single-cell construction of the polynomial set $G_1 \subseteq \mathbb{R}[\boldsymbol{x}_{[k-1]}]$ and the sample point $\boldsymbol{s}_{[k-1]}$, hence $\mathcal{C}^*$ is a $(k-2, k-1)$-proj pre-cell. Property (iii) of Algorithm 5 ensures that the pre-cell $\mathcal{C}$ on the right-hand side of line 9 is adjacent to $\mathcal{C}^*$, making their well-defined union possible. The closure of pre-cells under the $\cup_c$ operation then guarantees that $\mathcal{C}$ in line 10 is a $(k-2, k-1)$-proj pre-cell, thereby ensuring that $\mathcal{C}^N$ forms a $(k-2, k-1)$-proj pre-cell.

Next, we show the order-invariance of $g, p_1 := \texttt{Poly}(\theta_l)$ and $p_2 := \texttt{Poly}(\theta_u)$ in $\mathcal{C}^{BN}$. Property (v) of Algorithm 5 ensures $\boldsymbol{s}^*_{[k]} \in \mathcal{C}^B \times \phi_k$, by which Property 2 indicates that polynomials in $\texttt{SingleCellProj}(\{p_1, p_2\}, \boldsymbol{s}^*_{[k]})$ are order-invariant in $\mathcal{C}^B \times \phi_k$; Theorem 2 further guarantees polynomials in G_1 are order-invariant in $\mathcal{C}^*$. Consequently, $\texttt{SingleCellProj}(\{p_1, p_2, g\}, \boldsymbol{s}^*_{[k]}) = G_1 \cup \texttt{SingleCellProj}(\{p_1, p_2\}, \boldsymbol{s}_{[k]})$ is order-invariant in $\mathcal{C}^B \cap \mathcal{C}^*$, so $g, p1, p2$ are delineable over $\mathcal{C}^B \cap \mathcal{C}^*$. Since property (ii) of Algorithm 5 implies $\texttt{s\_interval}(\{p1, p2, g\}, \boldsymbol{s}^*_{[k]}) = \phi_k$, we obtain that g, p_1, p_2 are order-invariant in $(\mathcal{C}^B \cap \mathcal{C}^*) \times \phi_k$.

The following theorem shows the correctness of the main algorithm.

Theorem 6. *Let $\mathcal{C}_{in} := \mathcal{C}(F_k, \boldsymbol{s}_{[k]}) \times \phi_{k+1} \times \cdots \times \phi_n$ be a connected (k, n)-proj pre-cell, where $2 \le k \le n$. Then, $\mathcal{C}_{out} := \texttt{BigCellProj}(\mathcal{C}_{in})$ is a $(k-2, n)$-proj pre-cell wherein every polynomial in F_k is order-invariant.*

Proof. Following the single-cell construction, the output $\mathcal{C}^B$ of Algorithm 3 is a $(k-2, k-1)$-proj pre-cell, and Theorem 5 indicates that $\mathcal{C}_i$ is a $(k-2, k-1)$-proj pre-cell for $i = 1, 2, \ldots, m$. By Theorem 4, their intersection $\mathcal{C}^B \cap_c \mathcal{C}_1 \cap_c \cdots \cap_c \mathcal{C}_m$ is consequently a $(k-2, k-1)$-proj pre-cell. Since $\mathcal{C}^B$ is consistent with ϕ_k, we know $\mathcal{C}_{out}$ is a pre-cell. Furthermore, $\texttt{Poly}(\theta_l)$ and $\texttt{Poly}(\theta_u)$ are order-invariant in $\mathcal{C}^B \times \phi_k$. According to Theorem 5, we know that g_i is order-invariant in $\mathcal{C}^B \cap \mathcal{C}_i$, and $G_\perp$ is order-invariant in $\mathcal{C}_\perp$. We conclude that all polynomials in F_k are order-invariant over $\mathcal{C}_{out}$.

4.4 Detecting Mergeable Adjacent Cells

Given a polynomial set $F \subseteq \mathbb{R}[\boldsymbol{x}_{[k]}]$, a boundary polynomial set $G \subseteq \mathbb{R}[\boldsymbol{x}_{[k-1]}]$, a sample point $\boldsymbol{s}_{[k]} \in \mathbb{R}^k$, a root symbolic interval $\phi_k = [\![\theta_l, \theta_u]\!]$ and a $(k-2, k)$-proj pre-cell $\mathcal{C}$. Intuitively, we detect mergeable adjacent cells satisfying the following conditions, and then sample a point $\boldsymbol{s}^i_{[k]}$ from each candidate cell.

- The k-th dimension of each candidate cell is the root symbolic interval ϕ_k, *i.e.*, $\boldsymbol{s}^i_{[k]}$ satisfies $\texttt{s\_interval}(F \cup \{\texttt{Poly}(\theta_l), \texttt{Poly}(\theta_u)\}, \boldsymbol{s}^i_{[k]}) = \phi_k$;
- The $(k-1)$-th dimensions of candidate cells form an adjacent sequence, *i.e.*, the corresponding sample points are adjacent (Definition 10);
- Every polynomial in F is order-invariant in every candidate cell; and
- Every sample point is in the pre-cell $\mathcal{C}$.

Definition 10 (Adjacency). *Let $\boldsymbol{s}^1, \boldsymbol{s}^2 \in \mathbb{R}^k$ be sample points, $f \in \mathbb{R}[\boldsymbol{x}_{[k-1]}]$ be a polynomial, and $G \subseteq \mathbb{R}[\boldsymbol{x}_{[k-1]}]$ be a finite set of polynomials. The sample points $\boldsymbol{s}^1, \boldsymbol{s}^2$ are called* adjacent w.r.t. f *if $\boldsymbol{s}^1_{[k-2]} = \boldsymbol{s}^2_{[k-2]}$, and there exists a positive integer i such that $s^1_{k-1} = \texttt{Root}(f, \boldsymbol{s}_{[k-2]}, i)$, while $f(\boldsymbol{s}_{[k-2]}, x)$ has no other real root between s^1_{k-1} and s^2_{k-1}. The sample points $\boldsymbol{s}^1, \boldsymbol{s}^2$ are called* adjacent w.r.t. G *if they are adjacent w.r.t. the product polynomial $\prod_{g \in G} g$.*

Due to page limitation, the algorithm `AdjacentCellSampler` is described in the Appendix.

Theorem 7. *Let* $F, G \subseteq \mathbb{R}[\boldsymbol{x}_{[k]}]$ *be polynomial sets,* $\boldsymbol{s}_{[k]} \in \mathbb{R}^k$ *and* ϕ_n *a root symbolic interval, where* $\boldsymbol{s}_{[k]}$ *is consistent with* ϕ_k*. Then,* `AdjacentCellSampler`$(F, G, \boldsymbol{s}_{[k]}, \phi_k)$ *satisfies properties* (i)*-*(v) *in Algorithm 5.*

Proof. Property (i) is satisfied since $\boldsymbol{s}_{[k]}$ is the initial element in *sampleList*. Property (v) holds since the intersection in line 7 and the conditional statements in and line 13–14. The conditional statement in line 16 ensures the validity of properties (ii) and (iv). Finally, property (iii) is satisfied by our specific sample point ordering in the construction of *sampleList*, *i.e.*, new sample points from right-adjacent cells are appended to the right end, and then sample points from left-adjacent cells are appended to the left end, thus preserving the required adjacency.

Definition 11 (Full-Cell Projection Operator). *The operator* `FullCellProj` *is said to be a* full-cell projection operator *if for any polynomial set* $F \subseteq \mathbb{R}[\boldsymbol{x}_{[n]}]$ *on level* n*, and sample points* $\boldsymbol{s}_{[n]}, \boldsymbol{s}^*_{[n]} \in \mathbb{R}^n$ *satisfying* $\texttt{s\_interval}(F, (\boldsymbol{s}_{[n-1]}, s^*_n)) = \texttt{s\_interval}(F, \boldsymbol{s}_{[n]})$*, the following inclusion holds*

$$\texttt{SingleCellProj}(F, \boldsymbol{s}^*_{[n]}) \subseteq \texttt{FullCellProj}(F, \boldsymbol{s}_{[n]}) \subseteq \mathbb{R}[\boldsymbol{x}_{[n-1]}].$$

Remark 3. The McCallum's operator $\texttt{Proj}_M$ is an instance of `FullCellProj`. In implementation, we take a specific variant of $\texttt{Proj}_M$ designed for our algorithm as `FullCellProj`, which is

$$\underset{Full}{\texttt{Proj}}(F, x_n, \boldsymbol{s}) = \bigcup_{f \in F} \{\texttt{coeff}(f, x_n), \texttt{disc}(f, x_n)\} \cup \{\texttt{res}(\texttt{Poly}(\theta_l), \texttt{Poly}(\theta_u), x_n)\}$$
$$\cup \{\texttt{res}(p, \texttt{Poly}(\theta_l), x_n) \mid p \in F\},$$

where $[\![\theta_l, \theta_u]\!] = \texttt{s\_interval}(F, x_n, \boldsymbol{s})$.

5 Case Studies

We implemented the BigCell algorithm using Mathematica 2023 and conducted experiments on a set of representative examples. To compare with $\texttt{Proj}_N$, we also implemented $\texttt{Proj}_N$ using Mathematica 2023. For each polynomial system, we enumerate all full-dimensional cells and record the number of such cells as well as the total computation time. The selected benchmarks include:

- **P-zxy–P-xyz**: This refers to the example in Sect. 3. We evaluate the algorithm under all six permutations of the variable ordering $\{x, y, z\}$, such as `zxy`, `zyx`, and so on. The suffix (e.g., `zxy`) indicates the variable order used in the projection and lifting phases.
- **Random-3-i**: This set contains randomly generated polynomial systems. Each system consists of three quadratic polynomials in three variables. The index i distinguishes different instances (e.g., `Random-3-1`, `Random-3-2`, etc.).

- **Random-4-i**: Similar to the previous set, but each system consists of four quadratic polynomials in three variables. These examples are used to evaluate the algorithm's performance on slightly more complex random inputs.

All implementations and example data are available on our GitHub repository[1]. For every example, we first use OpenCAD [12] to compute one sample point in each open cell. The second column of Table 1 shows the numbers of sample points (open cells). Then, we compute single-cell construction with every sample point and the system. The third and forth columns report the numbers of cells computed by our BIGCELL algorithm and the baseline method $\texttt{Proj}_N$ (N), respectively. The less the numbers, the larger the cells. The rightmost two columns report the timings on computing all cells for the system by $\texttt{Proj}_N$ and our algorithm, respectively.

Table 1. Comparison of cell counts and computation time across different methods.

Examples	#Cells (CAD)	#Cells (N)	#Cells (BigCell)	Time(s) (N)	Time(s) (BigCell)
P-zxy	2564	352	209	34.0912	23.4164
P-zyx	604	75	51	1.6776	2.0144
P-yzx	364	35	19	0.4669	0.3986
P-yxz	476	43	34	0.7509	0.9234
P-xzy	2726	361	237	34.5344	31.7121
P-xyz	680	95	83	2.7404	5.1881
Random-3-1	242	116	71	2.2458	2.0894
Random-3-2	112	18	10	0.1336	0.0768
Random-3-3	509	140	62	4.9717	2.2525
Random-3-4	236	72	37	1.3097	3.0979
Random-3-5	580	204	89	7.6894	4.7481
Random-4-1	492	230	142	7.0886	17.5752
Random-4-2	1020	422	240	31.4073	21.7111
Random-4-3	2452	278	152	45.1191	38.8471
Random-4-4	902	464	211	23.7943	16.1810
Random-4-5	744	263	186	10.2071	14.2727

Experiments show that BIGCELL consistently constructs fewer cells and often runs faster. In a minority of cases, fewer cells are constructed, but the total runtime increases. This is because BIGCELL introduces extra steps (e.g., detecting and merging adjacent pre-cells) when constructing a single cell. In the majority of cases, BIGCELL substantially reduces the total number of cells to be constructed, so the overall execution time is shorter. Furthermore, integrating BIGCELL into a CDCL-style SMT-NRA solver for end-to-end evaluation is ongoing and it can be expected that the performance will be more convincing since fewer cells lead to less backtracking, especially for unsatisfiable formulas.

---

[1] https://github.com/Ntimesp/BigCell.

6 Conclusion

In this paper, we proposed a novel single-cell construction algorithm aimed at computing larger conflict regions, thus reducing the backtracking frequency in SMT(NRA) solving. During the construction process, we may merge more adjacent cells and minimize the number of discriminants and resultants required. Experimental results show that, compared to existing algorithms, our method effectively produces larger cells and achieves shorter timings in many cases.

Acknowledgements. The authors thank the anonymous reviewers for their constructive and valuable comments and suggestions. The authors also thank Haokun Li and Rizeng Chen for insightful discussions. This work was supported by the National Key R&D Program of China (No. 2022YFA1005102 and No. 2024YFA1014000).

Appendix A: The algorithm `AdjacentCellSampler`

Algorithm 5: AdjacentCellSampler

Input : a polynomial set $F \subseteq \mathbb{R}[\boldsymbol{x}_{[k]}]$, a polynomial set $G \subseteq \mathbb{R}[\boldsymbol{x}_{[k-1]}]$, a sample point $\boldsymbol{s}_{[k]} \in \mathbb{R}^k$, and a $(k-2,k)$-proj precell $\mathcal{C} = \mathcal{C}(P, \boldsymbol{s}_{[k-2]}) \times \phi_{k-1} \times \phi_k$, where $s_{k-1} \in \phi_k(\boldsymbol{s}_{[k-2]})$ and $s_k \in \phi_k(\boldsymbol{s}_{[k-1]})$.

Output: a list of sample points $sampleList := [\boldsymbol{s}^1_{[k]}, \ldots, \boldsymbol{s}^m_{[k]}]$, where

(i) $\boldsymbol{s}^1_{[k]} = \boldsymbol{s}_{[k]}$;

(ii) $\texttt{s\_interval}(F \cup \texttt{Poly}(\phi_k), \boldsymbol{s}^i_{[k]}) = \phi_k$;

(iii) $\forall\, k, \exists\, i \leq k$, such that $\boldsymbol{s}^i_{[k]}$ and $\boldsymbol{s}^{k+1}_{[k]}$ are adjacent w.r.t. G; and

(iv) for each polynomial f in F, $\texttt{order}_{\boldsymbol{s}^1_{[k]}}(f) = \cdots = \texttt{order}_{\boldsymbol{s}^m_{[k]}}(f)$.

(v) $\forall\, 1 \leq i \leq m$, $s^i_{k-1} \in \phi_k(\boldsymbol{s}^i_{[k-2]})$, $s^i_k \in \phi_k(\boldsymbol{s}^i_{[k-1]})$(i.e. $\boldsymbol{s}^i_{[k]} \in \mathcal{C}$).

$sampleList \leftarrow [\boldsymbol{s}_{[k]}]$

if $\llbracket^1 = [$ *and* $\rrbracket^1 =]$ **then return** $sampleList$

Compute $\texttt{Isolate}(G, \boldsymbol{s}_{[k-1]})$ and suppose we get $[\theta_1, \ldots, \theta_m]$

if $m = 0$ **then return** $sampleList$

else $\psi_{k-1} \leftarrow \texttt{s\_interval}(G, \boldsymbol{s}_{[k-1]})$

$invlList \leftarrow [(-\infty, \theta_1), [\theta_1, \theta_1], (\theta_1, \theta_2), \ldots, [\theta_m, \theta_m], (\theta_m, +\infty)]$ instantiated by $\boldsymbol{s}_{[k-2]}$

Substitute every interval in $invList$ with its intersection with $\phi_{k-1}(\boldsymbol{s}_{[k-1]})$ and remove empty intervals in $invList$

$i \leftarrow$ index of the interval in $invList$ covered by $\psi_{k-1}(\boldsymbol{s}_{[k-2]})$

$invList_1 \leftarrow invList[i+1:]$

$invList_2 \leftarrow$ reverse of $invList[:i-1]$

/* Searching all right adjacent cells, and then searching all left adjacent cells */

for $j = 1, 2$ **do**

  for $\psi_0 = \llbracket \theta_l, \theta_u \rrbracket$ *in* $invList_j$ **do**

    $d_1 \leftarrow$ an arbitrary real number in ψ_0

    $d_2 \leftarrow$ an arbitrary real number in $\phi_k(\boldsymbol{s}_{[k-2]}, d_1)$

    $\boldsymbol{s}'_{[k]} \leftarrow (\boldsymbol{s}_{[k-2]}, d_1, d_2)$

    if $\texttt{s\_interval}(F \cup \texttt{Poly}(\phi_k), \boldsymbol{s}'_{[k]}) = \phi_k$ *and* $\forall f \in F, \texttt{order}_{\boldsymbol{s}_{[k]}}(f) = \texttt{order}_{\boldsymbol{s}'_{[k]}}(f)$ **then** Append $\boldsymbol{s}'_{[k]}$ to $sampleList$

    else Break

return $sampleList$

References

1. Brown, C.W.: Improved projection for cylindrical algebraic decomposition. J. Symb. Comput. **32**(5), 447–465 (2001)
2. Brown, C.W.: QEPCAD B: a program for computing with semi-algebraic sets using CADs. ACM Sigsam Bull. **37**(4), 97–108 (2003)
3. Brown, C.W.: Constructing a single open cell in a cylindrical algebraic decomposition. In: Proceedings of the 38th International Symposium on Symbolic and Algebraic Computation, pp. 133–140 (2013)
4. Collins, G.E.: Quantifier elimination for real closed fields by cylindrical algebraic decomposition: a synopsis. ACM SIGSAM Bull. **10**(1), 10–12 (1976)
5. de Moura, L., Jovanović, D.: A model-constructing satisfiability calculus. In: Giacobazzi, R., Berdine, J., Mastroeni, I. (eds.) VMCAI 2013. LNCS, vol. 7737, pp. 1–12. Springer, Heidelberg (2013). https://doi.org/10.1007/978-3-642-35873-9_1
6. Hong, H.: An improvement of the projection operator in cylindrical algebraic decomposition. In: Proceedings of the International Symposium on Symbolic and Algebraic Computation, pp. 261–264 (1990)
7. Li, H., Xia, B.: Solving Satisfiability of Polynomial Formulas by Sample-Cell Projection. arXiv preprint arXiv:2003.00409 (2020)
8. McCallum, S.: An improved projection operation for cylindrical algebraic decomposition. In: Caviness, B.F., Johnson, J.R. (eds.) Quantifier Elimination and Cylindrical Algebraic Decomposition. Texts and Monographs in Symbolic Computation, LNCS, pp. 242–268. Springer, Vienna (1998). https://doi.org/10.1007/978-3-7091-9459-1_12
9. Nalbach, J., Ábrahám, E.: Merging adjacent cells during single cell construction. In: Boulier, F., Mou, C., Sadykov, T.M., Vorozhtsov, E.V. (eds.) Computer Algebra in Scientific Computing. CASC 2024. LNCS, vol. 14938, pp. 252–272. Springer, Cham (2024). https://doi.org/10.1007/978-3-031-69070-9_15
10. Nalbach, J., Ábrahám, E., Specht, P., Brown, C.W., Davenport, J.H., England, M.: Levelwise construction of a single cylindrical algebraic cell. J. Symb. Comput. **123**, 102288 (2024)
11. Sebastiani, R.: Lazy satisfiability modulo theories. J. Satisf. Boolean Model. Comput. **3**(3–4), 141–224 (2007)
12. Strzeboński, A.: Solving systems of strict polynomial inequalities. J. Symb. Comput. **29**(3), 471–480 (2000)
13. Tarski, A.: A decision method for elementary algebra and geometry. In: Caviness, B.F., Johnson, J.R. (eds.) Quantifier Elimination and Cylindrical Algebraic Decomposition. Texts and Monographs in Symbolic Computation, LNCS, pp. 24–84. Springer, Vienna (1998). https://doi.org/10.1007/978-3-7091-9459-1_3

Formal Modeling of Reinforcement Learning Systems with SMT

Tianyi Ding, Yuxin Lin, and Meng Sun(✉)

Peking University, Beijing, China
{dingty,linyuxin}@stu.pku.edu.cn, sunmeng@math.pku.edu.cn

Abstract. The widespread deployment of reinforcement learning (RL) systems in real-world applications necessitates rigorous guarantees of their correctness. In the RL system, an agent iteratively interacts with the environment, with the objective of maximizing cumulative rewards. These interactions involve constraints of states, actions, and rewards, where any violation of these constraints indicates a system-level error. In this paper, we propose an SMT-based framework for the formal modeling of RL systems. Our method encodes constraints for RL components as SMT formulas, and cumulative reward maximization as an optimization objective, enabling automated verification of constraint satisfiability through SMT solvers. We evaluate our formal modeling approach through experiments conducted on a popular RL environment. Experimental results validate the effectiveness of our method in identifying constraint violations and ensuring behavioral correctness.

Keywords: Reinforcement Learning · SMT · Formal Modeling

1 Introduction

Reinforcement learning is an important branch in the field of machine learning that studies how agents learn optimal strategies through interactions with their environment in order to achieve long-term goals. In this paradigm, an agent is equipped with the capability to discern the environmental state, execute actions that influence this state, and acquire rewards subsequent to each action. Unlike supervised and unsupervised learning methodologies, RL is particularly suited for addressing challenges that involve sequential decision-making processes.

Reinforcement learning is a rapidly evolving field whose potential for real-world applications continues to be explored and realized as algorithms and computational power advance. Reinforcement learning has been widely applied in various fields, including gaming [1–3], robotics [4,5], autonomous driving [6,7], healthcare [8,9], natural language processing [10–12], recommendation systems [13–15], and so on. However, due to potential errors in reinforcement learning systems, agents may exhibit undesirable behaviors that pose risks to human life and property. Ensuring the safety of RL systems is therefore critical, as incorrect decisions can have harmful consequences. Early research in RL primarily focused

É. André et al. (Eds.): ICFEM 2025, LNCS 16229, pp. 348–365, 2026.
https://doi.org/10.1007/978-981-95-4213-0_19

on algorithmic improvements and performance optimization, with less emphasis on safety considerations. Recent progress in RL has led to a growing attention to the urgent need for safety research in this field.

Formal methods, with their rigorous mathematical foundations, provide a systematic way to specify, model, and analyze the behavior of complex systems, thereby providing strong guarantees of safety and reliability. Consequently, the testing and verification of RL systems using formal methods has emerged as a new research trend. Fulton et al. explored the integration of formal methods with reinforcement learning to achieve safe control, combining proof and learning techniques [16]. Chen focused on the formal modeling and automatic generation of test cases for autonomous vehicles, enhancing their safety and validation processes [17]. Lu et al. introduced a novel mutation testing framework specifically designed for reinforcement learning systems, enhancing their robustness and safety [18]. Bacci presented a new formal verification techniques of deep reinforcement learning agents based on abstract interpretation [19]. Varshosaz et al. developed a formal specification and testing of reinforcement learning systems and algorithms, with a focus on temporal difference learning [20]. Gross and Spieker employed probabilistic model checking to verify the stochastic RL policies [21]. However, dynamic environment and partial observability inherent in many RL systems remain a fundamental challenge to providing safety and reliability guarantees for RL.

Formal verification with Satisfiability Modulo Theories (SMT) solvers has shown promising results in prior work. Zhang et al. presented an SMT-based approach for the modeling and verification of cloud applications [22]. Zhang et al. utilized the Z3 solver for the formal modeling and verification of the global robustness of feed-forward neural networks [23]. Amir et al. proposed an SMT-based approach for verifying binarized neural networks [24]. A key advantage of SMT-based techniques is their ability to combine first-order logic with arithmetic constraints while accommodating dynamic and partially known environments.

In this paper, we leverage SMT to formally model reinforcement learning (RL) systems. We present a step-by-step formalization of the key components of RL system and demonstrate how they can be encoded as SMT constraints. Our framework can handle both dynamic and partially known environments. To illustrate the model, we employ a classic RL environment, FrozenLake, provide an implementation using Z3 in Python, and design a scheme of test cases correspondingly. This enables automated satisfiability checking of RL systems through SMT solvers.

The rest of this paper is organized as follows. In Sect. 2, we introduce the basics, including mathematical framework of Markov process, reinforcement learning, and Satisfiability Modulo Theories. In Sect. 3, we propose a formal modeling of the reinforcement learning systems where constraints are formulated as an SMT formula. In Sect. 4, we illustrate our formal model with FrozenLake environment and design a systematic suite of test cases to evaluate the correctness and adaptability of our SMT-based formal model. Finally, we conclude this paper in Sect. 5.

2 Preliminaries

In this section, we introduce the background knowledge, including Markov Process (MP), Markov Reward Process (MRP), Markov Decision Process (MDP), RL and SMT. In reinforcement learning, MPs, MRPs and MDPs form the theoretical foundation for understanding agent decision-making in dynamic environments. These mathematical frameworks formally characterize the interactions between agents and their environments, facilitating the systematic analysis and design of reinforcement learning algorithms.

2.1 Markov Process

A *Markov process* (or *Markov chain*) is a stochastic process in which the current state fully encapsulates all necessary information for predicting future states, rendering past states irrelevant. Formally, a process is *Markovian* if the conditional probability distribution of future states depends solely on the present state, independent of prior history. This property is expressed mathematically as $P(s_{t+1} \mid s_t) = P(s_{t+1} \mid s_1, s_2, \cdots, s_t)$, where P is the probability function, and $s_1, s_2, ..., s_t, s_{t+1}$ denote the sequence of *states.* A Markov process is memoryless and can be formally defined as a tuple $(S, \mathcal{P})$, where S is the state space, and $\mathcal{P}$ is the *transition probability function.* Denote by $\mathcal{P}(s' \mid s) := P(s_{t+1} = s' \mid s_t = s)$, where s is the current state, and s' is the next state.

2.2 Markov Reward Process

A *Markov reward process* extends a Markov process by incorporating a reward function $\mathcal{R}$ a discount factor γ. Formally, an MRP is defined as a tuple $(S, \mathcal{P}, \mathcal{R}, \gamma)$, where S is the state space, $\mathcal{P}$ is the transition probability function, $\mathcal{R}(s) = \mathbb{E}[r_{t+1} \mid s_t = s]$ is the *reward function* representing the expected reward when transitioning from state s, and $\gamma \in [0, 1]$ is the *discount factor.*

The *return* U_t represents the cumulative discounted rewards from time t onward, i.e., $U_t = r_{t+1} + \gamma r_{t+2} + \gamma^2 r_{t+3} + \cdots$, where the discount factor γ serves two key purposes. The purposes are (i) preventing infinite returns in cyclic (looping) state sequences, and (ii) reflecting uncertainty about future rewards, as long-term predictions are less reliable. A higher γ (closer to 1) increases the emphasis on long-term rewards. The *state value function* $\mathcal{V}(s) := \mathbb{E}[U_t \mid s_t = s]$ quantifies the expected return when starting from state s. Using the Bellman equation, the state value function decomposes into $\mathcal{V}(s) = \mathcal{R}(s) + \gamma \sum_{s' \in S} \mathcal{P}(s' \mid s) \mathcal{V}(s')$, where the first term is the expectation of immediate reward, and the second term is the discounted expected value of future states.

2.3 Markov Decision Process

A *Markov decision process* extends a Markov Reward Process by incorporating an action space A. Formally, an MDP is defined as a tuple

$(S, A, \mathcal{P}, \mathcal{R}, \gamma)$, where S is the state space, A is the *action space*, $\mathcal{P}(s' \mid s, a) = P(s_{t+1} = s' \mid s_t = s, a_t = a)$ is the state transition probability function, $\mathcal{R}(s, a) = \mathbb{E}[r_t \mid s_t = s, a_t = a]$ is the reward function, and $\gamma \in [0, 1]$ is the discount factor.

The agent's behavior is determined by its *policy* π, which defines a probability distribution over actions for each state. Specifically, $\pi(a \mid s) = P(a_t = a \mid s_t = s)$, where $\pi(a \mid s)$ is the probability of selecting action a in state s. The policy π depends only on the current state s and is independent of time or historical information. Although the policy itself is static at any given time, the agent can update π iteratively during learning.

2.4 Reinforcement Learning

Reinforcement learning is typically formalized using MDPs, where an agent interacts with an environment through sequential decision-making. As illustrated in Fig. 1, RL operates through cyclic interactions between an agent and its environment. The process unfolds as follows.

1. **State Observation:** The agent perceives the environment's current state s_t, which fully characterizes the observable dynamics at time t.
2. **Action Execution:** Based on s_t, the agent selects an action a_t from its policy $\pi(a \mid s)$, which perturbs the environment.
3. **State Transition:** The environment transitions to a new state s_{t+1} according to the dynamics model $\mathcal{P}(s_{t+1} \mid s_t, a_t)$, which may be stochastic.
4. **Reward Feedback:** The agent receives an immediate reward $r_{t+1} = \mathcal{R}(s_t, a_t)$, providing a scalar performance metric.

This interaction loop generates trajectories $s_0, a_0, r_1, s_1, \ldots$, with the agent's objective being to maximize $\mathbb{E}[\sum_{k=0}^{\infty} \gamma^k r_{t+k+1}]$ through policy optimization.

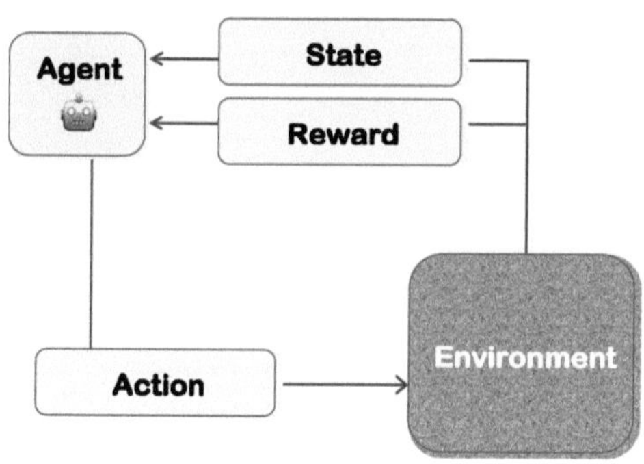

Fig. 1. Reinforcement learning interaction framework. The agent interacts with the environment by observing states, taking actions, and receiving rewards, forming a closed feedback loop for sequential decision-making.

2.5 Satisfiability Modulo Theories

The satisfiability problem of logical formulas has been an important issue in the fields of theoretical computer science and artificial intelligence. Scholars around the world have done a lot of research work in this area, especially on the satisfiability problem of propositional logic, i.e., Boolean Satisfiability Problem (SAT). SAT is a classical decision problem in propositional logical reasoning, and it is also the first problem proved to be NP-hard, which has been attracting a lot of attention. However, with the deepening of research, it has been found that SAT has great limitations in its expressive power and scope of application. Therefore, SMT began to attract great interest in recent years. The research object of SMT is the logical combination of various domain knowledge, often expressed as first-order logical formulas. Unlike SAT which determines the satisfiability of Boolean formulas, Satisfiability Modulo Theories (SMT) studies the problem of determining the satisfiability of a first-order logic formula under a background theory. Common theories include arithmetic, bitvectors, arrays, difference logic, strings, and equality with uninterpreted functions. SMT has a higher level of abstraction and stronger expressive ability. It can be seen as an extension of SAT by replacing certain Boolean variables in SAT with theoretical predicates.

3 Formal Modeling of Reinforcement Learning System and Environment

In this section, we aim to construct a formal model of reinforcement learning system and its environment based on SMT. We start with a formal specification of RL system in Sect. 3.1 and proceed to formalize the key components of the RL system with SMT from Sect. 3.2 to Sect. 3.6. Section 3.7 unites all constraints and presents the complete modeling. Here, we only provide the general constraints that exist for all RL systems. In the real life examples of RL system, there are far more constraints from the environment setting. We will illustrate a classic example FrozenLake in Sect. 4.1.

3.1 Formal Specification

With the introduction of MDP in Sect. 2.3, we can formulate the reinforcement learning system as a tuple $(S, A, \mathcal{P}, \mathcal{R}, \gamma)$, where S is the finite state space, A is the finite action space, $\mathcal{P} : S \times A \times S \rightarrow [0, 1]$ is the transition probability function, $\mathcal{R} : S \times A \rightarrow \mathbb{R}$ is the reward function, and $\gamma \in [0, 1]$ is the discount-rate parameter.

3.2 State

In RL system, the initial state s_0 is either deterministic or uniformly distributed over the state space. In the first case, s_0 needs to be picked from the state space S, i.e., $s_0 \in S$.

At any following time-step $t > 0$, the agent's state s_t should also be contained in the state space. Thus, we extend the above constraint to

$$\forall t \in \mathbb{N}, s_t \in S.$$

3.3 Action

Similarly, action a_t at any time-step t should be contained in the action space A, i.e.,

$$\forall t \in \mathbb{N}, a_t \in A.$$

As stated in Sect. 2.3, actions are decided according to the policy. $\pi(a \mid s)$ gives the probability of the agent performs action a if the agent observes state s, i.e.,

$$\forall t \in \mathbb{N}, a_t \sim \pi(\cdot \mid s_t).$$

With any state $s_t \in S$, the probability of the agent taking any possible action $a \in A$ should be summed to 1, i.e.,

$$\forall t \in \mathbb{N}, \sum_{a \in A} \pi(a \mid s_t) = 1.$$

3.4 Transition Probability Function

Transition probability $\mathcal{P}(s \mid s_t, a_t)$ is the probability of state s is observed as next state s_{t+1} if the agent takes action a_t at state s_t. For any time-step t, the probability of transferring to any possible state $s \in S$ should be summed to 1, i.e.,

$$\forall t \in \mathbb{N}, s_{t+1} \sim \mathcal{P}(\cdot \mid s_t, a_t),$$

$$\forall t \in \mathbb{N}, \sum_{s \in S} \mathcal{P}(s \mid s_t, a_t) = 1.$$

3.5 Reward

The environment rewards r_{t+1} after the agent takes action a_t at state s_t, i.e.,

$$\forall t \in \mathbb{N}, r_{t+1} = \mathcal{R}(s_t, a_t).$$

The utility function $U = \sum_{t=0}^{\infty} r_t$ represents the sum of the rewards after a series of actions $a_0, a_1, \ldots$ However, directly summing up rewards leads to an unbiased infinite time series, and an infinite loop of states is generated. So we need to introduce discount-rate parameter γ in the utility function. We multiply the reward of afterwards states by γ and define this function as cumulative reward.

Definition 1 (Cumulative Reward). *Given a series of rewards $r_0, r_1, \ldots$ and a discount-rate parameter γ, the cumulative reward is $\sum_{t=0}^{\infty} \gamma^t r_t$.*

Remark 1. In reinforcement learning cases, the learning process is usually finite, thus the series of rewards is finite. Consider the finite reinforcement learning sequence $s_0, a_0, r_1, s_1, a_1, r_2, ..., s_{n-1}, a_{n-1}, r_n, s_n$. In this case, the process is terminated at state s_n, so we treat subsequent rewards $r_{n+1}, r_{n+2}, ...$ as 0. The subsequent states stay unchanged and subsequent actions are empty or denoted as "STAY", i.e.,

$$\forall t > n, r_t = 0, s_t = s_n, a_t = \emptyset.$$

3.6 Trajectory of RL System

A reinforcement learning process can be represented as a sequence of actions, rewards and states. In a reinforcement learning system, for each moment t, the agent observes the state of the environment s_t and takes an action a_t, then the environment gives the agent a reward r_{t+1}. Thus the trajectory of reinforcement learning can be represented by the sequence

$$s_0, a_0, r_1, s_1, a_1, r_2, s_2, a_2, r_3, \ldots$$

To formalize this sequence, we define three predicates, named *StatetToAction*, *ActionToReward* and *RewardToState* respectively.

- *StateToAction*(s, a) denotes action a is taken by the agent with respect to the environment state s;
- *ActionToReward*(a, r) denotes the environment gives a reward r as feedback after the agent takes action a;
- *RewardToState*(r, s) denotes the environment state becomes s after it rewards r to the agent.

We can see that the sequence of the trajectory for reinforcement learning is equivalent to the following constraints.

$$\forall t \in \mathbb{N}, \mathit{StateToAction}(s_t, a_t),$$
$$\forall t \in \mathbb{N}, \mathit{ActionToReward}(a_t, r_{t+1}),$$
$$\forall t \in \mathbb{N}, \mathit{RewardToState}(r_{t+1}, s_{t+1}).$$

3.7 Complete Description of Formal Modeling

In Sect. 3.1–3.6, we give formal description of each element in the reinforcement learning system. Here, we integrate these elements together to give a complete description of the formal modeling of the reinforcement learning system.

The goal of reinforcement learning system is to obtain a policy that maximizes cumulative reward. In the pursuit of maximization, the reinforcement learning system needs to satisfy the constraints in Sect. 3.1–3.6 at all times. Therefore, the RL system (terminated at state s_n) is formulated as an SMT formula as (1).

$$
\begin{aligned}
\max_{\pi} \quad & \sum_{t=0}^{\infty} \gamma^t r_t, \\
s.t. \quad & \forall t \in \mathbb{N} \quad s_t \in S \\
& \wedge \forall t \in \mathbb{N} \quad a_t \in A \\
& \wedge \forall t \in \mathbb{N} \quad a_t \sim \pi(\cdot \mid s_t) \\
& \wedge \forall t \in \mathbb{N} \quad \textstyle\sum_{a \in A} \pi(a \mid s_t) = 1 \\
& \wedge \forall t \in \mathbb{N} \quad s_{t+1} \sim \mathcal{P}(\cdot \mid s_t, a_t) \\
& \wedge \forall t \in \mathbb{N} \quad \textstyle\sum_{s \in S} \mathcal{P}(s \mid s_t, a_t) = 1 \\
& \wedge \forall t \in \mathbb{N} \quad r_{t+1} = \mathcal{R}(s_t, a_t) \\
& \wedge \forall t > n, \quad r_t = 0, s_t = s_n, a_t = \emptyset \\
& \wedge \forall t \in \mathbb{N} \quad StateToAction(s_t, a_t) \\
& \wedge \forall t \in \mathbb{N} \quad ActionToReward(a_t, r_{t+1}) \\
& \wedge \forall t \in \mathbb{N} \quad RewardToState(r_{t+1}, s_{t+1}).
\end{aligned}
\tag{1}
$$

Our approach is applicable to settings where a complete transition model is unavailable. To address this model-free or partially-known challenge, we formally treat the unknown components of the environment's dynamics as uninterpreted functions (UFs) within the SMT framework. This abstraction allows us to specify the structural and logical relationships between states, actions, and rewards without requiring exact probabilistic or functional definitions for every transition. State-of-the-art SMT solvers, such as Z3 and CVC5, provide native and efficient support for reasoning with uninterpreted functions. Consequently, the solver does not require the concrete implementation of these functions; instead, it deduces the satisfiability of the logical system based on the axioms and constraints we provide. This enables us to verify critical properties by checking the satisfiability of the resulting formula. For the known portions of the model, we employ precise theories, resulting in a hybrid model that combines both exact and abstracted knowledge, which is an advantage over purely probabilistic methods.

4 Experiments

We utilize one of the traditional RL environments, FrozenLake, as an example to illustrate our SMT-based formal modeling and instantiate the modeling through Z3 Python interface.

4.1 Formal Modeling

In a FrozenLake environment, a lake is divided into a grid of cells, some of which are holes and the others are safe ice. The agent starts from a safe ice and tries to find a walkable path to the goal tile without falling into holes. Either falling in a hole or arriving at the final goal tile, causes the process to an end.

Considering a FrozenLake environment of 4×4 grid as in Fig. 2, we can formulate this problem as $(S, A, \mathcal{P}, \mathcal{R}, \gamma)$. Here, the state space S is the set of 16 cells

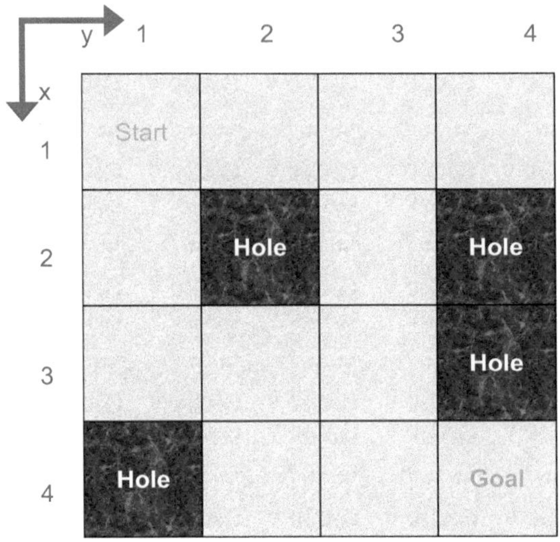

Fig. 2. A 4×4 FrozenLake environment.

and is defined as $S = \{(x, y) \mid x \in [1..4], y \in [1..4]\}$. We assume that the starting point is $(1, 1)$, the goal tile is $(4, 4)$, and the holes are $\{(2, 2), (2, 4), (3, 4), (4, 1)\}$. The remaining cells and $(1, 1)$ are safe frozen ice, i.e.,

$$\begin{aligned} S_{Start} &= \{(1, 1)\}, \\ S_{Goal} &= \{(4, 4)\}, \\ S_{Hole} &= \{(2, 2), (2, 4), (3, 4), (4, 1)\}, \\ S_{Frozen} &= S - S_{Goal} - S_{Hole}. \end{aligned}$$

The action space A is composed of one step towards each of the 4 directions (right, left, up, down) and remain at the current tile and is defined as $A = \{a_r, a_l, a_u, a_d, a_s\}$.

We assume that arriving at the goal tile gives a reward of 1; falling in a hole gives a reward of -1, which is actually a penalty; and walking on a frozen ice gives no reward or penalty. The reward $r(s)$ can be expressed as

$$r(s) = \begin{cases} 1 & if \quad s \in S_{Goal}, \\ -1 & if \quad s \in S_{Hole}, \\ 0 & if \quad s \in S_{Frozen}. \end{cases}$$

We can describe the environment setting with Z3 in Python as follows:

```
from z3 import *
# Declare State space
rows, cols = 4,4 # dime of grids
def rc_to_id(r, c): return (r-1)*cols + (c-1) # (r,c) to state id
def id_to_rc(s): return (s // cols + 1, s % cols + 1) # id to (r,c)
```

```
S = list(range(rows*cols)) # State set :[0,...,15]
start = rc_to_id(1,1)   # state 0
holes = [rc_to_id(2,2), rc_to_id(2,4), rc_to_id(3,4), rc_to_id(4,1)]
goal  = rc_to_id(rows, cols)  # state 15
end = holes + [goal]
# Declare Action space
A = {"UP":0, "DOWN":1, "RIGHT":2, "LEFT":3, "STAY":4}
# Declare Reward function
r_state = {s: 0 for s in S}
r_state[goal] = 1
for h in holes: r_state[h] = -1
opt = Optimize()
```

Suppose the total number of steps $H = 30$, we could state the constraints by part:

• **State**: the state of agent must be one of the 16 grids, i.e., $\forall t \in [0..H], s_t \in S$. The initial state $s_0 = (1, 1) \in S_{Start}$.

```
# state sequence
x = [[Bool(f"x_{t}_{s}") for s in S] for t in range(H+1)]
# initial state
opt.add(x[0][start] == True)
for s in S:
    if s != start:
        opt.add(x[0][s] == False)
# exactly one state is true at each time step
def exactly_one(bools):
    opt.add(Or(bools)) # at least 1 true
    for i in range(len(bools)):
        for j in range(i+1, len(bools)):
            opt.add(Not(And(bools[i], bools[j])))  # at most 1 true
for t in range(H+1):
    exactly_one(x[t])
```

• **Action**: the agent performs one of the possible actions i.e., $\forall t \in [0..H], a_t \in A$.

```
# action sequence
a = [Int(f"a_{t}") for t in range(H)]
# a_t in A
for t in range(H):
    opt.add(Or([a[t] == k for k in A_ids]))
```

• **Transition Probability Function**: on a frozen lake in real life, human might not always head towards the direction they intended to because of the wind or the slipperiness of the ice surface. We can choose whether to simulate this slippery in the model through using a deterministic or a stochastic environment.

In the deterministic setting, there is no slipperiness. The next state is determined with the knowledge of the agent's current state and the chosen action. In other words, if the agent moves upward, its next state must be in the cell above the current one, i.e., $\mathcal{P}(s_{t+1} \mid s_t, a_t) = 1$ if $a_t = a_u$ and $s_{t+1} = (s_t[x] - 1, s_t[y])$. However, we need to consider the case that the agent is on the boundary of the grid, where no further movement beyond the edge is allowed. In such cases, the agent remains in the current state if the intended action would result in leaving the boundary. We use the *min* or *max* function to execute this setting in the formalization. Therefore, x of the next state in the above example will be $max(s_t[x] - 1, 1)$. Thus, $\forall t \in [0..H]$,

$$a_t = a_u \rightarrow \mathcal{P}(s_{t+1} \mid s_t, a_t) = \begin{cases} 1 & if \quad s_{t+1} = (max(s_t[x] - 1, 1), s_t[y]), \\ 0 & otherwise. \end{cases}$$

$$a_t = a_d \rightarrow \mathcal{P}(s_{t+1} \mid s_t, a_t) = \begin{cases} 1 & if \quad s_{t+1} = (min(s_t[x] + 1, 4), s_t[y]), \\ 0 & otherwise. \end{cases}$$

$$a_t = a_l \rightarrow \mathcal{P}(s_{t+1} \mid s_t, a_t) = \begin{cases} 1 & if \quad s_{t+1} = (s_t[x], max(s_t[y] - 1, 1)), \\ 0 & otherwise. \end{cases}$$

$$a_t = a_r \rightarrow \mathcal{P}(s_{t+1} \mid s_t, a_t) = \begin{cases} 1 & if \quad s_{t+1} = (s_t[x], min(s_t[y] + 1, 4)), \\ 0 & otherwise. \end{cases}$$

$$a_t = a_s \rightarrow \mathcal{P}(s_{t+1} \mid s_t, a_t) = \begin{cases} 1 & if \quad s_{t+1} = s_t, \\ 0 & otherwise. \end{cases}$$

Based on this property of the transition probability function, we can define a transition function $\mathcal{T} : S \times A \rightarrow S$ to represent the next state given the current state and intended action, i.e., $s_{t+1} = \mathcal{T}(s_t, a_t), \forall t \in [0..H]$. Specifically,

$$\mathcal{T}(s_t, a_t) = \begin{cases} (max(s_t[x] - 1, 1), s_t[y]) & if \quad a_t = a_u, \\ (min(s_t[x] + 1, 4), s_t[y]) & if \quad a_t = a_d, \\ (s_t[x], max(s_t[y] - 1, 1)) & if \quad a_t = a_l, \\ (s_t[x], min(s_t[y] + 1, 4)) & if \quad a_t = a_r \\ s_t & if \quad a_t = a_s \end{cases}$$

In the stochastic setting, it is possible that the agent goes in directions that are perpendicular to the intended direction as shown in Fig. 3 [25]. If the agent observes state $(3, 3)$ and selects to move upward, the possible next states are $(2, 3)$, $(3, 2)$, and $(3, 4)$. The probabilities of other states are all 0. Thus, the transition probability function in a stochastic environment is

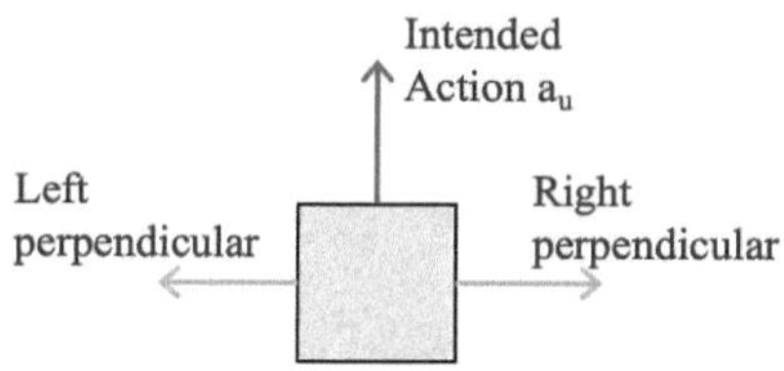

Fig. 3. Transition probability function in a stochastic environment.

$$a_t = a_u \rightarrow \mathcal{P}(s_{t+1} \mid s_t, a_t) \begin{cases} > 0 & if \quad s_{t+1} \in \quad \{(max(s_t[x]-1,1), s_t[y]), \\ & \qquad (s_t[x], min(s_t[y]+1,4)), \\ & \qquad (s_t[x], max(s_t[y]-1,1))\}; \\ = 0 & otherwise. \end{cases}$$

$$a_t = a_d \rightarrow \mathcal{P}(s_{t+1} \mid s_t, a_t) \begin{cases} > 0 & if \quad s_{t+1} \in \quad \{(min(s_t[x]+1,4), s_t[y]), \\ & \qquad (s_t[x], min(s_t[y]+1,4)), \\ & \qquad (s_t[x], max(s_t[y]-1,1))\}; \\ = 0 & otherwise. \end{cases}$$

$$a_t = a_l \rightarrow \mathcal{P}(s_{t+1} \mid s_t, a_t) \begin{cases} > 0 & if \quad s_{t+1} \in \quad \{(s_t[x], max(s_t[y]-1,1)), \\ & \qquad (max(s_t[x]-1,1), s_t[y]), \\ & \qquad (min(s_t[x]+1,4), s_t[y])\}; \\ = 0 & otherwise. \end{cases}$$

$$a_t = a_r \rightarrow \mathcal{P}(s_{t+1} \mid s_t, a_t) \begin{cases} > 0 & if \quad s_{t+1} \in \quad \{(s_t[x], min(s_t[y]+1,4)), \\ & \qquad (max(s_t[x]-1,1), s_t[y]), \\ & \qquad (min(s_t[x]+1,4), s_t[y])\}; \\ = 0 & otherwise. \end{cases}$$

As stated in Sect. 3.3, the transition probabilities of the agent going to all states at a times-step must sum to 1, i.e., $\sum_{s \in S} \mathcal{P}(s \mid s_t, a_t) = 1$. Furthermore, when current state is stuck in a hole or the goal tile, the system enforces $\mathcal{P}(s_{t+1} \mid s_t, a_t) = 1$, ensuring termination persists in both deterministic and stochastic environments.

Due to the inability of SMT solvers like Z3 to handle probability natively, our model is restricted to deterministic RL systems. The implementation of deterministic transition function and related constraints is detailed below:

```
def next_state_expr(s, a):
    r, c = id_to_rc(s)
    up    = rc_to_id(max(r-1,1), c)
```

```
    down  = rc_to_id(min(r+1,rows), c)
    left  = rc_to_id(r, max(c-1,1))
    right = rc_to_id(r, min(c+1, cols))
    base_next = If(a == A["UP"], up,
                If(a == A["DOWN"], down,
                If(a == A["LEFT"], left,
                If(a == A["RIGHT"], right,
                s))))
    return If(s == goal, goal,
           If(Or([s == h for h in holes]), s,
           base_next))
for t in range(H):
    for s in S:
        ns = next_state_expr(s, a[t])
        opt.add(Implies(x[t][s], Or([And(ns == j, x[t+1][j]) for j in
            S])))
```

• **Reward**: the process is ended if the agent arrives at a hole or the goal, i.e., $s_n \in S_{End}$, where

$$S_{End} = S_{Goal} \cup S_{Hole} = \{(4,4),(2,2),(2,4),(3,4),(4,1)\}.$$

After arriving at the termination state, the agent will always stay in that state, choose action a_s, and will not accumulate nonzero rewards repetitively. The objective function aims to maximize the accumulative rewards over H time steps.

```
reward_seq = []
for t in range(H+1):
    for s in S:
        reward_seq.append(If(x[t][s], r_state[s]*(gamma**t), 0))
# constraint after entering S_end
for t in range(H):
    cond = Or([x[t][s] for s in end])
    opt.add(Implies(cond, a[t] == A["STAY"])) #all action stay
for t in range(H+1):
    cond = Or([x[t][s] for s in end])
    for k in range(t+1, H+1):
        opt.add(Implies(cond, reward_seq[k] == 0)) #all reward 0
# max objective function
total_reward = Sum(reward_seq)
opt.maximize(total_reward)
if opt.check() == sat:
    m = opt.model()
```

In our modeling, the agent is discouraged from walking into the holes by the assignment of negative rewards. Alternatively, a strict safety constraint can be explicitly imposed to prohibit the agent from entering holes.

4.2 Test Cases

To assess the correctness and adaptability of our SMT-based formal model, we devise a systematic suite of test cases. These test scenarios are designed to verify that the formal model is valid and robust when key elements of the RL system are varied. Specifically, we consider (i) relocating the start state, goal state, and holes to different positions; (ii) increasing the number of holes; (iii) altering the size and shape of environment; (iv) checking the reward of optimized policy; and (v) introducing dynamic holes. These cases collectively help demonstrate that our formal model accommodates diverse environment settings.

Relocate Start, Goal, and Hole States. By default, we select the upper-left corner of the grid as the start state and the lower-right corner of the grid as the end state. To examine whether the formal model continues to function correctly when key environment components are altered, we exhibit four test cases in Table 1: **TC-1** corresponds to the default case described in Fig. 2; **TC-2** retains the locations of the goal tile and holes but randomly selects a start tile from the remaining safe tiles; **TC-3** keeps the location of start tile and holes fixed while randomly choosing the tile for the end state; **TC-4** preserves the start and goal tiles but randomly choosing four of the remaining tiles as holes, where in this instance we consider a special case that the holes chosen unintentionally block the agent's path to the goal.

Table 1. Representative test cases of relocating the special states.

Test-ID	[r,c]	Start	Goal	No. of holes	Holes
TC-1	$[4,4]$	$(1,1)$	$(4,4)$	4	$(2,2),(2,4),(3,4),(4,1)$
TC-2	$[4,4]$	$(1,3)$	$(4,4)$	4	$(2,2),(2,4),(3,4),(4,1)$
TC-3	$[4,4]$	$(1,1)$	$(4,2)$	4	$(2,2),(2,4),(3,4),(4,1)$
TC-4	$[4,4]$	(1,1)	$(4,4)$	4	$(2,1),(2,2),(2,3),(2,4)$

Variation in Number of Holes. The above TC-4 changes the location of holes, but preserves the number of holes. Here, we want to further evaluate whether the formal model works when increasing the number of holes as shown in Table 2: **TC-5** and **TC-6** both add 1 hole to TC-1 but at different place; **TC-7** adds 3 more holes to TC-1.

Scalability of Environment. To evaluate the scalability of our model, the environment's dimension and layout are altered. As detailed in Table 3, **TC-8** and **TC-9** expand the grid to 6×6 and 9×9, respectively, while **TC-10** further assesses the adaptability of the model with a nonsquare rectangle grid.

Table 2. Representative test cases of changing the number of holes.

Test-ID	[r,c]	Start	Goal	No. of holes	Holes
TC-5	[4, 4]	(1,1)	(4, 4)	5	(2, 2), (2, 4), (3, 4), (4, 1), (4, 2)
TC-6	[4, 4]	(1,1)	(4, 4)	5	(2, 2), (2, 4), (3, 4), (4, 1), (2, 3)
TC-7	[4, 4]	(1,1)	(4, 4)	7	(2, 2), (2, 4), (3, 4), (4, 1), (4, 2), (2, 3), (1, 4)

Table 3. Representative test cases of changing dimension and shape of environment.

Test-ID	[r,c]	Start	Goal	No. of holes	Holes
TC-8	[6, 6]	(1, 1)	(6, 6)	4	(2, 2), (2, 4), (3, 4), (4, 1)
TC-9	[9, 9]	(1, 1)	(9, 9)	4	(2, 2), (2, 4), (3, 4), (4, 1)
TC-10	[4, 6]	(1, 1)	(4, 6)	4	(2, 2), (2, 4), (3, 4), (4, 1)

Reward Maximization. To verify that the optimized policy maximizes the cumulative reward, we compare it against several manually constructed deterministic state sequences. The optimized policy π^* of TC-1, obtained with running our model, produces the state trajectory of $(1,1),(2,1),(3,1),(3,2),(3,3),(4,3),(4,4)$. All test cases in Table 4 maintain the same environment setting as TC-1 and are omitted for brevity. The sequences for **TC-11** and **TC-12** should achieve accumulative rewards equivalent to that of the optimized policy; **TC-13** is expected to accumulate a lower reward than the optimized policy, as it uses more steps to reach the goal state.

Table 4. Representative test cases of reward maximization.

Test-ID	...	State Sequence	Accumulative Reward
TC-11	...	(1, 1), (2, 1), (3, 1), (3, 2), (3, 3), (4, 3), (4, 4)	=optimized π^*
TC-12	...	(1, 1), (1, 2), (1, 3), (2, 3), (3, 3), (4, 3), (4, 4)	=optimized π^*
TC-13	...	(1, 1), (1, 2), (1, 3), (2, 3), (3, 3), (3, 2), (4, 2), (4, 3), (4, 4)	<optimized π^*

Dynamic Obstacles. The current setting of our model assumes the holes are static. However, real-world environments contain dynamic obstacles. For example, in the Freeway environment [21], the RL agent controls a chicken running across a highway to get to the other side, while avoiding collusion with moving cars. **TC-14** and **TC-15** in Table 5 extend our modeling to incorporate dynamic holes.

Table 5. Representative test cases of dynamic obstacles.

Test-ID	[r,c]	Start	Goal	No. of holes	Holes
TC-14	[4, 4]	(1, 1)	(4, 4)	4	hole at (r,c) moves to (r+1,c)
TC-15	[4, 4]	(1, 1)	(4, 4)	4	hole at (r,c) moves to (r,c+1)

4.3 Scalability

To evaluate the scalability of our SMT model, we investigate how the size of the environment influences computational performance. We set the number of holes to 3 and time step to 30, fix the upper-left corner to be the start state and the lower-right corner to be the goal state, and randomly sample three tiles from the remaining area to serve as holes.

As shown in Fig. 4, our analysis reveals that the solving time increases as the size of the environment grows. This trend might stem from larger state space introduces a greater number of possible paths. Consequently, while effective for modeling and verification in moderate-sized RL systems, computational efficiency remains a challenge for scaling to very large or high-dimensional RL systems.

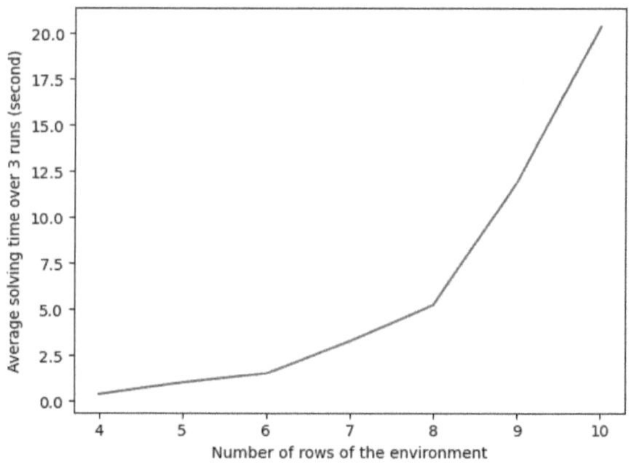

Fig. 4. Solving time of the model increases as the size of the environment.

5 Conclusion

In this paper, we introduced an SMT-based formal modeling of the Reinforcement Learning systems, aiming to guarantee the safety and reliability, which are crucial for widespread real-worl deployment.

Specifically, we have presented a step-by-step formal modeling of the key components RL system with SMT and illustrated our approach using a traditional RL environment FrozenLake. This setting involves additional constraints, which we have specified in detail. To evaluate the correctness and adaptability of our model, we designed test cases and implemented them using the Z3 solver. The proposed approach lays a solid foundation for broader area of RL verification and has the potential to significantly improve the safety and reliability of RL systems. This work opens new possibilities for safe and reliable deployment of RL systems.

In the future, we aim to apply our approach to more complex and realistic RL environments, and integrate it with other verification techniques like probabilistic model checking to overcome the limitation of handling stochastic policies. We also plan to evaluate our approach on larger-scale real-world RL applications to demonstrate its practical value and effectiveness.

Acknowledgment. This work was supported by the NSFC under Grant 62172019, and the National Key R&D Program of China under Grant 2022YFB2702200, 2022YFA1005102 and 2024YFA1014000.

References

1. Silver, D., et al.: Mastering the game of go with deep neural networks and tree search. Nature **529**(7587), 484–489 (2016)
2. Silver, D., et al.: Mastering Chess and Shogi by Self-Play with a General Reinforcement Learning Algorithm. arXiv preprint arXiv:1712.01815 (2017)
3. Bostrom, A., et al.: AlphaStar: Grandmaster Level in StarCraft II using Multi-Agent Reinforcement Learning. arXiv preprint arXiv:1911.08265 (2019)
4. Ng, A.Y., Schojet, R., DeLeon, M., Thrun, S.: Playing catch with a robot hand. In: Proceedings of the 2009 IEEE/RSJ International Conference on Intelligent Robots and Systems, pp. 1532–1537 (2009)
5. Raffin, E., et al.: Dactyl: Mastering the Dexterous Manipulation of Real Objects. arXiv preprint arXiv:2011.04962 (2020)
6. Kiran, B.R., et al.: Deep reinforcement learning for autonomous driving: a survey. IEEE Trans. Intell. Transp. Syst. **23**(6), 4909–4926 (2021)
7. Sallab, A.E., Abdou, M., Perot, E., Yogamani, S.: Deep Reinforcement Learning Framework for Autonomous Driving. arXiv preprint arXiv:1704.02532 (2017)
8. Krause, J., Lu, Y., Sun, W., Sun, M., Huang, X.: DeepMind's AI Predicts Hospital patient Deaths with 70
9. Jumper, J., et al.: AlphaFold: a solution to a 50-year-old grand challenge in biology. Nature **586**(7827), 546–551 (2020)
10. Li, J., Monroe, W., Ritter, A., Galley, M., Gao, J., Jurafsky, D.: Deep reinforcement learning for dialogue generation. arXiv preprint arXiv:1606.01541 (2016)
11. Keneshloo, Y., Shi, T., Ramakrishnan, N., Reddy, C.K.: Deep reinforcement learning for sequence-to-sequence models. IEEE Trans. Neural Netw. Learn. Syst. **31**(7), 2469–2489 (2019)
12. Uc-Cetina, V., Navarro-Guerrero, N., Martin-Gonzalez, A., Weber, C., Wermter, S.: Survey on reinforcement learning for language processing. Artif. Intell. Rev. **56**(2), 1543–1575 (2023)

13. Huang, L., Fu, M., Li, F., Qu, H., Liu, Y., Chen, W.: A deep reinforcement learning based long-term recommender system. Knowl.-Based Syst. **213**, 106706 (2021)
14. Lei, Y., Pei, H., Yan, H., Li, W.: Reinforcement learning based recommendation with graph convolutional Q-Network. In: Proceedings of the 43rd International ACM SIGIR Conference on Research and Development in Information Retrieval, pp. 1757–1760 (2020)
15. Javed, U., Shaukat, K., Hameed, I.A., Iqbal, F., Alam, T.M., Luo, S.: A review of content-based and context-based recommendation systems. Int. J. Emerg. Technol. Learn. (iJET) **16**(3), 274–306 (2021)
16. Fulton, N., Platzer, A.: Safe reinforcement learning via formal methods: toward safe control through proof and learning. In: Proceedings of the AAAI Conference on Artificial Intelligence, vol. 32 (2018)
17. Chen, W.: Formal Modeling and Automatic Generation of Test Cases for the Autonomous Vehicle. Ph.D. thesis, Université Paris-Saclay (2020)
18. Lu, Y., Sun, W., Sun, M.: Towards mutation testing of reinforcement learning systems. J. Syst. Architect. **131**, 102701 (2022)
19. Bacci, E.: Formal Verification of Deep Reinforcement Learning Agents. Ph.D. thesis, University of Birmingham (2022)
20. Varshosaz, M., Ghaffari, M., Johnsen, E.B., Wąsowski, A.: Formal specification and testing for reinforcement learning. Proc. ACM Program. Lang. **7**(ICFP), 125–158 (2023)
21. Gross, D., Spieker, H.: Probabilistic model checking of stochastic reinforcement learning policies. arXiv preprint arXiv:2403.18725 (2024)
22. Zhang, X., Sun, M.: SMT-based modeling and verification of cloud applications. In: Xia, Y., Zhang, L.J. (eds.) Services – SERVICES 2019. SERVICES 2019. LNCS, vol. 11517, pp. 1–15. Springer, Cham (2019). https://doi.org/10.1007/978-3-030-23381-5_1
23. Zhang, Y., Wei, Z., Zhang, X., Sun, M.: Using Z3 for Formal Modeling and Verification of FNN Global Robustness. arXiv preprint arXiv:2304.10558 (2023)
24. Amir, G., Wu, H., Barrett, C., Katz, G.: An SMT-based approach for verifying binarized neural networks. In: Groote, J.F., Larsen, K.G. (eds.) Tools and Algorithms for the Construction and Analysis of Systems. TACAS 2021. LNCS, vol. 12652, pp. 203–222. Springer, Cham (2021). https://doi.org/10.1007/978-3-030-72013-1_11
25. Maucher, J.: Example Q-Learning (2022). https://hannibunny.github.io/mlbook/rl/QLearnFrozenLake.html. Accessed 16 Sep 2021

Towards High-Level SMT Program Modeling: Bounded Integers, Simplified Structs, and Metaprogramming

Xiangyu Li(✉)

School of Mathematical Sciences, Peking University, Beijing, China
xyli@stu.pku.edu.cn

Abstract. Formal SMT modeling of programs remains less intuitive than programming, despite shared logical foundations. This paper argues that three high-level features, (1) bounded arbitrary-precision integers, (2) simplified struct syntax, and (3) template metaprogramming, are essential to bridge this gap. Unlike shallow SMT-LIB wrappers or direct SMT-LIB usage, these features enable program-like modeling with automated constraint propagation and compile-time code generation, thereby lowering the learning curve and boosting productivity. We also identify key compiler challenges unique to implementing these features.

Keywords: Satisfiability Modulo Theories · Modeling Language · Compiler · Language Design

1 Introduction

Although built on shared logical foundations, formal modeling of programs often proves less intuitive than the act of programming. Beyond the inherent complexity of mathematics, we argue that formal language design significantly impacts usability. While many formal methods require substantial human interaction, SMT's automatable nature under decidable theories makes its usability gap uniquely addressable. Yet current SMT modeling languages lag far behind programming languages.

SMT-LIB [2] provides a standard interface instrumental for solver interoperability. It separates modeling and solving concerns, leading solvers such as Z3 [14], CVC5 [1], Yices [5] and Alt-Ergo [4] to adopt a front-end/back-end architecture. SMT-LIB's theory-centric design is suitable for its primary purpose of interfacing SMT solvers, but it fractures data types (e.g., Arithmetic Integers vs. BitVectors) despite functional overlaps.

This standard resembles compiler intermediate representations (IR) like LLVM [8], but unlike compiler front ends that hide machine-level complexities and support developer-friendly high-level features, the interfaces of the aforementioned SMT solvers remain low-level wrappers. The common solution, programming language binding, suggests that a significant subset of software programs

É. André et al. (Eds.): ICFEM 2025, LNCS 16229, pp. 366–372, 2026.
https://doi.org/10.1007/978-981-95-4213-0_20

should be automatically translatable to SMT models. However, existing solutions do not comprehensively hide theory-combination complexities or enable type-safe code reuse to the extent required for intuitive program modeling.

To bridge this gap, we propose a higher-level language layer atop SMT-LIB. We address three core limitations: in Sect. 2, we explain how to model bounded arbitrary-precision integers in SMT models, which unifies arithmetic and bitwise operations; next, we provide insights on simplifying SMT modeling of common programming data structures in Sect. 3; finally in Sect. 4, we suggest that a Turing-complete metaprogramming mechanism should exist for the SMT front end to enhance code reusability. While an integral part of the MedTiny [10] project, these contributions stand independently given SMT-LIB's standard basis. Implementing these high-level abstractions requires solving challenges absent in typical compilers, which we summarize in Sect. 5.

2 Bounded Arbitrary-Precision Integer

Newer programming languages address the disparity between mathematical integers and machine representations by either introducing arbitrary-precision conventions through official library built-ins like BigInteger since Java 1.2 [6] or via changes to language standards like Python 3 [18]. What makes programming easier is that arbitrary-precision integers are mathematically idealized but also allow bitwise operations by generalizing signed two's complement integer representation conventions. The ability to use bitwise operators on numbers is significant in the engineering domain, exemplified by algorithms such as the fast inverse square root algorithm [11].

SMT-LIB offers two choices for representing integer values: Arithmetic and BitVector. Arithmetic can represent mathematical integers, with various theories to apply, while BitVector addresses common machine number representations: signed and unsigned two's complement convention. In SMT-LIB, converting an Arithmetic Integer to a BitVector requires providing a fixed constant length for the bit vector [13]. This implies that, without external knowledge of the bit vector length a priori, arbitrary-precision integer types with dynamic bit lengths fall outside the expressivity of the current SMT-LIB standard.

We propose enforcing bound specification when bitwise operators are used. Unlike parametric bit vector theories [15] that introduce undecidability, this bounded approach maintains decidability while aligning with programmer intuition. The compiler is responsible for inferring and propagating the minimum bit vector length (*minbvl*) following the rules shown in Table 1, thus preserving all significant bits, though conservatively.

Practically, theory combination overhead is not inherent to all programs: it arises only when both arithmetic and bitwise operations coexist. The compiler intelligently minimizes this overhead through three operational modes:

- **Pure Arithmetic Mode**: When no bitwise operators exist, all values are maintained within the Arithmetics, leveraging efficient integer/real solvers.

Table 1. Minimum bit vector length (*minbvl*) tracking rules.

<table>
<tr><th>Description</th><th>Expression</th><th>Result Min BV Length</th></tr>
<tr><td>Constant</td><td>a</td><td>$\log_2 |a|$</td></tr>
<tr><td>Bounded Integer Variable</td><td>x: int lb..ub</td><td>$\max(\log_2 |lb|, \log_2 |ub|)$</td></tr>
<tr><td>Exponentiation</td><td>x**y</td><td>minbvl(x)*$2^{minbvl(y)}$</td></tr>
<tr><td>Addition and subtraction</td><td>x+y, x-y</td><td>max(minbvl(x), minbvl(y))+1</td></tr>
<tr><td>Multiplication</td><td>x*y</td><td>minbvl(x)+minbvl(y)</td></tr>
<tr><td>Integer Division</td><td>x/y</td><td>minbvl(x)</td></tr>
<tr><td>Remainder</td><td>x%y</td><td>minbvl(y)</td></tr>
<tr><td>Value Comparison</td><td>x > y x<=y x==y x!=y</td><td rowspan="2">1</td></tr>
<tr><td>Logical Opeartor</td><td>x&&y x||y</td></tr>
<tr><td>Conditional Operator</td><td>z?x:y</td><td rowspan="2">max(minbvl(x),minbvl(y))</td></tr>
<tr><td>Bitwise Binary Operators</td><td>x&y x|y x^y</td></tr>
<tr><td>Negation and Bitwise Not</td><td>-x ~x</td><td>minbvl(x)</td></tr>
</table>

- **Pure BitVector Mode**: For code using only bitwise operations on bounded variables, fixed-size bit vectors suffice.
- **Hybrid Mode**: This mode applies only when both bitwise and arithmetic operations appear, and the bounded conversion strategy is employed:
  1. Begin in Arithmetic theory.
  2. Convert signed integer to bit vector at bitwise operator boundaries.
  3. Convert bit vector results back to Arithmetic integers.

  For example, in hybrid mode, the compiler translates the expression `x|y` to

  (sbv_to_int (bvor (int_to_bv minbvl(x|y) x) (int_to_bv minbvl(x|y) y))

  where `minbvl(x|y)` is an inferred constant following rules in Table 1.

Users may manually optimize via techniques like componentization and abstraction, but this tiered approach defaults to minimal overhead while maintaining programming-language semantics. This automation hides Arithmetic/BitVector complexities from users, requiring only that variable bounds be marked.

3 Simplified Struct Syntaxes

Modern programming languages converge on supporting arrays and structs as basic composite types with concise syntaxes. While SMT-LIB supports arrays, it offers only algebraic datatypes (a superset of basic structs) through a verbose, Lisp-style S-expression-based declaration process [12]. Lisp's heavy reliance on parentheses and the program-as-data principle imposes a high cognitive load [17], contributing to its decline in popularity. By choosing S-expressions, SMT-LIB inherits both their power and a learning curve that is even steeper, compounding the theory-centric aspect of SMT solving.

Language bindings mitigate verbosity but introduce new limitations. Consider Z3's Python bindings: despite simplifying arithmetic, bitwise, and array indexing operators by overloading, struct handling remains shallow because the dot syntax makes field names global identifiers, risking naming collisions. Constraints derived from Sect. 2's integer bounds can also be propagated through nested structs in this simplified syntax. For example:

```
typedef date = {year: int 1970..2100, month: int 1..12, day: int 1..31};
date newdate, olddate;
newdate = olddate + {year=1, month=1, day=1}; // Element-wise addition
```

Constraints should be automatically added for all `newdate` calculations by traversing the struct, generating the following SMT-LIB constraints:

```
(assert (and (>= (+ olddate.year 1) 1970) (<= (+ olddate.year 1) 2100)))
(assert (and (>= (+ olddate.month 1) 1) (<= (+ olddate.month 1) 12)))
(assert (and (>= (+ olddate.day 1) 1) (<= (+ olddate.day 1) 31)))
```

This constraint propagation feature extends SMT-LIB. While it matches Ada's static bound checking ability [7], SMT solvers offer much more flexibility than merely checking bounds.

4 Template Metaprogramming

Repetitive model or constraint patterns necessitate metaprogramming, which involves generating code during compilation. Metaprogramming exceeds macro capabilities by supporting full programmatic logic, whereas modern macros typically perform only text replacement once. However SMT-LIB is already a Lisp extension and Lisp is known for its powerful metaprogramming capability, its niche and untyped syntax yields to the current programming language binding solutions. C++ templating presents a superior option to programming language binding, offering type-safe, full Turing-complete metaprogramming capabilities [19]. Template expansion terminates at compile-time before solver invocation, thereby preserving SMT's decidability guarantees. Furthermore, numerous parametric or templated formal methods [3,15,20,21] demonstrate that this concept is easily understandable and extends formal modeling power in a reasonable direction.

Unlike C++'s organic evolution, this SMT metaprogramming design defaults to `constexpr`-like behavior, since SMT mostly reasons about values. Extensions like static `for` [10] (e.g. unrolling `for i in 0..N`) further reduce external programming language binding needs.

5 Future Work

The high-level SMT modeling features proposed in Sects. 2, 3, and 4 present significant implementation difficulties not typically covered in compiler courses or textbooks. We have been constructing a modified visitor pattern framework [9] to generalize these non-conventional compiler front-end algorithms:

1. **Theory-Aware Lowering**: Unlike LLVM, where lowering sacrifices some abstractions for optimization, SMT solver front ends must preserve high-level constructs to leverage solver theories. While bit-level integer expansion by division and modulo operations and array selection and store expansion by conditionals are always possible, such an expanded SMT model may degrade performance to an SAT-solver level, exponentially increasing solve time.
2. **Control-Flow-Sensitive AST Traversal**: Program execution order differs from abstract syntax tree(AST) traversal order. In standards prior to C++11, template metaprogramming code has to be constructed significantly differently from run-time code to work around lazy evaluation. Taking the recursive factorial as an example:

   $$\text{factorial (n): RETURN (n == 0) ? 1 : (n} * \text{factorial(n} - 1))$$

   `factorial(0)` would still evaluate the recursive branch before condition evaluation and resolution under standard depth-first traversal generated by frameworks like ANTLR [16], potentially causing an infinite loop.
3. **Multi-AST Traversal** The front ends of simpler languages only require the ability to traverse one AST, but simultaneous traversal of two or more trees is essential for propagating nested constraints, as demonstrated by the `date` example in Sect. 3. For instance, the constraints are obtained by traversing the type of the left-side `newdate`, while the constrained elements are derived from the corresponding portions of the right-side expression.

6 Conclusion

In this paper, we introduce three essential features to lift the level of SMT modeling of programs, collectively bridging the programming intuition and formal verification. As part of ongoing doctoral research, a unified front-end framework for high-level formal language compilation is proposed to open avenues for generalizing common verification techniques.

Acknowledgements. This research was sponsored by the National Key R&D Program of China (2022YFB2702200), NSFC under Grant No. 62172019.

References

1. Barbosa, H., et al.: CVC5: a versatile and industrial-strength SMT solver. In: Fisman, D., Rosu, G. (eds.) Tools and Algorithms for the Construction and Analysis of Systems. TACAS 2022. LNCS, vol. 13243, pp. 415–442. Springer, Cham (2022). https://doi.org/10.1007/978-3-030-99524-9_24

2. Barrett, C., Stump, A., Tinelli, C.: The smt-lib standard: version 2.0. In: Proceedings of the 8th International Workshop on Satisfiability Modulo Theories (Edinburgh, UK), vol. 13, p. 14 (2010). https://smt-lib.org/
3. Chatterjee, K., Goharshady, A., Goharshady, E., Karrabi, M., Zikelic, D.: Sound and complete witnesses for template-based verification of ltl properties on polynomial programs. In: Platzer, A., Rozier, K.Y., Pradella, M., Rossi, M. (eds.) Formal Methods. FM 2024. LNCS, vol. 14933, pp. 600–619. Springer, Cham (2025). https://doi.org/10.1007/978-3-031-71162-6_31
4. Conchon, S., Iguernlala, M., Mebsout, A.: Altgr-ergo, a graphical user interface for the smt solver alt-ergo. Electron. Proc. Theor. Comput. Sci. **239**, 1–13 (2017). https://doi.org/10.4204/EPTCS.239.1
5. Dutertre, B.: Yices 2.2. In: Biere, A., Bloem, R. (eds.): Computer-Aided Verification (CAV'2014). LNCS, vol. 8559, pp. 737–744. Springer, Cham (2014). https://doi.org/10.1007/978-3-319-08867-9_49
6. Gosling, J., et al.: The Java Language Specification. Oracle, java se 21 edition edn. (2023). https://docs.oracle.com/javase/specs/jls/se21/html/index.html
7. ISO/IEC JTC 1/SC 22/WG 9: Ada 2012 Language Reference Manual. International Standard ISO/IEC 8652:2012, International Organization for Standardization (ISO) (2012). http://www.ada-auth.org/standards/ada12.html
8. Lattner, C., Adve, V.: LLVM: a compilation framework for lifelong program analysis and transformation. In: International Symposium on Code Generation and Optimization, pp. 75–88. San Jose, CA, USA (Mar 2004). https://doi.org/10.1109/CGO.2004.1281665
9. Li, X.: MedTiny Python Implementation. https://github.com/xyli-pku/MedTiny-Python
10. Li, X., Zhang, Y., Luan, X., Xue, X., Sun, M.: Medtiny: enhanced mediator modeling language for scalable parallel algorithms. In: 2023 IEEE 23rd International Conference on Software Quality, Reliability, and Security Companion (QRS-C), pp. 451–460 (2023). https://doi.org/10.1109/QRS-C60940.2023.00075
11. Lomont, C.: Fast inverse square root. Technical report, Purdue University (2003)
12. McCarthy, J.: Recursive functions of symbolic expressions and their computation by machine, Part I. Commun. ACM **3**(4), 184–195 (1960). https://doi.org/10.1145/367177.367199
13. Microsoft Research: Z3 Guide: Bitvectors (2024). https://microsoft.github.io/z3guide/docs/theories/Bitvectors/
14. de Moura, L., Bjørner, N.: Z3: an efficient SMT solver. In: Ramakrishnan, C.R., Rehof, J. (eds.) Tools and Algorithms for the Construction and Analysis of Systems. TACAS 2008. LNCS, vol. 4963, pp. 337–340. Springer, Berlin, Heidelberg (2008). https://doi.org/10.1007/978-3-540-78800-3_24
15. Niemetz, A., Preiner, M., Reynolds, A., Zohar, Y., Barrett, C., Tinelli, C.: Towards satisfiability modulo parametric bit-vectors. J. Autom. Reason. **65**(7), 1001–1025 (2021). https://doi.org/10.1007/s10817-021-09598-9
16. Parr, T.: The Definitive ANTLR 4 Reference, 2nd edn. Pragmatic Bookshelf, Raleigh (2013)
17. Touretzky, D.S.: Common LISP: A Gentle Introduction to Symbolic Computation. Dover Publications, Garden City (2013)
18. Van Rossum, G., Drake, F.L.: Python 3 Reference Manual. CreateSpace, Scotts Valley, CA (2009). https://doi.org/10.5555/1593511
19. Vandevoorde, D., Josuttis, N.M., Gregor, D.: C++ Templates: The Complete Guide, 2nd edn. Addison-Wesley Professional, Boston (2017)

20. Wang, J., et al.: Scenario-based flexible modeling and scalable falsification for reconfigurable CPSs. In: Gurfinkel, A., Ganesh, V. (eds.) Computer Aided Verification. CAV 2024. LNCS, vol. 14683, pp. 329–355. Springer, Cham (2024). https://doi.org/10.1007/978-3-031-65633-0_15
21. Wang, P., Yang, T., Fu, H., Li, G., Ong, C.H.L.: Static posterior inference of bayesian probabilistic programming via polynomial solving. Proc. ACM Program. Lang. **8**(PLDI) (2024). https://doi.org/10.1145/3656432

Formal Modelling of Fault Tolerant Robotic Missions

Manon Lecart and Elena Troubitsyna(✉)

KTH – Royal Institute of Technology, Stockholm, Sweden
{lecart,elenatro}@kth.se

Abstract. Safety-critical autonomous robotic systems should be able to reliably execute their missions despite changes in the operating environment and system failures. Due to complex hierarchical architecture, efficient and correct implementation of fault tolerance is a challenging engineering issue. The states of the robots and progress of mission execution should be monitored at different layers and mission planning and execution should be adapted accordingly. In this paper, we formalise the main properties of fault-tolerant mission execution in Event-B. It allows us to derive a complex hierarchical architecture of fault tolerance mechanisms in a systematic correct-by-construction manner. The approach enhances design of robotic systems with mechanisms for monitoring mission progress and adaptation triggered whenever the progress is hindered by failures.

1 Introduction

Autonomous robotic systems are increasingly used to perform safety-critical missions. To successfully complete the missions allocated on them, the robots should be able to adapt not only to the changes in their operating environment but also to the failures in their function. Hence, achieving fault tolerance constitutes an important goal in designing robotic system.

However, the architecture of a robotic system is complex and divided into several layers. The layered architecture enables a separation of concerns from strategic mission planning and adaptation to assigning individual tasks to the robots and monitoring of their health. Designing such complex multi-layered fault tolerance mechanisms is complex and error-prone. To facilitate this task, we propose to formalise mission coordination in Event-B.

Event-B is a formal state-based approach to correct-by-construction system development [1]. The approach is supported by the Rodin platform – an integrated development environment for formal specification and proof-based verification in Event-B.

In this paper, we present several specification and refinement patterns supporting a rigorous construction of a hierarchy of monitors supporting fault-tolerant mission coordination and execution. We demonstrate how to formalise the relationships between the mission execution progress, task execution and

É. André et al. (Eds.): ICFEM 2025, LNCS 16229, pp. 373–390, 2026.
https://doi.org/10.1007/978-981-95-4213-0_21

health of robots. Formal modelling allows us to derive the conditions that should be monitored at different layers of system architecture to ensure that mission execution progressing correctly and adaptation is triggered whenever the progress is hindered by failures.

The paper is structured as follows: in Sect. 2, we introduce a reference layered architecture of a robotic system and define its main concepts. In Sect. 3, we overview our modelling framework – Event-B. In Sect. 4, we present our specification and refinement patterns for modelling fault tolerance of autonomous robotic systems. In Sect. 5, we discuss the results of the formal development. In Sect. 6, we overview the related work. Finally, in Sect. 7, we discuss the proposed approach and conclude.

2 Architecture of Autonomous Robotic Systems

The behaviour of a robotic system is a composition of task-oriented functions defined by the system mission and event-oriented reactions. The system mission defines a sequence of tasks to be performed to achieve a goal of the mission. The event-oriented behaviour is driven by the events occurring in the system environment as well as internal states. Hence, the system architecture includes several task-oriented and event-oriented loops. It allows the system, on the one hand, to progress in the mission execution and, on the other hand, to react to different internal and external events and adapt accordingly.

Typically, an architecture of a robotic system consists of three layers: decision, execution and functional layers. The decision layer takes a mission definition as an input and produces the task plan to execute it. It also supervises execution of the tasks and reacts to the events from the execution layer below.

The execution layer controls and coordinates the execution of the functions distributed among the robots according to the task requirements.

The functional layer includes the closed control loops of basic robot capabilities including image processing, motion control, etc. They rely on robot sensors and actuators. The overall system architecture is shown in Fig. 1.

Formally, we define the mission as follows:

Definition 1. Let T be a set of tasks in the mission. Let $t_{init} \in T$ be the initial task of the mission and $t_{fin} \in T$ be the final task of the mission. Let the partial function (denoted $\nrightarrow$) $status \in T \nrightarrow STATUS$, where $STATUS = \{completed, failed, ready\}$ designate the status of task execution. The mission is completed if $\forall t \in T : status(t) = completed$.

Definition 2. The mission scenario is a sequence defined over the set of tasks T included in the mission. The function (denoted $\rightarrow$) $next \in T \rightarrow T$ identifies the next task executed in the scenario. A task is said to be ready for execution if all the previous tasks in the scenario were successfully completed, i.e., $\forall t \in T,\ (status(t) = ready) \Rightarrow (\forall t' \in T,\ t = next(t') \Rightarrow status(t') = completed)$.

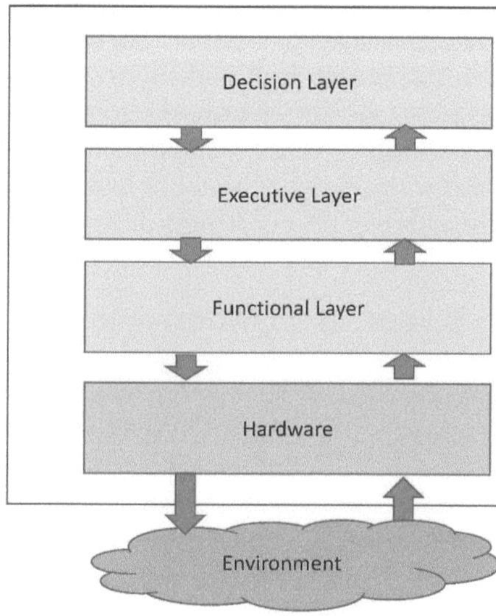

Fig. 1. Generic architecture of a robotic system

The definitions above establish a basis for designing the mission monitor at the decision layer. Namely, the decision layer chooses the next task to be executed if the execution of the previous tasks has been successfully completed. If a failure is reported by the execution layer, the decision layer can either abort the mission or choose an alternative mission scenario to execute.

At the execution layer, the task execution monitor assigns tasks to execute to the robots. The relation (denoted $\leftrightarrow$) $requirements \in TASKS \leftrightarrow CAPABILITIES$ associates each task with a set of capabilities required to perform it. It checks that for each task requested to be executed by the decision layer, the required set of capabilities can be provided by the currently operational idle robots.

We can define the status of the tasks at the execution layer as follows: Let $curr\_task$ be the task requested for execution by the decision layer. Let $ROBOTS$ be the set of system robots and $robots \subseteq ROBOTS$ be the subset of currently operational robots and *capabilities* is the set of their capabilities. Then the execution layer monitor assigns the task status *ready* if it receives a confirmation from the functional layer that the currently operational robots are capable of executing the current task, i.e., $requirements(curr\_task) \subseteq capabilities$. The status of the current task changes to *blocked* if $requirements(curr\_task) \not\subseteq capabilities$, i.e., among the robots there are no ones that possess required capabilities.

The monitor at the functional layer is responsible for monitoring health of a robot chosen to execute the current task. The monitor checks that there is at least one robot that has the required capabilities and assigns a task to execute to it. Robot's capabilities can be classified to sensing and acting. If a robot fails and loses some of its capabilities, the monitor should try to find another robot which can perform the current task, i.e., performs re-assigning a task as a result of failure the condition $requirements(curr\_task) \not\subseteq capabilities(curr\_robot)$ becomes satisfied. In this case, the monitor at the functional layer notifies the monitor at the execution layer that the current task is blocked.

3 Overview of the Event-B Framework

Event-B [2] is a state-based framework that promotes the correct-by-construction approach to system development and formal verification by theorem proving. In Event-B, a system specification is defined as an *abstract state machine* [2]. It encapsulates the model state, represented by a collection of variables, and defines operations on the state. Hence, it describes the dynamic behaviour of a modelled system. A machine part of specification has an accompanying component – *context*. It includes user-defined sets and constants. Their properties are defined as model axioms.

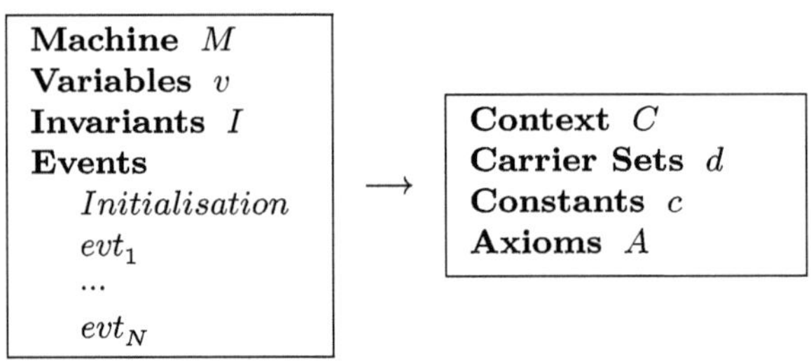

Fig. 2. Event-B machine and context

A general form of Event-B system specification is shown in Fig. 2. The machine is uniquely identified by its name M. The state variables, v, are declared in the **Variables** clause and initialised in the **Initialisation** event. The variables are strongly typed by the constraining predicates I given in the **Invariants** clause. The invariant clause usually also contains some other predicates, which define the essential properties (e.g., safety invariants) that should be preserved during the system execution.

The dynamic behaviour of the system is defined by a set of atomic **Events**. Generally, an event has the following form:

$$e \,\widehat{=}\, \textbf{any}\ a\ \textbf{where}\ G_e\ \textbf{then}\ R_e\ \textbf{end},$$

where e is the event's name, a is the list of local variables. The *guard* G_e is a predicate over the local variables of the event and the state variables of the system. The body of an event is defined by a *multiple* (possibly nondeterministic) assignment over the system variables. In Event-B, an assignment of an event e is semantically defined as a next-state relation R_e. We can distinguish between two types of assignments: deterministic and non-deterministic ones. In a standard form, a deterministic assignment is defined as an expression E over the variables of the machine: $x := E(x, y)$, where x and y are the variables of the machine. A non-deterministic assignment $x :\mid some\_condition(x, y, x')$ represents the fact that the state variable x gets non-deterministically updated by the value x', which may depend on the initial values of the variables x and y in such a way that *some_condition* is satisfied.

The guard G_e defines the conditions under which the event e is *enabled*, i.e., its body can be executed. If several events are enabled at the same time then any of them can be chosen for execution non-deterministically. If an event does not have the local variables then **any** clause is omitted.

To support precise modelling, Event-B specifications make use of set theory and relational notation. In addition to the standard set-theoretical notations (e.g., $\in$, $\subseteq$, $\cup$, $\cap$, $\varnothing$, etc.), the operator $\setminus$ is used to denote set subtraction. $T_1 \times T_2$ is a cartesian product of two types (sets) T_1 and T_2, i.e., $T_1 \times T_2 = \{t_1 \mapsto t_2 \cdot t_1 \in T_1 \wedge t_2 \in T_2\}$. The notation $\mathbb{P}(T)$ stands for the powerset (set of all subsets) type over elements of the type T, while $T_1 \leftrightarrow T_2$ denotes a relation between elements of two types (sets), i.e., $R \in T_1 \leftrightarrow T_2 \Leftrightarrow R \in \mathbb{P}(T_1 \times T_2)$. Moreover, *dom* and *ran* are respectively the relation domain and range operators. Functions are treated as special cases of relations, and Event-B distinguishes several categories: partial functions ($T_1 \nrightarrow T_2$), total functions ($T_1 \rightarrow T_2$), injections ($T_1 \rightarrowtail T_2$) and partial injections ($T_1 \rightarrowtail\!\!\!\!\!\nrightarrow T_2$), surjections ($T_1 \twoheadrightarrow T_2$) and partial surjections ($T_1 \nrightarrow\!\!\!\!\twoheadrightarrow T_2$).

The Event-B framework employs a top-down refinement approach to system development. The development typically starts from an abstract specification that nondeterministically defines the most essential functional requirements. In a sequence of refinement steps, we gradually reduce nondeterminism and introduce detailed design decisions. It enables an incremental construction of complex specifications, increases a degree of automation of the underlying proof-based verification and facilitates structured modelling of system requirements.

Event-B employs a proof-based approach to verifying correctness. The consistency of Event-B models, i.e., verification of well-formedness and invariant preservation as well as correctness of refinement steps is demonstrated by discharging a number of verification conditions – proof obligations. There are two main types of proof obligations for demonstrating correctness of a specification: invariant preservation and feasibility. Invariant preservation means that the invariant is preserved by an execution of each event and the initialisation. To verify *invariant preservation* for an event e, we should prove the following logical formula:

$$A(d,c),\ I(d,c,v),\ G_e(d,c,x,v),\ R_e(d,c,x,v,v')\ \vdash\ I(d,c,v'), \tag{INV}$$

where A are the model axioms, I are the model invariants, d and c are the model constants and sets respectively, x are the event's local variables and v, v' are the variable values before and after event execution.

The proof obligation of initialisation event simply requires to demonstrate that axioms and postcondition of initialisation establish invariant:

$$A(d,c),\ R_{Init}(d,c,v') \ \vdash \ I(d,c,v'). \tag{INIT}$$

Another type of proof obligations – feasibility – verifies well-formedness of the specification. Formally, for each event e of the model, its feasibility means that whenever the event is enabled, its next state relation is well-defined, i.e., there exists some reachable after-state:

$$A(d,c),\ I(d,c,v),\ G_e(d,c,v) \ \vdash \ \exists\, v' \cdot R_e(d,c,v,v'). \tag{FIS}$$

To verify correctness of a refinement step, one needs to discharge a number of proof obligations for a refined model. They aim at verifying that the refinement step is performed in a correctness-preserving way, i.e., the refined specification does not introduce a behaviour that contradicts a more abstract specification. The main proof obligations are guard strengthening and action simulation.

Let us introduce a shorthand $H(d,c,v,w)$ that stands for the hypotheses $A(d,c)$, $I(d,c,v)$ and $I'(d,c,v,w)$, where I and I' are respectively the abstract and the refined invariants, while v, w are respectively the abstract and concrete variables.

When refining an event, its guard can only be strengthened:

$$H(d,c,v,w),\ G'_e(d,c,w) \ \vdash \ G_e(d,c,v), \tag{GRD}$$

where G_e, G'_e are respectively the abstract and concrete guards of the event e.

The *simulation* proof obligation (SIM) requires to show that the action (i.e., the modelled state transition) of a refined event is not contradictory to its abstract version:

$$H(d,c,v,w),\ G'_e(d,c,w),\ R'_e(d,c,w,w') \ \vdash \ \exists v'.R_e(d,c,v,v') \ \wedge \ I'(d,c,v',w'), \tag{SIM}$$

where R_e, R'_e are respectively the abstract and concrete next-state relations of the same event e, w and w' are the concrete variable values before and after this event execution. The full definitions of all the proof obligations are given in [2].

The Rodin platform [18] is an integrated toolbox for automating formal modelling and verification in Event-B. The platform provides us with the facilities for creating and editing models as well as model animation. Moreover, it also generates and tries to automatically prove the required proof obligations. If the automatic proving does not succeed for some of the proof obligations then the integrated interactive provers are used to run human-assisted proving.

In this paper, we have chosen the Event-B framework for specifying and verifying the architecture of the robotic system. Our choice has been motivated by two main factors: availability of mature automated tool support and scalability of the framework. Since Event-B relies on theorem proving rather than state-space exploration, it is free of state explosion problem, which is acute for multi-robotic systems. In the next section, we present our formal development of the system architecture in Event-B and verification of its properties.

4 Specification and Refinement of Fault Tolerance Monitors

In this section, we present our approach to the development of multi-layered fault tolerance mechanism for a generic autonomous system. Our approach aims at providing a systematic support for specifying conditions for monitoring progress of mission execution and adaptation at the decision layer, then monitor for task execution at the execution layer and finally a robot health monitor at the functional layer.

We aim at achieving an encapsulation of the behaviour pertaining to the corresponding layer and defining explicit conditions that should be monitored to achieve fault tolerance and correctness in mission execution.

4.1 Robot State Machine

Our development starts from modelling a generic behavioural pattern of an individual robot during the execution of a mission. We model this by defining a generic abstract state machine, represented in Fig. 3. The robot starts as healthy (`ok`) and idle when no task is yet assigned to it (state `ok_idle`). Once the task to be executed is assigned to it, it becomes busy (`ok_busy`). During the execution the robot might experience failures resulting in loss of its capabilities. There are two types of possible failures: sensor failure (`sen_fail_busy`), and actuator failure (`act_fail_busy`). Failures might be recoverable, in which case the robot goes back to `ok_busy` and might still complete task execution. If failure is unrecoverable then the robot fails (`fail_idle`).

Since the behaviour of a robot on the functional layer can be represented by the control loops consisting of sensing and actuation, its capabilities are generalised as sensing and actuation. Correspondingly, failure result in lost of some or all of them.

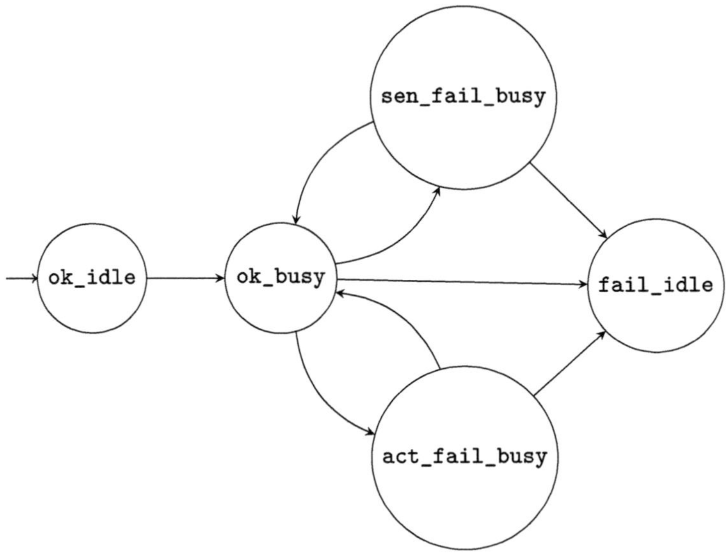

Fig. 3. Abstract state machine of a robot during the execution of a mission

4.2 Refinement Pattern

In this section, we present a pattern-based refinement strategy for formally modelling robotic systems capable of executing structured missions. Our development leverages the refinement paradigm of Event-B to incrementally introduce key functional concerns: robot states, capabilities, task execution and status, and mission decomposition. Each refinement step contributes to progressively elaborating system behaviour and its correctness assumptions while preserving invariants and safety properties.

Robot Status Control Pattern
The initial specification models the robot's operational lifecycle using a finite set of discrete status values. We define an abstract type $ROBOTS$ to represent the robots available. A variable $curr\_robot \in ROBOTS$ is introduced to represent the robot whose behaviour we are currently modelling.

To formulate the state machine presented in Fig. 3, we introduce an abstract type $STATUS$ defining the different states in which a robot can be: $STATUS = \{OK\_IDLE, OK\_BUSY, ACT\_FAIL\_BUSY, SEN\_FAIL\_BUSY, FAIL\_IDLE\}$. Moreover, since multiple robots can be modelled at the same time, we introduce a variable $curr\_status \in ROBOTS \nrightarrow STATUS$, a partial function mapping robots to their current operational status. Note that $curr\_status$ is a partial function, meaning that the set of relevant robots is $dom(curr\_status) \subseteq ROBOTS$, where dom denotes domain of a function.

A set of abstract events, described in Fig. 4, defines transitions between operational modes, including fault occurrences (**actuator_fail** and **sensor_fail**), fault recovery (**actuator_ok** and **sensor_ok**), and transitions to terminal failure

```
start ≙
  when curr_status = ∅
  then curr_status := {curr_robot ↦ OK_IDLE}
  end
get_busy ≙
  when curr_robot ∈ dom(curr_status) ∧
       curr_status(curr_robot) = OK_IDLE
  then curr_status(curr_robot) := OK_BUSY
  end
actuator_fail ≙
  when curr_robot ∈ dom(curr_status) ∧
       curr_status(curr_robot) = OK_BUSY
  then curr_status(curr_robot) := ACT_FAIL_BUSY
  end
actuator_ok ≙
  when curr_robot ∈ dom(curr_status) ∧
       curr_status(curr_robot) = ACT_FAIL_BUSY
  then curr_status(curr_robot) := OK_BUSY
  end
sensor_fail ≙
  when curr_robot ∈ dom(curr_status) ∧
       curr_status(curr_robot) = OK_BUSY
  then curr_status(curr_robot) := SEN_FAIL_BUSY
  end
sensor_ok ≙
  when curr_robot ∈ dom(curr_status) ∧
       curr_status(curr_robot) = SEN_FAIL_BUSY
  then curr_status(curr_robot) := OK_BUSY
  end
ok_to_fail ≙
  when curr_robot ∈ dom(curr_status) ∧
       curr_status(curr_robot) = OK_BUSY
  then curr_status(curr_robot) := FAIL_IDLE
  end
actfail_to_fail ≙
  when curr_robot ∈ dom(curr_status) ∧
       curr_status(curr_robot) = ACT_FAIL_BUSY
  then curr_status(curr_robot) := FAIL_IDLE
  end
senfail_to_fail ≙
  when curr_robot ∈ dom(curr_status) ∧
       curr_status(curr_robot) = SEN_FAIL_BUSY
  then curr_status(curr_robot) := FAIL_IDLE
  end
```

Fig. 4. Initial robot state machine

(**ok_to_fail**, **actfail_to_fail**, and **senfail_to_fail**). The **start** event models the start of the mission and puts robots in OK_IDLE mode. This pattern captures the fundamental life cycle of a robotic agent.

Capability Modelling Pattern

We refine the abstract state machine by adding *CAPABILITIES*, an abstract type allowing us to model the functional abilities of a robot, which may be affected by its operational status. The context constant $status\_cap \in STATUS \leftrightarrow CAPABILITIES$ defines a relation constraining which capabilities are available in each status mode. We add axioms in the context to add those constraints (the notation $r[S]$ denotes the relational image of set S by relation r):

axm1: $status\_cap[\{OK\_IDLE\}] = status\_cap[\{OK\_BUSY\}]$

axm2: $status\_cap[\{ACT\_FAIL\_BUSY\}]$
$\subseteq status\_cap[\{FAIL\_IDLE\}]$

axm3: $status\_cap[\{SEN\_FAIL\_BUSY\}]$
$\subseteq status\_cap[\{FAIL\_IDLE\}]$

The variable $curr\_cap \in ROBOTS \nrightarrow \mathbb{P}(CAPABILITIES)$, where $\mathbb{P}$ denotes a powerset, is introduced to map each robot to a set of capabilities. The set of relevant robots, i.e., $dom(curr\_status)$, becomes $dom(curr\_cap)$: this is added as a machine invariant to ensure that all variables relevant to the robots are always defined and updated.

inv1: $dom(curr\_status) = dom(curr\_cap)$

As a robot can lose or regain capabilities along its life cycle depending on what state it is in, we write an invariant to ensure that a robot's capabilities are always consistent with its status.

inv2: $curr\_robot \in dom(curr\_status)$
$\Rightarrow curr\_cap(curr\_robot)$
$\subseteq status\_cap[\{curr\_status(curr\_robot)\}]$

Failure and recovery events are refined to reflect degradation and restoration of capabilities. The events **actuator_fail** (and similarly **sensor_fail**) non-deterministically removes a subset of capabilities from the robot, while **actuator_ok** (and similarly **sensor_ok**) adds capabilities back, ensuring that the resulting capability set remains valid under the current status via guards involving $status\_cap$. These refinements are described in Fig. 5.

```
actuator_fail refines actuator_fail ≙
  any   lost_cap, new_cap
  when  curr_robot ∈ dom(curr_status) ∧
        curr_status(curr_robot) = OK_BUSY ∧
        lost_cap ∈ ℙ(CAPABILITIES) ∧
        curr_cap(curr_robot)  lost_cap ⊆ status_cap[{ACT_FAIL_BUSY}] ∧
        new_cap = curr_cap(curr_robot)  lost_cap
  then  curr_status(curr_robot) := ACT_FAIL_BUSY
        curr_cap(curr_robot) := new_cap
  end
actuator_ok refines actuator_ok ≙
  any   add_cap, new_cap
  when  curr_robot ∈ dom(curr_status) ∧
        curr_status(curr_robot) = ACT_FAIL_BUSY ∧
        add_cap ∈ ℙ(CAPABILITIES) ∧
        curr_cap(curr_robot) ∪ add_cap ⊆ status_cap[{OK_BUSY}] ∧
        new_cap = curr_cap(curr_robot) ∪ add_cap
  then  curr_status(curr_robot) := OK_BUSY
        curr_cap(curr_robot) := new_cap
  end
```

Fig. 5. Refinement of the **actuator_fail** and **actuator_ok** events

This pattern enables reasoning about the functional impact of faults and lays the foundation for task-capability matching in subsequent refinements.

Task Assignment Pattern

We refine the model by introducing task-level control, allowing robots to be assigned individual tasks. We introduce an abstract type *TASKS*, and a relation $requirements \in TASKS \leftrightarrow CAPABILITIES$ which maps each task to the set of capabilities required to perform it. We also introduce a new variable $curr\_task \in ROBOTS \nrightarrow TASKS$ to track each robot's active task. As in the previous refinement, an invariant is added to constraint the function's domain.

inv3: $dom(curr\_status) = dom(curr\_task)$

The **start** event is extended to assign an initial task to the robot. A new event **pick_up_task** allows a robot to adopt a new task and replace the value of its current task with a different task. This new event is described in Fig. 6.

```
pick_up_task ≘
  any   new_task
  when  new_task ∈ TASKS ∧
        curr_robot ∈ dom(curr_task) ∧
        curr_task(curr_robot) ≠ new_task
  then  curr_task(curr_robot) := new_task
  end
```

Fig. 6. **pick_up_task** event

Task Status Tracking Pattern

We enrich the model by introducing task status management. For a given task, a given robot can either have *completed* the task, be *ready* to complete the task, or be unable to complete the task and therefore be *blocked*. We define the abstract type $TASK\_STATUS = \{READY, COMPLETED, BLOCKED\}$ and we introduce a variable $task\_status \in (ROBOTS \times TASKS) \leftrightarrow TASK\_STATUS$ to record the execution status of robot-task pairs.

For every task a robot is assigned to during the execution, a status must be defined. This is described by the following invariant.

inv4: $curr\_robot \in dom(curr\_task)$
$\Rightarrow (curr\_robot \mapsto curr\_task(curr\_robot)) \in dom(task\_status)$

Here $\mapsto$ denotes an ordered pair. Note that the status of a pair $robot \mapsto task$ is only relevant if *robot*'s assigned task takes the value *task* at some point in the execution.

The event **pick_up_task** is refined by a guard which ensures that a robot is never assigned a task it has already completed. The event now also defines a status ($READY$) for the pair formed by the robot and its newly assigned task. The

```
pick_up_task refines pick_up_task ≙
  any   new_task
  when  new_task ∈ TASKS ∧
        curr_robot ∈ dom(curr_task) ∧
        curr_task(curr_robot) ≠ new_task ∧
        (curr_robot ↦ new_task) ↦ completed ∉ task_status
  then  curr_task(curr_robot) := new_task
        task_status := task_status ⩤ {(curr_robot ↦ new_task) ↦ READY}
  end
complete_task ≙
  when  curr_robot ∈ dom(curr_task) ∧
        (curr_robot ↦ curr_task(curr_robot)) ↦ READY ∈ task_status ∧
        requirements[{curr_task(curr_robot)}] ⊆ curr_cap(curr_robot)
  then  task_status := task_status ⩤ {(curr_robot ↦ curr_task(curr_robot))
                                        ↦ COMPLETED}
  end
blocked_task ≙
  when  curr_robot ∈ dom(curr_task) ∧
        (curr_robot ↦ curr_task(curr_robot)) ↦ READY ∈ task_status ∧
        requirements[{curr_task(curr_robot)}] ⊈ curr_cap(curr_robot)
  then  task_status := task_status ⩤ {(curr_robot ↦ curr_task(curr_robot))
                                        ↦ BLOCKED}
  end
```

Fig. 7. Refinement incorporating task statuses

new events **complete_task** and **blocked_task** check whether the robot's capabilities satisfy the task's requirements and update the execution status accordingly. These refinements are described in Fig. 7.

These refinements establish the link between abstract capabilities and functional task execution. This pattern also enables explicit progress tracking and is critical for managing mission-level sequencing in the final refinement.

Mission Decomposition Pattern

Until this point in the specification robots were assigned tasks arbitrarily, with no condition on their current or previous tasks' completion. This final refinement aims at modelling the sequencing of the tasks that a robot has to complete. We introduce mission-level control, allowing robots to execute complex missions composed of multiple interdependent tasks.

We introduce an abstract type *MISSIONS*. Each mission is associated with a sequence of tasks defined by the total function $decompose \in MISSIONS \rightarrow ((TASKS \rightarrowtail\!\!\!\!\!\!\shortmid\;\; TASKS) \cap (TASKS \twoheadrightarrow\!\!\!\!\!\!\shortmid\;\; TASKS))$. For every $mission \in MISSIONS$, $decompose(mission)$ models the mission's *next* function defined in Definition 2 in Sect. 2. This theoretical definition defined the *next* function as a total function on the set of tasks included in the mission, but since there is a final task (which has no next task) in the mission's sequence, a total function is not adequate to model the function in the Event-B specification. Therefore $decompose(mission)$ is a partial function, which is both surjective and injective: a given task can only have at most 1 previous task and at most 1 following task in the mission's sequence. Note that $decompose(mission)$ is a partial function ; this means that $dom(decompose(mission))$ is a subset of *TASKS*. The *decompose*(*mission*) function thus provides the list of tasks to be executed in the mission, along with the order in which they must be executed.

We add 3 other axioms to further define the *decompose* function and specify the constraints regarding the beginning and the end of a mission's task sequence:

$$\textbf{axm4:}\ \forall mission \cdot mission \in MISSIONS \Rightarrow (\exists\ task \cdot\ task \in dom(decompose(mission)) \land task \notin ran(decompose(mission)))$$

$$\textbf{axm5:}\ \forall mission \cdot mission \in MISSIONS \Rightarrow (\exists\ task \cdot\ task \in dom(decompose(mission)) \land task \in ran(decompose(mission)))$$

$$\textbf{axm6:}\ \forall mission \cdot mission \in MISSIONS \Rightarrow (\forall x \cdot \forall y \cdot x \mapsto y \in decompose(mission) \Rightarrow x \neq y)$$

Axiom **axm4** ensures that every mission has a first task, which has no predecessor in the mission's sequence. Similarly, axiom **axm5** ensures that every mission has a last task. Axiom **axm6** forbids any task to be its own predecessor or follower in a mission's sequence. This is necessary to maintain the task execution order in the events.

A robot's current mission is recorded in the machine via the new variable $curr\_mission \in ROBOTS \nrightarrow MISSIONS$. Like for the previous variables, we add a constraint to its domain.

$$\textbf{inv5}:dom(curr\_mission) = dom(curr\_task)$$

Invariants are added to ensure that a robot always executes its mission's tasks and only those, and that it executes them in order.

$$\textbf{inv6:}\ curr\_robot \in dom(curr\_task) \Rightarrow curr\_task(curr\_robot) \in dom(decompose(curr\_mission(curr\_robot))) \cup ran(decompose(curr\_mission(curr\_robot)))$$

$$\textbf{inv7:}\ curr\_robot \in dom(curr\_task) \Rightarrow (\forall prev\_task \cdot (prev\_task \mapsto curr\_task(curr\_robot)) \in decompose(curr\_mission(curr\_robot)) \Rightarrow (curr\_robot \mapsto prev\_task) \mapsto completed \in task\_status)$$

The model is refined to ensure that a robot can only proceed to a new task if all its immediate predecessors (as specified by the mission decomposition) have been completed. This is enforced through both the previously mentioned invariants and strengthened guards on the **pick_up_task** event, which requires that the current task be completed and that it is the unique predecessor of the new task. The refinement of the **pick_up_task** event is described in Fig. 8. The start event is extended to assign an initial mission and ensures the starting task is indeed the first in the mission sequence.

pick_up_task refines **pick_up_task** $\widehat{=}$
any new_task
when $new\_task \in TASKS \wedge$
$curr\_robot \in dom(curr\_task) \wedge$
$curr\_task(curr\_robot) \neq new\_task \wedge$
$(curr\_robot \mapsto new\_task) \mapsto completed \notin task\_status \wedge$
$curr\_task(curr\_robot) \in dom(decompose(curr\_mission(curr\_robot))) \wedge$
$(curr\_robot \mapsto curr\_task(curr\_robot)) \mapsto completed \in task\_status \wedge$
$(curr\_task(curr\_robot)) \mapsto new\_task \in decompose(curr\_mission(curr\_robot)) \wedge$
$(decompose(curr\_mission(curr\_robot))^{-1})[\{new\_task\}] = \{curr\_task(curr\_robot)\}$
then $curr\_task(curr\_robot) := new\_task$
$task\_status := task\_status \Leftarrow \{(curr\_robot \mapsto new\_task) \mapsto READY\}$
end

Fig. 8. Refinement of the **pick_up_task** event

We have specified the behaviour and properties of monitors that can ensure that the coordination of mission execution progresses according to the plan not only under nominal conditions but also when the robots fail and alternative robots can be deployed.

5 Discussion

5.1 Proof Efforts

Verification of correctness in Event-B is proof-based. The proof efforts were greatly facilitated by the Rodin platform which generated the proof obligations and attempted to discharge them automatically.

The development generated 108 proof obligations. Around 50% of them have been proved automatically by the Rodin platform. The rest of the proof obligations had to be discharged manually in the Rodin interactive proving environment. However, out of those, only two were rather non-trivial. Thus, only around 2% of the generated proof obligations required actual manual proving. This can be explained by the fact that our development was carried out in small refinement steps which mostly focused on superposition refinements. The non-trivial proof obligations were associated with complex nested data structures, which we used in the specification.

5.2 Multi-Layered Monitoring Architecture

Our formal development establishes a basis for defining a hierarchy of monitors enabling fault-tolerant mission execution. Below we outline the behaviour and properties of the monitors derived from our specifications.

Functional Layer Monitor. At the functional layer, the monitor should react on failures and recoveries of agent robots. It periodically checks the health of each robot and updates their statuses. The consistency of the status of the robots and its capabilities is guaranteed by **inv1** and **inv2**. If a failure of currently active robot is detected then the monitor sends a notification to execution layer to reallocated task execution to another robot. The dynamic behaviour of the monitor consists of updating the statuses of the robots as outlined in Fig. 4 and 5.

Executive Layer Monitor. The functional layer monitor encapsulates the states of the robot agents and sends the notification events to executive layer in case a robot has successfully completed a task or failed to complete it because it lost a required capability. Correspondingly, the monitor at the executive layer tries to re-allocate a task to another robot. The abstract specification of this behaviour is presented in Fig. 6 and refined in Fig. 7. Invariants **inv3** and **inv4** ensure that an idle robot with required capabilities is chosen. Upon successful completion of a task, a new task can be chosen and allocated on an appropriate robot until the entire mission is completed. However, if no robot is capable to execute a task in a mission, the mission execution becomes blocked and decision layer is notified about it.

Decision Layer Monitor. The executive layer monitor encapsulates the statuses of tasks execution and sends the notifications to the decision layer only in case the mission is completed or further progress of the mission becomes impossible and alternative mission plan should be chosen. The invariants **inv5** and **inv6** defines the correctness conditions for the mission decomposition into task. Moreover, **inv7** defines overreaching all three layers condition connecting the progress of mission execution with the availability of robots with required capabilities.

Architecture Construction via Refinement Process. Our formal development can be seen as a process of incremental construction of system architecture. We started from the specification of functional layer monitor, then by superposition, built a specification of executive layer monitor and then further refined the specification to define the decision layer monitor. It allowed us to gradually increase complexity inherent to hierarchical fault tolerance mechanisms. The main advantage of such an approach is in guaranteeing correctness of intertwined fault tolerance mechanisms and clean separation of concerns according to the architectural layer. However, our development could also benefit from the explicit decomposition of the entire system specification into the specifications of corresponding components and defining the communication protocol between them. We will experiment with it in the future work.

6 Related Work

The problem of engineering reliable autonomic robotic systems has received significant research attention. In particular, a great number of research publications in robotic systems has focused on a development of underling system architectures, robot control and navigation [4,5,10,14,15].

A systematic study is presented in recent work [3] where the authors overview the state of the art in managing safety for mobile robotic systems.

A variety of software engineering techniques and tools are used to engineer dependable robotic systems [14], including model checking [8,12], theorem proving techniques [16], runtime verification [6], simulation [21], etc.

The possible integration of formal methods with different approaches that complement each other for applying in the robotics domain is discussed, e.g., in works [7,9,13]. For instance, in work [17] the RoboChart framework is presented that combines formalised state machines and automatic implementation of robotic controllers. In our work, we use formal modelling to derive the system architecture and demonstrate how to implement the monitors at different architectural levels to achieve fault tolerance in mission execution.

Macek et al. [11] have proposed a layered architectural solution for robot navigation. They focus on a problem of safe navigation of a vehicle in an urban environment. Similarly to our approach, they distinguish between managing a mission at a decision layer – a global route planning and interconnection with executive and functional layers, which, in their work, are responsible for collision avoidance control. However, in their work, they focus on the safety issues associated with the navigation of a single vehicle and do not consider the problem of achieving fault tolerance in mission execution.

Zhu et al. [20] proposed the robot motion planning that integrated with the task assignment, thus the robots start to move once the overall task is given. The robot navigation can be dynamically adjusted to guarantee that each target location has the desired number of robots, even under uncertainties such as when some robots break down. The overall idea is similar to ours, however, we focus on formal modelling of fault tolerance monitors at different architectural levels.

Weyns et al. in [19] proposed the FORMS model (FOrmal Reference Model for Self-adaptation) that allows designers to describe and evaluate alternative design choices for self-adaptive systems. The reference model defines a vocabulary of adaptive primitives that can be used to precisely define complex self-adaptive systems. The formally specified model allows engineers to precisely define the main characteristics of self-adaptive software systems and reason about them. In our work, we relied on formal development to derive monitors for mission progress monitoring and adaptation at different levels of abstracton. We have provided a corresponding interpretation of the generic robotic system architecture, formalised them in the refinement process and demonstrated how to verify the properties of the derived architecture.

7 Conclusions

In this paper, we formalised and formally verified the properties of fault tolerant mission orchestration in multi-layered robotic architecture. Our approach allows the designers to built fault tolerant robotic systems in a systematic manner by supporting separation of concerns for each architectural layer. In our approach, the decision layer is responsible for the mission execution at the strategic level, i.e., in case due to failures the mission cannot be continued using the original plan, it decides on an alternative mission plan. The execution layer monitors the progress of task execution and notifies the decision layer only about the success or unrecoverable failures of tasks composing the mission. The functional layer monitors the health of the components and performs error recovery by assigning the task execution of alternative robots based on their capabilities. It notifies the execution layer about unrecoverable failures or success of execution.

We used Event-B as a formal modelling framework due to its scalability and availability of automated tool support. The framework allowed us to express complex safety and fault tolerance-related properties of monitors at different levels of system architecture. Moreover, supported formalising and verifying relationships between fault tolerant monitors at all architectural layers via defining relationships between the states of mission and tasks execution and robot's health.

As a future work, we are planning to use our formalisation as a basis for creating a domain-specific language for designing and verifying correctness and reliability of mission planning. Moreover, we are planning to extend our models with a wider set of fault tolerance mechanisms.

References

1. Abrial, J.R.: The B-Book: Assigning Programs to Meanings. Cambridge University Press, Cambridge (2005)
2. Abrial, J.R.: Modeling in Event-B. Cambridge University Press, Cambridge (2010)
3. Bozhinoski, D., Ruscio, D.D., Malavolta, I., Pelliccione, P., Crnkovic, I.: Safety for mobile robotic systems: a systematic mapping study from a software engineering perspective. J. Syst. Softw. **151**, 150–179 (2019). https://doi.org/10.1016/j.jss.2019.02.021
4. Brambilla, M., Ferrante, E., Birattari, M., Dorigo, M.: Swarm robotics: a review from the swarm engineering perspective. Swarm Intell. **7**(1), 1–41 (2013)
5. Bullo, F., Frazzoli, E., Pavone, M., Savla, K., Smith, S.L.: Dynamic vehicle routing for robotic systems. Proc. IEEE **99**(9), 1482–1504 (2011)
6. Falcone, Y., Jaber, M., Nguyen, T.-H., Bozga, M., Bensalem, S.: Runtime verification of component-based systems. In: Barthe, G., Pardo, A., Schneider, G. (eds.) SEFM 2011. LNCS, vol. 7041, pp. 204–220. Springer, Heidelberg (2011). https://doi.org/10.1007/978-3-642-24690-6_15
7. Farrell, M., Luckcuck, M., Fisher, M.: Robotics and integrated formal methods: necessity meets opportunity. In: Furia, C.A., Winter, K. (eds.) IFM 2018. LNCS, vol. 11023, pp. 161–171. Springer, Cham (2018). https://doi.org/10.1007/978-3-319-98938-9_10
8. Halder, R., Proença, J., Macedo, N., Santos, A.: Formal verification of ros-based robotic applications using timed-automata. Form. Methods Softw. Eng. 44–50. IEEE (2017)
9. Hinchey, M., Rash, J., Rouff, C., Truszkowski, W., Vanderbilt, A.: Requirements of an integrated formal method for intelligent swarms. In: Proceedings of the 10th International Workshop on Formal Methods for Industrial Critical Systems, pp. 33–59. Wiley-Blackwell (2012)
10. Iocchi, L., Nardi, D., Salerno, M.: Reactivity and deliberation: a survey on multi-robot systems. In: Balancing Reactivity and Social Deliberation in Multi-Agent Systems. BRSDMAS 2000. LNCS, vol. 2103, pp. 9–34. Springer, Berlin, Heidelberg (2001). https://doi.org/10.1007/3-540-44568-4_2

11. rt Macek, K., Vasquez, D., Siegwart, R.: Safe vehicle navigation in dynamic urban scenarios. In: Proceedings of the 11th International IEEE Conference on Intelligent Transportation Systems, pp. 482–489. IEEE (2008)
12. Konur, S., Dixon, C., Fisher, M.: Formal verification of probabilistic swarm behaviours. In: Dorigo, M., et al. (eds.) ANTS 2010. LNCS, vol. 6234, pp. 440–447. Springer, Heidelberg (2010). https://doi.org/10.1007/978-3-642-15461-4_42
13. Li, W., Miyazawa, A., Ribeiro, P., Cavalcanti, A., Woodcock, J., Timmis, J.: From formalised state machines to implementations of robotic controllers. Distrib. Auton. Robot. Syst. **6**, 517–529 (2018)
14. Luckcuck, M., Farrell, M., Dennis, L.A., Dixon, C., Fisher, M.: Formal specification and verification of autonomous robotic systems: a survey. CoRR **abs/1807.00048** (2018)
15. Macharet, D.G., Campos, M.F.M.: A survey on routing problems and robotic systems. Robotica **36**(12), 1781–1803 (2018). https://doi.org/10.1017/S0263574718000735
16. Mitsch, S., Ghorbal, K., Platzer, A.: On provably safe obstacle avoidance for autonomous robotic ground vehicles. In: Robotics: Science and Systems IX (2013)
17. Ribeiro, P., Miyazawa, A., Li, W., Cavalcanti, A., Timmis, J.: Modelling and verification of timed robotic controllers. In: Polikarpova, N., Schneider, S. (eds.) IFM 2017. LNCS, vol. 10510, pp. 18–33. Springer, Cham (2017). https://doi.org/10.1007/978-3-319-66845-1_2
18. Rodin: Event-B platform (2007). http://www.event-b.org/
19. Weyns, D., Malek, S., Andersson, J.: FORMS: unifying reference model for formal specification of distributed self-adaptive systems. TAAS **7**(1), 8:1–8:61 (2012). https://doi.org/10.1145/2168260.2168268
20. Zhu, A., Yang, S.X.: A neural network approach to dynamic task assignment of multirobots. IEEE Trans. Neural Netw. **17**(5), 1278–1287 (2006). https://doi.org/10.1109/TNN.2006.875994
21. Zhu, X., Liu, Z., Yang, J.: Model of collaborative UAV swarm toward coordination and control mechanisms study. Procedia Comput. Sci. **51**(C), 493–502 (2015). https://doi.org/10.1016/j.procs.2015.05.274

Author Index

É. André et al. (Eds.): ICFEM 2025, LNCS 16229, pp. 391–392, 2026.
https://doi.org/10.1007/978-981-95-4213-0

W

X

Y

Z

MIX
Papier aus verantwortungsvollen Quellen
Paper from responsible sources
FSC® C105338

If you have any concerns about our products,
you can contact us on
ProductSafety@springernature.com

In case Publisher is established outside the EU,
the EU authorized representative is:
Springer Nature Customer Service Center GmbH
Europaplatz 3, 69115 Heidelberg, Germany

Printed by Libri Plureos GmbH
in Hamburg, Germany